# Frommer's 96

# The Bahamas
## Including Turks & Caicos

### by Darwin Porter
### & Danforth Prince

Macmillan • USA

## MACMILLAN TRAVEL

A Simon & Schuster Macmillan Company
1633 Broadway
New York, NY 10019

ISBN 0-02-860646-9
ISSN 1068-9338

Editor: Margaret Bowen
Map Editor: Douglas Stallings
Design by Michele Laseau
Digital Cartography by John Decamillis
                    Ortelius Design

### SPECIAL SALES

Manufactured in the United States of America

# Contents

## 12   Turks & Caicos Islands   299

# List of Maps

## INVITATION TO THE READER

In researching this book, I discovered many wonderful places—hotels, restaurants, shops, and more. I'm sure you'll find others. Please tell us about them, so we can share the information with your fellow travelers in upcoming editions. If you were disappointed with a recommendation, we'd love to know that, too. Please write to:

Darwin Porter
*Frommer's Bahamas '96*
Macmillan Travel
1633 Broadway
New York, NY 10019

## AN ADDITIONAL NOTE

Please be advised that travel information is subject to change at any time—and this is especially true of prices. We therefore suggest that you write or call ahead for confirmation when making your travel plans. The authors, editors, and publisher cannot be held responsible for the experiences of readers while traveling. Your safety is important to us, however, so we encourage you to stay alert and be aware of your surroundings. Keep a close eye on cameras, purses, and wallets, all favorite targets of thieves and pickpockets.

## WHAT THE SYMBOLS MEAN

### ✪ Frommer's Favorites

Hotels, restaurants, attractions, and entertainments you should not miss.

### ⑤ Super-Special Values

Hotels and restaurants that offer great value for your money.

The following abbreviations are used for credit cards:

| | | | |
|---|---|---|---|
| AE | American Express | EU | Eurocard |
| CB | Carte Blanche | JCB | Japan Credit Bank |
| DC | Diners Club | MC | MasterCard |
| DISCM | Discover | V | VISA |
| ER | enRoute | | |

# The Best of
# the Bahamas

The Bahamas contain some 700 islands and a land area of over 5,000 square miles. The sprawling archipelago includes the Turks and Caicos islands in the south, but these have a separate government. Most of the population is centered on the major islands of New Providence and Grand Bahama.

With so many islands, visitors have a lot of options. One can choose a fast-paced destination with high-rise hotels and casinos; a sleepy, New England-style village of clapboard cottages; or perhaps something in between. The island you pick depends on who you are and what you like to do—swim in turquoise waters, hike in forests laced with rare vegetation, fish for marlin, or just sit by the pool with a tropical drink and the novel you've been meaning to read all year.

Everyone's taste is different. Do you prefer swanky accommodations rather than simple? Do you crave privacy or a house-party atmosphere? And during your holiday will you miss your VCR, or do you only hope for a hammock and the shade of a palm tree?

If you've come for an active vacation, you'll find plenty of possibilities, including snorkeling, scuba diving, golf, tennis, hiking, and windsurfing.

Whether you want a rustic room overlooking the sea, a honeymoon retreat, or the perfect place to bring children, this chapter will help you pick the island and facilities that best suits your needs.

For a thumbnail portrait of each island, see "Islands in Brief" in Chapter 2.

## 1 The Best Beaches

Good beaches can be found on virtually every island of the Bahamas, although in some cases, you might have to walk, drive, or bicycle a short distance from your hotel or guest house to reach them.

- **Ten Bay Beach,** Eleuthera. This beach was one of the reasons the exclusive Cotton Bay Club was built here. Ten Bay Beach lies a short drive south of Palmetto Point, just north of Savannah Sound. Since the Cotton Bay Club was closed for renovations at press time, the white sands and turquoise waters will be even more idyllic for vacationers.
- **Grace Bay Beach,** Providenciales. Its 12 miles of pale sands are considered one of the premier attractions of Provo. It's so

spectacular that increasing numbers of resorts (including Club Med) have developed along its edge.

- **Pink Sands Beach,** Harbour Island. Its color is a pale pink and it stretches for three miles, past a handful of low-rise hotels and private villas. When visitors leave the turquoise waters and pink sands, they can ramble along the streets of a village whose clapboard-covered roofs are pure New England.
- **Cabbage Beach,** Paradise Island. If Las Vegas were a seaside resort, its beaches would probably resemble Cabbage Beach. The sands are broad (but slope in some places rather steeply) and stretch for at least two miles. Palms, sea grapes, and casuarinas line its edge. You get the feeling that many of the sunbathers dozing on the sands are recovering from the previous evening's revels. It's likely to be rather crowded near the megahotels that form the core of Paradise Island, but escapists can usually find something approaching solitude on the beach's isolated northwestern extension (Paradise Beach), where the only access is by boat or on foot.
- **Old Fort Beach,** New Providence. This beach lies near the relatively unpopulated western tip of the most strategically important island in the Bahamas. It's probably the least developed major beach on New Providence. Many of its most ardent devotees are homeowners from nearby Lyford Cay, whose homes are among the most expensive in the Bahamas. Least crowded times are weekdays. Windiest times are throughout the winter. Calmest times (best suited for waterskiing) are during the summer. Sands are white, waters are turquoise.
- **MacTaggart's Beach,** Rose Island. A short boat ride from the piers and congestion of downtown Nassau will bring you to this beach. Its pristine condition remains intact because of the difficulty of reaching it. If you should hire a boat (or participate in any of Nassau's guided boat tours), know in advance that the only amenities you'll find are those you bring with you, Robinson Crusoe–style.
- **Tahiti Beach,** Hopetown, Abaco. Its isolation at the far end of Elbow Cay island ensures that only a handful of people will ever visit its cool waters and white sands. Access is possible only by foot, by riding a rented bicycle across sand and gravel paths from Hopetown, or by private boat. (The Abacos are considered the sailing capital of the Bahamas, and you'll never lack for boats to carry you there.)
- **Saddle Cay,** the Exumas. Most of the Exumas are oval-shaped islands strung end to end like the links of a 130-mile chain. One notable exception is Saddle Cay, whose horseshoe-shaped curve lies near the Exuma's northern tip. Don't even think of getting here except by boat. Once you reach it, however, you'll find an unspoiled setting without a trace of the modern world, and lots of other cays and islets for stranding yourself on, shipwreck-style, for a few hours.
- **Cable Beach,** New Providence. This beach got its name when the first underwater cable was laid in 1892, linking it (and the Bahamian capital of New Providence) to the mainland of Florida. During the 1930s, it enjoyed a certain vogue because of a nearby racetrack. Cable Beach is one of the best-accessorized beaches in the Bahamas, with easy access to shops, casinos, restaurants, water sports, and bars.
- **Xanadu Beach,** Grand Bahama Island. Grand Bahama Island boasts about 60 miles of sandy shoreline. The most convenient to the resort hotels of Freeport is Xanadu Beach. Shuttle-bus service connects the beach with several nearby hotels. The beach offers at least a mile of white sand and a (usually) gentle surf.

It's among the most-visited beaches on the island. If you're looking for more privacy, seek out any of the beaches stretching for many miles in either direction.

## 2  The Best Honeymoon Resorts

A resort that's suitable for a honeymoon should offer stunning natural beauty, a lot of privacy, and a cheerful, supportive staff. There are hundreds of resorts that might fit the bill, but I present my top choices here.

In recent times, as wedding ceremonies have become increasingly expensive and complicated, more and more couples are exchanging their vows in the Caribbean. Many resorts will arrange everything from the preacher to the flowers, so I've included in the following list some resorts that provide wedding services.

For more information about the various options and the legal requirements for marriages in the Bahamas, refer to Chapter 3, "Planning a Trip to the Bahamas."

- **Carnival's Crystal Palace Resort & Casino,** New Providence. If you're bored with the idea of honeymooning in an isolated village, with just you, your loved one, the moon, and the stars, head to this megacomplex of electronic razzamatazz, where bright lights, bright colors, and a mind-boggling assortment of diversions will help you while away your time.
- **Le Meridien Royal Bahamian,** New Providence. It's quiet and dignified, with roots firmly planted in Cable Beach's British heritage. Peacocks stroll within carefully clipped gardens, but if you want to casino- and restaurant-hop, the diversions of one of the largest resort complexes in the Bahamas lie within a 10-minute walk.
- **Ocean Club,** Paradise Island. It's elegant, low-key, and low-rise, with a well-deserved sense of exclusivity. The clientele is likely to include many older couples who might be celebrating second (or third) honeymoons. The Ocean Club's formal terraced gardens were inspired by the club's founder (an heir to the A&P fortune), and are probably the most impressive in the Bahamas.
- **Villas on Coral Island,** Silver Cay, off the coast of Nassau. The most obvious virtues of these units include private plunge pools, Italian marble accents, and lots of space. More subtle is their carefully controlled access to the booming nightlife and casino options of the New Providence mainland. The setting is a small offshore cay whose ambience encourages couples (especially honeymooners) to disappear inside their villas for entire days at a time.
- **Graycliff,** Nassau, New Providence. It's the only member of the prestigious Relais & Châteaux chain in the Bahamas. Its origins are at least 200 years old, and although many of the accommodations are much newer, each is permeated with an antique charm. The setting, in a garden in the heart of downtown Nassau, allows greater access to everyday Bahamian life than a megaresort would.
- **Xanadu Beach Resort & Marina,** Grand Bahama Island. Despite its contemporary exterior, the public rooms of this resort contain many expensive accessories that might have been chosen by a reclusive billionaire. In fact, the builder of this resort was Howard Hughes, who lived in its penthouse for many years. With some of the best architecture on Grand Bahama Island, it's closely linked to the goings-on of the island's restaurants, beaches, and casinos. The comfortable, contemporary bedrooms are suitable for an extended honeymoon for almost anyone.

- **Green Turtle Club & Marina,** Green Turtle Cay, Abaco. Honeymooners appreciate this resort's winning combination of yachting atmosphere and well-manicured comfort. The setting is small (31 rooms) and civilized in an understated, unflashy way. When you want a change of pace, you can stroll through the clapboard-covered village of New Plymouth. (New Plymouth is accessible either by motor launch or, even better, by a 45-minute walk across windswept scrublands, which seem far removed from everything.)
- **Bluff House Club & Marina,** Green Turtle Cay, Abaco. Its name derives from its position on a low cliff above a beach. The architecture focuses on privacy, with a rustic, seafaring decor that has its own kind of elegance. If you're at all intrigued by the sea, Bluff House might be very appropriate.
- **Stella Maris Inn,** Long Island. The Stella Maris is the social highlight of Long Island. Sailing is important here, as is diving and a "get away from it all" sense of escapism. European flair is added by a clientele who hail in many cases from Germany. The island itself is often cited as the most beautiful in the Bahamas. Honeymooners usually fit into the grand scheme of things perfectly.
- **Bahamas Princess Resort & Casino,** Grand Bahama Island. Your marriage might have an auspicious beginning at a resort whose architecture includes minarets. Whether you consider it kitsch or old-fashioned fun, there's no escaping the presence of enough accessories and diversions to keep your honeymoon whirring along as smoothly as a roulette wheel. Casinos and beach life are only a shuttle-bus ride away.

## 3  The Best Family Vacations

If you've ever traveled with a family, you'll know that children, especially small or loud children, aren't welcome everywhere. But those hotels that do welcome families with children tend to go all out to make them feel wanted, with everything from playgrounds to babysitters.

- **Villas on Coral Island,** Silver Cay, off the coast of New Providence. Adults appreciate its seclusion on a private cay, and children appreciate its access to a nearby marine park and the Coral Island aquariums. And no one can deny the appeal of a private plunge pool for your family.
- **Ramada Turquoise Reef Resort & Casino,** Provo, Turks and Caicos Islands. A luxury resort with oversized oceanfront rooms, this hotel aggressively pursues the family trade. This is a very activity-oriented resort—it even stages treasure hunts for kids. Babysitting can also be arranged.
- **Radisson Cable Beach,** Cable Beach, New Providence. A family could opt to never leave the grounds of this resort during their stay. The pool area features the most lavish artificial waterfall this side of Tahiti. The health club at the nearby Crystal Palace can be used by guests and their children, and the list of in-house activities includes dancing lessons.
- **Radisson Grand Hotel,** Paradise Island. This hotel offers activities for children aged 5–13 in its Camp Caribbean. Babysitting can be arranged, and older children have free use of bicycles. Also, right on the beach in front of the hotel is a water-sports center that offers banana boat rides for kids. All rooms have balconies.
- **Atlantis Paradise Island Resort & Casino,** Paradise Island. This is one of the largest hotel complexes in the world, with 1,200 bedrooms, endless rows of

shops, and water sports galore. Children will enjoy observing the canals that slice through the sand and limestone of this resort.

- **Pirate's Cove Holiday Inn,** Paradise Island. With 18 stories, this pirate-themed hotel is the tallest in the Bahamas. The pool was inspired by a tropical lagoon, and the bar that dispenses drinks to adults is modeled on a 95-foot pirate ship. There's a day camp for children (Captain Kid's), and even the game room bears the name and accessories of a pirate's den. If parents want to escape from all this saber rattling, there are lots of quiet escape hatches for them as well.

- **Bahamas Princess Resort and Casino,** Grand Bahama Island. Many of its clients come just to gamble and get a suntan, but others bring their children. To divert them, the hotel maintains a pair of playgrounds and a swimming pool inspired by a tropical oasis, and offers children's platters in some of the restaurants. The architecture features lots of "Aladdin and His Lamp" accessories, such as minarets above a decidedly non-Islamic setting. A shuttle bus makes frequent trips to and from the nearest beach.

- **Castaways Resort,** Grand Bahama Island. This is a relatively modest resort. The pagoda-capped lobby is set a very short walk from the ice-cream stands, souvenir shops, and fountains of the International Bazaar. Children under 12 stay free in their parent's room, and the in-house lounge presents limbo and fire-eating shows several evenings a month.

- **Sun Club Resort,** Grand Bahama Island. A small, family-run establishment, the Sun Club Resort is considered excellent value for those traveling with children. Roll-away beds are provided for free, and kids 12 and under stay with their parents for free. Kids can play on an immaculate lawn, and there's also a pool. Older children can rent bicycles on the premises. Each of the rooms has a kitchen. There's a Laundromat too.

- **Club Med,** Eleuthera. With 300 rooms, this is one of the largest hotels on Eleuthera. There's a miniclub for child minding, which parents use as a means of escaping for a few hours on the beach; a staff that dresses up as clowns during children's parties; and a miniclub that teaches teenagers how to snorkel and sail. At the end of each week, children and adults participate in a "circus workshop," with trapeze and trampoline acts, funny costumes, and lots of greasepaint.

## 4  The Best Places to Get Away from It All

Activity and a fast pace might be the last thing you're seeking in the Caribbean. You may just plain want to escape from the world. Assuming that you don't feel any urgent need to visit a casino or disco, here is a list of practically perfect options:

- **Meridian Club,** Pine Cay. This cluster of vacation homes is the only real development on an 800-acre island covered with shrubs and low trees. With most of the island devoted to the preservation of bird-and-animal life, it is truly a drop out and disappear sort of place. Communications with the outside world are deliberately limited, and the only socializing you're likely to find will be with occupants of the island's 30 or so privately owned homes.

- **Dunmore Beach Club,** Harbour Island. It's one of the less expensive all-inclusive resorts of the Bahamas. Because of its limited number of accommodations, its atmosphere is akin to a private house party in a New England summerhouse. Each of the dozen or so lodgings is positioned for privacy, and you can escape to the nether regions of the local beach if you're looking to get away from it all.

- **Club Med,** San Salvador. This was the first large resort to be built on one of the Bahamas' most isolated islands. Site of Columbus's first landfall in the New World, it's unusually luxurious, and unusually isolated, for a typical Club Med. The sheer difficulty of reaching it, however, adds to the get-away-from-it-all mystique.
- **Green Turtle Club,** Green Turtle Cay. Secluded and private, this mariner's retreat consists of tasteful one- to three-bedroom villas with full kitchens. It opens onto a small private beach with a 35-slip marina, which is the most complete yachting facility in the archipelago. Many rooms open onto poolside, and there's a dining room decorated in Queen Anne style. The hotel is popular with celebrities.
- **Fernandez Bay Village,** Cat Island. It contains only about a dozen stone and timber villas, the closest thing to urban congestion Cat Island ever sees. The beach bar is suitably raffish and has a thatch roof, which evokes the South Pacific. There's only one phone at the entire resort, and your bathroom shower will probably open to a view of the sky.

## 5  The Friendliest Islands

Open-minded visitors with a sense of humor will almost always have a good rapport with locals regardless of which destination they choose. Remember, though, that islands known for friendliness are usually the smaller ones that don't have much tourism.

- **Harbour Island,** off the coast of Eleuthera. During the 18th century, this town was famous for boatbuilding. Its colonial charm is evident in the rows of handsome clapboard-sided cottages, neat picket fences, and the capital (Dunmore Town), whose populace barely numbers 1,000. Drinks are consumed on verandas. People are friendly and crime is low.
- **Elbow Cay/Hope Town,** the Abacos. Access to this town requires a 20-minute boat ride from the airport at Marsh Harbour. Although it's only a short passage across usually calm waters, many visitors imagine that they've gone back a century in time. Bougainvillea flames on picket fences, and a stark lighthouse on the town's highest bluff looks like a scene from a Winslow Homer painting. While not necessarily chatty, the townspeople will greet you with respect and usually look out for your well-being. Most full-time residents are white, the descendants of 18th-century British Loyalists who fled the North American mainland shortly after the American Revolution.
- **Cat Island,** the Southern Bahamas. Life here is slow paced, and during some seasons, access by air occurs only two or three times a week. Islanders live by fishing and whatever will grow in the thin, sandy soil. A churchgoing ethic on Cat Island was reinforced here for many years by the presence of legendary monk, Father Jerome Hawes, a semirecluse, who almost single-handedly built one of the most famous abbeys in the Bahamas.
- **The Exumas.** Their sheer size (365 tiny islands strung over a distance of 177 miles) and the titanic force of the sea that surrounds them produces a rawboned kind of grit that encourages neighbors to look out for each other. Residents display a genuine curiosity about outsiders.

- **Providenciales/Provo,** Turks and Caicos Islands. It's the most international island in the Turks and Caicos, with a polyglot group of residents who hail from virtually every country of Europe and North America. Blessed with some of the finest beaches in the Western Hemisphere, the islanders have a buoyant enthusiasm.

## 6 The Best Food

Despite the epic difficulties of running a restaurant in the Bahamas, some islands enjoy better culinary reputations than others. For more information on cuisine in the Bahamas, refer to "Food & Drink" in Chapter 2.

- **Nassau/Cable Beach,** New Providence. The sheer volume of restaurants on this most crowded of Bahamian islands ensures a brisk competition for diners. Nassau and Cable Beach contain a staggering number of simple restaurants that offer grilled fish, surf and turf, and burgers. Upscale restaurants include Graycliff, Sun And . . . , Café de Paris, and Sole Mare.
- **Paradise Island.** Hotels will offer a choice of at least two (and sometimes two dozen) eating areas whose main difference is their degree of formality. If you want a club sandwich, a salad, or a steak, you won't have to look very far to find an emporium that will prepare it for you. If you're looking for something more esoteric, with enhanced service, consider such upscale eateries as the dining room of the Ocean Club, the Café Martinique, and the Villa d'Este.
- **Freeport,** Grand Bahama Island. Dozens of restaurants offer burgers and salads and steaks. Ethnic restaurants are also plentiful. Among the most upscale of the island's restaurants are the Escoffier Grill Room, the Rib Room (whose theme is that of an English hunting lodge), Don Luigi's, Luciano's, and the culinary showcase of the Lucayan Beach Resort, the Monte Carlo, and the Crown Room.

## 7 The Best Shopping

U.S. citizens are allowed to leave the Bahamas with $600 worth of goods untaxed.

- **New Providence/Paradise Island.** Most of the shopping in the Bahamas is centered in Nassau, where large numbers of cruise-ship passengers comb the stores. Specialty stores seem to crop up virtually everywhere, with a dense concentration on Bay Street between Rawson Square and the British Colonial Hotel, and along the side streets radiating off Bay Street. Especially numerous are stores selling such European crystal and porcelain as Wedgwood, Royal Doulton, Royal Copenhagen, Lalique, and Baccarat. Many stores sell cashmere sweaters from England. Anglophiles will never lack for souvenirs (decorative spoons, beer mugs, cuff links) that commemorate England. Other stores focus on Bahamian coins and stamps, antique prints, and nautical engravings. And there's never a lack of locally made souvenirs from the Straw Market, which sprawls along several colorful blocks along Bay Street, near the cruise-ship piers. Don't worry if your wardrobe is missing a swimsuit, sundress, or T-shirt. Everywhere you turn, you'll find hundreds of outlets selling warm-weather clothing.
- **Freeport,** Grand Bahama Island. Its stores are not the most upscale you might have ever seen, but there's a wide choice of merchandise, including all kinds of jewelry (Colombian Emeralds), goods patterned on English models (John Bull),

leather from exotic importers (Fendi), porcelain figurines (Lladro Gallery), and virtually every perfume ever distilled (the Perfume Factory, Parfums de Paris).

## 8 The Best Nightlife

It's sleepy time in most of the Out Islands (or so-called Family Islands) such as Spanish Wells, Andros, and the Berry Islands. Except for Provo, the serious partyer will also want to avoid Turks and Caicos.

- **Paradise Island.** Casinos whirl until dawn. Showgirls with sequins and feathers strut their stuff on cabaret stages. Discos beckon with electronic rhythms, and if you tire of the crowd at one bar, you only need to follow a trail of lights to find another.
- **Nassau/Cable Beach,** New Providence. New Providence offers many theme bars, casinos, and nightlife options. But nowhere else in the Bahamas offers as wide a choice of discos, local bars, and nocturnal diversions as Nassau.
- **Freeport/Lucaya,** Grand Bahama Island. There are casinos, cabarets, and floor shows. Bars and restaurants proliferate (and karaoke is big here). And the shops remain open conveniently late. Of the three nightlife meccas in this section, Freeport probably offers the greatest number of diversions for families.

## 9 The Best Gambling

Here is a list of islands that simply wouldn't be the same without their glittering casinos.

- **Paradise Island/Cable Beach,** New Providence. Until the development of Cable Beach as a formidable gambling emporium in its own right, Paradise Island ruled almost without competitors as the midwinter gambling mecca for casino lovers who either found Atlantic City too cold or Las Vegas too far away. In the 1980s, Cable Beach (a strip of massive hotels) was developed to challenge the reigning favorite. Today, both areas cater to everyone from the "high rollers" to grandmothers from Iowa who never leave the slot machines. Both of the major casinos (the Atlantis Paradise Island Resort on Paradise Island and the casino run by Carnival's Crystal Palace on Cable Beach) are vast emporiums and each has at least one cluster of slot machines that remain open 24 hours a day. Both require that players be 21 years of age. Dozens of shops, bars, and restaurants line every path leading to the casinos.
- **Freeport/Lucaya,** Grand Bahama Island. The largest of the island's casinos is the 20,000-square-foot Princess Casino, which is capped with somewhat startling Moorish domes. In its center rises one of my favorite vantage points, an enormous circular bar that is raised above the activities of the floor below. The array of slot machines is dazzling. In Lucaya, the main casino activities occur within the Lucayan Beach Casino. Both establishments offer free casino training for novices.

## 10 The Best Budget Islands

Here is a list of some of the least expensive islands:

- **Grand Turk,** Turks and Caicos Islands. Although there are some very comfortable low-rise hotels on the island, it never benefited from the spectacular amount of money that was spent on the development of Provo. Rooms usually cost around $110 or less per night, and evening meals range from $15 to $25 each.

- **Eleuthera.** Because of this island's changing fortunes, hotel-and-restaurant tabs are likely to be competitive. Most accommodations are not luxurious, but you might overlook this if costs are a serious consideration. If you're looking for family-style lodging, you might opt for any of the simple guest houses that line the island's long and narrow shores. Among these are Edwina's Place at Rock Sound, Hilton's Haven Motel and Restaurant at Tarpum Bay, and the Cigatoo Inn at Governor's Harbour.

- **Andros.** It's the largest, least-frequently explored, and most mysterious island in the Bahamas. About a half-dozen hamlets line its edges, each of which offers very simple accommodations. Food is about as basic as you'll get anywhere, and often only Bahamian regional items are available. But if you're willing to go through the inconvenience of getting there, and if all you're looking for is a beach and some palm trees, Andros is about as cost conscious as you'll ever get.

- **Exumas.** The entire chain contains only about 3,800 residents, many of whom grow onions or fish for a living. Unless you charter a boat to take you to some of the chain's 365 isolated cays (which is an expensive proposition), you'll probably spend your time on one of the Exumas' three or four larger islands. George Town in particular (the largest town in the Exumas) offers several opportunities for cost-conscious vacations.

- **Cat Island,** the Southern Bahamas. The local populace makes its living by farming and fishing. Hotels are anything but glamorous. And costs are proportionately low. Although Cat Island is the sixth-largest island in the Bahamas, it's undeveloped, underpopulated, and lined with beautiful white-sand beaches.

## 11 The Best Dive Sites

Scuba diving is a year-round undertaking in the Bahamas, where shallow, sunlit seas and thousands of reefs are packed with underwater life. All of the major islands offer diving excursions, lessons, and equipment rentals. Intermediate and advanced divers can participate in night dives.

- **Andros.** The barrier reef off the coast of Andros, the third largest in the world, is a famous destination for scuba enthusiasts. Marine life abounds.

- **Bimini.** Although most outsiders appreciate Bimini for its game-fishing options, its charms are increasingly obvious to scuba divers, too. Its allure includes the wreck of a motorized yacht, the *Sapona* (owned by Henry Ford), which sank in shallow waters off the coast of Bimini in 1929. Three miles of offshore reefs attract millions of fish.

- **Eleuthera.** This island contains all the underwater coral and fish a diver would expect, as well as handful of bizarre underwater experiences like the "Current Cut," an exciting underwater gulley that carries divers for a 10-minute ride on a swiftly flowing underwater current. (A boat usually retrieves divers at the end.) There are also four wrecked ships that lie in less than 40 feet of water. The most unusual of these contains the engine of a steam locomotive that was being transported on a barge in 1865, reportedly after being sold by the American Confederacy to raise cash for their war effort.

- **Grand Bahama Island.** The island is ringed with reefs, and dive sites are plentiful. What makes the island a cut above many others is the presence of a world-class dive operator, UNEXSO (Underwater Explorer's Society), whose teaching methods are well regarded.

- **Long Island,** the Southern Bahamas. Shallow-water snorkeling is considered spectacular on virtually all sides of the island, and in deeper waters offshore, teams of experienced divers make regular excursions in underwater cages to feed swarms of mako, bull, and reef sharks. Dive sites abound.

- **New Providence.** Many ships have sunk near Nassau in the past 300 years; the numerous wrecks are well-known to the dive outfitters here. Other attractions are underwater gardens of elk-horn coral and dozens of reefs teeming with underwater life.

- **San Salvador,** the Southern Bahamas. Ironically, the life teeming below the seas surrounding this isolated island is more robust than the dry, salty soil of the island's surface. There are nearly 80 well-known dive sites here, most on the leeward side of the island where the waves are usually the least powerful. The island's largest resort (Club Med) offers a complete array of dive facilities, including a much-valued decompression chamber.

- **Turks and Caicos Islands.** This cluster of islands contains a rich assortment of underwater sites, including sea lanes where boaters and divers often sight whales during April. There's also a collection of unusual underwater wrecks (such as the HMS *Endymion*, which sank during a storm in 1790), and many miles of reefs with every kind of marine life. Off Grand Turk, divers appreciate the many miles of "drop-off" diving, where the sea walls descend rapidly to the uncharted depths known as blue holes. The dive sites here are relatively unexplored.

## 12  The Best Snorkeling

The Bahamas is among the top places in the world for snorkeling. Even the tiniest hotel is likely to have equipment on hand. The snorkeling excursions of the following islands tend to be better organized and more frequent than those at islands with fewer tourists. Keep in mind, though, that such outlying islands as Eleuthera and the Abacos offer a wealth of snorkeling options as well.

- **New Providence/Paradise Island.** The waters that ring this densely populated island are among the most frequently explored in the Bahamas. The action is usually centered around the Rose Island Reefs, a series of well-known underwater wrecks, Gambier Deep Reef, Booby Rock Channel, and the Goulding Reef Cays. Virtually every resort hotel on the island offers equipment, often with a motorboat ride to the site.

- **Grand Bahama Island.** There are boats departing from hotel piers at frequent intervals for supervised snorkeling excursions around the island. There are miniflotillas, including glass-bottomed boats; sailboats offering free use of snorkeling equipment; and yachts with everything from dinner cruises to snorkeling junkets. The island is also home to UNEXSO, a scientific research group that dispenses advice to many dive-boat operations about the island's snorkeling sites. Great dive sites around Grand Bahama Island include the Wall, the Caves, the site of a long-ago marine disaster known as Theo's Wreck, and Treasure Reef.

## 13  The Best Golf Courses

Some of the world's most famous golf architects, including Robert Trent Jones, Sr., and Dick Wilson, have designed challenging courses.

- **Paradise Island Golf Club,** Paradise Island. Eighteen holes, par 72, a design by Dick Wilson, and easy access to the gaming casinos, bars, and restaurants of one of the country's biggest casino complexes are the distinguishing features of this golf course.
- **South Ocean Golf & Beach Resort,** Nassau. Set on the underpopulated south-western side of the island, it's so isolated from the congested sections of Nassau that golfers can imagine themselves on a remote island. The terrain is hilly and dotted with palm trees. This course is considered more challenging than its competitor on Paradise Island.
- **Bahama Princess and Golf Club,** Grand Bahama Island. This megaresort offers two different golf courses (the Princess Ruby and the Princess Emerald), both of which are par 72. Terrain is rolling and sandy, a welcome relief from the glitter and asphalt-covered boulevards that flank them.
- **Fortune Hills Golf & Country Club,** Grand Bahama Island. This course at Richmond Park has only nine holes (and a par-36 rating), but it nonetheless does a brisk business. On the premises is a bar, a restaurant, and a pro shop.
- **Lucayan Park Golf & Country Club,** Grand Bahama Island. Part of the Lucayan Beach casino-and-restaurant complex, this golf course provides an escape from the congested regions of Lucaya and Freeport.
- **Cable Beach Golf Club,** New Providence. Set on the low hills of north-central New Providence, this is the oldest golf course on the Bahamas. It was once the private retreat of British expatriates in the 1930s. Today, it's owned by the same folks who market the vast casino complexes of Cable Beach and managed by a corporate namesake of Arnold Palmer. It features a series of small ponds and water traps, a par-72 degree of difficulty, and more than 7,000 yards of well-maintained greens and fairways.
- **Provo Golf Club,** Turks and Caicos Islands. Its arrival on the arid surface of Provo is considered a major feat of landscape architecture. The design features a desert-inspired mixture of limestone and sand interspersed with greenery and relatively narrow fairways. The course is categorized as a challenging par 72.

## 14  The Best Tennis Facilities

Tennis is a popular sport in the Bahamas. The preferred hours of play tend to be early in the morning and in the evening, when it's cooler. If tennis is your passion, consider any of the resorts listed below. And when you're booking your holiday, ask about a "tennis package," which some resorts offer; it usually includes rooms and often meals at discounted rates.

- **Nassau/Paradise Island,** New Providence. New Providence has at least 80 tennis courts, and Paradise Island has about 30 of its own. If your hotel doesn't have courts of its own (which is unlikely), the desk personnel will probably be well-informed about where you can turn for a volley or two. Both islands pride themselves on the various tennis tournaments that are held here at regular intervals. There's sometimes a small fee imposed for illuminating a court for night play.

- **Grand Bahama Island.** Scattered among the various resorts of this tourist mecca are at least 20 different courts. Even if you're not registered at one of the hotels that maintain them, you'll usually be able to play for between $5 and $10 per hour. Many are illuminated for night play.
- **The Abacos.** There's more to do in the Abacos than sail. Scattered among the cays and the Abaco "mainland" are about a dozen tennis courts, which are usually maintained by various hotels.
- **Eleuthera.** This long, skinny island contains about 20 tennis courts, all set in the grounds of various hotels. Some are illuminated for night play, and most welcome nonresidents onto their premises to use the courts for a fee if they aren't otherwise occupied.
- **Provo,** Turks and Caicos Islands. Provo has approximately 20 tennis courts. Many of these are on the grounds of island hotels. The island places a heavy emphasis on tennis as a diversion for its residents and visitors.

## 15  The Best Hiking

For anyone interested in active vacations, the islands present some exciting prospects for hiking expeditions.

- **San Salvador,** the Southern Bahamas. The best way to appreciate the charms of this small island (where Columbus first landed in the New World) is with a handful of walking tours. Highlights include a series of brackish inland lakes, the ghostly ruins of an 18th-century plantation house (Watling's Castle), white crosses commemorating the arrival on the island of Christopher Columbus in 1492, a lighthouse built in 1856 (which is still entirely hand operated), and pristine panoramas loaded with bird-and-marine life. During your hikes, consider bringing your snorkeling equipment for spontaneous swimming en route. Also, one of the island's best observation platforms is a lookout tower that lies about a half mile east of the Riding Rock Inn, near the airport on the island's western coast.
- **Lucayan National Park,** Grand Bahama Island. The 40-acre Lucayan National Park offers visitors a view of undisturbed nature that is very far removed from the casinos and cabaret shows. It lies about 25 miles east of Freeport beside the island's main east-to-west traffic artery. The landscape is mostly covered with stunted pines and gnarled palmettos, except for a grove of more verdant trees at the entrance to each of the park's caves. The largest cave contains spiral staircases that lead visitors down into a freshwater world inhabited by shrimp, mosquito fish, fruit bats, freshwater eels, and a species of crustacean (*Spelionectes lucayensis*) that has never been found anywhere else in the world. A series of paths in the park lead to various flora and fauna, including rare varieties of orchids, sea turtles, hummingbirds, and barn owls.

## 16  The Best Fishing

The Bahamas are probably the best-known sportfishing region in the world—the waters abound with barracuda, tuna, amberjack, bonefish, wahoo, marlin, tarpon, and kingfish.

- **Bimini.** All kinds of fish seem to flourish in the deep waters around Bimini, but the most sought-after trophy is the marlin, whose image appears on the $100 Bahamian bill. As many as 40 annual fishing tournaments are held every year in the Bahamas, many of which transform Bimini into a mini–Olympic village where fish are hunted by a daunting armada of well-equipped fishing boats. Bimini was novelist Ernest Hemingway's favorite place to fish.
- **Andros.** The fishing is good everywhere in the Bahamas, but bonefish seem to thrive in the shallow, sunlit waters off Andros Island. It isn't the best tasting fish in the islands (it's mostly cartilage and bones), but aficionados say that it puts up one of the strongest fights of any fish in the world.

## 17  The Best Sailing

Most large hotels in the Bahamas will have small sailboats (especially Sunfish, Sail-fish, and small, one-masted catamarans) available for their guests. Windsurfers are also widely available.

- **The Exumas.** The Exumas are the setting for the famed April Family Island Regatta, the most attended sailing event in the Bahamas. In winter, Elizabeth Harbour is a mecca for yachties who explore the deserted islands and cays nearby, along with secluded bays, safe anchorage harbors, and secret coves. Even in winter, unless the weather turns unexpectedly bad (and usually foul weather days are short lived), the seas are balmy, the temperatures ideal. Clear skies and smooth waters make for ideal sailing conditions. Yacht magazines praise the Exumas for having the finest cruising areas in the Bahamas. Most marine supply facilities are in George Town, the capital. All of them, including Exuma Docking Services (☎ **809/336-2578**), are located at the marina.
- **The Abacos.** Vying with the Exumas as the most perfect sailing area not only in the Bahamas but in the world, the Abacos are known among yachties for their many anchorages, sheltered coves, and plentiful marine facilities. Sailing traditions in the Abacos date from the 18th century. Boats in all shapes and sizes can be chartered for a week or longer, with or without a crew. Major charter centers are found at Marsh Harbour and Hope Town. Make arrangements for rentals with Abaco Bahamas Charters (☎ toll free **800/626-5690**) in Hope Town, or the Bahamas Yachting Service (☎ **305/484-5246,** or toll free **800/327-2276**) in Marsh Harbour.

## 18  The Best Offbeat Experiences

If you'd like to do something unusual, consider any of the adventures listed below.

- **Sea Kayaking,** the Exumas. A modern sea kayak is a folding boat so small that a passenger can experience the movement of the sea at very close range. Since 1976, several tour operators have led kayak expeditions around the 365 islands and cays of the Exumas. Some tours feature a week of kayaking and camping on the remote islands of the Exumas. For more information, contact Ecosummer Expeditions, 1516 Duranleau St., Vancouver, B.C., Canada V6H 3S4. ☎ toll free **800/688-8605.**
- **Marooned on Bowe Cay,** the Exumas. Sandy, scrub-covered Bowe Cay, which has no residents, is set offshore from Great Exuma Island. Visitors fly to George

Town, then climb into a powerboat for a 45-minute ride to a shed-roofed, screened-in cabana (built in the early 1990s, it's the only structure on the island). You'll find the barest of worldly necessities; these include solar panels that power the lights, a stereo, and a freezer. There's also fishing gear, a gas-powered grill, and a two-way radio for emergencies. With the boat transfer from Great Exuma included, Bowe Cay rents for about $1,500 per week for two occupants. If you want to bring a group, the owners can provide tents for up to eight visitors, but the rustic charms of the 200-acre island are best appreciated by two. For information, call toll free **800/992-0128.**

- **Mail Boats to the Out Islands.** The Bahamas hires about 30 different mail boats, which service at least 17 very remote islands. Itineraries depend on the priorities of the captain and crew, and are affected by the weather. The mail boats make a real difference in the quality of life for the scattered communities of the archipelago, especially since the mail will accompany deliveries of goats, chickens, hardware, and food staples. Nassau is the embarkation point for every boat in the network. Passage from Nassau to, say, Governor's Harbour on Eleuthera costs about $25 each way, and takes about a full day. If you're committed to roughing it, you might be able to commandeer a mattress onboard, depending on the facilities in each of these privately owned boats. For more information, call the Bahamas Tourist Office at **800/422-4262** or the dockmaster at the Nassau piers at **809/393-1064** for current schedules of mail-boat departures. This is an adventure for someone with no expectations of luxury and lots of time to spend dealing with local (and sometimes bizarre) bureaucracies.

- **Visiting a Loyalist Town.** There are about a half dozen of them scattered throughout the Bahamian archipelago, each founded under difficult circumstances by disgruntled British colonists who did not regard the independence of the United States as a joyful event. Clapboard-sided houses resemble the saltbox cottages of New England, bougainvillea climbs up porch trellises, and the social fabric is intertwined with the sea. Life is gentle, detached from the outside world, and rather charmingly old-fashioned. Many visitors appreciate the Loyalist towns even more after the touristic frenzy of Nassau or Freeport. Suitable choices would include Harbour Island, Spanish Wells, George Town, or Marsh Harbour/Green Turtle Cay.

- **Diving the Wall off Grand Turk,** Turks and Caicos Islands. Some divers have compared this experience to jumping off a clifftop in the Swiss Alps. This is considered one of the most unusual experiences in the world of scuba. It occurs underwater, in a position only 300 yards from the shoreline of Grand Turk, where waters suddenly drop to uncharted depths of more than 7,000 feet below sea level. Only experienced divers should attempt this. Along the descent, one observes colonies of black coral, rare forms of anemone, purple sponges, rare gorgonia, endless forms of coral, and thousands of fish, the species of which change as one descends.

# Getting to Know
## the Bahamas

**A**fter George Washington visited the Bahama Islands, he wrote that they were the "Isles of Perpetual June"; I can't think of a better description.

Today the 760-mile-long chain of islands, cays, and reefs collectively called the Bahamas is designated by many as the playground of the Western world. The chain stretches from Grand Bahama Island, whose western point is almost due east of Palm Beach, Florida, about 75 miles away, to Great Inagua, southernmost of the Bahamas, lying some 60 miles northeast of Cuba and less than 100 miles north of Haiti. (The self-proclaimed Haitian king, Henri Christophe, is believed to have built a summer palace here in the early 19th century.)

There are 700 of these islands, many of which bear the name *cay*, pronounced *key*. (*Cay* is the Spanish word for small island.) Some, such as Andros, Grand Bahama, Great Abaco, Eleuthera, Cat Island, and Long Island, are fairly large, while others are tiny enough to seem crowded if more than two persons visit at a time.

## 1 Islands in Brief

**THE ABACO ISLANDS**    This long, arching archipelago attracted revolutionary war Loyalists in the 18th century, who settled at Hope Town and New Plymouth. After the failure of their farms, the Loyalists became formidable shipbuilders.

Never more than 15 miles long at their widest point, the Abacos extend for about 130 miles. They include such large islands as Great Abaco and Little Abaco (which are known collectively as the chain's "mainland") and a string of other islets and cays. Green Turtle Cay is one of the most attractive centers for tourism in the Bahamas, and Great Guana Cay is the longest of the Abaco's many islands. Marsh Harbour, on the Abaco "mainland," is the third-largest town in the Bahamas, with an estimated population of 3,500.

Although most North American urbanites would consider the Abacos as small-town fare, the islands shelter 10,000 year-round residents, making it one of the largest population centers of the Atlantic islands. Beaches and coves are suitably scenic, and the island's inland areas are thickly forested with pine.

# The Bahamas

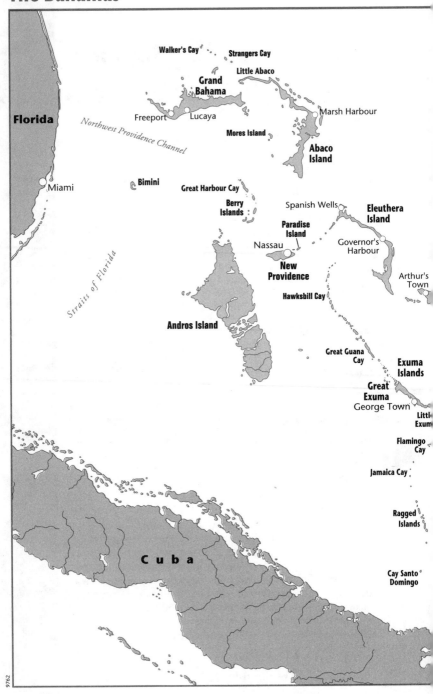

Walker's Cay

Strangers Cay

Little Abaco

**Grand Bahama**

Freeport  Lucaya  Marsh Harbour

Florida

Northwest Providence Channel

Mores Island

**Abaco Island**

Miami  Bimini

Great Harbour Cay

**Berry Islands**

Spanish Wells  **Eleuthera Island**

**Paradise Island**

Nassau  Governor's Harbour

**New Providence**

Arthur's Town

Straits of Florida

Hawksbill Cay

**Andros Island**

Great Guana Cay  **Exuma Islands**

**Great Exuma**

George Town  Little Exuma

Flamingo Cay

Jamaica Cay

**Ragged Islands**

**C u b a**

Cay Santo Domingo

9762

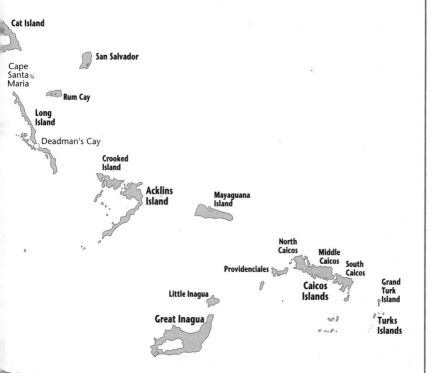

*Atlantic*

*Ocean*

**Cat Island**

**San Salvador**

Cape
Santa
Maria

**Rum Cay**

**Long
Island**

Deadman's Cay

**Crooked
Island**

**Acklins
Island**

**Mayaguana
Island**

**North
Caicos**

**Middle
Caicos**

**South
Caicos**

Providenciales

**Grand
Turk
Island**

**Caicos
Islands**

**Little Inagua**

**Great Inagua**

**Turks
Islands**

**ACKLINS ISLAND & CROOKED ISLAND**   What's most surprising about them is their large size (190 square miles) and their low population density. Both islands are home to a mere 1,000 souls. They lie in the remote southern hinterlands of the Bahamas, closer to Cuba than Florida. Columbus wrote in 1493 of the rich aromas that wafted toward his ships, and consequently dubbed them the "Fragrant Islands." Despite their imagined fertility, all of the plantations established by 18th-century British loyalists went bankrupt. Today, most of the island's populace makes its living from the sea and, to a very limited extent, tourism.

One noteworthy (and fragrant) export is the pungent bark of the cascarilla tree, which is used in medicines and as a flavoring for liqueurs. Waters offshore are very clear, with good snorkeling and a worthy assortment of beaches.

**ANDROS**   It's the largest island in the Bahamian chain. Most of its surface is composed of mangrove marshes. Bahamians refer to these marshes as the "Mud" and to the island's dense groves of pine and mahogany as the "Yard." Some portions of its interior have never been explored. Divers and snorkelers appreciate the enormous coral reef (third largest in the world) that flanks the island's eastern shore. The interior boasts many species of unusual birds and orchids.

A handful of settlements (whose total population numbers around 8,000) lie scattered around Andros's coast (Congo Town, Nicholl's Town, Cargill Creek, and Andros Town), but overall, the island is unpopulated. Considering its proximity to South Florida, many visitors find this astonishing.

**BERRY ISLANDS**   Lying between Nassau and the coast of Florida, these islands comprise only about 30 square miles of land. They're composed of about 30 islets and cays and rows of barely submerged rocks. The chain contains only a few hotels and restaurants, and there's a full-time population of only about 500 people. Most of them live on the largest island, Great Harbour, which measures only 6 by $2^1/2$ miles.

**BIMINI**   It's one of the smallest islands in the Bahamas, and lies close enough to Miami (just 50 miles away) to be distinctly separate from the other islands of the archipelago. It's divided into two islands, whose area totals 9 square miles. The smaller of these, North Bimini, is better developed than South Bimini. Throughout Bimini, there's a slightly rundown Florida-resort type of atmosphere mingled with some small-town charm. The yachts and fishing boats, which dock at the island's marinas, are among the most luxurious in the Western Hemisphere.

**CAT ISLAND**   With an eel-like shape, Cat Island is only a few miles wide and 48 miles long. It's one of the most fertile of the Bahamian islands, a fact that permits much of its populace to grow pineapples and tomatoes for a living. Only one road interconnects the villages that dot the island's surface. Largest of these villages is Arthur's Town, a sunflooded cluster of clapboard- and cement-sided buildings that seem to slumber in the salty air.

**EAST CAICOS**   Part of the Caicos archipelago, this island is almost completely uninhabited, with a uniformly low elevation above the sea and a landscape of scrubs and stunted trees. Birds, reptiles, and marine life find it rewarding. Head here only if you have sufficent food and water and love roughing it.

**ELEUTHERA**   Long and slender, this is probably the most historic of the Family Islands. A string of satellite islands, including Spanish Wells and Harbour Island, lie off its coast. The long length of the island, and the long distances between the island's communities, require access via three different airports (Rock South, Governor's Harbour, and North Eleuthera). With a colonized history dating back to the arrival of the first English settlers in 1648, Eleuthera is one of the most interesting islands in the country. Its name derives from the Greek word for freedom.

**THE EXUMAS**   Set in the middle of the Bahamas, the 365 islands of the Exumas form a long string. Most of them are uninhabited, but the largest (Great Exuma Island) is home to about 3,000 people. The chain's largest town is George Town, with around 1,000 inhabitants and a lively (sometimes raucous) nightlife. Today, fishing and tourism are the most visible means of support for local residents. Opportunities for sailing, fishing, and snorkeling are bountiful in the waters that ring the Exumas, and the scrub- and pine-covered surfaces of the tiny islands are among the region's most unspoiled terrain.

**GRAND BAHAMA ISLAND**   Until the hotel developments of the 1950s, Grand Bahama Island was sparsely populated. The name derives from the Spanish term *gran bajamar* ("great shallows"), which refers to the shallow reefs and sandbars that have, over the centuries, destroyed everything from Spanish galleons to English clipper ships. (Although many of their onboard treasures were pillaged, those in deeper waters are still being found.) Thanks to the tourist development schemes of such U.S. financiers as Howard Hughes, Grand Bahama boasts one of the most industrialized economies and one of the best-developed tourist infrastructures of any island in the Bahamas. It has experienced a more rapid population growth since the 1960s than any other island of the Bahamas. Casinos, beaches, and restaurants are plentiful. Visitors can escape the island's towns and head across casuarina-dotted scrublands to explore the island's isolated western end.

**GRAND TURK**   Grand Turk is the farthest island from Florida. Ringed with abundant marine life, it totals 9 square miles and houses 4,000 residents. Most of the island's surface is flat, rocky, and dry. Donkeys and cattle often graze beside the rutted roads that crisscross the island. The atmosphere is that of a small town, despite the presence of Cockburn Town, the capital of Turks and Caicos.

**INAGUA ISLAND**   Set very close to the eastern tip of Cuba, Inagua is the most southerly island of the Bahamas and the third largest in the nation.

Its scrub-dotted flatlands are baked white by the sun and the high salt content of the soil. Most of the population of around 1,200 people make their living harvesting salt from marsh areas. Pink flamingos thrive here. A handful of simple, no-frill inns provide overnight accommodations.

**LONG ISLAND**   Named for its length, this island is 58 miles long. Despite a promising early start (Columbus told the queen of Spain that it was the most beautiful island he'd ever seen), it languishes today in comparative obscurity. Most of its populace of 4,500 people earns a living building boats, fishing, farming, and conducting diving excursions to its spectacular offshore reefs. With only about 90 hotel rooms available on the entire island, Long Island remains undeveloped and inconvenient to reach. It's a haven for rugged travelers from as far away as Europe.

**MAYAGUANA ISLAND**   Located between the Bahamian islands and the Caicos, Mayaguana has 110 square miles of land, but only about 600 residents. This combination guarantees long panoramas of scrubland, whose hardy, salt-resistant plants thrive despite the high temperatures that are the norm here throughout the spring, summer, and early autumn. The island's largest settlement is a weather-beaten hamlet on the island's south coast (Abraham's Bay), which is rarely visited except by mariners. Mayaguana is sometimes a stopover for yachts from Miami headed south.

**MIDDLE (GRAND) CAICOS**    This is the largest (48 square miles) island of the Turks and Caicos, although, ironically, it's home to only about 300 people. Few of the attempts to colonize this place were ever successful, although archaeologists are usually absorbed in the artifacts that remain from long-ago-vanished Lucayan Indians, marooned sailors, and stranded slaves. Large sections of the island are marshland favored by aquatic birds and reptiles. Geologists appreciate the island's eerie collection of caves.

**NEW PROVIDENCE/NASSAU/CABLE BEACH**    It isn't the largest of the Bahamian Islands, yet New Providence is the historic core of the Bahamian nation, with a strong maritime tradition and the largest population of any island in the country. Home to about 125,000 residents, it offers groves of pines and casuarinas; sandy, flat soil; the closest thing in the Bahamas to urban sprawl; and superb anchorages, which are sheltered from rough seas by Paradise Island. New Providence contains the country's busiest airport, hundreds of villas owned by foreign investors, and two concentrations of resort development—Cable Beach and Nassau. On the islands northern coast, both are loaded with hotels and recreational diversions.

**NORTH CAICOS**    Only a narrow saltwater channel separates it from the previously described Middle Caicos. Large, flat, and dotted with mangrove swamps and thriving vegetation, it offers good beaches and excellent bonefishing for the hardy souls who brave the inconvenience of getting there. Only about 1,200 people, scattered amid a quartet of sunbaked villages, make this island their home. Large sections of the island are protected as nature reserves.

**PARADISE ISLAND**    It has one of the most colorful histories, and some of the least interesting architecture, of any resort island in the world. Elongated and narrow, its sands and shoals form a seawall for the wharves and piers of Nassau (New Providence Island), which rise across a narrow channel only 600 feet away. Inch for inch, it's probably the most intensely marketed piece of real estate in the world.

Owners of the 685-acre island have included brokerage mogul Joseph Lynch (of Merrill Lynch) and Huntington Hartford, heir to the A&P supermarket fortune. More recent investors have included Merv Griffin. After a merry-go-round of ownership changes, the island is today a carefully landscaped residential/commercial complex with good beaches, lots of glitter, and many diversions. All of these cater to a clientele from around the world, many of whom devote part of each day to the casinos.

**PINE CAY**    Pine Cay is the largest and most visible of the cays that stretch between North Caicos and Provo. Sparsely inhabited, with 800 acres and only about 35 carefully planned private homes under the administration of the Meridien Club, it's the relaxed but expensive enclave of European and North American investors. The island has its own landing strip, its own electrical generators, some remarkably good architecture, and sweeping stretches of beach. Reminders of bygone eras include ruins of Loyalist plantations built in the 18th century and petroglyphs carved by stranded sailors. The landscape is rocky, relatively flat, and arid.

**PROVO (PROVIDENCIALES)**    Its fine beaches and undeveloped coastline were a tourist development waiting to happen. In the late 1970s, such hotel megaliths as Club Med poured money into increasingly popular low-rise ecoconscious resorts. One of the larger islands of the Turks and Caicos, Provo is green but arid, with miles of scrubland and stunted trees covering the island's low, undulating hillsides. The population of Provo has grown in the last decade to around 6,000 persons, many of whom work in the tourist industry. Their differing nationalities (French, Canadian, German, American, and British) compose one of the most multinational communities in the archipelago.

**SALT CAY**  For years most of its income derived from salt harvested from the sunbaked flats on the island's coast. With only 3¹/₂ miles of surface, and very fine beaches, it has experienced a recent influx of mariners and hotel owners. Salt Cay lies 9 miles southwest of Grand Turk; in recent years it has developed a corps of devotees. The most famous resort on the island is the Windmills at Salt Cay; others on the island are atmospheric but somewhat scruffy.

**SAN SALVADOR**  Current scholarship believes this island was the first landmass Columbus reached during his voyage to the New World in 1492. Rising to heights of 140 feet above sea level, the island boasts fine beaches, a scrub-covered landscape dotted with lakes containing both fresh and brackish water, and a landmass that measures 6 by 12 miles. Its height has always made it a useful navigational aid for mariners negotiating local sea lanes, and for several decades, lighthouses have been maintained to assist them. A single badly rutted road skirts the island's 35-mile perimeter. Only 500 residents lived here before several new hotels were built (including a Club Med), but with its new-found fame and good beaches, the island will probably undergo further development.

**SOUTH CAICOS**  The reefs that surround it are treacherous, although Cockburn Town (the island's only port) is considered by yachters to have the best and largest natural harbor in the Turks and Caicos. Small fishing craft are used to explore and fish in the island's dozens of jagged coves. There aren't many acceptable hotels here, and only about 1,400 residents (clustered around Cockburn Town) occupy this 8¹/₂ mile long island. Much of the interior is scrubland and marshes, with lots of reptiles and birds. The island's airport accepts short-haul

---

### ❷ Did You Know?

- Although disputed by some historians, Christopher Columbus made his first footprints in the New World on the Bahamian island of San Salvador, 200 miles southeast of Nassau.

- Following in the footsteps of Columbus, Ponce de León arrived in the Bahamas searching for the legendary Fountain of Youth, which led to the discovery of Florida and the Gulf Stream.

- The Bahamians once earned a comfortable living bootlegging liquor to the United States during the Prohibition era.

- In 1856, about half of the able-bodied men of the colony lived off the shipwrecking industry.

- In 1940, the duke of Windsor (formerly King Edward VIII) arrived in Nassau to rule an impoverished colony of 65,000 people after briefly presiding over an empire numbering hundreds of millions.

flights (and many privately owned aircraft) from Florida, the Turks and Caicos, and the Bahamas. The beaches of South Caicos are small and unremarkable. Its offshore reef, however, makes the island a worthy goal for divers.

## 2  Junkanoo & Folklore

No descendants of the early inhabitants of the Bahamas, the Lucayans (Arawak Indians), survive. A few of today's Bahamians can trace their ancestry back to the Eleutherian Adventurers, others to Loyalists of American Revolution times and to southern Americans who fled after the Civil War, all of whom brought slaves to the islands. Some Bahamians of today can claim descent from pirates and privateers. Of the overall population of some 200,000 people, African-Bahamians are in the great majority and hold positions of leadership in all areas.

The language of the Bahamas is English. Bahamians speak it with a lilt and with more British Isles influence than American. There are some words left from the Arawak Indian tongue (like *cassava* and *guava*), and African words and phrases add to the colorful speech patterns.

When examining the social life of the Bahamas, it's important to note the broad differences between life in Nassau and Freeport and the less frenetic life in the Out Islands. The Out Islands are to the Bahamas what the remote and rural countryside is to other countries.

### JUNKANOO

No Bahamian celebration is as extroverted as the Junkanoo, the special rituals originated during the colonial days of slavery, when African-born newcomers could legally drink and enjoy themselves only on strictly predefined days of the year. As celebrated in the Bahamas, Junkanoo is a close relative of Carnival in Rio and Mardi Gras in New Orleans. Its major difference lies in the ornamentation of the costumes and the timing: Junkanoo reaches its apex the day after Christmas, a reminder of the medieval English celebration of Boxing Day on December 26.

The costumes of the Junkanoo in olden days were crafted from crepe paper, often in primary colors, stretched over wire frames. One sinister offshoot to the celebrations was that the Junkanoo costumes and masks were used to conceal the identity of anyone seeking vengeance on a white or on another slave. Although funds for Junkanoo festivals are more plentiful now than before, the finest costumes can cost up to $10,000, and are sometimes sponsored by local bazaars, lotteries, and charity auctions. More prevalent, however, are the vibrant colors and costumes worn by everyday revelers, whose sensual and humorous participation in the Junkanoo is one of the high points of the Bahamian calendar.

### FOLKLORE

Many different factors contributed to the formation of a potent and vital body of myth within the Bahamas. Among the strongest factors were the nation's unusual geography, its noteworthy history, and the often turbulent mingling of cultures. Some tales are a mélange from about a half-dozen different oral traditions, including those of England, Africa, France, and neighboring islands of the Caribbean. Storytelling is a fine art, with a tradition that remains the strongest on the Family Islands, where television (and electricity) were introduced only a few years ago.

Obeah, which has been defined as a mixture of European superstitions, African (especially Yoruban) religion, and Judeo-Christian beliefs, retains similarities to the voodoo of Haiti, the Santeria of Cuba and Brazil, and the Shango of Trinidad. Steeped in the mythic traditions of West Africa, it has held an increased importance for Bahamians as a part of their national heritage.

An obeah practitioner may chant, sing, or "go into a trance" to communicate with another dimension of reality. The most common method of obeah practice in the Bahamas today involves "fixing" a person with a spell, which can be "cleared" either by another obeah practitioner or by a formal medical doctor. Much more serious is to be "cursed" by an obeah master, the effect of which can be lifted only by that same person. Magic is divided into black and white spheres, with white magic being the more potent and the less evil.

Ghosts or spirits are known as "sperrids," and necromancy—the habit of soliciting communications from the dead—is a ritualistic form of obeah used to get information that can be used either for good or for evil. According to tradition, the sperrids dwell in the fluffy tops of the silk cotton trees that are widespread throughout the Bahamas. This belief is probably imported from African traditions, where many tribes worship the cotton tree as the abode of the spirits of the dead. Although sperrids wander at will throughout the earth, causing mischief and unhappiness wherever they go, only the obeah man or woman can channel their power.

On some islands (including remote Cat Island), residents believed that a "working witch" could be hired to perform tasks. The most common form of a witch was that of a cat, rabbit, snake, or rat. Folk tales abound with stories referring to the mythical powers of these witch-animals. Especially fearsome was any short, fat snake with a ribbon tied around it, a sure sign that the reptile was actually a witch in disguise.

# 3  Architecture & the Arts

## ARCHITECTURE

The unique geography and history of the Bahamas contributed to a distinctive architectural style (the Bahamian clapboard house) that is today one of the most broadly copied in the tropics. Ironically, it wasn't until the early 19th century that this design began to become perfected and standardized.

The earliest clapboard-sided houses were usually angled to receive the trade winds. Large window openings and high ceilings increased airflow, while awning-style push-out shutters shaded the windows and helped direct breezes indoors even during rainstorms. Unlike larger and more impressive houses, where foundations were massive edifices of coral, brick, or stone, the first floors of Bahamian cottages were elevated on low stilts or light masonry pilings to further allow air to circulate. Raising the building also kept the floor joists, beams, and planking above floodwaters during a hurricane surge.

Ruggedly built of timbers whose ends were often pegged (not nailed) together, and pinned to stone pilings several feet above the ground, Bahamian-style clapboard houses have survived when many rigid and unyielding stone-built structures collapsed during hurricanes. Modern engineers claim that the flexibility of these structures increases their stability in high winds.

Within the Bahamas, some of the best-preserved and most charming examples of the Bahamian cottage style can be found in Harbour Island, off the coast of Eleuthera, and to a lesser extent, Spanish Wells and Green Turtle Cay.

# MUSIC

The Bahamas maintains great pride in its original musical idioms, often comparing their vitality to the more famous musical traditions of Jamaica, Puerto Rico, and Trinidad. Other than the spirituals whose roots were shared by slaves in colonial North America, by far the most famous musical products of the archipelago are Goombay and its closely linked sibling, Junkanoo.

**GOOMBAY**   Goombay music is an art form whose melodies and body movements are always accompanied by the beat of goatskin drums and, when available, the liberal consumption of rum. Goombay is a musical combination of Africa's tribal heritage (especially that of the Egungun sect of the Yoruba tribe) mingled with the Native American and British colonial influences of the New World. Although its appeal quickly spread to such other islands as Bermuda, it is within the Bahamas where the traditions of Goombay remain the strongest.

The most outlandish moments of the Goombay world occur the day following Christmas (Boxing Day). Dancers outfit themselves in masquerade costumes whose bizarre accessories and glittering colors evoke the plumage of jungle birds. Once dismissed by the British colonials as the pastime of hooligans, Goombay is now the most widespread and broad-based celebratory motif in the Bahamas, richly encouraged by the island's political and business elite. Goombay musicians and dancers are almost always male, enjoying a tradition whereby men and boys from the same family pass on the rhythms and dance techniques from generation to generation. Goombay signifies at the same time the Bantu word for "rhythm" as well as a specific type of African drum.

Today, Goombay has a gentle, rolling rhythm, a melody produced either by a piano, a guitar, or a saxophone, and the enthusiastic inclusion of bongos, maracas, and rhythm ("click") sticks. Lyrics, unlike the words that accompany reggae, are rarely politicized, dealing instead with topics that might have been referred to in another day as "saucy." Later, the sounds of Goombay would be commercialized and adapted into the louder and more strident musical form known as Junkanoo.

**JUNKANOO**   Until the 1940s, Junkanoo referred almost exclusively to the yuletide procession where elaborate costumes were paraded down the main streets of towns accompanied solely by percussion music. (During the days of slavery, Christmas was the most important of the four annual holidays granted to slaves, and the one that merited the most exuberant celebrations.) The rhythms of Junkanoo, understandably, soon became hypnotic, growing with the enthusiasm of the spectators and the uninhibited movements of the dancers. Essential to the tradition were the use of traditional goatskin drums, cowbells, and whistles. Theories differ as to the origins of Junkanoo's name, but possible explanations include a derivation from the Creole patois of neighboring Haiti's *gens inconnus,* translated as "unknown persons" because of the masks worn by the dancers.

## Impressions

*Look from your door, and tell me now*
*The colour of the sea.*
*Where can I buy that wondrous dye*
*And take it home with me?*
                    —Bliss Carman, a 19th-century poet who visited the Bahamas

Around World War II, a series of Bahamian musicians fleshed out the percussion rhythms of the yuletide Junkanoo parade with the use of piano, electric bass, and guitar. This sparked the beginning of its development into what is today the most prevalent musical form in the Bahamas.

## LITERATURE

The greatest literary figure inspired by the Bahamas was not Bahamian at all. He was Ernest Hemingway. The Bahamas figured in some of his fiction, notably *Islands In the Stream.* Hemingway preferred Bimini because of its fishing, and he was the first person the locals had seen land a bluefin tuna on rod and reel. Papa stayed at Helen Duncombe's Compleat Angler Hotel, which today has much Hemingway memorabilia.

Hemingway went to Bimini first in 1934 on his boat, *Pilar,* bringing the writer John Dos Passos, among others. He was also there in 1937, working on revisions for his manuscript, *To Have And Have Not.* But the Bahamians remember him mainly for *Islands in the Stream.* No writer before or since has captured in fiction the seedy charm of Bimini's Alice Town.

There are no Hemingways around anymore, but novelists still use the Bahamas as a backdrop for their fiction. Instead of fishing, however, there is usually a drug-scene theme. Typical of this genre is *Bahama Blue* by D. C. Poyer, the adventure of Lyle "Tiller" Galloway. Poyer, the author of *Hatteras Blue,* obviously loves the sea but hates the drug runners who use it. In his book, the hero sets off to make a 400-foot dive to recover 50 tons of cocaine thought to lie off the coast of the Bahamas. It's a thriller, and certainly evocative of the nineties in the Bahamas.

# 4  Sports A to Z

The 700 islands in the Bahamian archipelago—fewer than 30 of which are inhabited—are surrounded by clear waters ideal for fishing, sailing, and scuba diving. (Detailed recommendations and often the costs of these activities are previewed under the individual destinations listings.) The country's perfect weather and its many cooperative local entrepreneurs allow easy access to more than 30 sports throughout the islands.

For sports-related **information** about any of the activities listed below, call toll free **800/32-SPORT.**

**DIVING**   The unusual marine topography of the Bahamas offers an almost astonishing variety of options for snorkelers and scuba enthusiasts. Throughout the more than 700 islands, there are innumerable reefs, drop-offs, coral gardens, caves, and shipwrecks. In many locations, visitors feel that they are the first human beings ever to explore the site. Andros Island boasts the third-largest barrier reef in the world. Chub Cay in the Berry Islands, and Riding Rock, San Salvador, also offer premium spots to take a plunge in an underwater world teeming with aquatic life. The intricate layout of the Exumas includes virtually every type of underwater dive site, very few of which have ever been explored at all. The Abacos, famous for its yachting, and the extensive reefs off the coast of Freeport, are also rich sources for dive sites. Freeport, incidentally, contains the country's most famous and complete diving operation, UNEXSO, offering an 18-foot-deep training tank, a diving museum, and the popular "Dolphin Experience," in which visitors are allowed to pet, swim, snorkel, and dive with these remarkable animals.

Since fewer than 30 of the Bahamian islands are inhabited, diving can usually occur in unspoiled and uncrowded splendor. Visitors need not be highly experienced to share in the underwater fun. Most Bahamian resorts offer diving programs for novices, usually enabling a beginner to dive with a guide after several hours of instruction. (This is usually conducted either in a swimming pool, with scuba equipment, or from the edge of a beach.) A license, proving the successful completion of a predesignated program of scuba study, is legally required for solo divers. Many resort hotels and dive shops offer the necessary training as part of 5-day training courses whose successful completion is rewarded with the issuance of a PADI- or NAUI-approved license.

Visitors are urgently cautioned never to attempt diving beyond their level of skill, and to observe accepted safety standards.

**FISHING**    The shallow waters between the hundreds of cays and islands of the Bahamas are some of the most fertile fishing grounds in the world. Hundreds of spots have proven beneficial for the capture of fish, even waters where marine traffic is relatively congested. Grouper, billfish, wahoo, tuna, and dozens of other species also thrive in Bahamian waters, with dozens of charter boats available for deep-sea fishing. Reef fishing, either from small boats or from shorelines, is popular everywhere, with grouper, snapper, and barracuda being the most commonly caught species. Specialists, however, or serious amateurs of the sport, often head for any of the following points:

Hemingway's old haunt, the island of Bimini, is known as the "Big-Game Fishing Capital of the World," where anglers can successfully hunt for swordfish, sailfish, and marlin. Bimini maintains its own Hall of Fame where many a proud angler has had his or her catch honored. Annual highlights include the Bimini Billfish Championship in May and the Hemingway Championship Tournament in July. World records for the size of catches don't seem to last long here, being quickly surpassed.

Walker's Cay in the Abacos and Chub Cay in the Berry Islands are famous for both deep-sea and shore fishing. Some anglers, who return to these cays year after year, claim that part of the appeal of these cays is the reduction of stress. Grouper, jacks, and snapper are plentiful. Even spearfishing without scuba gear is common and popular.

Andros is the site of the world's best bonefishing. Bonefish (also known as "gray fox") are medium-sized fish that feed in shallow, well-illuminated waters. Known as some of the most tenacious fish in the world, they struggle ferociously against anglers who pride themselves on using light lines from shallow-draft boats.

Cargill Creek Lodge (☎ 809/368-5129) and Lighthouse Yacht Club & Marina (☎ 809/368-2305) specialize in fishing adventures off some of the most remote and sparsely populated coastlines in the country. An annual highlight for this type of fishing is held every October, during Andros Island's Bonefish Bonanza.

*Note:* Taking sponges or turtles from Bahamian waters is strictly prohibited. The Ministry of Agriculture, Fisheries, and Local Government keeps a close eye on catches of crayfish (spiny lobster), and export of conch meat is prohibited. Stone crab cannot be caught within two miles off Bimini or Grand Bahama.

**GOLF**    Since the introduction of golf to the Bahamas in the 1930s, the islands have lured both stars and "duffers" in increasing numbers. The richest pickings are offered on Grand Bahama Island, home to three courses that have been designated as potential PGA tour stops. The Princess Resort and Casino boasts two challenging and spectacular courses, the Princess Ruby and the Princess Emerald, site of the Bahamas National Open. The oldest course on Grand Bahama Island is the Lucayan Park Golf & Country Club, a heavily wooded course designed for precision golf with elevated greens and numerous water hazards.

Quality golf in the Bahamas, however, is not restricted to Grand Bahama Island. The Cable Beach Golf Club, part of the Radisson Cable Beach Casino & Golf Resort on New Providence, is the oldest and best-established golf course in the country, and remains very popular today. New Providence has two additional courses, including the widely publicized Paradise Island Golf Club, whose unusual obstacles—a lion's den and a windmill—have challenged the skill of both Gary Player and Jack Nicklaus. It also boasts the world's largest sand trap.

Golf is also available at courses in the Abacos (Treasure Cay) and on Eleuthera (Cotton Bay). Designs are challenging, with many panoramic water views and water obstacles.

**SAILING**  The Bahamas, rivaled only by the Virgin Islands and, perhaps, the Grenadines, are probably the most sought-after yachting destinations in the Atlantic. Its 700 islands and well-developed marinas provide a spectacular and practical backdrop for sailing enthusiasts. The miniarchipelago of the Abacos, sometimes referred to as "The Sailing Capital of the World," is especially popular.

Don't be dismayed if you don't happen to own a yacht. All sizes and types of craft, from dinghies to blue-water cruisers, are available for charter. Crew and

---

### Hemingway in Bimini

It's one of the oddest pieces of real estate in the Atlantic. Less than a few hundred feet wide in many places, with a surface area of only 9 square miles, Bimini has always floated like a magic lure, only 50 miles from some of the most crowded seashores in the United States. Even during the 1930s, it was famous as an alter ego to such stateside islands as Key West. Soaked with liquor during U.S. Prohibition (it served as a depot for outlawed contraband), and widely recognized as a storage depot for illegal drugs, it's one of the most controversial and raffish islands in the Western Hemisphere.

Thanks to American writer Ernest Hemingway, the appeal of its raunchy, no-holds-barred landscapes became well-publicized throughout North America.

Hemingway's first boat (*the Pilar*) was a diesel-powered tub he skippered with fellow writer John Dos Passos for the express purpose of reaching Bimini. One of the bloodiest of his many self-destructive acts occurred off the coast of Bimini when, struggling to aim a revolver at the thrashing jaws of a captured mako shark, he accidentally shot himself in both legs. Among his best catches were a 785-pound mako shark and a 514-pound tuna, both captured off the coast of Bimini. Some of his most famous fistfights? On Bimini, one with wealthy publisher Joseph Knapp, another with a series of black contenders who stood to earn $250 if they could stay in the ring with him for three 3-minute rounds. (No one ever collected the money.) Hemingway revised the manuscript of *To Have and Have Not* on Bimini in 1937. The town that inspired his evocative description of the seaport in *Islands in the Stream* was Alice Town, the still-seedy but raffish capital of Bimini.

captain are optional. Even if your dreams involve the seagoing life for only an afternoon or less, many hotels offer sightseeing cruises aboard catamarans or glass-bottom boats, often with the opportunity to snorkel or swim in the wide open sea.

Regattas and races for both sail and power craft are held throughout the year. The Exumas host the Cruising Yacht Regatta in George Town every March, and another regatta limited to boats crafted in the Bahamas in April. The Abacos hosts both the Green Turtle Cay Boating Fling in June and Regatta Week at Marsh Harbour in July. Also important are the Boating Fling at Port Lucaya, Freeport, scheduled in June, and the All-Eleuthera Regatta in August.

**TENNIS**    Most tennis courts are part of large resorts, and are usually free for the use of registered guests. Nonguests are welcome, but are sometimes charged a small fee. Larger resorts usually offer on-site pro shops and professional instructors. Court surfaces range from clay or asphalt to such technologically advanced substances as Flexipave and Har-Tru. New Providence, with more than 80 tennis courts, wins points for offering the greatest number of choices. At least 21 of these lie on Paradise Island. Also noteworthy are the many well-lit courts at the Radisson Cable Beach Casino & Golf Resort. After New Providence, Grand Bahama has the largest number of courts available for play—almost 40 in all. The Burger Tennis Classic is held every August at the Bahamas Princess Country Club. Within the Family Islands, tennis courts are available on Eleuthera, the Abacos, the Berry Islands, and the Exumas.

# 5  Cuisine

There *is* a bona fide Bahamian cuisine, but you'll sometimes have to leave the deluxe hostelries of Freeport/Lucaya, New Providence (Nassau and Cable Beach), or Paradise Island to find it. Once you reach the Family Islands, it's a different story. Of course, they too have continental chefs, but in many places, especially at the little local restaurants previewed in this guide, you get to eat what the Bahamians eat.

Count yourself fortunate if you get a continental or Bahamian chef who really decides to make use of local fish and seafood. Grilled fish can be a delight. Most meats are frozen, however, and often imported from the United States, although chicken can be homegrown.

## THE CUISINE

**SOUP**    Bahamian fish chowder can be prepared in any number of ways. Old-time Bahamian chefs tell me that it's best when made with grouper. To that they add celery, onions, tomatoes, and an array of flavorings that might include A-1 sauce (or Worcestershire, or both), along with thyme, cooking sherry, a bit of dark rum, and lime juice.

Increasingly rare these days, turtle soup was for years a mainstay of the Family Islands (called Out Islands back then). Turtle soup and other turtle dishes still appear on some local menus. However, if you have alternatives, it would be better to choose another dish. Turtles are considered an endangered species by environmentalists.

**CONCH**   The national food of the Bahamas is conch (pronounced "konk"). The firm white meat of this mollusk—called the "snail of the sea"—is enjoyed throughout the islands. Actually, its taste is somewhat bland, but not when Bahamian chefs finish with it. Locals eat it as a snack (usually served at happy hour in taverns and bars), as a main dish, as a salad, or as an hors d'oeuvre.

The Pacific coast resident will think it tastes like abalone. The conch does not have a fishy taste, like halibut, and it has a chewy consistency, which means that a chef must pound it to tenderize it, the way one might pound wienerschnitzel. Every cook has a different recipe for making conch chowder. A popular version includes tomatoes, potatoes, sweet peppers, onions, carrots, salt pork or bacon, bay leaf, thyme, and (of course) salt and pepper.

Conch fritters, shaped like balls, are served with hot sauce, and are made with finely minced sweet peppers, onions, and tomato paste, among other ingredients. Like most fritters, they are deep-fried in oil.

Conch salad is another local favorite, and again it has many variations. Essentially, it is uncooked conch that has been marinated in Old Sour (a hot pepper sauce) to break down its tissues and to add extra flavor. It is served with diced small red (or green) peppers, along with chopped onion. The taste is tangy.

Cracked conch (or fried conch, as the old-timers used to call it) is like a breaded veal cutlet in preparation. Pounded hard and dipped in batter, it is then sautéed. Conch is also served steamed, in a creole sauce, curried, "scorched," creamed on toast, and stewed. Instead of conch chowder, you might get conch soup. You'll also see "conch burgers" listed on menus.

**SEAFOOD**   The most expensive item you'll see on nearly any menu in the Bahamas is the spiny local lobster. A tropical cousin of the Maine lobster, it is also called crayfish or rock lobster. Only the tail is eaten, however. You get fresh lobster only when it's in season, from the first of April until the end of August. Otherwise it's frozen.

Bahamian lobster, in spite of its cost, is not always prepared well. Sometimes a cook leaves it in the oven for too long, and the meat becomes tough and chewy. But when prepared right, such as is done by the famed Graycliff Restaurant in Nassau, it is perfection and worth the exorbitant cost.

The Bahamian lobster lends itself to any international recipe for lobster, including Newburg or thermidor. It can be served in a typical local style: curried, with lime juice and fresh coconut among the other ingredients.

After conch, grouper is the second most consumed fish in the Bahamas. It's served in a number of ways, often batter dipped, sautéed, and called "fingers" because of the way it's sliced. The fish is often steamed and served in a spicy creole sauce. Sometimes it comes dressed in a sauce of dry white wine, mushrooms, onions, and such seasonings as thyme. Because the fish has a mild taste, the extra flavor of the other ingredients is needed.

Baked bonefish is also common, and it's very simple to prepare. The bonefish is split in half and seasoned with a hot pepper sauce, Old Sour, and salt, then popped into the oven to bake until ready.

Baked crab is one of the best-known dishes of the Bahamas. A chef mixes the eggs and meat of both land or sea crabs with seasonings and bread crumbs. The crabs are then replaced in their shells and baked.

You'll also encounter yellowtail, "goggle eyes," jacks, snapper, grunts, and margot, plus many more sea creatures.

**POULTRY, MEATS & VEGGIES**   Chicken is grown locally in the Bahamas, especially on Eleuthera. Popular "chicken souse" is a dish made with chicken, onion, sweet peppers, bay leaves, allspice, and other ingredients left up to a cook's imagination. It's simmered in a pot for about an hour, then lime juice is added and it's simmered a little longer. Pig's feet souse is also a favorite dish.

Goats and sheep are also raised in the Family Islands. Somehow either meat on a menu appears as "mutton," and it's often curried. Wild boar is caught on some of the Family Islands, and game birds such as ducks and pigeons are shot. Raccoon stew is also eaten.

Most meats, including pork, veal, and beef, are imported. However, even here, Bahamian cooks show their ingenuity by giving these meats interesting variations. For example, at a Family Island inn, I recently enjoyed pork that had been marinated with vinegar, garlic, onion, celery tops, cloves, mustard, and Worcestershire sauce, then baked and served with gravy. Even a simple baked ham is given a Bahamian touch with the addition of fresh pineapple, coconut milk, and coconut flakes, along with mustard, honey, and brown sugar.

Many vegetables are grown in the Bahamas; others are imported. If it's a cucumber, you can be almost certain it's from one of Edison Key's farms in North Abaco. They not only supply cucumbers to their own country, but it's estimated that they also have captured about 5% of the stateside market. Bahamians also grow their own sweet potatoes, corn, cassava, okra, and peppers (both sweet and hot), among other produce.

**PEAS 'N' RICE & JOHNNYCAKE**   If mashed potatoes are still the "national starch" of America, then peas 'n' rice perform that role in the Bahamas. Peas 'n' rice, like mashed potatoes themselves, can be prepared in a number of ways. A popular method is cooking pigeon peas (which grow on pods on small trees) or black-eyed peas with salt pork, tomatoes, celery, uncooked rice, thyme, green pepper, onion, salt, pepper, and whatever special touch a chef wants to add. When served as a side dish, Bahamians most often sprinkle hot sauce over the concoction.

Johnnycake, another famed part of the Bahamian table, dates from the early settlers, who most often were simple folk and usually poor. They existed mainly on a diet of fish and rice, supplemented by johnnycake. This is a pan-cooked bread made with butter, milk, flour, sugar, salt, and baking powder. (Originally it was called "Journey Cake," which was eventually corrupted to johnnycake.) Fishermen could make this simple bread on the decks of their vessels. They'd build a fire in a box that had been filled with sand to keep the flames from spreading to the craft.

**DESSERTS**   Guava duff is the dessert specialty of the Bahamas, although one cook confided to me, "It takes too long, and we don't like to make it anymore unless there's a special call for it."

The dessert, resembling a jelly roll, is made with guava pulp that has been run through a food mill or sieve. Nobody seems to agree on the best method of cooking it. One way is to cream sugar and butter and add eggs and such spices as cinnamon and cloves, or nutmeg. The flour is made into a stiff dough and mixed with the guava pulp, which is then placed in the top of a double boiler and cooked over boiling water for hours. It can also be boiled or steamed, and there are those who insist it should be baked. The guava duff is served with hard sauce.

In addition to guava duff, there are lots of other tasty desserts and breads, including coconut tarts, coconut jimmie, benne seedcakes, and potato bread.

**TROPICAL FRUITS**  Bahamians are especially fond of fruits, and they make inventive dishes out of them, including soursop ice cream and sapodilla pudding. Guavas are used to make their famous guava duff dessert, which has already been described. The islanders also grow and enjoy melons, pineapples, passion fruit, mangoes, and other varieties.

Perhaps their best-known fruit is the papaya, which is called pawpaw or "melon tree." It's made into a dessert or a chutney, or eaten for breakfast in its natural state. It's also used in many lunch and dinner recipes. An old Bahamian custom of using papaya as a meat tenderizer has, at least since the seventies, invaded the kitchens of North America. Papaya is also used to make fruity tropical drinks, such as a Bahama Mama shake. And if you see it for sale in a local food store, take home some "Goombay" marmalade, made with papaya, pineapple, and green ginger.

## DRINKS

**WATER**  The Bahamians don't need to post "Please Don't Drink the Water" signs, although in some outlying areas it might be in short supply. New Providence and Grand Bahama have ample pure water, filtered and chlorinated. In other islands, only Marsh Harbour on Great Abaco Island has chlorinated and piped water, but you will find potable water at all resorts. In addition, bottled water is available at all tourist facilities and at stores and supermarkets.

On many of the Family Islands rainfall is a main source of water for drinking and other household uses. This is caught and kept in the cisterns that most houses have. In this land of no factories and no polluted air, you can be sure it's safe to drink the water.

**RUM, LIQUEURS & SPECIALTY DRINKS**  Rum was known to the ancient Romans—it was even known to the ancient Chinese—but it is today mostly associated with the islands stretching from the Bahamas to the Caribbean. Although rum came north from Cuba and Jamaica, the people of the Bahamas quickly adopted it as their national alcoholic beverage. And using their imagination, they "invented" several local drinks, including the Yellow Bird, the Bahama Mama, and the Goombay Smash.

The Yellow Bird is made with crème de banana liqueur, Vat 19 rum, orange juice, pineapple juice, apricot brandy, and Galliano; whereas a Bahama Mama is made with Vat 19, citrus juice (perhaps pineapple as well), bitters, a dash of nutmeg, crème de cassis, and a hint of grenadine. The Goombay Smash is usually made with coconut rum, pineapple juice, lemon juice, Triple Sec, Vat 19, and a dash of simple syrup.

Nearly every bartender in the islands has his or her own version of planter's punch. A classic recipe is to make it with lime juice, sugar, Vat 19, plus a dash of bitters. It's usually served with a cherry and an orange slice. If you want a typically Bahamian liqueur, try Nassau Royale. Nassau Royale is used to make an increasingly famous drink, the C. C. Rider, which also includes Canadian Club, apricot brandy, and pineapple juice.

# 3

# Planning a Trip to the Bahamas

The Bahamas, as a country, are completely different from the United States. You are indeed "going abroad." But unlike a trip from the U.S. mainland to Europe, you can be in the Bahamas sipping a Goombay Smash after only a 35-minute jet hop—from Miami, that is.

Travel agents who keep up-to-the-minute schedules and rates can inform you about the latest package deals if you're contemplating either a summer or winter holiday. Fortunately, many of these package deals aren't offered just in the slow season, the summer, but appear frequently throughout the winter, except during the heavily booked Christmas period.

In this chapter I concentrate on what you need to do before you go. In addition to helping you decide when to take your vacation, I answer questions about what to pack, where to get information, and what documents you need to obtain. I also offer sample itineraries, alternative travel options, and tips for special travelers.

## 1 Visitor Information, Entry Requirements & Money

### VISITOR INFORMATION

To obtain information on the Bahamas before you go, see your travel agent or the **Bahamas Tourist Office** nearest you. In the **United States,** offices are found in *Atlanta* at 2957 Clairmont Rd., Suite 150, Atlanta, GA 30345 (☎ **404/633-1793**); in *Chicago* at 8600 W. Bryn Mawr Ave., Suite 820, Chicago, IL 60631 (☎ **312/693-1500**); in *Dallas* at World Trade Center, 2050 Stemmons Freeway, Suite 116, Dallas, TX 75258 (☎ **214/742-1886**); in *Fort Lauderdale,* Bahamas Out Islands Promotion Board, 1100 Lee Wagener Blvd., Fort Lauderdale, FL 33315 (☎ **305/359-8099**); in *Los Angeles* at 3450 Wilshire Blvd., Suite 208, Los Angeles, CA 90010 (☎ **213/385-0033**); in *Miami* at 255 Alhambra Circle, Suite 425, Coral Gables, FL 33134 (☎ **305/444-4860**); in *New York* at 150 E. 52nd St., New York, NY 10022 (☎ **212/758-2777**); and in *Washington, D.C.,* at 1730 Rhode Island Ave. NW, Washington, DC 20036 (☎ **202/659-9135**).

In **Canada,** offices are found in Montreal at 1130 Sherbrooke St. W., Montreal, PQ H3A 2MI (☎ **514/448-5116**); and in

Toronto at 121 Bloor St. E., Suite 1101, Toronto, ON M4W 3M5 (☎ **416/ 968-2999**).

In **England,** contact the office at 10 Chesterfield St., London W1X 8AH (☎ **0171/629-5238**).

A good travel agent can be a source of information. If you use one, make sure the agent is a member of the American Society of Travel Agents (ASTA). If you get poor service from an agent, you can write to the **ASTA Consumer Affairs,** 1101 King St., Alexandria, VA 22314 (☎ **703/739-2851**).

## ENTRY REQUIREMENTS
### DOCUMENTS

To enter the Bahamas, citizens of the United States coming in as visitors for a period not to exceed eight months need bring only proof of citizenship, such as a passport, a birth certificate, or a voter registration card. The latter two require a photo ID. Onward or return tickets must be shown to immigration officials in the Bahamas.

The Commonwealth of the Bahamas does not require visas. On entry to the Bahamas, you'll be given an Immigration Card to complete and sign. The card has a carbon copy that you must keep until departure, at which time it must be turned in. Also, a departure tax is levied before you can exit the country (see "Taxes" under "Fast Facts" later in this chapter).

*Note:* It's good policy to make copies of your most valuable documents, including your passport, before you leave home. Make a photocopy of the inside page of your passport, the one with your photograph. In case of loss abroad, you should also make copies of your driver's license, an airline ticket, strategic hotel vouchers, and any other sort of identity card that might be pertinent. You should also make copies of any prescriptions you take. Place one copy in your luggage and carry the original with you. Leave the other copy at home. The information on these documents will be extremely valuable should you encounter loss or theft abroad.

## CUSTOMS

Visitors leaving Nassau or Freeport/Lucaya for most U.S. destinations clear U.S. Customs and Immigration before leaving the Bahamas. Charter companies can make special arrangements with the Nassau or Freeport flight services and U.S. Customs and Immigration for preclearance. No further formalities are required upon arrival in the United States once the preclearance has taken place in Nassau or Freeport.

### BRINGING IT ALL HOME

**U.S. Customs**   When you return home you may take $600 worth of merchandise duty free if you've been outside the United States for 48 hours or more and have not claimed a similar exemption within the past 30 days. Articles valued above the $600 duty-free limit but not over $1,000 will be assessed at a flat duty rate of 10%. Gifts for your personal use, not for business purposes, may be included in the $600 exemption. Unsolicited gifts totaling $50 a day may be sent home duty free. You are limited to one liter of wine, liqueur, or liquor. Five cartons of cigarettes can be brought home duty free. U.S. Customs preclearance is available for all scheduled flights. Passengers leaving for the United States must fill out written declaration forms before clearing U.S. Customs in the Bahamas. The forms are available at hotels, travel agencies, and airlines in the Bahamas.

Collect receipts for all purchases made in the Bahamas. *Note:* If a merchant suggests giving you a false receipt, misstating the value of the goods, beware—the merchant might be an informer to U.S Customs. You must also declare all gifts received during your stay abroad.

If you purchased such an item during an earlier trip abroad, carry proof that you have already paid Customs duty on the item at the time of your previous reentry. To be extra careful, compile a list of expensive carry-on items and ask a U.S. Customs agent to stamp your list at the airport before your departure.

If you're concerned and need more specific guidance, write to the U.S. Customs Service, 1301 Constitution Ave., P.O. Box 7407, Washington, DC 20229, requesting the free pamphlet *Know Before You Go.*

**Canadian Customs** For total clarification, write for the booklet "I Declare," issued by Revenue Canada, 875 Heron Rd., Ottawa, ON K1A OL5. Canada allows its citizens a $300 exemption, and they are allowed to bring back duty free 200 cigarettes, 2.2 pounds of tobacco, 40 imperial ounces of liquor, and 50 cigars. In addition, they are allowed to mail gifts to Canada from abroad at the rate of $60 (CDN) a day, provided they are unsolicited and aren't alcohol or tobacco (write on the package: "Unsolicited gift, under $60 value"). All valuables should be declared on the Y-38 form before departure from Canada, including serial numbers, as in the case of, for example, expensive foreign cameras you already own. *Note:* The $300 exemption can be used only once a year and only after an absence of seven days.

**British Customs** On returning from the Bahamas, if you either arrive directly in the U.K. or arrive via a port in another EC country where you did not pass through Customs controls with all your baggage, you must go through U.K. Customs and declare any goods in excess of the allowances. These are: 200 cigarettes or 100 cigarillos or 50 cigars or 250 grams of tobacco; two liters of still table wine and one liter of spirits or strong liqueurs over 22% volume, or two liters of fortified or sparkling wine or other liqueurs, or two liters of additional still table wine; 60cc/ml of perfume; 250cc/ml of toilet water and £136 worth of all other goods, including gifts and souvenirs. (No one under 17 years of age is entitled to a tobacco or drinks allowance.) Only go through the Green "nothing to declare" channel if you're sure that you have no more than the Customs allowances and no prohibited or restricted goods. For further details on U.K. Customs, contact H.M. Customs and Excise Office, New King's Beam House, 22 Upper Ground, London SE1 9PJ (☎ 0171/382-5468).

**Australian Customs** The duty-free allowance in Australia is $400 (AUS) or, for those under 18, $200 (AUS). Personal property mailed back from the Bahamas should be marked "Australian goods returned," to avoid payment of duty, providing it is what it says on the package. Upon returning to Australia, citizens can bring in 200 cigarettes or 250 grams of tobacco and 1 liter of alcohol. If you're returning with valuable goods you already own, such as expensive foreign-made cameras, you should file form B263. A helpful brochure, available from Australian consulates or Customs offices, is called *Customs Information for Travellers.*

**New Zealand Customs** The duty-free allowance is $700 (NZ). Citizens over 17 years of age can bring in 200 cigarettes or 50 cigars or 250 grams of tobacco (or a mixture of all three if their combined weight doesn't exceed

250 grams), plus 4.5 liters of wine or beer or 1.125 liters of liquor. New Zealand currency does not carry import or export restrictions. A Certificate of Export listing already-owned values taken out of the country allows you to bring them back in without paying duty. Most questions are answered in a free pamphlet available at New Zealand consulates and Customs offices called *New Zealand Customs Guide for Travellers,* Notice No. 4.

**Irish Customs**   Irish citizens may bring in 200 cigarettes or 100 cigarillos or 50 cigars or 250 grams (approximately 9 ounces) of tobacco, plus 1 liter of liquor exceeding 22% by volume (such as whisky, brandy, gin, rum, or vodka), or 2 liters of distilled beverages and spirits with a wine or alcoholic base of an alcoholic strength not exceeding 22% by volume, plus 2 liters of other wine and 50 grams of perfume. Other allowances include duty-free goods to a value of IR £34 per person or IR £17 per person for travelers under 15 years of age.

# MONEY
## CASH/CURRENCY

The legal tender is the Bahamian dollar (B$1), which is on a par with the U.S. dollar. Both U.S. and Bahamian dollars are accepted on an equal basis throughout the Bahamas. There is no restriction on the amount of foreign currency brought into the country by a tourist. Currency transfers must be handled through banks, as there are no provisions for Western Union–type money cabling. If you wish to send home for funds, you can do so by telephoning, cabling, or writing to your stateside bank with the request that a specified sum be transmitted to a bank in the Bahamas. Traveler's checks are accepted by most large hotels and stores, but you may have trouble getting a personal check honored.

### A Note on Currency for British Travelers

Here is how the British pound is converted from U.S. or Bahamian dollars. The Bahamian dollar—no longer pegged to pound sterling—has the same value as the U.S. dollar.

| The U.S. Dollar & the British Pound | | | |
|---|---|---|---|
| U.S.$ | U.K.£ | U.S.$ | U.K.£ |
| 1 | .63 | 75 | 47.25 |
| 2 | 1.26 | 100 | 63.00 |
| 3 | 1.89 | 125 | 78.75 |
| 4 | 2.52 | 150 | 94.50 |
| 5 | 3.15 | 175 | 110.25 |
| 6 | 3.78 | 200 | 126.00 |
| 7 | 4.41 | 225 | 141.75 |
| 8 | 5.04 | 250 | 157.50 |
| 9 | 5.67 | 300 | 189.00 |
| 10 | 6.30 | 350 | 220.50 |
| 15 | 9.45 | 400 | 252.00 |
| 25 | 15.75 | 450 | 283.50 |
| 50 | 31.50 | 500 | 315.00 |

| What Things Cost in the Bahamas | U.S. $ |
|---|---|
| Taxi from airport to Nassau's center | 19.00 |
| Local phone call in pay phone | .25 |
| Double room at Graycliff (deluxe) | 255.00 |
| Double room at British Colonial Beach Resort (moderate) | 129.00 |
| Double room at El Greco (budget) | 87.00 |
| Continental breakfast in a hotel | 6.50 |
| Lunch for one at the Europe (moderate)* | 12.00 |
| Lunch for one at the Bahamian Kitchen (budget)* | 10.00 |
| Dinner for one at Buena Vista (deluxe)* | 50.00 |
| Dinner for one at Green Shutters (moderate)* | 25.00 |
| Dinner for one at Bayside Buffet Restaurant (budget)* | 19.95 |
| Bottle of beer | 3.00 |
| Coca-Cola in a café or bar | 1.50 |
| Coffee in a café | 1.50 |
| Roll of ASA 100 color film, 36 exposures | 7.25 |
| Movie ticket | 4.00–6.00 |
| Show at the Palace Theater | 30.00 |

*Includes tax and tip, but not wine.

## TRAVELER'S CHECKS

Traveler's checks are the safest way to carry cash while traveling. Most banks will give you a better rate on traveler's checks than for cash. Each of the agencies listed below will refund your checks if they are lost or stolen, provided you produce sufficient documentation. When purchasing your checks, ask about refund hot lines: American Express has probably the greatest number of offices around the world.

**American Express** (☎ toll free **800/221-7282** in the U.S. and Canada) is one of the largest and most immediately recognized issuers of traveler's checks. No commission is charged to members of the American Automobile Agency or to holders of certain types of American Express credit cards. The company issues checks denominated in U.S. dollars, Canadian dollars, British pounds sterling, Swiss francs, French francs, German marks, Japanese yen, and Dutch guilders. The vast majority of checks sold in North America are denominated in U.S. dollars. For questions or problems which arise outside the United States or Canada, contact any of the company's many regional representatives.

**Citicorp** (☎ toll free **800/645-6556** in the U.S. and Canada or call **813/623-1709** collect from anywhere else in the world) issues checks in U.S. dollars, British pounds, German marks, Japanese yen, and Australian dollars.

**Thomas Cook** (☎ toll free **800/223-7373** in the U.S. and Canada, otherwise call **609/987-7300** collect from other parts of the world) issues MasterCard traveler's checks denominated in U.S. dollars, Canadian dollars, French francs, British pounds, German marks, Dutch guilders, Spanish pesetas, Australian dollars, and Japanese yen. Depending on individual banking laws in each of the various states, some of the above-mentioned currencies might not be available at every outlet.

**Interpayment Services** (☎ toll free **800/221-2426** in the U.S. or Canada or call **212/858-8500** collect from other parts of the world) sells VISA checks which are issued by a consortium of member banks and the Thomas Cook organization. Traveler's checks are denominated in U.S. or Canadian dollars, British pounds, and German marks.

## CREDIT CARDS

Credit cards are in wide use in the Bahamas. VISA and MasterCard are the major cards used, although American Express and, to a lesser extent, Diners Club are also popular.

# 2  When to Go

## CLIMATE

The temperature in the Bahamas varies to a surprisingly slight degree, averaging between 75 and 85 degrees Fahrenheit in both winter and summer, although there can be really chilly days, especially in the early morning and at night. However, the Bahamian winter is usually like a perpetual May.

The tropic of Cancer crosses the Bahamian archipelago at about the halfway mark, passing through Great Exuma and the northern part of Long Island. Thus there is some variation between the mean temperatures in the northernmost and southernmost parts of the islands, but the climate overall is mild. The Gulf Stream sweeps along the western shores with its clear, warm waters, and the prevailing trade winds blow steadily in from the southeast.

### THE HURRICANE SEASON

The curse of Bahamian weather, the hurricane season lasts—officially at least— from June 1 to November 30. But there is no cause for panic. More tropical cyclones pound the U.S. mainland than hurricanes devastate the Bahamas. Hurricanes are, in fact, infrequent in the Bahamas. However, when one does come, satellite forecasts generally give adequate warnings so that precautions can be taken in time.

If you're heading for the Bahamas during the hurricane season, you can call your nearest branch of the National Weather Service. In your phone directory, look it up under the U.S. Department of Commerce listing. You can also obtain current weather information on many destinations, including the Bahamas, by dialing a toll-charge call (95¢ per minute): **900/WEATHER** from any push-button phone in the United States.

### The Bahama's Average Temperatures & Rainfall

|          | Jan | Feb | Mar | Apr | May | June | July | Aug | Sept | Oct | Nov | Dec |
|----------|-----|-----|-----|-----|-----|------|------|-----|------|-----|-----|-----|
| Temp. °F | 70  | 70  | 72  | 75  | 77  | 80   | 81   | 82  | 81   | 78  | 74  | 71  |
| °C       | 21  | 21  | 22  | 24  | 25  | 27   | 27   | 28  | 27   | 26  | 23  | 22  |
| Rainfall"| 1.9 | 1.6 | 1.4 | 1.9 | 4.8 | 9.2  | 6.1  | 6.3 | 7.5  | 8.3 | 2.3 | 1.5 |

## HOLIDAYS

Public holidays observed in the Bahamas are *New Year's Day, Good Friday, Easter Monday, Whitmonday* (seven weeks after Easter), *Labour Day* (the first Friday in June), *Independence Day* (July 10), *Emancipation Day* (the first Monday in August),

*Discovery Day* (October 12), *Christmas,* and *Boxing Day* (the day after Christmas). When a holiday falls on Saturday or Sunday, it is usually marked on the following Monday by the closing of stores and offices.

## THE BAHAMAS CALENDAR OF EVENTS

January

☼ **Junkanoo**

This Mardi Gras–like festival begins two or three hours before dawn on New Year's Day. Throngs of cavorting, music-making, costumed figures prance through Nassau. Freeport/Lucaya, and the Family Islands. Elaborate headdresses and festive apparel are worn by jubilant men, women, and children as they celebrate their African heritage. Mini-Junkanoos in which visitors can participate are regular events.

**Where:** Best in Nassau, but also observed throughout the islands. **When:** New Year's Day. **How:** Local tourist offices will advise the best locations to see the festivities.

April

☼ **The Bahamas Family Island Regatta**

Featuring Bahamian craft sloops, these celebrated boat races began in 1954. Held in Elizabeth Harbour, the races are divided into five separate levels. The Regatta program also features a variety of onshore activities including basketball, a skipper's party, and a Junkanoo parade.

**Where:** At George Town in the Exumas. **When:** Late April. **How:** Call toll free **800/32-SPORT** for exact dates and information.

June

- **The Goombay Summer Festival** incorporates the sounds of Junkanoo and the rhythm of Goombay in a 4-month, round-the-clock celebration for the enjoyment of summer visitors. The start date of the Goombay Festival varies, so check with the Bahamas Tourist Office nearest you. It begins some time in June.

July

- **Independence Week** is marked throughout the islands by festivities, parades, and fireworks to celebrate the independence of the Commonwealth of the Bahamas, with the focal point being Independence Day, July 10.

October

- **Discovery Day.** The New World landing of Christopher Columbus, supposedly on an island that the Arawak Indian residents called Guanahani, is celebrated throughout the Bahamas. Columbus renamed Guanahani San Salvador, and, naturally, the town has a parade every year on this day. October 12.

November

- **Guy Fawkes Day.** The best celebrations are in Nassau. Nighttime parades through the streets are held on many of the islands, culminating in the hanging and burning of Guy Fawkes, an effigy of the British malefactor who was involved in the Gunpowder Plot of 1605 in London. Usually takes place around November 5, but check with island tourist offices.

December
- **Junkanoo Boxing Day.** High-energy Junkanoo parades and celebrations are held throughout the islands on December 26th. Many of these activities are repeated on New Year's Day (see January above).

## 3 Health, Insurance & Other Concerns

### HEALTH

Medical facilities in the Bahamas are considered excellent. Physicians and surgeons in private practice are readily available in Nassau, Cable Beach, and Freeport/Lucaya. In the Family Islands, there are 13 health centers. Satellite clinics are held periodically in small settlements by health personnel, and there are 36 other clinics, making a total of 49 health facilities throughout the outlying islands. For the names and telephone numbers of specific clinics, refer to the individual island listings. Where intensive or urgent care is required, patients are brought by the Emergency Flight Service to Princess Margaret Hospital in Nassau.

There is a government-operated hospital, Rand Memorial, in Freeport, plus government-operated clinics on Grand Bahama Island. Nassau and Freeport/Lucaya also have private hospitals.

Dentists are plentiful in Nassau, but somewhat less so on Grand Bahama. You'll find two dentists on Great Abaco Island, one at Marsh Harbour, another at Treasure Cay, and one on Eleuthera.

Some of the big resort hotels have in-house physicians or can quickly secure one for you. Staffs are also knowledgeable as to where to go for dental care.

It's a good idea to carry all your vital medicines and drugs (the legal kind) with you in your carry-on luggage, in case your checked luggage is lost. If your medical condition is chronic, always talk to your doctor before leaving home. He or she may have specific advice to give you, depending on your condition. For conditions such as epilepsy, a heart ailment, diabetes, or some other affliction, wear Medic Alert's Identification Tag, which will immediately alert any doctor as to the nature of your trouble. The tag provides the number of Medic Alert's 24-hour hot line, so that a foreign doctor can obtain medical records for you. For a lifetime membership, the cost is a well-spent $35 if the tag is steel, $45 if silver plated, and $60 if gold plated. There is also an annual fee of $15. Contact the **Medic Alert Foundation,** P.O. Box 1009, Turlock, CA 95381-1009 (☎ toll free **800/432-5378**).

At some point in a vacation, most visitors experience some diarrhea, even those who follow the usual precautions. This is often the result of a change in diet and eating habits, not usually from bad or contaminated food and water. Mild forms of diarrhea usually pass quickly without medication. As a precaution, take along some antidiarrhea medicine, moderate your eating habits, and drink only mineral water until you recover. Always drink plenty of fluids during the course of your disturbance to prevent dehydration. Consuming more than your usual intake of salt will help your body retain water. Eat only simply prepared foods at such times, such as plain bread (no butter) and boiled vegetables or some broth. Avoid dairy products at the time, except yogurt. If symptoms persist, you may have dysentery, especially if you notice blood or mucus in your stool. At this point you should consult your doctor.

## OTHER TIPS

Although **tap water** is generally considered safe to drink, if you have a delicate stomach it is better to avoid it and drink mineral water instead. This applies even to iced drinks. Stick to beer, hot tea, or soft drinks. Why risk a vacation with a stomach upset?

One of the most dangerous things you can catch in the Bahamas is a **sunburn,** especially if you're coming from a winterly climate and haven't been exposed to the sun in some time. Take precautions: Wear sunglasses, a hat (wide-brimmed if possible), a cover-up for your shoulders, and a sunscreen lotion. Experts also advise that you should limit your time on the beach the first day.

**Mosquitoes** exist, but rarely are they the dangerous malaria-carrying kind. Nevertheless, they are still a nuisance. Spray yourself with your favorite bug repellent if need be.

**Vaccinations** aren't required to enter the Bahamas if you're coming from a "disease-free" country such as the United States, Britain, or Canada.

Take along an adequate supply of any **prescription drugs** that you need and a written prescription that uses the generic name of the drug as well—not the brand name.

## INSURANCE

Insurance needs for the traveler abroad fall into three categories: Health and accident, trip cancellation, and lost luggage.

First, review your present policies before traveling internationally—you may already have adequate coverage between them and what is offered by credit-card companies. Many credit-card companies insure their users in case of a travel accident, providing a ticket was purchased with their card. Sometimes fraternal organizations have policies that protect members in case of sickness or accidents abroad. Many homeowners' insurance policies cover theft of luggage during foreign travel and loss of documents—your airline ticket, for instance. Coverage is usually limited to about $500. To submit a claim on your insurance, remember that you'll need police reports.

Some policies (and this is the type you should have) provide advances in cash or transfers of funds so that you won't have to dip into your precious travel funds to settle medical bills.

If you've booked a charter fare, you will probably have to pay a cancellation fee if you cancel a trip suddenly, even if it is due to an unforeseen crisis. It's possible to get insurance against such a possibility. Some travel agencies provide such coverage, and often flight insurance against a cancelled trip is written into tickets paid for by credit cards from such companies as VISA or American Express. Many tour operators or insurance agents provide this type of insurance.

Among the companies offering insurance policies are:

**Access America,** 6600 W. Broad St., P.O. Box 11188, Richmond, VA 23230 (☎ **804/285-3300** or toll free **800/284-8300** in the U.S.), offers a comprehensive travel insurance and assistance package, including medical expenses, on-the-spot hospital payments, medical transportation, baggage insurance, trip-cancellation/interruption insurance, and collision-damage insurance for a car rental. Their 24-hour hot line connects you to multilingual coordinators who can offer advice and help on medical, legal, and travel problems. Varying coverage levels are available.

**Wallach and Co.,** 107 W. Federal St., Middleburg, VA 22117-0480 (☎ **703/ 687-3166** or toll free **800/237-6615** in the U.S.), offers coverage for between 10 and 120 days at $3 per day; this policy includes accident and sickness coverage to the tune of $100,000. Medical evacuation is also included, along with $25,000 accidental death and dismemberment compensation. Provisions for trip cancellation can also be written into this policy at a nominal cost.

**Mutual of Omaha** (Tele-Trip), Mutual of Omaha Plaza, Omaha, NE 68175, offers insurance packages priced from $115 per couple for a 3-week trip. Included in the packages are travel-assistance services and financial protection against trip cancellation, trip interruption, flight-and-baggage delays, accident-related medical costs, accidental death and dismemberment, and medical evacuation coverages. A deluxe package costing $213 per couple offers double the coverage of the standard policy mentioned above. Application for insurance can be made over the phone for major credit card holders (☎ toll free **800/228-9792**).

**Travelers Insurance PAK,** Travel Insured International, Inc., P.O. Box 280568, East Hartford, CT 06128 (☎ **203/528-7663** or toll free **800/243-3174**), offers illness and accident coverage costing from $10 for 6 to 10 days. For lost or damaged luggage, $500 worth of coverage costs $20 for 6 to 10 days. You can also purchase trip-cancellation insurance for $5.50 per $100 of coverage to a limit of $10,000 per person.

**INSURANCE FOR BRITISH TRAVELERS** Most big travel agents offer their own insurance, and will probably try to sell you their package when you book a holiday. Think before you sign. Britain's Consumers' Association recommends that you insist on seeing the policy and reading the fine print before buying travel insurance.

You should also shop around for better deals. You might contact **Columbus Travel Insurance Ltd.** (☎ **0171/375-0011** in London) or, for students, **Campus Travel** (☎ **0171/730-3402** in London). Columbus Travel will sell travel insurance only to people who have been official residents of Britain for at least a year.

## 4 Tips for the Disabled, Seniors, Singles, Families & Students

### FOR THE DISABLED

Some 30 hotels and resorts have made provisions for the physically handicapped that allows full or limited use of the accommodations and facilities, including easy use of dining rooms, nightclubs, pool areas, and the like. Such accommodations can be found in Nassau and Cable Beach, and on Paradise Island, Grand Bahama, the Abacos, Andros, Cat Island, Eleuthera, Great Inagua, Long Island, and Spanish Wells. Some other small hotels, guest houses, and cottages have also made provisions for comfortable stays by the physically handicapped. Ask your travel agent.

There are many agencies that provide advance data to help you plan your trip. One is the **Travel Information Service,** MossRehab Hospital, 1200 W. Tabor Rd., Philadelphia, PA 19141, which provides information to telephone callers only. Call **215/456-9603** for assistance with your travel needs. You can obtain a copy of *Air Transportation of Handicapped Persons,* published by the U.S. Department of Transportation. The copy is sent free by writing for Free Advisory Circular No.

AC12032, Distribution Unit, U.S. Department of Transportation, Publications Division, M-4332, Washington, DC 20590.

You may want to consider joining a tour specifically for disabled visitors. Names and addresses of such tour operators can be obtained by writing to the **Society for the Advancement of Travel for the Handicapped,** 347 Fifth Ave., Suite 610, New York, NY 10016 (☎ 212/447-7284). Yearly membership dues in this society are $45 or $25 for senior citizens and students. Send a stamped self-addressed envelope.

You might also consider the **Federation of the Handicapped** (FEDCAP), 154 W. 14th St., New York, NY 10011 (☎ 212/727-4200), which offers summer tours for its members, who pay a yearly membership fee of $4.

The **Information Center for Individuals with Disabilities,** Fort Point Place, 27–43 Wormwood St., Boston, MA 02210 (☎ 617/727-5540), is another good source. It has lists of travel agents who specialize in tours for the disabled.

For the blind or visually impaired, the best source is the **American Foundation for the Blind,** 15 W. 16th St., New York, NY 10011 (☎ 212/620-2147 or toll free 800/232-5463 for ordering of information kits and supplies). It offers information on travel and various requirements for the transport and border formalities for seeing-eye dogs. It also issues identification cards to those who are legally blind.

One of the best organizations serving the needs of the disabled (wheelchairs and walkers) is **Flying Wheels Travel,** 143 W. Bridge St., P.O. Box 382, Owatoona, MN 55060 (☎ toll free 800/535-6790 or 507/451-5005), offering various escorted tours and cruises internationally.

For a $20 annual fee, consider joining **Mobility International USA,** P.O. Box 10767, Eugene, OR 97440 (☎ 503/343-1284). It answers questions on various destinations and also offers discounts on videos, publications, and programs it sponsors.

Finally, a bimonthly publication, **Handicapped Travel Newsletter,** keeps you current on accessible sights worldwide for the disabled. To order an annual subscription for $15 call 903/677-1260.

**FOR BRITISH TRAVELERS   RADAR** (the Royal Association for Disability and Rehabilitation), Unit 12, City Forum, 250 City Rd., London EC1V 8AF (☎ 0171/250-3222), publishes two annual holiday guides for the disabled. *Holidays and Travel Abroad* costs £5, while *Holidays in the British Isles* costs £7. RADAR (whose patroness is Elizabeth, the Queen Mother), also provides a number of holiday fact sheets on such subjects as sports and outdoor holidays, insurance, financial arrangements for the disabled, and accommodations within nursing-care units for groups or for the elderly. Each of these fact sheets is available for 75p. Fact sheets or the above-mentioned holiday guides can be mailed to you outside the U.K. for a nominal mailing fee.

Another good service is the **Holiday Care Service,** 2 Old Bank Chambers, Station Road, Horley, Surrey RH6 9HW (☎ 01293/774-535; fax 01293/784-647), a national charity that advises on accessible accommodations for elderly and disabled people. Annual membership costs £25. Once someone is a member, he or she can receive a newsletter and access to a free reservations network for hotels throughout Britain and—to a lesser degree—Europe and the rest of the world. The organization's Holiday Care Awards recognize people, hotels, and travel wholesalers in the tourism industry who provide excellent service for persons with disabilities.

If you're flying, the airlines and ground staff will help you on and off planes and reserve seats for you with sufficient leg room, but it is essential to arrange for this assistance in advance by contacting your airline.

## FOR SENIORS

Many discounts are available for seniors, but be advised that you have to be a member of an association to obtain certain discounts.

For information before you go, obtain a copy of *101 Tips for the Mature Traveler,* available from **Grand Circle Travel,** 347 Congress St., Suite 3A, Boston, MA 02210 (☎ **617/350-7500** or toll free **800/221-2610** in the U.S.). This travel agency also offers escorted tours and cruises for seniors.

**SAGA International Holidays** is well-known for its all-inclusive tours for seniors, preferably those 60 years old or older. Both medical and trip-cancellation insurance are included in the net price of any of their tours except for cruises. Contact SAGA International Holidays, 222 Berkeley St., Boston, MA 02116 (☎ toll free **800/343-0273**).

Information on travel for seniors is also available from the **National Council of Senior Citizens,** 1331 F St. NW, Washington, DC 20004 (☎ **202/347-8800**). A nonprofit organization, the council charges a membership fee of $12 per couple, for which you receive a monthly newsletter and membership benefits, including travel services. Benefits of membership include discounts on hotels, motels, and auto rentals, and also includes supplemental medical insurance for members.

**Mature Outlook,** 6001 N. Clark St., Chicago, IL 60660 (☎ toll free **800/336-6330**), is a travel organization for people more than 50 years of age. Members are offered discounts at ITC-member hotels and will receive a bimonthly magazine. The annual membership fee of $9.95 entitles its members to discounts and in some cases free coupons for reduced merchandise from Sears Roebuck & Co. Savings are also offered on selected auto rentals and restaurants.

## FOR SINGLES

Jens Jurgen matches single travelers with like-minded companions; he charges $99 for a 6-month listing. Applicants desiring a travel companion fill out a form stating their preferences and needs. They then receive a minilisting of potential partners who might be suitable. Companions of the same or opposite sex can be requested. A bimonthly newsletter, averaging 46 pages, also gives numerous money-saving travel tips for solo travelers. A sample issue is available for $5. For an application and more information, write to Jens Jurgen, **Travel Companion,** P.O. Box P-833, Amityville, NY 11701 (☎ **516/454-0880**).

**Singleworld,** 401 Theodore Fremd Ave., Rye, NY 10580 (☎ **914/967-3334** or toll free **800/223-6490**), offers a selection of cruises and tours for single travelers. Tours and cruises fall into three categories: 20s to 30s, 40s plus, and "all ages." Annual dues are $25.

Since single supplements on tours carry a hefty price tag, some tour companies will arrange for you to share a room with another single traveler of the same gender. One such company that offers a "guaranteed-share plan" is **Cosmos Tourama,** with offices at 5310 S. Federal Circle, Littleton, CO 80123 (☎ toll free **800/221-0090**).

**Grand Circle Travel,** 347 Congress St., Boston, MA 02210 (☎ **617/350-7500** or toll free **800/221-2610**), offers escorted tours and cruises for retired people, including singles. Once you book one of their trips, membership is included; in addition, you get vouchers providing discounts for future trips.

## FOR FAMILIES

The Bahamas are a wonderful choice for a family vacation. The smallest toddlers can spend blissful hours in the shallow seawater or in pools constructed with them in mind, while older children can enjoy boat rides, horseback riding, and hiking. Many resort hotels have play directors and supervised activities for the young of various age groups. However, here are some tips for making your trip a surefire success.

- Take along a "security blanket" for your child. This might be a pacifier, a favorite toy or book, a baseball cap, or a favorite T-shirt.
- Take protection from the sun. For tiny tots, this should include a sun umbrella, while the whole family will need sunscreen and sunglasses.
- Take along anti-insect lotions and sprays. You'll probably need both of these to repel mosquitoes and sand fleas as well as to ease the itching of insect bites.
- Arrange ahead for necessities, such as a crib and a bottle warmer, as well as cots for larger children. Find out if the place where you're staying stocks baby food, and if not, take it with you.
- Draw up guidelines on bedtime, eating, keeping tidy, being in the sun, even shopping and spending—it might make everybody's vacation more enjoyable.
- Lastly, don't forget the thermometer, basic first-aid supplies, medications your doctor may suggest, swimsuits, beach-and-pool toys, water wings for tiny mites, flip-flops for everybody, and terry-cloth robes.

*Family Travel Times* is published quarterly by TWYCH, Travel With Your Children, and includes a weekly call-in service for subscribers. Subscriptions cost $55 a year and can be ordered by writing to TWYCH, 45 W. 18th St., seventh floor, New York, NY 10011 ( ☎ **212/206-0688**). An information packet describing TWYCH's publications that includes a recent sample issue is available by sending $3.50 to the above address.

Babysitters can be found for you by most hotels.

## FOR STUDENTS

Bona fide students can avail themselves of a number of discounts on travel. The most wide ranging travel service for students is provided by **Council Travel,** 205 E. 42nd St., New York, NY 10017 (☎ **212/661-1414** or toll free **800/ GET-AN-ID**). In addition to its New York office, Council Travel has 37 other offices throughout the United States. This outfit runs a travel-related service for students, providing details about budget travel, study abroad, working permits, and insurance. It also compiles a number of helpful publications, including *Student Travels,* which features information on study and work opportunities abroad. It's distributed free, except for the $1 postage. Council Travel also issues a useful International Student Card (ISIC) for $16.

## 5  Alternative/Adventure Travel

## EDUCATIONAL/STUDY TRAVEL

The best information is available from the **Council on International Educational Exchange** (CIEE), 205 E. 42nd St., New York, NY 10017 (☎ **212/661-1450**);

see "For Students" in "Tips for the Disabled, Seniors, Singles, Students & Families," above. Request a copy of the 606-page *Work, Study, Travel Abroad: The Whole World Handbook* ($14.45 by mail), with more than 1,000 study opportunities abroad.

**Elderhostel,** 75 Federal St., Boston, MA 02110-1941 (☎ 617/426-7788), established in 1975, maintains an array of postretirement study programs, several of which are in the Bahamas. Its Europe programs include airfare; its Bahamian programs do not. Most courses last two or three weeks and are a good value, considering that hotel accommodations in student dormitories or modest inns, all meals, and tuition are included. Courses involve no homework, are ungraded, and center mostly on the liberal arts. In no way is this to be considered a luxury vacation, but rather an academic fulfillment of a type never possible for senior citizens until several years ago. Participants must be age 60 or older. However, if two members go as a couple, only one member needs to be 60 or over. Write for their free newsletter and a list of upcoming courses and destinations.

## HOMESTAYS OR VISITS

**Friendship Force,** 57 Forsyth St. NW, Atlanta, GA 30303 (☎ 404/522-9490), is a nonprofit organization existing for the sole purpose of fostering and encouraging friendship among people worldwide. Dozens of branch offices throughout North America arrange visits en masse, usually once a year. Each participant is required to spend two weeks in the host country, one full week of which will be as a guest in the home of a family.

## HOME EXCHANGES

If you don't mind "staying put," you can avail yourself of a "house swap"—as it's often called. It certainly keeps costs low if you don't mind a stranger living in your mainland home or apartment. Sometimes the exchange includes use of the family car.

Many directories are published detailing the possibilities for this type of service.

**The Invented City,** 41 Sutter St., Suite 1090, San Francisco, CA 94104 (☎ 415/673-0347), is an international home-exchange agency. Home-exchange listings are published three times a year, in February, May, and November. A membership fee of $50 allows you to list your home, and you can also give your preferred time to travel, your occupation, and your hobbies.

**Intervac U.S.,** P.O. Box 590504, San Francisco, CA 94119 (☎ 415/435-3497 or toll free 800/756-HOME in the U.S.), is part of the largest worldwide home-exchange network. It publishes four catalogs a year, containing more than 9,400 homes in more than 36 countries. Members contact each other directly. The $65 cost, plus postage, includes the purchase of three of the company's catalogs (which will be mailed to you), plus the inclusion of your own listing in whichever one of the three catalogs you select. If you want to publish a photograph of your home, it costs $11 extra. Hospitality and rentals are also available.

## PEOPLE-TO-PEOPLE

Visitors to Nassau on New Providence Island and Freeport/Lucaya on Grand Bahama Island have a unique opportunity. A program called People-to-People, thought up by the Bahamas Ministry of Tourism, gives visitors a chance to sample some "real" Bahamian culture. You will be introduced to a Bahamian family or couple, and they will show you how they live, take you to their churches and social functions, introduce you to their special cuisine. The staff tries to match you up with a host or hostess who might have interests similar to yours. To coordinate a People-to-People visit often takes several days, so visitors or their travel agents are encouraged to request the adventure before arrival. However, arrangements can also be made through the hotel where you are staying. You can get a form in advance by writing to the Ministry of Tourism, P.O. Box N-3701, Nassau, the Bahamas. If you're already in Nassau, go to one of the Tourist Information Centres, which are at the airport, at Prince George Dock, and at Rawson Square, or telephone **809/326-5371.** If you are planning to go to Freeport/Lucaya, the form can be mailed to the Ministry of Tourism, P.O. Box F-251, Freeport/Lucaya, the Bahamas. In Freeport/Lucaya, you can fill out the form at the Tourist Information Centre at the International Bazaar or phone **809/352-8044.**

## YOGA RETREATS

The only ashram in the Bahamas or the Caribbean that practices authentic Indian yoga is **Sivananda Ashram Yoga Retreat,** P.O. Box N-7550, Paradise Island, the Bahamas (☎ **809/363-2902;** fax 809/363-3783). The central core here is a clapboard building that contains dormitories, the kitchen, and the al fresco dining area. Communal meditation every day at 6am takes place either on the beach or at an open-air temple by the bay. Guests are expected to attend 8am and 4pm yoga classes. Breakfast at 10am is followed by free time until 4pm, when additional yoga lessons are held. An early dinner (6pm) is followed by an evening of meditation or an inspirational film.

About 75% of the guests here are North Americans, many of whom check in for one of the specialized workshops that include fasting clinics and 4-week yoga seminars. No smoking, drinking, or drugs are allowed here. Rates here are the cheapest on the island. In winter, beach huts cost $85 single or $60 per person double, with meals and classes included in all rates. Under the same arrangements, shared dormitory rooms go for $55 per person. If you bring your own tent, you are charged $50 per person. In the off-season, a single beach hut goes for $75, or else $50 per person based on double occupancy. Shared dormitory rooms cost $45 per person, or else $40 per person if you bring your own tent. From late November through Easter, all units are heavily booked, so reserve as early as possible.

## 6  Getting There

## BY PLANE

The Bahamas receives flights from many different states and countries. Nassau, followed by Freeport, is the busiest and most popular point of entry, with connections on to many of the more remote Family Islands. If you're headed for one of the Family Islands (formerly known as the Out Islands), refer to the "Getting There" section that appears at the beginning of my review of each island chain.

You face a choice of booking a seat on a regularly scheduled flight or on a charter flight, the latter being somewhat cheaper. On a regular flight, you can usually cancel or alter your flight dates without penalty; on a charter you do not have such leeway.

Flight time to Nassau from Miami is about 35 minutes; from New York to Nassau, 2¹/₂ hours; from Atlanta to Nassau, 2 hours 5 minutes; from Philadelphia,

2 hours 45 minutes; from Charlotte, about 2 hours 10 minutes; from central Florida around 1 hour 10 minutes; and from Toronto, about 3 hours.

## THE MAJOR AIRLINES

From the U.S. mainland, about a half-dozen carriers fly nonstop to the country's major point of entry and busiest airline hub, Nassau International Airport. A handful of others fly to the archipelago's second most populous city of Freeport. Despite the touristic allure of the Family Islands, only a handful of carriers (see below) fly directly to any of them.

**American Airlines** (☎ toll free **800/433-7300**) flies to Nassau nonstop from Miami. There is no nonstop flight between New York and Nassau on American. One must fly to Miami and change planes there. Flights from Miami are especially plentiful, with more than a dozen daily departures. American Eagle also offers about half a dozen daily flights between Miami and Freeport.

**Delta** (☎ toll free **800/221-1212**) offers several connections to the Bahamas, including twice daily flights from Atlanta. There's also a daily nonstop flight between LaGuardia airport in New York and Nassau. Delta also has a daily flight (nonstop) to Nassau from both Orlando and Fort Lauderdale. There are also two flights a day between Fort Lauderdale and Nassau and two flights a day between Orlando and Nassau on Comair, a partially owned subsidiary of Delta. Comair also has three flights a day between Orlando and Freeport and four daily flights between Fort Lauderdale and Freeport.

The national airline of the Bahamas, **Bahamasair** (☎ toll free **800/222-4262**), flies to the Bahamas from Miami, landing at either Nassau (with between 8 and 10 nonstop flights daily) or Freeport (with 3 nonstop flights daily). Bahamasair also has connections of about 5 to 7 flights a week from Fort Lauderdale to either Nassau or Freeport.

**USAir** (☎ toll free **800/428-4322**) offers five nonstop flights a week between Tampa and Nassau and a daily nonstop flight between Philadelphia and Nassau. There's also a daily direct flight from Baltimore that stops briefly in Charlotte, North Carolina, before continuing nonstop to Nassau.

Canadians often opt for flights to the Bahamas on **Air Canada** (☎ toll free **800/776-3000**), which flies nonstop from Toronto to Nassau two times a week.

As a former British colony and a present member of the British Commonwealth, the Bahamas continues to offer strong tourist appeal to Britain-based travelers. Most of them usually opt for transatlantic passage aboard **British Airways** (☎ toll free **800/247-9297**), which flies every day nonstop from London's Heathrow to Miami. Sometimes it has two flights a day. From there, a staggering number of convenient connections are available to Nassau and many other points within the archipelago on several different carriers.

### Flying to the Family Islands Directly from Florida

Many frequent visitors to the Bahamas do everything they can to avoid the congestion, inconvenience, and uncertain connections of the country's busiest airline hub, Nassau International Airport. (I highly recommend avoiding it if you possibly can.) Three U.S.-based airlines are available to cater to these needs. They include: **American Eagle,** an affiliate of American Airlines (☎ toll free **800/433-7300**), offers frequent service from Miami's international airport to such Family Island outposts as the Abacos, Eleuthera, and the Exumas. **USAir** (☎ toll free **800/428-4322**) flies nonstop every day from Fort Lauderdale, Florida, to

Eleuthera, usually making stops at both Governor's Harbour and North Eleuthera. It also flies every day from West Palm Beach to the Abacos, stopping in both Treasure Cay and Marsh Harbour. Another capable carrier is the Fort Lauderdale–based **Paradise Island Airlines** (☎ **305/895-1223** or toll free **800/432-8807**). It offers frequent flights from the Florida mainland to the company's private landing strip on Paradise Island. Nonstop flights to Paradise Island originate in West Palm Beach, Fort Lauderdale, and Miami's international airport.

**Chalk's International Airline** (☎ toll free **800/4-CHALKS**) stakes a claim as the oldest airline in the world in continuous service. Containing 17 passengers, each of the company's planes are amphibious aircraft that take off and land in calm waters near the company's port-side terminals. From the Florida mainland, nonstop flights depart from both Miami's Watson Island Airport and Fort Lauderdale's Jet Center Airport for both Bimini and Paradise Island. (The airline also offers charter flights to virtually anywhere in the Bahamas.)

## REGULAR FARES

The best strategy for securing the lowest airfare is to shop around. Keep calling the airlines. Peak season, which means winter in the Bahamas, is the most expensive time to go; basic season, during the summer months, offers the least expensive fares. Shoulder season refers to the spring and fall months in between.

Most airlines offer an assortment of fares from first class to business class to economy. The latter is the lowest-priced regular airfare carrying no special restrictions or requirements. Most airlines also offer promotional fares, which carry stringent requirements such as advance purchase, minimum stay, and cancellation penalties. The most common such fare is the APEX (Advance Purchase Excursion). Land arrangements (that is, prebooking of hotel rooms) are often tied in with promotional fares offered by airlines.

## OTHER GOOD-VALUE CHOICES

**BUCKET SHOPS (CONSOLIDATORS)**   In their purest sense, bucket shops act as clearinghouses for blocks of tickets that airlines discount and consign during normally slow periods of air travel. In the case of the Bahamas, that usually means from mid-April to mid-December. Charter operators (see below) and bucket shops used to perform separate functions, but many outfits perform similar functions these days.

Tickets are sometimes—but not always—priced at up to 35% less than the full fare. Terms of payment can vary—anywhere, from, say, 45 days prior to departure to last-minute sales offered in a final attempt by an airline to fill an empty craft. Tickets can be purchased through regular travel agents, who usually mark up the ticket 8% to 10%, maybe more, thereby greatly reducing your discount.

Bucket shops abound from coast to coast, but to get you started, here are some recommendations. Look also for their ads in your local newspaper's travel section.

One of the biggest U.S. consolidators is **Travac,** 989 Sixth Ave., New York, NY 10018 (☎ **212/563-3303** or toll free **800/TRAV-800** in the U.S.), which offers discounted seats throughout the U.S. on airlines that include TWA, United, and Delta. Another Travac office is at 2601 E. Jefferson St., Orlando, FL 32803 (☎ **407/896-0014**).

In New York try **TFI Tours International,** 34 W. 32nd St., 12th floor, New York, NY 10001 (☎ **212/736-1140** in New York State or toll free **800/745-8000** elsewhere in the U.S.). This tour company offers services to 177 cities worldwide.

For the Midwest, explore the possibilities of **Travel Avenue,** 10 S. Riverside Plaza, Suite 1404, Chicago, IL 60606 (☎ toll free **800/333-3335** in the U.S.), a national agency whose headquarters are here. Its tickets are often cheaper than most shops, and it charges the customer only a $25 fee on international tickets, rather than taking the usual $10 commission from an airline. Travel Avenue rebates most of that back to the customer—hence, the lower fares.

In New England, a possibility is **TMI** (Travel Management International), 39 JFK St. (Harvard Square), third floor, Cambridge, MA 02138 (☎ toll free **800/245-3672** in the U.S.), which offers a wide variety of discounts, including youth fares, student fares, and access to other kinds of air-related discounts as well.

**CHARTER FLIGHTS**   Now open to the general public, charter flights allow visitors to the Bahamas to travel at rates cheaper than on regularly scheduled flights. Many of the major carriers offer charter flights to the Bahamas at rates that are sometimes 30% (or more) off the regular fare.

There are some drawbacks to charter flights that you need to consider. Advance booking, for example, of up to 45 days or more may be required. You could lose most of the money you've advanced if an emergency should force you to cancel a flight. However, it is now possible to take out cancellation insurance against such an event.

Unfortunately, on the charter flight you are forced to depart and return on a scheduled date. In most cases, unless you've arranged special insurance with the charter operator in advance, it will do no good to call the airline and tell them you're in the hospital with yellow fever! If you're not on the plane, you can kiss your money good-bye.

Since charter flights are so complicated, it's best to go to a good travel agent and ask him or her to explain to you the problems and advantages. Sometimes charters require ground arrangements, such as the prebooking of hotel rooms.

The most visible agent for the booking of charter flights to the Bahamas is **Nassau/Paradise Island Express.** P.O. Box 3429, Secaucus, NJ 07096 (☎ toll free **800/722-4262**). The company prebuys blocks of seats aboard airplanes owned by either Continental or Carnival Airlines on flights headed between Newark, New Jersey, and Nassau. The company then resells the seats at prices that sometimes represent savings over most traditional tickets on conventional airlines. Airfare can be sold alone, but about 65% of the company's ticket sales are sold in conjunction with hotel packages at New Providence, Paradise Island hotels, and Freeport/Lucaya.

One highly specialized airline, established during the 1980s, is **Carnival Airlines** (☎ toll free **800/437-2110**), an affiliate of Carnival Cruise Lines. Although to the annoyance of potential clients, their toll-free number is often busy, they succeed in flying planeloads of clients in close cooperation with the country's biggest hotel, the Crystal Palace, whose rooms the airline is specifically designed to fill. Air-only fare is also available, especially from JFK. Two flights to Nassau are also available from Fort Lauderdale.

One reliable charter-flight operator is **Council Charter,** run by the Council on International Educational Exchange, 205 E. 42nd St., New York, NY 10017 (☎ **212/661-0311** or toll free **800/800-8222**), which arranges charter seats on regularly scheduled aircraft.

One of the biggest New York charter operators is **Travac,** 989 Sixth Ave., New York, NY 10018 (☎ **212/563-3303** or toll free **800/TRAV-800** in the U.S.)

Other Travac offices are at 2601 E. Jefferson St., Orlando, FL 32803 (☎ **407/ 896-0014**).

**REBATORS**    To confuse the situation even more, in the past few years rebators have also competed in the low-cost airfare market. Rebators are outfits that pass along part of their commission to the passenger, although many of them assess a fee for their services. Although they are not the same as travel agents, they can sometimes offer roughly similar services. Sometimes a rebator will sell you a discounted travel ticket, and also offer discounted land arrangements, including hotels and car rentals. Most rebators offer discounts averaging anywhere from 10% to 25%, plus a $20 handling charge.

Specializing in clients within the Midwest, **Travel Avenue,** 10 S. Riveside Plaza, Suite 1404, Chicago, IL 60606 (☎ **312/897-1116** or toll free **800/333-3335**), is said to be one of the oldest agencies of its kind. It offers up-front cash rebates on every airfare over $300 it sells. In a style similar to a discount brokerage firm, they pride themselves on NOT offering travel counseling. Instead, they sell airline tickets to independent travelers who have already worked out their travel plans. Also available are tour-and-cruise fares, plus hotel reservations, usually at prices less expensive than if you have prereserved them on your own.

Another major rebator is **Smart Traveller,** 3111 SW 27th Ave., P.O. Box 330010, Miami, FL 33133 (☎ **305/448-3338** or toll free **800/448-3338**). The agency also offers discounts on packaged tours.

**PROMOTIONAL FARES**    Airlines do announce promotional fares to the Bahamas. You'll need a good travel agent, or you'll have to do a lot of investigating yourself to learn what's available at the time of your intended trip.

**TRAVEL CLUBS**    A club supplies an unsold inventory of tickets discounted in the usual range of 20% to 60%. Some of the deals involve cruise ships and complete tour packages. After you pay an annual fee to join, you are given a hot-line number to call when you're planning to go somewhere. Many of these discounts become available several days in advance of an actual departure, though sometimes you have as much as a month's notice. Some of the best of these clubs nationwide include the following.

**Moment's Notice,** 425 Madison Ave., New York, NY 10017 (☎ **212/ 486-0500**), charges $25 per year for a membership that allows spur-of-the-moment participation in dozens of tours. Each is geared for impulse purchases and last-minute getaways, and each features air-and-land packages which sometimes represent substantial savings over what you'd have paid through more conventional channels. Although membership is required for participation in the tours, anyone can call the company's hot line (☎ **212/750-9111**) to learn what options are available. Most of the company's best-valued tours depart from New Jersey's Newark airport.

**Sears Discount Travel Club,** 3033 S. Parker Rd., Suite 900, Aurora, CO 80014 (☎ toll free **800/255-1487** in the U.S.), offers members, for $50, a catalog (issued four times a year), maps, discounts at select hotels, and a limited guarantee that equivalent packages will not be undersold by any other travel organization. It also offers a 5% rebate on the value of all airline tickets, tours, and hotel-and-car rentals which are purchased through them. (To collect this rebate, participants are required to fill out some forms and photocopy their receipts and itineraries.)

## FLIGHTS FROM THE U.K.

Though there are no direct flights to the Bahamas, **British Airways** (☎ **081/ 897-4000** in London) flies directly to Miami, Florida, daily. There, passengers take connecting flights to the various islands. British Airways agents make reservations for the connecting flights.

## BY CRUISE SHIP

Most cruises today appeal to the middle-income voyager who probably has no more than one week (or two at the most) to spend cruising at sea. Some 300 passenger ships sail the Caribbean and the Bahamas all year, and in January and February that figure may go up another hundred or so.

Most cruise-ship operators suggest the concept of a "total vacation." Some promote activities "from sunup to sundown," while others suggest the possibility of "having absolutely nothing to do but lounge." Cruise ships are self-contained resorts, offering everything on board but actual sightseeing once you arrive in a port of call.

If you don't want to spend all your time at sea, some lines offer a fly-and-cruise vacation. Terms vary widely under this arrangement. You spend a week cruising, another week staying at an interesting hotel at reduced prices. These total packages cost less (or should!) than if you'd purchased the cruise and air portions separately.

Miami is the "cruise capital of the world," and vessels also leave from New York, Port Everglades, Los Angeles, and other points of embarkation.

If you want to keep costs at a minimum, ask for one of the smaller, inside cabins when booking space on a cruise ship. If you're the type who likes to be active all day and for most of the night, you need not pay the extra money, which can be considerable, to rent luxurious suites aboard these seagoing vessels. Nearly all cabins rented today have a shower and a toilet, regardless of how cramped and confining the bathroom is. If you get a midship cabin, you are less likely to experience severe rolling and pitching.

Prices vary so widely that I cannot possibly document them here. Sometimes the same route, stopping at the identical ports of call, will carry different fares.

Unfortunately, the one ingredient needed for a successful cruise is the hardest to know in advance—and that's the list of your fellow passengers. The right crowd can be a lot of fun. A group incompatible with your interests can leave you sulking in your cabin.

**Vacations to Go,** 2411 Fountain View, Houston, TX 77057 (☎ toll free **800/ 338-4962**), established in 1984, specializes in establishing contacts between cruise lines and cruise participants and discounted prices. Annual membership costs $19.95 per family and provides access to catalogs and news briefs about cost-conscious cruises to the Bahamas, the Caribbean, and the Mediterranean.

Here's a rundown of some of the major cruise lines serving the Bahamas; pick up a copy of *Frommer's Cruises* for more detailed information.

If you've never taken an ocean cruise before, you may find the Miami-to-Nassau cruise, lasting three to four days, a good and proper introduction to cruising. Not only that, it's far kinder to your pocketbook than the more extended cruises to the Caribbean.

In a class by itself is the **American Canadian Caribbean Line, Inc.,** P.O. Box 368, Warren, RI 02885 (☎ **401/247-0955** in Rhode Island or toll free

**800/556-7450** outside Rhode Island). The company has been recognized for the quality of its ecological and historical tours by both the National Geographic Society and the Library of Congress. Designed with a shallow draft of only 6 feet, the three small cruise ships can accommodate 78 to 92 passengers and can land on isolated shorelines without the pier-and-wharf facilities required for the disembarkation of larger cruise ships. Thanks to a specially designed 40-foot bow ramp, passengers can disembark directly onto the sands of some of the most obscure but pristine islands in the Bahamas—places that would otherwise require the chartering of a private yacht to reach.

Tours through the Bahamas are usually offered only in March, April, and November. They always last for 12 days, begin and end in either Nassau or Freeport, and include stopovers at outlying islands, which usually include San Salvador, Norman's Cay, Sampson's Cay, Crooked Island, Staniel Cay, the Exumas, and Provo in the Turks and Caicos Islands. Priced at from $1,300 to $2,299 per person, double occupancy, the cruise is entitled "The Columbus Discovery Tour" and follows in the footsteps of the 15th-century explorer, with lots of bird-watching, snorkeling, nature appreciation, and conviviality thrown in. Appealing to mature travelers, the line is proud of its lack of on-board casinos, flashing lights, and disco music. Its BYOB policy, where passengers' private supplies of liquor are marked for their exclusive use, is cited as one of the greatest incentives for enhanced socializing. The line enjoys a 65% repeat business, one of the highest in the industry.

**Carnival Cruise Lines** (☎ **305/599-2600** or toll free **800/327-9501**), operating from such ports as Miami, is an enormous company with seven relatively youthful ships, ranging from medium sized (37,000 tons) to gargantuan (70,000 tons). Although the oldest of these entered service in 1982 (and was renovated in 1989), four of the newest were launched since 1990. Cruises tend to feature non-stop activities, lots of casino glitter, and the hustle and bustle of armies of clients and crew members embarking and disembarking at every conceivable port. Specific ships include the *Tropicale,* the *Festivale,* and the *Celebration* (all midsized). Much larger are the company's quartet of 70,000-ton superships, which include the *Ecstasy,* the *Fantasy,* the *Fascination,* and the *Sensation.* Their overall effect is sometimes compared to a floating theme park, loaded with whimsy, and with lots of emphasis on partying in a style you might have expected in Atlantic City. Lots of single passengers opt for this line, where the average onboard age is a relatively youthful 42. Featured are 3- or 4-day trips to Nassau and Freeport (Grand Bahamas Island). For example, the *Fantasy* leaves Port Canaveral in Florida on Thursday and Sunday, and the *Ecstasy* leaves from the Port of Miami on Friday and Monday.

**Dolphin Cruise Lines** (☎ **305/358-2111** or toll free **800/222-1003**) sails a trio of ships (*Dolphin IV, Ocean Breeze,* and *Seabreeze*) that are among the oldest in the industry, each built between 1955 and 1958. Each has been refurbished, and today they ply the waters between the ports of southern Florida, Nassau, and San Juan. Ships range from small to medium sized, weighing in at anywhere from 13,000 to 21,000 tons. Nothing on board any of these ships is particularly fancy, but no one seems to mind in view of the good value each cruise represents. *Dolphin IV* leaves every Friday from the Port of Miami and heads for a 3-day cruise of Nassau and Blue Lagoon Island, carrying 588 passengers.

**Fantasy Cruise Lines** (☎ **305/262-6677** or toll free **800/423-2100**) has two ships (the *Amerikanis* and the *Britanis*) that are carefully refurbished older models, built in 1932 and 1952, respectively, and as such are two of the oldest cruise ships in the market. Each also has a distinctive personality of its own, a quality sometimes missing from newer ships. The line is known for serving extremely good food for such a cost-conscious company. Each of its cruises specializes in mass-market, relatively inexpensive 7-day cruises originating in either San Juan or Miami. The cruises tend to appeal to senior citizens, families, students, and virtually anyone else traveling on a budget. There's lots to do onboard, including organized group games and trivia contests. With each of the vessels weighing in at no more than 26,000 tons, the two ships are considered small to moderate sized. Its 926-passenger *Britanis* leaves every Friday from Miami for a 2-day trip to Nassau.

**Majesty Cruise Line** (☎ **305/536-0000** or toll free **800/532-7788**) is a company whose U.S. port of embarkation is almost always Miami, and whose one ship (the *Royal Majesty,* 32,400 tons) was specifically built in 1992 for continuous 3- or 4-day circuits whose outer limits are usually Nassau, Key West, and the coastal resorts of Mexico. Majesty is usually considered the upscale twin of the less glamorous (and less expensive) Dolphin Cruise Lines, with whom it shares the same owners. Carrying 1,056 passengers, the *Royal Majesty* offers 3-day trips to Nassau from the Port of Miami.

**Norwegian Cruise Line** (☎ **305/447-9660** or toll free **800/327-7030**) operates popular 3- and 4-day cruises out of Miami, stopping first at Nassau, then at a private Family Island, then Freeport, before returning to Miami. The line carries more passengers than any other cruise line in North America. Its "Bahamarama cruises," as they are called, are among the most popular in the industry. Its 1,534-passenger *Seeward* operating out of Miami departs every Friday.

**Premier Cruise Lines,** the official cruise line of Walt Disney World (☎ toll free **800/473-3262**), has three ships, the *Atlantic,* the *Oceanic,* and the *Majestic,* each of which has a distinctive red hull and an onboard program which makes great efforts to cater to children. (When the *Oceanic* was christened in 1986, the character who broke the champagne bottle on the crimson hull was outfitted like Minnie Mouse.) The line, which is said to have invented family cruising in the mid-1980s, devotes most of its marketing effort to attracting intergenerational business. Adults appreciate such activities as bridge tournaments and fitness facilities. Overall, however, the themes are geared to family fun, so if you don't really want to share your recreational activities with children, you might consider looking for another cruise line. Its ships make 3- or 4-day loops from Port Everglades or Port Canaveral, stopping at Freeport/Lucaya on Grand Bahamas Island and Nassau.

**Royal Caribbean Cruise Line** (☎ **305/539-6000**). This company led the industry in the development of megaships. Three of this company's six vessels weigh in at 73,000 tons and are among the largest anywhere. These include *Majesty of the Seas, Monarch of the Seas,* and *Sovereign of the Seas.* The remaining three are *Nordic Empress, Song of America,* and *Sun Viking.* A house-party theme tends to permeate the onboard ambience of these ships, although it's a bit less frenetic than that found aboard the megaships of other cruise lines. The company is well run, and there are enough onboard activities to suit virtually any taste or age level. Though accommodations and accoutrements are more than adequate, they are not to be considered as upscale. Its *Nordic Empress* leaves Miami every Monday and Friday for 3-day cruises to Nassau and Coco Cay. Four-day cruises to Nassau, Coco Cay, and Freeport/Lucaya are also offered.

## BY CHARTERED BOAT

For those who can afford it, this is one of the most luxurious ways to arrive in the Bahamas. On your private boat, you can island-hop at your convenience. Well-equipped marinas are on every major island and many cays. There are designated ports of entry at Great Abaco (Marsh Harbor), Andros, the Berry Islands, Bimini, Cat Cay, Eleuthera, Great Exuma, Grand Bahama Island (Freeport/Lucaya), Great Inagua, New Providence (Nassau), Ragged Island, and San Salvador.

Vessels must check with Customs at the first port of entry and receive a cruising clearance permit to the Bahamas. Carry it with you and return it at the official port of departure.

You should buy *The Yachtsman's Guide to the Bahamas,* which is available from Tropic Isle Publishers. Edited by Meredith H. Fields, this is the *only* guide covering the entire Bahamas and Turks and Caicos Islands. Copies of the book are available at major marine outlets, bookstores, and by mail direct from the publisher for $28.95, U.S. postpaid: **Tropic Isle Publishers, Inc.,** P.O. Box 610938, North Miami, FL 33261-0938 (☎ **305/893-4277**).

Experienced sailors and navigators, with a sea-wise crew, can charter "bareboat," a term meaning a rental with a fully equipped boat but with no captain or crew. You're on your own, and you'll have to prove you can handle it before you're allowed to take out such craft. Even if you're your own skipper, you may want to take along an experienced yachtsperson familiar with local waters, which may be tricky in some places.

Four to twelve people often charter yachts varying from 50 to more than 100 feet, and split the cost among them. The Bahamas, as will be pointed out many times, offer among the most beautiful and romantic cruising grounds in the world, especially around such island chains as the Exumas, the Abacos, and Eleuthera.

Most yachts are rented on a weekly basis, with a fully stocked bar, plus equipment for fishing and water sports. People taking bareboat charters can save money and select menus more suited to their tastes by doing their own provisioning.

**Windjammer Barefoot Cruises Ltd.,** P.O. Box 120, Miami Beach, FL 33119 (☎ **305/534-7447** or toll free **800/327-2601**), offers 6- and 13-day sailing adventures on classic "tall ships" through the Caribbean. *Flying Cloud* island-hops the British Virgin Islands, *Yankee Clipper* travels the Grenadines and Tobago cays, *Polynesia* sails through the West Indies, *Fantome* sails the Bahamas during the summer months and the West Indies during the winter, and *Mandalay* takes a leisurely 13-day cruise through the Grenadines. The supply ship, *Amazing Grace,* carries 96 passengers island-hopping from Freeport to Grenada. Rates start at $650. Air-sea package deals are offered. All ships are registered in Honduras and comply with international safety standards.

**Sunsail,** 2 Prospect Park, 3347 NW 55th St., Fort Lauderdale, FL 33309 (☎ **305/484-5246** or toll free **800/327-2276**), specializes in yacht chartering from one of its bases in Marsh Harbour, Great Abaco, the Bahamas. Bareboat and crewed yachts between 32 and 56 feet are available from a well-maintained fleet of sailing craft. The charter manager suggests that 4- to 6-month advance reservations (which require a 25% deposit of the total rental fee) are a good idea for locked-in dates. Clients whose schedules are more flexible usually need only reserve about a month ahead of time. Insurance and full equipment will be included in the rates.

## BY PACKAGE TOUR

If you want everything done for you, and want to save money as well, consider traveling to the Bahamas on a package tour. General tours appealing to the average voyager are commonly offered, but many of the tours have a special focus—tennis, golf, scuba and snorkeling, etc. The costs of transportation (usually an airplane fare), a hotel room, food (sometimes), and sightseeing (sometimes) are combined in one package, neatly tied up with a single price tag. Transfers between your hotel and the airport are often included. Many packages carry several options, including the possibility of low-cost car rentals.

There are disadvantages, too. First, you generally have to pay the cost of the total package in advance. Then, you may find yourself in a hotel you dislike immensely, yet you are virtually trapped there. The single traveler, regrettably, usually suffers too, since nearly all tour packages are based on double occupancy.

Also, I find that many package deals to the Bahamas contain more hidden extras than they should. The list of "free" offerings sometimes sounds better than it is. Forget about that free rum punch at the manager's cocktail party and peruse the fine print to see if your deal includes meals and other costly items.

Choosing the right tour can be a bit of a problem. It's best to go to a travel agent, tell him or her what island (or islands) you'd like to visit, and see what's currently offered.

Also, consider hiring the services of **Tourscan, Inc.,** P.O. Box 2367, Darien, CT 06820 (☎ **203/655-8091** or toll free **800/962-2080**). Tourscan researches the best value vacation at each hotel and condo. Two catalogs are printed each year. Each lists a broad choice of hotels on most of the islands of the Bahamas, in all price ranges. Catalogs cost $4 each, the price of which is credited to any Tourscan vacation. Prices are based on travel from New York, Newark, Baltimore, Philadelphia, and Washington, D.C., although the company will arrange trips originating from any location in the United States or abroad on request.

Another good deal might be a combined land-and-air package offered by one of the major U.S. carriers. Call their toll-free numbers: **American Fly-Away Vacations** (☎ **800/321-2121**); **Delta's Dream Vacations** (☎ **(800/872-7786**); **TWA Getaway Vacations** (☎ **800/GETAWAY**); and **United Airlines Vacations** (☎ **800/328-6877**).

The best diving cruises are packaged by **Oceanic Society Expeditions,** Fort Mason Center, Building E, San Francisco, CA 94123 (☎ **415/441-1106** or toll free **800/326-7491**). Whale-watching jaunts and some research-oriented trips are also a feature. Another specialist in this field is **Tropical Adventures,** 111 Second Ave. N., Seattle, WA 98109 (☎ **206/441-3483** or toll free **800/247-3483**). Its packages to Saba are a particular delight.

**Horizon Tours,** 1010 Vermont Ave. NW, Suite 202, Washington, DC 20005 (☎ **202/393-8390** or toll free **800/395-0025**), specializes in all-inclusive resorts on the islands of the Bahamas, Jamaica, Aruba, and Puerto Rico.

**Club Med,** Club Med Sales, P.O. Box 4460, Scottsdale, AZ 85258 (☎ toll free **800/258-2633**), has various all-inclusive options throughout the Caribbean and the Bahamas.

Advertising more packages to the Bahamas and the Caribbean than any other agency is **Liberty Travel,** with offices in many states. One base is Spring Street, Ramsey, NJ 07446 (☎ **201/934-3500**).

**Frontiers International,** 100 Logan Rd. (P.O. Box 959), Wexford, PA 15090 (☎ 412/935-1577 in Pennsylvania or toll free **800/245-1950** elsewhere in the U.S.), features fly-and-spin fishing tours of the Bahamas and is considered a specialist in its limited field.

**FOR BRITISH TRAVELERS**   Package tours to the Bahamas can be booked through **Harlequin Worldwide,** 2 North Rd., South Ockendon, Essex RM15 6QJ (☎ **01708/852-780**). This agency offers both air-and-hotel packages not only to Nassau, but to such Out Islands as Eleuthera, Cat Island, Long Island, and Pirates Cove. Another specialist is **Kuoni Travel,** Kuoni House, Dorking, Surrey RH5 4AZ (☎ **01306/742-222**), offering both land-and-air packages to the Bahamas, including such destinations as Nassau and Freeport, but also to some places in the Out Islands. They also offer packages for self-catering villas on Paradise Island.

# 7  Getting Around

If your final destination is Paradise Island, Freeport, or Nassau (Cable Beach), and you plan to go there by plane, you'll have little trouble in reaching your destination.

However, if you're heading for one of the Family Islands, you face more exotic choices, not only of airplanes but also of other means of transport, including a mail boat, the traditional connecting link among the old Out Islands in days of yore.

As mentioned, each section on one of the Family Island chains has specific transportation information, but in the meantime, I'll give you a general overview.

## BY PLANE

The national airline of the Bahamas, **Bahamasair** (☎ toll free **800/222-4262**), serves 19 airports on 12 Bahamian islands, including Abaco, Andros, Cat Island, Eleuthera, Long Island, and San Salvador. Many of the Family Islands have either airports or airstrips, or are within a short ferry ride's distance of one.

## BY MAIL BOAT

Before the advent of better airline connections, the traditional way of exploring the Family Islands—in fact, about the only way unless you had your own craft—was by mail boat. This 125-year-old service is still available, but it's recommended only for those who have unlimited time and a sense of adventure. You may ride with cases of rum, oil drums, crawfish pots, live chickens, even an occasional piano.

The boats, 19 of them comprising the "Post Office Navy," under the Direction of Bahamian Chief of Transportation, are often fancifully colored, high sided, and somewhat clumsy in appearance, but the little motor vessels chug along, serving the 30 inhabited islands of the Bahamas. Schedules can be thrown off by weather and other causes, but most morning mail boats depart from Potter's Cay (under the Paradise Island Bridge in Nassau) or from Prince George Wharf. The voyages last from 4$^1$/$_2$ hours to most of a day, sometimes even overnight. Check the schedule of the particular boat you wish to travel on with the skipper at the dock in Nassau.

Tariffs charged on the mail boats are considerably less than for air travel. Many of the boats offer two classes of passenger accommodations, first and second. In first class you get a bunk bed and in second you may be entitled only to deck space. The bunk beds are actually usually reserved for the seasick, but first-class passengers sit in a fairly comfortable enclosed cabin, at least on the larger boats.

For information about mail boats to the Family Islands, contact the **Dockmasters Office** in Nassau, under the Paradise Island Bridge on Potter's Cay (☎ **809/393-1064**).

## BY TAXI

Taxis are plentiful in the Nassau/Cable Beach/Paradise Island area and in the Freeport/Lucaya area on Grand Bahama Island. These cabs, for the most part, are metered. See "Getting Around" in the section on each island.

In the Family Islands, however, you will not be so richly blessed. In general, taxi service is available at all air terminals, at least if those air terminals are of the status of "port of entry" terminals. They are also available in the vicinity of most marinas.

Taxis are usually shared, often with the local residents. Family Island taxis aren't metered, so you must negotiate the fare before you get in. Cars are often old and badly maintained, so be prepared for a bumpy ride over some rough roads if you've selected a particularly remote hotel.

## BY CAR

**RENTALS**   Some judicious research may reveal that renting a car is less expensive than you may have thought, especially if you consider the high cost of transportation by taxi or the inconvenience of traveling by bus. Blithe spirits will also appreciate the freedom of reaching that out-of-the-way beach or secluded cove.

Of all the locations in the Bahamas, the airports at Nassau (New Providence Island) and Freeport (Grand Bahama Island) have the most North American car-rental companies. Of course, they compete with a handful of local car-rental companies, some of which may charge a few dollars less.

Most readers prefer to do business with one of the major firms, since they offer toll-free reservation services and, generally, better-maintained vehicles.

Reserving a car in Nassau or Freeport is just a matter of making a toll-free phone call in advance from wherever you live. Renting a car in the Family Islands, however, may be more difficult. If you plan to remain near your hotel, you'll probably be better off just using taxis.

Each of the major firms quotes an unlimited-mileage rate, which varies slightly with the time of year. Each company's system is slightly different, although after the first week the per-day rate is usually less expensive than the daily rate for rentals of less than a week. Of course, there are extra charges, which the fine print of a rental contract will reveal. These sometimes include a small refueling service charge, which applies if the renter returns the car with less fuel than when he or she originally rented it. More important, a renter is able to arrange additional insurance in the form of a collision damage waiver (CDW). Without the waiver, depending on the company, a renter is liable for the first several hundred dollars' worth of damage to the car in the event of an accident. If the waiver is purchased, the driver waives all financial responsibility in the event of an accident. The amount of liability varies from company to company. If in doubt, I suggest you purchase the waiver.

Each company has a different age limit for its drivers. All require a minimum age of between 21 and 25, and some won't rent a car to anyone over 70. Underage drivers can sometimes rent from an agency upon payment of a substantial cash (not credit card) deposit. Of course, a valid driver's license must be presented when the rental contract is issued.

For more information about rentals in Nassau or Freeport, you can call the international departments of **Budget Rent-a-Car** (☎ toll free **800/472-3325**), **Hertz** (☎ toll free **800/654-3001**), and **Avis** (☎ toll free **800/331-2112**). Budget rents only in Nassau.

**GASOLINE**    "Petrol" is easily available in Nassau and Freeport. In the Family Islands, where the cost of gasoline is likely to vary from island to island, you should plan your itinerary based on information as to where you'll be able to get fuel. Usually the major towns of the islands have service stations. You should have no problems on New Providence or Grand Bahama unless you start out with a nearly empty tank.

**DRIVING REQUIREMENTS**    A visitor may drive on his or her home driver's license for up to three months. Longer stays require a Bahamian driver's license. Insurance against injury or death liability is compulsory.

*A word of warning:* British tradition lives on in the Bahamas. You must drive on the left!

**ROAD MAPS**    As you emerge at one of the major airports, including those of Nassau (New Providence) and Freeport (Grand Bahama Island), you can pick up island maps that are quite sufficient for routine touring around those islands. However, if you plan to do extensive touring in the Family Islands, you should go first to a bookstore either in Nassau or Freeport and ask for a copy of *Atlas of the Bahamas,* sponsored by the Ministry of Education in Nassau. It provides touring routes (outlined in red) through all the major Family Islands. Once you arrive on these remote islands, it may be hard to obtain maps.

**BREAKDOWNS/ASSISTANCE**    There are no emergency numbers to call. Before setting out in a rented car, ask the rental company what number you should call in case of a breakdown. Usually it's the car-rental firm itself, which will send someone to help you.

## HITCHHIKING

Even though technically illegal, this is a commonplace method of travel, particularly in the Family Islands, where there is a scarcity of vehicles. It's a less desirable practice in Nassau, Cable Beach, and Freeport/Lucaya, and it's unheard of on Paradise Island. Please know in advance that *Frommer's The Bahamas* does not endorse hitchhiking, not only in the islands but anywhere else in the world. It's too risky these days.

## SUGGESTED ITINERARIES

Travelers on a short visit to the Bahamas. might want to skip this section and refer to the more "concentrated" sightseeing, as outlined in Chapters 4, 5, and 6, for Nassau, Paradise Island, and Freeport.

### If You Have 1 Week

**Day 1**    Do as most visitors do the first day: don't do anything. Providing you took a morning flight to Nassau from an East Coast city such as New York, you will arrive in The Bahamas in time to clear Customs and have lunch at your hotel. Wind down by the pool at your hotel or at one of the sandy beaches along Cable Beach or Paradise Island, have dinner, and retire early to tackle the charms of New Providence Island the following day.

**Day 2**   Head for the center of Nassau; and take our walking tour of its attractions (see Chapter 4). After lunch in a local restaurant, go on a shopping spree looking for duty-free bargains. If you're still there at sunset, head for one of the local bars opening onto the water for a "sundowner," a time-honored custom in the islands.

**Day 3**   Devote most of the day to the beach at Paradise Island or pursue your favorite sport, such as golf, waterskiing, or parasailing. Try a local Bahamian restaurant for lunch and sample conch in its many variations. Pay a late-afternoon visit to the Botanical Gardens on Chippendale Road.

**Day 4**   Visit Coral World Bahamas on Silver Cay in the morning, have lunch at a restaurant along Cable Beach after getting in some sunning, then explore Ardastra Gardens in the afternoon. Head for the casinos of Cable Beach or Paradise Island that evening.

**Day 5**   Return to downtown Nassau for some final shopping before trying out a different beach, perhaps heading back to one on Paradise Island again. Have lunch at an open-air place near the water. In the afternoon see any sights on our list that you missed the first time, and then take in a Las Vegas–type revue on Paradise Island.

**Day 6**   If you have a week for the Bahamas, why not leave Nassau/Paradise Island now and spend the final two days at Freeport/Lucaya on Grand Bahama Island, which offers a different insight into the Bahamas. There are frequent air links between Nassau and Freeport. On Grand Bahama Island, check into a hotel—perhaps at Lucaya—and spend the rest of the day unwinding at the beach.

**Day 7**   Head for the International Bazaar for a morning of shopping, then explore the West End of the island by car in the afternoon. If time remains, see the Garden of the Groves and the Rand Memorial Nature Center. Then nightcap your Freeport visit by going to one of the casinos such as the Princess Casino or take in a cabaret show at one of the big hotels.

## If You Have 2 Weeks

**Days 1–7**   See above.

**Day 8**   Instead of flying back home, continue your exploration of the Bahamas. From either Freeport or Nassau, make connections to the Abaco Islands. Your best bet is to land on the east coast of Abaco where you can take a taxi to the dock for departures to Green Turtle Cay (New Plymouth). Select a resort on the island, either Green Turtle Club or Bluff House Club & Marina, relax, and wind down. It's always early to bed so you'll get plenty of rest.

**Day 9**   In the morning, explore the old town of New Plymouth and have lunch in one of the typical Bahamian restaurants. See the Albert Lowe Museum and perhaps enjoy some scuba or bonefishing in the afternoon. That evening, attend Miss Emily's Blue Bee Bar.

**Day 10**   Do what one does on Green Turtle Cay: relax, enjoy the sun, or engage in some sports. Have dinner at the Green Turtle Club.

**Day 11**   Return to the east coast of North Abaco and make flight connections south to Marsh Harbour. Overnight here at one of the inns, such as Abaco Towns by the Sea or the Great Abaco Beach Resort. Walk around the town and dine at one of the local Bahamian joints.

**Day 12** While still based at Marsh Harbour, take Albury's Ferry Service the next morning to spend the day at Man-O-War Cay, which is very quaint and old-fashioned. Enjoy a local lunch on the island, check out some of the little shops, and walk around the island. Return to Marsh Harbour for a conch dinner that night.

**Day 13** Leave Marsh Harbour for the 20-minute ferry ride to Elbow Cay, landing at Hope Town, another place-that-time-forgot hamlet of the Abacos.

**Day 14** Enjoy the beaches, go scuba diving (if that is your desire), and explore some of the local shops. Have lunch at the Abaco Inn. Climb to the top of the lighthouse for a sweeping view before contemplating your return home tomorrow.

## 8 Tips on Accommodations

The Bahamas offer a wide selection of accommodations, ranging from small private guest houses to large luxury resorts. Hotels vary in size and facilities, from deluxe (offering room service, sports, swimming pools, entertainment, etc.) to fairly simple hostelries.

There are package deals galore, and though they have many disadvantages, they are always cheaper than rack rates. (A rack rate is what an individual pays who literally walks in from the street.) Therefore it's always good to go to a reliable travel agent to find out what, if anything, is available in the way of a land-and-air package before booking into a particular accommodation.

There is no rigid classification of hotel properties in the islands. The word "deluxe" is often used—or misused—when "first class" might have been a more appropriate term. First class itself often isn't. For that and other reasons, I've presented fairly detailed descriptions of the properties, so that you'll get an idea of what to expect once you're there. However, even in the deluxe and first-class resorts and hotels, don't expect top-rate service and efficiency. "Things," as they are called in the islands, don't seem to work as well here as they do in certain fancy resorts of California, Florida, or Europe. Life here has its disadvantages. When you go to turn on the shower, sometimes you get water and sometimes you don't. You may even experience power failures.

Facilities often determine the choice of a hotel, and regardless of your particular interest, there is probably a hotel for you. All the big first-class resort hotels have swimming pools. Usually a beach is nearby if not directly in front of the hotel property. If you want to save money, you can book into one of the more moderate accommodations less desirably located. Then, often for only a small fee, you can use the facilities of the larger and more expensive resorts. However, don't try to "crash" a resort. It's better to be a paying customer. Often if you have lunch or patronize the bar, you can stick around and enjoy the afternoon. Policies vary from resort to resort: some are stricter than others.

The **winter season** in the Bahamas runs roughly from the middle of December to the middle of April, and hotels charge their highest prices during this peak period. Winter is generally the dry season in the islands, but there can be heavy rainfall regardless of the time of year.

During the winter months, make reservations two months in advance if you can, and if you rely on writing directly to the hotels, know that the mail service is unreliable and takes a long time. At certain hotels it's almost impossible to secure accommodations at Christmas and in February. Again, instead of writing or faxing to reserve your own room, it's better to book through a stateside representative.

The so-called **off-season** in the Bahamas—roughly from mid-April to mid-December (although this varies from hotel to hotel)—amounts to a sale. In most cases, hotel rates are slashed a startling *20% to 60%*. It's a bonanza for cost-conscious travelers, especially for families who can travel in the summer. Perhaps people think that the Bahamas are a caldron. This is not the case. The fabled Bahamian weather is balmy all year. The mid-80s prevail throughout most of the region, and trade winds make for comfortable days and nights, even in cheaper places that don't have air-conditioning. Truth is, you're better off in the Bahamas than suffering through a roaring August heat wave in Chicago or New York.

## THE BAHAMIAN GUEST HOUSE

The guest house is where many Bahamians themselves stay when they're traveling in their own islands. In the Bahamas, however, and to a very limited extent in the Turks and Caicos Islands, the term "guest house" can mean anything. Sometimes so-called guest houses are really like simple motels built around swimming pools. Others are small individual cottages, with their own kitchenettes, constructed around a main building in which you'll often find a bar and restaurant serving local food.

In the Family Islands of the Bahamas, the guest houses are not as luxurious for the most part as those of Bermuda. Although bereft of frills in general, the Bahamian guest houses I've recommended are clean, decent, and safe for families or single women. Many of these guest houses are very basic. Salt spray on metal or fabric takes a serious toll, and chipped paint is commonplace. Bathrooms can fall into the vintage category, and sometimes the water isn't heated—but when it's 85 to 92 degrees Fahrenheit outside, you don't need hot water.

On the other hand, some of these establishments are quite comfortable. Some are almost luxurious; and in addition to giving you the opportunity to live with a local family, they boast swimming pools, private baths in all rooms, and air-conditioning.

---

### What the Symbols Mean

**AP** (American Plan): Includes three meals a day (sometimes called full board or full pension).

**BP** (Bermuda or Bahamas Plan): Popularized first in Bermuda, this option includes a full American breakfast (sometimes called an English breakfast).

**CP** (Continental Plan): A continental breakfast (that is, bread, jam, and coffee) is included in the room rate.

**EP** (European Plan): This rate is always cheapest, as it offers only the room— no meals.

**MAP** (Modified American Plan): Sometimes called half board or half pension, this room rate includes breakfast and dinner (or lunch if you prefer).

## HOUSEKEEPING HOLIDAYS

Particularly if you're a family or a congenial group, a housekeeping holiday can be one of the least expensive ways to stay in the Bahamas. These types of accommodations are now available on all the islands discussed in this guide. Sometimes you can rent individual cottages; other accommodations are housed in one building. Some are private homes rented when the owners are away. All have small kitchens or kitchenettes where you can do your home cooking after shopping for groceries, which is one of the best ways to keep holiday costs at a minimum. Most of the self-catering establishments have maid service included in the weekly rental, and you're given a supply of fresh linen as well.

## RENTAL VILLAS & VACATION HOMES

You might rent a big villa, a good-sized apartment in someone's condo, or even a small beach cottage (more accurately called a "cabana").

Private apartments are also available, with or without maid service. This is more of a no-frills option than the villas and condos. The apartments may not be in buildings with swimming pools, and they may not have a front desk to help you.

Cottages, or cabanas, offer the most freewheeling lifestyle available in these categories of vacation homes. Many ideally open onto a beach, although others may be clustered around a communal swimming pool. Most of them are fairly simple, containing no more than a plain bedroom plus a small kitchen and bath. In the peak winter season, reservations should be made at least five or six months in advance.

Agencies specializing in these rentals include the following:

**At Home Abroad,** 405 E. 56th St., Suite 6-H, New York, NY 10022-2466 (☎ 212/421-9165), has a roster of private homes for rent, all with maid service included.

**VHR Worldwide,** 235 Kensington Ave., Norwood, NJ 07648 (☎ 201/767-9393), offers the most comprehensive portfolio of luxury villas, condominiums, resort suites, and apartments for rent not only in the Bahamas, but also in the Caribbean, Mexico, the United States, and Europe.

**Hideaways International,** 767 Islington St. (P.O. Box 4433), Portsmouth, NH 03801-4433 (☎ 603/430-4433 or toll free **800/843-4433** in the U.S.), publishes *Hideaways Guide,* a 140-page pictorial directory of home rentals throughout the region with full descriptions so you know what you're renting. Rentals range from cottages to staffed villas to whole islands! On most rentals you deal directly with owners. At condos and small resorts Hideaways offers member discounts. Other services include yacht charters, airline ticketing, car rentals, and hotel reservations. Annual membership is $99; a 4-month trial membership is $39.95.

**Rent-a-Home International,** 7200 34th Ave. NW, Seattle, WA 98117 (☎ 206/789-9377), specializes in condos and villas. It arranges weekly or longer bookings.

Sometimes local tourist offices will also advise you on vacation-home rentals if you write or call them directly.

## 9 Getting Married in the Bahamas

You might prefer a wedding beneath a palm tree instead of a snowbound setting in your hometown. If that's the case, a bevy of islanders can assist you with the legalities. Any large resort in the Bahamas, as well as the Ministry of Tourism's People-to-People program, will help you arrange the details.

Here's what's required: Both of you must be in the Bahamas at the moment you apply for your wedding license, the price of which is $40. If both of you are single and U.S. citizens, you must obtain an affidavit to that effect from the U.S. embassy in Nassau. (The price of this is $10 and will require presentation of proof of identity, such as a passport.) If it's applicable, you'll also need to show proof of divorce. Request a waiver of the 15-day residency requirement from the Registrar General, P.O. Box N-532, Nassau, the Bahamas. (This waiver will almost always be granted.) If all of the above-mentioned requirements are met, you can be married anytime after the third day of your arrival in the Bahamas. If either of you is under 18 years of age, parental consent is required. No blood test is necessary.

Once you're hitched, a wide array of hotels will present themselves as suitable settings for your honeymoon. The most alluring of these will probably lie within the Out Islands, and each will probably offer an array of honeymoon packages with various types of money-saving options.

## FAST FACTS: THE BAHAMAS

**American Express**   Representing American Express in the Bahamas are Playtours, Shirley Street, between Charlotte and Parliament Streets, Nassau (☎ **809/ 322-2931**), and Mundytours, Building 4 Regent Centre, Suite 20, Freeport (☎ **809/352-6641**). At either of these offices you can receive customer service and travel and tour arrangements. Hours are 9am to 5pm Monday through Friday. Traveler's checks are issued upon presentation of a personal check and an American Express card.

**Area Code**   The area code for the Bahamas is 809.

**Business Hours**   In Nassau, Cable Beach, and Freeport/Lucaya, commercial banking hours are 9:30am to 3pm Monday through Thursday, 9:30am to 5pm on Friday. Hours are likely to vary widely in the Family Islands. Ask at your hotel.

Most government offices are open Monday through Friday from 9am to 5pm. Most shops are open Monday through Saturday from 9am to 5pm.

**Camera & Film**   Purchasing film in Nassau/Paradise Island or Freeport/Lucaya is relatively easy. However, it might be well to stock up if you're going to some of the remote Family Islands and need a special kind of film.

**Car Rentals**   See "Getting Around" in this chapter.

**Climate**   See "When to Go" in this chapter.

**Crime**   See "Safety," below.

**Currency**   See "Visitor Information, Entry Requirements & Money" in this chapter.

**Customs**   To go through Bahamian Customs, you only need to do an oral baggage declaration, unless you're bringing in something on which duty must be paid. However, your baggage is subject to Customs inspection. Each adult visitor coming to the Bahamas is allowed 50 cigars, 200 cigarettes, or 1 pound of tobacco; 1 quart of spirits; and personal effects, articles that have been in the possession of the visitor before arrival.

The Bahamaian government has enacted strict laws regarding possession of dangerous drugs or firearms. Penalties for infractions are severe. Special authorization is necessary to bring firearms into the Bahamas, and licenses are required.

For more information on Customs once you return home, refer to "Information, Entry Requirements & Money" in this chapter.

**Documents Required**   See "Visitor Information, Entry Requirements & Money" in this chapter.

**Driving Rules**   See "Getting Around" in this chapter.

**Drug Laws**   Importation of, possession of, or dealing with unlawful drugs, including marijuana, is a serious offense in the Bahamas, with heavy penalties. Customs officers, at their discretion, may conduct body searches for drugs or other contraband goods.

**Drugstores**   Nassau and Freeport are amply supplied with pharmacies (see individual island listings). However, if you're traveling in the Family Islands, it is always best to carry your prescribed medication with you.

**Electricity**   Electricity is normally 120 volts, 60 cycles, AC. American appliances are compatible.

**Embassies & Consulates**   The U.S. embassy is on Queen Street, P.O. Box N-8197, Nassau (☎ 809/322-4753), and the Canadian consulate is on Shirley Street, Nassau (☎ 809/393-2123). The British High Commission is in the BITCO Building (third floor), East Street, Nassau (☎ 809/325-7471).

**Emergencies**   In Nassau, call the police at 919. You can report a fire at the same number. In the Freeport/Lucaya area, call the police at 911, or dial **809/352-8888** to report a fire. In the Family Islands, ask at your hotel—or the first responsible-looking person you see—to summon the nearest available help. If you are near a phone, call the operator and ask to be connected to the nearest police station.

**Etiquette**   It is customary to greet people in the Family Islands with a hello or some acknowledgment of their existence as you pass them on the road. People are often shy and will wait for you to make the first overture.

Many tourist boards are increasingly sensitive to the treatment of visitors because their fragile economies depend on how many people their islands attract. Rudeness, room burglaries, anything that results in unfavorable publicity can cause damage. As a result, many islands are taking steps to make their own people more aware of the importance of tourism, and to treat their guests well. Of course, many of the problems have come from the tourists themselves. The people of the Bahamas must be given their respect and dignity.

Many of the islanders are deeply religious, and they are offended by tourists who wear bikinis on expeditions in town. Always wear a cover-up at meals. Know that most of the people in the Bahamas are proud, very proper, and most respectable, and if you treat them as such, they will likely treat you the same way. Others—certainly the minority, but a visible minority—can be downright antagonistic. Some, in fact, are not to be trusted. But every country has its share of that type.

**Gambling**   Casino gambling is legal in the Bahamas for visitors. Bahamians and Bahamas residents are prohibited from gambling, although they can enter the casinos in the company of friends from elsewhere. Games offered are dice, roulette, blackjack, baccarat, wheel of fortune, and slot machines. There is a casino at Cable Beach on New Providence, one on Paradise Island, and two at Freeport/ Lucaya on Grand Bahama Island.

**Gasoline**   See "Getting Around" in this chapter.

**Hitchhiking**   See "Getting Around" in this chapter.

**Holidays**   See "When to Go" in this chapter.

**Hospitals**   See "Health, Insurance & Other Concerns" in this chapter.

**Information**   For tourist information before you go, see "Visitor Information, Entry Requirements & Money" in this chapter. For information while you're in the Bahamas, see the individual island listings.

**Language**   In the Bahamas locals speak English, but sometimes with a marked accent that often provides the clue to their ancestry—African, Irish, Scottish, or whatever.

**Legal Aid**   Being arrested at home or abroad isn't fun, and perhaps it's worse abroad. Most foreign arrests in the Bahamas involve drug offenses, either possession or dealing. If arrested, there is no legal aid service to refer to. You can apply for help at your consulate or embassy (see above), but don't expect much sympathy there. They will give you the name of some local attorney, and will notify your family—and that's about all. If you're involved in a serious driving offense, you can also contact your consulate, which will provide the name of an attorney to represent you. After that, you're on your own so far as public assistance is concerned.

**Liquor Laws**   Persons must be 21 years of age to order alcoholic drinks in the Bahamas.

**Mail & Postage Rates**   Only Bahamian postage stamps are acceptable. To send a postcard to the United States or Canada will cost 40¢. Airmail letters cost 45¢ per half ounce to the United States or Canada, but 50¢ to the U.K.

From the United States, mail to the Family Islands is sometimes slow. Airmail may go by air to Nassau and by boat to its final destination. If a resort has a U.S. or Nassau address, it is preferable to use it.

**Maps**   In Nassau and Freeport, ask at local tourist offices for maps to both the islands of New Providence and Grand Bahama Island. In Nassau, if available, ask also for a detailed street map of downtown Nassau.

**Newspapers & Magazines**   Three newspapers are circulated in Nassau and Freeport: the *Nassau Guardian,* the *Tribune,* and the *Freeport News.* Circulation in the Family Islands is limited and likely to be slow.

You can find the *New York Times,* the *Wall Street Journal, USA Today,* the *Miami Herald,* the *Times* of London, and the *Daily Telegraph* at newsstands in your hotel and elsewhere in Nassau, usually the day after they are published but sometimes later. Such U.S. magazines as *Time* and *Newsweek* are flown in from the mainland.

**Passports**   See "Visitor Information, Entry Requirements & Money" in this chapter.

**Pets**   A valid import permit is required to import any animal into the Bahamas. Application for such a permit must be made in writing, accompanied by a

$10 processing fee, to the Director of Agriculture, Department of Agriculture, P.O. Box N-3028, Nassau, the Bahamas (☎ **809/325-7502**), a minimum of three weeks in advance.

**Police**  In Nassau, call the police at 919; in Freeport/Lucaya, dial 911.

**Radio & TV**  Government-owned Radio Bahamas is run by the Broadcasting Corporation of the Bahamas and supported by advertising. ZNS-1, the most powerful of the three, is located in Nassau but can be heard throughout the country. ZNS-2 also operates out of Nassau, and ZNS-3 is based in Freeport. ZNS-1 broadcasts 24 hours a day.

ZNS TV transmits on Channel 13 in full color, for 6 hours a day Monday through Friday. On Saturday it transmits for 16 hours, on Sunday for 12. Most large hotels have cable television and can receive U.S. telecasts via Miami from all major networks. Islands nearest the United States receive TV without cable.

**Restrooms**  Adequate toilet facilities can be found at hotels, restaurants, and air terminals in the Bahamas that are frequented by the public, although they may turn out to be in short supply at some of the points of interest you may go to see. Also, if you're in some of the more remote Family Islands not well supplied with public places, you may have difficulty finding a toilet.

**Safety**  When going to Nassau (New Providence), Cable Beach, Paradise Island, or Freeport/Lucaya, exercise the kind of caution you would if visiting an American metropolis, such as Miami. Whatever you do, if you're approached by people peddling drugs, view them as if they had the bubonic plague. Americans and other foreigners have gotten into much trouble in the Bahamas by purchasing illegal drugs.

Women, especially, should take caution if walking alone on the streets of Nassau after dark, especially if those streets appear to be deserted. Pickpockets (often foreigners) work the crowded casino floors of both Paradise Beach and Cable Beach. See that your wallet or money, or whatever, is secured.

If you're driving a rented car, always make sure your car door is locked, and never leave possessions in view in an automobile. Don't leave valuables, such as cameras and purses, lying unattended on the beach while you go for a swim. If you have valuables with you, don't leave them unguarded in hotel rooms—especially jewelry. Many of the bigger hotels will provide safes. Keep your hotel-room doors locked. Bahamian tourist officials often warn visitors, "If you've got it, don't flaunt it." This will minimize the possibility of your becoming a victim of crime.

You're less likely to get mugged in the Family Islands, where life is generally more peaceful. There are some resort hotels that—even today—don't have locks on the doors (never a good policy, in my opinion).

However, drug dealers frequent many of the Family Islands, especially Bimini, because of its proximity to Miami. Take special care if you plan to vacation there. Transporting illegal drugs between Bimini and the Florida coastline is so commonplace that every day the boating set sees bales of marijuana floating on the water as they make the crossing. The marijuana is dumped when vessels are spotted by the Coast Guard as they approach American territorial waters.

**Taxes**  Departure tax is $15. International airline and steamship tickets issued in the Bahamas are subject to a nominal tax, which is written into the cost of the ticket. A 9% tax is imposed on hotel tariffs. There is no sales tax in this country.

**Telephone, Telex, & Fax**    Communications by telephone and cable to resorts in the Bahamas have improved recently, although some of the Family Islands are difficult to reach because of distance and equipment. In recent years, virtually every hotel in the Bahamas seems to have installed a fax machine. Direct distance dialing between North America and Nassau, Grand Bahama, the Abacos, Andros, the Berry Islands, Bimini, Eleuthera, Harbour Island, Spanish Wells, the Exumas, and Stella Maris on Long Island is available. Cables to the Bahamas are usually delivered by phone or by citizens band radio. Urgent telegrams are charged at double the full rate, although no urgent-rate messages to the U.S. mainland are accepted.

**Time**    Eastern standard time is used throughout the Bahamas. In recent years, eastern daylight time has been adopted during the summer to avoid confusion in scheduling transportation to and from the United States. April to October, EDT; October to April, EST.

**Tipping**    Many establishments add a service charge, but it's customary to leave something extra if service has been especially fine. If you're not sure whether service has been included in your bill, ask.

Bellboys and porters, at least in the upper-bracket hotels, expect a tip of $1 per bag. It's also customary to tip your chambermaid at least $2 per day—more if she or he has performed special services such as getting a shirt or blouse laundered. Most service personnel, including taxi drivers, waiters, and the like, expect 15% (perhaps 20% in deluxe restaurants).

**Tourist Offices**    See "Visitor Information, Entry Requirements & Money" in this chapter and also specific island chapters.

**Water**    See "Cuisine" in Chapter 2.

**Yellow Pages**    All Bahamian telephone numbers appear in one phone book, revised annually, with a helpful yellow pages in the rear.

# 4 New Providence (Nassau/Cable Beach)

The capital of the Bahamas, the historic city of Nassau, stands on the island of New Providence, less than an hour's flight from the United States. It offers the charm of an antique, and has a tropical indolence, yet it boasts up-to-date tourist facilities and modern hotels. Nassau lies on the north side of New Providence, which is 21 miles long and 7 miles wide at its greatest point.

## 1 Orientation

### ARRIVING

**BY PLANE**   After you land at the Nassau International Airport, you immediately face the problem of transportation to your hotel. If you're renting a car, you can drive there. If not, you'll find no inexpensive bus service waiting for you—you must take a taxi instead, unless you're being met by a special van. Typical taxi fares from the airport to Cable Beach are about $14; to the center of Nassau, about $19. If you're going to Paradise Island, see Chapter 5. Drivers expect to be tipped 15%, and some will remind you should you "forget." The airport where you'll land is not luxurious in any way and has very limited facilities, although you'll find a tourist kiosk dispensing some data.

**BY BOAT**   Nassau is one of the busiest cruise-ship ports in the world. For details on cruise-ship travel, see "Getting There" in Chapter 3. In recent years, Nassau has spent millions of dollars increasing its facilities so that now 11 cruise ships can pull into dock at one time! It would be your good fortune if the arrival of your ship wasn't with 10 other ships. Facilities in Nassau, Cable Beach, and Paradise Island become extremely overcrowded when major cruise ships dock. You'll have to stake out your space on the beach, and you will find shops and attractions overrun with visitors. However, don't despair. You can almost always get a taxi to take you where you want to go.

Most cruise-ship passengers dock right at Rawson Square, which is one of the best places to begin a tour of Nassau, as the square is the very center of the city and the shopping area. Unless you want to go to one of the beach strips along Cable Beach or Paradise Island, you don't need a taxi but can go on a shopping expedition right where you land. The Straw Market is nearby, at Market Plaza; Bay

---

## What's Special About New Providence

Beaches
- Saunders Beach, across from Fort Charlotte, the most popular weekend rendezvous for New Providence residents.
- Caves Beach, seven miles west of Nassau, a dreamy, crescent-shaped strip of sand opening onto clear water.
- Love Beach, across from Sea Gardens, a smooth stretch of sand lying east of Northwest Point.

Excursions
- Discovery Island, once the private stamping ground of the rich and famous—now a haven for picnickers and sun worshipers.

Shopping
- Straw Market, in the center of Nassau, a vast array of local crafts, mostly straw items.

Great Towns
- Nassau, capital of the Bahamas and major cruise port of call, still retaining much of its colonial charm.

Historic Shrines
- Queen's Staircase, the 65 most famous steps in the Bahamas, leading to Fort Fincastle.
- Fort Charlotte, off West Bay Street, begun in 1787—enough dungeons and underground passages to delight the kid in everybody.

Parks & Gardens
- Ardastra Gardens, five acres of lush tropical vegetation about a mile west of Nassau.
- Botanical Gardens, Chippendale Road, with more than 600 species of tropical flora.
- Coral Island Bahamas, on Silver Cay, a marine park with aquariums and attractions, including an Underwater Observatory.

---

Street (the main shopping artery) is close at hand, and the Nassau International Bazaar is at the intersection of Woodes Rogers Walk and Charlotte Street.

## TOURIST INFORMATION

The **Bahamian Ministry of Tourism** maintains a tourist information booth at the Nassau International Airport (☎ **809/377-6806** or **809/377-6782**); at Rawson Square (☎ **809/328-7810**) and at Bay Street (☎ **809/322-7500**), where many cruise ships dock. Hours are generally 8:30am to 4:30pm daily.

## CITY LAYOUT

**MAIN STREETS & ARTERIES**  The capital, Nassau, is the only city or town of any significance on New Providence. Known as Charles Town until 1695, it is still decidedly old-fashioned after all these years, and skyscrapers or other signs of modern urban life have been strictly controlled or prohibited altogether. Many of its Georgian houses are two centuries old or even older.

**Rawson Square** is the heart of Nassau, lying just a short walk from **Prince George Wharf,** where the big cruise ships, usually from Florida, berth. Here you'll see the Churchill Building, named for Britain's former prime minister, who loved to retreat to Nassau for holidays. The building contains the offices of the Bahamian prime minister along with other government ministries.

Busy **Bay Street,** the main shopping artery, begins on the south side of Rawson Square. This was the street of the infamous "Bay Street Boys," who once controlled all political and economic activity on New Providence.

On the opposite side of Rawson Square is **Parliament Square,** with a statute of a youthful Queen Victoria. Here are more government houses and the House of Assembly. This is the oldest governing body in continuous sessions in the New World. In the building behind the statue of the queen, the Senate meets. These are Neo-Georgian buildings, dating from the late 1700s and early 1900s. In back of the Senate is the Supreme Court. Bahamian judges, even in these hot climes, are bewigged, as in London.

The courthouse is separated by a little square from the Nassau Public Library and Museum, which opens onto Bank Lane. It was the former Nassau Gaol (jail). South of the library, across Shirley Street, are the remains of the Royal Victoria Hotel, which opened the year that the American Civil War (1861) was launched. It was once peopled by blockade runners and Confederate spies.

A walk down Parliament Street leads to the post office. Stamp collectors come here not only to buy stamps but to collect them, as some Bahamian stamps are considered collector's items.

Going south, moving farther away from the water, Elizabeth Avenue leads to the Queen's Staircase, one of the landmarks of Nassau. This leads to Bennet's Hill and Fort Fincastle. Each of the 65 steps of the stairway represent a year of Queen Victoria's reign.

If you return to Bay Street, you'll discover the **Straw Market,** where you can buy all sorts of souvenirs and certainly almost any item made of straw. You can even get your hair braided. At the intersection of Charlotte Street is another major shopping emporium, the **Nassau International Bazaar.**

If you continue east along Bay Street, you'll reach Paradise Bridge leading to Paradise Island. However, if you go west on Bay Street, you'll come to West Bay Street, which is the road that will take you to Cable Beach and the airport.

**FINDING AN ADDRESS**   In Nassau, and especially in the rest of the Bahamas, you will seldom if ever find street numbers on hotels or other businesses. Sometimes in the more remote places, you won't even find street names. Always get directions before heading somewhere in particular. You can always ask along the way, as Bahamians tend to be very helpful.

## 2  Getting Around

**BY SURREY**   The elegant, traditional way to see Nassau is in a horse-drawn surrey—the kind with the fringe on top and a wilted hibiscus stuck in the straw hat shielding the horse from the sun. Before you get in, you should negotiate with the driver and agree on the price. The average charge is $5 per person for a 25-minute ride. The maximum load is three adults plus one or two children under the age of 12. The surreys are available seven days a week from 9am to 4:30pm, except when horses are rested, from 1 to 3pm from May to October, and

# New Providence Island

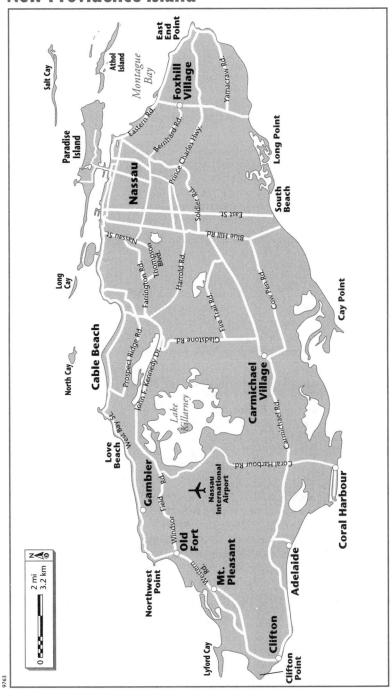

East End Point

Foxhill Village

Salt Cay

Athol Island

*Montague Bay*

Yamacraw Rd.

Eastern Rd.

Paradise Island

Bernhard Rd.

Prince Charles Hwy.

Long Point

Nassau

South Beach

East St.

Soldier Rd.

Long Cay

Nassau St.

Blue Hill Rd.

Farrington Rd.

Thompson Blvd.

Harrold Rd.

Fire Trail Rd.

Cow Pen Rd.

Cay Point

Cable Beach

Prospect Ridge Rd.

Gladstone Rd.

North Cay

John F. Kennedy Dr.

Carmichael Village

West Bay St.

*Lake Killarney*

Carmichael Rd.

Love Beach

Gambier

Field Rd.

Nassau International Airport

Coral Harbour Rd.

Coral Harbour

Windsor

Old Fort

Northwest Point

Western Rd.

Mt. Pleasant

Adelaide

Lyford Cay

Clifton

Clifton Point

N

2 mi
3.2 km

0

9763

from 1 to 2pm from November to April. You'll find the surreys at Rawson Square, off Bay Street.

**BY TAXI**   Taxis are more practical, at least for longer island trips, as the rates for New Providence, including Nassau, are set by the government. When you get in, you should find a working meter, as this is a requirement. For the first quarter mile, one or two passengers are charged $2, with 30¢ for each additional quarter mile. Each additional passenger is assessed another $2. Taxis can also be hired on the hourly rate of $23 to $25 for a five-passenger cab. Luggage is carried at a cost of 30¢ per piece. The radio taxi call number is **809/323-5111.**

**BY JITNEY**   The least expensive means of transport is by jitney, really VW mini-buses, which leave from the downtown Nassau area to outposts on New Providence, costing from 75¢ to $1 per ride. They operate daily from 6:30am to 7:30pm. Some hotels on Paradise Island and Cable Beach run their own jitney service free. However, jitneys and buses are not allowed to operate from the airport to Cable Beach, Nassau, or Paradise Island (the taxi union saw to that).

**BY BOAT**   Water taxis operate daily from 8:30am to 6pm at 20-minute intervals between Paradise Island and Prince George Wharf at a round-trip cost of $3 per person.

There is also ferry service from the end of Casuarina Drive on Paradise Island across the harbor to Rawson Square for a round-trip fare of $2 per person. The ferry operates daily from 9:30am to 4:15pm, with departures every half hour from both sides of the harbor.

**BY SCOOTER OR BICYCLE**   Motor scooters have become a favorite mode of transportation among tourists. The little mopeds with their white license tag and helmeted riders scoot all over New Providence. Unless you're an experienced moped rider, it's wise for you to stay on quiet roads until you feel at ease with your vehicle. Don't start out on Bay Street. Many hotels have rental vehicles on the premises. Average rental begins at $25 per half day or $40 per full day. If your hotel doesn't have this service, contact **Ursa Investment,** Prince George Wharf (☎ **809/326-8329**).

**BY CAR**   Four of the biggest U.S.-based car-rental companies maintain branches in New Providence, at the Nassau International Airport, across the street from the main terminal. These include **Avis** (☎ toll free **800/331-2112** or **809/326-6380** locally), **Budget Rent-a-Car** (☎ toll free **800/472-3325** or **809/377-7405** locally), **Hertz** (☎ toll free **800/654-3001** or **809/377-8684** locally), and **National** (☎ toll free **800/328-4567** or **809/377-7301** locally). Avis also maintains branches at the cruise-ship docks, and in downtown Nassau on Marlborough Street. National has a branch at Carnival's Crystal Palace Hotel, and Budget maintains a branch at Chalk's Airline Terminal for anyone arriving at Paradise Island Airport (☎ **809/363-3095**). In addition, Budget will send a driver anywhere on Paradise Island to pick you up and deliver you to its headquarters.

Rates among the various companies are approximately (but not exactly) the same, and insurance regulations are stricter at some than others. Weekly prices are usually calculated at six times the daily rate, so keeping a car for the seventh day usually works out free, although that gives you a price break only if you declare your intention to rent for a full week when you sign your rental contract.

At press time, among the four rental firms, Budget offered the least expensive rate, $282 a week, or $47 a day, and some of the most lenient restrictions for their cheapest, non-air-conditioned car. Drivers at Budget need to be 25 or older. The rental of a Budget car with automatic transmission and air-conditioning costs $378 a week, or $63 a day. The price for the rental of an equivalent car at Hertz is $59.95 a day or $359.70 a week. Avis and National both charge more, although it's always a good idea to ask both of them about discounts or promotional offerings before your trip.

Each of the companies offers additional insurance for $11.95 per day. Purchase of a collision damage waiver (CDW) will usually waive a customer's financial responsibility in the event of an accident, with the notable exception of policies offered by National. There, even with the purchase of this optional insurance, a driver still bears up to $1,000 worth of liability in the event of an accident. At all four companies, clients who do not buy the CDW are fully liable for the repair cost of all damages after an accident. (Certain clients arrange private insurance, including using policies that are affiliated with their credit cards.)

There's no tax on car rentals in Nassau. Drivers must present a valid driver's license, plus a credit card or a cash deposit.

*Drive on the left,* don't drink and drive, and pay extra attention when driving at night.

**ON FOOT**   This is the only way to see Old Nassau, unless you rent a horse and carriage. All the major attractions and the principal stores are close enough to walk to. You can even walk to Cable Beach or Paradise Island, although many prefer a taxi or bus to reach those destinations. Confine your walking to the daytime, and beware of pickpockets and purse snatchers. In the evening, avoid walking the streets of downtown Nassau, where muggings occur.

## FAST FACTS: New Providence

**American Express**   The local representative is Playtours, Shirley Street, between Charlotte and Parliament Streets, Nassau (☎ **809/322-2931**). Hours are Monday through Friday from 9am to 5pm.

**Area Code**   The area code for Nassau is **809.**

**Bookstores**   The largest on the island is the United Bookstore, with its major branch located two miles east of the center of town, at the Madeira Street Shopping Centre (☎ **809/322-8597**). Another branch, almost as big, lies in the heart of Nassau, within the Marathon Mall, at the corner of Robinson and Marathon (☎ **809/393-6166**). Yet a third branch lies three miles west of downtown Nassau on Thompson Boulevard, Oak Field (☎ **809/325-0316**).

**Business Hours**   See "Fast Facts" in Chapter 3.

**Car Rentals**   See "Getting Around" in this chapter.

**Climate**   See "When to Go" in Chapter 3.

**Currency**   See "Visitor Information, Entry Requirements & Money" in Chapter 3.

**Currency Exchange**   Americans need not bother to exchange their dollars into Bahamian dollars, because the currencies are on par. However, Canadians will need to convert their dollars, and Britishers their pounds, which can be done at local banks or sometimes at a hotel. Hotels, however, offer the least favorable rates.

**Dentist**   There are numerous dentists in Nassau, all of whom speak English, but for the best treatment go to the dental department of the Princess Margaret Hospital on Sands Road (☎ **809/322-2861**).

**Doctor**   For the best service, use a staff member of the Princess Margaret Hospital on Sands Road (☎ **809/322-2861**).

**Drugs**   The strict drug law of the Bahamas was cited under "Fast Facts" in the preceding chapter, but the warning bears repeating. The authorities do not smile on visitors possessing or selling marijuana or other narcotics, and offenders are speedily and severely punished. A normal lapse of three days between arrest and sentencing can be expected. Penalties are harsh.

**Drugstores**   Try Lightbourn's Pharmacy, Bay and George Streets (☎ **809/322-2095**), which is open Monday through Saturday from 9am to 5pm.

**Embassies & Consulates**   See "Fast Facts" in Chapter 3.

**Emergencies**   For the police or fire department, dial **919;** for an ambulance, call **809/322-2221** (if busy, try **809/322-2861**).

**Eyeglasses**   Both large and convenient to the center of Nassau is the Optique Shoppe, on Parliament Street at the corner of Shirley Street (☎ **809/328-2711**). Hours are Monday through Friday from 9am to 5pm and on Saturday from 9am to noon.

**Hairdressers & Barbers**   Try Cliffie's Unisex Beauty Salon, Market Street, corner of Bay Street (☎ **809/323-6253**), for both men and women. Hours are Monday through Saturday from 9am to 6:30pm. You might also try Mitzi's, Wong Shopping Plaza (☎ **809/328-1493**). It is open Monday, Wednesday, Thursday, and Friday from 7:30am to 4pm and on Saturday from 5:30am to 2pm.

**Holidays**   See "When to Go" in Chapter 3.

**Hospitals**   The government-operated Princess Margaret Hospital on Sands Road (☎ **809/322-2861**) is the leading hospital in the Bahamas. Its bed capacity is 455, and it has a well-qualified staff. The privately owned Doctor's Hospital, with 72 beds, is at 1 Collins Ave. (☎ **809/322-8411**).

**Hot Lines**   For the Drugs Action Service, dial **809/322-2308**.

**Information**   See "Tourist Information," above.

**Laundry & Dry Cleaning**   The Laundromat Superwash (☎ **809/323-4018**), at the corner of Nassau Street and Boyd Road, offers coin-operated laundry. It is open 24 hours a day, seven days a week. In the same building is the New Oriental Dry Cleaner (☎ **809/323-7249**). It is open Monday through Thursday 7:30am to 7pm, Friday and Saturday 7:30am to 8pm. Another dry cleaner lying a short drive north of the center of town is the Jiffy Quality Cleaner (☎ **809/323-6771**) at the corner of Blue Hill Road and Cordeaux Avenue. It is open Monday through Saturday from 7:30am to 7pm.

**Library**   The Nassau Public Library and Museum, Bank Lane (☎ **809/322-4907**), is housed in the former Nassau Gaol. The library and museum are open Monday through Thursday from 10am to 8pm, on Friday from 10am to 5pm, and on Saturday from 10am to 4pm. Admission is free.

**Lost Property**   There is no office for this. Call the police station and report your loss.

**Newspapers & Magazines**   See "Fast Facts" in Chapter 3.

**Photographic Needs**   The largest camera store in Nassau is John Bull, Bay Street (☎ **809/322-3328**), one block east of Rawson Square. It sells top-brand cameras, film, and other accessories. Camera experts are available for advice. It is open Monday and Thursday from 9am to 5pm; Tuesday, Wednesday, and Friday from 9am to 5:30pm; and Saturday from 8:30am to 5:30pm.

**Police**   Dial **919.**

**Post Office**   The Nassau General Post Office, at the top of Parliament Street on East Hill Street (☎ **809/322-3344**), is open Monday through Friday from 9am to 5pm, on Saturday from 9am to 1pm.

**Radio & TV**   See "Fast Facts" in Chapter 3.

**Religious Services**   Bahamians tend to be religious people, with a history of religious tolerance. Of the major faiths, the following churches are established here. *Anglican:* Christ Church Cathedral, King and George Streets (☎ **809/322-4186**); St. Matthews, Shirley Street and Church Lane (☎ **809/325-2191**). *Baptist:* Zion, East and Shirley Streets (☎ **809/325-3556**). *Roman Catholic:* St. Francis Xavier's Cathedral, West and West Hill Streets (☎ **809/323-3802**); Sacred Heart Church, East Shirley Street (☎ **809/326-6274**). *Methodist:* Trinity, Fredrick Street (☎ **809/325-2552**); Ebenezer, East Shirley Street (☎ **809/393-2936**). *Presbyterian:* St. Andrew's Kirk, Princes Street (☎ **809/322-4085**). *Lutheran:* Lutheran Church of Nassau, John F. Kennedy Drive (☎ **809/323-4107**).

**Restrooms**   These are generally inadequate. Visitors often have to rely on the facilities available at airports, hotels, restaurants, and other commercial establishments.

**Safety**   Women should avoid walking along the often nearly deserted streets of Nassau at night. Cable Beach and Paradise Island are much safer places to be in the evening. For more details, see "Safety" under "Fast Facts" in Chapter 3.

**Shoe Repair**   Head for Wilson's Shoe Repair, at the corner of East Street and Wulff Road (☎ **809/323-4250**). The shop is open Monday through Saturday from 9:30am to 7pm.

**Taxes**   There is no sales tax, as mentioned. All visitors leaving Nassau pay a $15 departure tax.

**Telephone, Telex & Fax**   Direct distance telephone dialing is available. Nearly all major hotels send telexes and faxes; if your hotel is too small to offer such services, go to the main post office (see above). To send a telegram, you can either call from your hotel (paying over the phone with a valid credit card) or visit in person the Bahamas Telecommunications Corp., John F. Kennedy Drive (☎ **809/323-4911**), located beside the main seafront road leading to the resort hotels of Cable Beach.

**Transit Information**   To summon a taxi, call **809/323-5111.** There is no central information number for the Nassau International Airport. If you want flight information, it is necessary to call individual airlines directly.

**Weather**   New Providence, which is fairly centrally located in the Bahamas, has temperatures in winter that vary from about 60 degrees to 75 degrees Fahrenheit daily. Summer variations are 78 degrees Fahrenheit to the high 80s.

## 3  Where to Stay

In the hotel descriptions that follow I've listed regular room tariffs, called "rack rates." In booking, however, always inquire about honeymoon specials, golf packages, summer weeks, and other discounts.

Hotels add a 4% room tax and a 4% to 6% "resort levy" to your rate. Sometimes this is quoted as part of the tariff, and at other times it is added when your final bill is presented. Always ask if the tax is included when you are quoted a rate. Many hotels also add a 15% service charge to your bill as well—so check these items out in advance so you won't be shocked when the final tab is presented.

Taxes and service are not included in the rates listed below unless otherwise noted. *Note:* For an explanation of our symbols for rates with meals included, see "Tips on Accommodations" in Chapter 3.

In general, hotels judged "expensive" charge from $190 to $315 a night for a double room in winter. "Moderate" hotels ask from $95 to $190 for a double, whereas "inexpensive" establishments want from $65 to $95 for a double. Anything under $55 a night for a double room is considered "budget." In the off-season (spring through autumn), expect reductions ranging from 20% to 60%.

## NASSAU
### EXPENSIVE

#### ✪ Graycliff
West Hill St., P.O. Box N-10246, Nassau, the Bahamas. ☎ **809/322-2796** or toll free 800/423-4095 in the U.S. Fax 809/326-6110. 14 rms. A/C MINIBAR TV TEL. Winter, $170 single; $255–$280 double; $290–$365 poolside cottage for two. Off-season, $120 single; $165–$210 double; $210–$290 poolside cottage for two. Breakfast from $8 extra. Rates include continental breakfast. AE, DC, MC, V. Free parking. Bus 10, 17.

This well-preserved example of Georgian colonial architecture stands deep in the heart of Old Nassau, across the street from Government House. The main house of Graycliff is some 250 years old, built by Capt. John Howard Graysmith, a pirate who was noted for his exploits against Spanish shipping and who was commander of the notorious *Graywolf,* which was scuttled off New Providence in 1726. By 1844 Graycliff was a hotel for "gentlefolk and invalids."

Over the years since then, when the house was sometimes a hotel, sometimes a private residence, a handsome swimming pool was added and extensive additions and renovations were made while keeping the main house intact. Both as hotel and home, the place has hosted the rich and famous. The duke and duchess of Windsor often visited here while he served as governor of the Bahamas and lived across the street. Sir Winston Churchill used to paddle around the swimming pool with a cigar in his mouth. Lord Mountbatten, Aristotle Onassis, even the Beatles were guests at Graycliff at one time or another.

The present owner, Enrico Garzaroli, brings his own aristocratic ways and tastes to this chic oasis, furnished with exceptional and luxuriously styled antiques. Today you're likely to run into Paul Newman, Perry Como, or Michael Caine.

**Dining/Entertainment:** The hotel boasts one of the finest restaurants in Nassau—also called Graycliff—certainly the most elegant (see "Where to Dine," below). Always reserve well in advance.

**Services:** Room service, concierge, babysitting, massage.

**Facilities:** Swimming pool.

*A church, a gaol and an assembly house make up the buildings of the town [Nassau].*

—A German visitor named Schoepf, 1784

### ✪ Villas on Coral Island

Silver Cay, P.O. Box N-7797, Nassau, the Bahamas. ☎ **809/328-1036** or toll free 800/328-8814 in the U.S. Fax 809/323-3202. 22 villas. A/C MINIBAR TV TEL. Winter, $245 single or double villa. Off-season, $210 single or double villa. Up to two children 12 or younger stay free in parents' villa. Rates include continental breakfast. AE, DC, MC, V. Free parking. Bus 10.

This resort lies isolated on the private island of Silver Cay (site of the underwater attraction Coral Island, reviewed later), midway between downtown Nassau and Cable Beach. When it opened in 1988, Silver Cay became yet another of the inhabited islands of the archipelago. You can cross a small bridge to the "mainland" (New Providence), but many guests find this little world sufficient unto itself. The private island becomes quite tranquil after the Coral Island sightseeing crowds have departed.

The villas, furnished in a light Caribbean motif with wicker furniture and tropical accents, open onto ocean views. Each villa has a king-size bed and a pull-out queen-size sleeping sofa, ideal for sharing the unit with children. The villas also have their own private swimming pools, as well as kitchens, microwaves, and bars. The bathrooms are sheathed in marble, and from your oval bathtub you can take in a view of the waves through a picture window.

**Dining/Entertainment:** Guests can lunch at Villas on Coral Island's oceanfront Clipper Restaurant. Many restaurants nearby offer dinner.

**Services:** Laundry, babysitting, room service, free daytime transportation to downtown or casino on Cable Beach.

**Facilities:** Each villa has a private swimming pool.

## MODERATE

### British Colonial Beach Resort

1 Bay St., P.O. Box N-7148, Nassau, the Bahamas. ☎ **809/322-3301** or toll free 800/528-1234 in the U.S. Fax 809/322-2286. 325 rms, 7 suites. A/C TV TEL. Winter, $129–$189 single or double; $229 suite. Off-season, $94–$144 single or double; $184 suite. Third and fourth persons sharing room $35 each. Continental breakfast $7 extra. (EP rates.) AE, DC, MC, V. Free parking. Bus 10, 17.

On eight tropical acres in the heart of Nassau, this hotel (the only major one in the downtown area) presides over Nassau's bayfront and is just steps away from the shopping area of Bay Street. Ever since 1922, it has been the most prominent building in the center of Nassau and has been renovated frequently throughout its long career. Nevertheless, whether or not you like this place may depend on your room assignment. Many of the large rooms have ocean views.

This Best Western–affiliated hotel is a monument to resort living and is spread out along the shore, so you won't even need to go off the premises. The dining facilities include Carib Café and Bayside Restaurant. There are three championship tennis courts lit for night play, an Olympic-size swimming pool, and a private white-sand beach. Deep-sea fishing, skin diving, and snorkeling can be arranged.

# Nassau Accommodations

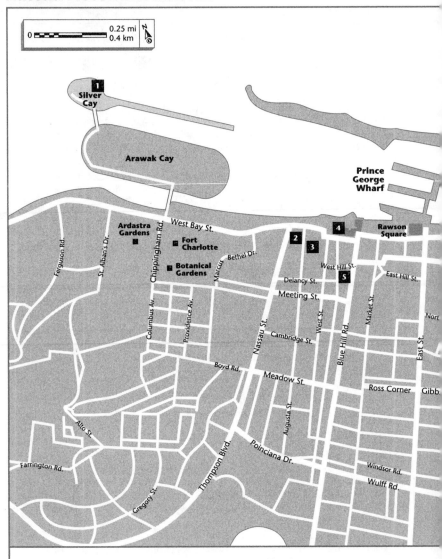

British Colonial Beach Resort **4**
El Greco Hotel **2**
Graycliff **5**
The Little Orchard **6**

Olympia Hotel **2**
Parthenon Hotel **3**
Villas on Coral Island **1**

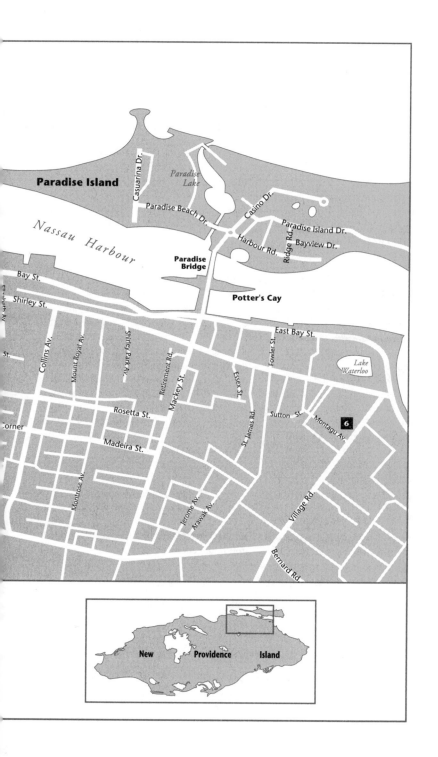

## INEXPENSIVE

### ⑤ El Greco Hotel

W. Bay St., P.O. Box N-4187, Nassau, the Bahamas. ☎ **809/325-1121.** Fax 809/325-1124. 25 rms, 1 suite. A/C TV TEL. Winter, $77 single; $87 double; from $150 suite. Off-season, $57 single; $67 double; from $110 suite. (EP rates.) AE, DC, MC, V. Free parking. Bus 10.

Across the street from Lighthouse Beach, within a 5-minute walk of the shops and restaurants of Bay Street, El Greco Hotel has a Spanish design. Rounded archways accent its facade, and black-painted iron chandeliers are found inside the reception area. The staff seems to care about the well-being of guests. The rooms are clustered around a tiny central swimming pool set within the vine-covered and hedge-trimmed confines of an Iberian-style courtyard. Many of the accommodations have separate sitting rooms, while each has a tile bath and Spanish-style furniture. You can walk to many places nearby for breakfast.

### ⑤ The Little Orchard

Village Rd., P.O. Box N-1514, Nassau, the Bahamas. ☎ **809/393-1297.** Fax 809/394-3526. 16 efficiencies, 12 cottages. A/C MINIBAR TV TEL. Winter, $70 single or double efficiency; $90 single or double cottage. Off-season, $60 single or double efficiency; $75 single or double cottage. Rates include tax and service. AE, DC, MC, V. Free parking. Bus 17.

Only 500 yards from Montagu Beach is an apartment/hotel complex offering individual cottage facilities grouped around a central swimming pool in a 2-acre semitropical garden. The cottages are in a residential part of Nassau, within 800 yards of a large supermarket and a 5-minute drive from tennis-and-squash courts and several island restaurants. All units have fully equipped kitchens, baths (some with balconies), and daily maid service. You can buy food at the market, then prepare your own breakfast the next morning. The establishment doesn't have an in-house restaurant, although the Tamarind Restaurant (under different management) lies next door. Guests can take bus no. 17, which stops near the hotel, if they want to go shopping in downtown Nassau (the bus service also runs to the foot of the bridge leading to Paradise Island). Later, economy-minded vacationers share stories at the convivial Tree Frog Bar, on the premises.

### Ocean Spray Hotel

W. Bay St., P.O. Box N-3035, Nassau, the Bahamas. ☎ **809/322-8032.** Fax 809/325-5731. 30 rms. A/C TV TEL. Winter, $55 single; $75 double. Off-season, $45 single; $65 double. (EP rates.) AE, MC, V. Free parking. Bus 10.

This modestly modern corner hotel is a short stroll from the shopping district and across the street from the beach. Bedrooms are conservative and neutral in decor, with twin beds, private baths, and wall-to-wall carpeting. Best known for its restaurant-bar Europe, which serves good imported wines and international specialties, the hotel has an informal atmosphere. Ocean Spray offers guests both beach and town, a winning combination in Nassau. You can order breakfast at several places nearby.

### Orange Hill Beach Inn

W. Bay St. just west of Blake Rd., Box N-8583, Nassau, the Bahamas. ☎ **809/327-7157.** 32 units (all with bath). A/C TV. Winter, $77 single; $93 double; $115 apartments with kitchens. Off-season discounts of $15 per unit. Breakfast $5 extra. AE, MC, V. Free parking.

Despite its location on the most densely populated island in the Bahamas, many visitors appreciate this place for the image it evokes of a family-run hotel deep within the Out Islands. It lies on 3$\frac{1}{2}$ carefully landscaped hillside acres, a 3-minute walk from a beach known for its snorkeling options, and about three miles west of the congestion of Cable Beach. Its owners are Judy and Danny Lowe, the Irish-Bahamian partnership whose diplomatic skill has been shown many times during their dealings with the more than 300 couples who have selected Orange Hill as the venue for their wedding ceremonies.

The establishment, which began life as a private home in the 1920s, became a hotel in 1979 after the Lowes added new wings, a swimming pool, and placed great emphasis on their scuba facilities. Much of the clientele here is European, especially during the summer months. On site are two bars, both serving sandwiches and salads throughout the day for anywhere from $3 to $5 each, and a restaurant which offers simple set-price dinners for between $13 and $19. Diving excursions to the rich marine fauna of New Providence's southwestern coast are among the most popular activities here, and sea kayaks can be rented on site.

## BUDGET

### Parthenon Hotel

17 West St., P.O. Box N-4930, Nassau, the Bahamas. ☎ **809/322-2643.** Fax 809/ 322-2644. 18 rms. A/C TV TEL. Winter, $54 single or double; $62 triple. Off-season, $44 single or double; $50 triple. Continental breakfast $4 extra. (EP rates.) AE, MC, V. Free parking. Bus 10.

The Parthenon is a small hotel only three minutes from Bay Street and the beaches. Although modern, it's styled in the old Bahamian way with continuous covered balconies overlooking a well-tended garden. The rooms are simple, nothing special, with basic, restrained decor and private baths. Fishing, golf, tennis, and water sports can be arranged. There is no restaurant or bar. Consider this place as a budget alternative only if you like to spend most of your time outdoors instead of lounging around a hotel room.

## CABLE BEACH

Cable Beach, the shoreline west of Nassau, is regarded by many as the ultimate island resort area, with broad stretches of beachfront, a wide array of sports facilities and entertainment, and an oceanfront of hotels.

The area was named for the telegraph cable laid in 1892 from Jupiter, Florida, to the Bahamas.

## EXPENSIVE

### ✪ Carnival's Crystal Palace Resort & Casino

W. Bay St., Cable Beach, P.O. Box N-8306, Nassau, the Bahamas, ☎ **809/327-6200,** or toll free 800/453-5301 in the U.S. Fax 809/327-6459. 767 rms, 109 suites. A/C TV TEL. Winter, $215–$315 single or double. Off-season, $170–$230 single or double. Year-round, from $400 suites. MAP rates $40–$60 per person daily. AE, DC, MC, V. Free parking. Bus 10.

Here you'll find the largest, most shamelessly glitzy (it's nicknamed the "Purple Palace"), and most strenuously promoted hotel in the Bahamian-Caribbean basin. Set on its own beachfront near a re-creation of a beached clipper ship (designed as a changing room), the hotel was the creation of Joe Farcus. The Crystal Palace incorporates five high-rise towers, a futuristic central core, and a cluster of gardens and beachfront gazebos—all interconnected with arcades, underground passages, and minipavilions. Most spectacular among the accommodations is a high-tech showplace suite (with a voice-controlled robot named Ursula in attendance who will do everything from serve drinks to reproduce the sound of thunder and lightning), which rents for $25,000 a night! The regular rooms are spacious, modern, well furnished, and comfortable, but nowhere near as opulent as the public rooms.

**Dining/Entertainment:** The complex contains eight specialty restaurants, six bars, a high-tech disco, a cabaret theater (the Palace Theater, recommended under "New Providence After Dark," below), and a casino. The restaurants run a wide culinary gamut. The most expensive and formal is the Sole Mare, serving Italian food. Other choices include a Chinese restaurant, between two and four seafood restaurants, a buffet restaurant, a pizza restaurant, a poolside grill, the Goombay Mama Snack Bar and Pizzeria, and a European restaurant called Le Grille.

**Facilities:** A swimming pool with a 100-foot water slide; complete array of water-sports facilities; 10 tennis courts and an 18-hole golf course; health club with sauna, massage facilities, and exercise machines.

### Forte Nassau Beach Hotel

P.O. Box N-7756, Cable Beach, Nassau, the Bahamas. ☎ **809/327-7711** or toll free 800/ 225-5843 in the U.S. Fax 809/327-7615. 401 rms, 9 suites. A/C MINIBAR TV TEL. Winter, $160–$230 single or double; $375–$750 suite. Off-season, $150–$185 single or double; $290–$500 suite. (EP rates.) AE, DC, MC, V. Free parking. Bus 10.

Part of its allure has been overshadowed by the glitzy hotels that rise from the shoreline a short walk away. But a crowd of loyal fans remain devoted to this British-based hotel. The hotel was built in the 1940s, with three separate wings in a gray-and-white twin-towered design and modified Georgian detailing and tile and marble-covered floors. In the early 1990s, its new owners, London-based Forte properties, invested $8.5 million in its restoration. Today, the place has been enhanced by landscaping and a series of Bahamian accessories that include ceiling fans and upholstered wicker furniture. Each of the accommodations contains a marble-sheathed bath with hair dryer and other accessories and Queen Anne reproductions.

**Dining/Entertainment:** The hotel offers at least four theme restaurants, one of which, the Beef Cellar, is reviewed under "Where to Dine," below. Nightlife possibilities include a waterside trip backward in time to the rock-and-roll era at the Nassau Beach Rock and Roll Café (see "Where to Dine," below).

**Services:** Concierge, laundry, babysitting.

**Facilities:** 3,000-foot white-sand beach; six all-weather tennis courts lit for night play with a resident pro for lessons; health club with weight-and-exercise machines; water sports; children's program.

### ✪ Le Meridien Royal Bahamian Hotel

W. Bay St., P.O. Box N-10422, Nassau, the Bahamas. ☎ **809/327-6400** or toll free 800/ 543-4300 in the U.S. Fax 809/327-6961. 145 rms, 21 suites. A/C MINIBAR TV TEL. Winter, $205–$300 single or double; $250–$315 villa suite. Off-season, $135–$220 single or double; $185–$235 villa suite. Breakfast $10 extra. (EP rates.) AE, DC, MC, V. Free parking. Bus 10.

This elegant and lavishly refurbished hotel was acquired in 1989 by the French-based Meridien hotel chain. Built as a private club in 1946 to shelter the rich and famous from prying eyes and outsiders, it became a hotel in 1967, the Balmoral Beach. The establishment still exudes a kind of timeless colonial charm. Each of the public rooms has been furnished with Chippendale reproductions, brass chandeliers, marble-and-carpeted floors, French settees, and, along the curved walls

# Cable Beach Accommodations

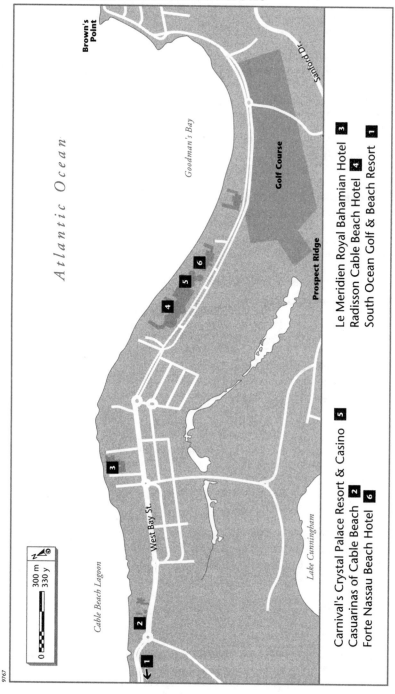

Atlantic Ocean

Brown's Point

Goodman's Bay

Cable Beach Lagoon

West Bay St.

Lake Cunningham

Prospect Ridge

Golf Course

Sanford Dr.

300 m
330 y

9767

Le Meridien Royal Bahamian Hotel **3**
Radisson Cable Beach Hotel **4**
South Ocean Golf & Beach Resort **1**

Carnival's Crystal Palace Resort & Casino **5**
Casuarinas of Cable Beach **2**
Forte Nassau Beach Hotel **6**

of one of the rose-colored salons, about a dozen bandy-legged desks for letter writing.

The central core of the property, known as the Manor House, has a courtyard where a stork fountain spits water at what might remind you of the facade of a Corinthian temple. The bedrooms are in the Manor House, while the suites are in outlying villas. Some of these suites have Jacuzzis and private pools, and some of the bathrooms are as spacious as many big-city apartments. The bedrooms have cove moldings, formal English furniture, and baths loaded with bathrobes, perfumed soaps, and cosmetics. Those rooms that face the ocean offer small curved terraces with ornate iron railings and views of an offshore sand spit still named Balmoral Island.

**Dining/Entertainment:** The establishment's premier restaurant, the Café de Paris, is recommended under "Where to Dine," below. The hotel has one of the most appealing bars in the Bahamas, the Balmoral Bar, where you can listen to live entertainment on Friday and Saturday nights.

**Services:** Complimentary shuttle bus to casino and nightlife options of nearby Crystal Palace complex.

**Facilities:** Sandy beach; hourglass-shaped swimming pool; complete spa facility equipped with masseurs and masseuses, exercise machines, and health programs; two lit tennis courts; complete array of water sports; access to golf facilities.

### Radisson Cable Beach Hotel

Cable Beach, W. Bay St., P.O. Box N-4914, Nassau, the Bahamas. ☎ **809/327-6000** or toll free 800/333-3333. Fax 809/327-6987. 669 rms, 31 suites. A/C MINIBAR TV TEL. Winter, $160–$190 single or double. Off-season, $135–$165 single or double. Year-round, $330–$1,000 suites. AE, DC, MC, V. Free parking. Bus 10.

The construction of this massive hotel in the early 1980s was a much-noted event that challenged the near monopoly of Paradise Island and gave to Cable Beach the razzmatazz that later became an indelible part of its image. Owned by the Bahamian government, but managed by a Florida-based hotel conglomerate (the Myers Group) with input from Radisson Hotels, the hotel lies a short walk from the larger and glitzier facilities at the Carnival Crystal Palace Resort & Casino. Designed in a horseshoe-shaped curve around a landscaped beachfront garden, the nine-story building has an Aztec-inspired facade of sharp angles and strong horizontal lines, evoking images of Las Vegas with its rows of fountains in front and acres of marble sheathing inside. Big enough to get lost in, but with plenty of intimate retreats and

---

### 🏨 Family-Friendly Hotels

**Villas on Coral Island**    *(see p. 77)* If your kids had to choose, they'd make it this place on Silver Cay, site of Coral Island. Two children 12 or younger stay free in parents' room.

**Forte Nassau Beach Hotel**    *(see p. 82)* Management actively seeks the family trade, offering a large children's activities program, including a play center with slides and swings, a video-game room, and a supervised recreation room.

**Radisson Cable Beach Hotel**    *(see p. 84)* A massive hotel on Cable Beach, dating from the 1980s, this has become a family favorite—largely because of its Camp Junkanoo, which offers daily supervised play for children 3 to 12.

an almost endless array of things to do, the hotel contains a four-story lobby with huge windows.

Each of the bedrooms is modern, comfortable, and standardized, with private balconies and big-windowed views of the garden or the beach.

**Dining/Entertainment:** The hotel contains five restaurants, the most glamorous of which is the Riviera Seafood Restaurant. Enchiladas and such fare are offered at Margaritaville. There's also a wide selection of bars. Beach parties and native reviews are often staged.

**Services:** 24-hour room service; babysitting at Camp Junkanoo, where supervised play is available for children 3 to 12; laundry; dry cleaning; beauty salon; concierge. Readers constantly complain of staff attitude and slow service at this sprawling resort.

**Facilities:** 18 tennis courts; boutiques; easy access to Crystal Palace casino.

## MODERATE

### ⑤ Casuarinas of Cable Beach

W. Bay St., P.O. Box N-4016, Nassau, the Bahamas. ☎ **809/327-8153** or toll free 800/327-3012 in the U.S. Fax 809/327-8152. 77 rms, 14 suites. A/C TV TEL. Winter, $95–$130 single or double; from $190 suite. Off-season, $65–$100 single or double; from $145 suite. Continental breakfast $3.50 extra. (EP rates.) AE, DC, MC, V. Free parking. Bus 10.

A well-managed Bahamian-owned hotel that grew over many years, this place now occupies land on both sides of the main road connecting Nassau with Cable Beach. The family-run apartment-hotel complex is the creation of Nettie Symonette, an enterprising woman who was the former general manager of the old Balmoral Beach Hotel before acquiring her own property.

Contained within clusters of brown-and-white buildings set amid casuarina trees, the establishment offers two swimming pools, a tennis court, and a restaurant (see "Where to Dine," below). It also has an outdoor roadside café set in a garden. You'll be offered a choice of accommodations. The less expensive rooms are clustered around their own swimming pool across the road from the beach. The more expensive rooms lie closer to the beach, also around their own swimming pool.

# LOVE BEACH
## EXPENSIVE

### Compass Point

W. Bay St., Gambia, Love Beach, New Providence, the Bahamas. ☎ **809/327-7309.** Fax 809/327-FAXX. 18 bungalows (all with bath). TV TEL. Winter, $150–$225 single or double without kitchenette, $300 single or double with kitchenette. Off-season, $100–$175 single or double without kitchenette, $250 single or double with kitchenette. Breakfast from $8 extra. AE, DC, MC, V. Free parking.

Charming, personalized, and "casually upscale," this is a well-crafted alternative to the megahotels of Cable Beach, which lie about six miles to the east. Scattered over two acres of some of the most expensive terrain in the Bahamas, the property lies beside one of the few sandy coves along the island's northwest. To accommodate it, one of a pair of cement-sided villas ("the Reefs" and "Press on Regardless," both originally built in the 1960s) was demolished.

The hotel was named by its owner, Christopher Blackwell (Jamaican-born entrepreneur who "discovered" Bob Marley), in 1994. It lies adjacent to one of the best-known recording businesses in the Caribbean, Compass Point Studios (a division of Island Records), with whom it shares some of its staff and some of its profitable and, depending on your point of view, very appealing attitudes about business and life.

Each accommodation is a private, fully detached bungalow painted in multicolored hues. About nine contain kitchenettes; each has exposed rafters, high ceilings, a half-dozen windows facing the ocean breezes, and all the privacy afforded by the verdant banana trees that ring each unit. Depending on their distance from the beach, some are raised on stilts, others hug close to the ground. On the premises is a tennis court, a swimming pool, a bar, and whatever Caribbean musician happens to be on the island at the time.

The establishment's restaurant (Compass Point), is recommended separately in "Where to Dine," below.

## SOUTHWESTERN NEW PROVIDENCE

### South Ocean Golf & Beach Resort

SW Bay Rd., P.O. Box N-8191, Nassau, the Bahamas. ☎ **809/362-4391** or toll free 800/ 223-6510. Fax 809/362-4728. 260 rms. A/C TV TEL. Winter, $155–$195 single or double. Off-season, $125–$165 single or double. Third person $30 extra per day. Continental breakfast $6 extra. (EP rates.) AE, DC, MC, V. Free parking. Transportation: "The Bahamas Experience Bus," charging $5 one-way into Cable Beach, Nassau, or Paradise Island.

Remotely situated on the pine-covered southwestern shore of New Providence, about a 45-minute drive southwest of Nassau, this is one of the most secluded resorts on the otherwise relatively congested island. It covers almost 180 rolling acres, including a challenging golf course and a sandy beach.

The resort's guest rooms are equally divided between older but still very comfortable units set inland in a garden around a swimming pool and newer, more plush units on the beach, the latter decorated in plantation-era style. Regardless of the location, each accommodation contains either one king-size or two double beds, a safe-deposit box, and in most cases a private terrace or balcony.

**Dining/Entertainment:** The resort's premier eatery is the Papagayo Italian restaurant. Less formal is the Casuarinas, as well as a beachfront snack bar. There's a manager's cocktail party and dancing one night a week.

**Services:** Guest-relations staff, room service during breakfast hours, babysitting.

**Facilities:** Beach, 18-hole golf course, two freshwater swimming pools, array of water-sports activities including scuba diving, four tennis courts (two lit at night), volleyball on the beach.

## 4 Where to Dine

In restaurants rated "very expensive," expect to spend from $50 to $75 for a meal; in "expensive," $25 to $30. In "moderate" restaurants, dinner goes for $15 to $20. Anything under $12 is considered "inexpensive." Drinks and a 15% service charge are extra.

## NASSAU
### VERY EXPENSIVE

#### ✪ Graycliff

W. Hill St. ☎**809/322-2796.** Reservations required. Jacket advised for men. Appetizers $7.50–$15; main courses $28.75–$80. AE, DC, MC, V. Lunch Mon–Fri noon–3pm; dinner daily 7–10pm. Bus 10, 17. CONTINENTAL.

Graycliff is the elegant and aristocratic dining choice of Nassau (also see "Where to Stay," above). In an antiques-filled colonial mansion, opposite Government House, Graycliff is owned by Enrico Garzaroli. The talented chefs produce a cuisine of culinary excellence, served at opulently set tables in a setting of charm and grace, surrounded by lush gardens.

The menu opens with caviar and gourmet terrines, including foie gras with truffles and a pâté of hare with pine kernels. The soups and pastas are outstanding, including chilled cream of cucumber and fettuccine Enrico. The chef is a master at the charcoal grill and spit, as my spit-roasted duckling flambé with apple brandy proved. Also offered are roast rack of lamb with herbs, chateaubriand with a perfectly made béarnaise sauce, and seafood pasta. The fish selection in general is outstanding, including grilled spiny lobster, panfried grouper, and grilled Dover sole. All main dishes are cooked *à la minute.*

The masterful array of Italian desserts includes soufflés, a chilled zabaglione, and assorted pastries. The wine is the best in all the Bahamas, with more than 175,000 bottles. Some often stunning vintages are priced at thousands of dollars. The collection of Cuban cigars here—almost 90 types—is considered the most varied in the world. Before dinner, try the charming balcony bar.

## EXPENSIVE

### Buena Vista

Delancy and Meeting Sts. ☎**809/322-2811.** Reservations recommended. Appetizers $6.50–$70; main courses $25–38; fixed-price dinner $44.50. AE, DC, MC, V. Dinner daily 7–10pm. Closed Sun Apr 15–Christmas. Bus 10, 17. CONTINENTAL.

Lying one block west of Government House is a 200-year-old colonial mansion set on five acres of tropical foliage, a dining choice of traditional elegance and fine eating. The house has had a long and colorful history and was once owned by a Presbyterian minister. Ever since it opened in the 1940s, it's been a favorite of the local banking and business community. When the weather's right, which is most of the time, tables are set out on the garden patio, surrounded by flowers and palms. You can also dine in the Verandah Room or the Victorian Room.

A wide variety of local seafood is offered, and in addition to haute cuisine, under the direction of host Stan Bocus and chef Jimmy Perez, the restaurant turns out a number of nouvelle cuisine dishes. There are daily specials, and a number of main dishes are for two, such as roast rack of lamb in the style of Provence. The chef also prepares excellent beef and veal dishes. You might begin your meal with the daily pasta; cream of garlic soup rates as a novelty dish. Caviar is the most expensive appetizer. Desserts include cherries jubilee or orange crêpes au Grand Marnier. Service is deft and efficient, but also polite. Delancy Street is opposite the cathedral close of St. Francis Xavier, only a short distance from Bay Street.

### ✪ Sun And . . .

Lake View Rd., off Shirley St. ☎**809/393-1205.** Reservations required. Jacket required for men. Appetizers $8–$65; main courses $27.50–$35. AE, MC, V. Dinner Tues–Sun 6:30–9:45pm. Closed Aug–Sept. Bus 10, 17. FRENCH/SEAFOOD.

One of the oldest in Nassau, this restaurant is located near Fort Montagu. Everybody has dined here—Sir Winston Churchill, the Gabors, even Queen Elizabeth and Prince Philip. More recent guests have included Eddie Murphy, Sean Connery, Diana Ross, and Julio Iglesias. The place became a bit of a local legend when it was run by Pete Gardner, a former Battle of Britain "ace." To get to the

# Nassau Dining

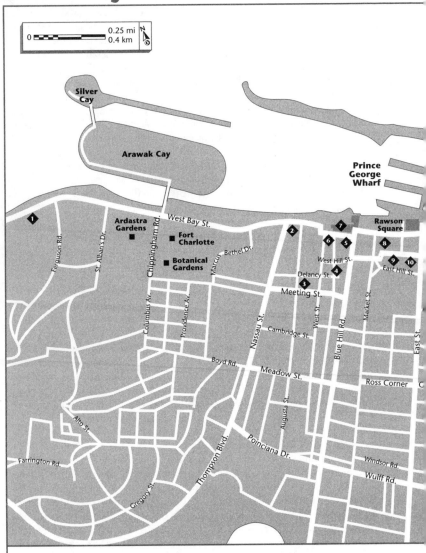

Bahamian Kitchen **8**

Bayside Buffet Restaurant **7**

Buena Vista **3**

Carib Café **1**

Cellar and Garden Patio **9**

Coconuts **13**

Coco's Café **5**

Europe **2**

Graycliff **4**

Green Shutters Restaurant **10**

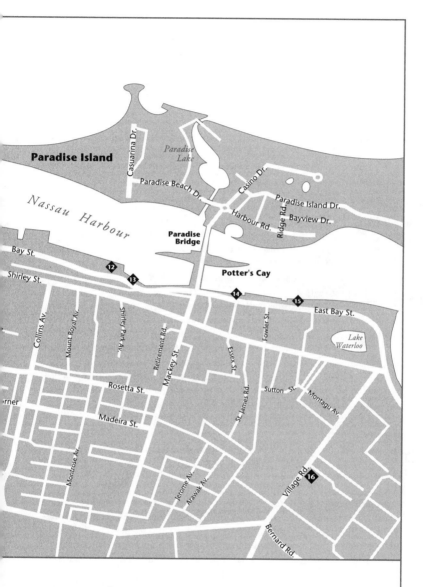

**Paradise Island**

*Paradise Lake*

Casuarina Dr.

Paradise Beach Dr.

Casino Dr.

Paradise Island Dr.

Ridge Rd.

Bayview Dr.

*Nassau Harbour*

Harbour Rd.

**Paradise Bridge**

Bay St.

**Potter's Cay**

Shirley St.

East Bay St.

Fowler St.

*Lake Waterloo*

Collins Av.

Mount Royal Av.

Shirley Park Av.

Retirement Rd.

Mackey St.

Essex St.

Sutton St.

Montagu Av.

Rosetta St.

Madeira St.

St. James Rd.

Montrose Av.

Jerome Av.

Arawak Av.

Village Rd.

Bernard Rd.

House of Wong ❿
Le Shack Bar & Grill ⓭
Passin' Jack ⓯
Piccadilly at 18 Parliament ❿
Poop Deck ⓮

Roscoe's at the Red Roof ⓬
Sun and ... ⓭
Tamarind Hill ⓰
Tony Roma's ❶

restaurant, you pass over a drawbridge between two pools and then enter a Spanish-style courtyard of a fine old Bahamian home, complete with fountains. You can order drinks in the patio bar, and then dine either inside or *al fresco* around the rock pool.

Beluga caviar is not only the most expensive appetizer but the most expensive item on the menu. However, you have a wide choice of more reasonably priced appetizers, including steamed mussels and Bahamian lobster cocktail. The chef has long been known for his conch chowder. Specialties include braised duckling with a raspberry sauce and lightly breaded veal chop sautéed in olive oil with a tomato Madeira sauce. Some main courses, including roast spring lamb, are prepared only for two guests. Soufflés are a specialty but you should order them in advance. One excellent soufflé is prepared with rum raisins and Black Label Bacardi.

## MODERATE

### ⑤ Carib Café

In the British Colonial Beach Resort, 1 Bay St. ☎ **809/322-3301.** Reservations recommended. Appetizers $4.95–$8.95; main courses $11.95–$21.95; lunch $10–$13.95. Lunch daily 11:30am–4pm; dinner daily 5–11:30pm. Bus 10, 17. STEAKS/SEAFOOD.

The most popular dining choice in this previously recommended landmark hotel, the Carib Café for years was known as Blackbeard's Forge, recalling the days when Nassau was a haven for buccaneers. Renovated in 1995, it has emerged as a lighter, more up-to-date restaurant, although steaks and seafood remain its specialty. It also remains a favorite of the cruise-ship crowd. Each of the wood-and-chrome tables has a box-shaped vent above to catch the smoke from its individual grill. You can feast on Bahamian conch chowder or onion soup, followed by sirloin steak, jumbo shrimp kabob, lobster tail, grouper filets, surf and turf, or breast of chicken, topped off by coconut-cream layer cake or walnut cake. On Wednesday night a seafood-and-steak buffet is presented for $25, including one hour of free rum punches, music, and entertainment. Call for a reservation if you'd like to attend.

### Cellar and Garden Patio

11 Charlotte St. ☎ **809/322-8877.** Reservations required for dinner. Appetizers $4–$6; lunch main courses $4.50–$12.50; dinner main courses $14–$27. AE, MC, V. Breakfast daily 9–11am; lunch daily 11am–3:30pm; dinner Mon–Sat 6–10pm. Bus 10, 17. BAHAMIAN/ENGLISH.

Located half a block from Bay Street in the downtown section, near the Straw Market and Rawson Square, this makes for a pleasant dining choice, not only because of its good food but also because of its garden-patio setting. Lunch, usually salads and sandwiches, is served in the outermost room, in an ambience midway between a Mediterranean cellar and an English pub. During dinner the setting moves to the lattice-rimmed courtyard, where glass-topped tables are set under cascading vines. Many diners, however, prefer the formal dining room in a charming, rustic cottage at the far end of the courtyard, which is open only in winter. Since only eight tables can be served here without cramping, dinner reservations are important.

The kitchen turns out at least half a dozen different kinds of quiche, including varieties made with tuna, conch, chicken, and lobster. For a main dish, selections featured are filet of grouper in a white wine sauce, shrimp scampi, lobster Newburg, pepper steak, New York sirloin, cracked conch, and a steak-and-mushroom pie cooked in Guinness.

## Coconuts

E. Bay Street. ☎ **809/325-2148.** Reservations recommended. Appetizers $4–$7; main courses $15–$28. AE, MC, V. Dinner only, daily 5:30–10:30pm (last order). INTERNATIONAL.

This is the gourmet, more upscale branch of a food-and-entertainment complex set within stone's throw of the edge of Nassau's harbor, a 5-minute walk to the west of the Paradise Island Bridge. (It's the companion restaurant of Le Shack Bar and Grill, which is recommended separately.) Coconuts prides itself on carefully prepared food served within either of two dining rooms, one of which overlooks the harbor (which I prefer), the other overlooking a garden.

The menu includes lots of fresh seafood culled from Bahamian waters, and steaks and chops which are usually imported from purveyors in Miami. Examples include at least three different preparations of lobster (panfried with onions in a black peppercorn sauce) broiled and served with lime-flavored butter; or minced with tomato sauce, peppers, and celery in the Bahamian style). Grouper comes in your choice of three different preparations; snapper is prepared amandine style; and sautéed scallops and shrimp are proposed "wedding party style" in a peppercorn sauce. There's always a featured "game fish of the day" (usually wahoo or blue marlin), seafood kabobs, and virtually anything a chef could concoct from a conch. Meat dishes include "ocean-view beef" (a glorified version of surf and turf), all kinds of steaks, filet of veal, lamb chops, and marina chicken (breast of fowl stuffed with pulverized crabmeat and herbs). After your meal, you might want to drop into Le Shack for a nightcap and a closeup view of whatever live band might be playing on the night of your visit.

## Europe

In the Ocean Spray Hotel, W. Bay St. ☎ **809/322-8032.** Reservations not required. Lunch appetizers $3.50–$6; lunch main courses $6–$14; set lunch $12; dinner appetizers $3.50–$8; dinner main courses $10.50–$24. AE, MC, V. Mon–Fri 8am–10pm, Sat 5–10pm. Bus 10. GERMAN/CONTINENTAL.

Europe, attached to a moderately priced hotel (see "Where to Stay," above), offers the best German specialties in Nassau. The restaurant is attracting more and more German visitors, but it also draws locals as well as North Americans. If you're driving, you'll find parking behind the restaurant.

You might begin with a hearty soup, perhaps lima bean and sausage. You can then go on to Bratwurst, a Wiener Schnitzel, perhaps pepper steak cognac. Sauerbraten is an eternal favorite, and the chef also prepares two kinds of fondue, both bourguignonne and cheese. Everybody's favorite dessert is German chocolate cake.

## ⓈGreen Shutters Restaurant

48 Parliament St. ☎ **809/325-5702.** Reservations not required. Appetizers $4.50–$6.50; lunch main courses $7.50–$10; dinner main courses $12–$22; fixed-price lunch $5.95. AE, MC, V. Lunch daily 11:30am–4pm; dinner daily 6–10:30pm. Bar open daily noon–1am. Bus 10, 17. ENGLISH/BAHAMIAN.

Rather like an English country pub, this spot serves three imported British beers as well as steak-and-kidney pie. It lies two blocks south of Rawson Square. You can dine either in the pub section with the regulars or in the mahogany-paneled restaurant. The menu is varied, offering fresh seafood complemented by traditional British fare: bangers and mash, shepherd's pie, and fish-and-chips. For dinner, roast prime rib with Yorkshire pudding and fresh key lime pie for dessert are winners. Bahamian specialties include grouper and conch salad. Vichyssoise, called "tater soup" here, and escargots with fresh spinach salad may also tempt you. The sandwiches at lunch are particularly good and well stuffed, including the triple-decker club. Courage beer is on tap, and the bartender also offers frozen daiquiris. The place has live music five nights a week.

## House of Wong

Marlborough St. ☎ **809/326-0045.** Reservations recommended. Appetizers $2.75–$43.75; main courses $6–$20. AE, MC, V. Lunch daily 11:30am–3pm; dinner daily 5:30–11pm. ASIAN.

In the heart of downtown Nassau, House of Wong is the latest reincarnation of the famed Mai Tai Chinese-Polynesian Restaurant which used to stand near Fort Montagu. Peter Wong and his family brought all their recipes for Polynesian, Szechuan, and Cantonese dishes, even some Hawaiian ones, to their new kitchen. This place is still considered the leading Asian restaurant in Nassau. Before your meal, try one of the exotic drinks that complement the Asian theme: Volcanic Flame (served with flaming rum), Lover's Paradise, or perhaps a Fog Cutter.

In the Polynesian mood? You might choose chow samsee, deviled Bahamian lobster, Mandarin orange duck, or sizzling steak. Szechuan dishes include hot shredded spiced beef, kung pao chicken ding, and lemon chicken. Among the Cantonese selections are chicken almond ding, moo goo gai pan, and sweet-and-sour chicken or pork. The restaurant also has take-out service. You get a lot of good food and polite service for the price.

## INEXPENSIVE

### ⑤ Bahamian Kitchen

Trinity Place, off Market St. ☎ **809/325-0702.** Reservations not accepted. Appetizers $3.50–$5; main courses $10.50–$24; lunches $6–$18. AE, DC, MC, V. Mon–Sat 11:30am–10pm, Sun 2–8:30pm. Bus 10, 17. BAHAMIAN.

Next to Trinity Church, this is one of the best places for good Bahamian cookery at modest prices. Specialties include lobster Bahamian style, fried red snapper, conch salad, stewed fish, steamed mutton, okra soup, and pea soup and dumplings. Most dishes are served with peas 'n' rice. You can order such old-fashioned Bahamian fare as stewed fish and corned beef and grits, all served with johnnycake. There is a take-out service if you're planning a picnic. The place is honest, decent, and upright.

### ⑤ Bayside Buffet Restaurant

In the British Colonial Beach Resort, 1 Bay St. ☎ **809/322-7479.** Reservations not required. Breakfast from $6.50; all-you-can-eat lunch buffet $10.95; all-you-can-eat dinner buffet $19.95. AE, DC, MC, V. Daily 7:30am–10pm (breakfast until 11:30am). Bus 10, 17. CONTINENTAL.

This restaurant is worth visiting almost as much for its view as for its good and reasonably priced buffets. The tall, 100-foot-long windows face Nassau's harbor and allow a panoramic view of cruise ships, yachts, and other boats around Prince George Wharf. Lunch and dinner feature prime rib, steamed shrimp, ham, turkey, roast pork loin, and fish. There are homemade pasta salads and crabmeat salad, as well as salads of greens, fresh vegetables, and other ingredients. The salad bar is arguably the best in town.

## Coco's Cafe

Marlborough St., corner of Bay St. ☎ **809/323-8778.** Reservations not required. American breakfast $4.95–$10.95; lunch appetizers $4.75–$6; lunch main courses $7.50–$20;

sandwiches $5–$7; dinner appetizers $6.50–$8; dinner main courses $8.50–$24. AE, MC, V. Breakfast daily 7:30–11am; lunch daily 11:30am–5pm; dinner daily 5–10:30pm. Bus 10, 17. BAHAMIAN/AMERICAN.

Across from the British Colonial Beach Resort, Coco's is a casual, informal café, decorated in a modern art deco style. It is a good choice for breakfast, lunch, or dinner. The drink menu lists every concoction from Bahama Mama to Goombay Smash, and the food menu is quite extensive, featuring hot and cold sandwiches, crab thermidor, cracked conch, and burgers. You might order that old budgeteer's favorite, grouper fingers, or perhaps a seafood lasagne. Cheesecake comes with a choice of toppings, or else you might opt for the rich chocolate or carrot cake.

### Piccadilly at 18 Parliament

18 Parliament St. ☎ **809/322-2836.** Reservations not required. Appetizers at lunch and dinner $4–$6; lunch main courses $6–$14; dinner main courses $9–$17. AE, MC, V. Lunch Mon–Sat 11am–3pm; dinner Mon–Sat 5–10pm. Bus 10. BAHAMIAN.

This downtown restaurant lies within the palm-studded tropical garden of Nassau's oldest continually operating hotel, the Parliament. Casually dressed diners come here for Bahamian seafood in a verdant setting. Appetizers include conch salad or snails in garlic butter. The fish is well prepared, especially the house special, grouper Florentine. Try also the cracked conch or the conch curry. Appropriate desserts include key lime pie, mud pie, or "bananas à la Dilly." There's a large tropical drink menu featuring frozen fruit daiquiris. Bahamian music is presented two nights a week (usually Wednesday and Saturday) from 7pm until closing.

### Le Shack Bar & Grill

E. Bay St. ☎ **809/325-2148.** Reservations not necessary. Burgers, sandwiches, and platters $4.50–$12.50. AE, MC, V. Daily 11am–midnight. BAHAMIAN/INTERNATIONAL.

Night owls appreciate Le Shack as a bar where live music reverberates five nights a week (for more information, see "New Providence After Dark" section of this chapter). Set within a 5-minute walk west of the Paradise Island Bridge, it's also suitable as a clean and well-managed lunch or dinner stopover where food prices are relatively reasonable. Cuisine features what the owners refer to as "portable food" (burgers, club sandwiches, chicken teriyaki platters, etc.), which you can eat sitting down, standing up, or dancing, burger in hand, whenever you feel inspired by the music. It's gazebolike setting perched on the sands above Nassau's harbor adds a lot to its appeal. Naturally, there's a full repertoire of sunset-colored drinks available to help you welcome the twilight of early evening.

### Tamarind Hill

Village Rd. ☎ **809/393-1306.** Reservations recommended. Appetizers $4.50–$6.50, sandwiches and burgers $5.75–$7.25; main courses $9.75–$21. AE, MC, V. Dinner only, nightly 5–10:15pm (last order). Bus route 17 (Soldier Road Bus). CARIBBEAN.

This is considered a favorite neighborhood restaurant for scores of Nassau residents who appreciate its charms and conviviality. It was named after the huge tamarind tree that grows in the front yard of a brightly painted building that was originally a private home in the 1960s. Set about a mile east of the Paradise Island Bridge, in a residential neighborhood uphill from Mont Ague Beach, it's outfitted with primitive paintings, potted plants, and flat, brightly painted metal sculptures inspired by aquatic themes. Menu items include at least a half-dozen types of burgers, sandwiches, and salads. More substantial fare includes grouper in a nut crust, Caribbean pork tenderloin stuffed with tropical fruit, fresh catch of the day prepared in any of about four different ways, cracked conch, conch fritters, and fresh salads prepared with wild raspberry dressings. The preferred drinks at the bar? A Tamarind Hill Cooler or a Tamarind Hill Smoothie, each of which costs $4.75.

### Tony Roma's

Saunders Beach, W. Bay St. ☎ **809/325-6502.** Reservations not required. Appetizers $3.50–$5.25; main courses $13–$22.95. AE, MC, V. Sun–Thurs 11am–midnight, Fri–Sat 11am–2am. Bus 10. RIBS.

On the main road between Nassau and Cable Beach, this place offers rib-sticking portions and good value. The stone-trimmed building affords views of Saunders Beach from its open-air veranda. Inside, the decor includes exposed paneling, captain's chairs, and ceiling fans.

The establishment bills itself as "the place for ribs," which is a good dish to order. Barbecued in a special sauce, they come in small (lunchtime) or large orders and can be accompanied by barbecued chicken as part of the same platter. Juicy sandwiches made from barbecued beef or London broil, about the best hamburgers on the island, Bahamian conch chowder, chef's or green salad, and panfried grouper are also offered. Every day a "Sunset Special" is offered between 4 and 6:30pm, costing only $9.95. For an appetizer, I always order the onion rings, which are served in a steaming loaf with a spicy sauce.

# CABLE BEACH
## Very Expensive

### ✪ Riviera Restaurant

Riviera Tower, in the Radisson Cable Beach Hotel, W. Bay St. ☎ **809/327-6000.** Reservations required. Jacket and tie required for men. Appetizers $5.75–$12.95; main courses $22–$37.95. AE, MC, V. Dinner Mon and Wed–Sat 6–10:30pm. Bus 10. SEAFOOD.

Considered the upscale restaurant in this previously recommended hotel, this restaurant lies one floor above the lobby. Decorated in a theme some diners describe as colonial New England–inspired, with tones of Newport blue and a big-windowed view of the beach and the sea, the Riviera serves an array of seafood specialties, such as Maryland crab cakes, shrimp and lobster ravioli, smoked Scandinavian salmon, tuna steak sautéed in a mustard sauce, and several different preparations of lobster. Desserts are sumptuous, including Bahamian guava duff, and might be followed with a Jamaican, Bahamian, Mexican, or calypso coffee, each liberally laced with the appropriate liqueur.

## Expensive

### Androsia Seafood Restaurant

In the Henrea Carlette Hotel, W. Bay St. ☎ **809/327-7085.** Reservations recommended. Appetizers $4.50–$7; main courses $19.50–$25. AE, MC, V. Dinner Mon–Sat 6pm–midnight. Bus 10. SEAFOOD.

In this restaurant housed in an unpretentious apartment hotel, German-born Siegfried von Hamm sets one of the finest tables on the island, featuring fresh seafood cooked to order, among other dishes. At a location west of the major Cable Beach hotels, Siegfried maintains both the cuisine and the ambience; he has elegantly fed everybody, including Sean Connery and Michael Caine. The decor of his restaurant is inviting, with nautical items, artwork, and captain's chairs and banquettes. Broiled local lobster is one of his most popular dishes, or you can order it thermidor style. Nassau-style grouper, a seafood platter, perfectly flavored

# Cable Beach Dining

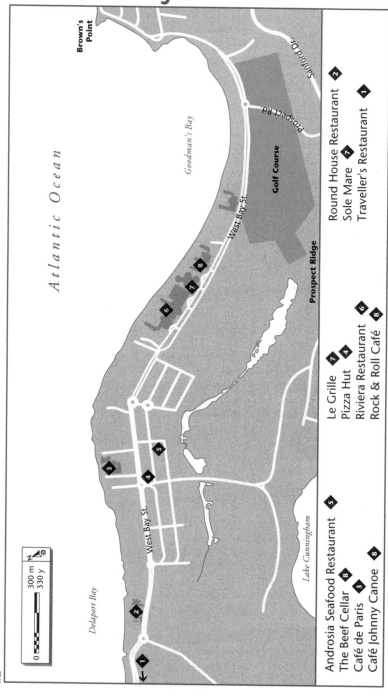

Androsia Seafood Restaurant 5
The Beef Cellar 8
Café de Paris 3
Café Johnny Canoe 8

Le Grille 7
Pizza Hut 4
Riviera Restaurant 6
Rock & Roll Café 8

Round House Restaurant 2
Sole Mare 1
Traveller's Restaurant 1

Atlantic Ocean

Brown's Point

Goodman's Bay

Golf Course

Prospect Rd

Sanford Dr.

West Bay St.

Prospect Ridge

Delaport Bay

West Bay St.

Lake Cunningham

300 m
330 y

9768

coq au vin, and filet mignon are all available. After one of the daily dessert specials, you can finish with one of Hamm's "coffee adventures."

### The Beef Cellar

In the Forte Nassau Beach Hotel. ☎ **809/327-7711.** Reservations recommended. Appetizers $3–$4.50; main courses $11–$29. AE, DC, MC, V. Dinner daily 6:30–10pm. STEAK/SEAFOOD.

This is the premier theme restaurant in the previously recommended Forte Nassau Beach Hotel. Located downstairs from the hotel's lobby, within a short walk of the glittering casino at the neighboring Carnival Crystal Palace Hotel, it features a warmly masculine decor of exposed stone and leather, two-fisted drinks, and tables that each have an individual charcoal grill set within easy reach of diners who prefer to grill their own steaks as part of the dining ritual. (If you prefer, the kitchen will do it for you instead.)

A limited but succulent choice of U.S.-bred beef is featured, including beef kabobs, New York sirloin, filet mignons, grilled veal loin chops, and surf and turf. Diners choose which of five different sauces they want to accompany their main courses. Salad and bread come with all main courses.

### Café de Paris

In Le Meridien Royal Bahamian Hotel, W. Bay St. ☎ **809/327-6400.** Reservations not required. Appetizers $5–$11.50; main courses $14.75–$29.50; three-course fixed-price dinner $24. AE, DC, MC, V. Bus 10. FRENCH/BAHAMIAN.

Café de Paris offers a tasteful, European-style setting and cuisine for clients seeking respite from the glitter of Cable Beach's Crystal Palace complex. The dress code is casual but elegant. Contained within the inner courtyard of the previously recommended Le Meridien Royal Bahamian Hotel, it offers a soothing French decor of fan-topped windows, views of a manicured garden, and such accessories as crisp napery and glistening silverware. Start with a Bahamian ceviche or perhaps local lobster bisque with brandy. An Abaco steamed conch salad also is featured as an appetizer. Among main dishes you can order mahimahi steak Exuma served with citrus wedges or a Royal Bahamian stir-fry with tenderloin tips, shelled prawns, ginger, and green papaya. An herb steamed halibut is served with a tomato basil coulis, or else you can order baked prawns with feta cheese. For dessert, try mango ice cream, a freshly baked thin apple tart, or a Royal Bahamian croissant pudding.

## MODERATE

### Round House Restaurant

In the Casuarinas of Cable Beach, W. Bay St. ☎ **809/327-8153.** Reservations not required. Appetizers $4.50–$6; main courses $12.50–$19. AE, DC, MC, V. Dinner Wed–Mon 6–9:30pm. Bus 10. BAHAMIAN/AMERICAN.

Nettie Symonette's restaurant has muted lighting and soft-grained paneling. It's a family affair, serving some of the best Bahamian cuisine on the island. The waiter will bring you a generous drink if you wish, after which you can enjoy a choice of steak, seafood, or other specialties. These might include New York strip, Eleuthera chicken, and shrimp creole, plus lobster and conch prepared in various ways. The health conscious will order from the "fit for life" menu. For dessert, try Nettie's guava duff if featured.

## INEXPENSIVE

### Café Johnny Canoe

In the Forte Nassau Beach Hotel, W. Bay St., Cable Beach. ☎ **809/327-3373.** Reservations not necessary. Breakfast $5–$7; appetizers $5–$7; main courses $6.75–$22. AE, MC, V. Daily 7:30am–midnight. INTERNATIONAL.

Although it's set on the less desirable side (i.e., the one facing West Bay Street) of the Forte Nassau Beach Hotel, that doesn't seem to diminish any of its allure. Within a yellow-painted interior accented with framed antique photographs of Old Nassau, you can order a wide range of the kind of dishes that everybody (including extended families) seems to like. These include burgers, all kinds of steaks, seafood, and chicken dishes, as well as two platters which the staff tells me are among the most popular anywhere, blackened grouper and barbecued ribs. On the opposite side of the French windows that illuminate the dining room, you'll find an outdoor terrace for sunlit (or starlit) meals. The weekly high point? Every Friday night, a miniature version of the Bahamian carnival parade (Junkanoo, starring a stylized representation of the mythical character of Johnny Canoe) promenades through the dining room, much to the delight of any children who happen to be present.

### Rock & Roll Café

Forte Nassau Beach Hotel, Cable Beach. ☎ **809/327-7711.** Reservations not necessary. Appetizers $5–$8; sandwiches and salads $7–$13; platters $9–$22. AE, MC, V. Daily noon–2am. INTERNATIONAL/ BAHAMIAN.

Set in an open-sided building midway between two of Cable Beach's resort hotels, this restaurant celebrates the combination of tropical weather, rock-and-roll music, and the music-related paraphernalia that would thrill any groupie who ever hung out for autographs after a rock concert. The decor is modeled on the Hard Rock Cafés you might have visited in London or New York, and includes a model of a World War II fighter plane suspended over the bar, framed publicity shots for rock-and-roll bands, and lots of nostalgia from the golden age of electronically amplified music. There's a view of the sea, an option of dining either indoors or on a beachfront terrace, and an array of drinks whose most popular choice has always been the strawberry daiquiri. Drinks range from $4 to $5 each; food includes club sandwiches, barbecued pork, stuffed potato skins, an array of sandwiches (both vegetarian and meat stuffed), platters of fish, and ice cream. The outdoor terrace (site of volleyball games and other tournaments) is often mobbed by college students, especially during spring break. (Ironically, the building that contains this place, Frilsham House, was originally owned by Lord Beaverbrook, the British newspaper magnate of the 1930s and 1940s, who would probably be horrified at the state of affairs going on there today.) At press time, anyone who enjoyed a meal here would receive free entrance to the Zoo, a separately recommended disco (see the "New Providence After Dark" section of this chapter) which is owned by the same management. Live rock-and-roll concerts and karaoke are frequently part of the agenda at this very popular restaurant.

## LOVE BEACH

### The Restaurant at Compass Point

W. Bay St., Gambia, Love Beach. ☎ **809/327-7309.** Reservations necessary. Lunch platters $6.50–$16; dinner appetizers $3.50–$7; dinner main courses $18–$27. AE, DC, MC, V. Lunch daily 11:30am–3pm; dinner daily 7:30–11pm. BAHAMIAN.

The beachfront, cement-sided building that contains the restaurant was originally built in the 1960s as an upscale private home. Today, it's surrounded by the multicolored, hexagonal-shaped bungalows of New Providence's newest hotel, Compass Point (see "Where to Stay," above), a short walk from what's probably the most famous recording studio (Compass Point Studios) in New Providence.

Menu items celebrate creative Bahamian cuisine and include such dishes as queen conch salad with sweet-fried plantain; Caesar salad with johnnycake croutons; grilled fresh snapper with avocado, mango, and sweet pepper relish; rack of lamb with guava and roasted garlic glaze; and blackened Exuma grouper with roasted pepper and pineapple coulis. Desserts are appropriately creative and suitably tropical, an example of which is Junkanoo pineapple and guava tart with passion-fruit sauce.

## SOUTHWESTERN NEW PROVIDENCE

### Traveller's Restaurant
W. Bay St., near Gambier. ☎ **809/327-7633.** Reservations not required. Appetizers $3–$4; lunch main courses $7–$15.50; dinner main courses $11.50–$17.50. AE, MC, V. Daily noon–10:30pm. Closed last two weeks in Sept. Western Transportation to and from Nassau, $1.75 each way. BAHAMIAN/SEAFOOD.

A Bahamian culinary tradition, this is the best bet for dining on local fare. Set in a grove of sea-grape and palm trees, facing the ocean, the place serves typical Bahamian fare and seafood. But that hasn't stopped the world, including celebrities such as Mick Jagger and Sidney Poitier, from beating a path to its door.

You can dine outside under a portico or on the terrace. If it's rainy (highly unlikely), you can go inside the tavern with its small bar and decor of local paintings. Many diners bring their swimsuits and use the white-sand beach across from the restaurant; others arrive in their own boats. In this laid-back atmosphere, you can feast on grouper fingers, barbecue ribs, steamed or curried conch, or minced crawfish, and finish perhaps with guava cake. The restaurant lies about nine miles west of the center of Nassau.

## SPECIALTY DINING
### HOTEL DINING

### Le Grille
In the Carnival's Crystal Palace Resort & Casino, W. Bay St., Cable Beach. ☎ **809/327-6200.** Reservations recommended. Appetizers $7.75–$14.50; main courses $26–$35. AE, DC, MC, V. Dinner Mon–Sat 6–11pm. Bus 10. INTERNATIONAL/STEAKS/SEAFOOD.

Considered the favorite of many casinogoers within the mammoth hotel that contains it, this elegantly decorated restaurant lies one floor above the gambling tables that provide its visual inspiration. Menu items include salads of native lobster; double lamb chops with rosemary and apricot sauce; double breasts of chicken with a ginger, green onion, and pineapple sauce; and a tempting array of steaks, chops, fish, and seafood.

### Sole Mare
In the Carnival's Crystal Palace Resort & Casino, W. Bay St. ☎ **809/327-6200.** Reservations required. Jacket and tie required for men. Appetizers $9–$90; main courses $19–$35. AE, DC, MC, V. Dinner Tues–Wed and Fri–Sun 6–11pm. Bus 10. ITALIAN.

This upscale restaurant is the culinary showcase of the previously recommended Crystal Palace megaresort, where eight other restaurants compete fiercely. It is set

## 👪 Family-Friendly Restaurants

**Green Shutters Restaurant** *(see p. 91)* This restaurant in downtown Nassau is noted for its well-stuffed sandwiches, potato skins, and wide selection of burgers. Kids also like its simple fare, including fried chicken and seafood kabobs, and especially the chocolate cake for dessert.

**Pizza Hut** *(see p. 100)* Just as they do back home, kids love to be taken to Pizza Hut. This worldwide chain member offers not only pizzas, but pastas and sandwiches as well.

**Bayside Buffet Restaurant** *(see p. 92)* In Nassau's British Colonial Hotel, of James Bond fame, children and their parents can enjoy all-you-can-eat lunch or dinner buffets. These meals are among the top bargains in town, and, besides that, you enjoy a panoramic view of the harbor.

on the second floor of the resort's Casino Tower, amid a stylishly up-to-date decor that features soft tones of lilac, mauve, and pink. A view of the sea complements the elegant menu items.

Only the very rich order beluga caviar as an appetizer. Otherwise, you might choose among spinach salad; apple-scented lobster bisque laced with cream and cognac; an array of pastas; salmon tartare; veal sautéed with endive, white wine, and capers; grilled tuna or beefsteak; a filet of whatever fresh fish is available that day; and freshly made dessert soufflés served with vanilla sauce.

## DINING WITH A VIEW

### Poop Deck

Nassau Yacht Haven Marina, E. Bay St. ☎ **809/393-8175.** Reservations not required. Bus 10, 17. Appetizers $3.75–$5; main courses $8.95–$27.50; fixed-price lunch $9.95; fixed-price dinner $12.95–$14.95. AE, MC, V. Lunch daily noon–5pm; dinner daily 5:30–10:30pm. BAHAMIAN.

This is a favorite with the yachting set, who find a perch on the second-floor open-air terrace, overlooking the harbor. The deck opens onto the yachts in the harbor, as well as Paradise Island. At lunch, you can order conch chowder, followed by beef burgers. In the evening, native grouper fingers are served with peas 'n' rice, or you might prefer Rosie's special chicken or Bahamian broiled crayfish. Stuffed deviled crab is another specialty, and the chef does a homemade lasagne with crisp garlic bread. The bar opens at 11:30am, and food is served all day.

## LOCAL FAVORITES

### Passin' Jack

In the Nassau Harbour Club Hotel, E. Bay St. ☎ **809/394-3245.** Reservations not required. Appetizers $3.50–$7; main courses $10–$15. AE, DC, MC, V. Breakfast daily 7–11am; lunch daily noon–3pm; dinner daily 6–10pm. Bus 17. BAHAMIAN/AMERICAN.

Located on the lobby level of an unpretentious modern hotel on Bay Street, a half-mile east of the Paradise Island Bridge, this likable restaurant was established in 1993. It's named after the schools of passin' jack (a cousin of the amberjack) that Bahamian fishermen have traditionally caught by the hundreds every September. In addition to well-flavored food, the restaurant offers a panoramic view over the Paradise Island Channel to one of the country's most mysterious houses, the enormous villa built by a reclusive Saudi sheik in the late 1980s. Menu items include grouper fingers, cracked conch, baby-back ribs, strip steak, filet mignon, and sandwiches. The house special drink (the "Passin' Jack Special") combines the best parts of a frozen rum runner with a frozen piña colada for one heady libation.

## FAST FOOD

### Pizza Hut
Delaport Point, W. Bay St., Cable Beach. ☎ **809/327-7293**. Reservations not required. Sandwiches, pizzas, and pastas $4.50–$16.50. AE, V. Mon–Thurs 11am–11pm. Fri–Sat 11am–midnight. Bus 10. PIZZAS/PASTAS.

Set in a small shopping center a short distance from the massive hotel complexes of Cable Beach, this unpretentious member of a worldwide chain offers a low-cost alternative for cost-conscious diners. No beer or wine is served, but pizzas come in three sizes, and lasagne and spaghetti, as well as sandwiches, are also available. There's space inside for seating, as well as a salad bar.

## SUNDAY BRUNCH

All the major hotels present rather lavish Sunday brunches, and you can partake of them, even if you're not registered at one of the big resort hotels. However, you should call in advance to see if there is space available, as restaurant managers like to give preference to registered guests.

For a real Bahamian breakfast, head for the previously recommended **Cellar and Garden Patio,** 11 Charlotte St. (☎ 809/322-8877), in the center of Nassau. It even serves the typically Bahamian breakfast of stewed fish and johnnycakes, long an island favorite. The cost is only $8. Breakfast is served on Sunday from 8 to 11am. Bus 10, 17.

## PICNIC FARE & WHERE TO EAT IT

You can find many places to buy picnic fare in New Providence. A longtime favorite for securing "the fixin's" is **Roscoe's at the Red Roof,** West Bay Street (☎ 809/322-2810). Located next to the water, a mile west of the Paradise Island Bridge, the shop offers more than 150 kinds of cheeses, smoked salmon cutlets, and the fixings for dozens of kinds of sandwiches. (Among the most popular is the crabmeat.) You'll also find smoked meats from Germany, exotic rye breads from Canada, and daily take-away specials of such foods as quiche and lasagne. There's a small cluster of tiny tables if you prefer to eat in. Sandwiches cost from $3 to $5 each. Roscoe's is open Monday through Friday from 8am to 5pm and Saturday 9am to 5pm.

If you have a kitchenette you might head for one of the fishing boats that moor beneath the Paradise Island Bridge and buy fresh lobster or conch to take home and transform into salad. You could also buy portions of johnnycake-to-go from the previously recommended **Bahamian Kitchen,** or stock up on cold cuts and soda at any of Nassau's supermarkets.

An ideal spot for a picnic would be **Fort Charlotte,** off West Bay Street on Chippingham Road (see below). After touring its dank dungeons, seek out a sunny spot on the grounds for your picnic, but remember not to litter.

Others prefer to take their picnic basket and head for the **Botanical Gardens** (see below). While you're enjoying your picnic, you can take in the lush tropical foliage. Children especially find the spot delightful.

## 5 What to See & Do

Most of Nassau can be covered on foot, beginning at Rawson Square in the center, where the stalls of the Straw Market are found. I also enjoy the native market on the waterfront, a short walk through the Straw Market. Here is where Bahamian fisherpeople unload a variety of produce and fish—crates of mangoes, oranges, tomatoes, and limes, plus lots of crimson-lipped conch.

Facing Rawson Square is a colonial-style structure, housing Parliament, the Law Courts (where wigged judges dispense standards of British justice), and the Senate. In the center is a statue of Victoria as a young queen.

At the top of George Street, Government House is the most imposing building of New Providence. It's the residence of the governor-general of the Bahamas. The duke and duchess of Windsor lived here during the war years, when he was governor. At the main entrance stands a much photographed 12-foot statue of Columbus, who landed at San Salvador (in the Bahamas) in 1492. Every visitor in town likes to attend the **Changing of the Guard** ceremony on alternate Saturdays at 10am.

At Elizabeth Avenue, turn right (away from the water) and walk uphill to the Queen's Staircase, 65 steps leading to Fort Fincastle (see below). These steps, hand hewn by slaves, were carved out of solid limestone in the 18th century to allow troops stationed at the fort to escape in case of danger.

## SUGGESTED ITINERARIES

For visitors with more leisurely time to see the Bahamas, ranging from one week to three weeks, refer to the slower-paced "Suggested Itineraries" in Chapter 3.

### If You Have 1 Day

**Day 1**    Far too little time, but that is often the curse of modern tourism. Go for an early morning swim on one of the beaches of New Providence, take our walking tour of the center of Nassau. Have lunch at a typically Bahamian restaurant in the city, then go on a boat ride from the harbor. Return in time to do some duty-free shopping and pay a visit to the Straw Market. That night, head for a glitzy casino or take in one of the Las Vegas–type revues at Cable Beach or Paradise Island.

### If You Have 2 Days

**Day 1**    Spend as above.
**Day 2**    Head for the beach again, or devote most of your morning to your favorite sport, such as golf or tennis. In the afternoon, see Coral World Bahamas. Still later in the afternoon, head for one of the local waterfront bars in Nassau for the time-honored custom of a sundowner.

### If You Have 3 Days

**Days 1–2**    Spend as above.
**Day 3**    In the morning explore Paradise Island (see Chapter 5). Have lunch on Paradise Island, then spend the afternoon exploring Ardastra Gardens. Go to a local club in the evening to hear some Goombay music.

**If You Have 5 Days**

**Days 1–3**   Spend as above.

**Day 4**   Have a leisurely morning at the major beach on Paradise Island (see Chapter 5). Return to Nassau for lunch in a local restaurant, then explore the shops in greater depth this time. In the afternoon, visit the Botanical Gardens.

**Day 5**   Spend most of the day visiting one of the offshore islands such as Blue Lagoon Island or Discovery Island (see "Easy Excursions," below), allowing for plenty of time on the beach. After resting at your hotel, plan a special dinner at one of Nassau's top restaurants, such as Buena Vista or Riviera Restaurant, then top off your vacation with some casino action and a show at either Cable Beach or Paradise Island.

# THE TOP ATTRACTIONS

## ✪ Ardastra Gardens

Chippingham Rd. ☎ **809/323-5806.** Admission $7.50 adults, $3.75 children. Daily 9am–5pm. Bus 10.

In almost five acres of lush tropical planting, about a mile west of downtown Nassau and near Fort Charlotte, are the Ardastra Gardens, where the main attraction is the parading flock of pink flamingos. The Caribbean flamingo, national bird of the Bahamas, had almost disappeared in the early 1940s but was brought back to significant numbers through efforts of the National Trust, and they now flourish in the rookery on Great Inagua. A flock of these exotic feathered creatures has been trained to march in drill formation, responding to the drillmaster's oral orders with long-legged precision and discipline. The Marching Flamingos perform Monday through Saturday at 11am, 2pm, and 4pm.

Other exotic wildlife to be seen at the gardens are boa constrictors (very tame), kinkajous (honey bears) from Central and South America, green-winged macaws, peacocks and peahens, blue-and-gold macaws, and capuchin monkeys, iguanas, hutias (a ratlike animal indigenous to the islands), ring-tailed lemurs, red-ruff

---

### ❓ Did You Know?

- New Providence Island was originally named Sayle's Island after its discoverer, Capt. William Sayle, who found refuge there during a storm.
- Cable Beach was given its name by W. B. C. Johnson in 1892; he wanted to publicize an underwater telegraph cable newly laid between Jupiter, Florida, and the Bahamas.
- An octagonal building in downtown Nassau—now the library—was originally built as a jail in 1797. Today's bookcase alcoves were once individual prison cells.
- The flamingo, the national bird of the Bahamas, has the unusual trait of holding its bent bill completely upside down when feeding.
- Residents of New Providence more than double the population of the rest of the Bahamas.
- The Royal Victoria Hotel (now in ruins) welcomed such prominent guests as Prince Albert and Winston Churchill.

lemurs, margays, brown-headed tamarins (monkeys), and a crocodile. There are also numerous waterfowl to be seen in Swan Lake, including black swans from Australia and several species of wild ducks.

You can get a good look at the flora of the gardens by walking along the signposted paths, as many of the more interesting and exotic trees bear plaques with their names. Guided tours of the gardens and the aviary are given Monday through Saturday at 10:15am and 3:15pm.

### Coral Island Bahamas

On Silver Cay just off W. Bay St. ☎ **809/328-1036.** Admission $16 adults, $11 children under 12. Daily 9am–6pm. It's directly off the main harbor entrance to Nassau on Silver Cay between downtown Nassau and Cable Beach. Bus 10.

Coral Island Bahamas is a marine park with a network of aquariums, landscaped park areas, lounges, a gift shop, and a restaurant, but the outstanding feature is the Underwater Observation Tower. You descend a spiral staircase to a depth of 20 feet below the surface of the water, where you can view tropical fish in their natural habitat, coral reefs, and abundant sea life, seen through 24 large clear windows. The tower rises 100 feet above the water, with two viewing decks plus a bar where you can have a drink while enjoying a panoramic view of Nassau, Cable Beach, and Paradise Island. Among the marine attractions are a reef tank, a shark tank, a turtle pool, and a stingray pool, plus 24 aquariums under one roof as well as tidal pools.

### Botanical Gardens

Chippingham Rd. ☎ **809/323-5975.** Admission $1 adults, 50¢ children. Mon–Fri 8am–4:30pm. Bus 10, 17.

More than 600 species of tropical flora are found on these 16 acres of grounds, near Fort Charlotte. The curator will answer your questions.

### Fort Fincastle

Elizabeth Ave. ☎ **809/322-2442.** Admission 50¢ adults and children. Mon–Sat 9am–4pm. Bus 10, 17.

Reached by climbing the Queen's Staircase (see above), this fort was constructed in 1793 by Lord Dunmore. Here you can take an elevator ride to the top and walk on the observation floor (a 126-foot-high water tower and lighthouse), enjoying a view of the harbor. The tower is the highest point on New Providence.

### Fort Charlotte

Off W. Bay St. on Chippingham Rd. ☎ **809/322-7500.** Admission free. Mon–Sat 8:30am–4pm. Bus 10, 17.

Begun in 1787 and built with plenty of dungeons, Fort Charlotte is worth a trip. The largest of Nassau's three major defenses, it used to command the western harbor. Named after King George III's consort, it was built by Governor Lord Dunmore, who was also the last royal governor of New York and Virginia. Its 42 cannons never fired a shot, at least not an invader. Within the complex are underground passages and a waxworks, which can be viewed on free tours.

### Fort Montagu

Eastern Rd. Admission free. No regular hours. Bus 10, 17.

Fort Montagu was built in 1741 and stands guard at the eastern entrance to the harbor of Nassau. It's the oldest fort on the island. The Americans captured it in 1776 during the War of Independence.

### Blackbeard's Tower

Yamacraw Hill Rd. Admission free. Open all day. Transportation: Jitney.

This historic mossy ruin stands five miles east of Fort Montagu. These crumbling remains of a watchtower are said to have been used by the infamous pirate Edward Teach in the 17th century.

### Junkanoo Expo

Prince George Wharf. ☎ **809/356-2731.** Admission $1 adults, 50¢ children. Daily 10am–4pm.

In case you miss the beginning of the real thing (at 2am on Boxing Day, December 26, following Christmas), you can relive the Bahamian Carnival at this expo. One of the city's newer museums, it lies in an old customs warehouse. All the glitter and glory of Mardi Gras comes alive in this museum, with its fantasy costumes used for the holiday bacchanal. A favorite venue of cruise-ship passengers, the museum, in costumes, masks, and other paraphernalia, re-creates the festivities.

### Pompey Museum

At Vendue House, W. Bay St. at George St. ☎ **809/326-2566.** Admission free. Mon–Fri 10am–4:30pm, Sat 10am–1pm. Bus 10, 17.

The building that contains Vendue House was originally built of imported brick in 1762. It served as the island's slave market until 1834, when the practice was outlawed throughout the British Empire by an act of Parliament. Named after the leader of a 19th-century slave revolt in the Exumas that almost toppled the ruling patriarchs, the Rolle family, it houses an exhibition on Bahamian life and the work of one of the country's most prolific artists, Amos Ferguson, called "the father of Bahamian art."

## WALKING TOUR
## Historic Nassau

**Start:** Rawson Square.
**Finish:** Prince George Wharf.
**Time:** 2 hours.
**Best Times:** Monday through Saturday between 10am and 4pm.
**Worst Times:** Sunday when many places are closed; and any day lots of cruise ships are in port.

Begin your tour at:

1. **Rawson Square,** the center of Nassau, some say its "very heart and soul." The square lies directly inland from Prince George Wharf, where many of the big cruise ships dock. On the square is the Churchill Building, where the controversial Lynden Pindling conducted his affairs as prime minister for 25 years before his ouster in 1992. The present prime minister and some other government ministries use the building today. Look for the statue in the square: it's of Sir Milo Butler, a former shopkeeper who became the first governor of the Bahamas when independence from Britain was granted in 1973.

   Across Rawson Square is:

2. **Parliament Square,** dominated by a statue of a youthful Queen Victoria before she got her dour, paunchy look. To the right of the statue stand more Bahamian government office buildings, and to the left is the House of

# Walking Tour–Historic Nassau

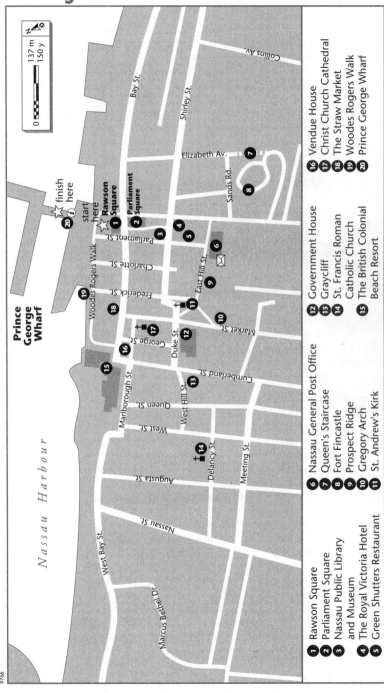

0  137 m
   150 y

Nassau Harbour

Prince George Wharf

finish here
start here

Rawson Square

Parliament Square

1 Rawson Square
2 Parliament Square
3 Nassau Public Library and Museum
4 The Royal Victoria Hotel
5 Green Shutters Restaurant
6 Nassau General Post Office
7 Queen's Staircase
8 Fort Fincastle
9 Prospect Ridge
10 Gregory Arch
11 St. Andrew's Kirk
12 Government House
13 Graycliff
14 St. Francis Roman Catholic Church
15 The British Colonial Beach Resort
16 Vendue House
17 Christ Church Cathedral
18 The Straw Market
19 Woodes Rogers Walk
20 Prince George Wharf

Church ✠   Post Office ⊠   Information ⓘ

9766

Assembly, the oldest governing body in continuous session in the New World. In the building in back of the statue, the Senate meets; this is a less influential body than the House of Assembly. Some of these Neo-Georgian style buildings date from the late 1700s and early 1800s.

The Supreme Court building stands next to the:

3. **Nassau Public Library and Museum** (actually opening onto Bank Lane), a building from 1797 that once was the Nassau Gaol (jail). In 1873, it became the public library. Just across Shirley Street from the library is:

4. **The Royal Victoria Hotel,** now in ruins. Once this was the haunt of Confederate spies, royalty, smugglers of all sorts, and ladies and gentlemen. Horace Greeley pronounced it "the largest and most commodious hotel ever built in the tropics," and many agreed with this American journalist. The hotel experienced its heyday during the American Civil War. It is said that at the Blockade Runners' Ball, some 300 guests consumed 350 magnums of champagne. Former guests have included two British prime ministers, Neville Chamberlain and the man who replaced him, Winston Churchill. Prince Albert, consort of Queen Victoria, also stayed here at one time. The hotel closed in 1971.

After imagining its former splendor, head south along Parliament Street.

🍵 **TAKE A BREAK**　If you'd like some time out, try the **5. Green Shutters Restaurant,** 48 Parliament St. (☎ 809/325-5702). This popular restaurant and English-style pub occupies a colonial house nearly two centuries old. People come here for their favorite pick-me-up or to enjoy a typical English lunch, perhaps shepherd's pie or other pub grub. It is lively both day and night, one of the few places where locals mingle happily with visitors. Lunch is served daily from 11:30am to 4pm; dinner is served daily from 6 to 10:30pm. The bar is open daily from noon to 1am.

At the end of Parliament Street stands:

6. **The Nassau General Post Office,** where you may want to purchase Bahamian stamps if you're a collector. You can also mail letters and packages.

Armed with your purchases of colorful Bahamian stamps, walk east on East Hill Street and turn left onto East Street, then right onto Shirley Street, and head straight on Elizabeth Avenue. This will take you to the landmark:

7. **Queen's Staircase,** leading to Bennet's Hill. In 1793, slaves cut these 65 steps out of sandstone cliffs. Upon their completion, they provided access from the center of Old Nassau to:

8. **Fort Fincastle,** built by Lord Dunmore in 1793, who had a talent for constructing unnecessary forts at great expense. Designed in the shape of a paddle-wheel steamer, the fort kept looking out for marauders who never came. It was eventually converted into a lighthouse, as it occupied the highest point on the island. The tower is more than 200 feet above the sea, providing a panoramic view of Nassau and its harbor.

A small footpath leads down from the fort to Sands Road. Once you reach it, head west (left) until you approach East Street again, then bear right. When you come to East Hill Street (again), go left, as you will have returned to the post office. Continue your westward trek along East Hill Street, which is the foothill of:

9. **Prospect Ridge.** This was the old dividing line between Nassau's rich and poor. The rich people (nearly always white) lived along the waterfront, often in

beautiful mansions, one once occupied by the British newspaper magnate, Lord Beaverbrook. The African Bahamians went "over the hill" to work in these rich homes during the day, but returned to Prospect Ridge to their own homes (most often shanties) at night. They lived in such places as seedy Grant's Town, originally settled in the 1820s by freed slaves. Near the end of East Hill Street, you come to:

**10. Gregory Arch.** This tunnel was cut through the hill in 1850; after its opening, working class African Bahamians didn't have to go "over the hill"—and steep it was—but could go through the arch to return to their villages.

At the intersection with Market Street, go right. On your right rises:

**11. St. Andrew's Kirk** (Presbyterian). Called simply the "Kirk," the church dates from 1810 but has seen many changes over the years. In 1864 it was enlarged, with the addition of a bell tower, among other architectural features. This church had the first non-Anglican parishioners in the Bahamas.

On a steep hill, rising to the west of Market Street, you see:

**12. Government House,** on your left, the official residence of the governor-general of the archipelago. This is the queen's representative to the Bahamas, and the post today is largely ceremonial, since the actual governing of the nation is in the hands of an elected prime minister. This pink-and-white neoclassical mansion dates from the dawn of the 19th century. Poised on its front steps is a rather jaunty statue of Christopher Columbus, which was presented to the then colony of the Bahamas by its ruling governor, Sir James Carmichael Smyth, who'd assumed the post in 1829.

Opposite the road from Government House on West Hill Street rises:

**13. Graycliff.** A Georgian building from the 1720s, this deluxe hotel and restaurant—a stamping ground of the rich and famous—was constructed by Capt. John Howard Graysmith in the 1720s. In the 1920s, it achieved fame—or perhaps notoriety—when it was run by Polly Leach, pal of gangster Al Capone. Later it was purchased by Lord and Lady Dudley, who erased the old memories and furnished it with grand flair and taste. It attracted such famous guests as the duke and duchess of Windsor and Winston Churchill.

Upon leaving Graycliff, you will see a plaque embedded in a hill. The plaque claims that this site is the spot where the oldest church in Nassau once stood.

On the corner of West Hill Street and West Street is Villa Doyle, former home of William Henry Doyle, chief justice of the Bahamian Supreme Court in the 1860s and 1870s.

Opposite it stands:

**14. St. Francis Roman Catholic Church,** constructed between 1885 and 1886. It was the first Catholic church in the Bahamas, and funds were raised from the Archdiocese of New York.

Continue along West Street until you reach Marlborough. Walk a short block that leads to Queen Street and go right, passing the front of the American embassy. At the corner of Queen Street and Marlborough rises:

**15. The British Colonial Beach Resort,** dating from 1923. It was for a time run by Sir Harry Oakes, once the most powerful man in the Bahamas and a friend of the duke of Windsor. His still unsolved murder in 1943 was called "the crime of the century." Constructed on the site of Fort Nassau, an old hotel on this spot was called simply Hotel Colonial—but it burned in 1922. The site has been used in some films, including James Bond thrillers. One part of the hotel fronts George Street where you'll find:

**16. Vendue House,** one of the oldest buildings in Nassau. It was once called the Bourse (Stock Exchange) and was the site of many slave auctions. It is now a museum.

**17. Christ Church Cathedral** is not far from Vendue House on George Street. Dating from 1837, this is a Gothic Episcopal cathedral, and is often the venue of many important state ceremonies, including the opening of the Supreme Court, with its procession of bewigged, robed judges followed by barristers— all accompanied by music from the police band.

   If you turn left onto Duke Street, and proceed along Market Street, you reach:

**18. The Straw Market,** opening onto Bay Street. A favorite of cruise-ship passengers, this market offers not only straw products, but all sorts of souvenirs and gifts. Bahamian women will not only weave you a basket, but braid your hair with beads if that is your desire.

   Next, take the narrow little Market Range, leading to:

**19. Woodes Rogers Walk,** named for the former governor of the colony, who fell on bad days and eventually ended in a debtors' prison in London before coming back as royal governor to Nassau. Head east along this walk for a panoramic view of the harbor, with its colorful mail and sponge boats. Its markets sell vegetables and fish and lots and lots of conch. The walk leads to:

**20. Prince George Wharf,** where the cruise ships dock. It was constructed in the 1920s, the heyday of American Prohibition, to provide more harbor space for the hundreds of bootlegging craft running the American blockade against liquor. It was named for the duke of Kent (Prince George) in honor of his visit here in 1928. Its most aristocratic vessel is always the yacht of Queen Elizabeth II, the HMS *Britannia,* which has been a frequent visitor, notably in 1985 when the queen arrived as the honored guest at a meeting of the leaders of the Commonwealth.

## ORGANIZED TOURS

There's a lot to see in Nassau, and tours have been arranged to suit your taste for seeing the colorful historic city as well as the outlying sights of interest.

   **Free Goombay Guided Walking Tours** are arranged by the Ministry of Tourism as a gesture of welcome to newcomers. They leave from the Tourist Information Booth on Rawson Square at 10am and again at 2pm; there are no tours on Thursday and on Sunday afternoon. Tours last for about 45 minutes and include descriptions of some of the city's most venerable buildings, with commentaries on the history, customs, and traditions of Nassau. The briskly informal tours require no advance reservations and few advance preparations. Call **809/326-9772** to confirm that tours are on schedule.

   **Majestic Tours,** Hillside Manor, P.O. Box N-1401, Cumberland, the Bahamas (☎ **809/322-2606**), offers a number of trips, both night and day, to many points of interest. A 2-hour city-and-country tour leaves daily at 2:30pm and goes to all points of interest in Nassau, including the forts, the Queen's Staircase, the water tower, the Straw Market (passing but not entering it), and other sights. The tour costs $18 per person.

   An extended city-and-country tour, also leaving daily at 2:30pm, includes the Ardastra Gardens on its route. The charge is $25 per person, half for children.

A combination tour, departing Tuesday, Wednesday, and Thursday at 10am, is just that—a combination of all the sights you see on the first tour listed above, plus the Botanical Gardens and lunch, at a cost of $33 per person, half for children.

Majestic has a nightclub tour Monday to Friday nights. They take you to one of Nassau's leading nightclubs to see an exotic floor show consisting of limbo, fire dancing, and other entertainment. Transportation to and from your hotel is included in the prices. The tour without dinner goes for $24 per person; with dinner included, $55 per person; half for children.

For information about these tours, as well as for reservations and tickets, many hotels have a Majestic Tours Hospitality Desk in the lobby, and others can supply you with brochures and information as to where to sign up.

## EASY EXCURSIONS

A short boat trip will take you to several small islands lying off the north coast of New Providence. One of these, **Blue Lagoon Island,** just three miles north of the Narrows at the eastern end of Paradise Island, has seven beaches. Nassau Cruises Ltd. (see "Boat Trips" under "Sports A to Z," below) will take you there to see the pirate's stone watchtower, to relax in a hammock under swaying palms, to party and dance at a pavilion, or just to stroll along narrow pathways edging the sea.

**Discovery Island,** renamed in honor of the 1992 quincentennial of Columbus's discovery of the Bahamas, used to be known as Balmoral Island, for it was the private stamping ground of the now defunct Balmoral Club. But all that changed long ago at this island, which is visible offshore from the hotels strung along Cable Beach. A haven for picnickers and sun worshipers, it is ringed by a superb beach, with a network of paths connected to the dock. There's even a lookout for "sundowners," as well as a bar and barbecue along with toilets and changing rooms. Recreational facilities include windsurfing, parasailing, snorkeling, waterskiing, and volleyball. The small sandy cay requires a 5- to 10-minute boat ride to reach it,

---

### ⭐ Frommer's Favorite New Providence Experiences

**Listening to the Sounds of Goombay.** At some local joint, you can enjoy an intoxicating beat and such island favorites as "Goin' Down Burma Road," "Get Involved," and "John B. Sail."

**A Ride in a Horse-Drawn Surrey.** If you'd like to see Nassau as the duke and duchess of Windsor did when he was governor, consider this unique form of transport. It's elegant, romantic, and nostalgic. Surreys await passengers at Rawson Square, in the exact center of Nassau.

**A Glass-Bottom Boat Ride.** Right in the center of Nassau's harbor, numerous craft wait to take you on enchanting rides through the colorful "sea gardens" off New Providence Island. In the teeming reefs offshore, you'll meet all sorts of sea creatures while an underwater wonderland unfolds before your eyes.

**An Idyllic Day on Blue Lagoon Island.** It's like an old Hollywood fantasy of a tropical island. Off the eastern end of Paradise Island, this Blue Lagoon has seven sandy beaches. Boats from Nassau Harbour take you there and back.

and a round-trip ticket costs $10 for adults and children. Boats depart daily from the water-sports kiosk at Carnival's Crystal Palace Resort & Casino every half hour from 9:30am to 4pm. For more information, call **809/327-6200.**

**Athol Island** and **Rose Island** are slivers of land poking up out of the sea northeast of the Prince George waterfront docks of Nassau. Shelling is one of the lures of these little islands. Do-it-yourself skippers can make the trip in motorboats.

You don't have to go to sea to reach **Potters Cay.** It's to be found under the Paradise Island Bridge, linked by causeway to Nassau, so you can walk to it. The attraction here is a fish-and-vegetable market, where you can sample some raw conch fresh from its shell.

# 6 Sports A to Z

One of the great sports centers of the world, Nassau (and the islands that surround it) is a marvelous place for swimming and sunning, snorkeling, scuba diving, boating, waterskiing, and deep-sea fishing, as well as tennis and golf.

At last count, there were 32 different sports being actively pursued in the Bahamas. You can learn more about any of them by calling the **Bahamas Sports and Aviation Information Center** (☎ **305/932-0051** or toll free **800/32-SPORT**) from anywhere in the continental United States. Call Monday through Friday from 9am to 5pm, EST. Or write the center at 19495 Biscayne Blvd., Suite 809, Aventura, FL 33180.

## BEACHES

On New Providence Island, the hotels at Cable Beach have their own stretches of sand, as do the hotels on Paradise Island. Of course, everyone wants to head for the famed and spectacular **Paradise Beach,** especially those occupants of downtown Nassau hotels. The beach can be reached by boat from the Prince George Wharf, costing $3 per person for a round-trip ticket. However, you must pay a separate $3 for admission to the beach, but this fee includes the use of a shower and locker. An extra $10 deposit is required for the safe return of towels. If you're traveling with children under 12, you pay $1 admission for each of them. It's also possible to drive to the beach across the Paradise Island Bridge for a toll of $2, 25¢ to walk.

To reach **Saunders Beach,** where many of the local people go on weekends, take West Bay Street toward Coral Island. This beach lies across from Fort Charlotte.

On the north shore, past the Cable Beach Hotel properties, is **Caves Beach,** some seven miles west of Nassau. It stands near Rock Point, right before the turnoff along Blake Road that leads to the airport.

Continuing west along West Bay Street you reach **Love Beach,** across from Sea Gardens, a good stretch of sand lying east of Northwest Point.

## BOAT TRIPS

Cruises from the harbors around New Providence Island are offered by a number of operators, with trips ranging from daytime voyages for diving, picnicking, sunning, and swimming to sunset-and-night cruises mainly for leisure activity.

### Flying Cloud
Paradise Island West Dock. ☎ **809/363-2208.**

This outfit features catamaran cruises carrying 50 people on day trips and sunset trips or a maximum of 30 for dinner. Snorkeling equipment is provided free. A half-day charter costs $30 per person, a 2¹/₂ hour sunset cruise goes for $25. The 3¹/₂ hour dinner cruise is $50 per person (half price for children). The 57-foot catamaran was designed and built by Gold Coast Yachts. Sailings are daily except Thursday and Sunday, departing at 9:30am and at 2pm. Round-trip transportation to the dock from your hotel is included.

## Majestic Tours Ltd.
Hillside Manor. ☎ **809/322-2606.**

Majestic Tours will book 3-hour cruises on two of the biggest catamarans in the Atlantic, offering you views of the water, sun, sand, and outlying reefs. *Yellow Bird* is suitable for up to 250 passengers, and *Tropic Bird* carries up to 170 passengers. They depart from Prince George's Dock. Ask for the departure point when you make your reservation. The cruises include a 1-hour stop on a relatively isolated portion of Paradise Island's Cabbage Beach. The cost is $15 per adult, with children under 12 paying $7.50 on either cruise. Departures are Tuesday at 1:15pm, Wednesday 9:45am and 1:15pm, Friday 1:15pm, and Saturday 9:45am and 1:15pm.

## Nassau Cruises Ltd.
Paradise Island Bridge. ☎ **809/363-3577.**

This company maintains a pair of three-deck motorized yachts, the *Calypso I* and *Calypso II*. Equipped with bars, they depart from a point just west of the toll booth on the Paradise Island Bridge. Daytime trips depart several days a week, depending on business, for the secluded beaches of an uninhabited cay (Blue Lagoon Island), a half-hour's sail east of Paradise Island. The 6-hour day sails, from 10am to 4pm, require advance reservations; they include a buffet lunch and cost $35 per person. The company also offers once-a-week dinner cruises every Thursday between 7 and 10pm. The price of $35 per person includes a steak-and-grouper dinner and a glass of wine. A half-day cruise from 1 to 4pm costs $20.

## Topsail Yacht Charters
British Colonial Hotel Dock. ☎ **809/393-0820.**

*Wind Dance* and *Liberty Call* leave for all-day cruises from this dock, offering many sailing-and-snorkeling possibilities. Topsail has added a third ketch to its fleet, the 54-foot *Riding High*, which is bigger than the 41-foot *Wind Dance* or the 36-foot *Liberty Call*. Cruise options are plentiful, including a half day of sailing, snorkeling, and exploring, costing $34. A full day goes for $149. Champagne-and-cocktail cruises in the evening are also popular, going for $35 per person. A private dinner cruise is a favorite for honeymooners—the 3-hour moonlit sail costs $350. All vessels are available for private charter.

## DEEP-SEA FISHING

Many sportspeople come to Nassau just to fish. May through September are the best months for the oceanic bonito and the black-fin tuna; June and July, for blue marlin; and November through May, for the amberjack found in reefy areas. The list seems endless. This is, of course, a costly sport. Arrangements can be made at big hotels. Prices are usually $300 for a half-day boat rental for parties of two to six or $600 for a full day's fishing. Some of the best charter operators are **Nassau Yacht Haven** (☎ **809/393-8173**), which has both a 35-foot boat and a 42-foot boat. Fishing is mainly close to shore. It takes 15 to 20 minutes to reach a drop-off where wahoo and barracuda abound. Another reliable operator is the

**Charter Boat Association** (☎ 809/363-2335), offering 8 to 10 boats in their fleet. This company offers both half-day and full-day rentals for vessels that can seat six comfortably. Each additional person is charged from $40 to $50 depending on boat size. Fishing choices are plentiful, and one may choose from trolling for wahoo, tuna, and marlin in the deep sea or casting in the shallows for snapper, amberjack, grouper, and yellowtail. Anchoring and bottom fishing offer calmer options.

## FITNESS CLUBS

The health spa in Le Meridien Royal Bahamian Hotel, Cable Beach, West Bay Street, (☎ 809/327-6400), is among the best in the country, and it is open to both hotel guests and visitors. It has state-of-the-art equipment, including Universal exercise machines, a sauna and steam room, whirlpool baths, Scandinavian-type massages, mud baths, an outdoor freshwater swimming pool, and an aerobics workout room. Entrance fee for nonresidents is $10 per day or free for residents. Advance notice should be given for mud baths priced at $25 for 30 minutes, facials at $25 for 30 minutes, and massages at $60 for 50 minutes. Hours are daily from 8am to 7:30pm.

The Palace Spa, in the Carnival Crystal Palace Complex, West Bay Street (☎ 809/327-6200), adjoining Radisson Cable Beach, is one of the best gyms on the island, with equipment such as a Stairmaster, cardiovascular exercise equipment, whirlpool, steam room, saunas, and free weights. You pay a $5 deposit for lockers and towels. Crystal Palace guests pay $10 per day or $35 per week, and nonguests are charged $15 per day or $40 per week. Sneakers and shorts are required in the fitness area, and children under 14 are not admitted. Hours are Monday through Friday from 6am to 9pm and Saturday and Sunday from 7am to 9pm.

## GOLF

Some of the best golfing in the Bahamas is found in Nassau.

### Cable Beach Golf Course

Cable Beach, W. Bay Rd. ☎ 809/327-6000.

This is a spectacular 18-hole, 7,040-yard, par-72 championship golf course. It's under the management of Radisson Cable Beach Hotel, but often used by guests of Carnival's Crystal Palace Resort & Casino. Greens fees are $50 for residents of Radisson, but $60 for all other players. Carts can be rented for $45.

### South Ocean Golf Course

SW Bay Rd. ☎ 809/362-4391.

One of the finest golf courses in the Bahamas is a 30-minute drive from Nassau on the southwest edge of the island. The course has palm-fringed greens and fairways. Overlooking the ocean, the 6,706-yard beauty has some first-rate holes with a backdrop of trees, shrubs, ravines, and undulating hills. The 18-hole, USPGA-sanctioned course, has a par of 72. Players are charged $45 for greens fees, plus $25 for a golf cart. It's best to phone ahead in case there's a golf tournament scheduled for the day you had planned to play.

## HORSEBACK RIDING

On the southwest shore, Happy Trails Stables, Coral Harbour (☎ 809/362-1820), offers a 1-hour, 20-minute horseback trail ride for $45 per person.

This includes free transportation to and from your hotel. The weight limit for riders is 200 pounds. The stables are signposted from the Nassau International Airport, a distance of two miles. Children must be eight or older. Reservations are required, especially during the holiday season.

## PARASAILING

This increasingly popular sport allows you to zoom up to 200 feet in the air, parachute style. Parasailing with Sea Sports, Forte Nassau Beach Hotel, West Bay Street, Cable Beach (☎ 809/327-7711), costs $35 for 5 to 6 minutes or $50 for 10 to 12 minutes.

## SAILING

At Sea Sports, Forte Nassau Beach Resort Club, West Bay Street (☎ 809/327-6058), you're offered your best bet in sailing rentals. A Hobie costs $40 for the first hour, lowered to $30 for each additional hour. A Sunfish rents for $30 per hour or $20 for each additional hour. A paddleboat costs $15 per half hour and a kayak can be rented for $10 per half hour.

## TENNIS

Courts are available at only some hotels. Guests usually play free or for a nominal fee, while visitors are charged.

Most of the courts at Cable Beach are under the auspices of the Radisson Cable Beach Hotel, Cable Beach, West Bay Street (☎ 809/327-6000). Residents of Radisson play for free until 4pm. After that, illumination costs $10 per hour. The night rate applies to all, regardless of which hotel one is registered at. During the day, any tennis player showing up who's not a guest at Radisson pays $3.50 per person.

Other hotels offering tennis courts include Forte Nassau Beach Hotel, West Bay Street, Cable Beach (☎ 809/327-7711), with six Flexipave night-lit courts and British Colonial Beach Resort, 1 Bay St., Nassau (☎ 809/322-3301), with three hard-surface lit courts.

## UNDERWATER SPORTS & WALKS

The following outfits cater to snorkelers and divers of all levels.

### Bahama Divers
E. Bay St. ☎ 809/393-5644.

Packages available here include a half day of snorkeling to offshore reefs, costing $20 per person, and a half-day scuba trip with preliminary pool instruction for beginners, costing $60. Half-day excursions for experienced divers to offshore coral reefs with a depth of 25 feet go for $35, and half-day scuba trips for certified divers to deeper outlying reefs, drop-offs, and blue holes cost $60. Participants receive free transportation from their hotel to the boats. Children must be eight or older. Reservations are required, especially during the holiday season.

### Hartley's Undersea Walk
E. Bay St. ☎ 809/393-8234.

An educational and exciting experience is offered by the Hartley's, who take you out from Nassau Harbour aboard the yacht *Pied Piper*. On the 3¹/₂-hour cruise, you're submerged for about 20 minutes, making a shallow-water descent to a point where you walk along the ocean bottom through a "garden" of tropical fish, sponges, and other undersea life. You'll be guided through the underwater world wearing a helmet that allows you to breathe with ease and to see. Entire families can make this walk, which costs $40 per person in groups of five. You don't even have to be able to swim to make this safe adventure. Two trips are operated at 9:30am and 1:30pm, Tuesday through Saturday. Arrive 30 minutes before departures.

### Stuart Cove's Dive South Ocean

Lyford Cay. ☎ **809/362-4171** or toll free 800/879-9832 in the U.S.

Stuart Cove's is about 10 minutes from top dive sites such as the coral reefs, wrecks, and an underwater airplane structure used in filming James Bond thrillers. The Porpoise Pen Reefs, named for Flipper, and steep sea walls are also on the diving agenda. An introductory scuba program costs $99, with morning two-tank dives priced at $65. All prices for boat dives include tanks, weights, and belts. An open-water certification course starts at $350. Escorted boat snorkeling trips cost $25. A special feature is a series of shark-dive experiences costing from $110. In one outing, Caribbean reef sharks swim among the guests. In one dive, called "Shark Arena," divers kneel down while a dive master feeds the sharks off a long pole. Another experience, a "Shark Buoy" in 6,000 feet of ocean, involves a dive among silky sharks at about 30 feet. They swim among the divers while the dive master feeds them.

## WINDSURFING

At Sea Sports, Forte Nassau Beach Resort Club, West Bay Street, Cable Beach (☎ **809/327-7711**), windsurfing equipment rents for $25 for the first hour and $15 for each additional hour. Guests of the Forte Nassau Beach Hotel can enjoy windsurfing free. If you rent a board for four hours, the total cost is $55. Lessons cost from $35 for one half hour of instruction.

# 7 Shopping

You can find a variety of bargains in Nassau—Swiss watches, Japanese cameras, French perfumes, Irish crystal and linens, and British china, usually, but not always, at prices below those charged in stores in the United States.

In 1992, the Bahamas abolished import duties on 11 categories of luxury goods, including china, crystal, fine linens, jewelry, leather goods, photographic equipment, watches, fragrances, and other merchandise. Antiques, of course, are exempt from import duty worldwide. How much you can take back home depends on your country of origin. Americans, for example, can bring back $600 worth of merchandise tax free, plus two liters of wine, if they've been away for 48 hours and have not claimed a similar exemption in the past 30 days. For more details, plus Customs requirements for some other countries, refer to "Customs" in Chapter 3.

The principal shopping area is a stretch of the main street of town, Bay Street, and its side streets downtown, as well as the shops in the arcades of hotels.

Bahamian shops offer so many bargains you may be tempted beyond what you are allowed to take home duty free, but sometimes you'll find the prices lower than back home even if you have to pay duty.

Don't try to bargain with the salespeople in Nassau stores as you would at the Straw Market (see "Markets," below). The price asked in the shops is the price you must pay, but you won't be pressed to make a purchase. The salespeople here are courteous and helpful in most cases.

Store hours are 9am to 5pm Monday through Saturday at most shops in Nassau. The Nassau Shop closes at noon on Thursday, and a few other places lock their doors at noon on Friday. No stores are open on Sunday, although the Straw Market does business seven days a week. You can have purchases mailed to wherever from many stores.

In lieu of street numbers along Bay Street (true in most cases), look for signs advertising the various stores.

# SHOPPING A TO Z

## ANTIQUES

### Marlborough Antiques

Corner of Queen and Marlborough Sts. ☎ **809/328-0502.**

Catering to the types of tastes you might have expected in London, this store maintains an inventory of such items as antique books, antique maps and engravings, English silver (both sterling and plate), and the kinds of unusual table settings (fish knives, etc.) which might have been better appreciated by other, more formal generations. Among the most appealing objects for nostalgia buffs are the store's collection of antique photographs of Old Bahamas, any of which might be treasured by an island historian. Also displayed are works by Bahamian artists Brent Malone and Maxwell Taylor.

## BRASS & COPPER

### Brass and Leather Shop

12 Charlotte St. ☎ **809/322-3806.**

With two branches on Charlotte Street, between Bay and Shirley Streets in Nassau, this shop offers English brass, handbags, luggage, briefcases, attachés, and personal accessories. Shop no. 2 has handbags, belts, scarves, ties, and small leather goods from such famous designers as Furla, Bottega Veneta, Pierre Balmain, and others.

## CIGARS

### Pipe of Peace

Bay St., between Charlotte and Parliament Sts. ☎ **809/325-2022.**

The Pipe of Peace is called the "world's most complete tobacconist," and here you can buy Cuban and Jamaican cigars; however, the Cuban cigars can't be brought back to the United States. For the smoker, the collection is amazing. The shop also sells such name-brand watches as Seiko and Girard-Perregaux, along with cameras, stereos, Dunhill and other lighters, and calculators.

## COINS & STAMPS

### Bahamas Post Office Philatelic Bureau

In the General Post Office, at the top of Parliament St. on E. Hill St. ☎ **809/322-3344.**

Here you'll find beautiful Bahamian stamps. Destined to become collector's items is a series of stamps, printed in lithography, and issued to commemorate the discovery of the New World. Called "Discovery stamps," they were first released on February 24, 1988. In all, there are four stamps, the first of a number of issues culminating in 1992. One stamp depicts Ferdinand and Isabella. Supplies are expected to dwindle drastically in the 1990s.

### Coin of the Realm
Charlotte St., just off Bay St. ☎ 809/322-4497.

This family-run shop lies in a lovely building more than two centuries old that was hewn out of solid limestone. The shop offers not only fine jewelry, but also mint and used Bahamian and British postage stamps, as well as rare and not-so-rare Bahamian silver and gold coins. It also sells old and modern paper currency of the Bahamas. Bahama pennies, the ones minted in 1806 and 1807, are now rare and expensive items.

## CRYSTAL & CHINA

### Bernard's China & Gifts Ltd.
Bay St. and Fifth Terrace, Centreville. ☎ 809/322-2841.

Bernard's has a wide selection of Wedgwood, Coalport, Royal Copenhagen, Royal Crown Derby, Royal Worcester, and Crown Staffordshire china; Baccarat, Lalique, Daum, and Schott Zwiesel crystal; and Ernest Borel and Seiko watches. You can also find jewelry and gift items here.

### Treasure Traders
Bay St. ☎ 809/322-8521.

This offers the biggest selection of gifts made of crystal and china in the Bahamas. All the big names in china are here, including Rosenthal and Royal Copenhagen. Counters contain crystal by Waterford, Lalique, Orrefors, and Daum. There are a multitude of designs, and the store sells not only traditional designs but also modern sculpted glass.

## DEPARTMENT STORES

### The Nassau Shop
284 Bay St. ☎ 809/322-8405.

Between Parliament Square and the British Colonial Beach Resort, the Nassau Shop is one of the largest department stores in the Bahamas, with lots of good buys if you shop and pick carefully. French perfume is a good value here, including Hermès. Piaget watches are for sale, as are Shetland pullovers and cardigans, for both men and women.

## FABRICS

### Bahamas Hand Prints
Corner of Mackey and Shirley Sts. ☎ 809/393-1974.

Visitors are invited to a display room and workshop to watch fabrics being screen printed and processed. You can buy goods by the yard or made up into ready-to-wear items for men, women, and children, including shirts, shorts, dresses, skirts, and tops. Place mats, tea towels, wall hangings, aprons, and pillow covers make good gifts to take home.

## FASHION

### Barry's Limited
George St. ☎ 809/322-3118.

Considered one of Nassau's more formal and elegant clothing stores, this shop sells garments made from lamb's wool, English cashmere, and the kinds of upscale garments you might wear to a meeting of your local bankers. Elegant sportswear (including Chinese-made Guayabera shirts) as well as leisure suits are also sold here. Most of the clothes are for men, but women often stop in for a look at the fancy handmade Irish linen handkerchiefs and such stylistic accessories as cuff links and studs.

## Cole's of Nassau

Parliament St. ☎ **809/322-8393.**

This boutique offers the most extensive selection of designer fashions in Nassau. Women can be outfitted from top to bottom in everything from swimwear to formal gowns, from sportswear to lingerie and hosiery. Gift items are also sold. Cole's also sells sterling-silver and costume jewelry. A second shop is at the Mall at Marathon, Marathon and Robinson Roads ( ☎ **809/393-3542**).

## Fendi

Charlotte St. at Bay St. ☎ **809/322-6300.**

This is Nassau's only outlet for the well-crafted Italian-inspired accessories (handbags, luggage, shoes, watches, cologne, wallets, and portfolios) endorsed by the famous leather-goods company. Its choice of gift items might solve some of your gift-giving quandaries.

## Mademoiselle, Ltd.

Bay St. at Frederick St. ☎ **809/322-5130.**

The store specializes in the kinds of resort wear which looks appropriate at either a tennis court or a cocktail party. Inventory includes garments by Andros fabric (the batik specialists), whose bright colors and free-form designs are well-known throughout the archipelago. Swimwear, sarongs, jeans, and halter tops are the rage here, as well as all the soaps, unguents, and paraphernalia (through their on-site "Body Shop" boutique) you'd need for herbal massages and beauty treatments. A less well-stocked branch of this store, with a higher percentage of Bahamian souvenirs, lies at Rawson Square ( ☎ **809/328-0433**), close to the cruise-ship docks.

# JEWELRY

## John Bull

At the corner of Bay and East Sts. ☎ **809/322-4252.**

One block east of Rawson Square, this fine store features a wide selection of watches, jewelry, cameras, perfumes, cosmetics, leather goods, and accessories. John Bull recently renovated its Bay Street store, expanding its jewelry department and adding a leather division featuring the wares of Dooney & Bourke and Prime Classe by Alviero Martini.

## Little Switzerland

Bay St. ☎ **809/322-8324.**

Little Switzerland offers a wide variety of jewelry, watches, china, perfume, crystal, and leather in top brands. Also sold are world-famous Swiss watches including Ebel, Rado, Omega, Baume & Mercier, and Tag-Heuer, plus such scents as Oscar de la Renta, Dior, and Chloe. Figurines from Royal Doulton and Lladró, as well as crystal by Schott Zwiesel and, of course, Waterford, will please your eye.

## The Treasure Box

Bay St. ☎ **809/322-1662.**

On the corner of Market Street, the Treasure Box offers "gifts from the sea"—that is, conch-shell and coral jewelry, including earrings, necklaces, and pillboxes.

## LEATHER

### Gucci

Saffrey Sq., Bay St., corner of Bank Lane. ☎ **809/325-0561.**

This shop, opposite Rawson Square, offers a wide selection of designer handbags, wallets, luggage, briefcases, gift items, scarves, ties, designer casual wear and evening wear for men and women, beach towels, umbrellas, shoes and sandals, all by Gucci of Italy. Also featured are Gucci watches and perfume—all at savings over most U.S. prices.

### Leather Masters

Parliament St. ☎ **809/322-7597.**

This well-known retail outlet carries an internationally known collection of leather bags, luggage, and accessories by Ted Lapidus, Lanvin, and Lancel of Paris, Etienne Aigner of Germany, and "i Santi" of Italy. Leather Masters also carries luggage by Piel and Marroquinnera of Colombia. Other displays are a handsome range of leather wallets by Bosca and pens, cigarette lighters, and watches by Colibri. Designer silk scarves and neckties, as well as sunglasses, carry the designer labels of Ted Lapidus and Giorgio Armani.

## LINENS

### The Linen Shop

Savoy Bldg., Bay St., between Charlotte and Frederick. ☎ **809/322-4266.**

The Linen Shop carries such select items as exquisite bed linen, Irish handkerchiefs, hand-embroidered women's blouses, tablecloths, and infant wear, as well as Japanese designer kimonos and children's pajamas.

## MAPS

### Balmain Antiques

Mason's Bldg., Bay St., near Charlotte St. ☎ **809/323-7421.**

A wide and varied assortment of 19th-century etchings, engravings, and maps, many of them antique and all reasonable in price, are sold here. It's usually best to discuss your interests with Mr. Ramsey, the owner, so he can direct you to the proper drawers. His specialties include the Bahamas, America at the time of the Civil War, and black history. You'll find the shop on the second floor, two doors east of Charlotte Street.

## MARKETS

The **Nassau International Bazaar** consists of some 30 shops selling international goods in a new arcade, pleasant for strolling and browsing at leisure. The $1.8-million complex sells goods from around the globe. The bazaar runs from Bay Street down to the waterfront (near the Prince George Wharf). The alleyways here have been cobbled and storefronts are garreted, evoking the villages of old Europe.

**Prince George Plaza,** Bay Street (☎ 809/322-5854 for information), is popular with cruise-ship passengers. Many fine shops selling such quality merchandise as Gucci are found here. You can patronize an open-air rooftop restaurant here, overlooking Bay Street.

The **Straw Market** in Straw Market Plaza on Bay Street is a must visit. Here you can watch the Bahamian craftspeople weave and pleat straw hats, handbags, dolls, place mats, and other items, including straw shopping bags for you to carry your purchases in. You can buy items ready-made or order special articles, perhaps bearing your initials, and you can have fun bargaining to get the stated prices reduced.

## Music

### Cody's Music and Video Center
E. Bay St., corner of Armstrong St. ☎ **809/325-8834.**

Considered one of the finest record stores in the Atlantic, Cody's specializes in the contemporary music of the Bahamas and the Caribbean. The father of owner Cody Carter was mentor to many of the country's first Goombay and Junkanoo artists. The store also sells videos, compact discs, and tapes.

## Perfumes & Cosmetics

### The Beauty Spot
Bay and Frederick Sts. ☎ **809/322-5930.**

The largest cosmetic shop in the Bahamas, this outlet sells duty-free cosmetics, including Lancôme, Chanel, YSL, Elizabeth Arden, Estée Lauder, and Biotherm, among others. It also operates facial salons.

### Cameo
W. Bay St. across from the Straw Market. ☎ **809/322-1449.**

Has the Bahamian sun wreaked havoc with your complexion? This store will provide you with the upscale unguents and creams you'll need to restore your skin to the texture and consistency of an English rose. Cameo is the exclusive agent for the Swiss-based La Prairie skin treatments. Their line of perfumes come from such names as Donna Karan, Givenchy, and an assortment of other French and Italian brands which aren't always marketed within the North American mainland.

### The Perfume Shop
Corner of Bay and Frederick Sts. ☎ **809/322-2375.**

In the heart of Nassau, within walking distance of the cruise ships, the Perfume Shop offers duty-free savings on world famous brand names in perfumes. Treat yourself to a flacon of Eternity, Giorgio, Poison, Lalique, Shalimar, or Chanel. Those are just a few of the scents for women. For men, there are such highly touted names as Drakkar Noir, Polo, and Obsession.

## Shoes

### Alexis
Corner of Rosetta and Montgomery Sts. ☎ **809/328-7464.**

Need a pair of leather pumps for an impromptu, spur-of-the-moment rendezvous with the prime minister and his wife? Stop by for a view of their selection of women's footwear by such shoemakers as Evan Picone, Timothy Hitsman, and Bandolino.

## 8  New Providence After Dark

Gone are the days of such famous native nightclubs as the Yellow Bird and the Big Bamboo, where tuxedo-clad gentlemen and elegantly gowned ladies drank and danced the night away. You still get dancing now, along with limbo and calypso, but for most visitors, the major attraction is gambling.

Cultural entertainment is limited for Nassauvians. The chief center for this is the **Dundas Center for the Performing Arts,** which sometimes stages ballets, plays, or musicals. Call **809/393-3728** to see if a production is planned at the time of your visit. Ticket prices depend on the event being staged.

## CASINOS

### ✪ Carnival's Crystal Palace Casino
W. Bay St., Cable Beach. ☎ **809/327-6459.** No cover.

This dazzling casino is part of Carnival's Crystal Palace Resort & Casino. It's a joint undertaking of Carnival Cruise Lines and the Continental Companies of Miami. The casino complex is a spectacular addition to the island's nightlife. In hues of purple, pink, and mauve, the 35,000-square-foot casino is filled with flashing lights. The gaming room features 750 slot machines in true Las Vegas style, along with 51 blackjack tables, 7 craps tables, 9 roulette wheels, a baccarat table, and 1 big six. An oval-shaped casino bar extends onto the gambling floor, and the Casino Lounge, with its bar and bandstand (offering live entertainment), overlooks the gaming floor. It is open daily from 10am to 4am.

## THE CLUB & MUSIC SCENE

### Fanta-Z
In Carnival's Crystal Palace Resort & Casino, W. Bay St., Cable Beach. ☎ **809/327-6200.** Cover $15, including two drinks.

Near the casino, and accessible only from there, is this two-story disco with a marble dance floor and tiers of laserlike lights perched above a wraparound balcony. A big-windowed view of the sea contrasts with the dazzlingly electrified interior. A mixed drink costs $4. The club reserves the right to refuse admittance to anyone in jeans or shorts. Open Thursday through Sunday from 9pm to 2am and Friday and Saturday from 9pm to 4am.

### Rock & Roll Café
In the Forte Nassau Beach Hotel, Cable Beach. ☎ **809/327-7711.** No cover.

Set on the beachfront of one of Cable Beach's more staid hotels, this loud and iconoclastic nightclub will warm the heart of any rock-and-roll lover. Patterned after the Hard Rock Café in London, it features an almost constant barrage of electronic music, a wide selection of beer and tropical drinks, and a noteworthy collection of rock-and-roll memorabilia. There's also a big-screen TV showing sporting events. Drinks cost from $4 to $5. See "Where to Dine," above, for more information. Open daily from noon to 2am.

### The Zoo
West Bay St. at Saunders Beach. ☎ **809/322-7195.** Cover Sun–Thurs $20; Fri–Sat $40.

Opened in 1994, and set midway between Cable Beach and the western periphery of Nassau, this is the largest and best-accessorized nightspot of its kind on New Providence. It's housed on two floors of what was built many years ago as a warehouse, although the architects who designed the place originally would never recognize it today. It contains two floors, five bars, an indoor/outdoor restaurant (Zooley's, open nightly from 6pm to 6am), and a sometimes crowded dance floor. Five different theme bars lie within this complex, each conceived in a radically different format. These include an underwater theme, a jungle theme, a *Gilligan's Island* theme, and a sports bar, which is complete with pool tables, wide-screen broadcasts of sporting events, and lots of suitably macho paraphernalia. The most raucous area of this complex is on street level, where people tend to drink and dance more enthusiastically than upstairs. If you're looking for a respite from the brouhaha below, climb a flight of stairs to the "VIP Lounge" (which is technically open to anyone even if you aren't a VIP), which offers stiff drinks and the chance for dialogue. Most of the complex is open nightly from 8pm to 4am, although the restaurant (Zooley's) begins serving salads, sandwiches, and platters every night from 6pm in the evening until dawn. Strawberry daiquiris and beer cost from $3.50 to $5 each.

## STAGE SHOWS

### Palace Theater

In Carnival's Crystal Palace Resort & Casino, W. Bay St., Cable Beach. ☎ **809/327-6200.** Admission for show and dinner, $45; show and two drinks, $30.

This 800-seat theater is considered one of the major nightlife attractions of the Bahamas. With simulated palm trees on each side and lots of glitz, it's an appropriate setting for the Las Vegas–style extravaganzas that are presented on its stage.

Dinner in the theater is a fixed-price affair with an international menu. Many guests, however, prefer to dine in one of the resort's eight other restaurants and arrive either before or after their meal to see the glittery shows. Reservations in advance are recommended, especially on Tuesday and Saturday nights, when many of the seats might be filled with cruise-ship passengers. On Sunday and Thursday, no dinner is offered, but shows are presented at 9pm only. On Tuesday and Saturday, dinner is at 6pm, with shows at 7:30, 9:30, and 11:30pm. On Wednesday and Friday, dinner is at 7pm, followed by shows at 9 and 11pm. The theater is closed Monday.

## THE BAR SCENE

### Banana Boat Bar

In the Forte Nassau Beach Hotel. ☎ **809/327-7711.**

This lobby bar is used primarily by guests of this previously described hotel, but it is open to all. A live Bahamian band plays nightly from 8pm, and it's one of the best places on Cable Beach for a drink and some light entertainment. Most drinks cost from $3.75, but they're reduced to half price at happy hour, 5 to 7pm. The bar is open daily from 4pm to either 11pm or midnight.

### Cudabay Bar

In the Nassau Harbour Club Hotel, E. Bay St. ☎ **809/393-0771.**

This is the bar which lies adjacent to a previously recommended dining choice, Passin' Jack. Many visitors appreciate it for its own merits and stop in for a drink without ever moving on to a meal at Passin' Jack. Outfitted in a Bahamian-American sports theme, with banners, prominent TV screens, and the kind of dart boards you might have expected at a British pub, it changes its venue from a drinking bar throughout the afternoon and early evening to something between a karaoke club and a disco later in the evening. Entrance is free, but rum punches cost around $3.50 each. It's open daily from 3pm to around 2am, or whenever the last client leaves.

### Le Shack

E. Bay St. ☎ **809/325-2148.**

Set within a 5-minute walk west of the Paradise Island Bridge, this is a gazebolike harbor-front bar whose main attraction is the live bands that perform here every Wednesday to Sunday from 8pm to midnight. The venue might include everything from reggae to soca to calypso to good old-fashioned rock and roll, depending on whoever happens to be playing at the time. Don't overlook this as a possible lunch or dinner stopover, as it shares its premises with Le Shack Bar & Grill and Coconuts Restaurant, both of which are separately recommended in "Where to Dine," above. Its bar is open daily from 11am till at least 1:30am, depending on the crowd.

## Palm Patio Bar

In the British Colonial Beach Resort, 1 Bay St. ☎ **809/322-3301.**

The Palm Patio Bar is a good rendezvous. Many scenes from the James Bond movie *Never Say Never Again* were shot here. There is live music every Friday, Saturday, and Sunday from 8:30pm to 1am. At those times, there is a two-drink minimum. Open daily from 5:30pm to midnight. Happy hour is Thursday and Friday from 5:30 to 7:30pm.

# Paradise Island 5

The choicest real estate in the Bahamas, Paradise Island was once known as Hog Island—it served as a farm for Nassau. Purchased for $294 by William Sayle in the 17th century, it later became the property of the A&P grocery chain heir, Huntington Hartford, in 1960. After paying out $11 million, he decided to rename the 4-mile-long sliver of land Paradise. (He eventually sold out his interests.)

Celebrated for its white-sand Paradise Beach, the island has beautiful foliage, including brilliant red hibiscus and a grove of casuarina trees sweeping down to form a tropical arcade. Just 600 feet off the north shore of Nassau, it has become one of the favorite vacation areas in the Western Hemisphere.

Long a retreat for millionaires, the island experienced a massive building boom in the 1980s, and its old Bahamian charm is now gone forever, as high-rises, condos, and the second homes of the wintering wealthy, plus casino gambling, take over.

Atlantis Paradise Island Resort & Casino, which is comprised of two towers (called Coral and Beach), the Paradise Club, and the Paradise Island Casino (see "Where to Stay," below), operates in one facility. Extending over several acres, it is considered the world's most complete island resort and casino; there's nothing in Europe, not even on the Riviera, and certainly nothing in the Caribbean, to match it.

## 1 Orientation

Although Paradise Island, for purposes of this guide, is treated as a separate entity, it is actually part of New Providence, to which it is connected by a bridge. Therefore, view this section as a "companion chapter" to the larger chapter preceding it on New Providence.

For "Fast Facts" information, such as how to find a hospital, and even for transportation data, such as how to get to Paradise Island from the Nassau International Airport, refer to the previous chapter. Except for the glittering casino at Paradise Island and a few minor attractions, you'll need to refer to the New Providence chapter for the major sightseeing attractions as well as the sports and recreation choices of the area.

## What's Special About Paradise Island

Beaches
- Paradise Beach, the white sandy beach that virtually put the resort on world tourist agendas.
- Cabbage Beach, another white sandy strip stretching along the northern shoreline.

Resorts
- Atlantis Paradise Island Resort & Casino, a self-contained world unto itself, with restaurants, a huge casino, and Las Vegas–style revues.

Sports & Outdoor Activities
- Paradise Island Golf Club, opened by Merv Griffin in 1989.

Parks & Gardens
- Versailles Gardens at the Ocean Club, a haven of tranquillity, with statues of luminaries ranging from Napoléon to Franklin D. Roosevelt.

Historic Shrines
- The Cloisters, the remains of a 14th-century stone monastery originally shipped from France to the United States by newspaper baron William Randolph Hearst.

# ARRIVING

**BY PLANE** If you'd like to fly directly to Paradise Island, airlines making this run include **Paradise Island Airlines** (☎ **809/363-3169** or toll free **800/432-8807** in the U.S.), with flights from Palm Beach, Fort Lauderdale, and Miami, and **Chalk's International Airline** (☎ toll free **800/4-CHALKS**), with service from Miami.

**The Airports** With the inauguration of the **Paradise Island International Airport** in 1989 (☎ **809/363-2845**), a 3,000-foot runway allows passengers to land directly on the island. This eliminates the Customs delays at Nassau International Airport, as well as the expensive 30-minute taxi ride. A U.S. Customs office (☎ **809/363-3383**) at Paradise Island clears passengers disembarking from international connections, mainly from Florida.

If you arrive at the Nassau International Airport (see Chapter 4 for information on flying to Nassau), there is no airline bus waiting to take you to Paradise Island unless you're on a package deal that includes transfers. If you're not renting a car, you'll need to take a taxi. Taxis in Nassau are metered. It will usually cost you $22 to go by cab from the airport to your hotel on Paradise Island. The driver will also ask you to pay the $2 bridge toll. Luggage is carried at the cost of 50¢ per piece.

**TOURIST INFORMATION** Paradise Island does not maintain a tourist office of its own, so refer to the tourist facilities in downtown Nassau (see "Orientation," at the beginning of Chapter 4). Also keep in mind that the concierges or the guest services staff at all Paradise Island hotels are knowledgeable about the local attractions.

**ISLAND LAYOUT** Paradise Island's finest beaches lie on the island's Atlantic (northern) coastline, whereas the docks, wharves, and marinas are located on the (southern) side. West and north of the roundabout lie most of the island's largest and glossiest hotels and restaurant facilities, as well as the famous casino and a lagoon with carefully landscaped borders. East of the roundabout, the landscape is less congested, accented with a handful of smaller hotels, a golf course, the Versailles Gardens, the Cloisters, the airport, and many of the island's privately owned villas.

## 2 Getting Around

Rather than renting a car, most visitors to Paradise Island prefer instead to walk around the island's most densely developed sections and hire a taxi or take the Casino Express (see below) for the occasional longer haul. At least two of the island's more far-flung hotels, including the Holiday Inn and the Ocean Club, maintain minivans to carry their guests to and from the casino. For information on **renting a car,** refer to "Getting Around," at the beginning of Chapter 4.

The most popular way to reach nearby Nassau is to walk across the $2-million toll bridge. Pedestrians pay 25¢ for the privilege.

**BY TAXI**   If you want to tour Paradise Island or New Providence by taxi, you can make arrangements. Taxis wait at the entrances to all the major hotels. The going hourly rate is about $20 to $23 in cars or small vans, depending on the size of the vehicle.

**BY BOAT**   If you're without a car and don't want to take a taxi or walk, you can go to Nassau by a **ferry** service. If you're already on Paradise Island, you may want to take a shopping stroll along Bay Street. If so, the ferry to Nassau leaves from behind the Café Martinique on Casino Drive. It runs every half hour, and the 10-minute ride costs $2 round-trip. Quicker and easier than a taxi, the ferry deposits you right at Bay Street. Service daily is from 9:30am to 4:15pm.

**Water taxis** also operate daily from 8:30am to 6pm at 20-minute intervals between Paradise Island and Prince George Wharf in Nassau. A round-trip fare is $3 per person.

**TRANSPORTATION FOR PARADISE ISLAND RESORT & CASINO GUESTS**   If you are a guest at one of the properties of Atlantis Paradise Island Resort & Casino, you can take a complimentary tour of the island, leaving Wednesday through Monday at 10 and 11am and at 2pm. There is no tour on Tuesday.

Also, a free bus service is offered daily to Rawson Square in Nassau. The bus departs from the Paradise Towers. Tickets can be obtained from the bell captain's desk.

**BY BUS**   No public buses are allowed on Paradise Island, unlike New Providence. However, a bus marked **Casino Express** runs frequently throughout the day and for most of the night, costing $1. It will take you virtually anywhere you want to go on Paradise Island, not just to the casino, in spite of its name.

## 3 Where to Stay

At hotels rated "very expensive," expect to spend from $275 to $575 a night for a double room. Most hotels on Paradise Island are in the "expensive" category, charging from $155 to $225 for a double room. Hotels classified as "moderate" charge from $95 to $150 a night for a double room. In the off-season (mid-April to mid-December), prices are slashed at least 20%—and perhaps a lot more. For "inexpensive" or "budget" accommodations, refer to the recommendations on New Providence Island (see Chapter 4). Paradise Island is not a budget destination!

## VERY EXPENSIVE

### ✪ Ocean Club

Ocean Club Dr., P.O. Box N-4777, Paradise Island, the Bahamas. ☎ **809/363-3000** or toll free 800/321-3000 in the U.S. Fax 809/363-2424. 71 rms, 15 suites, 5 private villas. A/C MINIBAR TV TEL. Winter, $275–$575 single or double; $875–$925 suite; $975 villa. Off-season, $200–$345 single or double; $525–$555 suite; $600 villa. Continental breakfast from $12 extra. AE, DC, MC, V. Free parking. Bus: Casino Express.

The Ocean Club is the most prestigious address on Paradise Island. Guests can revel in the casino and nightlife activities of the other parts of the resort a short distance away, yet they can return to the seclusion of this exclusive, small-scale hotel. This is also one of the best-developed tennis resorts in the Bahamas. The plushly comfortable rooms exude a contemporary dignity and have refrigerators, spacious tile baths, and tasteful colors and fabrics.

The real heart and soul of the resort lies in the surrounding gardens, which were designed by the island's former owner, Huntington Hartford. Formal gardens surround a French cloister set on 35 acres of manicured lawns. The 12th-century carvings are visible at the crest of a hill, across a stretch of terraced waterfalls, fountains, a stone gazebo, and rose gardens. Bigger-than-life statues dot the vine-covered niches on either side of this landscaped extravaganza. If you're visiting these gardens, begin your promenade at the large swimming pool whose waters feed the series of reflecting pools stretching out toward the cloister.

The white-sand beach that lies adjacent to the hotel is arguably the best in the Nassau/Paradise Island area. The walkways to the accommodations run down the verandas, which ring one of the garden courtyards. The repeat business at this posh resort runs a high 65%.

**Dining/Entertainment:** At night the Courtyard Terrace (see "Where to Dine," below) is illuminated by a pair of fountains.

**Services:** Concierge, babysitting, complimentary shuttle to casino and golf course.

**Facilities:** Beach, nine well-maintained tennis courts and full-time tennis pro.

## EXPENSIVE

### ✪ Atlantis Paradise Island Resort & Casino

Casino Dr., P.O. Box N-4777, Paradise Island, the Bahamas. ☎ **809/363-3000** or toll free 800/321-3000 in the U.S. Fax 809/363-3957. 1,089 rms, 62 suites. A/C MINIBAR TV TEL. Winter, $130–$275 single or double; from $325 suite. Off-season, $105–$225 single or double; from $275 suite. Extra person $55. Continental breakfast $12 extra. AE, DC, MC, V. Free parking. Bus: Casino Express.

The patriarch of the Paradise Island hotels still gives the newer establishments stiff competition. This resort is very much a self-contained world of its own, filled with so many entertainment and dining facilities that many visitors are not even tempted to leave the compound. Once owned in part by Merv Griffin, the property was acquired in May of 1994 by Sol Kerzner, who built the Sun City complex in South Africa. This South African company closed the resort for part of 1994 until $125 million in refurbishments could be made.

# Paradise Island Accommodations

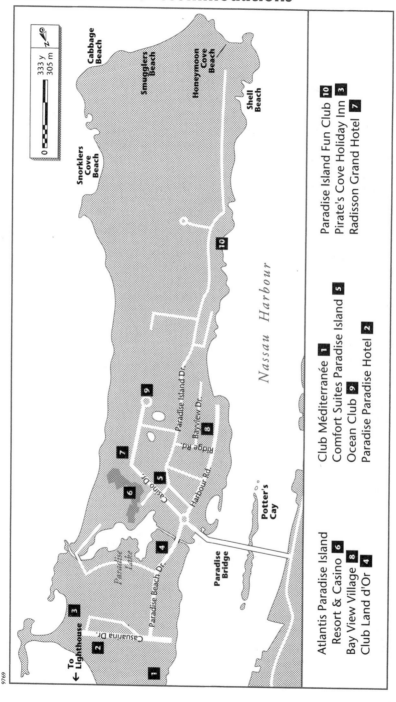

Atlantis Paradise Island
Resort & Casino **6**
Bay View Village **8**
Club Land d'Or **4**

Club Méditerranée **1**
Comfort Suites Paradise Island **5**
Ocean Club **9**
Paradise Paradise Hotel **2**

Paradise Island Fun Club **10**
Pirate's Cove Holiday Inn **3**
Radisson Grand Hotel **7**

Nassau Harbour

Potter's Cay

Paradise Bridge

Paradise Lake

To Lighthouse →

Casuarina Dr.
Paradise Beach Dr.
Casino Dr.
Harbour Rd.
Ridge Rd.
Bayview Dr.
Paradise Island Dr.

Cabbage Beach
Smugglers Beach
Homeymoon Cove Beach
Shell Beach
Snorklers Cove Beach

333 y
305 m
0

9769

Set atop a sandy, pine-dotted strip of land between three miles of beachfront and the calm waters of a saltwater lagoon, it is comprised of three structures interconnected by a series of passageways, arcades, and gardens. The focal point is the Paradise Island Casino (see "Paradise Island After Dark," below), on either side of which rise the two towers.

Accommodations in both towers are eminently comfortable and conservatively stylish, although rooms in the Reef Club are slightly larger, more recently renovated, and more expensive. The most expensive rooms are on the concierge floor of the Reef Club, where a staff checks guests in within a special reception area and provides enhanced service and amenities. Regardless of its location, each room contains a refrigerator, a balcony with water view, either two queen-size beds or one king-size bed, and dozens of amenities.

**Dining/Entertainment:** There are 12 gourmet and specialty restaurants, a dozen bars and lounges, and a full array of discos and nightlife possibilities.

**Services:** Hair-and-beauty salon, travel desk, room service, 24-hour medical service, concierge desk, babysitting, valet parking, in-house laundry, supervised children's program at Camp Paradise.

**Facilities:** Beach, health club and sauna, jogging path, all water sports; Paradise Island Golf Club with an 18-hole course located nearby; 14-acre waterscape; six exhibit lagoons with 100 species of tropical fish; five swimming pools (including a children's pool), 800 running feet of cascading waterfalls, quarter mile long Lazy River Ride for tubing, and predator lagoon alive with sharks, barracuda, and stingrays, with an underwater viewing tunnel.

## Bay View Village

Harbour Rd., P.O. Box SS-6308, Paradise Island, the Bahamas. ☎ **809/363-2555** or toll free 800/321-3000 in the U.S. Fax 809/363-2370. 30 units. A/C TV. $160 one-bedroom apartment for two; $230 penthouse apartment for three; $270 town house for four; $290–$320 villa for four; $420 penthouse for six. Off-season, $115 apartment for two; $168 penthouse apartment for three; $189 town house for four; $205–$220 villa for four; $294 penthouse for six. Continental breakfast $6 extra. AE, MC, V. Free parking. Bus: Casino Express.

More than 20 kinds of hibiscus and many varieties of bougainvillea beautify the four acres of this condominium complex. Although it is near the geographic center of Paradise Island, it's only a short walk to either the sands of Cabbage Beach or the harbor. Each accommodation has its own kitchen, patio or balcony, and daily maid service. The villas and town houses have dishwashers, and some have views of the harbor. A full-time maid or personal cook can be arranged on request. The units come in a wide variety of sizes and can hold up to six occupants. Rates are slightly less for weekly rentals. Penthouse apartments contain roof gardens opening onto views of the harbor. A minimarket and two coin-operated laundry rooms are on the property.

**Dining/Entertainment:** The restaurants, nightlife, and casino of Atlantis Paradise Island Resort & Casino are only a few minutes away.

**Services:** Laundry, babysitting.

**Facilities:** Three swimming pools, tennis court; facilities of the Paradise Island Resort & Casino are a few minutes away.

## Club Land'Or

Paradise Dr., P.O. Box SS-6429, Paradise Island, the Bahamas. ☎ **809/363-2400** or toll free 800/552-2839 in Virginia, or 800/446-3850 elsewhere in the U.S. Fax 809/363-3403. 72 apts. A/C MINIBAR. Winter, $205–$225 apartment for two. Off-season, $145–$170 apartment for two. AE, DC, MC, V. Free parking. Bus: Casino Express.

Across the saltwater canal from Atlantis Paradise Island Resort & Casino, these self-sufficient time-share apartments are in white concrete buildings set in a landscaped garden dotted with shrubs and reflecting pools. Although the club isn't located on the bay, the beach is a short drive away, and there's a small freshwater swimming pool as well as a promenade beside the canal for guests interested in sniffing the salt air. If you wish to visit the casino, you must drive to get there. Facilities include the Oasis lounge and the Blue Lagoon Restaurant. The management hosts energetic activities programs. Each of the accommodations includes a separate bedroom, a patio or balcony, a fully equipped kitchenette, and a living room. The rates depend on the view (garden or water). For reservations and information, contact the club's executive offices: 7814 Carousel Lane, Suite 200, Richmond, VA 23294 (☎ **804/346-8200** or the toll-free numbers given above).

## Club Méditerranée

Casuarina Dr., P.O. Box N-7137, Paradise Island, the Bahamas. ☎ **809/363-2640** or toll free 800/CLUB-MED in the U.S. Fax 809/365-3496. 352 rms. A/C. Winter, $1,200 per person weekly; Christmas and New Year's, $1,490 per person weekly. Off-season, from $800 per person weekly. Rates are all-inclusive. AE, MC, V. Free parking. Bus: Casino Express.

Club Med occupies 21 acres and is made up of two wings of three-story pastel bungalows curving above the 3-mile beach. Accommodations are twin-bedded rooms, small but comfortably furnished with white cane furniture and not a lot else. In the middle stands a Georgian-style mansion housing public rooms and restaurant facilities. A walk through the landscaped garden brings members harborside and to the main restaurant. This place accepts children under 12, but there are no special facilities for children. Mostly the place is for people without children. Honeymooners are attracted to the place in large numbers, along with many single people in their 30s.

**Dining/Entertainment:** Facilities include an intimate restaurant (offering both indoor and outdoor dining), a disco, a beach bar, and an open-air theater/dance floor/bar complex.

**Facilities:** Swimming pool; 20 tennis courts, with 8 lit at night; fitness center; aerobics classes.

## ✪ Radisson Grand Hotel

Casino Dr., P.O. Box SS-6307, Paradise Island, the Bahamas. ☎ **809/363-2011** or toll free 800/333-3333 in the U.S. Fax 809/363-3193. 306 rms, 36 suites. A/C MINIBAR TV TEL. Winter, $159–$219 single or double; from $350 suite. Off-season, $125–$189 single or double; from $275 suite. Continental breakfast $6 extra. Wintertime packages available. AE, DC, MC, V. Free parking. Bus: Casino Express.

The Radisson has a dramatic 14-story exterior with spacious balconies that afford sweeping water views from each of the plushly furnished bedrooms. The architects chose to build this palace on an uncluttered 3-mile stretch of beach so that guests leaving the shelter of the poolside terrace could settle almost immediately onto one of the waterside chaise longues. The Radisson is within walking distance of the casino, restaurants, and nightlife facilities of the Paradise Island Casino properties.

Welcoming drinks are served while you relax on comfortable chairs near the waterfall of the soaring reception area, with its plant-rimmed lagoon. All the accommodations here are deluxe and decorated tastefully. In the Radisson Towers, the 12th and 14th floors are really grand. There, continental breakfast is served in a panoramic private breakfast room, complete with silver tureens and fine porcelain.

**Dining/Entertainment:** The premier restaurant of the Radisson is the Rôtisserie, which serves haute cuisine nightly from 6:30 to 10:30pm. Other dining choices include the multilevel Verandah Restaurant and its adjoining terrace, where you can dine within view of the sea. Sunbathers in need of a poolside drink will be served at their chaise longues by waiters, and burgers as well as lobster or chicken salads are available all day at the Grand Bar and Grille. After dark, the most elegant disco on Paradise Island is Le Paon (see "Paradise Island After Dark," below).

**Services:** Babysitting, room service, valet.

**Facilities:** Beach, swimming pool, four tennis courts, fleet of boats for various water pursuits.

## MODERATE

### Comfort Suites Paradise Island

1 Paradise Island Dr., P.O. Box SS-6202, Paradise Island, the Bahamas. ☎ **809/363-3680** or toll free 800/228-5150. Fax 809/363-2588. 150 junior suites. A/C MINIBAR TV TEL. Winter, $149–$199 single or double. Off-season, $120–$175 single or double. Rates include continental breakfast. AE, DC, MC, V. Free parking.

Opened in 1991, and a favorite with honeymooners, this three-story resort hotel enjoys a low-rise position across the street from the Atlantis Paradise Island Resort & Casino. Although there's both a pool bar and restaurant on the premises, guests are granted signing privileges at each of the drinking-and-dining spots, as well as the pool, beach, and sports facilities of the nearby megaresort. Accommodations are priced by their views over the island, the pool, or the garden. They contain kitchens and have such amenities as a minibar, in-room safe, clock radio, coffeemaker, hair dryer, and a contemporary tropical decor.

**Dining/Entertainment:** A swim-up bar at a poolside pavilion lies adjacent to Crusoe's Restaurant, which serves an international cuisine. There's also easy access to dozens of other restaurants on Paradise Island.

**Services:** Tour desk and guest relations staff.

**Facilities:** Bicycle rentals.

### Paradise Island Fun Club

Harbour Rd., P.O. Box SS-6249, Paradise Island, the Bahamas. ☎ **809/363-2561.** Fax 809/363-3803. 237 rms, 5 suites. A/C TV TEL. Dec 26–Jan 5 and Feb 7–23, $198 single; $145 per person double; $135 per person triple or quad. The rest of the year, $149 single; $129 per person double; $119 per person triple or quad. Year-round, $458 one-bedroom suite for

---

### 🎎 Family-Friendly Hotels

**Radisson Grand Hotel**    *(see p. 129)* A high-rise hotel, with a panoramic view of the beach, the Radisson offers family packages that reduce its regular rates substantially. In summer and during Easter and Christmas, activities for children from 5 through 13 are organized at Camp Caribbean.

**Pirate's Cove Holiday Inn**    *(see p. 131)* Many repeat visitors consider this favorite, opening onto Pirate's Cove Beach, the most family-oriented hotel on the island. It's an activity-packed resort, with much fun planned for children ages 4 through 12.

**Atlantis Paradise Island Resort & Casino**    *(see p. 126)* This place is an extravaganza with fun for all ages, and families are delighted with its activity-oriented Camp Paradise (ages 4 to 12), which operates year-round.

two; $558 two-bedroom suite for two. Rates include meals, drinks, tips, and taxes. AE, DC, MC, V. Free parking.

This is one of only two all-inclusive resorts (the other being Club Med) on Paradise Island. Selecting it allows one of the most cost-conscious vacations on the island. The hotel lies on 21 acres of low-lying sandy ground near the island's southeastern end, facing the narrow channel which separates Paradise Island from Nassau. In 1991, the owners spent $3 million on renovations. Bedrooms are tastefully restful, filled with wicker furniture and pastel tones of green, with views over the gardens or onto the boats that moor offshore.

In 1991, the owners imported many tons of sand to improve the beach, although surf lovers usually opt for a 5-minute walk to the island's north shore, where the beach is broader and waves are bigger.

**Dining/Entertainment:** Both the Captain's Table and the Terrace Restaurant serve an ongoing series of buffets, with once-a-week limbo parties and nightly bouts of Bahamian music. There are also three bars and a karaoke disco.

**Services:** Complimentary snorkeling trip, sunset cruise, and beach excursion three times a week; organized games, aerobics classes.

**Facilities:** Minigym with exercise bicycles, table tennis, toys for children, L-shaped swimming pool.

## Paradise Paradise Hotel

Casuarina Dr., P.O. Box SS-6259, Paradise Island, the Bahamas. ☎ **809/363-3000** or toll free 800/321-3000 in the U.S. Fax 809/363-2540. 100 rms. A/C MINIBAR TV TEL. Winter, $95–$135 single or double. Off-season, $85–$110 single or double. Extra person $45. AE, DC, MC, V. Free parking. Bus: Casino Express.

This pleasantly unpretentious hotel, lying on the western tip of the island, is a rambling, veranda-lined building. Half the accommodations offer direct access to the beach, which lies on the far side of a cluster of trees. In many ways, being here is like living in a forest. Rooms are rather basic, encased in whitewashed concrete walls with a blue-on-blue decor; perhaps by the time of your arrival some of the time-worn furnishings will have been replaced. The hotel restaurant is a short distance away, in a teepee-shaped building directly on the beach. Guests are not locked into any meal plan, although many of them opt to arrange one of the resort's dine-around plans. The hotel also offers free transportation by shuttle bus to the casino and its adjacent bars and restaurants. Included free are a variety of water sports: sailing, snorkeling, windsurfing, and waterskiing.

## Pirate's Cove Holiday Inn

Casuarina Dr., P.O. Box SS-6214, Paradise Island, the Bahamas. ☎ **809/363-2101** or toll free **800/HOLIDAY** in the U.S. Fax 809/363-2206. 479 rms, 87 suites. A/C TV TEL. Rates: Winter, $119–$149 single or double. Off-season, $79–$129 single or double. Year-round, $149–$295 suite. Continental breakfast $5.50 extra. AE, DC, MC, V. Free parking. Bus: Casino Express.

This 18-story resort lying on a crescent-shaped private beach, Pirate's Cove, is the tallest in the Bahamas. That may or may not be what you had in mind for a beachside vacation. Rising above a forest of pine trees, the hotel is especially popular with families because of its Captain Kids day camp with supervised activities for children 4 to 12. When not occupied there, kids can have fun at the Pirate's Den game room and the video arcade. Special activities in the evening are sometimes staged for children so parents can dine alone. The swimming pool area has as its centerpiece a 95-foot-long replica of *Bonnie Anne,* a pirate ship that once terrorized the waters around Nassau. Rooms are bright and cheery, often taking as their color scheme the turquoise waters of Paradise Island or perhaps the shell pink of the islander's favorite food: conch.

**Dining/Entertainment:** Restaurants include Matilda's poolside snack bar for hamburgers, cold beer, and tropical drinks and the garden-style Calico Jack's for breakfast or lunch. The Paradise Grill offers seafood-and-beef specialties. A musical group provides dance tunes every night until 1am. Weekly buffets and poolside parties occur regularly.

**Services:** Laundry, babysitting, room service (7am to 11pm).

**Facilities:** Two tennis courts and a full-time pro; crab races and other organized games and contests; two Jacuzzis, exercise/fitness room, water-sports center.

# 4 Where to Dine

Paradise Island offers an array of the most glittering and also the most expensive restaurants in the Bahamas. If you're on a strict budget, cross over the bridge into downtown Nassau, which has far more reasonable places at which to eat. Meals on Paradise Island may be expensive, but they're also unimaginative, sometimes in the extreme.

Surf and turf appears with too much frequency for some. The greatest collection of restaurants is owned by the Atlantis Paradise Island Resort & Casino. They are all near the casinos. There are other good ones outside this complex, including the Courtyard Terrace at the Ocean Club (one of the most prestigious) and the Rôtisserie at the Radisson Grand Hotel, which is that hotel's showcase restaurant.

## EXPENSIVE

### ✪ Café Martinique

In Atlantis Paradise Island Resort & Casino, Casino Dr. ☎ **809/363-3000.** Reservations required. Appetizers $8.50–$13.50; main courses $31–$38; Sun brunch $30. AE, DC, MC, V. Dinner daily 7–11pm; brunch Sun 11:30am–2:30pm. Bus: Casino Express. FRENCH/CONTINENTAL.

This is one of the choicest restaurants in the Bahamas, serving everything from beef Wellington to cherries jubilee. James Bond dined here in *Thunderball*. Patrons select tables either inside or outdoors. The best French and continental food on Paradise Island is served here, and it is backed up by a well-stocked cellar.

When you sit down, enjoying the *fin de siècle* decor that suggests the Moulin Rouge of Paris, you are presented with a list of dessert soufflés. The chef is justifiably proud of these delicacies, but because of the time and preparation involved, they can't be ordered at the last minute; therefore many people order the dessert first, especially the soufflé Grand Marnier and the soufflé au chocolat.

Then it's on to a dazzling menu, with an appealing list of hors d'oeuvres likely to include everything from escargots bourguignonne to foie gras with truffles. Fish dishes are limited, but select, including fresh Bahamian grouper. For a main course, you might like the grenadine de veau au calvados, which is prepared perfectly here, or chateaubriand with béarnaise sauce, or perhaps a rack of lamb roasted with herbs in the style of Provence. Café Bahamian is a nice finish. Diners once glided in here by boat, but nowadays they cross the bridge. Jackets are required for men.

The café also serves a deluxe Sunday brunch. Enticing arrays of fresh fruits, salads, cold meats, smoked fish, and cheeses are laid out, along with hot dishes and

# Paradise Island Dining

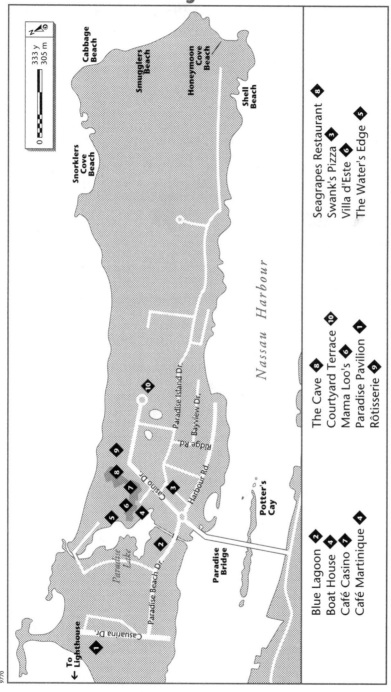

a dessert selection. A complimentary glass of champagne or a mimosa is served with the brunch.

## ✪ Courtyard Terrace

In the Ocean Club, Ocean Club Dr. ☎ **809/363-3000.** Reservations required. Appetizers $10.50–$75; main courses $22–$34. AE, DC, MC, V. Dinner daily 7 and 9pm seatings. Bus: Casino Express. CONTINENTAL/BAHAMIAN.

When the moon is right, an evening meal here can be the closest thing to paradise on the island, although the cuisine may not be the island's finest. You dine amid palms and flowering shrubs in a flagstone courtyard surrounded with colonial verandas flanked by a fountain. A musical group on one of the upper verandas wafts music down to the patio below. This isn't the most glittering dining room on the island, but in many ways it is the most sophisticated. Men are requested to wear jackets and ties, and women should bring some kind of evening wrap in case it becomes chilly. Specials include beefsteak tartare, prime sirloin, lobster quiche, chateaubriand, Nassau grouper, shrimp Provençale, roast rack of lamb, and calves' liver lyonnaise.

## Mama Loo's

In the Coral Towers, Atlantis Paradise Island Resort & Casino, Casino Dr. ☎ **809/363-3000.** Reservations recommended. Appetizers $6.50–$8.75; main courses $17.50–$27. AE, DC, MC, V. Dinner only, Tues–Sun 6:30–11pm. CHINESE/CARIBBEAN.

Its decor might remind you of a British colonial enclave in Hong Kong around the turn of the century. There's a bar that appeals to many clients who never intend to dine here, but if you're in the mood for a Chinese meal worthy of the best Chinese restaurants in New York City, you'll be ushered to a table in a dining room inspired by the decors of Asia. High-back wicker chairs, spinning ceiling fans, flaming torches from an overhead chandelier, and lots of potted palms add exoticism to a menu that includes dishes from the Szechuan, Cantonese, Polynesian, and Caribbean repertoire. A specialty is Mama Loo's stir-fried lobster with ginger and scallions. There's also curried conch, an array of Chinese soups, curried salads, twice-barbecued pork, deboned duckling Imperial, spicy Paradise chicken, and Szechuan shrimp. Meals can be accompanied by tea or by any of several deceptively potent tropical drinks.

## Rôtisserie

In the Radisson Grand Hotel, Casino Dr. ☎ **809/363-2011.** Reservations recommended. Appetizers $5.50–$13.50; main courses $22–$29.50. AE, DC, MC, V. Dinner daily 6:30–10pm. Bus: Casino Express. STEAK/SEAFOOD/INTERNATIONAL.

The premier restaurant of this deluxe hotel is deliberately understated, with oversize rattan chairs and exposed stone. Here you will enjoy what might be the thickest cuts of steak and prime rib in the Bahamas. From behind a glass window, a team of uniformed chefs prepares the grills to your specifications. You can also order surf and turf or spit-roasted chicken. Should you want seafood, they'll tempt you with Bahamian grouper cooked creole style or perhaps swordfish steak.

## ✪ Villa d' Este

Bird Cage Walk, Coral Towers, Casino Dr. ☎ **809/363-3000.** Reservations required. Appetizers $7.50–$9; main courses $22–$24. AE, DC, MC, V. Dinner Thurs–Tues 6:30–11pm. Bus: Casino Express. ITALIAN.

Nassau's most elegant Italian restaurant offers classic dishes prepared with skill and served with flair. Italian murals decorate the walls. The restaurant takes its name from the world-famed hotel on Lake Como, although the cuisine doesn't begin to equal that gathering place of the world's elite. Freshly made fettuccine Alfredo, prepared here nigh unto perfection, can be served as a first course or as a main dish. A good-tasting Florentine version of minestrone is also served. Main dishes include several chicken and veal dishes, including deviled chicken and scaloppine alla parmigiana. Desserts feature a selection of pastries from the trolley. Many guests finish their meal with an espresso.

### The Water's Edge

At the Atlantis Paradise Island Resort & Casino, Casino Dr. ☎ **809/363-3000.** Reservations recommended. Appetizers $5.25–$10; main courses $21–$32. AE, DC, MC, V. Dinner only, daily 6:30–10pm. MEDITERRANEAN/CALIFORNIAN.

This is one of the first restaurants conceived by Atlantis Paradise Island in 1994 after they committed themselves to a total refurbishment of the old Merv Griffin resort. Considered one of the most upscale of the many eateries within the resort, it was designed with a trio of 15-foot waterfalls that splash into an artificial lagoon just outside the dining room's windows. Huge chandeliers illuminate a dining room whose theatricality is enhanced by a view of an open kitchen, where a battalion of chefs work to create such dishes as peppered roast loin of pork; an unusual collection of antipasto misto; roasted eggplant dip; seared tenderloin of beef with hot chili oil, local greens, and cilantro; mussels à la Provençale steamed in white wine sauce; an Iberia-inspired version of shrimp with garlic, olives, and red-pepper flakes. Dessert is a succulent version of flamed banana with vanilla ice cream and almonds.

## MODERATE

### Blue Lagoon

In the Club Land'Or, Paradise Dr. ☎ **809/326-2400.** Reservations required. Appetizers $5.25–$8.75; main courses $18–$50. AE, DC, MC, V. Dinner daily 5–10pm. Bus: Casino Express. SEAFOOD.

Lying across the lagoon from Atlantis Paradise Island Resort & Casino, this restaurant is located two floors above the reception of the Club Land'Or. A view of the harbor and Paradise Lake, as well as music from an island combo, will complement your meal—served by candlelight. The nautical decor includes polished railings and lots of full-grain hardwood. Menu items are stone crab claws in cocktail sauce, Nassau conch salad, Caesar salad for two, broiled grouper amandine, seafood brochette, and other dishes. Meat specialties include steak au poivre with brandy sauce, duck à l'orange, and chicken chasseur. Dessert might include crêpes Suzette for two or a Tía María parfait.

### Boat House

In Atlantis Paradise Island Resort & Casino, Casino Dr. ☎ **809/363-3000.** Reservations recommended. Three-course fixed-price menus $35.50–$42. AE, DC, MC, V. Dinner Thurs–Tues 6:30 and 9pm seatings  Bus: Casino Express. STEAKS.

The Boat House is located next to the Paradise Lagoon near the Café Martinique. Behind its nautical facade, the richly polished leather and hardwood contribute to a fun, clubhouse ambience. You cook your own dinner on the charcoal grill that's the focal point of each group of diners. The bartender serves generous drinks to accompany the top-quality meats, which are the house specialty.

The menu is limited to a choice of four main courses, each of which is priced as part of a full meal. Choices include a well-marbleized New York sirloin, prime filet mignon, sea and steer (filet mignon with half a Bahamian lobster tail), or gulf shrimp kabob marinated in a special sauce. Each main course is accompanied with Bahamian conch chowder to which a generous splash of sherry is added at your table. Also offered are a crisp Boat House salad and a baked potato or rice. Cheesecake, raisin fudge, and coffee are also included in the meal.

## INEXPENSIVE

### Café Casino
In the Paradise Island Casino, Casino Dr. ☎ **809/363-3000.** Reservations not required. Appetizers $3.50–$7.50; main courses $11–$25. AE, DC, MC, V. Daily 11:30am–11pm; late snacks daily 11pm–7am. Bus: Casino Express. AMERICAN.

If you want a late-night snack or a break from the gaming tables, you have only to walk to the far end of the casino to find this coffee shop. Its menu includes pizza and well-stuffed sandwiches—corned beef, pastrami, and Reubens—as well as many kinds of salad. You can order soup-and-sandwich meals or full dinners, which might include lasagne bolognese, deep-fried grouper fingers, or beef brochette with rice.

### The Cave
At the Atlantis Paradise Island Resort & Casino, Paradise Dr. ☎ **809/363-3000.** Reservations not necessary. Lunch platters $2.75–$9. AE, DC, MC, V. Daily 11am–5pm. BURGERS, SALADS, SANDWICHES.

Except for its location near the beach of the most lavish hotel and casino complex on Paradise Island, this might be considered little more than a burger-and-salad joint. Indeed, the menu focuses on the kinds of beach food you'd feel comfortable consuming in a bathing suit, but the decor manages to instill a sense of wonder in any child, as well as within the childlike persona that lurks within even the most jaded of adults. To reach it, you'll pass beneath a simulated rock-sided tunnel illuminated with flaming torches worthy of a pirate rendezvous. You'll ascend into an open-air setting whose view of the beach inspires some children to scan the seafront for Spanish galleons that might be hauling gold back to the Old World. The repertoire of this establishment's ice creams is suitably creamy for mid-afternoon cool-offs.

---

### 🏠 Family-Friendly Restaurants

**The Cave**    *(see p. 136)* At the Atlantis Paradise Island Resort & Casino, one of the most popular lunchtime venues is run by this casino complex. For burgers, salads, and sandwiches, kids enter a simulated rock-sided tunnel with flaming torches for their midday meal. Later they might return before it closes at 5pm for an ice cream.

**Swank's Pizza**    *(see p. 137)* At the Paradise Shopping Center, this fast-food place is considered the least expensive place for family dining on Paradise Island. Pizzas are prepared in familiar ways, but if your child is daring he or she will order a slice with Bahamian conch.

**Seagrapes Restaurant**    *(see p. 137)* Off the lobby of Beach Towers, this tropical restaurant serves three meals a day. It's especially known for its low-price buffet lunches and dinners. Barbecued ribs, shrimp creole, and apple pie appear on the menu.

### ⑤ Paradise Pavilion

In the Paradise Paradise Beach Resort, Casuarina Dr. ☎ **809/363-3000.** Reservations not required. Appetizers $3.50–$6.95; main courses $13.50–$26.50. AE, DC, MC, V. Daily 6pm–9:45 pm. Bus: Casino Express. STEAKS/SEAFOOD.

With its beachfront location and barbecue specialties, this is a good choice for those who want a casual ambience with ocean views, good value, and good food. The restaurant is in a thatch-roofed pavilion directly on the beach. The menu includes steaks, barbecued chicken, Bahamian lobster tails, succulent ribs, and a variety of appetizers, soups, salads, and desserts. You might try the Paradise mud pie or key lime pie.

### ⑤ Seagrapes Restaurant

In Beach Towers. ☎ **809/363-3000.** Reservations not required. Breakfast buffet $14.95; lunch buffet $15.95; dinner buffet $29.95. AE, DC, MC, V. Breakfast daily 7–11am; lunch daily 12:30–3pm; dinner daily 6–10:30pm. Bus: Casino Express. INTERNATIONAL.

In this pleasantly decorated tropical restaurant, you can have buffet lunches and dinners. Access to the salad bar is a treat, and some patrons consider this to be a full meal. Tropical foods from around the world are featured, including Cuba and the Caribbean and also Cajun dishes. The restaurant, seating 200 to 300 diners at a time, overlooks the lagoon and has a marketplace look, with little stalls and different stations making up the buffet offerings.

### Swank's Pizza

In the Paradise Island Shopping Centre. ☎ **809/363-2765.** Reservations not required. Pizzas $4–$25; sandwiches $4–$4.25; breakfast specials from $5.25. AE, MC, V. Daily 7:30am–11pm. Bus: Casino Express. PIZZA.

You'll find Swank's at the beginning of the driveway leading to the casino and its nearby hotels. It offers simple breakfasts, as well as a variety of pizzas, including a Bahamian one with conch, from $13.50. Salads, such as conch or chicken, are available, as is cheesecake for dessert. The place is informal, and no one minds if you want only a snack.

## 5  What to See & Do

To prevent guests from getting bored with "just going to the beach," most of the big hotels here have activity-packed calendars, especially for that occasional windy, rainy day that comes in winter. Hordes of Americans can be seen taking group lessons in such activities as backgammon, whist, tennis, and cooking and dancing Bahamian style. They are even taught how to mix tropical drinks, such as a Goombay Smash or a Yellow Bird.

### The Cloister

Ocean Club, Ocean Club Dr. ☎ **809/363-3000.**  Free admission. Open Anytime. Bus: Casino Express.

In front of the Ocean Club, a 14th-century cloister built by Augustinian monks in France was reassembled stone by stone. Huntington Hartford, the A&P heir, purchased the cloister from the estate of William Randolph Hearst at San Simeon in California. Regrettably, when the newspaper czar originally bought the cloister, it had been dismantled in France for shipment to America. The parts were not numbered. Arriving unlabeled on Paradise Island, the cloister baffled the experts until artist and sculptor Jean Castre-Manne set about to reassemble it piece by piece. It took him two years, and what you see today, presumably, bears some similarity to the original. The gardens, extending over the rise to Nassau Harbour, are filled with tropical flowers and classic statuary.

## Versailles Gardens at the Ocean Club

Ocean Club Dr. ☎ **809/363-3000.** Free admission. Open Anytime. Bus: Casino Express.

Paradise Island Drive will take you to the "garden of tranquillity" on Paradise Island, the Versailles Gardens of the exclusive Ocean Club (see previous hotel recommendation). Once owned by Huntington Hartford, the A&P heir, the seven terraces of the club are a frequent venue today for Bahamian or foreign weddings. Statues of some of Hartford's favorite people are found in the gardens, including Mephistopheles, Franklin D. Roosevelt, and even Napoléon.

## ✪ Atlantis Paradise Island Resort & Casino

Casino Dr. ☎ **809/363-3000.** No cover. Open 24 hours. Bus: Casino Express.

Regardless of where you're staying—even at the remotest hotel on New Providence (see Chapter 4), you'll want to visit this lavish hotel, restaurant complex, casino, and entertainment center. It is *the* big attraction of Paradise Island. Of course, the rich and famous have visited before you. Donald Trump tried his luck at running the place before he finally passed it along to former talk show host and TV producer, Merv Griffin, who sold it in 1994. The new owner is Sol Kerzner, who built the fabled Sun City complex in South Africa.

You could spend all day here—and all night, too—wandering through the glitzy shopping malls; sampling the international cuisine of the varied restaurants; gambling in the casino at roulette wheels, slot machines, and blackjack tables; or seeing Las Vegas–type revues. During the day you can dress casually, but at night you should dress up a bit, especially if you want to patronize one of the better restaurants. (See individual restaurant listings in "Where to Dine," above.)

The most crowded time to visit is between 8 and 11pm any night of the week. There is no cover to enter: you pay just for what you gamble away (and that could be considerable), eat, drink, or watch in the case of a show, although some entertainment in the bars is free except for the price of the liquor.

# 6  Sports A to Z

Visitors interested in something more than lazing on the beaches have only to ask hotel personnel to make the necessary arrangements. Guests at Atlantis Paradise Island Resort & Casino (☎ **809/363-3000**), for example, can have a surprising catalog of diversions without so much as leaving the hotel property. They can splash in private pools (one with a swim-up bar), play tennis, Ping-Pong, and shuffleboard, ride the waves, snorkel, or rent sunfish, sailfish, jet skis, banana boats, and catamarans from contractors located in kiosks in the hotel's lobby.

## BEACHES

For comments about the beach at **Paradise Island,** refer to "Beaches" under "Sports A to Z" in Chapter 4. The island has a number of smaller beaches as well, including **Pirate's Cove Beach** and **Cabbage Beach,** both of them on the north shore of Paradise Island.

## FISHING

Sports anglers can fish for grouper, dolphin, red snapper, crabs, even lobster close to shore. Farther out, in first-class fishing boats fitted with outriggers and fighting chairs, they troll for billfish or the giant marlin that Hemingway used to pursue regularly in the Bahamas.

The best way to "hook up" with this activity is to go to the activities desk of your hotel. All hotels have contacts with local fishermen who take their clients out for a half or full day's fishing.

## GOLF

### ✪ Paradise Island Golf Club
Paradise Island Dr. ☎ **809/393-3625.**

This superb club at the east end of the island has an 18-hole championship course. Designed by Dick Wilson, it has a fully stocked pro shop. From May through November, greens fees are $45 for 18 holes or $22.50 for 9 holes; in winter, the rate is $100, including the cart. Golfers, who have included Jack Nicklaus, Gary Player, and other stars, face the challenge of shooting a ball through the twirling blades of a small windmill, through a waterpipe, over or around a lion's den, and other such obstacles. The 14th hole of the 6,771-yard, par-72 course has the world's largest sand trap: the entire left side over the hole is white-sand beach.

## PARASAILING

For a sport combining the gliding power of a sea gull with the aquatic skill of an osprey, try parasailing. It's sometimes the highlight of a vacation here—for daredevils. After donning water skis, you're connected to a powerboat that circles around in the shallow offshore waters, where a modified parachute takes you aloft. With Paradise Para-Sail, Coral Towers (☎ **809/363-3000,** ext. 6123), a 6- to 8-minute ride costs $30 per person.

## SCUBA DIVING & SNORKELING

Anyone in search of more ambitious water sports can sign up through **Atlantis Paradise Island Resort & Casino** (☎ **809/363-3000**) for powerboat sightseeing or catamaran sailing. Experienced crews also run guests four or five miles out to reefs, where they strap on snorkel masks or scuba gear.

---

### ✪  Frommer's Favorite Paradise Island Experiences

**Dazzling Stage Shows.** In the Las Vegas tradition, some of the world's greatest show biz extravaganzas are staged at the red-and-gold Cabaret Theatre of the Paradise Island Casino.

**Watching the Sunset at the Cloister.** Here amid the reassembled remains of a 14th-century French stone monastery, once owned by William Randolph Hearst, you can enjoy one of the most beautiful pink-and-mauve sunsets in all the Bahamas.

**A Day at Paradise Beach.** It's acclaimed as not only one of the best beaches in the Bahamas, but in the Caribbean as well. The beach is dotted with *chikees* (thatched huts) for when you've had too much of the sun.

**A Night at the Casino.** The Paradise Island Casino has been called one giant "pleasure palace." Many visitors arrive on the island just to test their luck in this 30,000-square-foot casino. The nearby "Bird Cage Walk" is home to some of the finest restaurants in the Bahamas.

---

### ❓ Did You Know ?

- Sack races, tightrope walkers, ventriloquist shows, dancing lessons, fireworks, and "all-you-can-eat" fruit attracted early visitors to the island.
- In 1930, the island was the exclusive haunt of the Porcupine Club, which only allowed "multimillionaires" to join (the Morgans, Astors, Mellons, and the like).
- The Mary Carter Paint Company once owned Paradise Island.
- Huntington Hartford, playboy and art collector, bought Paradise Island for $11 million. It was this A&P heir who changed its name from Hog Island to Paradise Island.
- The island's major attraction, the Cloister, was brought stone by stone from a monastery near Lourdes, France, by American newspaper magnate William Randolph Hearst. But he forgot to include the written instructions on how to reassemble them!
- The eccentric multimillionaire Howard Hughes once took an entire upper floor of what is now Atlantis Paradise Island Resort & Casino to "hide out."

---

## TENNIS

Hotels with courts are: Atlantis Paradise Island Resort & Casino (☎ **809/363-3000**), with nine hard-surface courts; Pirate's Cove Holiday Inn (☎ **809/326-2101**), with four night-lit asphalt courts; and the Radisson Grand Hotel (☎ **809/326-2011**), with four night-lit Har-Tru courts, and lessons available.

### Ocean Club Courts
In the Ocean Club, Ocean Club Dr. ☎ **809/363-3000.**

Many visitors come to Paradise Island just for tennis, which can be played day or night on the nine Har-Tru courts near the Ocean Club. Guests booked into the cabanas and villas of the club can practically roll out of bed onto the courts. Although beginners and intermediate players are welcome, the courts are often filled with first-class competitors. Two major tennis championships a year are played at the Ocean Club courts, drawing players from the world's top 20.

## 7 Shopping

For really serious shopping, you'll want to cross over the Paradise Island Bridge into Nassau (see Chapter 4). However, many of Nassau's major stores, as previewed below, also have shopping outlets on Paradise Island.

### Greenfire Emeralds Ltd.
In the Beach Towers, Casino Dr. ☎ **809/363-2748.**

For a rich collection of emeralds and jewelry from Colombia, as well as other precious and semiprecious stones and pearls from around the world, you can't go wrong by shopping at Greenfire Emeralds Ltd., also agents for Seiko watches.

### Jewels of the Sea
In the Pirate's Cove Holiday Inn. ☎ **809/363-2100.**

Original designs in coral and natural pearls are spread out before you, including earrings, necklaces, and bracelets crafted from Bahamian conch shells.

## John Bull

In Atlantis Paradise Island Resort & Casino, Casino Dr. ☎ **809/363-3956.**

Known for its Bay Street store and as a pioneer seller of watches throughout the Bahamas, John Bull sells watches, cameras, jewelry, and designer accessories.

## Mademoiselle

In the Coral Towers, Casino Dr. ☎ **809/363-3000.**

For chic women's clothing in both Bahamian and foreign styling, this is an excellent place to shop. Mademoiselle specializes in women's sportswear up to size 14. Designs are usually in brightly colored cottons. For this category of clothing, it's a good choice. You can find other branches of this charming store at Pirate's Cove Holiday Inn (☎ **809/326-3154**), Paradise Village (☎ **809/326-3102**), and Beach Towers (☎ **809/363-3000**).

# 8 Paradise Island After Dark

Among all the islands of the Bahamas, nightlife reaches its zenith on Paradise Island. There is no other spot with the diversity of attractions, especially after dark, that this self-contained playground can offer. The best choices are covered below.

## A CASINO

### ✪ Paradise Island Casino

In Atlantis Paradise Island Resort & Casino, Casino Dr. No cover. ☎ **809/363-3000.**

All roads on the island eventually lead to the focal point of the nightlife: the extravagantly decorated casino run by Sun International. It's a pleasure palace in the truest sense of the term. No visit to Nassau would be complete without a promenade through the Bird Cage Walk, where assorted restaurants, bars, and cabaret facilities make this one of the single most visited attractions anywhere outside the United States. For sheer gloss, glitter, and show-biz-oriented extravagance, this 30,000-square-foot casino, with adjacent attractions, is the place to go.

The gaming tables, open daily from 10am to 4am, provide the main attraction in the enormous room, where Doric columns, a battery of lights, and a mirrored ceiling vie with the British colonial decor. Some 1,000 whirring and clanging slot machines operate 24 hours a day.

From 10am until early the following morning, the 60 blackjack tables, the 10 roulette wheels, and the 12 tables for craps, 3 for baccarat, and 1 for big six are seriously busy with the exchange of large sums of money. Open 24 hours.

## A REVUE

### Cabaret Theatre

In Atlantis Paradise Island Resort & Casino, Casino Dr. ☎ **809/363-3000.** Dinner show, $48; "cocktail show" (including two drinks), $30.

The best days of vaudeville are extravagantly brought back in the $2-million production that is presented between one and three times a night Monday through Saturday in the Cabaret Theatre. Visitors usually purchase tickets in advance at the booth adjacent to the casino.

The show employs an army of magicians, acrobats, jugglers, and comedians, as well as five complete theater sets, one with a skating rink. There's also a trio of "felines": a lion, a panther, and a tiger. Certainly not the least of all, a carefully choreographed set of routines is performed, sometimes with a trapeze, by a bevy of jewel- and feather-bedecked showgirls.

Dinner is served between 5:30 and 7pm, depending on that night's schedule. Most guests, however, opt for a meal at one of the resort's other restaurants and then head for the show afterward. Dinner shows are presented Monday at 8pm, Tuesday through Friday at 7pm, and Saturday at 5:30pm. Shows with drinks only are offered Monday at 10pm, Tuesday, Wednesday, and Friday at 9pm and 11pm, Thursday at 9pm only, and Saturday at 7:15pm, 9:30pm, and 11:30pm. No shows are presented on Sunday.

## A COMEDY CLUB

### Joker's Wild
Adjacent to the casino of the Atlantis Paradise Island Resort & Casino. ☎ **809/363-3000.** Admission $10.

This is one of the only comedy clubs in the Bahamas, with a repertoire of funny people who work hard to make their casino-loving clients laugh. It lies adjacent to the largest casino on Paradise Island, amid a cabaret-style setting whose accessories include depictions of everything from conch shells to tropical birds. Performances begin Tuesday to Sunday at 9:30pm, and last for about an hour and 20 minutes. At least three different comedians will appear on any given night, hailing from the Bahamas as well as ports as far away as London and New York. Scotch and soda costs $5.

## A DISCO

### Le Paon (The Peacock)
In the Radisson Grand Hotel, Casino Dr. ☎ **809/363-2011.** No cover, but the two-drink minimum costs $10.

This spacious, multilevel disco is in the back of the hotel's main lobby. If you're with a group of friends, you may want to establish your headquarters in the circular banquette in the middle of the floor, close to the dancing area. The bar is long and provides views of the ocean. Open Friday and Saturday from 9pm to 2am.

## THE BAR SCENE

There are so many different nightspots at Atlantis Paradise Island Resort & Casino, Casino Drive (☎ **809/363-3000**), that a visit to each of them could occupy an entire evening for anyone who wanted to "discover" the perfect tropical libation. Drinks in each of these places cost from $4 each.

One of the best vantage points for a view of both the entrance of the casino and Bird Cage Walk is the cozy **Gallery Bar** in Beach Towers. It offers seating in low-slung, comfortable chairs and an English-club atmosphere. Hours are from 11am to 4pm daily.

If you're looking for a taste of Polynesia, head for the bar in **Mama Loo's restaurant** (see "Where to Dine," above), off the casino's arcade, where fruited cocktails exude a hint of the Pacific.

Daytime drinkers can enjoy a drink at the swim-up bar in the pool of the **Coral Towers** before moving on to the **Sports Bar,** whose scope encompasses the floor of the casino. Also here are a thatched hut beside the pool, which dispenses waterside drinks, and the Beach Bar.

# Grand Bahama (Freeport/Lucaya) 6

**O**n Grand Bahama Island, Freeport/Lucaya was once just a dream, just a forest of pine trees that almost overnight turned into one of the world's major resorts. The resort was the dream of Wallace Groves, a Virginia-born financier who saw the prospects of developing the island into a miniature Miami Beach. Today, with El Casino, the International Bazaar, high-rise hotels, golf courses, marinas, and a bevy of continental restaurants, that dream has been realized.

Originally, Freeport was developed as an industrial free zone in 1956. Groves wanted to attract international financiers who could appreciate the fact that Grand Bahama was less than 80 miles from Florida and only three hours by air from New York.

The Lucaya district was born eight years later, as a resort center along the coast. It has evolved into a comfortable blend of residential and tourist facilities. As the two communities grew, their identities became almost indistinguishable. But elements of their original purposes still exist today: Freeport is the downtown attracting visitors with commerce, industry, and its own resorts, while Lucaya is called the garden city, pleasing residents and vacationers alike with its fine sandy beaches.

A major sports center, Freeport/Lucaya has six championship golf courses on the island, plus a nine-hole executive layout. Water sports—skiing, skin diving, swimming, fishing, sailing—abound. With some 40 tennis courts on the island, there's plenty of opportunity to hit the ball. There are also riding stables and jogging tracks.

Grand Bahama Island is the northernmost and fourth-largest landmass in the Bahamas. Lying 76 miles east of Palm Beach, it is 73 miles long and 4 to 8 miles wide. Nearly everything here is new, including the people. Before the development boom, the population numbered only 4,000. Historically, not much had happened since Ponce de León is believed to have landed here searching for the Fountain of Youth.

## 1 Orientation

For a general discussion of traveling to the Bahamas, refer to Chapter 3.

## What's Special About Grand Bahama

Beaches
- Xanadu Beach, one of Grand Bahama's premier beaches, with a mile of white sand. Convenient to the Lucaya hotels.
- Taino Beach. Smith's Point, and Fortune Beach—a trio of good sandy beaches, adjacent to one another, lying east of Freeport.
- Gold Rock Beach, only 20 minutes from the Lucayan hotels, a pleasant beach that's a favorite with families on a picnic.

Great Towns
- Freeport, with its glitzy casinos and International Bazaar, the capital of Grand Bahama.
- Lucaya, separated by a 4-mile stretch from Freeport, a beach resort known for its wide selection of hotels and white sands.

Parks & Gardens
- Rand Memorial Nature Centre, a 100-acre site, close to Freeport, with unspoiled forests and trails home to 5,000 different species of birds.
- Garden of the Groves, a scenic preserve of waterfalls, flowering shrubs, and some 10,000 trees.

Shopping
- International Bazaar, one of the world's great shopping emporiums, right in the heart of Freeport.

Sports & Outdoor Activities
- Snorkeling and scuba diving with the Underwater Explorers Society, one of the premier facilities for such in the Bahamas.
- The Dolphin Experience, an underwater explorer's fantasy—where dolphins and humans get to know each other.

## ARRIVING

**BY PLANE**   A number of airlines fly to Freeport from points within the continental United States. Since Nassau provides the country's most important air link to the rest of the world, many visitors arrive in Nassau, then change to one of the five daily flights operating between Nassau and Freeport on Bahamasair (☎ toll free 800/222-4262). Aircraft contains 50 passengers each, take 40 minutes en route, and charge $128 round-trip.

**BY CRUISE SHIP**   Because of its proximity to the Florida coastline, Freeport is popular with cruise ships that depart and return from the U.S. mainland on the same day. The most visible of these short-term cruises are run by **Palm Beach Cruise Line**, 2790 N. Federal Hwy., Boca Raton, FL 33431 (☎ **407/394-7450** or toll free **800/841-7447**), which offers them every Monday, Tuesday, Thursday, and Saturday, departing from the port of West Palm Beach at 8:30am and returning there by midnight the same day.

Passengers can stay on Grand Bahama for a few days or make the most of three hours ashore in Freeport (just enough time for some shopping, a margarita, and a visit to the casino) before cruising back to Florida. The cost for this cruise ranges from $64 to $89 per person, plus $36 in port taxes for each visitor. The cost includes three meals, a shipboard cabaret show and video movies, an onboard swimming pool, and live calypso entertainment. If you want to rent a cabin for the course of the day (for midafternoon naps or whatever), you can arrange for one for an additional charge ranging between $25 and $125, depending on size and location. Other onboard facilities include a casino, bingo games, and skeet shooting, all of which you pay for separately.

The ship used by Palm Beach Cruise Line is the *Viking Princess,* built in Helsinki in 1964 and fully refurbished in 1988. For those passengers wishing to use the *Princess* as a relaxed means of starting and ending a short vacation on Grand Bahama, Palm Beach Cruise Line can arrange discounted hotel accommodations in Freeport.

Other cruise lines offering 3- or 7-day jaunt tours of the Bahamas and the Caribbean often make stops at Grand Bahama. Among the largest of these companies is **Carnival Cruise Lines,** 3655 NW 87th Ave., Miami, FL 33178 (☎ **305/ 599-2600**), and **Norwegian Cruise Lines,** 97 Merrick Way, Coral Gables, FL 33134 (☎ toll free **800/327-7030**), both of which offer large ships and lots of onboard activities.

**SeaEscape,** 8751 W. Broward Blvd., Suite 300, Plantation, FL 33324 (☎ **305/ 476-9900**), sails from Fort Lauderdale to Freeport. Cruises carry 1,200 passengers and depart from the Port Everglades Terminal in Fort Lauderdale, landing at Freeport Harbour. Sailing time is about five hours each way, and the cost is $119 per person on Monday, Wednesday, and Sunday, plus $49 port charges. On Friday the charge is $99 plus $49 in port charges. Departures range between 7 and 8am, depending on the day of the week. The ship contains a full casino, three restaurants, a disco, two bars, and a limbo bar beside the swimming pool.

**TOURIST INFORMATION**   Assistance and information are available at the Grand Bahama Tourism Board, International Bazaar in Freeport (☎ **809/ 352-6909**). Another information booth is at Port Lucaya (☎ **809/373-8988**), and yet another is at the Freeport International Airport (☎ **809/352-2052**). Hours are 8:30am to 5pm Monday through Friday and 10am to 2pm on Saturday.

**ISLAND LAYOUT**   Getting around Freeport/Lucaya is fairly easy because of its flat terrain. Although Freeport and Lucaya are frequently mentioned in the same breath, newcomers should note that whereas Freeport is a landlocked collection of hotels and shops rising from the island's center, Lucaya is a waterfront collection of hotels, shops, and restaurants clustered next to a saltwater pond on the island's southern shoreline. Both were conceived as separate developments during their inception, but over the years, expansion has somewhat blurred their borders.

**Freeport** lies midway between the northern and southern shores of Grand Bahama Island. Bisected by some of the island's largest roads, it contains the biggest hotels, as well as two of the most-visited attractions in the country, the Bahamas Princess Resort & Casino and the International Bazaar, a shopping complex. The local straw market, where inexpensive souvenirs of your visit to the Bahamas can be bought, lies just to the right of the entrance to the International Bazaar.

In addition to its hotels, Freeport contains many banks, small local businesses, and government offices, most of which lie along East Mall Drive, a short walk from the bazaar. Most of these businesses and organizations are centered around Churchill Square. Lying west of the International Bazaar, flanking both sides of

West Sunrise Highway, are two of the island's four golf courses, the Emerald and Ruby—(see "Sports A to Z" below).

To reach **Port Lucaya** from Freeport, head east from the International Bazaar along East Sunrise Highway, then turn south at the intersection with Seahorse Road. Within about 2¹/₂ miles, it will lead to the heart of the Lucaya complex, Port Lucaya.

Set between the beach and a saltwater pond, Port Lucaya's architectural centerpiece is Count Basie Square. (It's named for the great entertainer, who used to have a home on the island.) Within a short walk to the east and west, along the narrow strip of sand between the sea and the saltwater pond, rise most of the hotels of Lucaya Beach as well as the headquarters for the famed Underwater Explorers Society (see "Sports A to Z," below).

Heading west of Freeport and Lucaya, the West Sunrise Highway passes industrial complexes such as the Bahamas Oil Refining Company. At the junction with Queen's Highway, you can take the road northwest all the way to the **West End,** a distance of some 30 miles from the center of Freeport. Along the way you pass Freeport Harbour, where cruise ships are docked. Just to the east of this harbor lies Hawksbill Creek, a village known for its fish market. After passing this, you go through quaint villages with names like Eight Mile Rock and Bootle Bay Village. West End used to be a haven for bootleggers running liquor to the United States during the Prohibition era.

Much less explored is the **East End** of Grand Bahama, a distance of some 45 miles from the center of Freeport, and reached by going along the Grand Bahama Highway, which in spite of its name is rather rough in parts. Allow about two hours of driving time to reach the East End. The Rand Memorial Nature Centre lies about 3 miles east of Freeport. About 10 miles east of Freeport is the Lucaya National Park. Past the park is Gold Rock, a U.S. missile-tracking station. About 5 miles along the highway lies the hamlet of Free Town. East of Free Town is the village of High Rock, known for its Emmanuel Baptist Church. From here, the road gets considerably rough, finally ending in MacLean's Town, which celebrates Columbus Day every year with a conch-cracking contest. From here, it's possible to take a water taxi ride across Runners Creek to an exclusive club, Deep Water Cay, which is patronized mainly by fisherfolk, although open to the public.

**FINDING AN ADDRESS**  In Freeport/Lucaya, but especially on the rest of Grand Bahama Island, you will almost never find a street number on a hotel or a store. Sometimes in the more remote places, you won't even find a street name. In lieu of numbers, locate places by prominent landmarks or hotels.

# 2 Getting Around

**BY TAXI**  The government sets the taxi rates, and the cabs are metered (or should be). A trip from the airport to one of the hotels in Freeport or Lucaya costs about $10. (No buses connect the airport with the hotels.) The cost is $2 for the first quarter mile, plus 30¢ for each additional quarter mile. You can call for a taxi, although most of them wait at the major hotels or the cruise-ship dock to pick up passengers. One major taxi company is **Freeport Taxi Company,** Old Airport Road (☎ 809/352-6666). You can also call **Grand Bahama Taxi Union** at **809/352-7101.**

**BY BUS**   There is a public bus service from the International Bazaar to downtown Freeport and from the Pub on the Mall to the Lucaya area. The typical fare is $1. A private company, **Franco's People Express,** runs a twice-daily service from the International Bazaar and Lucaya Beach to West End, costing $8 round-trip. Check with the tourist office (see "Tourist Information," above) for bus schedules. There is no number to call for information.

**BY LOCAL AIR SERVICE**   You can charter a plane for sightseeing tours above Grand Bahama from **Major's Airline,** Freeport International Airport (☎ **809/352-5778**). Airborne excursions over the lagoons, golf courses, and outlying reefs to the island, suitable for between one and five passengers, costs around $260 per hour. The airline has regular flights to Bimini, costing $90 round-trip, and to Walker's Cay, $82 round-trip.

A competitor is **Taino Air Service,** Freeport International Airport (☎ **809/352-8885**). Flying 18-passenger propeller planes, they offer trips from Freeport to Eleuthera (Governor's Harbour and North Eleuthera) for $80 each way. Flights are on Thursday, Friday, and Sunday. On Thursday, Friday, and Sunday, there are flights to South Andros for $85 each way, Central Andros for $77 each way, and North Andros for $77 each way. From Freeport to Great Abaco (Marsh Harbour) the cost is $60 each way.

**BY CAR**   Your need for a car will be less intense on Grand Bahama than in Nassau because of the self-contained nature of many of the island's major hotels. Still, if you want to explore, and drive yourself, you can try **Avis** (☎ toll free **800/331-2112** or **809/352-7666** locally), **Hertz** (☎ toll free **800/654-3001** or **809/352-9250** locally), or **National** (☎ toll free **800/328-4567** or **809/352-9308** locally). Each of these companies maintains offices in small bungalows outside the exit of the Freeport International Airport.

*Note:* Regarding Budget Rent-a-Car, know in advance that for many years a Bahamas-based car-rental company, without authorization, copied Budget's name and logo and plastered them on billboards around Grand Bahama, despite much confusion from prospective renters, many lawsuits, and much consternation from Budget in Chicago. Although their advertising is less visible in recent years than in the past, know that if you decide to rent from the company calling itself Budget in Freeport, your rental will not be subject to the insurance-policy safeguards or the maintenance standards of the reputable and well-respected U.S.-based Budget Rent-a-Car.

Avis, Hertz, and National each charge a daily or weekly rate, with unlimited mileage included. The arithmetic usually works out that the per-day rate is reduced for rentals of a week or more. You usually get the cheapest tariff by reserving a car several days in advance.

Although conditions are subject to change, Hertz offers the least expensive rates—an air-conditioned car with automatic transmission for $359.70 per week, with unlimited mileage included. On Grand Bahama Island, the Hertz affiliate is sometimes known among locals as Red Cap Car Rentals.

The cheapest car at Avis also contains air-conditioning and automatic transmission, but rents for a whopping $419.70 per week, with unlimited mileage. National charges $479.95 per week for its least expensive car, probably a Ford Tempo.

Each of the three companies offers an optional collision damage waiver (CDW), priced at between $10 and $11.95 a day. Unless you have it, you'll be liable for up to the full value of damages in case of an accident. Its purchase from Avis and

Hertz eliminates any and all financial responsibility after an accident. Purchase of a CDW at National, however, will still leave you with up to $1,000 worth of liability for repair damages in the event of an accident.

Use of some kinds of credit cards that carry automatic insurance provisions sometimes works to the advantage of certain renters, although those provisions must be verified in advance directly with the issuer of the credit card.

**ON FOOT**    You can explore the center of Freeport or Lucaya on foot, but if you want to make excursions into the East End or the West End you'll either need a car or public transportation (highly erratic), because the distances are too far.

**BY BICYCLE OR MOTORSCOOTER**    Bicycles and motorscooters are good means of transport here. Try **Honda Cycle Shop,** Queen's Highway (☎ **809/352-7035**). A two-seater scooter requires a $100 deposit and rents from $40 per half day, whereas a one-seater also requires a $100 deposit but costs $35 per day. Bicycles require a $50 deposit and cost $15 per day, but only $12 for a half day (four hours). Gas is provided and there's no charge for mileage. The rental agency also supplies helmets for drivers and passengers, which are required by law. The operator of the vehicle must also have a valid driver's license. The establishment is open daily from 9am to 5pm.

## FAST FACTS: Grand Bahama

**American Express**    The local representative is Mundytours, Block 4 Regent Centre, Suite 20, Freeport (☎ **809/352-4444**). Hours are 9am to 5pm Monday through Friday.

**Area Code**    The area code for Grand Bahama is 809.

**Babysitters**    See "Fast Facts" in Chapter 3.

**Bookstores**    The Freeport Book Centre, 14 West Mall (☎ **809/352-3759**) has a good selection of books. Open Monday, Tuesday, and Thursday from 9am to 5:30pm, Wednesday 9am to 1pm, and Saturday 9am to 4:30pm.

**Business Hours**    See "Fast Facts" in Chapter 3.

**Car Rentals**    See "Getting Around" earlier in this chapter.

**Climate**    See "When to Go" in Chapter 3.

**Currency**    See "Visitor Information, Entry Requirements & Money" in Chapter 3.

**Currency Exchange**    Americans need not bother to exchange their dollars into Bahamian dollars, as the currencies are on par. However, Canadians will need to convert their dollars or Britishers their pounds, which can be done at local banks or sometimes at a hotel. Hotels, however, offer the least favorable rates.

**Dentists**    A reliable dentist is Dr. Larry Bain, Sun Alliance Building, Pioneer's Way, Freeport (☎ **809/352-8492**).

**Doctors**    For the fastest and best services, use a member of the staff at the Rand Memorial Hospital (see "Hospitals," below).

**Drugs**    The strict drug laws of the Bahamas were cited under "Fast Facts" in Chapter 3, but the warning bears repeating. Offenders are speedily and severely punished.

**Drugstores**    For prescriptions and other pharmaceutical needs, go to Mini Mall, 1 West Mall, Explorer's Way, where you'll find L.M.R. Prescription Drugs (☎ **809/352-7327**), next door to Burger King. Hours are Monday to Saturday from 8am to 9pm.

**Embassies & Consulates**    See "Fast Facts" in Chapter 3.

**Emergencies**    For police, call **911**; for fire, call **809/352-8888**; for an ambulance, call **809/352-2689**; and for Air-Sea Rescue, call **809/352-2628** or **911.**

**Eyeglasses**    The biggest specialist in eyeglasses and contact lenses is the Optique Shoppe, 7 Regent Centre, downtown Freeport (☎ **809/352-9073**). Hours are Monday through Friday from 9am to 5pm and Saturday from 9am to noon.

**Hairdressers & Barbers**    Many of the island's large hotels maintain barbershops and beauty shops. One of the most visible is Cheetah Chic Beauty Salon, Sea Horse Plaza (☎ **809/373-5213**). This outlet cuts men's as well as women's hair.

**Holidays**    See "When to Go" in Chapter 3.

**Hospitals**    If you have a medical emergency, contact the Rand Memorial Hospital, East Atlantic Drive (☎ **809/352-6735**; ambulance emergency, **809/352-2689**). This is a government-operated 90-bed hospital.

**Information**    See "Tourist Information," above.

**Laundry & Dry Cleaning**    Freeport's hotels almost universally provide both laundry and dry-cleaning services. You can also take your dry cleaning or laundry to Jiffy Cleaners and Laundry, West Mall at Pioneer's Way (☎ **809/352-7079**).

**Library**    Grand Bahama's library is the Sir Charles Hayward Library, the Mall (☎ **809/352-7048**), which allows temporary visitors to browse through its books and periodicals.

**Lost Property**    There is no office for this. You must call the police station and report your loss.

**Newspapers & Magazines**    The *Freeport News* is an afternoon newspaper published Monday through Saturday except holidays. The two dailies published in Nassau, the *Tribune* and the *Nassau Guardian,* are also available here, as are some New York and Miami papers, especially the *Miami Herald,* usually on the date of publication. American newsmagazines, such as *Time* and *Newsweek,* are flown in on the day of publication.

**Photographic Needs**    Virtually every major hotel in Grand Bahama offers kiosks for the sale and processing of film. If your hotel doesn't have such a service, head for the shopping arcade in the Bahamas Princess Resort and Casino. Otherwise, there are several within the International Bazaar.

**Police**    In an emergency, dial **911.**

**Post Office**    The main post office is on Explorers Way in Freeport (☎ **809/352-9371**). Airmail is delivered daily; surface mail, weekly. Open Monday through Friday from 9am to 5:30pm.

**Radio & TV**    See "Fast Facts" in Chapter 3.

**Religious Services**    Grand Bahama has a large number of houses of worship. Of the major faiths, the following are established in Freeport/Lucaya:

*Anglican* at Christ the King, East Atlantic Drive and Pioneer's Way ( ☎ 809/ 352-5402); *Baptist* at First Baptist Church, Columbus Drive and Nansen Avenue ( ☎ 809/352-9224); *Lutheran* at Our Saviour Lutheran Church, East Sunrise Highway ( ☎ 809/373-3500); *Methodist* at St. Paul's Methodist Church, East Sunrise Highway and Beachway Drive ( ☎ 809/373-1888); *Presbyterian* at Lucaya Presbyterian Kirk, West Beach Road and Kirkwood Place, Lucaya ( ☎ 809/373-2568); and *Roman Catholic* at Mary Star of the Sea, East Sunrise Highway and West Beach Road ( ☎ 809/373-3300).

**Restrooms**   These are generally inadequate. Visitors often have to rely on the facilities available at hotels, restaurants, cafés, and other commercial establishments.

**Safety**   Naturally, you should safeguard your valuables and take all the discretionary moves on Grand Bahama you would when traveling anywhere. Avoid walking—or jogging—along lonely roads. There are no particular "danger zones," but stay alert since Grand Bahama is a center for drugs and crime.

**Shoe Repairs**   If you lose a heel or need a repair, head for Simmon's Shoe Repair, 4 Sunrise Shopping Centre ( ☎ 809/373-1714). Hours are Monday through Saturday 9am to 8pm.

**Taxes**   There is no city tax other than the 4% national tax already mentioned, which is imposed on hotel rates. There is also a 4% to 6% "resort levy." All visitors leaving Freeport also pay a $15 departure tax.

**Taxis**   See "Getting Around" earlier in this chapter.

**Telephone, Telexes, & Faxes**   Direct distance telephone dialing is available. Nearly all major hotels send telexes and faxes, but if yours is too small to offer such services, go to the main post office (see above). To send a telegram, head for or call the Freeport branch of the Bahamas Telecommunications Company, West Mall at Pioneer's Way ( ☎ 809/352-6220).

**Transit Information**   To call for airport information, dial **809/352-6020;** to summon a taxi, call **809/352-6666;** for bus schedules, call the tourist office at **809/352-8044.**

**Water**   It is generally considered safe to drink, but if you have a delicate stomach you may want to confine yourself to bottled water.

**Weather**   Grand Bahama, in the north of the Bahamas, has temperatures in winter that vary from about 60 to 75 degrees Fahrenheit daily. Summer variations range from 78 degrees Fahrenheit to the high 80s. In Freeport/Lucaya, phone **809/352-6675** for weather information.

## 3 Where to Stay

Your choice is between hotels in the Freeport area, near the Princess Casino and the International Bazaar, or at Lucaya, closer to the beach.

*Remember:* In most cases, a 4% room tax, a resort levy of 4% to 6%, and a 15% service charge will be added to your final bill. Be prepared.

Hotels rated "expensive" usually charge from $125 to $195 for a double room. Those viewed as "moderate" ask anywhere from $100 to $125 for a double room. Establishments judged "inexpensive" get $100 or under for a double. These are high-season (December through April) tariffs.

For an explanation of what the rate symbols mean, see "Tips on Accommodations" in Chapter 3.

# FREEPORT
## EXPENSIVE

### ✪ Bahamas Princess Resort and Casino

The Mall at W. Sunrise Hwy., P.O. Box F-2623, Freeport, Grand Bahama, the Bahamas. ☎ **809/352-6721** for the Princess Country Club, 809/352-9661 for the Princess Tower, or toll free 800/223-1818 in the U.S. Fax 809/352-4485. 942 rms, 23 suites. A/C TV TEL. Winter, $145–$155 Country Club single or double; from $240 suite; $165–$195 Tower single or double; from $290 suite. Off-season, $105–$115 Country Club single or double; from $200 suite; $125–$160 Tower single or double; from $240 suite. MAP $50 extra per person daily. Up to two children under 12 stay free in parents' room. AE, DC, MC, V. Free parking. Freeport bus.

The star of Freeport's resort hotels is a multimillion-dollar resort/golf/convention complex set into 2,500 acres of tropical grounds. There are in fact two "Princesses," the Princess Country Club and the Princess Tower. Combined, they form the largest resort in the Freeport/Lucaya area. Ten minutes from the airport, near the International Bazaar, the resort also has one of the largest casinos in the country.

First, the **Princess Country Club.** The hotel's design is not unlike an enormous low-rise wagon wheel, with a Disneyland type of minimountain at its core, surrounded by an extravagant swimming pool with cascading waterfalls. There's an arched bridge allowing guests to pass over the water between the rocks. The hotel is so spread out that guests often complain jokingly that they need ground transport to reach their bedrooms, a total of 561, plus 4 suites. Nine wings radiate from the pool, sheltering buildings that are only two or three stories high (some are sold as time-share units with kitchenettes). Accommodations come in several classifications. However, even the standard rooms are well equipped, with two comfortable double beds, dressing areas, and tile baths. Both the Country Club and the Tower also rent out a number of lavishly furnished—and expensive —suites.

The **Princess Tower,** lying across the Mall from its larger sibling, is smaller, containing 19 suites and 381 luxuriously furnished, large units, adjoining the Princess Casino and the International Bazaar. The Tower rises 10 floors and stands on 7¹/₂ acres of landscaped grounds. The Arabic motif, set by the Moorish-style tower, with turrets, arches, and a white dome, is continued through the octagon-shaped lobby. Guest rooms are designed in both "tropical and traditional," as they say here, each containing two double beds and individual climate control.

**Dining/Entertainment:** Dinner choices at the Princess Country Club include the Rib Room, the most deluxe establishment at the Country Club, and Guanahani's, which offers smoked ribs and other dishes in a setting overlooking the waterfall. Guests can order three meals a day at the Patio, which also has a view over the pool. The tropical John B offers lunch, dinner, and late-night snacks, such as hamburgers and quiche.

At the Princess Tower, two of the best restaurants, Morgan's Bluff and La Trattoria, are recommended separately (see "Where to Dine," below). You can select either the Lemon Peel or the outdoor La Terraza, which in season has a breakfast buffet spread out. Also noteworthy is the Crown Room, set adjacent to the casino, where continental cuisine is served amid an elegant decor. In the Palm Pavilion, *Goombaya!* is presented, a buffet dinner and show staged at 6:30pm on Wednesday and Saturday, costing $30 per person. Tribal dances depict the heritage of the Bahamian people.

**Services:** Babysitting, massage, room service (7am to 10pm), concierge, and guest relationships desk.

**Facilities:** Two 18-hole championship golf courses nearby; 12 tennis courts (8 lit at night); two swimming pools (one Olympic size); Jacuzzi; nearby private beach with white sand and shuttle-bus service to hotel; full program of water sports, including deep-sea fishing.

### ✪ Xanadu Beach Resort and Marina

Sunken Treasure Dr., P.O. Box F-2438, Freeport, Grand Bahama, the Bahamas. ☎ **809/352-6782.** Fax 809/352-5799. 139 rms, 47 1-bedroom suites. A/C TV TEL. Winter, $125–$130 single or double; $165–$195 suite. Off-season, $89–$99 single or double; $115 suite. Continental breakfast $6.25 extra. (EP rates.) AE, DC, MC, V. Free parking. Freeport bus.

Originally built as condominiums and later inhabited by the reclusive millionaire Howard Hughes, this symmetrical tower reopened in 1986 after months of costly renovations. It sits amid a complicated series of marinas and peninsulas, a few steps from a wide sandy beach. The hotel, just 10 minutes from the international airport, was inspired by the line from Coleridge: "In Xanadu did Kubla Khan a stately pleasure dome decree." In 1969, when it opened, it was an exclusive private club and you were likely to see Sammy Davis, Jr., and Frank Sinatra walking through the lobby.

Carefully balanced with evenly spaced rows of carved balconies, the hotel boasts the kind of pyramid-shaped roof you'd expect on a Tibetan monastery. Rooms are attractively and comfortably furnished, among the finest at the resort.

**Dining/Entertainment:** The premier restaurant is Escoffier, serving dinner only (continental cuisine). The hotel also offers the Casuarina Café and Bar and the Ocean Front Bar and Grill.

**Services:** Babysitting, room service.

**Facilities:** Tennis courts, swimming pool, and easily booked water sports on premises; golf course nearby.

## INEXPENSIVE

### Castaways Resort

International Bazaar, P.O. Box F-2629, Freeport, Grand Bahama, the Bahamas. ☎ **809/352-6682.** Fax 809/352-5087. 130 rms. A/C TV TEL. Winter, $75–$98 single or double. Off-season, $65–$75 single or double. Continental breakfast $5 extra. (EP rates.) AE, MC, V. Free parking. Freeport bus.

Castaways is located at the International Bazaar and Princess Casino. The hotel has pagoda roofing and an indoor and outdoor Caribbean garden lobby, and is surrounded by well-kept gardens. Accommodations, decorated in cool greens or blues and whites, have one king-size bed or two double beds in the typical roadside motel style. In the lobby you'll find a gift shop, a clothing shop, a game room, and tour desks. The Flamingo Restaurant features Bahamian and American specialties. There is a swimming-pool area with a wide terrace and a pool bar that serves sandwiches and cool drinks. A disco, Yellow Bird, stays open until 3am. The manager's cocktail party, a complimentary feature, is held on Monday. Services include a laundry room, babysitting, and continuous free transportation to Xanadu Beach, five minutes away. At the hotel's Yellow Bird Night Club, shows Monday through Saturday feature limbo dancers, fire-eaters, and all that jazz.

**Family-Friendly Hotels**

**Bahamas Princess Resort & Casino**   *(see p. 151)* This massive hotel doesn't just attract Atlantic City types headed for the casino. It also does a large family-oriented business year-round. Two children's playgrounds with supervised activities are available.

**Castaways Resort**   *(see p. 152)* Right at the International Bazaar, this family favorite lets children under 12 stay free in rooms with their parents. There's a large swimming pool plus a free shuttle to Xanadu Beach.

**Sun Club Resort**   *(see p. 153)* This well-maintained and economical resort rents units with kitchenettes where families prepare light meals. Special reduced rates are available for accommodations with three or four guests.

## Lakeview Manor Club

Cadwallader Jones Dr., P.O. Box F-2699, Freeport, Grand Bahama, the Bahamas. ☎ **809/352-9789.** Fax 809/352-2283. 52 apts. A/C TV TEL. Year-round, $75 double studio, $450 double studio per week; $100 double one-bedroom apartment, $600 double one-bedroom apartment per week. (EP rates.) AE, MC, V. Free parking. Closed one week in Nov. Freeport bus.

Today this resort is classified as a time-sharing project, but it was originally built as private apartments. It offers luxurious one-bedroom and studio apartments, each with well-chosen furniture, a private balcony, and a kitchen. The club overlooks the fifth hole of the PGA-approved Ruby Golf Course. It stands away from the beach, but is ideal for golfers or for anyone to whom a sea view isn't important. There is no bar or restaurant on the premises, but the hotel maintains a daily complimentary shuttle bus that travels to the dining, drinking, and shopping facilities of the International Bazaar and beach areas. The resort features tennis courts, a swimming pool, reduced greens fees, and other extras. This place offers bargain headquarters for those seeking tranquillity. Laundry facilities are available.

## Running Mon Marina & Resort

Box F-2663, 208 Kelly Court, Freeport, the Bahamas. ☎ **809/352-6834.** Fax 809/352-6835. 32 rms (all with bath). A/C TV TEL. Winter, $99 single or double. Off-season, $78 single or double. Breakfast $4–$6 extra. AE, DC, MC, V. Free parking. The hotel maintains free shuttle-bus service to and from the International Bazaar and the beach near the Xanadu Hotel.

Its showcase and centerpiece is a 66-slip marina which was originally developed in the late 1960s. In 1991, the owners added a 32-room hotel and a nautically decorated restaurant as an incentive to the marine facilities which had by that time become extremely well known. All bedrooms within this two-story pink-sided hotel face the marina, and each is simply but comfortably outfitted with flowered draperies, an unstocked refrigerator, and wicker furniture. The complex lies within a 5-minute drive east of the Xanadu Beach Hotel, within a flat and sandy landscape pierced with a labyrinth of man-made saltwater lagoons. There's a diving facility on-site, and a full-service restaurant (the Mainsail) where sandwiches and platters at lunch cost from $4 to $15 and main courses at dinner cost from $12 to $16.

## ⊛ Sun Club Resort

Settlers Way, P.O. Box F-1808, Freeport, Grand Bahama, the Bahamas. ☎ **809/352-3462** or toll free 800/327-0787 in the U.S. Fax 809/352-6835. 42 rms. A/C MINIBAR TV. Winter,

# Grand Bahama Accommodations

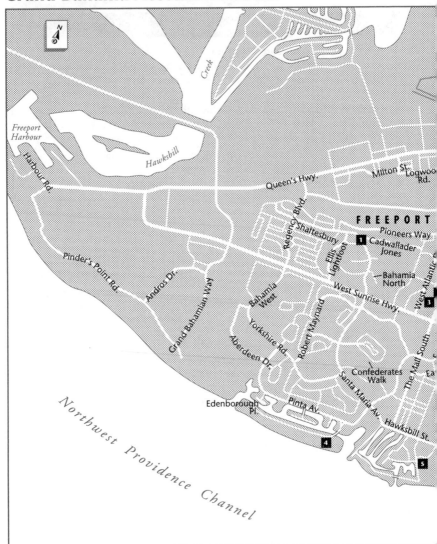

Atlantik Beach Hotel **9**

Bahamas Princess
   Resort and Casino **3**

Castaways Resort **2**

Club Fortuna Beach **11**

Coral Beach **7**

Lakeview Manor Club **1**

Lucayan Beach Resort & Casino **10**

Radisson Resort on Lucaya Beach **8**

Running Mon Marina & Resort **5**

Silver Sands Sea Lodge **6**

Sun Club Resort **12**

Xanadu Beach Resort and Marina **4**

9771

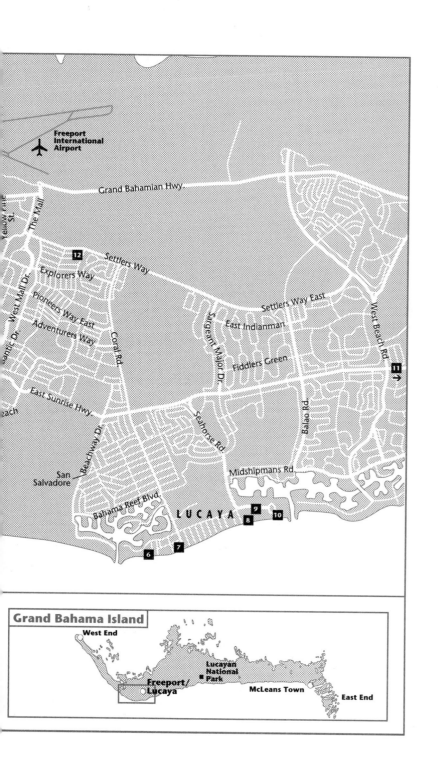

Freeport
International
Airport

Grand Bahamian Hwy.

The Mall

Yellow Pine St.

12

Settlers Way

Explorers Way

West Mall Dr.

Pioneers Way East

Adventurers Way

Coral Rd.

lantic Dr.

East Sunrise Hwy.

Beach

Settlers Way East

East Indianman

Sargeant Major Dr.

Fiddlers Green

West Beach Rd.

11

Balao Rd.

Beachway Dr.

San
Salvadore

Seahorse Rd.

Midshipmans Rd.

Bahama Reef Blvd.

L U C A Y A

6

7

8

9

10

## Grand Bahama Island

West End

Lucayan
National
Park

Freeport/
Lucaya

McLeans Town

East End

$70 single; $80 double; $90 triple; $100 quad. Off-season, $50 single; $60 double; $70 triple; $80 quad. Units with kitchenette $15 per day extra. Children under 12 stay free in parents' room. (EP rates.) AE, MC, V. Free parking. East End bus.

Clean and well maintained, this small-scale resort sits at the edge of a busy traffic intersection and remains a family favorite. In the rear of the building, behind a vine-covered entrance arbor, is a quiet enclave of greenery, encompassing a tennis court, a pool, and a clubhouse with a bar. The establishment is often completely booked. Each room, decorated in vibrant colors, has simple furniture. Some units also contain kitchenettes. A complimentary bus travels every hour to the beach throughout most of the day.

# LUCAYA
## EXPENSIVE

### Atlantik Beach Hotel
Royal Palm Way, P.O. Box F-531, Lucaya, Grand Bahama, the Bahamas. ☎ **809/373-1444** or toll free 800/622-6770 in the U.S., 800/848-3315 in Canada. Fax 809/373-7481. 123 rms, 52 suites. A/C TV TEL. Winter, $110–$145 single; $130–$170 double; $170–$360 suite. Off-season, $100–$140 single; $120–$155 double; $155–$330 suite. Rates include American breakfast. AE, DC, MC, V. Free parking. Lucaya bus.

After a $5-million renovation, this Swiss International Hotel is better than ever, the only high-rise in the area. Combining European flair with tropical style, the high-rise opens onto a palm-shaded beach six miles east of Freeport. In a family-oriented environment, the hotel rents rooms that are well furnished with a view of either the ocean or yacht harbor. The suites are actually junior apartments, each equipped with a kitchenette.

**Dining/Entertainment:** Special features include a shopping arcade, a lounge, and an espresso bar. There are several places to dine, including the Butterfly Brasserie coffee shop and Alfredo's Restaurant, for Italian cuisine.

**Services:** Shuttle bus to nearby golf course, laundry, babysitting, room service, beauty salon, massages.

**Facilities:** 18-hole golf course, the only windsurfing school on the island, complete water-sports facility, boating, deep-sea fishing, tennis, large pool.

### Lucayan Beach Resort & Casino
Royal Palm Way, P.O. Box F-40336, Lucaya, Grand Bahama, the Bahamas. ☎ **809/373-7777** or toll free 800/772-1227 in the U.S. Fax 809/373-6916 or 305/471-5658 in Miami. 243 rms. A/C TV TEL. Winter, $160–$190 single or double. Off-season, $140–$165 single or double. Special package rates available. MAP $35 extra per person daily. AE, MC, V. Free parking. Lucaya bus.

Set on a 16-acre spit of land midway between the open sea and a protected inlet, this low-rise hotel is often heavily booked in winter. It contains one of the island's two casinos and lies within walking distance of the Port Lucaya Marketplace. The accommodations are in two wings that stretch toward a garden filled with tropical trees and shrubs. Each room has a veranda and all the comforts you'd expect from a major international hotel.

**Dining/Entertainment:** The hotel has a casino, a collection of popular restaurants, and a cabaret act. The gourmet restaurant, Monte Carlo, and the cabaret are reviewed separately (see "Where to Dine" and "Grand Bahama After Dark," below).

**Services:** Room service, laundry, babysitting, daily activities program for children.

**Facilities:** Sweeping expanse of pristine beachfront, pool, host of water-related activities (sailing, snorkeling, and waterskiing), tennis courts, nearby golf course.

## MODERATE

### Radisson Resort on Lucaya Beach

Royal Palm Way, P.O. Box F-2496, Lucaya, Grand Bahama, the Bahamas. ☎ **809/373-1333** or toll free 800/333-3333. Fax 809/373-8662. 500 rms. A/C TV TEL. Winter (including continental breakfast), $110–$140 single; $120–$150 double. Off-season, $90–$120 single; $100–$130 double. AE, DC, MC, V. Free parking. Lucaya bus.

Formerly the Holiday Inn, this hotel opens onto a white-sand beach, a short walk from the Lucayan Beach Casino and across from the Port Lucaya Marketplace. Its rooms have been renovated, and most of them have private balconies with a view of the ocean. A limited number of rooms for the disabled are available.

**Dining/Entertainment:** Bahamian and international dishes are served at the Garden Patio Coffee Shop and Matilda's Poolside Snack Bar. Theme evenings and dancing in the Poinciana Lounge round out the entertainment.

**Services:** Room service, laundry, babysitting.

**Facilities:** Beach, tennis courts, freshwater swimming pool, kiddie pool, children's playground, beauty salon; sailing and deep-sea fishing charters can be arranged.

### Silver Sands Sea Lodge

Royal Palm Way, P.O. Box F-2385, Lucaya, Grand Bahama, the Bahamas. ☎ **809/373-5700.** Fax 809/373-1039. 88 apts, 11 suites. A/C MINIBAR TV TEL. Winter, $105 single or double; $120 one-bedroom suite. Off-season, $95 single or double; from $100 one-bedroom suite. MC, V. Free parking. Lucaya bus.

This lodge, 7 miles east of the Freeport International Airport, consists of three buildings clustered around two swimming pools. A condominium complex, about three-quarters of its accommodations are available for rent. Set 100 yards from a white-sand beach are modern studio apartments, plus one-bedroom first-class suites, all with a view of the pool area, the marina, or garden. All the spacious units have balconies and fully equipped kitchens. There is full maid service. Although swimming and snorkeling are possible from the nearby beach, most serious water-sports enthusiasts head for the facilities at the Radisson Resort at Lucaya Beach, three-quarters of a mile to the east. The lodge, however, has two hard-surface tennis courts ($6 per hour), two paddleball courts, two shuffleboard courts, and a poolside snack bar. The main restaurant, La Phoenix (see "Where to Dine," below), is one of the best in the Freeport/Lucaya area.

## INEXPENSIVE

### Coral Beach

Royal Palm Way, P.O. Box F-2468, Lucaya, Grand Bahama, the Bahamas. ☎ **809/373-2468.** Fax 809/373-5140. 10 units. A/C MINIBAR TV. Winter, $84.50 single; $98.80 double; $113.10 triple. Off-season, $62.90 single; $77.20 double; $91.50 triple. (Rates include taxes.) AE, MC, V. Free parking. Lucaya bus.

Built in 1965 as an upscale collection of privately owned condominiums, this peacefully isolated property sits amid well-maintained gardens and groves of casuarinas in a residential neighborhood. Some of the apartments and rooms contain verandas and all have kitchens where you can prepare your own breakfast. More suitable for older travelers, the complex rents large but rather severely furnished units. No entertainment is provided, but you're within walking distance of more glamorous facilities, including the Port Lucaya Marketplace and the Lucayan Beach Resort & Casino (a 5-minute taxi ride away). On the premises is a sandy and well-maintained beach, as well as a swimming pool.

# SOUTHEASTERN GRAND BAHAMA
## MODERATE

### Club Fortuna Beach

1 Dubloon Rd., P.O. Box F-2398, Freeport, Grand Bahama, the Bahamas. ☎ **809/ 373-4000.** Fax 809/373-5555. 204 rms. A/C. Winter, $206–$280 single; $294–$400 double; $382–$520 triple; $470–$640 quad. Off-season, $117–$220 single; $210–$315 double; $273–$408 triple; $336–$502 quad. Children 1 and under free. Children 2–12 $50 per day in parents' room (maximum of two). (Rates include meals, land, and water sports.) AE, MC, V. Free parking. Transportation: Taxi.

Of the many resorts on Grand Bahama Island, this is the most finely tuned to the Italian aesthetic. Established in 1993, it lies six miles east of the International Bazaar in the southeastern part of the island, amid an isolated landscape of casuarinas and scrubland. Vaguely modeled on lines similar to those of Club Med, it caters to a mostly European clientele (mostly Italian) who appreciate the 35 secluded acres of beachfront and the barrage of organized sports activities that are included in the price. At press time, because of their newness, the gardens and landscaping lacked the lushness you might have expected, although as the property matures, this should improve.

Bedrooms lie within a series of two-story sherbet-colored outbuildings. About three-quarters of the bedrooms have ocean views, the others overlook the garden. Each has a private balcony, a private safe, and two queen-size beds. Singles, however, can book one of these rooms but they are charged 40% more than the per-person double-occupancy rate.

**Dining/Entertainment:** All meals are served buffet style in a pavilion near the beach. Nightly entertainment is provided by Bahamian and Italian performers. There is a disco and a few bars.

**Services:** Italian language lessons, babysitting, laundry, massage.

**Facilities:** Sailing, windsurfing, weight training, volleyball, tennis, daily aerobics classes, outings to a nearby golf course, exercise room, children's playground, beauty salon.

# 4  Where to Dine

In restaurants classified as "expensive," expect to spend from $35 per person for dinner, excluding drinks, tip, and the 15% service charge. "Moderate" means $25 to $30 dinners, and a place charging under $20 for dinner is considered "inexpensive."

# FREEPORT
## EXPENSIVE

### Crown Room

In the Princess Casino, the Mall at W. Sunrise Hwy. ☎ **809/352-6721.** Reservations recommended. Appetizers $5.95–$28.50; main courses $22.95–$36. AE, DC, MC, V. Tues–Sat 6:30pm–midnight. Freeport bus. INTERNATIONAL.

The Crown Room is for those who prefer casino dining. It looks like a chic dining room on an art deco ocean liner, with pink-marble accents, brass-trimmed walls, and rose-colored mirrors. Eight hot and cold hors d'oeuvres, ranging from liver pâté to shrimp deJonge, are featured. Among the main dishes are lobster, fettuccine, rack of lamb, filet mignon, roast prime rib of beef, and medallions of veal. Desserts range from crêpes Casino to selections from the pastry trolley.

## ✪ Guanahani's Restaurant

In the Princess Country Club, the Mall at W. Sunrise Hwy. ☎ **809/352-6721.** Reservations recommended. Appetizers $4.25–$8.50; main courses $15.95–$23.95; three-course early bird dinner $14. AE, DC, MC, V. Dinner Sun–Thurs 5:30–10:30pm. Freeport bus. BARBECUE/SEAFOOD.

This attractive place is easy to find, as it lies within the poolside arcade of this previously recommended hotel. Surprisingly, it closes on Friday and Saturday nights when all other restaurants in Freeport are open. To enter, you cross over a small drawbridge. The decor is country-style tropical, with massive brass chandeliers and lots of exposed wood. The establishment prepares island roasts and barbecues by marinating top-quality meats and then roasting them for hours in specially constructed barbecue ovens. The house specialty is hickory-smoked ribs. Other choices include scampi, sirloin steak, beef brisket, and Bahamian lobster. To get the early bird special, you must dine between 5:30 and 6:30pm.

## ✪ The Rib Room

In the Princess Country Club, the Mall at W. Sunrise Hwy. ☎ **809/352-6721.** Reservations required. Appetizers $4.50–$10.25; main courses $19.50–$29.50; early bird fixed price meal $23 (6 to 7pm only). AE, DC, MC, V. Dinner Thurs–Mon 6–11pm. Freeport bus. SEAFOOD/STEAK.

At the Rib Room, which is among the gourmet dining rooms in the big hotels, you'll be delighted with the British hunting lodge decor and service. You can choose from broiled Bahamian lobster, native grouper, succulent shrimp, steak au poivre, steak Diane, or rack of lamb for two. Blue-ribbon prime rib of beef with Yorkshire pudding is also served. There is an excellent wine list to complement your meal.

## Ruby Swiss Restaurant

W. Sunrise Hwy. at W. Atlantic Ave. ☎ **809/352-8507.** Reservations required for dinner. Lunch appetizers $1.50–$3.50; lunch main courses $4.25–$14.75; dinner appetizers $3.50–$12.50; dinner main courses $13.50–$28.50; late-night main courses $4.50–$25. AE, DC, MC, V. Lunch daily 11am–4pm; dinner daily 6–10:30pm; late-night snacks daily 11pm–6am. Lucaya bus. INTERNATIONAL.

Airy and imaginative, this restaurant which opened in 1986 contains two bars (one, rescued from a Victorian building, is an antique), an inviting dining room, and a less formal eating area. Lunch includes pâté maison, seafood or Caesar salads, burgers, and Reuben or club sandwiches. Dinner might include lobster cocktail, seafood platter, scampi with garlic, catch of the day, creole-style shrimp, or filet Stroganoff. Viennese strudel is a dessert specialty. Late-night snacks include omelets, sandwiches, and burgers.

# MODERATE

## Morgan's Bluff

In the Princess Tower, the Mall at W. Sunrise Hwy. ☎ **809/352-9661.** Reservations recommended. Appetizers $3.75–$9.50; main courses $15.50–$26. AE, DC, MC, V. Dinner only, Thurs–Sat 6–9pm. Freeport bus. SEAFOOD.

Near the reception desk of the previously recommended Princess Tower, this restaurant looks a bit like a high-tech pirate's lair. Painted an enticing shade of

# Grand Bahama Dining

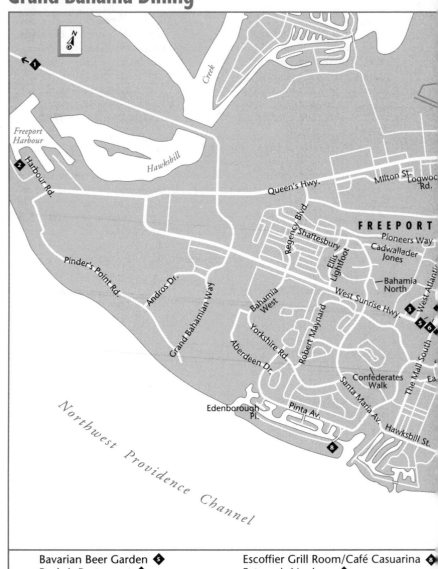

Bavarian Beer Garden **5**
Becky's Restaurant **5**
Britannia Pub **13**
Buccaneer Club **1**
Café Michel **5**
Captain's Charthouse Restaurant **17**
China Temple **5**
Crown Room **5**
Don Luigi's **12**

Escoffier Grill Room/Café Casuarina **8**
Fatman's Nephew **14**
Geneva's **4**
Guanahani's Restaurant **5**
Japanese Steak House **5**
La Phoenix **11**
La Trattoria **5**
Luciano's **14**
Monte Carlo **15**
Morgan's Bluff **5**

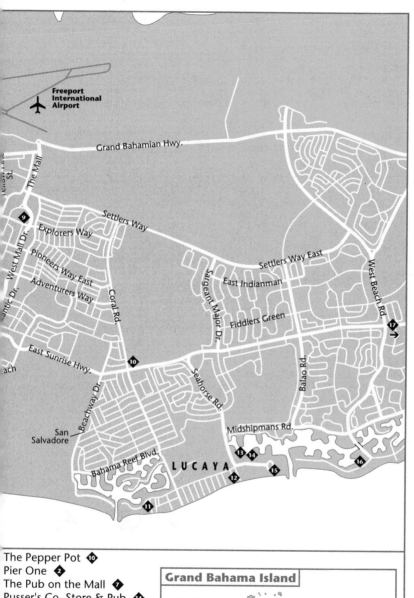

Freeport
International
Airport

Grand Bahamian Hwy.

The Mall

St.

Settlers Way

Explorers Way

West Mall Dr.

Pioneers Way East

antic Dr.

Adventurers Way

Coral Rd.

Settlers Way East

Sargeant Major Dr.

East Indianman

Fiddlers Green

West Beach Rd.

East Sunrise Hwy.

ach

Beachway Dr.

Seahorse Rd.

Balao Rd.

San
Salvadore

Midshipmans Rd.

Bahama Reef Blvd.

LUCAYA

 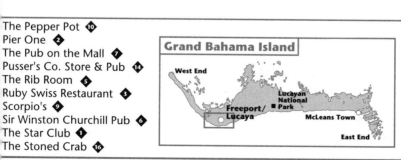
Grand Bahama Island

West End

Lucayan
National
Park

Freeport/
Lucaya

McLeans Town

East End

coral, and accented with huge tropical murals, it offers such seafood specialties as lobster thermidor, a captain's platter of mixed seafood, cracked conch, lobster bisque, seafood crêpes, and clams Benedict.

### La Trattoria

In the Princess Tower, the Mall at W. Sunrise Hwy. ☎ **809/352-9661.** Reservations recommended. Appetizers $3.75–$7.25; main courses $14.95–$22; fixed-price three-course dinner (5:30–6:30pm) $13.95. AE, DC, MC, V. Dinner daily 5:30–10:30pm. Freeport bus. ITALIAN.

The open parasols near the entrance remind one of a café terrace you might find in Capri. Budgeteers are encouraged to dine before 6:30pm, when a fixed-price bargain is offered. After 6:30pm, regular à la carte meals include five versions of pizza and nine kinds of pasta, such as fettuccine Alfredo and spaghetti alla carbonara. You can follow any of these with a Caesar salad, saltimbocca, and veal alla milanese. Finish with either a cappuccino or espresso.

## INEXPENSIVE

### 🟢 Geneva's

Kipling Lane, the Mall at W. Sunrise Hwy. ☎ **809/352-5085.** Reservations not required. Appetizers $3.50–$6; main courses $8.95–$15.95. No credit cards. Sun–Wed 7am–midnight, Thurs–Sat 7am–1am. Freeport bus. BAHAMIAN.

This restaurant is owned and operated by Geneva Monroe and her sons Francis and Robert. The kitchen prepares such Bahamian staples as conch (stewed, cracked, fried, or as chowder) and grouper prepared in every imaginable way. A Bahama Mama, the rum-laced house specialty drink, costs $4.

### The Pub on the Mall

Ranfurley Circus, Sunrise Hwy. ☎ **809/352-5110.** Reservations recommended. Lunch and dinner appetizers $3.50–$9; lunch main courses $6–$12; daily special one-course platter lunch $5.50; dinner main courses $10–$25. AE, MC, V. Prince of Wales Lounge, lunch daily 11:30am–4pm. Baron's Hall Grill Room and Silvano's Italian Restaurant, dinner Mon–Sat 5:30–11pm. Freeport bus. INTERNATIONAL.

Contained on the same floor of the same building, administered by the same management, you'll find three distinctive eating areas, each imbued with a separate theme. All of them lie opposite the International Bazaar and attract many locals. The Prince of Wales Lounge evokes medieval Britain and serves a lunchtime menu

---

### 🅗 Family-Friendly Restaurants

**Morgan's Bluff**  *(see p. 159)* This family restaurant, named after the 17th-century pirate Sir Henry Morgan, has a nautical decor and red neon "portholes." In the Princess Tower, it offers seafood specialties that appeal to most members of the family. Casual dress is the rule.

**Pier One**  *(see p. 180)* In the West End, children and their families "walk the plank" to reach this dining room resting on stilts above the water. Kids are thrilled by the nearby shark pool.

**Japanese Steak House**  *(see p. 163)* In a setting of umbrellas, lanterns, and rice-paper doors, tables are set for families who sit, Japanese style, on the floor. Hibachi meals are served by kimono-clad waitresses. Families on a budget opt for the "early bird" specials.

of shepherd's pie, fish-and-chips, platters of roast beef or fish, and real English ale. The more elaborate Baron's Hall Grill Room serves an evening menu of certified Angus beef, fish, fowl, and prime rib. Silvano's serves copious portions of pasta, veal, and beefsteaks.

### Scorpio's

W. Mall Dr. at Explorer's Way. ☎ **809/352-6969.** Reservations not necessary. Breakfast from $3.75; lunch platters $5–$19.50; dinner appetizers $1.25–$3.75; dinner main courses $8.75–$23. AE, MC, V. Breakfast daily 7–11am; lunch daily noon–4:30pm; dinner daily 4:30pm–1am. Bar daily 7am–3am. BAHAMIAN.

Named after the astrological sign of its Bahamas-born owner, this restaurant offers a welcome respite from too constant a diet of the burgers and pizza that seem to prevail within downtown Freeport. It lies at a busy traffic junction, within a cement-sided building painted both inside and outside in a medley of earth-toned colors. There's a bar inside, where tropical drinks (especially rum punch) seem to be the most popular libations, and a respectable dining room where the staff wears uniforms of black and white. Menu items include the full repertoire of Bahamian cuisine, including lobster salads, steaks, steamed chicken, peas 'n' rice, and virtually anything a chef could concoct from a conch.

## THE INTERNATIONAL BAZAAR
### MODERATE

### ⊛ Becky's Restaurant

International Bazaar. ☎ **809/352-8717.** Reservations not required. Bahamian or American breakfasts $3.95; sandwiches and salads, $2.95–$12.50; dinner main courses $5.95–$14.95. No credit cards. Daily 7am–10pm. International Bazaar bus. BAHAMIAN/AMERICAN.

This pink-and-white restaurant offers authentic Bahamian cuisine prepared in the time-tested style of the Family Islands. Owned by Becky Tucker and Berkeley Smith, the place offers a welcome respite from the relentless glitter of the nearby casino.

Breakfasts are either all-American or Bahamian and are available all day. Also popular are such dishes as minced lobster, curried mutton, fish platters, baked or curried chicken, conch salads, and an array of U.S.-inspired dishes. Soup is included with the purchase of any main course.

### Café Michel

International Bazaar. ☎ **809/352-2191.** Reservations recommended for dinner. Lunch main courses $5–$8; dinner appetizers $3.75–$6.50; dinner main courses $11.50–$25. AE, MC, V. Mon–Sat 8am–4pm and 5–10pm. International Bazaar bus. CONTINENTAL.

Set amid the bustle of the International Bazaar, this open-air coffeehouse and restaurant is decorated in earth tones with exposed brick and parasols. Many of the local shopowners come here for coffee, as well as platters, salads, and sandwiches throughout the day. In the evening, a more formal aura takes hold, when Bahamian-born chefs prepare seafood platters, grouper, lobster, duck in orange sauce, and steaks.

### ⊛ Japanese Steak House

International Bazaar. ☎ **809/352-9521.** Reservations not required. Appetizers $3.50–$6; main courses $10–$22; early bird special (5–8:30pm) $14.95. AE, MC, V. Dinner daily 5–10:30pm. International Bazaar bus. JAPANESE.

Here you'll find a touch of Asia in the tropics. Kimono-clad waitresses serve such specialties as sukiyaki steak and teppanyaki steak. The restaurant's most expensive dish—and a favorite—is hibachi-grilled New York strip steak and a lobster tail. Most dinners include soup, salad, and five different vegetables as well as rice. However, if you want to save money, go for the early bird special. Main dishes include Japanese pepper steak and teriyaki pork loin.

## INEXPENSIVE

### Bavarian Beer Garden
International Bazaar. ☎ **809/352-5050.** Reservations not required. Pizza, hamburgers, and sausages $3.50–$4.50, beer from $3.25. No credit cards. Daily 10:30am–9pm. International Bazaar bus. GERMAN/BAHAMIAN.

Its tables are reassuringly battered, and its owners may or may not have ever been to Germany, but the Teutonic aura of a Bavarian beer garden thrives here. Set beneath the Moorish-style arches of the International Bazaar, the place features at least a dozen kinds of imported beer, recorded versions of oom-pah-pah music, such German fare as knockwurst, bockwurst, and sauerkraut, and a selection of pizzas.

### China Temple
International Bazaar. ☎ **809/352-5610.** Reservations not required. Appetizers $3–$4.50; main courses $8.75–$15; fixed-price three-course dinner $13.75; lunch from $6.50. AE, MC, V. Mon–Sat 10:30am–10:30pm. International Bazaar bus. CHINESE.

A restaurant that also prepares take-out orders, the China Temple has outdoor café tables, or you can retreat inside. The bargain dining spot of the bazaar, it has a classic Chinese "chop suey menu," with all the standard items such as sweet-and-sour fish.

# LUCAYA
## EXPENSIVE

### Don Luigi's
In the Radisson Resort on Lucaya Beach, Royal Palm Way. ☎ **809/373-1333.** Reservations recommended. Appetizers $3.50–$9; main courses $17–$26. AE, MC, V. Tues–Sun 5–10pm (last order). INTERNATIONAL.

Despite its Italian-sounding name, this restaurant serves a mostly international menu with only a handful of Italian-derived dishes. Renovated in 1994, it has a floral decor, an absence of windows, and a candlelit formality which is enhanced by a staff wearing black-and-white uniforms and chef's aprons. Menu items include Bahamian grouper broiled with green peppers and local herbs, sirloin steak, surf and turf, breast of chicken "hunter's style" with mushroom sauce, rack of lamb, and Bahamian lobster. The pasta selection? Fettuccine Alfredo. The restaurant lies one flight below the lobby level of one of Lucaya's most visible hotels.

### Escoffier Grill Room/Café Casuarina
In the Xanadu Beach Resort, Sunken Treasure Dr., Lucaya. ☎ **809/352-6782.** Reservations recommended for dinner. Lunch platters (Café Casuarina) $8.25–$11.50; dinner appetizers $3–$10.50, dinner main courses $12–$40, dinner all-you-can-eat buffet $17.20. AE, MC, V. Lunch (in Café Casuarina) daily noon–5pm; dinner (in Escoffier Grill) daily 6–10:30pm, dinner buffet (in Escoffier Grill) nightly 6:30–8:30pm. INTERNATIONAL.

The food here is competently prepared and served with a flourish, but the allure for many diners at these restaurants involves the legend of reclusive billionaire Howard Hughes, owner and sometime resident of the hotel which contains them during the 1970s. His tastes affected the decor of the more formal of the two restaurants, the Escoffier Grill, whose walls are sheathed in burnished mahogany and brass. If you drop in for lunch, you'll dine within an airy café set behind big windows with a view of the resort's swimming pool. Dinners (within the Escoffier Grill) feature an all-you-can-eat buffet whose culinary theme (Italian, Bahamian, international, etc.) changes every night. Items on the à la carte menu include minced lobster, grilled or blackened swordfish, grouper amandine, smoked salmon, chateaubriand, and batter-fried cracked conch. There's a rumor that the ghost of Howard Hughes himself sometimes enters the restaurant and consumes a simple meal after wandering through the upper corridors of the hotel.

### Monte Carlo

In the Lucayan Beach Resort & Casino, Royal Palm Way. ☎ **809/373-7777.** Reservations recommended. Appetizers $6.50–$14.25; main courses $19–$36. AE, MC, V. Dinner Sun–Thurs 6–11pm, Fri–Sat 6pm–midnight. Closed Tues in summer. Lucaya bus. CONTINENTAL.

A few steps from the entrance to the busy Lucayan Casino, this is the most elegant—and most expensive—restaurant in the previously recommended hotel. Its minimalist decor includes a collection of gray-and-white tables and framed silk scarves. A uniformed staff caters to your needs during your meal, which might include a creamy lobster bisque with dumplings, many different preparations of lobster, bay scallops with garlic and provençal-herbs, and several beef, veal, and chicken dishes. Chef's specialties include chateaubriand and rack of lamb, both served to two diners. Dessert might be a baked Alaska or a Sachertorte.

### ✪ The Stoned Crab

At Taino Beach, Lucaya. ☎ **809/373-1442.** Reservations required. Appetizers $6.95–$18; main courses $17–$37.50. AE, MC, V. Dinner daily 5–10:30pm. Transportation: Taxi. SEAFOOD.

This restaurant with its 14-story pyramid roof, opening onto Taino Beach, is the favorite of well-heeled local residents and always the one likely to be recommended by a hotel reception desk when you ask "Where do you go to get the best food on the island." Guests can dine inside or on the beach patio. This place fills up at night, not only with visitors, but also with local residents who know about the large portions and the fine seafood.

To get you going, try the conch chowder. The snow crab claws are sweet and delicate. The restaurant specializes in a number of other crab dishes, including crab Andrew and a crab-and-avocado cocktail. Dolphin (the fish, not the mammal) is regularly featured, as is the game fish wahoo. Fresh, not frozen, fish are used whenever possible. Accompaniments include a salad, as well as home-baked raisin bread. You can finish your meal with Irish coffee. You might also order a carafe of the house wine; the restaurant has a very nice burgundy bottled under its own label in France. The bartender's special is a "Stoned Crab" drink based on various liqueurs, fruit juices, and rum. At night, taxis are usually lined up outside to drive you off to the Princess Casino.

## MODERATE

### Britannia Pub

King's Rd. on Bell Channel. ☎ **809/373-5919.** Reservations not required. Appetizers $3.25–$5.50; main courses $4.75–$16. DC, MC, V. Daily 4pm–4am. Freeport bus. BAHAMIAN/GREEK.

This mock-Tudor structure is one of Grand Bahama's most convivial bars. Patrons gather at the bar to watch sports on TV, and English beer is available on draft. The pub is also a restaurant, and meals might include lobster tails, grouper meunière, cracked conch, moussaka, or barbecued ribs.

### Captain's Charthouse Restaurant

E. Sunrise Hwy. and Beach Dr. ☎ **809/373-3900.** Reservations not required. Appetizers $6.95–$8.50; main courses $12.95–$26.95. AE, DC, MC, V. Dinner daily 5–11pm. INTERNATIONAL.

In a relaxed, treetop-level dining room, guests can select from prime rib of beef, teriyaki steak, chateaubriand for two, lobster thermidor, grouper filet, and other seafood selections, along with homemade bread and a "do-it-yourself" salad bar. Portions are large, but if you still have an appetite, the homemade desserts include key lime pie. A happy hour is held in the Mates Lounge from 5 to 7pm, with complimentary hors d'oeuvres. Entertainment is also presented nightly. Courtesy transportation to and from your hotel is offered.

# PORT LUCAYA
## EXPENSIVE

### ✪ Luciano's

Market Place, Port Lucaya. ☎ **809/373-9100.** Reservations required. Appetizers $4.50–$13.95; main courses $14.50–$23.95. AE, MC, V. Dinner daily 5:30–11pm. Lucaya bus. FRENCH/ITALIAN.

Luciano's is one of the most upscale Italian restaurants on Grand Bahama. Although it is found upstairs from a Pizza Hut, all thoughts of fast food are abandoned as you enter its rarefied precincts, decorated in a gray-and-pink color scheme. You can go early and enjoy an apéritif in the little bar inside or on the wooden deck overlooking the marina. Food is freshly prepared and beautifully served. You might begin with oysters Rockefeller or smoked salmon. Fish and shellfish are regularly featured and imaginatively prepared. Steak Diane is one of Luciano's classics. Veal Luciano's is the finest milk-fed veal sautéed with shrimp and plump pieces of lobster.

## INEXPENSIVE

### Fatman's Nephew

Market Place, Port Lucaya. ☎ **809/373-8520.** Reservations not required. Appetizers $3–$4.50; main courses $6.50–$26. AE, MC, V. Mon and Wed–Sun noon–11pm, Sun and Thurs 5pm–1am. Lucaya bus. BAHAMIAN.

This restaurant lies on the second floor above Pusser's Co. Store & Pub, overlooking the marina at Port Lucaya. Guests can enjoy drinks or meals inside a well-decorated main dining room; but most diners prefer to eat on a large deck where they can survey the action below. As you climb the steps, you'll see "today's catch" posted on blackboard menus. Dishes are likely to include about a dozen kinds of game fish, such as wahoo and Cajun blackened kingfish. If you don't want fish, try the curried chicken. I suggest you begin your meal with either a freshly made conch salad or conch chowder.

# SPECIALTY DINING
## HOTEL DINING

### La Phoenix

In the Silver Sands Sea Lodge, Royal Palm Way. ☎ **809/373-5700.** Reservations recommended. Appetizers $4–$8.50; main courses $15–$22. MC, V. Dinner daily 6:30–11pm. Lucaya bus. SEAFOOD.

Amusing, witty, and nautically inspired, this highly recommendable restaurant sits above the reception area of a previously endorsed hotel. An eclectic decor of driftwood paneling, Bahamian paintings, plants, and intimate table groupings provides for fun evenings. Specialties include seafood stew, fresh lobster kabob, sirloin kabob, and chicken Kiev, climaxed by either Nassau or Irish coffee.

## DINING WITH A VIEW

### Pusser's Co. Store & Pub

Market Place, Port Lucaya. ☎ **809/373-8450.** Reservations not accepted. Lunch appetizers $3–$7. lunch main courses $5–$18; dinner appetizers $3.50–$6.95, dinner main courses $9.95–$24.50. AE, MC, V. Daily 11am–midnight. Lucaya bus. CONTINENTAL/BAHAMIAN/ENGLISH.

Pusser's is the most popular place to hang out at this shopping-and-dining complex. While a robot piano player hammers out golden oldies, you can dine indoors in air-conditioned comfort or outside at a table overlooking the yachts in the marina, one of the best views on Grand Bahama.

There's an open grill turning out your favorite foods, and plenty of stained glass, polished brass, and pub artifacts. For lunch most guests select either a New York–style sandwich, such as a Reuben or hot pastrami, or an English pie, ranging from shepherd's to fisherman's. You can also order fish-and-chips. Dinners are more elaborate, including a wide list of appetizers. English pies include steak and ale, along with chicken asparagus. For the main course, you can order the catch of the day, calves' liver, lamb chops, or pork chops. For dessert, try either Pusser's pecan pie or key lime pie.

## LOCAL FAVORITES

### Sir Winston Churchill Pub

East Mall, next to the Straw Market and the International Bazaar. ☎ **809/352-8866.** Reservations not required. Pizzas $8–$20; salads and sandwiches $4–$6. AE, MC, V. Daily 11am–3am. Freeport bus. INTERNATIONAL.

In spite of its name, this has become mainly a pizzeria. In an upstairs location, it is often visited by the casino crowd when they grow bored with the slot machines. Don't expect much here in the way of cuisine, although it remains an enduring watering hole with many repeat visitors. Try one of about a dozen different pizzas or a selection of salads and sandwiches.

## FAST FOOD

### The Pepper Pot

E. Sunrise Hwy. at Coral Rd. ☎ **809/373-7655.** Reservations not accepted. Breakfast $5; appetizers $5.50–$6; main courses $7.50–$12.50. No credit cards. 24 hours. Transportation: Taxi. BAHAMIAN.

This might be the only establishment on Grand Bahama that specializes in Bahamian take-out food. You'll find it after about a 5-minute drive east of the International Bazaar, in a tiny shopping mall. You can order take-out portions of the best carrot cake on the island, as well as conch chowder, fish and pork chops, chicken souse, cracked conch, sandwiches and hamburgers, and an array of daily specials. The owner is Ethiopian-born Wolansa Fountain.

# 5  What to See & Do

Except for the coral, rock, and pines, there isn't much on Grand Bahama that's very old, unless you count some of the Native Lucayan artifacts. However, the efforts toward beautification have paid off in interesting botanical gardens and parks where you can see tropical plants in their glory in the right seasons. Also, plant preservation has become important here.

## SUGGESTED ITINERARIES

### If You Have 1 Day

**Day 1**   After a leisurely breakfast, head for the International Bazaar and shop until noon. Lunch at one of the restaurants at the bazaar, then head for Xanadu Beach at Lucaya in the afternoon. That evening, attend a casino and/or see one of the Las Vegas–type revues.

### If You Have 2 Days

**Day 1**   Spend as above.

**Day 2**   Visit the Underwater Explorers Society and participate in their unique "Dolphin Experience." In the afternoon get in some beach time and explore the Port Lucaya Marketplace.

### If You Have 3 Days

**Days 1–2**   Spend as above.

**Day 3**   Explore the West End of Grand Bahama on a leisurely visit. Stop in at Hawksbill Creek to see the fish market, then head for Eight Mile Rock and eventually the West End, site of a Prohibition-era rum-boat boomtown.

---

## ❷  Did You Know?

- Grand Bahama was once settled by a primitive tribe called Siboney that disappeared upon the arrival of the Native Lucayans.
- Ponce de León arrived seeking the Fountain of Youth but found only one *vieja* (old woman), all that was left of the once-proud Lucayans.
- Grand Bahama—from the Spanish *gran bajamar*—means literally "vast underwater."
- It is believed that Grand Bahama was the only land base many notorious pirates ever had—they spent the rest of their time aboard pirate ships.
- A Spanish treasure ship, discovered in 1965 off Grand Bahama, contained 10,000 silver coins valued at from $2 to $9 million.
- Eccentric millionaire Howard Hughes once lived in a "sealed-off" environment on the 12th and 13th floors of the Xanadu Beach Hotel.

---

### ⊙ Frommer's Favorite Grand Bahama Experiences

**Frolicking with Dolphins.** Swimmers and snorkelers interact with bottle-nosed dolphins as part of a "familiarization program." Your session is videotaped, and, for most visitors, it provides a lifetime souvenir of an unforgettable experience.

**Cycling Freeport/Lucaya.** Good roads and a pancake-flat terrain make cycling around these two resorts easy on the body. After your explorations, bike to Fortune Beach, one of the best beaches on the island.

**Discovering Rand Memorial Nature Centre.** Walk along the nature trails of this 100-acre site with a knowledgeable guide who describes the exotic flora and fauna of his homeland. Keep your eyes peeled for the rich bird life, ranging from olive-capped warblers to the West Indian flamingo.

---

### If You Have 5 Days

**Days 1–3**   Spend as above.

**Day 4**   In the morning, explore Rand Memorial Nature Centre and return to the International Bazaar for a look at more shops. Discover another beach in the afternoon, perhaps Fortune Beach. Before returning to the casinos at night, dine at the Stoned Crab.

**Day 5**   Spend the day exploring the East End of the island, all the way to McLean's Town, at the far-eastern tip of Grand Bahama. Go shelling; get in some beach time, then return in time for a sundowner and a panoramic sunset.

## SIGHTS

### Garden of the Groves

Intersection of Midshipman Rd. and Magellan Dr. ☎ **809/352-4045.** $5 for adults or children. Garden, Mon–Fri 9am–4pm, Sat–Sun and holidays 10am–4pm. Palmetto Café, Mon–Fri 9am–3pm, Sat 10am–noon. Transportation: Taxi and local tours.

The prime attraction of Grand Bahama is this 11-acre garden, which honors its founder, Wallace Groves, and his wife, Georgette. Seven miles east of the International Bazaar, this scenic preserve of waterfalls and flowering shrubs has some 10,000 trees.

Tropical birds flock here, making this a lure for bird-watchers and ornithologists. There are free-form lakes, footbridges, ornamental borders, lawns, and flowers. A small nondenominational chapel, open to visitors, looks down on the garden from a hill. The Palmetto Café (☎ **809/373-5668**) serves snacks and drinks, and a Bahamian straw market is at the entrance gate.

### Hydroflora Garden

On East Beach at Sunrise Hwy. ☎ **809/352-6052.** $3 adults, $1.50 children. Daily 9–5pm. Transportation: Taxi.

At this artificially created botanical wonder, you can see 154 specimens of plants that grow in the Bahamas. A special section is devoted to bush medicine, widely practiced by Bahamians (who have been using herbs and other plants to cure everything from sunburn to insomnia since the Native Lucayans were here centuries ago). Guided tours cost $2 per person.

## ○ Lucaya National Park

Midshipman Rd. (For information, contact the Rand Nature Centre. ☎ **809/352-5438.**) Admission free. Open daily 24 hours. Directions: Drive east along Midshipman Rd., passing Sharp Rock Point and Gold Rock, about 12 miles from Lucaya.

This 40-acre park, filled with mangrove, pine, and palm trees, contains one of the loveliest, most secluded beaches on Grand Bahama. The long, wide, dune-covered stretch of sandy beach is found by following a wooden path winding through the trees. As you wander through the park, you'll cross Gold Rock Creek, fed by a spring from what is said to be the world's largest underground freshwater cavern system. Two of the caves can be seen, they were exposed when a portion of ground collapsed. The pools there are composed of six feet of freshwater atop a heavier layer of saltwater. Spiral wooden steps have been built down to the pools. There are 36,000 passages in the cavern system, some of which may be opened to scuba diving by the time you visit.

The freshwater springs once lured Native Lucayans, those Arawak-connected tribes who lived on the island and depended on fishing for their livelihood. They would come inland to get fresh water for their habitats on the beach. Lucayan bones and artifacts, such as pottery, have been found in the caves as well as on the beaches.

## Rand Nature Centre

E. Settlers Way. ☎ **809/352-5438.** Guided tours, $5 adults, $3 children (5–12); free 4 and under. Self-guided tours, $3 adults, $2 children (5–12); free 4 and under. Mon–Sat 9am–4pm; guided tours at 10am and 2pm Mon–Fri, Sat 10am only.

This 100-acre pineland sanctuary, located 2 miles east of the center of Freeport, is the regional headquarters of the Bahamas National Trust, a nonprofit conservation organization. Forest nature trails highlight native flora and "bush medicine" and provide opportunities for bird-watching. Wild birds abound at the park, and a freshwater pond is home to a flock of West Indian flamingos, the national bird of the Bahamas. Other features of the nature center include native animal displays, a replica of a Lucayan Indian village, an education center, and a gift shop selling nature books and souvenirs.

# ORGANIZED TOURS

Several informative tours of Grand Bahama Island are offered. One reliable company is **H. Forbes Charter Co.,** the Mall at West Sunrise Highway, Freeport (☎ 809/352-9311). From its headquarters in the lobby of the Bahamas Princess Country Club, it offers half- and full-day bus tours. The most popular option is the half-day Super Combination Tour, priced at $16 per adult and $12 per child under 12. It includes guided visits to the botanical gardens, drive-through tours of residential areas, the island's commercial center, and stops at the island's deep-water harbor. Shopping and a visit to a wholesale liquor store are included in the price. Tours depart Monday through Saturday at 9am and 1pm for a duration of three hours.

A full-day tour, the Grand Bahama Day Trip includes everything mentioned above, as well as an excursion to the island's barren but beautiful West End. Departing Tuesday, Thursday, and Saturday at 9am, it costs $25 per adult and $15 per child under 12 and returns to Freeport around 4:30pm. Advance reservations are necessary. Tours are usually operated from Blue Bird buses holding between 48 and 52 passengers.

## 6  Sports A to Z

### BEACHES

Grand Bahama has some 60 miles of white-sand beaches rimming the blue-green waters of the Atlantic. The heaviest concentration of beaches is in the Lucaya area, site of the major resort hotels. Most of these resorts have their own beaches, with a fairly active program of water sports. The mile-long **Xanadu Beach,** at the Xanadu Beach Resort in the Freeport area, is one of the premier beaches. The resort beaches tend to be the most crowded in winter.

Other island beaches include **Taino Beach,** site of the Stoned Crab restaurant, lying to the east of Freeport, plus **Smith's Point** and **Fortune Beach,** the latter considered by some as the finest beach on Grand Bahama. Another good beach, about a 20-minute ride east of Lucaya, is **Gold Rock Beach,** a favorite picnic spot with the locals, especially on weekends.

### BOAT CRUISES

*Mermaid Kitty*
Port Lucaya Dock. ☎ **809/373-5880.**

Any tour agent can arrange for you to go out on this vessel, supposedly the world's largest twin-diesel-engine glass-bottom boat. You'll get an excellent view of the beautiful underwater life that lives off the coast of Grand Bahama. Departures are from the Lucayan Bay Hotel at 10:30am and 12:30 and 2:30pm. The tour lasts 1¹/₂ hours and costs $15 for adults, $8 for children.

### THE DOLPHIN EXPERIENCE

✪ **Underwater Explorers Society, (UNEXSO)**
Next to Port Lucaya, opposite Lucayan Beach Casino. ☎ **809/373-1250.**

A group of bottle-nosed dolphins are involved in a unique dolphin/human familiarization program at Dolphin Experience, located at UNEXSO. This "close encounter" program allows participants to observe these intelligent and friendly animals close up and hear an interesting talk by a member of the animal-care staff. This is not a swim-with-the-dolphins type of program, but you can step onto a shallow wading platform and interact with the dolphins. This is an educational adventure for all ages. The animals are released daily to swim with scuba divers in the open ocean. The informational close encounter program, which includes a close-up observation of the dolphins, costs $25. Most diving with the dolphins is in the open ocean, costing $105. There are several versions daily. Most Dolphin Experience sessions are videotaped with copies available to participants for $35. Because of the popularity of the program, advance reservations are essential. In the United States, call **305/351-9889** or toll free **800/992-DIVE.**

### FITNESS CENTERS

**Princess Fitness Centre**
In the Princess Country Club, Bahamas Princess Resort and Casino, the Mall at W. Sunrise Hwy. ☎ **809/352-6721,** ext. 4606.

For complete fitness services, try this health club, which is open to both guests and nonguests. It offers sauna, facials, massages, and use of an exercise room with body-building equipment. It is open Monday through Friday from 10am to 6pm and on Saturday and Sunday from 10am to 4pm.

## GOLF

This island boasts more golf links than any other island in the Bahamas or the Caribbean. The courses are within seven miles of one another, and you won't have to wait to play. All courses are open to the public year-round, and clubs can be rented from all pro shops on the island.

### Fortune Hills Golf & Country Club
Richmond Park, Lucaya. ☎ **809/373-4500.**

Designed as an 18-hole course, the back 9 were never completed. You can replay the front 9 for 18 holes and a total of 6,916 yards from the blue tees. Par is 72. Greens fees are $16 for 9 holes, $26 for 18. Electric carts cost $22 and $30 for 9 and 18 holes, respectively. The nearest hotels are the Atlantik Beach, Radisson Resort on Lucaya Beach, and Lucayan Beach. The location is 5 miles east of Freeport.

### Lucayan Park Golf & Country Club
Lucaya Beach. ☎ **809/373-1066.**

This is the best-kept and most manicured course on Grand Bahama. Greens are fast, and there are a couple of par 5s more than 500 yards long. It totals 6,824 yards from the blue tees and 6,488 from the whites. Par is 72. Greens fees are $27 for 9 holes or $36 for the day. A golf cart costs $22 for 9 holes or $44 for 18 holes.

### Princess Emerald Course
The Mall South. ☎ **809/352-6721.**

This is one of two courses owned and operated by the Bahamas Princess Resort and Casino (see below for the Princess Ruby Course). The Emerald Course was the site of the Bahamas National Open some years back. The course has plenty of trees along the fairways as well as an abundance of water hazards and bunkers. The toughest hole is the ninth, a par 5 with 545 yards from the blue tees to the hole. Greens fees are $46 for 9 holes or $63 for 18 holes.

### Princess Ruby Course
W. Sunrise Hwy. ☎ **809/352-6721.**

This championship course was designed by Joe Lee in 1968 and was the recent site of the Michelin Long Drive competition. Greens fees are $46 for 9 holes, $63 for 18 holes, including electric carts. It's a total of 6,750 yards if played from the championship blue tees.

## HORSEBACK RIDING

### Pinetree Stables
N. Beachway Dr., Freeport. ☎ **809/373-3600.**

Pinetree offers trail rides to the beach Tuesday through Sunday at 9am, 11am, and 2pm. The cost is $35 per person for a ride lasting $1^1/_2$ hours. Lessons in dressage and jumping are available for $35 for 45 minutes of instruction.

## SNORKELING & SCUBA

### Paradise Watersports
Sunken Treasure Dr., Xanadu Beach. ☎ **809/352-2887.**

At the Xanadu Beach Resort and Marina, this outfit offers a variety of activities. With snorkeling trips, you cruise to a coral reef on a 48-foot catamaran for $18 per person; snorkeling gear costs $9 per hour. Paddleboats rent for $7 for a half hour, $10 per hour. Waterskiing is priced at $15 for a 15-minute ride. Parasailing costs $25 for a 5-minute ride. Their sunset cruise, at $20 per person, includes dance music, unlimited Bahama Mamas (the drink, that is), and cheese and crackers. A glass-bottom-boat ride costs $15 for adults and $8 for children under 12 for a cruise lasting 1 1/2 hours.

### Underwater Explorers Society (UNEXSO)
Lucaya Beach. ☎ **809/373-1244.**

UNEXSO is one of the premier facilities for diving and snorkeling throughout the Bahamas and Caribbean. There are three dive trips daily, including reef trips, shark dives, wreck dives, and night dives. Also, this is the only facility in the world where divers can dive with dolphins in the open ocean (see "The Dolphin Experience," above). Also, a popular 3-hour learn-to-dive course is offered every day. Over UNEXSO's 28-year history, more than 50,000 people have completed this course. For $89, students learn the basics in UNEXSO's training pools. Then, the same day, they dive the beautiful shallow reef with their instructor. For experienced divers, a guided reef dive is $35, a three-dive package is $89, and a 7-day pass (up to three dives per day) is $299. A snorkeling trip to the reef costs $18, all equipment included, and a half-hour snorkeling lesson is $10.

## SPORTFISHING

In the waters off Grand Bahama you can fish for barracuda, snapper, grouper, yellowtail, wahoo, and kingfish, along with other denizens of the deep.

### Reef Tours, Ltd.
Port Lucaya Dock. ☎ **809/373-5880.**

Reef Tours offers the least expensive way to go deep-sea fishing around Grand Bahama Island. Adults pay $60 if they fish, $40 if they only go along to watch. Departures for the half-day excursion are at 8:30am and 1pm seven days a week. Included in the cost are bait, tackle, and ice.

### Running Mon Marina
208 Kelly Court, Bahama Terrace. ☎ **809/352-6833.**

A half day's deep-sea fishing costs $60 per person, and a full day costs $120 per person. It takes six people to make up the party.

## TENNIS

### Bahamas Princess Resort and Casino
The Mall at W. Sunrise Hwy.

This resort almost has the monopoly on tennis courts. At its Princess Country Club (☎ **809/352-6721**), there are six hard-surface courts. Guests and nonguests are charged $7 per hour. Lessons are also available. At the Princess Tower (☎ **809/352-9661**), there are three clay and three hard-surface courts, all of which are lit for night play. The charge for both guests and nonguests is $7 ($17 at night).

### Lucayan Beach Resort
Royal Palm Way. ☎ **809/373-6545.**

There are four hard courts (not illuminated). Free for guests, these courts cost nonresidents $10 per hour.

### Radisson Resort on Lucaya Beach
Royal Palm Way. ☎ **809/373-1333.**

This resort has four hard-surface courts, costing $10 per hour for guests and nonguests alike. There is no night play.

## WINDSURFING

### Atlantik Beach Hotel
Royal Palm Way. ☎ **809/373-1444.**

Courses are offered here for beginners, advanced, and freestyle. Each course is eight hours and costs $150. Windsurfing boards and equipment rent for $25 per hour or $40 per day.

## 7 Shopping

There's no place in the Bahamas for shopping quite like the International Bazaar, where the goods of the world come together for you to browse among. In the nearly 100 fascinating shops, you're bound to find something that is both a discovery and a bargain. Here are displayed African handcrafts, Chinese jade, British china, Swiss watches, Irish linens, and Colombian emeralds—and that's just for starters. The price tags on goods you find here will probably be from 10% to 40% below those on the same merchandise at home.

At the **Straw Market,** beside the International Bazaar, are items with a special Bahamian touch—colorful baskets, hats, handbags, and place mats—all of which make good gifts and souvenirs of your trip.

Shopping hours in Freeport/Lucaya are 9:30am to 3pm Monday through Thursday, 9:30am to 5pm on Friday. Many shops are closed on Saturday and Sunday. However, in the International Bazaar hours vary widely. Most places there are open Monday through Saturday. Some begin business daily at 9:30am, others don't open until 10am. Closing time ranges from 5:30 to 6pm.

## THE INTERNATIONAL BAZAAR

One of the world's most unusual shopping marts, the International Bazaar, at East Mall Drive and East Sunrise Highway, covers 10 acres in the heart of Freeport. There is a major bus stop at the entrance of the complex. Unfortunately, buses aren't numbered, but those marked ✪ INTERNATIONAL BAZAAR will take you right to the gateway. Visitors walk through the much-photographed Toril Gate, a Japanese symbol of welcome, into a miniature world's fair setting. Continental cafés and dozens of shops loaded with merchandise await visitors. The bazaar blends architecture and cultures from some 25 countries. The place was re-created with cobblestones, narrow alleys, and authentically reproduced architecture.

On a street patterned after the Ginza in Tokyo, just inside the entrance to the bazaar, is the Asian section. A rich collection of merchandise from the Far East is here, including cameras, handmade teak furniture, fine silken goods, and even places where you can have clothing custom-made. If browsing among the jade figurines and kimonos makes you think of Japanese food, drop in at the Japanese Steak House (see "Where to Dine," above), for sushi or other delicacies.

To the left you'll find the Left Bank of Paris, or a reasonable facsimile, with sidewalk cafés where you can enjoy a café au lait and perhaps a pastry under shade trees. In the Continental Pavillion, there are leather goods, jewelry, lingerie, and gifts at shops with names such as Love Boutique.

A narrow alley leads you from the French section to East India, where shops sell such exotic goods as taxi horns and silk saris. Moving on from the India House, past Kon Tiki, you arrive in Africa, where you can purchase carvings or a colorful dashiki.

For a taste of Latin America and Iberia, make your way to the Spanish section, where serapes and piñatas hang from the railings. Imports are displayed along the cobblestoned walks. You may enjoy stopping in a Hispanic restaurant, such as Café Valencia.

Many items sold in the shops here are said to be about 40% less costly than if you bought them in the United States, but don't count on that. You can have purchases sent anywhere you wish.

Here is a description of various shops in the bazaar.

## ART

### Flovin Gallery
Arcade. ☎ **809/352-7564.**

This gallery sells original Bahamian and international art, frames, lithographs, posters, and sculptures. It also offers handmade Bahamian straw dolls, coral jewelry, and other gift items. Another branch is at Port Lucaya (see below).

### Garden Gallery
Arcade. ☎ **809/352-9755.**

The Garden Gallery features paintings and prints by local Bahamian and international artists. It also sells Bahamian craft souvenirs.

## CRYSTAL & CHINA

### Island Galleria
Arcade. ☎ **809/352-8194.**

China by Wedgwood, Rosenthal, and Aynsley, and crystal by Waterford, are the major lure of this store. Bahamian paintings are in the art gallery in the back room.

### Midnight Sun
Arcade. ☎ **809/352-7515.**

This is the best bet for exquisite crystal and china. Its high-quality dinnerware from well-known manufacturers is displayed in twin boutiques. It offers Baccarat, Hummel, and Daum, among others.

## FASHIONS

### London Pacesetter Boutique
Arcade. ☎ **809/352-2929.**

Here you'll find stylish sportswear, Pringle and Braemar cashmere sweaters, Gottex swimwear, and assorted European fashions.

### The Sweater Shop
Island Galleria. ☎ **809/352-8194.**

The Sweater Shop features men's and women's sweaters in lambswool, cashmere, and cotton from such countries as Scotland and Italy. Cotton sweaters, made in Italy, were especially created for the Bahamas market.

## JEWELRY

### Casa Simpatica
Spanish Section. ☎ **809/352-6425.**

This shop sells gold, silver, and gemstone jewelry. Discounts range as much as 40% and beyond. Semiprecious beads and coral items are made in the Bahamas. There is also a large selection of Japanese watches.

## Colombian Emeralds International
South American Section. ☎ 809/352-5464.

Here you'll find emeralds, as well as gold-and-silver jewelry, and watches from Japan and Switzerland. In the Jewelry Factory, local craftspeople set gemstones in jewelry while explaining the process. The shop is also the authorized agent for Ebel, Omega, Seiko, Citizen, Tissot, and other well-known watches.

## Ginza
Far East Section. ☎ 809/352-7515.

Ginza specializes in 14- and 18-karat gold chains. It also sells Mikimoto pearls, bracelets, and rings, some with gemstones. Its watches include those from Baume & Mercier, Pulsar, Seiko, and Rolex. It also has a Cartier leather collection and top-brand cameras.

## Sea Treasures
Spanish Section. ☎ 809/352-2911.

Sea Treasures sells jewelry inspired by the sea and handcrafted on the island. Prices go from $25 to $3,000. The staff will show you 14-karat gold necklaces and bracelets, along with diamonds, topazes, pearls, and both pink and black coral.

## LLADRÓ FIGURINES

### Lladró Gallery
In the International Bazaar. ☎ 809/352-2660.

Lovers of Lladró figurines welcome the chance to add to their collections by visiting what's probably the best-stocked emporium of Lladró on Grand Bahama Island. If you appreciate the elongated limbs and wistful mannerisms of characters within the 17th-century paintings of El Greco, you'll probably appreciate Lladró. Also in stock are a less extensive collection of figures by Swarovski and a limited collection of Waterford crystal.

## MISCELLANY

### Far East Traders
Island Galleria. ☎ 809/352-8194.

In the Hong Kong section, Far East Traders sells linens, exotic gifts, decorative ornaments, silk coats, hand-embroidered dresses and blouses, coral jewelry, and freshwater pearls.

### The Old Curiosity Shop
Arcade. ☎ 809/352-8008.

This shop specializes in antique English bric-a-brac, including original and reproduction items: Victorian dinner rings and cameos, antique engagement rings, lithographs, old and new silver and porcelain, and brass candlesticks and trivets.

## PERFUMES & FRAGRANCES

### Les Parisiennes
Moroccan Section. ☎ 809/352-5380.

This outlet offers a wide range of perfumes (the latest from Paris). It also sells Lancôme cosmetics and skin-care products.

### The Perfume Factory Fragrance of the Bahamas
At the rear of the International Bazaar. ☎ **809/352-9391.**

This shop is housed in a model of an 1800 mansion, through which visitors are invited on a guided tour and can see the mixing of fragrant oils. There's even a "mixology" department where you can create your own fragrance, with several oils from which to select. The shop's well-known products include Island Promises, Goombay, Paradise, and Pink Pearl (which has conch pearls in the bottle).

### Parfum de Paris
French Section. ☎ **809/352-8164.**

Here you'll find practically all existing French perfumes and colognes. Discounts are often granted with prices up to 40% less than in the United States.

## SHOES

### Gemini
In the International Bazaar. ☎ **809/352-4809.**

Although most of its inventory consists of stylish (usually Italian-made) shoes for women, this store is also well stocked with the kinds of accessories that might help coordinate outfits that a woman already owned. These include handbags, wallets, belts, T-shirts, and a wide collection of jewelry (some of it gold plated) inspired by the aesthetic of Chanel.

## STAMPS & COINS

### Bahamas Coin and Stamp Ltd.
Arcade. ☎ **809/352-8989.**

This shop sells stamps, coins, commemorative medallions, and uncirculated coin sets. It has Bahamian and world stamps, along with $100 gold coins, British half sovereigns, and gold jewelry.

## PORT LUCAYA MARKETPLACE

The first of its kind in the Bahamas, Port Lucaya on Seahorse Road was named after the original settlers of Grand Bahama. This is a shopping and dining complex set on six acres near the Lucayan Beach Resort & Casino, Radisson Resort on Lucaya Beach, and Atlantik Beach Hotel. Free entertainment, such as steel-drum bands and strolling musicians, adds to a festival atmosphere.

The complex rose on the site of a former Bahamian straw market, but the craftspeople and their straw products are back in full force after being temporarily dislodged.

Full advantage is taken of the waterfront location. Many of the restaurants and shops overlook a 50-slip marina, home of a "fantasy" pirate ship featuring lunch and dinner/dancing cruises. A variety of charter vessels are also based at the Port Lucaya Marina. Dockage at the marina is available to visitors coming to shop or dine by boat.

A boardwalk along the water makes it easy to watch the frolicking dolphins and join in other activities at the Underwater Explorers Society (UNEXSO). (For more information, see "Sports A to Z.")

Merchandise in the shops of Port Lucaya ranges from leather to lingerie and wind chimes. Traditional and contemporary fashions are featured for men, women, and children.

### Coconits by Androsia
Port Lucaya. ☎ **809/373-8387.**

This is the Port Lucaya outlet of the famous batik house of the Andros Islands. Its designs and colors capture "the spirit of the Bahamas." Fabrics are handmade on the island of Andros, and the store sells quality, 100% cotton resort wear including simple skirts, tops, and jackets for women.

### Flovin Gallery II
Port Lucaya. ☎ **809/373-8388.**

A branch of the art gallery at the International Bazaar, this gallery sells a collection of oil paintings (both Bahamian and international), along with lithographs, posters, and sculptures. It also features a number of gift items.

### Pusser's Co. Store & Pub
Port Lucaya. ☎ **809/373-8450.**

This establishment is exceptional. In addition to its pub and restaurant (see "Where to Dine") it is also part nautical museum. It's a shopping adventure, with Pusser's own line of travel-and-sports clothing in classical designs, along with fine ship models, antiques, and other nauticalia.

## 8  Grand Bahama After Dark

Grand Bahama has Las Vegas–type revues, casino action, dance clubs, and native entertainment such as steel bands. Many of the resort hotels stage their own entertainment at night, and the hotel shows are open to the general public.

## LOCAL CULTURAL ENTERTAINMENT

The nonprofit repertory company, the **Freeport Players' Guild,** Regency Theatre (☎ **809/352-5533**), offers about four plays during its September-to-June season. The **Grand Bahama Players,** Regency Theatre (☎ **809/373-2299**), is a local amateur group which also uses the Regency Theatre for its productions. Works by Bahamian, West Indian, and North American playwrights are presented. Sometimes performances are staged at the International Bazaar. Call for information. Performances of both of the above groups are advertised in local papers.

## CASINOS

### Lucayan Beach Casino
In the Lucayan Beach Resort, Royal Palm Way. ☎ **809/373-7777.**

The center of casino action at Lucaya Beach, this casino is as large as its competitor (see below). With 20,000 square feet, it offers 550 super slots. Happy hour lasts daily from 4 to 7pm. Novices can take free gaming lessons daily at 11am or 7pm. The casino is open daily from 9am to 3am. Entrance is free.

### Princess Casino
The Mall at W. Sunrise Hwy. ☎ **809/352-7811.**

Most of the nightlife in Freeport/Lucaya centers around this glittering, giant, Moroccan-style palace, one of the largest casinos in the Bahamas and the

Caribbean. Under this Moorish-domed structure, visitors play games of chance and attend Las Vegas–type floor shows. They can also dine in the gourmet restaurant, the Crown Room (see "Where to Dine"). The casino is open daily from 9am to 4am. Entrance is free.

# CABARET

### Casino Royale Showroom

In the Bahamas Princess Resort and Casino, the Mall at W. Sunrise Hwy. ☎ **809/352-6721.** Cover (including two drinks) $25.

The shows here come and go, but there are usually Las Vegas–type revues. Expect more than a dozen performers who cavort in Goombay-inspired colors with lots of glitter and a smattering of toplessness. Advance reservations are a good idea. Two shows a night are presented from Tuesday to Sunday, with the first at 8:30 and the second at 10:45pm. Usually closed for two weeks during the month of September.

### Flamingo Showcase Theatre

In the Lucayan Beach Resort, Royal Palm Way. ☎ **809/373-7777.** Cover (including two drinks) $29.95.

If you're staying at Lucaya, you'll want to attend the Flamingo Showcase Theatre. The Las Vegas–type revues here are among the best in the Bahamas. Performances are Monday through Saturday at 8 and 10pm. Reservations are required. A dinner-and-show package includes a buffet dinner, costing $39.95 per person, except on Thursday when it's a steak-and-lobster buffet.

# A DISCO

### Club Estee

Port Lucaya Marketplace, Royal Palm Way. ☎ **809/373-2777.** Cover $5–$8, depending on the venue. Drinks from $3.50 each.

This is considered the most energetic and interesting disco on Grand Bahama Island, reigning almost without competition except for the bar-and-music facilities of the island's large resorts. It contains all its attractions on one sprawling level of a building outfitted in a brightly colored tropical theme. There's one enormous dance floor, two bars (one very large, the other intimate), and a changing array of virtually every kind of amplified and highly danceable music.

The club was named, incidentally, after the mother (Estee) of its Swiss-born owner, Liliane Miller. It is open Tuesday to Sunday from 9pm until very late.

# THE CLUB & MUSIC SCENE

### Yellow Bird Show Club

In the Castaways Resort, International Bazaar. ☎ **809/373-7368.** Cover (including two drinks and the tip) $20.

In the rear of the Castaways Resort, this spot offers an evening of Bahamian entertainment, with steel drums, the limbo, conga drums telling stories, the fire dance, and glass eating. The show even presents its highly stylized version of the Caribbean Queen of Calypso. From Monday through Saturday, doors open at 9pm, with show time at 10pm. You can disco here after the show.

## 9  An Easy Excursion

One of your most refreshing days on Grand Bahama can be spent by escaping from the plush hotels and casinos of Freeport/Lucaya and heading to West End, 28 miles from Freeport. At this old fishing village you'll get glimpses of how things used to be before package-tour groups began descending on Grand Bahama.

To reach West End, you head north along Queen's Highway, going through Eight Mile Rock and on to the northernmost point of the island. West End has several good restaurants, so you can plan to make a day (or a night) of it.

A lot of the old buildings of the village now stand dilapidated, but a nostalgic air prevails. Many old-timers remember when rum boats were busy and the docks buzzed with activity day and night. This was from about 1919 to 1933, when Prohibition reigned in the United States—but not with great success. West End was so close to the U.S. mainland that rum-running became a lucrative business, with booze flowing out of West End into Florida at night. Al Capone is reputed to have been a frequent visitor.

Villages along the way to West End have colorful names, such as Hawksbill Creek. For a preview of some local life, try to visit the fish market along the harbor here. You'll pass some thriving harbor areas, too, but the vessels you'll see will be oil tankers, not rumrunners.

Eight Mile Rock is a hamlet of mostly ramshackle houses that stretch along both sides of the road for—you guessed it—eight miles. At West End, you come to an abrupt stop. Then it's time to visit the weathered old Star Club (see below). If you stick around till night, you're likely to hear some calypso music nearby. You can also enjoy a meal at the Buccaneer Club before heading back to Freeport/Lucaya to catch the last show at the casino.

## WHERE TO DINE

### Buccaneer Club

Deadman's Reef. ☎ **809/349-3794.** Reservations required. Appetizers $3.50–$7; main courses $16.50–$27. AE, MC, V. Dinner Tues–Sun 5–10:30pm. West End bus. CONTINENTAL.

The Buccaneer Club is a tropical version of a German beer garden. The whimsical decor was created by Heinz Fischbacher and his Bahamian wife, Kitty. The compound is ringed with stone walls, within which are palm-dotted terraces where foot-stomping Alpine music provides lots of fun for the yachting crowd you'll see here. The collection of inner rooms contains mismatched crystal chandeliers, pine trim, and a beer-hall ambience that's unique in the Bahamas. Main dishes are likely to include beef tenderloin, wienerschnitzel, breaded shrimp, veal Oskar, and surf and turf. Twice a week, the Fischbachers have beach parties, which cost $35 per person. The price includes transportation from hotels, an hour-long open bar, a buffet, a beer-drinking contest, crab races, limbo dancing, and lively games of musical chairs.

### Pier One

Freeport Harbour. ☎ **809/352-6674.** Reservations recommended for dinner. Appetizers (lunch and dinner) $3.75–$14.50; lunch main courses $4.50–$24.50; dinner main courses $15.95–$38.50. AE, MC, V. Lunch Mon–Sat 11am–4pm; dinner daily 4–10pm, Sun 3–10pm. West End bus. BAHAMIAN/INTERNATIONAL.

Many people head here because it's close to the cruise-ship dock—this is the first Bahamian restaurant many visitors see. It rises on stilts a few steps from the water's edge. A footbridge leads into an interior loaded with nautical artifacts. Don't overlook the high-ceilinged bar as a place for a round of drinks before your meal. There are several dining rooms, the most desirable of which overlooks schools of fish. The lunch fare includes a delectable version of a cream-based clam chowder, lobster soup, fresh oysters, the fresh fish of the day, and pan-fried grouper. Dinner specialties include baked stuffed flounder, coconut-flavored shrimp, shrimp curry, and roast prime rib. For dessert, you might try Italian rum cake or key lime pie.

## The Star Club

Bayshore Rd. ☎ **809/346-6207.** Reservations not required. Appetizers $2–$3.50; main courses $8–$15. No credit cards. Daily 24 hours. West End bus. AMERICAN.

When it was built in the 1940s, this was the first hotel on Grand Bahama. Today it contains the only 24-hour-a-day bar and snack bar on the island, which sometimes encourages people from the casino to motor out here after a night at the tables. There's also a pool hall with taped music. You'll probably be able to strike up a conversation with Austin Henry Grant, Jr., a former Bahamian senator who owns the place, and his wife, Anne. Mr. Grant knew many of the famous guests who stayed here incognito in the 1940s, when West End enjoyed a cachet that it has since lost. A full range of drinks is available as well as Bahamian chicken in the bag, hamburgers, cheeseburgers, fish-and-chips, and "fresh sexy" conch prepared as chowder, fritters, or salads. Drinks cost $3.

# 7

# Bimini, The Berry Islands & Andros

In this chapter we begin a journey through the Family Islands—a very different world from that found in the major tourist meccas of Nassau, Cable Beach, Paradise Island, and Freeport/Lucaya.

Bimini, the Berry Islands, and Andros are each quite different. Bimini is famous and overrun with tourists, particularly in summer, but visitors practically have the Berry Islands to themselves. These two islands are to the north and west of Nassau and might be called the "westerly islands," as they, along with Grand Bahama, lie at the northwestern fringe of the Bahamas. As such, they are the closest islands to the Florida coastline.

In contrast, the much larger Andros is located southwest of Nassau. In many ways Andros is the most fascinating. Actually a series of islands, it is laced with creeks and densely forested inlands, once said to have been inhabited by mysterious creatures.

## 1 Bimini

Bimini is known as the big-game fishing capital of the world, and fishing is excellent throughout the year in flats, on the reefs, and in the streams. Ponce de León didn't find the legendary Fountain of Youth on Bimini, but Ernest Hemingway came to write and fish and publicize Bimini around the world with his novel *Islands in the Stream.* He also wrote much of *To Have and Have Not* on Bimini.

Fifty miles east of Miami, Bimini consists of a number of islands, islets, and cays, including North and South Bimini, the targets of most visitors. You'll most often encounter the word "Bimini," but it might be more proper to say the "Biminis" since North Bimini and South Bimini are two distinct islands, separated by a narrow ocean passage. There is ferry service between the two. Tourist facilities are on North Bimini, mostly in Alice Town, its major settlement.

Guided by native fishers, visitors can go bonefishing or deep-sea fishing. Divers find the reefs laced with conch, lobster, coral, and many tropical fish. Sightseers are allowed to visit the Lerner Marine Laboratory for Marine Research on North Bimini.

Off North Bimini, in 30 feet of water, are some large hewn-stone formations. Many people believe them to be from the lost continent of Atlantis.

## What's Special About Bimini, The Berry Islands & Andros

Beaches
- The eastern shore of Andros, stretching for some 100 miles, is an almost uninterrupted palm grove opening onto beaches of white or beige sand. Snorkelers find a colorful underwater world.

Great Islands
- Bimini, former stamping ground of Ernest Hemingway and the big-game fishing capital of the Bahamas.
- Andros, largest of the Bahamian islands (40 miles wide, 100 miles long) and the least explored archipelago. It's also the bonefish capital of the Bahamas.
- The Berry Islands, two dozen little cays—most of them uninhabited except by rare birds using them as nesting grounds.

A Coral Reef
- The Andros Barrier Reef, the second largest in the world, easily accessible from the shore.

Literary Shrines
- The Compleat Angler, Bimini, a museum of writer Ernest Hemingway's memorabilia from his Bimini days in the 1930s.
- The End of the World Bar, Bimini, which the late Congressman Adam Clayton Powell used as a hangout in the 1960s. Now a "mandatory" watering hole for all visitors.

Special Events
- The annual Bacardi Rum Billfish Tournament and the Hemingway Billfish Tournament brings world anglers to Bimini in March.

Bimini's location off the Florida coastline is at a point where the Gulf Stream meets the Bahama Banks. That has made Bimini a favorite cruising ground for America's yachting set, who follow the channel between North and South Bimini into a spacious, sheltered harbor where they can stock up on food, drink, fuel, and supplies at well-equipped marinas.

Hook-shaped North Bimini is $7^1/2$ miles long. Combined with South Bimini, it makes up a landmass of only 9 square miles. That's why Alice Town looks so crowded. Another reason is that a large part of Bimini is privately owned, and in spite of pressure from the Bahamian government, the landholders have not sold their acreage yet—so Bimini can't "spread out" until they do.

At Alice Town, the land is so narrow that you can walk "from sea to shining sea" in just a short time. Most of Bimini's population of some 1,600 people live in Alice Town. Other hamlets include Bailey Town and Porgy Bay.

South Florida visitors flock to Bimini in the summer months; winter, especially the season from mid-December to mid-March, is quieter. Fishers, as mentioned, and divers are attracted to Bimini, and have been for years. But in recent years Bimini is attracting more and more visitors who don't care about sports at all. If you're not a fisherperson or scuba diver, one of the most interesting experiences in Bimini is to cruise the cays that begin south of South Bimini. Each has its own special interest, beginning with Turtle Rocks and stretching to South Cat Cay (the latter of which is uninhabited). Along the way you'll pass Holm Cay, Gun Cay, and North Cat Cay.

If you go to Bimini, you'll hear a lot of people mention Cat Cay, and you may want to go there. You can't stay overnight on the island, which lies eight miles off South Bimini, unless you are a member of **Cat Cay Yacht Club,** with headquarters at 1100 Lee Wagener Blvd., Suite 101, Fort Lauderdale, FL 33315 (☎ **305/ 359-8272**). The initiation fee is $10,000. This is a privately owned island, attracting titans of industry and such famous families as the Goulds. It is for the exclusive use of Cat Cay Club members and their guests, who enjoy a golf course, a large marina, white-sand beaches, and club facilities such as restaurants and bars. Many wealthy Americans maintain homes on the island, which has a private airstrip (Chalk's International flies into the cay from Fort Lauderdale and Miami).

Don't confuse Cat Cay with Cat Island, far to the south (see Chapter 11).

## GETTING THERE

*Note:* A passport or a birth certificate with picture ID is required for entry to Bimini. An outbound (return) ticket must be presented to Bahamian Customs before you will be allowed entry. Passengers returning from Bimini to the United States also must pay a $15 departure tax.

**BY PLANE**   Although it lies closer to the Florida coastline than any of the other Bahamian islands, many Americans fly to Bimini, often by chartering a small aircraft or by flying their own plane. The island's only airstrip is at the southern tip of South Bimini, a time-consuming transfer and ferryboat ride away from Alice Town on North Bimini, site of most of the archipelago's hotels and yacht facilities.

The best way to avoid this transfer is with the small Chalk's International Airlines (previously recommended in Chapter 3), located at 1100 Lee Wagener Blvd., Fort Lauderdale, FL 33315 (☎ toll free **800/4-CHALKS**). Chalks has a fleet of 17-passenger amphibious aircraft that land in the waters near Alice Town three times a day. The 20- to 30-minute flights depart from the calm waters near Watson Island Terminal, near downtown Miami, twice a day. A round-trip ticket costs $154.95. There is a baggage allowance of only 30 pounds per passenger. If you're carrying heavy travel or fishing gear, you'll be hit with overweight charges. In addition, Chalk's doesn't allow any hand luggage on board. Every piece of your luggage must be checked and weighed in.

**BY BOAT**   In olden days, long before anyone ever heard of Chalk's International Airlines, the traditional way of going from Nassau to Bimini was by a slow-moving boat. That sea trip still exists. You can go by sea on the MV *Bimini Mack,* leaving from Potter's Cay Dock in Nassau and stopping at Cat Cay and Bimini. The vessel leaves Nassau weekly but with no set schedule. For details about departure, call the dockmaster at Potter's Cay Dock in Nassau (☎ **809/393-1064**).

## GETTING AROUND

If you've taken my advice and traveled lightly to Bimini, you can walk to your hotel from the point where the Chalk's seaplane lands in Alice Town. If not, then a small minibus will transport you for $3 per person. If you arrive at the small airport on South Bimini, it is a $5 taxi and ferry ride to Alice Town.

Very few visitors need a car on Bimini—in fact, there are no car-rental agencies. Most people walk to where they want to go. The walk is up and down King's Highway, which has no sidewalks. It's so narrow that two automobiles have a tough time squeezing by.

# The Biminis & Andros

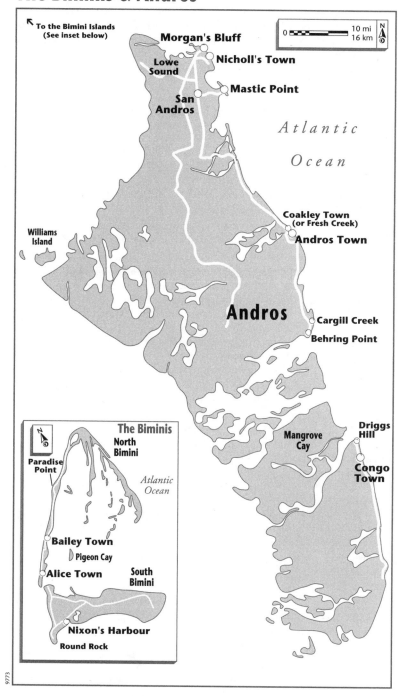

**To the Bimini Islands**
(See inset below)

0    10 mi
16 km

N

Morgan's Bluff

Nicholl's Town

Lowe
Sound

Mastic Point

San
Andros

*Atlantic*

*Ocean*

Williams
Island

Coakley Town
(or Fresh Creek)

Andros Town

**Andros**

Cargill Creek

Behring Point

Driggs
Hill

Mangrove
Cay

Congo
Town

## The Biminis

N

North
Bimini

Paradise
Point

*Atlantic
Ocean*

**Bailey Town**

Pigeon Cay

**Alice Town**

South
Bimini

**Nixon's Harbour**

Round Rock

9773

This highway, lined with low-rise buildings, splits Alice Town on North Bimini. If you're a beachcombing type, stick to the side bordering the Gulf Stream. It's here you'll find the best beaches. The harborside at Alice Town contains a handful of inns (many of which are reviewed below), along with marinas and docks unloading supplies. You'll see many Floridians arriving on yachts.

## FAST FACTS: Bimini

**Banks**   The Royal Bank of Canada has a branch office in Alice Town (☎ **809/ 347-3031**), open Monday and Friday 9am to 3pm and Tuesday, Wednesday, and Thursday 9am to 1pm.

**Churches**   Houses of worship include the largest congregation, Mount Zion Baptist, P.O. Box 645 (☎ **809/347-2056**), and the Anglican Church Rectory, P.O. Box 666 (☎ **809/347-2268**).

**Clothing**   If you're going to Bimini in the winter months, you'd better take along a windbreaker for those occasional chilly nights.

**Customs & Immigration**   The Chalk's plane from Miami stops right near the Alice Town office of Customs and Immigration (☎ **809/368-2030**) for the Bahamas. There's only one Immigration officer, plus another Customs official.

In Miami you will have been handed a Bahamian Immigration Card, which you should have filled out. You must carry proof of your citizenship. For U.S. visitors, that most ideally would be a passport, but a voter-registration card or a birth certificate will also do. The latter two require photo ID. Regrettably, many passengers cross over from Miami with only a driver's license, which will not be accepted by Immigration. Customs may or may not examine your baggage.

**Drugs**   The rumrunners of the Prohibition era have now given way to a more deadly criminal: the smuggler of illegal drugs into the United States from the Bahamas. Because of its proximity to the U.S. mainland, Bimini, as is no secret to anyone, is now a major drop-off point for drugs, many of which have found their way here from Colombia, South America. If not intercepted by the U.S. Coast Guard, those drugs will find their way to the Florida mainland and eventually to the rest of the United States.

Buying and/or selling illegal drugs such as cocaine and marijuana in the Bahamas is an extremely risky business. You may be approached several times by pushers in Bimini, but make sure you don't get "pushed" into jail. If caught with any illegal drugs in Bimini, or elsewhere in the Bahamas, you will be apprehended and will face immediate imprisonment.

Incidentally, all sorts of undercover agents, particularly U.S. narcotics agents, are likely to be found on Bimini, often bearded and sometimes looking like a 1967 "hippie," blending well into the social landscape.

**Emergencies**   To call the police or report a fire, dial **919.**

**Laundry**   Most of the housekeeping staffs of the major hotels, for a fee, will be glad to do your laundry for you.

**Mail**   If you're sending mail back to the United States, I suggest you skip the Bahamian postal service entirely and drop your letter off at Chalk's Airlines special basket. You can use U.S. postage stamps, and your mail will reach its mainland target far quicker than by the usual route.

**Medical Care**   There are a doctor, nurses, and a dentist on the island, as well as the North Bimini Medical Clinic (☎ **809/347-3210**). However, for a medical emergency, patients are usually airlifted to either Miami or Nassau. Helicopters can land in the well-lit baseball field on North Bimini.

# WHERE TO STAY

Accommodations in Bimini are extremely limited, and it's almost impossible to get a room during one of the big fishing tournaments unless you've reserved way in advance. Inns are cozy and simple, many often family owned and operated (chances are, your innkeeper's name will be Brown). Furnishings are often time worn, the paint chipped. No one puts on airs here: the dress code, even in the evening, is very simple and relaxed. From where you're staying in Alice Town, it's usually easy to walk to another hotel for dinner or drinks.

For an explanation of rate symbols, refer to "Tips on Accommodations" in Chapter 3.

## MODERATE

### ✪ Bimini Big Game Fishing Club & Hotel

King's Hwy., P.O. Box 609, Alice Town, Bimini, the Bahamas, or P.O. Box 523238, Miami, FL 33152. ☎ **809/347-3391, 305/447-7480** in Miami, or toll free 800/327-4149 in the U.S. Fax 809/347-3392. 35 rms. 12 cottages, 4 penthouse apts. A/C TV TEL. Year-round, $149–$159 single or double; $178 cottage for one or two; $298 penthouse. Extra person $22. Continental breakfast $6 extra. (EP rates.) AE, MC, V. Free parking.

Run by the Bacardi rum people, this is the premier place for accommodations in Bimini. Filled with anglers and yachties, the hotel is the largest place to stay on the island. It's a self-contained world with well-furnished guest rooms in the main building, surrounded by cottages and luxurious penthouse apartments, the latter often housing VIPs. The general manager, Curtis Carroll, is the most experienced hotelier on the island, and he will see to your requests and help you ease your adjustment to Bimini, especially if you want to know about fishing in all its many forms.

Established in 1946, the hotel places most of its accommodations in its central structure, where each unit is large and equipped with two beds. Everything is clean and comfortable, and the rooms have patios or porches opening onto a marina and the club's swimming pool. The ground-floor cottages are even more spacious than the standard bedrooms and have tiny kitchenettes with refrigerators—but cooking is strictly forbidden. If you want to charcoal-broil your catch of the day, you will have to use one of the outdoor grills.

A freshwater swimming pool is set aside for guests so that it won't be overrun with day-trippers. Guests can also play tennis. Even if you didn't arrive by yacht, you may want to stroll over to the dockmaster's office and look at those who did. This 100-slip marina is where incoming yachts must clear Bahamian Customs and Immigration.

The hotel is also the best place to go for food on the island, plus it's an entertainment hub (see "Where to Dine" and "Bimini After Dark," below). Usually the best anglers at the big-game fishing tournaments stay here, and during the tournaments it's next to impossible to get a room without reservations long in advance.

### Bimini Blue Water Resort Ltd.

King's Hwy., P.O. Box 601, Alice Town, Bimini, the Bahamas. ☎ **809/347-3166.** Fax 809/347-3293. 10 rms, 2 suites. A/C TV. Year-round, $90 single or double; $190 suite; $285 Marlin Cottage. (EP rates.) AE, MC, V. Free parking.

Blue Water, essentially a resort complex for sportfishers, is one of the finest in the Bahamas, with complete dockside services, containing 32 modern slips. It has as its main building a white frame waterfront Bahamian guest house, the Anchorage, where Michael Lerner, the noted fisherman, used to live. It's at the top of the hill, with a dining room and bar from which you can look out onto the ocean. Its regular bedrooms contain double beds, wood-paneled walls, and white furniture. Picture-window doors lead to private balconies. A swimming pool, set amid a tropical garden with an adjoining refreshment bar, is also available.

The Marlin Cottage, although much altered, was one of Hemingway's retreats in the 1930s, and he used it as a main setting in *Islands in the Stream*. It has three bedrooms, three baths, a large living room, and two porches. In honor of his memory, the hotel sponsors the Hemingway Billfish Tournament every March.

## INEXPENSIVE

### ⑤ Compleat Angler Hotel

King's Hwy., P.O. Box 601, Alice Town, Bimini, the Bahamas. ☎ **809/347-3122** (or contact Chalk's International Airlines, Watson Island, Miami, FL 33132, for reservations). Fax 809/347-3293. 12 rms. A/C. Year-round, $65 single; $75–$80 double. AE, DC, V. Free parking.

Right on the main street, and affiliated with Bimini Blue Water Resort, this small and time-worn hotel was built in the 1930s, when big-game fishing was at its peak. The building is designed like an old country house, with Bahamian timber. The wood on the face of the building is from rum barrels used during the Prohibition era. Ernest Hemingway made the hotel his headquarters on and off from 1935 to 1937 while he was stalking marlin, and the room in which he stayed is still available to guests. He penned parts of *To Have and Have Not* here. At the bar, Ossie Brown, bartender, host, and manager, will be helpful. You can swim, dine, shop, or fish right at your doorstep, and fishing charters can be booked at the hotel. *Note:* Because of the famous, noisy bar on the premises, this hotel is only suitable for night owls.

# WHERE TO DINE

## EXPENSIVE

### ✪ Gulfstream Restaurant

In the Bimini Big Game Fishing Club & Hotel, King's Hwy., Alice Town. ☎ **809/347-3391.** Reservations recommended for dinner. Appetizers $3.50–$14; main courses $13.50–$28. AE, MC, V. Breakfast daily 7:30–10:30am; dinner Wed–Mon 7–10:30pm. AMERICAN/CONTINENTAL.

This place consistently serves the finest food on the island in its curved dining room opening onto the pool. Murals from Phil Brinkman depict scenes relating to the legend and lore of Bimini. A good wine list complements the many dishes served. Dinner includes many island specialties such as crisp homemade Bimini bread and freshly caught kingfish, along with broiled local lobster and grouper meunière. Instead of french fries, why not go Bahamian and order peas 'n' rice with your meal? If you're tired of fish, the kitchen will usually serve you a steak, roast prime rib of beef, or lamb chops.

## MODERATE

### Big Game Sports Bar

In the Bimini Big Game Fishing Club & Hotel, King's Hwy., Alice Town. ☎ **809/347-3391.**
Reservations not required. Appetizers $2.50–$5.50; main courses $12.50–$19. AE, MC, V.
Lunch daily noon–4:30pm. SEAFOOD.

During lunch the popular bar serves conch, a Bahamian delicacy, in many ways
including conch fritters, conch salad, conch chowder, and cracked conch, which
is breaded like veal cutlet alla milanese. But conch pizza is the specialty. You can
also order grouper fingers, barbecued back ribs, hamburgers, sandwiches, or a daily
special. Tables overlook the marina and the flats beyond.

### Red Lion Pub

King's Hwy., Alice Town. ☎ **809/347-3259.** Reservations not required. Appetizers $3–$5;
main courses $13–$17. No credit cards. Lunch Mon only, 11:30am–3pm; dinner Tues–Sun
6–10pm; pub Tues–Sun 11am–2pm and 5–11:30pm. BAHAMIAN.

This centrally located restaurant is far larger than its simple facade would imply.
In a relaxed, friendly atmosphere, it's one of the best places on the island to retreat to after a day of fishing and sailing. The dining room is in a large extension
of the original pub, overlooking the marina in back. Above the cash register hangs
a photograph of Stephanie Saunders, daughter of owner Dolores Saunders, who
won the title of Miss Bimini in 1977. The well-prepared meals include the local
fish of the day, cracked conch, barbecued ribs, baked grouper in foil, followed by
either key lime pie or banana cream pie.

### ⑤ Anchorage Dining Room

King's Hwy., Alice Town. ☎ **809/347-3166.** Reservations not required. Appetizers $2.50–
$6.50; main courses $13–$22. AE, MC, V. Lunch daily noon–4pm; dinner daily 6–10pm.
SEAFOOD/BAHAMIAN.

This dining room overlooks the harbor of Alice Town. At night, if you're seeking atmosphere "at the top of the hill," it has the jump on every other establishment. You can see the ocean through picture windows. Have a before-dinner drink
in the bar. The modern, paneled room is filled with captain's chairs and Formica
tables. You might begin your dinner with conch chowder, then follow with one
of the tempting seafood dishes, including spiny broiled lobster or perhaps a chewy
cracked conch. They also do fried Bahamian chicken and a New York sirloin.

# WHAT TO SEE & DO

At the southern tip of North Bimini, **Alice Town** is all that many visitors ever see
of the island. The hotel center of Bimini, it can be thoroughly explored in an hour
or two.

Nothing is spick-and-span in Alice Town. First timers are warned not to judge
the Bahamas by Bimini. A yachting guide poses a question: "Would you judge the
rest of America if you visited only Miami?"

If you're traversing the island, you may want to stop off at the **Bimini Straw
Market,** speak with some of the Bahamians, and perhaps pick up a souvenir.

**King's Highway** runs through the town and continues north. It's lined
with houses painted in such colors as gold, lime, buttercup yellow, and pink—
gleaming in the bright sunshine.

At some point you may notice the ruins of Bimini's first hotel, the Bimini Bay
Rod and Gun Club. Built in the early 1920s, it did a flourishing business until a
hurricane wiped it out later in that decade. It was never rebuilt.

If you're on the trail of Papa Hemingway, you'll want to visit the **Compleat Angler,** King's Highway (☎ 809/347-3122), where there is a museum of Hemingway memorabilia. The collection of prints and writings describes the times he spent in Bimini, mainly from 1935 to 1937. The prints are posted in the sitting room downstairs. In case you didn't read it, Hemingway devoted part of his novel *Islands in the Stream* to Bimini. Much of this memorabilia makes interesting browsing. There is a wide variety of books by Hemingway in the library collection.

If you want to cross over to **South Bimini,** like Ponce de León looking for that Fountain of Youth, you can take a ferry, costing $3 and leaving every 20 minutes from Government Dock. The ferry ride takes about 10 minutes or so.

Once you land on South Bimini, you can rent a taxi to see the island's limited attractions for about $15. There's not a lot to see, but you are likely to hear some "tall tales" worth the cab fare.

One of the chief points of interest can be reached only by boat. It's the *Sapona,* which was built by Henry Ford during World War I. This huge concrete ship lies between South Bimini and Cat Cay. It was once a private club and a rumrunner's storehouse in the Roaring Twenties. The 1929 hurricane blew it ashore, and in World War II, U.S. Navy pilots used it as a practice bomb range. Now spearfishers are attracted to the ruins, looking for the giant grouper. The dive operations on Bimini include it in their repertoire.

In terms of **shopping** in Bimini, the Bimini Big Game Fishing Club & Hotel, King's Highway, has some of the best duty-free liquor buys in town. If you're a souvenir collector, ask at the front office for T-shirts, sunglasses, coffee mugs, and Big Game Club hats.

---

## Island in the Stream

Nevil Norton Stuart, a Bahamian, came to Bimini in the late 1920s and purchased the Fountain of Youth, a Prohibition era bar. He renamed it the Bimini Big Game Fishing Club. In 1940 Stuart reclaimed land in Bimini harbor, constructed a marina, and added several cottages along with a desalination plant. Thus began the legend of one of the most highly publicized sportfishing meccas in the world.

Film stars, including Judy Garland and Sir Anthony Hopkins, among others, have lodged at the club. Martin Luther King, Jr., visited twice. Of course, no one immortalized the island as much as Hemingway, who called it "My Island in the Stream."

Today the complex has grown to more than 50 rooms, including cottages and penthouses, and it's owned by the rum makers, Bacardi International. In the 100-slip marina can be found enormous sportfishing boats, costing more than several million dollars, proudly standing alongside simple outboard powered runabouts.

Today the club hosts many fishing tournaments throughout the year, including the Bacardi Rum Billfish Tournament in March. This week-long world-class event attracts the biggest names in sportfishing, and is regarded by many fishers as the event of the year to win.

## SPORTS A TO Z

**SNORKELING & SCUBA**   This has become an increasingly popular sport in the last 20 years. Visitors can snorkel above a wonderland of black coral gardens and reefs, or go scuba diving, exploring the wrecks and the blue holes, plus a mystery formation on the bottom of the sea that many people claim is part of the lost continent of Atlantis. A cliff extends 2,000 feet down in Bimini waters—known for a breathtaking drop-off at the rim of the continental shelf, an underwater mountain. A major attraction for snorkelers and divers, not to mention fish, is the *Sapona*, lying hard aground in 15 feet of water ever since it was blown there by a hurricane in 1929. In the heyday of the Roaring Twenties, the ship served as a private club and speakeasy.

### Bimini Undersea Adventures
King's Hwy., Alice Town. ☎ **809/347-3089.**

The people to see here are Bill and Nowdla Keefe. Full-day snorkeling trips cost $25. Scuba rates are $30 for a one-tank dive, $59 for a two-tank dive, and $79 for a three-tank dive. Night dives go for $40. All-inclusive dive packages are also available. For further information or reservations, the Keefes can be reached by mail at P.O. Box 21766, Fort Lauderdale, FL 33335 (☎ **305/359-0065** or toll free **800/327-8150**).

**SPORTFISHING**   Bimini is called the "Big Game Fishing Capital of the World," and Ernest Hemingway, above all others, has given fame to the sport practiced here. But Zane Grey came this way, too, as did Howard Hughes. Richard Nixon used to fish here aboard the posh cruiser of his friend Bebe Rebozo. In the trail of Hemingway, fishers today still flock to cast lines in the Gulf Stream and the Bahama Banks.

Of course, everyone's after the "big one," and a lot of world records have been set in this area: marlin, sailfish, swordfish, wahoo, grouper, and tuna. Fishing folk can spin cast for panfish and can boat snapper, yellowtail, and kingfish. Many experts consider stalking bonefish, long a pursuit of baseball great Ted Williams, to be the toughest challenge in the sport.

Five charter boats are available in Bimini for big-game and little-game fishing, with some center-console boats rented for both bottom and reef angling. At least eight bonefishing guides are available, and experienced fishers who have made repeated visits to Bimini know the particular skills of each of these men who take you for a half or full day of "fishing in the flats," as bonefishing is termed. Most skiffs hold two anglers, and part of the fun in hiring a local guide is to hear their fish stories and other island lore. If they tell you that 16-pound bonefish have turned up, don't think it's invented. Such catches have been documented.

Reef-and-bottom fishing are easier than bonefishing, and can be more productive. There are numerous species of snapper and grouper to be found, as well as amberjack. This is the simplest and least expensive boat fishing, as you need only a local guide, a little boat, tackle, and a lot of bait. Sometimes you can negotiate to go out bottom fishing with a Bahamian, but chances are he'll ask you to pay for the boat fuel for his trouble. That night, back at your Bimini inn, the cook will serve you the red snapper or grouper you caught that day.

Most hotel owners will tell you to bring your own fishing gear to Bimini. A couple of small shops sell some items, but you'd better bring major equipment with you. Bait, of course, can be purchased locally.

---

### Myths of Bimini

Bimini has long been shrouded in myths, none greater than the one claiming that the lost continent of Atlantis lies off the shores of North Bimini. This legend grew because of the weirdly shaped rock formations that lie submerged in about 30 feet of water near the shoreline. Pilots flying over North Bimini have reported what they envision as a "lost highway" under the sea. This myth continues, and many scuba divers are attracted to North Bimini to explore these rocks.

   Ponce de León came to South Bimini looking for that legendary Fountain of Youth. He never found it, but people still come to South Bimini today in search of it. Near the turn of the century it was reported that a religious sect came here to "take the waters." Supposedly there was a bubbling fountain, or at least a spring, in those days. If you arrive on South Bimini and seem interested enough, a local guide (for a fee) will be only too happy to show you "the exact spot" where the Fountain of Youth once bubbled.

---

### Bimini Big Game Fishing Club & Hotel
King's Hwy., Alice Town. ☎ **809/347-2391.**

   Here you can charter a 41-foot Hatteras at $750 for a full day of fishing, $400 for a half day. A Bertram, either 31 or 28 feet, will cost $550 for a full day, $400 for a half.

### Bimini Blue Water Marina
King's Hwy., Alice Town. ☎ **809/347-3166.**

   This place offers a 28-foot Bertram with tackle and crew for $600 or $350 for a full or half day, respectively.

   **TENNIS**   You'll find hard-surface courts at the Bimini Big Game Fishing Club & Hotel (☎ **809/347-2391**), King's Highway, which are complimentary and reserved for hotel guests and members. The courts are lit for night play, and you can purchase balls at the club.

## BIMINI AFTER DARK
   You can dance to a Goombay beat or try to find some disco music. Most people have a leisurely dinner, drink a lot in one of the local taverns, and go back to their hotel rooms by midnight so they can get up early to continue pursuing the elusive "big one" the next morning. Every bar in Alice Town is likely to claim that it was Hemingway's favorite. He did hit quite a few of them, in fact. Most drinks cost $3.50, and there's rarely a cover charge anywhere unless some special entertainment is being offered.

### The Compleat Angler Hotel
King's Hwy., Alice Town. ☎ **809/347-3122.**

   This is the favorite watering hole for every visiting Hemingway buff. Ossie Brown, the bartender (he's also the manager), is said to make the best planter's punch in the Bahamas, and he challenges anyone to make a better one. Nightly entertainment by a calypso band turns this place into a real island hot spot, featuring Goombay drinks from 9pm to 1am. The place, as mentioned, is filled with Hemingway memorabilia, and it's open daily from 11am "until . . ."

## ✪ End of the World Bar
King's Hwy., Alice Town. No phone.

One of the almost mandatory requirements, to firmly establish you on Bimini soil, is to have a drink in this bar. When you get here, you may think you're in the wrong place—it's just a waterfront shack with sawdust on the floor. It was the late congressman from New York, Adam Clayton Powell, who put this bar on the map in the 1960s. Between stints in Washington battling Congress and preaching at the Abyssinian Baptist Church in Harlem, the controversial congressman might be found sitting at a table here. Regardless of what Powell's fellow congressmen thought of him, he was a hero locally, and many people of Bimini still remember him. While the bar doesn't attract the media attention it did in Powell's heyday, it's still going strong as a local favorite, and everybody takes a felt marker and signs his or her name. It's open daily from 11am to 3am.

## Bimini Big Game Fishing Club & Hotel
King's Hwy., Alice Town. ☎ **809/347-3391.**

Beginning at midmorning and lasting until midnight at least, the bars of this previously recommended hotel are the most frequented places in town. Tall tales of the big one that got away fill the air. The Big Game Sports Bar (see "Where to Dine," above) starts serving its famed conch pizza at noon. No less than four TV sets are positioned for your favorite sports program, or you may want to enjoy a hand of cards. It's the best room in which to entertain yourself during those lazy days in Bimini. The Barefoot Bar, open from midmorning to late afternoon, is the poolside bar, serving favorite island drinks and ice cold beers. Off the main dining room of the Gulfstream Restaurant is the Gulfstream Bar, featuring Ratti, the island's best known calypsonian, singing the songs of the island and strumming them on a guitar. Naturally, since Bacardi owns the place, all the rum punches are made with Bacardi rums.

# 2 The Berry Islands

A dangling chain of cays and islets on the eastern edge of the Great Bahama Bank, the unspoiled and serene Berry Islands begin 35 miles northwest of New Providence (Nassau), 150 miles east of Miami. This 30-island archipelago is known to sailors, fishers, yachtspeople, Jack Nicklaus, and a Rockefeller or two, as well as the beachcombers who explore its uninhabited reaches.

As a center of fishing, the Berry Islands are second only to Bimini. At the tip of the Tongue of the Ocean, called TOTO, world-record-setting big-game fish are found, along with endless flats (the shallow bodies of water near the shore where bonefish congregate). In the "Berries" you can find your own tropical paradise islet, enjoying, totally isolated and sans wardrobe, the white-sand beaches and palm-fringed shores. Some of the best shell collecting in the Bahamas is found on the beaches of the Berry Islands and in their shallow-water flats.

The main islands are, beginning in the north, Great Stirrup Cay, Cistern Cay, Great Harbour Cay, Anderson Cay, Haines Cay, Hoffmans Cay, Bond's Cay, Sandy Cay, Whale Cay, and Chub Cay.

The largest island within the Berry Islands is Great Harbour Cay, which sprawls over 3,800 acres of sand, rock, and scrub. The development here received a great deal of publicity when Douglas Fairbanks, Jr., was connected with its investors. It became a multimillion-dollar resort for jet-setters who occupied waterfront town houses and villas overlooking the golf course or marina. There are 7 1/2 miles of almost solitary beachfront. Once Cary Grant, Brigitte Bardot, and other stars romped on this beach.

Bond's Cay, a bird sanctuary in the south, and tiny Frazer's Hog Cay (stock is still raised here) are both privately owned. An English company used to operate a coconut and sisal plantation on Whale Cay, also near the southern tip.

Sponge fishermen and their families inhabit some of the islands. One of the very small cays, lying north of Frazer's Hog Cay and Whale Cay, has, in my opinion, the most unappetizing name in the Bahamian archipelago: Cockroach Cay.

## GETTING THERE

Great Harbour Cay is an official point of entry for the Bahamas if you're **flying** from a foreign territory such as the United States. You can fly to the Great Harbour Cay airstrip. Trans Island Airways (☎ **809/377-7172**) offers two flights a day from Nassau to Great Harbour Cay.

If you're contemplating the mail-boat sea-voyage route, the MV *Champion II* leaves Potter's Cay Dock in Nassau weekly on Tuesday at 7pm, heading for the Berry Islands. Inquire at the Potter's Cay Dock for an up-to-the-minute report (contact the dockmaster at **809/393-1064**).

**ESSENTIALS**   The Great Harbour Cay **Medical Clinic** is at Bullock's Harbour on Great Harbour Cay (☎ **809/367-8400**). The **police** station is also at Bullock's Harbour, Great Harbour Cay (☎ **809/367-8344**).

## GREAT HARBOUR CAY
### WHAT TO SEE & DO

The largest concentration of people—an estimated 500 residents—live on the most populated island of the Berry chain, Great Harbour Cay. Its main settlement is Bullock's Harbour, which might be called the "capital of the Berry Islands." The cay is about 1 1/2 miles wide and some 8 miles long. There isn't much in town: a grocery store and some restaurants. Most visitors arrive to stay at the Great Harbour Cay Yacht Club & Marina (see "Where to Stay & Dine," below),outside of town. Fisherpeople are especially fond of the place.

Reached from Miami, 150 miles to the west, in about an hour, or in half a day by powerboat, Great Harbour Cay lies between Grand Bahama Island and New Providence (Nassau), and is 60 miles northwest of Nassau. Unlike most islands in the Bahamas, the island isn't flat but contains rolling hills.

Deep-sea fishing possibilities abound here, including billfish, dolphin, king mackerel, and wahoo. Light-tackle bottom fishing is also good, netting yellowtail snapper, barracuda, and triggerfish, as well as plenty of grouper. Bonefishing here is considered among the best in the world.

The Great Harbour Cay marina is called "world class," with some 80 slips and all the amenities. Some of Florida's fanciest yachts pull in here. When you tire of fishing, there are eight miles of white-sand beaches. There is also a nine-hole golf course, designed by Joe Lee, plus four clay tennis courts.

### WHERE TO STAY & DINE

#### Great Harbour Cay Yacht Club & Marina

Great Harbour Cay, Berry Islands, the Bahamas (mailing address: 1441 E. Maple, Suite 300, Troy, MI 48083). ☎ **809/367-8838** or toll free 800/343-7256; 313/689-1580 in Michigan. Fax 809/367-8115. 18 units. A/C TV. Year-round, $90–$290 single or double. AE, MC, V. Free parking.

The two-level waterfront town houses here overlook the marina, each with its own private dock, topped off with a garage and patio. Town houses have a light, airy feeling, with some 1,600 square feet of living space. Each has two bedrooms and 2¹/₂ baths and is suitable for up to six people. Fully equipped kitchens are featured. Beach villas, covered in cedar shakes, have tile floors and a Mediterranean-type decor. They can be rented in various configurations—from studio apartments to two-bedroom units. Daily maid service is included.

Dining facilities include the Wharf, serving breakfast and lunch; Basil's Bar and Restaurant at the end of the marina, serving three meals a day; and the Tamboo Club, at the west end of the marina—open Wednesday through Monday for drinks and dinner only.

## CHUB CAY

Named after a species of fish that thrives in nearby waters, Chub Cay is a name well-known to sportfishing enthusiasts. A self-contained hideaway with a devoted clientele, it's the southernmost of the Berry Islands, separating the mainland of South Florida from the commercial frenzy of Nassau.

It originated in the late 1950s as the strictly private (and rather Spartan) enclave of Texas-based anglers and investors. It was originally uninhabited, but over the years, a staff was imported, dormitory-style housing was built for them, and the island's most famous feature (its state-of-the-art, 90-slip marina) was constructed within the 979-acre island's most prominent feature, a sheltered lagoon.

After recovering from severe damage inflicted in 1992 by Hurricane Andrew, Chub Cay is little more than a tranquil, scrub-covered sand spit with awesome amounts of marine hardware, a dozen well-accessorized private homes, the above-mentioned marina, and a complex of buildings devoted to the Chub Cay Inn (see below). Today, membership in the Club begins at around $2,000 a year and grants reduced rental of marina slips, boat repairs, and rental of hotel rooms and villas. Nonmembers, however, are welcome to use the facilities and rent rooms at the rates listed below.

There's a liquor store and a yachties' commissary on the island, an outlet for the sale of marine supplies, and a concrete runway for landing anything up to and including a 737. Most visitors reach Chub Cay by private yacht from the Florida mainland, but if you prefer to charter your fishing craft on Chub Cay, you'll find a miniarmada of suitable craft at your disposal. Island Express Airlines (☎ 305/359-0380) flies to Chub Cay from Fort Lauderdale at least five times a week (daily except Wednesday and Thursday), charging just under $200 per person round-trip. Charter flights can be arranged with the help of the Chub Cay Inn's desk staff. If you opt to fly here, travel light; there's a baggage allowance of no more than 50 pounds per passenger.

The water temperature around Chub Cay averages a tepid 80 to 85 degrees Fahrenheit year-round, even at relatively deep depths. There's only a small tide change, and under normal conditions, there is no swell or noticeable currents in offshore waters.

Many divers have waxed enthusiastic over the dive spots of Chub Cay, including Chub Wall and Mamma Rhoda Rock. Despite the dozens of examples of rare coral that ring the island, remember that it's forbidden by Bahamian authorities to bring back coral as souvenirs. In fact, it violates local ecological laws to take anything from the sea for purposes other than obtaining food.

It is said that one of the reasons why fishing is so good near Chub Cay is because bait fish and lures are scented by hungry pursuers swimming in from TOTO

(Tongue of the Ocean). They include dolphins, mako sharks, barracudas, wahoos, and the 300-pound blue marlins described by Hemingway in *Islands in the Stream*. Unknown to these big fish, yet another hunter of the human kind is waiting.

## WHERE TO STAY & DINE

### Chub Cay Inn

Chub Cay, Berry Islands, the Bahamas. ☎ **809/325-1490** or toll free 800/662-8555. Fax 809/322-5199. (For expedition of all forms of mail, write Chub Cay Club, P.O. Box 661067, Miami Springs, FL 33266. ☎ **305/445-7830**.) 8 rms, 8 villas, 2 town houses. A/C MINIBAR TV. Year-round, $150 single or double; $300 one-bedroom villa for two with kitchen; $400 two-bedroom villa for four with kitchen; $450 duplex town house for four with kitchen; $500 three-bedroom villa for up to six with kitchen. Discounts available for stays of a week or more. AE, MC, V. Free parking.

Simple, breezy, uncluttered, and comfortable, these air-conditioned accommodations are the only available option on all of Chub Cay. It prides itself on its marina, its freshwater swimming pool, and the many sandy beaches nearby. Throughout the resort, there's a nautical, laid-back kind of feeling, and a clublike atmosphere. Don't expect inspired architecture: Buildings throughout the islands are functional, weatherproof, and not particularly stylish. Most, but not all, have been repaired from the damage of the 1992 hurricane. None of the rooms has a phone, although there are phone facilities available at the reception desk. Their absence enhances the feeling of isolation, a welcome relief to many of the escapist clients.

**Dining/Entertainment:** There's a restaurant (the Harbour House), with its own bar, as well as the Cay Bar set beside the pool, and the Hilltop Bar on the island's highest elevation. This contains a TV for sports broadcasts, pool tables, and occasional bouts of live music.

**Services:** Fishing guides, diving guides, laundry, babysitting.

**Facilities:** Scuba diving, snorkeling, Laundromat, tennis courts, swimming pool, shopping boutique.

## 3 Andros

The largest island in the Bahamas, Andros is also one of the largest unexplored tracts of land in the Western Hemisphere. Mostly flat, its 2,300 square miles are riddled with lakes and creeks, and most of the local population, who still indulge in fire dances and go on wild boar hunts on occasion, live along the shore.

One of the most mysterious islands in the Bahamas, Andros is 100 miles long and 40 miles wide. Its interior is a dense, tropical forest, really rugged bush and mangrove country. The marshy and relatively uninhabited west coast is called the "Mud," and the east coast is paralleled for 120 miles by the second-largest underwater barrier reef in the world. The reef drops to over a mile into the Tongue of the Ocean, or TOTO. On the eastern shore, this "tongue" is 142 miles long and 1,000 fathoms deep.

Lying 170 miles southeast of Miami and 30 miles west of Nassau, Andros, although spoken as if it were one island, is actually three major land areas: **North Andros, Middle Andros,** and **South Andros.** Ferries, operated free by the Bahamian government, ply back and forth over the waters separating Mangrove Cay from South Andros. At the end of the road in North Andros, private arrangements can be made to have a boat take you over to Mangrove Cay. In spite of its size, Andros is very thinly populated, its residents numbering around 5,000, although the tourist population swells it a bit. The temperature range here averages from 72 degrees to 81 degrees Fahrenheit.

The Spaniards, who came this way in the 16th century looking for slaves, called the island La Isla del Espíritu Santo or the "Island of the Holy Spirit," but the name didn't catch on, although it came from the belief that the Holy Spirit dwells over water, with which Andros is abundantly supplied—Andros constantly ships the precious liquid to water-scarce New Providence (Nassau) in barges.

The name used for the island today is believed by some experts to have come from Sir Edmund Andros, a British commander.

You won't find the western side of Andros much written about in yachting guides, as it is almost unapproachable by boat because of the tricky shoals. The east coast, however, is studded with little villages, and hotels have been built here that range from simple guest cottages to dive resorts to fishing camps. "Creeks" (I'd call them rivers) intersect the island at its midpoint. Called "bights," in the main they have three channels. Their width ranges from 5 to 25 miles, and they are dotted with tiny cays and islets. There are miles of unspoiled beach along the eastern shore.

Few people draw comparisons between overly developed Paradise Island and underdeveloped Andros. However, their tourism industry has a common ancestor, Dr. Axel Wenner-Gren, a Swedish industrialist who invested in what was then Hog Island (renamed Paradise Island). Dr. Wenner-Gren also built the Andros Yacht Club, to the south of Fresh Creek on Andros. That now defunct club began to attract the island's first tourists following World War II.

The fishing at Andros is famous, establishing records for blue marlin caught offshore. Skindivers report that the coral reefs are among the most beautiful in the world.

*A word of warning:* Be sure to bring along plenty of mosquito repellent.

## GETTING THERE

**BY PLANE**   Reaching Andros is not that difficult. **Bahamasair** (☎ **800/ 222-4262** in the U.S.) has flights to the airports at Andros Town and San Andros twice daily. Four weekly flights land at Congo Town on South Andros. It is only a 15-minute flight from Nassau to, say, Andros Town. There is also a small airstrip on Mangrove Cay. Flight schedules are subject to change.

If you're going to Small Hope Bay Lodge, there is a 1-hour flight service from Fort Lauderdale to Andros Town.

*Warning:* Make sure you know where you're going in Andros. For example, if you land in South Andros and you've been booked in a hotel at Nicholl's Town, you'll find connections nearly impossible at times (both ferryboats and a rough haul across a bad highway).

Taxi drivers—what few there are—know when the planes from Nassau are going to land, and they drive out to the airports, hoping to drum up some business. Taxis are most often shared. A typical fare from Andros Town Airport to Small Hope Bay Lodge is about $20.

**BY BOAT**   Many locals, along with a few adventurous visitors, use the mail boats as a means of reaching Andros; the trip takes five to seven hours across some beautiful waters.

North Andros is serviced by the MV *Lisa J. II,* a mail boat departing from Potter's Cay Dock in Nassau, heading for Morgan's Bluff, Mastic Point,

## The Three-Toed Bahamian Elf

One of the legends of the island is that aborigines live in the interior. These were thought to be a lost tribe of Native Arawaks—remnants of the archipelago's original inhabitants, who were exterminated by the Spanish centuries ago. However, low-flying planes, looking for evidence of human settlements, have not turned up any indication to support this far-fetched assertion. But who can dispute that chickcharnies (red-eyed Bahamian elves with three toes, feathers, and beards) live on the island? Even the demise of Neville Chamberlain's ill-fated sisal plantation was blamed on these mischievous devils.

The chickcharnie once struck terror into the hearts of superstitious islanders. They were supposed to live in the depths of the Androsian wilderness, making their nests in the tops of two intertwined palm trees. Tales are told of how many a woodsman in the old days endured hardship and misery because he thoughtlessly felled the trees that served as stilts for a chickcharnie nest. Like the leprechauns of Ireland, the chickcharnies belong solely to Andros. They are the Bahamian version of the elves, goblins, fairies, and duppies of other lands. Children may be threatened with them if they fail to behave, and business or domestic calamity is immediately attributed to their malevolent activities.

The origin of the legend is shrouded in mystery. One story has it that the tales began in the late 19th century when a Nassau hunting enthusiast who wanted to protect his duck-hunting grounds in Andros invented the malicious elves to frighten off unwanted interlopers. Another has it that the myth was brought to the Bahamas by bands of Seminoles fleeing Florida in the early 1880s to escape the depredations of white settlers. Some of the Seminoles settled on the northern tip of Andros. But the most probable explanation is one that traces the chickcharnie to a once-living creature—an extinct 3-foot-high flightless barn owl (*Tyto pollens*)—which used to inhabit the Bahamas and West Indies.

According to the Bahamas National Trust, the local conservation authority, such a bird, "screeching, hissing and clacking its bills in characteristic barn owl fashion, hopping onto its victims or pouncing on them from low tree limbs, would have been a memorable sight. And a frightening one."

The species may have survived here into historical times, and Andros, being the largest Bahamian landmass, was probably able to sustain *Tyto pollens* longer than the smaller islands. It is probable that the early settlers on Andros encountered such beasts, and it's possible that *Tyto pollens* was the inspiration for the chickcharnie.

In any event, chickcharnie tales are still told in Andros, and there is no doubt that they will live on as a fascinating part of the Bahamas' cultural legacy.

and Nicholl's Town. It departs Nassau on Wednesday, returning to Nassau on Tuesday.

To reach Central Andros, you have to take the MV *Central Andros Express*, departing from Potter's Cay Dock, in Nassau. The boat goes to Fresh Creek, Behring Point, Blanket Sound, and Stafford Creek, leaving Nassau on Wednesday. It returns to Nassau on Sunday.

For details about sailing and costs, contact the dockmaster at Potter's Cay Dock in Nassau (☎ **809/393-1064**).

## GETTING AROUND

Transportation can be a big problem on Andros. If you have to go somewhere, it's best to use one of the local taxi drivers.

**BY CAR** What cars there are to rent are in North Andros. These are few and far between, owing to the high costs of shipping cars to Andros. The weather also takes a great toll on the cars that are brought in (the salt in the air erodes metal), so no car-rental agencies are represented. Your best bet is to ask at your hotel to see what's available. It's not really recommended that you drive on Andros because roads are mainly unpaved and in bad condition, and gasoline stations are scarce. However, if you'd like to give a car a try, call **Bereth Rent-A-Car,** Fresh Creek (☎ **809/368-2102**), or **Basil Martin,** Mastic Point (☎ **809/329-3169**). Expect to spend from $60 a day, maybe a lot more.

**BY SCOOTER OR BICYCLE** If you'd like to attempt traversing the roads of Andros on a scooter or bicycle, call **Small Hope Bay Lodge,** Fresh Creek (☎ **809/ 368-2014**), and see if one is available for rent.

## FAST FACTS: Andros

**Banks** These are rare on Andros. There is one, the Canadian Imperial Bank of Commerce (☎ **809/329-2382**), in San Andros. It is open Wednesday from 10am to 2pm.

**Clothing** Dress is casual, and don't come to Andros expecting to catch up on your dry cleaning. If you need shirts and blouses washed and ironed, ask at your hotel. Even if they don't have a service themselves, they usually know someone in the community who "takes in wash."

**Hairdressers & Barbers** Women should be prepared to do their own hair, unless someone at a hotel tells them about a local woman "who's studying to be a beautician." Men can get a haircut—and that's it.

**Mall** The island has no big post office as such, although there is a post-handling office in the Commissioner's Office in Nicholl's Town on North Andros (☎ **809/329-2034**). Hotel desks will sell you Bahamian stamps. Make sure you mark cards and letters airmail; otherwise, you'll return home before they do. Each little hamlet in Andros has a store that serves as the post office.

**Medical Care** Government-run clinics are at North Andros (☎ **809/ 329-2121**); at Central Andros (☎ **809/368-2038**); and at South Andros (☎ **809/329-4620**). Bring along whatever drugs (legal ones) or medicines you'll need while visiting Andros. Local supplies are very limited.

**Police** Call the police on North Andros at **919;** on Central Andros at **809/ 368-2626;** and on South Andros at **809/369-0083.**

**Religious Services** Protestant denominations are represented on the island. If you want to attend, ask at your hotel where the nearest place of worship is. Outsiders are usually warmly welcomed and received in local congregations.

**Telephone** Service is available only at the front desks of hotels.

**Traveler's Checks** Your hotel probably will be able to cash traveler's checks for you, but if not, there is one bank on Andros (see "Banks," above).

## WHERE TO STAY

Chances are your hotel will be in North Andros, in either Andros Town or Nicholl's Town.

**North Andros** is the most developed of the three major Andros islands. **Nicholl's Town** is a colorful old settlement with some 600 people and several places serving local foods. Most visitors come to Nicholl's Town to buy supplies at a shopping complex.

Directly to the south is **Mastic Point,** which was founded in 1781. If you ask around, you'll be shown to a couple of concrete-sided dives that offer spareribs and Goombay music. To the north of Nicholl's Town is **Morgan's Bluff,** namesake of Sir Henry Morgan (a pirate later knighted by the British monarch).

**Andros Town,** with its abandoned docks, is another hamlet, lying about a 29-mile drive south of Nicholl's Town. The major reason most visitors come to Andros Town is either to stay at the Small Hope Bay Lodge or to avail themselves of its facilities. The biggest retail industry, Androsia, is in the area, too. The scuba diving—minutes away on the barrier reef—is what lures the world to this tiny place. Many people come here just for the shelling.

On the opposite side of the water is **Coakley Town.** If you're driving, before you get to Andros Town you may want to stop and spend some restful hours on the beach at the hamlet of Staniard Creek, another old settlement on Andros. There's a South Seas aura here.

Now moving south to the second major landmass, **Central Andros** is smaller than either North or South Andros. It's also the least built-up. The island is studded with hundreds upon hundreds of palm trees. Queen's Highway runs along the eastern coastline, but the only thing about this road that's regal is its name. In some $4^1/_2$ miles you can practically travel the island. Talk about sleepy—this place drowses, and for that very reason many people come here to get away from it all. They don't find much in the way of accommodations. There are a few guest houses a half mile from the Mangrove Cay Airport. Boating, fishing, scuba diving, and snorkeling are the popular sports practiced here.

Another hamlet (don't blink as you pass through or you'll miss it) is **Moxey Town,** where you'll see conch being unloaded from the fishing boats.

The third and last major land area, **South Andros** is the home of the wonderfully named Congo Town. The pace here is that of an escargot on a marathon. The Queen's Highway, lined in part with pink-and-white conch shells, runs for about 25 miles or so. The island, as yet undiscovered, has some of the best beaches in the Bahamas, and you can enjoy them almost by yourself.

*Note:* For an explanation of the rate symbols, refer to Chapter 3, "Tips on Accommodations."

## NORTH ANDROS

### Cargill Creek

#### Cargill Creek Lodge

Cargill Creek, Andros, the Bahamas. ☎ **809/368-5129.** Fax 809/368-5046. 11 rms, 3 cottages. A/C TV. Year-round, $165 single; $290 double. (AP rates.) AE, MC, V. Free parking. Closed July–Aug.

One of the best accessorized hotels in the Andros, this 1990 fishing lodge opened on a 7-acre tract containing many fruit trees. At times its guests of flyfishermen and spin fishermen look like one of those famed Ernest Hemingway look-alike contests staged every year in Key West, Florida. The hotel complex consists of white stucco buildings with marine blue trim set directly on the waterfront. Accommodations are furnished with Florida tropical pieces. Cottages contain two full bedrooms, two baths, and a sitting room.

Meals are served in a pleasantly airy restaurant, trimmed with Andros cedar and set close to the waterfront pier and pool with patio. A sample dinner menu might include conch fritters, broiled grouper with a green salad, and rice and pigeon peas, followed by pineapple upside-down cake.

The resort specializes in guided bonefishing on the flats in and around the bights of Andros. Trips can be arranged on-site or as part of a fishing/hotel package that costs about $300 per person. For reservations call the lodge Monday through Saturday from 9am to 5pm.

## Andros Town

### Landmark Hotel & Restaurant

Andros Town, Andros, the Bahamas. ☎ and Fax **809/368-2082.** 15 rms. A/C TV TEL. Winter, from $60 single or double. Off-season, $45 single or double. (EP rates.) No credit cards. Free parking.

The unpretentious Landmark offers the most comfortable rooms in Andros Town. Each is sheathed in planks of pinewood, complete with modern windows, big closets, a private bath, and balcony. Calabash Bay Beach is within a 5-minute walk of the hotel, and guests rarely lack for companionship because of the lively bar and restaurant (Carmetta's) on the premises. The house drink, the Andros Special, is memorable. Full meals are served throughout the day, with lunches priced at around $10 and dinners at around $18. This is one of the most popular nightlife spots on the island. Some of its patrons are nightclubbing students from Andros Island's branch of the Marine Biology Studies Center.

### ✪ Lighthouse Yacht Club & Marina

Andros Town, Andros, the Bahamas. ☎ **809/368-2308** or toll free 800/835-1019. Fax 809/368-2300. 20 rms. A/C TV. Year-round, $130 single or double. MAP $40 per person extra. AE, MC, V. Free parking.

One of the newest resorts on Andros, this complex lies at the mouth of Fresh Creek, featuring an 18-slip marina. A favorite of the yachting crowd, who desperately needed such a place in Andros, the hotel rents comfortably furnished bedrooms, each with air-conditioning and a private bath. Scuba divers, snorkelers, and fishers make ample use of the beach and the offshore waters, as the hotel lies near one of the world's largest barrier reefs and the deep Tongue of the Ocean. Fishing charters are readily available, and scuba diving and snorkeling can easily be arranged. The package rates offered by the hotel, in addition to room and meals, include airport pick up. The hotel also has a swimming pool and a good restaurant, serving Bahamian and American dishes. In addition to the marina, the hotel also offers tennis courts.

## Fresh Creek

### ⑤ Chickcharnie Hotel

Fresh Creek, Andros Town, Andros, the Bahamas. ☎ **809/368-2025.** 19 rms (8 with bath). Year-round, $45 single or double without bath, $60–$75 single or double with bath. Breakfast $6 extra. (EP rates.) No credit cards. Free parking.

Charmingly named after those mischievous Bahamian elves, this hotel is three miles east of the Andros Town Airport on the waterfront. A simple concrete structure, the hotel attracts fisherpeople and an occasional business traveler. Eight of the rooms have air-conditioning, private baths, and TVs with satellite hookups. The other rooms have sinks with hot and cold running water, access to a bathroom off the hallway, and ceiling fans. Island-born Charles Gay, the owner, maintains a grocery store on the ground floor of the building. In the hotel's spartan dining room, three meals are served daily. Fish, chicken, lobster, or conch dinners cost from $13 to $19 per person.

If you'd like to go fishing, the best person to contact is Bill Braynen (the hotel will make the arrangements). He owns 10 boats, charging from $120 for a half day or $220 for a full day in a medium-size bonefishing craft. The cost is $300 for a full day of fishing above the reefs in a 25-foot boat.

## ✪ Small Hope Bay Lodge

(c/o P.O. Box 21667, Fort Lauderdale, FL 33335). ☎ **809/368-2014** or toll free 800/223-6961 in the U.S. and Canada. Fax 809/368-2015. 20 cabins. Winter, $150 single; $300 double. Off-season, $140 single; $280 double. (AP rates.) AE, MC, V. Free parking. Closed Sept to mid-Nov.

At Fresh Creek, one of the most important underwater centers in the Bahamas, is this intimate and cozy beachside cottage colony, engulfed by tall coconut palms. Canadian-born Richard Birch created the resort, which now is the oldest dive operation on the island. Its name comes from a prediction (so far, accurate) from pirate Henry Morgan, who claimed there was "small hope" of anyone finding the treasure he'd buried on Andros. There is a spacious living and dining room where guests congregate for conversations and meals. Andros Town Airport is a 10-minute taxi ride from the lodge. The beach is at the doorstep. Cabins are made of coral rock and Andros pine, decorated with batik Androsia fabrics. Honeymooners like to order breakfast served on their water bed.

For groups of three or more, the resort has a limited number of family cottages, featuring two separate rooms connected by a single bath. Single travelers have a choice of staying in a family cottage with private accommodations (which is the same as per-person double occupancy) or staying in a regular cottage with private bath, to which $45 per person is added nightly.

The bar is an old boat, dubbed *Panacea*. The food is wholesome, plentiful, and good—conch chowder, lobster, hot johnnycake. The chef will even cook your catch for you. Lunch is a buffet; dinner, a choice of seafood and meat every night. Children dine in the game room. A picnic lunch can be prepared for those who request it. Drinks are offered on a rambling patio built out over the sea where conch fritters are served. Nightlife is spontaneous—dancing in the lounge or on the patio, watching underwater movies and slides, or playing the club's guitar yourself. Definitely don't wear a tie at dinner.

When you're making a reservation, inquire about special dive packages. This is the lodge's specialty (see "Sports A to Z," below). The owners have been diving for three decades, and they have sufficient equipment, divers, boats, and flexibility to give guests any diving they want, whether it be shallow or deep. If you'd rather fish, the lodge can "hook" you up with an expert guide, especially for bonefishing.

## Nicholl's Town

### Andros Beach Hotel

Nicholl's Town, Andros, the Bahamas. ☎ **809/329-2582** or toll free 800/327-8150 in the U.S. 10 rms, 3 cottages. $95 single or double; from $110 cottage for two. AE, MC, V. Free parking.

Built on four acres of palm-dotted sandy beachfront, this one-story red-brick hotel lies adjacent to a white sandy beach, close to some of the best diving along Andros Island's legendary barrier reef. Its restaurant attracts residents of the hotel as well as nonresidents and locals looking for a solidly established place for lunch or dinner.

Damaged by the 1992 hurricane, it was restored and improved. The hotel has its own pool and dock and occasional live entertainment on Saturday nights. Each unit has a private patio, two double beds, and a private bath. The establishment's dive facility is especially noteworthy.

## Conch Sound Resort Inn

P.O. Box 23029, Nicholl's Town, Andros. ☎ **809/329-2060** or 809/329-2341. 6 rms (all with bath), 6 cottages with kitchens. A/C TV. Year-round, $80 single or double; $190–$200 single or double occupancy of a cottage with kitchen. Breakfast $5–$7 extra. No credit cards. Free parking.

This is a carefully maintained motel and cottage complex set within a pine forest on the northern outskirts of Nicholl's Town, a 5-minute walk to the beach. Built in 1988, the establishment consists of a compound of coral-colored cement-block buildings that include a half-dozen motel rooms and a half-dozen cottages with kitchens. Furnishings are for the most part formica-covered pieces inspired by art deco models, with vertical venetian blinds shielding the windows from prying eyes. Each room has its own satellite reception on its TV. Maid service and complimentary shuttle-bus service to and from the local airport are included in the price. There's a restaurant and bar on the premises open daily from 9am to midnight. Your host is Ms. Lovan Miller; she is assisted by her parents, Emmeth and Dolores.

# Behring Point

## Charlie's Haven

Behring Point, Andros, the Bahamas. ☎ **809/368-4087.** 10 rms. A/C MINIBAR. Year-round, from $95 single; $125 double. (AP rates.) No credit cards. Free parking.

About 25 miles from Andros Town Airport and near what are said to be some of the best bonefishing banks in the world, this is a remote outpost for fishers who like the rustic but comfortable hospitality. Many anglers have tried other fishing spots in the Bahamas, but since they found this place they return here again and again. It is the very isolation and rather rawboned qualities that appeal to many patrons, most of whom are men, although families sometimes come, too. As you can imagine, many tall tales of fish that got away are swapped over the informal meals served here. There's occasionally live entertainment, as well as a separate bar area. The concrete building sits on the edge of the sound separating North Andros from Mangrove Cay. The air-conditioned bedrooms have ceiling fans, simple white walls, and a minimum of furniture.

Fishing can be arranged with Charles Smith, patriarch of the family that owns the hotel and one of the region's most respected bonefishing guides. Mr. Smith's sons, some or all of whom you're likely to meet here, include Benry, Andy, and Prescott.

## Nottages Cottages

Behring Point, Andros, the Bahamas. ☎ **809/368-4293.** 10 rms, 1 cottage. A/C TV. Year-round, from $100 per person AP double; from $200 EP cottage for four. No credit cards. Free parking.

Set on a knoll above the waterway separating North Andros and Mangrove Cay, this clean guesthouse (owned by Daisy Nottage) is fronted with a garden of croton and hibiscus. A favorite with bonefisherpeople, it has as its social center a blue-and-white dining room where Bahamian food is served to guests and visiting nonresidents. You can stay in one of the motel-like rooms whose glass windows face the sea, or in an outlying cottage equipped with a kitchenette.

## SOUTH ANDROS

### ✪ Emerald Palms By-the-Sea

Driggs Hill, P.O. Box 800, South Andros, the Bahamas. ☎ **809/369-2661** or toll free 800/ 742-4276. Fax 809/369-2667. 20 rms. A/C MINIBAR TV. Year-round, $90 single; $110 double. MAP $30 per person extra. AE, MC, V. Free parking.

Staying here at this laid-back place is a lot like staying at a beachside ranch. The accommodations are set on five miles of beachfront on an island containing 10,000 palm trees. The hotel is informally casual—a place to get away from urban life for a sojourn on a white-sand beach. Guests are treated like members of the family.

Scattered over the palm-studded property are a freshwater swimming pool, a tennis court, and shuffleboard. The cocktail lounge offers live musical entertainment, and there's sometimes a live local show. The dining room features Bahamian seafood. Outdoor steak barbecues and seafood buffets are sometimes held. The rooms are large and situated directly on the sands of the beach. This resort has some of the fanciest decorations in Andros, and some of the most special amenities, including VCRs, lanai-style rooms, four-poster beds with plantation house mosquito netting—all in all, a relaxed tropical ambience. South Bight marina is 1¹/₂ miles away, serving as a yacht anchorage for anyone who wants to arrive by boat. The hotel is 2 miles from the Congo Town Airport, and you can rent a car or bicycle if you wish.

# WHERE TO DINE

Andros follows the rest of the Bahamas in its cuisine (see "Food & Drink" in Chapter 2). Conch, in all its many variations, is the staple of most diets, along with heaping peas 'n' rice and johnnycake, pig souse, or chicken souse.

The best places to dine are at the major hotels, including those previously recommended: the **Chickcharnie Hotel,** Fresh Creek, near Andros Town (☎ 809/ **368-2025**); and if you're in South Andros, **Emerald Palms By-the-Sea,** outside Congo Town (☎ 809/369-2661). Most guests book into these hotels on the Modified American Plan, which frees them to shop around for lunch. At any of these hotels a dinner will run around $25 to $30 per person.

If you're touring the island during the day, you'll find some local spots that serve food. If business has been slow at some of these little places, you might find nothing on the stove. You take your chance.

## NORTH ANDROS

### Cargill Creek

#### Dig-Dig's Restaurant

Cargill Creek. ☎ **809/368-5097.** Reservations required for dinner. Main courses $15–$18. No credit cards. Lunch or dinner by prearrangement only. AMERICAN/BAHAMIAN.

If you're heading south, you might want to know about one of the most charming restaurants in the region. Set in a pleasant and cozy pink house, ringed with a garden beside the main highway, this establishment is inextricably tied to the personalities of its owners, Elizabeth ("Liz") and Alton Bain. The cuisine reflects the national origins (Canada and the Bahamas, respectively) of the two, and includes cracked conch, grouper cutlets, crayfish, and chicken. An appetizer is included with the main course. Your menu will be prearranged, and your arrival will probably be celebrated with a jug of the house special drink (a mixture of gin, sweetened condensed milk, and fresh coconut water) set beside your waiting table. Because they get so little business in these parts—especially from drop-in clients searching for a luncheon or dining spot—the owners ask you to call them if you'd like to have them prepare a lunch or dinner for you.

### Nicholl's Town

#### Big Josh Seafood Restaurant and Lounge
Lowe Sound. ☎ **809/329-7517.** Reservations not required. Appetizers $3; main courses $7–$15. AE. Daily 7am–11pm. SEAFOOD.

If you're on the trail of the bonefishermen who hang out at Lowe Sound you'll find good local dishes at this place. The restaurant was established years ago by the late Joshua Bootle, a legendary bonefishing guide. The restaurant is managed today by his widow, Malvese, who still does most of the cooking herself. She turns out her own versions of chicken, pork, steak, crayfish, and conch—but mostly the catch of the day.

## WHAT TO SEE & DO

Andros is vastly unexplored—and with good reason. Getting around takes some doing. Roads—what roads there are—are badly maintained and potholed, except for the main arteries. Sometimes you're a long way between villages or settlements, and if your car breaks down, all you can do is stop and wait, hoping someone will come along and give you a ride to the next settlement, where (you pray) there will be a skilled mechanic. If you're striking out on an exploration, make sure you have a full tank, as service stations are not plentiful.

All of Andros certainly can't be explored by car, although there is a dream that as Andros develops, it will be linked by a road and causeways stretching some 100 miles or more. Most of the driving and exploring is confined to North Andros, and there only along the eastern sector, going by Nicholl's Town, Morgan's Bluff, and San Andros.

If you're driving in Central Andros or South Andros, motorists must stay on the rough Queen's Highway. The road in the south is paved and better than the one in Central Andros, which should be traveled only in an emergency or by a local.

Drivers from all over the world come to explore the ✪ **Andros barrier reef,** running parallel to the eastern shore of the island. After Australia's Great Barrier Reef, this is the largest in the world, but unlike the one in Australia, some 200 miles off the coast, the barrier reef of Andros is easily accessible, beginning a few hundred yards offshore.

One side of the reef is a peaceful haven for snorkelers and scuba divers, who report that the fish are tame (often a grouper will eat from your hand, but don't try it with a moray eel). The water here is from 9 to 15 feet deep. On the other side of the reef it's a different story. The water plunges to a depth of a full mile into the awesome TOTO (Tongue of the Ocean). One diver reported that, as an adventure, diving in the ocean's "tongue" was tantamount to a flight to the moon.

Much marine life thrives on the reef, and it attracts nature lovers from all over the world. The weirdly shaped coral formations alone are worth the trip. This is a living, breathing garden of the sea, and its caves are often called "cathedral-like."

For many years the U.S. Navy has conducted research at a station on the edge of TOTO. The research center is at Andros Town. It is devoted to oceanographic, underwater weapons, and antisubmarine research. Called AUTEC (Atlantic Undersea Testing and Evaluation Centre), this is a joint U.S. and British undertaking.

When this station first opened, Androsians predicted that the naval researchers would turn up "Lusca." Like the Loch Ness monster, Lusca had been reported as having been sighted by dozens of locals. The sea serpent was accused of sucking both sailors and their vessels into the dangerous "blue holes" around the island's coastline. No one has captured Lusca yet, but the blue holes do exist, including the most famous—made so by Jacques Cousteau—Uncle Charlie's Blue Hole, which is mysterious and fathomless. The other blue holes are almost as incredible. Essentially, these are narrow circular pits that plunge straight down as much as 200 feet through rock and coral into murky, difficult-to-explore depths. Most of them begin under the level of the sea, although others appear unexpectedly (and dangerously) in the center of the island, usually with warning signs placed around the perimeter.

One of these holes, called Benjamin's Blue Hole, is named after its discoverer, George Benjamin. In 1967 he found stalactites and stalagmites 1,200 feet below sea level. What was remarkable about this discovery is that stalactites and stalagmites are not created underwater. This has led to much speculation that the Bahamas are actually mountaintops, all that remains of a mysterious continent (Atlantis?) that sank beneath the sea in dim, unrecorded times. Although Cousteau came this way to make a film, making the blue holes of Andros internationally famous, most of them, like most of the surface of the island itself, remain unexplored. Tour boats leaving from Small Hope Bay Lodge (see "Sports A to Z" below) will take you to these holes.

Near Small Hope Bay at Andros Town you can visit the workshop where **Androsia batik** is made (that same Androsia batik sold in the shops of Nassau and other towns). Androsia's artisans create their designs using hot wax on fine cotton and silk fabrics. The fabrics are then made into island-style wear, including blouses, skirts, caftans, shirts, and accessories. All hand painted and hand signed, the resort wear comes in dazzling red, blue, purple, green, and earth tones. You can visit the factory in Andros Town (☎ **809/368-2020**), Monday through Saturday from 8am to 4pm.

**Morgan's Bluff,** at the tip of North Andros, lures men and women hoping to strike it rich. Sir Henry Morgan, the pirate, is supposed to have buried a vast treasure here, which remains undiscovered to this day. Many have searched for it.

Typical of discoveries that continue to make Andros mysterious is **Red Bay Village,** where inhabitants were found in recent times living as a tribe. Their leader was "the chief," and old rituals were religiously followed. The passage of time had made little difference to these people. Now the world comes to their door, and changes are inevitable, although the people still follow their longtime customs. The village, it is believed, was settled sometime in the 1840s by Seminoles and blacks fleeing slavery in Florida. Their location is a small community lying off the northwestern coast of Andros. A causeway now connects them to the mainland, and sightseers can visit. Red Bay Village can be reached by road from Nicholl's Town and San Andros. You should be polite and ask permission before indiscriminately photographing these people.

Bird-watchers are attracted to Andros for its varied **bird population.** In the dense forests, in trees such as lignum vitae, mahogany, madeira, "horseflesh," and pine, lives a huge feathered population: many parrots, doves, and marsh hens. (Ever hear a whistling duck?)

Botanists are lured here by the **wildflowers** of Andros. It is said that some 40 to 50 species of wild orchids thrive here, some that are found nowhere else. New discoveries are also being made, as more and more botanists study the rich vegetation of Andros.

One custom in Andros is reminiscent of the Tennessee Williams drama *Suddenly Last Summer.* This is the catching of land crabs, which leave their burrows and march relentlessly to the sea to lay their eggs. This annual ritual occurs between May and September. However, many of these hapless crabs will never have offspring; both visitors and Androsians walk along the beach with baskets and catch the crustaceans before they reach the sea. Later, they clean them, stuff them, and bake them for dinner.

## SPORTS A TO Z

Golf and tennis fans should go elsewhere, but those who want some of the best bonefishing and scuba diving in the Bahamas should flock to Andros.

### FISHING

As mentioned previously, Andros is called the "Bonefish Capital of the World." The actual capital is Lowe Sound Settlement, a tiny hamlet with only one road. It lies four miles north of Nicholl's Town. Fishing enthusiasts come here to hire bonefish guides.

Regardless of what area you're staying in—North Andros, Central Andros, or South Andros—someone at your hotel can arrange for you to go fishing.

#### Charlie's Haven

Behring Point, North Andros. ☎ **809/368-4087.**

Already recommended as a rustic hotel, Charlie's Haven is one of the best places for fishing. Bonefishing trips are arranged for $130 for a half day, $240 for a full day. Deep-sea fishing is also available.

#### Small Hope Bay Lodge

Andros Town, North Andros. ☎ **809/368-2014.**

This lodge also arranges fishing. A guide will take you to where there is superb bonefishing and tackle and bait are provided.

### SCUBA & SNORKELING

As mentioned several times, scuba divers and snorkelers are attracted to Andros because of the barrier reef, which lies on the eastern shore along the Tongue of the Ocean. Blue holes, coral gardens, drop-offs, wall-and-reef diving, and wrecks make it even more enticing. The best dive operations are previewed below.

#### Andros Beach Hotel

Nicholl's Town, North Andros. ☎ **809/329-2582.**

This resort takes advantage of the proximity to the Andros Barrier Reef, offering a complete dive package with a full array of options. Simple rentals of the equipment you need can be arranged if you're qualified, although many guests prefer the complete package, with transportation included. A handful of experienced instructors and guides will show you sections of the barrier reef and the Tongue of the Ocean.

When not included in the price of a package, single-tank dives cost $40, two-tank dives go for $60, and three-tankers cost $80. Half-day snorkeling trips cost $25 per person.

For additional information, write to **Andros Undersea Adventures,** P.O. Box 21766, Fort Lauderdale, FL 33335. In Florida, call **305/462-3400.** Outside of Florida, call **800/327-8150** toll free in the United States and Canada.

## Small Hope Bay Lodge

Fresh Creek, Andros Town, North Andros. ☎ **809/368-2014** or toll free 800/223-6961 in the U.S. and Canada.

This lodge lies a short distance from the barrier reef, with its still-unexplored caves and ledges. A staff of trained dive instructors at the lodge caters to levels of expertise from beginners to experienced divers (the staff members have various credentials, including certification from some of the world's professional diving organizations). Snorkeling expeditions can be arranged as well as scuba outings, and the staff claims to be able to teach novices to dive even if they can't swim, beginning with the steps off the establishment's docks. Visibility underwater exceeds 100 feet on most days, with water temperatures ranging from 72 to 84 degrees Fahrenheit.

Without hotel accommodations, half-day excursions to the reef, with snorkeling gear included, cost $10; with scuba gear, $40. Scuba instruction is free. Night dives cost $50 per person and require a minimum of six participants. To stay at the hotel here for five nights and six days, all-inclusive (meals, tips, taxes, airport transfers, and three dives a day), costs $1,000 per person. All guests are allowed access to the beachside hot whirlpool as well as to all facilities, such as free use of Sunfish, Windsurfers and bicycles.

# The Abaco Islands

# 8

The northernmost of the Bahamas—called the "top of the Bahamas"—the Abacos form a boomerang-shaped miniarchipelago 130 miles long, consisting of both Great Abaco and Little Abaco as well as a sprinkling of cays (pronounced "keys"). The location, at least of the Abaco airports, is 200 miles east of Miami and 75 miles north of Nassau.

Ponce de León landed here in 1513, looking for the Fountain of Youth. Visitors, many of them retired Americans, still arrive searching—if not for eternal youth, at least for a pleasant way of life that has disappeared from much of the world.

Fisherpeople find some of the finest offshore fishing in the Bahamas, and yachtspeople call this the "world's most beautiful cruising grounds" (a title also bestowed upon the Exumas—I'll grant them a tie). In the interior are wild boar, and, I am told, wild ponies, although I've never seen the latter.

The Abacos, with many first-rate resorts, are the leading and most visited attraction in the Bahamas, after Nassau, Paradise Island, and Freeport/Lucaya. The weather is about 10 degrees Fahrenheit warmer than in southern Florida, but if you visit in January or February, don't expect every day will be beach weather. Remember, Miami and Fort Lauderdale, even Key West, can get chilly at times. When winter squalls hit, temperatures can drop to the high 40s in severe cases. Spring in the Abacos, however, is one of the most glorious and balmy seasons in all the islands. In summer it gets very hot around noon, but if you act as the islanders do and find a shady spot, the trade winds will cool you off.

Fishing, swimming, and boating—especially boating—are the top sports on the Abacos. There are also diving, golf, and tennis. If you're a boating type, the favorite pastime is to rent a small boat, pack a picnic (or have it done for you), and head for one of the cays just big enough for two.

Excellent marine facilities, with guides, charter parties, and boat rentals are available on Great Guana Cay, Green Turtle Cay, Hope Town, Marsh Harbour, Treasure Cay, and Walker's Cay. Sunfish, Sailfish, Hobie Cats, and Morgan bareboats are available. In fact, Marsh Harbour is the bareboat-charter center of the northern Bahamas.

## What's Special About the Abaco Islands

Beaches
- Treasure Cay Beach, widely recognized as one of the world's 10 finest beaches—$3^1/_2$ miles of white powdery sand.

Intriguing Towns
- Man-O-War Cay, a real Bahamian Loyalist village populated by descendants of early settlers.
- Elbow Cay and Hope Town, evocative of Nantucket, but also like a leap back to the 18th century.
- Green Turtle Cay and New Plymouth, the northernmost of Abaco's Loyalist villages—clapboard houses, gingerbread trim, and a Puritan past.
- Treasure Cay, in the northern half of Great Abaco, a haven for tourists drawn to its golf course and $3^1/_2$ mile white sandy beach.

A Funky Bar
- Miss Emily's Blue Bee Bar, the most famous "watering hole" in the Family Islands, with a Goombay Smash that is compared to atomic fission.
- Elbow Cay Lighthouse, the most famous in the Bahamas, candy striped, and kerosene powered, rising 120 feet. Most photographed landmark in the Family Islands.
- The Sea of Abaco, turquoise waters between Great and Little Abaco and the offshore cays. Hailed as not only the finest sailing area in the Bahamas, but in the Caribbean as well.

Special Events
- Regatta Week in July at Marsh Harbour, the premier yachting event in the Abacos, attracting sailboats and their crews from around the world.
- Treasure Cay, host of two of the most popular tournaments in the Bahamas: the Treasure Cay Billfish Championship in April and the Treasure Cay Invitational in May.

Anglers from all over the world come to test their skill against the blue marlin, kingfish, dolphin, yellowfin tuna, sailfish, wahoo, amberjack, and grouper. Fishing tournaments abound at Walker's Cay. There are plenty of Boston Whalers for bottom fishing and Makos for reef fishing and trolling. Many cruisers for deep-sea fishing can be rented.

Scuba divers can dive to the depths with UNEXSO (Underwater Explorers Society) and discover the Abacos' caverns, inland "blue holes," coral reefs and gardens, along with marine preserves and wrecks. Night dives are featured. Top-rated dive centers can be found at Marsh Harbour, Hope Town, Treasure Cay, and Walker's Cay, all offering NAUI/PADI instructors and a full line of equipment sales, rentals, and air fills.

*Note:* For an explanation of rate symbols, refer to "Tips on Accommodations" in Chapter 3.

## A LITTLE HISTORY

Once the waters around the Abacos swarmed with Robert Louis Stevenson–type pirates and treasure ships. It is estimated that 500 to 600 Spanish galleons—many

# The Abacos

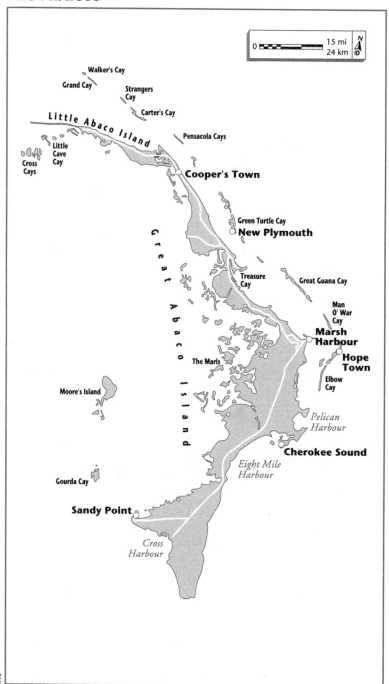

Walker's Cay
Grand Cay
Strangers Cay
Carter's Cay
Little Abaco Island
Pensacola Cays
Little Cave Cay
Cross Cays
**Cooper's Town**
Green Turtle Cay
**New Plymouth**
Great Abaco Island
Treasure Cay
Great Guana Cay
Man O' War Cay
**Marsh Harbour**
The Maris
**Hope Town**
Elbow Cay
Moore's Island
*Pelican Harbour*
**Cherokee Sound**
*Eight Mile Harbour*
Gourda Cay
**Sandy Point**
*Cross Harbour*

0    15 mi
24 km

N

treasure laden—went to their watery graves in and around the Abaco reefs. To this day, an occasional old silver coin or a doubloon is found along the beaches, particularly after a storm.

Many of the Bahamians who live in the Abacos are descendants of Loyalists who left New England or the Carolinas during the American Revolution. An Elizabethan accent still exists in their speech. They founded towns like New Plymouth and Hope Town, which are reminiscent of New England fishing villages. Many of these early settlers were shipbuilders, and to this day many Abaconians claim that the finest island boats are those built with Abaco pine by the Man-O-War Cay artisans. This is still the boatbuilding center of the Bahamas, and it is also rather grandly acclaimed as "the finest sailing capital" in the world.

Other early settlers were farmers who, when they found that they could not make a living in that line—the soil wasn't fertile enough—turned to wrecking (the business of salvaging ships that were wrecked or foundered on the reefs). Since there wasn't a lighthouse in the Abacos until 1836, many vessels crashed on the shoals and rocks, and salvagers legally claimed the cargoes, at the same time saving the lives of crews and passengers when possible. However, this enterprise became so profitable that some unscrupulous wreckers deliberately misled ships to their doom and became rich from the spoils.

Most of the "Tories"—descendants of the British Loyalists—still live on Elbow Cay, Green Turtle Cay, and Man-O-War Cay. From a sightseeing point of view, these are the main islands of the Abacos to visit, having more interest, in my opinion, than the Abaco "mainland." The first timer will likely head for Treasure Cay, Marsh Harbour, even Walker's Cay or Green Turtle Cay, but repeat visitors gravitate to more esoteric destinations.

## GETTING THERE

**BY PLANE**    Three airports service the Abacos: Marsh Harbour (the major one), Treasure Cay, and Walker's Cay. The official points of entry are Marsh Harbour, Treasure Cay, Walker's Cay, and Green Turtle Cay (New Plymouth). Green Turtle Cay doesn't have an airstrip, but many people of the yachting set clear Customs and Immigration there.

Many visitors arrive from Nassau or Miami on **Bahamasair** (☎ toll free **800/ 222-4262**). Flight schedules change frequently in the Bahamas, but you can usually get a daily flight out of Nassau, going first to Marsh Harbour, then on to Treasure Cay. If you're in Miami, you can usually get a morning flight to Marsh Harbour. There is also service from Miami on to Treasure Cay.

**American Eagle** (☎ toll free **800/433-7300**) flies from Miami nonstop to the Abacos, touching down at both Marsh Harbour and at Treasure Cay.

**USAir** (☎ toll free **800/428-4322**) has one flight daily from Fort Lauderdale to Treasure Cay, and also flies in on direct flights from Orlando.

**BY BOAT**    **Premier Cruise Line,** P.O. Box 573, Cape Canaveral, FL 32920 (☎ **407/783-5061** or toll free **800/327-7113**), sails its *Majestic* on 3- and 4-day jaunts to the Abacos. Departures are from Port Canaveral in Florida on Thursday and Sunday. Cruise-ship passengers get to explore Green Turtle Cay, Great Guana Cay, Man-O-War Cay, and Treasure Cay, which are the sightseeing highlights of the Abacos.

The mail boat MV *Deborah K* leaves from Potter's Cay Dock in Nassau, going to Cherokee Sound, Green Turtle Cay, Hope Town, and Marsh Harbour.

It departs on Wednesday at 6pm, and the trip to the Abacos takes 12 hours. The return is on Monday at 9pm.

In addition, the MV *Champion II* also heads out from Potter's Cay Dock in Nassau on Tuesday at 10am, calling first at Sandy Point, then Moore's Island and Bullock's Harbour, before returning to Nassau on Thursday at 10am (trip time: 11 hours). For details of sailings and costs, passengers should get in touch with the dockmaster at Potter's Cay Dock in Nassau (☎ **809/393-1064**).

## GETTING AROUND

**BY TAXI**   Unmetered taxis, often shared with other passengers, meet all arriving planes. They will take you to your hotel if it's on the Abaco "mainland"; otherwise, they will deposit you at a dock where you can hop aboard a water taxi to one of the neighboring offshore islands such as Green Turtle Cay or Elbow Cay. Most visitors use a combination taxi and water taxi ride to reach the most popular hotels. From Marsh Harbour Airport to Hope Town on Elbow Cay costs about $11 for the transfer. From the Treasure Cay Airport to Green Turtle Cay, there is a transportation charge of about $13. Elbow Cay costs about $10 for the transfer. From the Treasure Cay Airport to Green Turtle Cay, there is a transportation charge of $13.

It's also possible to make arrangements for a taxi tour of Great Abaco or Little Abaco. These, however, are expensive. You don't really see that much either. It's much better to go sightseeing in one of the Loyalist settlements, such as New Plymouth. That you can do on foot.

**BY CAR**   If you want to risk the Abacos' potholed roads, you can rent a car, usually for $70 a day. Try **H & L Car Rentals,** Don MacKay Boulevard, Marsh Harbour (☎ **809/367-2840**), which is open Monday through Saturday from 7am to 6pm.

**BY FERRY**   Mostly, you'll probably use **Albury's Ferry Service** (☎ **809/367-3147**). Its departures from Marsh Harbour coincide with incoming and outgoing flights. It provides ferry connections to Elbow Cay (Hope Town) and Man-O-War Cay, a 20-minute trip to each destination. The round-trip fare is $12 if you return the same day. The boats run from Hope Town and from Man-O-War Cay to Marsh Harbour at 8am and 1:30pm daily, making the run from Marsh Harbour to the two island ports at 10:30am and 4pm. On Monday, Thursday, and Saturday there is also a departure from Marsh Harbour at 11:30am. For car-ferry service to Green Turtle Cay, refer to the write-up on that cay below.

## 1 Spanish Cay

Set 12 miles northwest of Green Turtle Cay, this island was named after the pair of Spanish galleons that sank offshore during the 17th century. Originally owned by Queen Elizabeth II, the island was purchased in the 1960s by Texas-based investor (and former owner of the Dallas Cowboys) Clint Murchinson. After his death in the early 1980s, two successive Florida conglomerates poured time, money, and landscaping efforts into developing the island as a site for upscale private homes.

Although its vegetation began with little more than stunted shrubs and sea grapes, today, the narrow, 3-mile-long, 185-acre island is forested with 6,000 palms, descendants of the original 800 specimens brought in by Murchinson in the 1970s. Unusual among the coral-and-sand islands of the northern Bahamas, Spanish Cay is relatively vertiginous, rising to a panoramic altitude of 65 feet above sea level. The little island has five beaches and about 7 miles of shoreline. Most residents of the inn (see below) and the island's private homes maneuver their way along the island's paved roads by electric-powered golf carts.

The island contains a 70-slip state-of-the-art marina, 4 private homes, and a collection of 13 garden suites available to overnight guests. The island also has a pair of restaurants (each with its own bar), the more upscale of which (the Wrecker's Raw Bar) is built on stilts above the tidal flats of the island's Atlantic shore. Among other amenities are a 5,000-foot airstrip, a complete PADI-certified dive shop, a handful of sailing vessels for excursions above the legendary coral reefs of the Sea of Abaco, and a congenial staff, which for the most part is ferried in every day from the nearby community of Cooperstown. Most visitors arrive by private boat, chartered aircraft, or by the occasional flights from Fort Lauderdale on Island Express Airlines. Other options include flying to Treasure Cay on Bahamasair, then arranging water transport from there through the hotel.

## WHERE TO STAY & DINE

### ✪ The Inn at Spanish Cay

Spanish Cay, Abacos. ☎ **809/365-0083.** Fax 809/365-0466. (For information, contact Investco, Inc., 325 Nottingham Blvd., Suite 2, West Palm Beach, FL 33405. ☎ 407/655-0172). 13 garden suites (most with kitchen), 4 private homes. A/C MINIBAR. $200 one-bedroom suite; $275 two-bedroom suite with kitchen; $325 three-bedroom suite with kitchen. Rental of homes for between 6 and 12 occupants, $3,500–$5,500 per week. MC, V. Free parking.

Pending an eventual purchase of a home or building site, these accommodations offer some of the most secluded, off-the-beaten-track lodgings in the northern Bahamas. Furnishings in the suites include tropical fabrics and lots of rattan and wicker. Decoration in the private homes includes whatever struck the fancy of the individual (absentee) homeowner, but tends to include summery, easy-to-care-for decors inspired by Florida models.

Dining options include more formal meals in the Wrecker's Raw Bar, where lunches cost from $10 to $14 each, and dinners go for around $25 per person. Less expensive casual fare (sandwiches, salads, and platters) are served near the marina, overlooking the Sea of Abaco, within the Point House.

## 2 Walker's Cay

This is the northernmost and outermost of the Abaco chain of islands, and one of the smallest, lying at the edge of the Bahama Bank. The cay produces its own fresh water and electricity. Coral reefs surrounding this island drop off to depths of some 1,000 feet. It's known around the world as one of the best deep-sea fishing resorts, and has been featured on the ABC-TV network's *American Sportsman* on several occasions. It is usually mentioned as being the "Top of The Bahamas."

Ponce de León is said to have stopped here in 1513 looking for fresh water. That was just six days before he discovered Florida. From the 17th century, this was a place known to pirates, who stored their booty here. It became a bastion for blockade-runners during the American Civil War, and later it was a hideout for rumrunners in the days of U.S. Prohibition.

To service those who want to reach the island, Walker's Cay Hotel and Marina operates its own plane service, Walker's International (☎ **305/359-1400** or toll free **800/432-2092**). The airline makes the 45-minute flight daily from Fort Lauderdale to Walker's Cay.

## WHERE TO STAY & DINE

### Walker's Cay Hotel and Marina

Walker's Cay, Abaco, the Bahamas. ☎ **305/359-1400** in Fort Lauderdale or toll free 800/432-2092 in the U.S. and Canada. Fax 305/359-1400. 62 rms. 3 villas. A/C. Sept 11–Feb, $100–$120 single or double; from $200 villa. Mar–Sept 10, $130–$150 single or double; from $260 villa. MAP $37.50 per person extra. (EP rates.) AE, DC, MC, V. Free parking.

This resort has the largest full-service, privately owned marina in the Abacos, and each year runs what has become the largest deep-sea fishing tournament in the Bahamas. The hotel has attractively furnished villas and bedrooms, each with a view of the ocean from its own private terrace. Of course, the villas and ocean-view suites are more expensive. In winter, rates are lower than in summer (usually the reverse in the Bahamas).

If you're planning a winter visit, ask a travel agent (or call directly) to see if the resort will still be offering its "Discover Us Package." Its most recent one (good through the winter until the end of February) included three days and two nights, with round-trip airfare from Fort Lauderdale or West Palm Beach, for $339 per person. To write for a reservation, address your letter to Walker's Cay Hotel and Marina, 700 SW 34th St., Fort Lauderdale, FL 33315.

**Dining/Entertainment:** The food is good (everything is imported), with an assortment of American and Bahamian specialties. The chef bakes his own bread and pastries, and there is also an excellent wine selection. Bahamian lobster and conch fritters are invariably featured, along with fresh fish. The Lobster Trap lounge evokes the early Bahamas of Hemingway, and the Conch Pearl and dining terrace overlook the sea. In season, guests can dance to disco music in the Lobster Trap Lounge, at Marina North Dock.

**Services:** Laundry, babysitting.

**Facilities:** Two all-weather tennis courts; every kind of water sport from scuba to ski; freshwater and saltwater swimming; some of the finest offshore fishing in the Bahamas, just five minutes from the 75-slip marina (many world records have been set here).

## 3 Green Turtle Cay (New Plymouth)

Three miles off the east coast of Great Abaco, Green Turtle Cay is the jewel of the archipelago, a little island with an uneven coastline, deep bays, sounds, and good beaches, one of the best stretching for 3,600 feet. There are green forests, gentle hills, and secluded inlets. The island is 3½ miles long and half a mile across, and lies some 170 miles due east of Palm Beach, Florida.

Water depths seldom exceed 15 to 20 feet inside the string of cays that trace the outer edge of the Bahama Bank. It is the reefs outside the cays that provide the abundance of underwater flora and fauna that delight snorkelers and anglers. The coral gardens that make up an inner and an outer reef teem with colorful sea life, and shelling on the beaches and offshore sandbars is considered among the finest in the Bahamas.

If you have a boat, you can explore such deserted islands as Fiddle Cay to the north and No Name Cay and Pelican Cay to the south of Green Turtle Cay.

New Plymouth, at the southern tip of the cay, is an 18th-century settlement that has the flavor of a New England sailing port back in the days when such towns were filled with boatbuilders and fishermen. Much of the masonry of the original town was made from lime produced from conch shells, broken up, burned, and sifted for cement. Records say that the alkali content was so high that it would burn the hands of the masons who used it.

Clapboard houses with gingerbread trim line the narrow streets of the little town, which once had a population of 1,800 people, now shrunk to 400. Green Turtle Cay became known for the skill of its shipbuilders, although the industry, like many others in the area, failed when total emancipation of the slaves came in the Bahamas in 1838.

---

## Far From The Madding Crowd

The settlers of New Plymouth were Loyalists who found their way here from other parts of the Abacos shortly before the end of the 18th century, with some "new" blood thrown in when émigrés from Eleuthera moved to Marsh Harbour and other Abaconian settlements. The people today are mostly named Curry, Lowe, Russell, Roberts, and especially Sawyer. Because they all came from the same rootstock—English, Welsh, and Scottish—and because of a long history of intermarriage, many of the faces are amazingly similar: deeply tanned, often freckled skin, blue eyes, and red or blond hair. The people here are friendly but not outgoing, having lived for generations far from the madding crowd.

One morning I spent an hour with a lifelong resident. The next morning, encountering what I took to be the same man on the ferryboat, I resumed our conversation, only to learn I was talking to a different man entirely. "No relation," he said, until chided by a woman passenger, which elicited from him, "Well, I think my mother's cousin did marry . . ."

The insularity of these people has also caused their speech patterns to retain many facets of those their forebears brought from the mother country, with even a smattering of cockney to flavor it. Many drop their initial letter *h*, using it instead at the beginning of words that start with vowels. You may hear someone ordering " 'am" and with it some "heggs." Also, the letter *v* is often pronounced *w*, and vice versa.

Many of the inhabitants of New Plymouth today are engaged in turtling, lobstering, shark fishing, and sponging. New Plymouth is a so-called "sister city" to Key West, Florida, and if you have ever visited there, you'll see startling similarities between the American people of "conch" descent and the Abaconians, even to their wrecking history, fishing industries, and appearance.

A big event in the day-to-day life of the people of New Plymouth is the arrival at the Government Dock of the mail boat from Nassau. People gather there also whenever the ferryboat is arriving or leaving, just to keep tabs on what's going on.

There is no auto traffic in New Plymouth except for a few service vehicles—but who needs a car? You can walk all the way around the village in a fairly brief stroll.

Parliament is the village's main street, and you can walk its entire length in only 10 minutes, perhaps acknowledged only by a few clucking hens. Many of the houses have front porches, usually occupied in the evening with people enjoying the breezes.

## GETTING THERE

Most guests fly to Treasure Cay Airport, where a taxi will take them to the ferry dock for departures to Green Turtle Cay (New Plymouth).

At the dock, you may have to wait a while for the ferry (which has no phone), or have one called for you. It's about a 10-minute ride to Green Turtle Cay from the dock. The ferry will take you to the Green Turtle Club, if you're staying there, or to New Plymouth. This land-and-sea transfer costs $13 per person.

## FAST FACTS: Green Turtle Cay (New Plymouth)

**Banks**   Service is limited. Barclay's Bank PLC operates a branch (☎ 809/365-4144), open only from 10am to 1pm on Tuesday and Thursday.

**Churches**   The people of New Plymouth, for the most part, are deeply religious. With such a small population, they manage to support five churches. The Anglican church is the oldest, dating from 1786.

**Crime**   There's no crime in New Plymouth, unless you import it yourself. There is a little jail made of stone, which makes visitors chuckle: the doors have fallen off. No one can remember when, if ever, it held a prisoner.

**Medical Care**   If you need medical attention on Green Turtle Cay, there is a clinic (☎ 809/365-4028), run by a nurse.

**Post Office**   Green Turtle Cay's post office (☎ 809/365-4242) is entered through a pink door. It has the only public telephone on the island. Hours are Monday through Friday 9am to noon and 1 to 5pm.

**Shopping**   In New Plymouth, there are several gift shops, and well-stocked grocery stores feature freshly baked Bahamian bread.

## WHERE TO STAY
### EXPENSIVE

#### ✪ Green Turtle Club

Green Turtle Cay, Abaco, the Bahamas. ☎ **809/365-4271.** Fax 809/365-4272. 28 rms, 3 suites. A/C. Winter, from $140 single or double; $160 poolside suite for two; $260 villa for two. Off-season, $115 single or double; $135 poolside suite for two; $195 villa for two. Prices higher at Christmas. Children under 12 stay free in parents' room. Extra person $20. MAP $36 per adult extra. $25 per child extra. AE, MC, V. Free parking. Closed end of Aug to mid-Nov. Most guests arrive at Treasure Cay Airport, then take a taxi (there are usually plenty there) to the ferry dock, where a water taxi will take you to the club.

The Green Turtle Club is where such celebrities as Christopher Reeve, Tanya Tucker, and former president Jimmy Carter have gone for a retreat from the pressures of daily life. It is the only four-star resort in the Abacos. The resort was built on a half-moon-shaped beach off which yachts of all sizes ride at anchor. The flag-festooned bar is the social center of the resort. Today its ambience is very much that of a clubhouse, lodge, and country club, capped with heavy rafters and flanked on one side by a panoramic veranda and on the other by a pine-covered dining room.

The Green Turtle Yacht Club has its base here. It's associated with the Birdham Yacht Club, one of the oldest in England, and with the Palm Beach Yacht Club.

Members have their own villas right on the water, often with private docks, although temporary guests will be lodged in exceptionally spacious bungalows set on the side of the hill. There are no locked doors on this tree-dotted estate. Also, the only telephone is the one in the main office, where the polite staff can organize a full array of sporting as well as sightseeing excursions.

Some guests choose to walk the several miles into New Plymouth, or you can take a boat. The waters around the resort are shallow enough that landlubbers can spot schools of fish and sometimes even a green turtle paddling along above the sandbanks. Nature has blessed the resort with enough visual splendor to more than make up for its relative isolation.

There's an unmistakably British note here—both in the evening meals which begin with before-dinner cocktails beside a roaring fire in the bar (in chilly weather only, of course), and in the courteous staff, who offer assistance yet don't intrude on anyone's tranquillity. Arrangements can be made for a boat trip into New Plymouth, and laundry service is available. There's a swimming pool dug into one of the flower-dotted hillsides in case swimmers don't want to bathe in the turquoise waters off the hotel's beach.

## MODERATE

### ✪ Bluff House Club & Marina

Green Turtle Cay, Abaco, the Bahamas. ☎ **809/365-4247.** Fax 809/365-4248. 14 rms, 11 suites and villas. A/C. Year-round, $80–$90 single or double; $95–$110 suite; $125–$140 one-bedroom villa for two; $200–$235 two-bedroom villa for four; $280–$330 three-bedroom villa for six. (EP rates.) MAP $34 per person extra. MC, V. Free parking.

Managed by English-born Martin Havill, Bluff House has 12 acres fronting the Sea of Abaco on one side and the harbor of White Sound on the other. The house sits atop an 80-foot-high peninsula that rises from its own private pink powder sandy beach—backed by 40 acres of palm, oak, and pine-forested jogging trails. It is a 5-minute boat ride from the village of New Plymouth, and a boat takes guests to the village three mornings a week for sightseeing and shopping and also for a Saturday-night dance.

The main building has paneled and glass walls, slow-whirling tropical fans, wicker furnishings, and polished wooden floors. A wide wooden deck surrounds the swimming pool, sheltered by palms and with a panoramic view of the surrounding waters and the sunsets.

The hotel offers beach or hillside villas and split-level suites as well as hotel rooms, plus complete seclusion and views. Favored units are spacious "tree houses" with private porches and balconies. Inside, the decor has floral bedcovers and tropical furniture. The resort is open year-round.

**Dining/Entertainment:** Breakfast and dinner (including complimentary wine) are served in the main Club House, where cocktails and fresh hors d'oeuvres are offered before a candlelit dinner that features local conch, grouper, snapper, and lobster, as well as roast duck à l'orange. The Beach Club, open daily, serves luncheons featuring Bahamian cracked conch and fresh grouper, as well as hamburgers and other American favorites.

**Services:** Babysitting, laundry.

**Facilities:** Full service 15-slip marina, boats for rent, swimming pool, tennis court; free use of rackets, balls, and snorkeling equipment; gift shop/boutique; arrangements made for reef fishing, deep-sea fishing, bonefishing, and a snorkeling/fishing picnic during which your guide will take you diving for seafood to be cooked at lunch.

## New Plymouth Inn

New Plymouth, Green Turtle Cay, Abaco, the Bahamas. ☎ **809/365-4161**; 305/665-5309 in Florida. Fax 809/365-4138. 9 rms. Year-round $110–$120 single or double. (MAP rates.) No credit cards. Free parking. Closed Sept–Oct.

This restored New England–Bahamian-style inn stands next door to the former home of Neville Chamberlain, the prime minister of Great Britain on the eve of World War II. It has colonial charm, a Loyalist history, cloistral gardens, and a patio pool, and it's in the heart of New Plymouth village. It was one of the few buildings in town to survive the 1932 hurricane. The inn is run by Wally Davies, an expert diver and swimmer. He has turned New Plymouth Inn into a charming oasis, refurbishing the 150-year-old building with taste and care.

The inn has wide, open verandas, intricate cutout wooden trim, and an indoor A-frame dining room. The comfortable hammock on the front porch is constantly fought over. The light and airy rooms are kept spotlessly clean, and each has a private bath and shower. Some units are air-conditioned. Many of the same guests have come back every year since the inn opened in 1974.

**Dining/Entertainment:** Out on the veranda, you can smell night-blooming jasmine mixing with fresh-baked island bread. Island candlelit dinners of fresh native lobster, snapper, conch, and vintage wines are served. Roasts, steaks, chops, and imported beer in frosty steins are also part of the menu. The bar and lounge, which overlook the garden's small freshwater swimming pool, are the social center of the establishment. The Sunday brunch is the most popular on the island, costing only $10 per person.

**Facilities:** Swimming pool; nearby tennis; fishing and snorkeling can be arranged.

## COTTAGE RENTALS

### Coco Bay Cottages

Green Turtle Cay, Abaco, the Bahamas. ☎ **809/365-4464** or toll free 800/752-0166. Fax 809/365-4390. 4 cottages. Dec 15 to Labor Day, $900–$1,100 per week for two. Off-season, $800–$1,000 per week for two. Extra person $100 per week. No credit cards. Docking free.

On the north end of Green Turtle Cay, at a point where 500 feet of land separate the Atlantic from the Sea of Abaco, this cottage complex is ideal for those who'd like to anchor in for a while. It enjoys a 70% repeat clientele. Furnished in a refreshing style of Caribbean furnishings and pastel colors, the oceanfront property occupies 5 acres. Each of the cottages has two bedrooms and a living and dining room with a fully equipped kitchen and microwave. Refurbished in 1988, they have been much improved over the years. Linens and kitchen utensils are provided. Cooling is by ceiling fans and trade winds. Guests come directly to the property by water taxi from the airport dock. They have a selection of two different beaches, and three well-stocked stores can be found in New Plymouth for guests who want to cook their own meals.

### Deck House

White Sound, Green Turtle Cay, Abaco, the Bahamas. ☎ **513/821-9471** in Cincinnati, Ohio (for information, write to Dorothy Lang, 535 Hickory Hill Lane, Cincinnati, OH 45215). 2 units. Year-round, $850 per week for four; $1,150 per week for six. No credit cards.

Deck House lies on the leeward side of the island at the entrance to White Sound. Rented weekly as a complex, it can house up to six people. It consists of two bedrooms and two baths, plus a small guest house for two with bath—in other words, it houses three couples "with privacy." There is a living room, plus a kitchen.

Linens and all utensils are provided. Out back is a sundeck. Owners A. V. and Dorothy Lang prefer bookings from Saturday noon to Saturday noon. Incidentally, a maid comes in Saturday to put things in order. As an added bonus, the Langs include a 30-horsepower Malibu, a Butterfly, and the use of a Sunfish at no additional charge.

## WHERE TO DINE

The hotels previously recommended have the best food on the island. But if for a change of pace you'd like to escape for either lunch or dinner, I recommend the following small dining rooms in New Plymouth.

### ❺ Laura's Kitchen

Parliament St. ☎ **809/365-4287.** Reservations recommended for dinner. Appetizers $3.25–$6; main courses $10–$13. No credit cards. Lunch daily 11am–3pm; dinner daily 5:30–8:30pm. Closed Sept. BAHAMIAN.

On the main street of town, across from the Albert Lowe Museum, this family-owned operation occupies a well-converted white Bahamian cottage. Owner Laura Sawyer serves lunch and dinner in a decor that might best be described as pleasant, cozy, and homey. Chicken is the specialty, as are cracked conch and fried fish.

### Rooster's Rest Pub and Restaurant

Gilliam's Bay Rd. ☎ **809/365-4066.** Reservations recommended for dinner. Main courses $9–$14; lunch burgers and snacks $3–$6.50. No credit cards. Lunch Mon–Sat 11:30am–3:30pm; dinner Mon–Sat 7:30–10pm. BAHAMIAN.

Rooster's serves good Bahamian food, including lobster, conch, and fresh fish. The cook also prepares some tasty ribs. The establishment lies just beyond the edge of town. All main courses in the evening are served with peas 'n' rice, cole slaw, and potato salad.

## WHAT TO SEE & DO

New Plymouth celebrated its bicentennial in 1984 by opening a **Memorial Sculpture Garden** in the center of town across from the New Plymouth Inn. A monument honors American Loyalists and also some of their notable descendants, including Albert Lowe, a pioneer boatbuilder and historian. The garden is designed in the pattern of the Union Jack.

### Albert Lowe Museum

Parliament St. ☎ **809/365-4094.** Admission $3 adults, $1.50 children. Mon–Sat 9–11:45am and 1–4pm.

More than anything else I've seen in the Bahamas, this museum gives a view of the rawboned and sometimes difficult history of the Family Islands. You could easily spend a couple of hours reading the fine print of the dozens of photographs that show the hardship and the valor of citizens who changed industries as often as the economic circumstances of their era dictated.

There's a garden in the back of the beautifully restored Loyalist home where the caretaker will give you a guided tour of the stone kitchen, which occupants of the house used as a shelter when a hurricane devastated much of New Plymouth in 1932. Inside the house a narrow stairway leads to a trio of bedrooms that reveal the simplicity of 18th-century life on Green Turtle Cay. Amid Victorian settees, irreplaceable photographs, and island artifacts, you'll see a number of handsome ship models, the work of Albert Lowe, for whom the museum was named.

Also displayed are paintings by Alton Lowe, son of the former boatbuilder and founder of the museum. Cherub-faced and red-haired, Alton, who now resides in Miami most of the time, has for some time been one of the best-known painters in the Bahamas. His works hang in collections all over the world. Many of Alton Lowe's paintings have been used as the background for Bahamian postage stamps, blowups of which are displayed in the museum. Whoever guides you on your tour might open the basement of the house for you as well, where you'll see some of Alton Lowe's work, as well as that of other local painters, for sale.

## SPORTS A TO Z

Some critics have hailed the yearly **Regatta Week** at Marsh Harbour as the "premier annual yachting event in the Abacos." Every year, it's held sometime between Independence Day in the United States and Independence Day in the Bahamas (July 4 and July 10). The events include sailboat races in many categories, with crews from around the world competing.

Another event that draws visitors is the **Green Turtle Club Fishing Tournament,** held sometime in May. In 1984, the winner hooked a 500-pound blue marlin that was so heavy the competing participants from other boats generously came aboard the winning craft to bring the fish in.

For **tennis,** the choice is very limited. There's a court at Bluff House (☎ 809/365-4247), where guests play for free and nonresidents are charged $10 per hour.

The previously recommended Bluff House Club & Marina (☎ **809/365-4247**) is the place to go for scuba facilities. It also offers snorkeling and "diving with the dolphins." The hotel also has access to a 29-foot "sportsfish" boat, with all equipment included. **Bonefishing** is on a smaller boat. Each trip takes about four hours, and the schedule depends completely on the tide. Bonefish are said to be, pound for pound, the strongest, most "fighting" fish in the Bahamas.

If you want to go **deep-sea fishing,** the people to see are the Sawyer family, two brothers and a father. Referrals are usually made through the Green Turtle Club (☎ **809/365-4271**), or you can call directly at **809/365-4173.** Prices are negotiated.

## GREEN TURTLE CAY AFTER DARK

### Miss Emily's Blue Bee Bar
Victoria St. No cover. ☎ **809/365-4181.**

This bar is likely to be the scene of the liveliest party in the Family Islands at any time of day. Despite its simplicity, this family-run bar is one of the most famous places east of Miami. When I was last there, an energetic party was developing just before lunch, as a yachtswoman from West Virginia was demonstrating the frug she'd learned long ago in college, to enthusiastic applause. This and more are likely to be happening at this hallowed bar, where the walls near the bar area are covered with the business cards of past clientele, including Glen Campbell, Jimmy Buffet, and the late Lillian Carter.

The Goombay Smash, the specialty here (which costs $4), has been called "Abaco's answer to atomic fission," and its recipe includes secret proportions of coconut rum, "dirty" rum, apricot brandy, and pineapple juice.

The owner (she's really Mrs. Emily Cooper) is filled with humor and anecdotes. Failing health makes it impossible for her to always be on duty at the bar, but she has taught her daughter, Violet Smith, how to make the secret recipe. Tips at the

# The Lost Settlement

The first settlement in the Abacos was a village that no longer exists—Carleton—to the north and a little east of Treasure Cay (then called Lovel's Island). It was separated from the cay by Carleton Creek, a rivulet that flowed to join the sea. The little town was abandoned some 200 years ago and largely forgotten until 1979, when the site of the settlement was discovered and artifacts were found by archaeological excavation. In a bicentennial ceremony in 1983, a point of land near the site was designated Carleton Point, and a bronze plaque was placed there describing Carleton's brief history.

Loyalist refugees, fleeing the United States in 1783 following the formation of the new country and the withdrawal of British troops from the former colonies, migrated to the Bahamas, some settling in the Abacos, which were uninhabited at the time. Their aim was grandiose—they thought they could establish a colony that would become a new agricultural/mercantile empire under the protection of the British Crown.

Carleton, named for Sir Guy Carleton, who had been British commander in chief in New York, did not fulfill the dreams of the colonists. They staked out claims to land, but they learned, as had other settlers in other parts of the Bahamas, that this was not farming country. They built ships, but could not produce cargoes for them. The town initially had a population of 600 people, but civil strife and a devastating hurricane added to their woes, and soon some two-thirds of the settlers moved 18 miles to the southeast to found Marsh Harbour. Others moved to Cocoa Plum Creek and elsewhere, and some left the Bahamas. By 1800 Carleton had ceased to exist.

The Loyalists remaining in the Abacos were joined by migrants from Harbour Island on Eleuthera, who taught them to fish and even how to farm the rough acreage, and this union formed the nucleus from which today's Abaconians descend.

bar go to St. Peter's Anglican Church. No food is served here. The bar is open Monday to Saturday from 10am until late.

### Rooster's Rest Pub and Restaurant
Gilliam's Bay Rd. $2 cover. ☎ **809/365-4066.**

An out-of-the-way nightspot, and recommended separately as a restaurant, Rooster's attracts a crowd including both yachting people and locals, who gather here every Friday and Saturday night. "The Gully Roosters" perform on weekends, "the best time to go," according to New Plymouth residents. Beer costs $3.50 per bottle. Not visible from most of Parliament Street, the pub-restaurant is at the far side of a hill beyond the edge of town. The place is open daily from 10:30am to 10pm on quiet nights, later when there's activity.

## 4 Treasure Cay

Treasure Cay, called Lovel's Island in records as far back as the 1780s, was once separated from the Abaco mainland by Carleton Creek. Over the years, however, landfill operations have joined the two, although Treasure Cay retains the name. It now contains one of the most popular and elaborate resorts in the Family Islands. On the east coast of Great Abaco, it boasts not only 3½ miles of private sandy beach but also one of the finest marinas in the Commonwealth, with complete docking and charter facilities.

Before the opening of the tourist complex, the cay was virtually unsettled. So the resort has become the "city," providing its thousands of visitors with all the supplies they need, including medical goods, grocery-store items (liquor, naturally), and even bank services. The real estate office peddles the condos, and the builders predict that they will one day reach a capacity of 5,000 guests. What is hoped is that many visitors will like Treasure Cay so much that they'll buy into it.

## WHERE TO STAY & DINE

### Treasure Cay Beach Hotel & Villas

Treasure Cay, Abaco, the Bahamas. ☎ **809/367-2570** or toll free 800/327-1584. Fax 809/367-3362. For reservations, Treasure Cay Services, Inc., 2301 S. Federal Hwy., Fort Lauderdale, FL 33316 (☎ 305/525-7711). 64 rms, 36 suites and villas. A/C TV TEL. Winter, $80 single; $90 double; $100 suite for one; $125 suite for two; $350 villa for up to four. Off-season, $60 single; $70 double; $90 suite for one; $100 suite for two; $200 villa for up to four. MAP $34 per person extra. (EP rates.) AE, DC, MC, V. Free parking.

The foundation for this resort was laid in 1962, when the potential of its position near one of the finest beaches in the world was recognized by groups of international investors. One of the most popular in the Family Islands, the resort has attracted celebrities, including George C. Scott, who filmed the *Day of the Dolphin* here. In 1990, about a dozen of the most fully developed acres were sold to Jamaican hotel mogul Butch Stewart, who laid much-delayed plans to build a Bahamian branch of Sandals around what had once been the resort's main core.

However, the vast majority of the peninsula (1,200 acres), as well as the marina facility, all of the villas, 80 privately owned condominiums, the tennis courts, and several blocks of other housing remains under the ownership of the original investors. Guests sometimes rent electric golf carts (priced at around $25 a day) or bicycles, which enable them to more easily visit the far-flung palm and casuarina groves of this sprawling compound.

Today, the resort encourages a healthy blend of ownership by many different international investors, who own some of the villas and most of the condominiums. Mingling with them around the grounds are temporary hotel clients, who appreciate the *House and Garden* look of the architecture, the tropical plantings, the beachfront, an excellent golf course, and the marina facilities. Most accommodations overlook the dozens of sailing craft moored in the marina, and are simply furnished in conservatively modern tropical motifs. Villas usually contain private kitchens and two bedrooms.

**Dining/Entertainment:** The restaurant, the Spinnaker, serves an international cuisine, and two bars are in operation. Occasional evening musical entertainment is offered.

**Services:** Small-boat rentals, fishing guides for sportfishing and bonefishing, all-day or all-afternoon snorkeling excursions by boat, activities director.

**Facilities:** 150-slip marina, 18-hole golf course, scuba charters, golf-cart rentals, full array of water sports including parasailing, bicycle rental, eight tennis courts, and ferryboat running to Green Turtle Cay three times a day.

## SPORTS A TO Z

The **Treasure Cay Golf Club,** (☎ **809/367-2570**), Treasure Cay, offers 6,985 yards of fairways and was designed by Dick Wilson. Greens fees are $40 for 18 holes.

Full-service facilities for a variety of **water sports** are offered at the Treasure Cay Marina (☎ **809/367-2570**). Fishing boats with experienced skippers will guide anglers to tuna, marlin, wahoo, dolphin, barracuda, grouper, yellowtail, and snapper. Treasure Cay's own bonefish flats are just a short cruise from the marina. A full day of bonefishing costs $190, a half day $130; a sportfishing boat goes for $285 for a half day, $395 for a full day.

In addition, sailboat, Hobie Cat, and windsurfing board rentals can be arranged, as well as rental of snorkeling gear and **bicycles.** The marina has showers, fish-cleaning facilities, 24-hour weekday laundry service, and water and electricity hookups.

# 5 Marsh Harbour

The largest town in the Abacos, Marsh Harbour on Great Abaco is the third largest in the Bahamas. The first settlers were a group of Loyalists who were among those who tried to start a town called Carleton near Treasure Cay. The Abaconians who live here are usually shy but gracious.

Marsh Harbour is also a shipbuilding center, but tourism accounts for most of its revenues. The town has a shopping center and various other facilities not found in many Family Island settlements. You'll even spot the green turrets of a "castle" here, which was designed and constructed by Evans Cottrell, who wrote *Out Island Doctor.*

The shoreline provides one of the finest anchorages in the Family Islands, which is probably what lured the first settlers here 200 years ago. There are good water-taxi connections, making this a center for exploring some of the offshore cays, including Man-O-War and Elbow Cay. Its international airport serves not only the resorts at Marsh Harbour but those at Elbow Cay (Hope Town).

I prefer to treat Marsh Harbour more as a refueling depot than a sightseeing attraction, as there are far more colorful towns in the Abacos and the offshore cays. However, because of its location—roughly in the center of the island—you may want to use it as a base, since it has a number of good inns. Several places will rent you a bike if you want to pedal around the town.

## FAST FACTS

**Banks**    If you're going to be in the Abacos for an extended vacation, Marsh Harbour can serve your banking needs in an emergency. Some cays have banks that operate only three hours a week. In Marsh Harbour, try Barclays Bank, on Don MacKay Boulevard (☎ **809/367-2152**). Hours are Monday through Thursday 9:30am to 3pm and Friday 9:30am to 5pm.

**Car Rentals**    See "Getting Around" at the beginning of this chapter.

**Drugstore**    For your pharmaceutical needs, go to the Chemist Shop Pharmacy, Don MacKay Boulevard (☎ **809/367-3106**). Hours are Monday through Saturday 8:30am to 5:30pm.

**Medical Care**    The best medical clinic in the Abacos is in Marsh Harbour, the Great Abaco Clinic, Steede Bonnet Road (☎ **809/367-2510**).

**Police**    Dial **809/367-2560.**

**Post Office**    Marsh Harbour's post office (☎ **809/367-2571**) is on Don MacKay Boulevard.

**Shopping**    If you'd like to shop for gifts or souvenirs, the best place is the Loyalist Shoppe, Don MacKay Boulevard (☎ **809/367-2701**), which has leather goods from England and Italy, pottery, crystal, bone china, cosmetics, souvenirs, and gift items. It is open Monday through Saturday from 9am to 5pm.

## WHERE TO STAY

For an explanation of rate symbols, see "Tips on Accommodations" in Chapter 3.

### EXPENSIVE

#### ✪ Abaco Towns by the Sea

P.O. Box 486, Marsh Harbour, Abaco, the Bahamas. ☎ **809/367-2227** or toll free 800/ 322-7757 in the U.S. Fax 215/938-0656 in the U.S. 64 units. A/C. Year-round, $100–$170 unit for one to six. AE, MC, V. Free parking.

If you like this resort complex, you can purchase time shares. Set on sandy soil on a hilly terrain, it offers lagoon-type beaches looking out over the Sea of Abaco. A cluster of white stucco villas are grouped in a flowering landscape that includes bougainvillea, coconut palms, hibiscus, and banana trees scattered over a property considered deluxe for the area. Since any unit can accommodate up to six, this could be an economical choice, depending on the size of your party. Each accommodation offers two bedrooms, a combined living and dining area, a modern kitchen (with microwaves and dishwashers), and ceiling fans. Linens, bath, and beach towels are provided, and maid service is available for another $15 per day.

**Dining/Entertainment:** A poolside bar and grill is available, but you can easily walk to several restaurants nearby for more elaborate dinner fare. Live entertainment and dancing are featured three nights a week.

**Services:** Daily activities program, including visits to islands offshore, snorkeling, scuba, fishing, and golf.

**Facilities:** Swimming pool; lit tennis courts; boutique; bicycle, scooter, and car rentals; nearby sailing and powerboat rentals; jet skis, Sunfish, and sailboards.

#### ✪ Great Abaco Beach Hotel

P.O. Box 511, Marsh Harbour, Abaco, the Bahamas. ☎ **809/367-2158** or toll free 800/ 468-4799 in the U.S.; 305/359-2720 in Florida. Fax 809/367-2819. 80 rms, 6 villas. A/C TV TEL. Winter, $165 single or double; $300–$375 villa for four. Off-season, $95 single or double; $200–$300 villa for four. Continental breakfast $5 extra. (EP rates.) AE, MC, V. Free parking.

Created by a former pilot who served with Canadian forces in World War II, this resort attracts guests interested in diving and fishing. The resort is in two parts: the hotel with handsomely furnished rooms, with views opening onto the Sea of Abaco, plus the Boat Harbour Marina, with slips for 180 boats and full docking facilities. Each room is furnished in a tropical motif. There are also six villas, each with two bedrooms and two baths, plus a kitchen and living room area, along with private decks. To reach the place, you can take a taxi from Marsh Harbour Airport, a distance of four miles.

**Dining/Entertainment:** The resort boasts the most diverse dining options in Marsh Harbour, and you may want to patronize the place even if you're not a guest. Chief of these is Island Oasis (see separate recommendation below). Other drinking and dining choices include the Flamingo Room, serving an international cuisine in an octagon-shaped dining room overlooking the hotel's swimming pool and the Sea of Abaco. Below Decks serves snacks, including pizza. A band plays on weekends. Penny's Pub is a popular gathering place with the nautical set, and

Billfish Bar & Grill is a cabana-style restaurant at the marina, offering such fare as grilled "catch of the day" and hamburgers.

**Services:** Laundry.

**Facilities:** Two swimming pools, 150-slip marina, two tennis courts, fishing charters, diving trips, boat rentals, car-and-bicycle rentals, sightseeing tours.

## MODERATE

### Different of Abaco

Casuarina Point, P.O. Box AB-20092. Abaco, the Bahamas. ☎ **809/366-2150.** Fax 809/327-8152. 8 rms (all with bath). A/C. $200 single; $225 double. Rates include all meals. No credit cards. Free parking.

Set within the hamlet of Casuarina Point, 18 miles south of Marsh Harbour, this is a small, family-managed bonefishing club built at the edge of a saltwater marsh favored by birds, wild hogs, and iguana. Built in 1993, it's surrounded by a wide deck and a garden and contains a bar and restaurant where the only food available is the Bahamian fare that the staff will recite to you before you sit down for your meal. (The dining room's theme revolves around the primitive household implements that the owner, Nettie Symonette, has hung on her walls. Nonresidents are welcome to drop in for two-course meals priced at from $16 to $18 each.) Each of the bedrooms contains a screened-in porch, a ceiling fan, and simple, slightly battered furnishings. If you opt for a stay at this hotel, you'll be exposed to the inner workings of a closely knit, isolated community of residents firmly committed to preserving their environment. The place is not luxurious, and it probably won't be to everyone's liking, but its allure is most obvious to bonefishing enthusiasts. The hotel is intricately associated with several bonefishing guides in the neighborhood, any of whom can arrange full day fishing excursions for around $250 per couple. (Not all equipment is included in this fee. Be sure you understand all aspects of the arrangements before you commit yourself to a full-fledged fishing expedition here.)

## INEXPENSIVE

### ⊛ Conch Inn Resort & Marina (The Moorings)

P.O. Box AB20469, Marsh Harbour, Abaco, the Bahamas. ☎ **809/367-4000.** Fax 809/367-4004. 9 rms (all with bath). A/C TV. Year-round, $85 single or double. Extra person $10. Breakfast from $7 extra. AE, MC, V. Free parking.

Set at the junction of Bay Street and the southeastern edge of the harbor, this is a low-slung, one-story hotel whose premises are leased on a long-term basis by one of the world's largest yacht chartering companies, the Moorings. Its exterior is painted in white with pink-and-blue trim, and its bedrooms are earth-toned hideaways that contain both a queen-size bed and a double bed, a table, and two chairs. Roll-aways are available for extra occupants. All rooms overlook the yachts bobbing at any of 75 slips in the nearby marina.

Clients at this hotel include scuba aficionados and repeat visitors sailing Florida-based yachts who appreciate the opportunity to tie in for fuel, ice, fresh water, and use of the Laundromat, hotel rooms, restaurant, and bar. On the premises are an open-air swimming pool fringed with palm trees and a nearby branch of the Dive Abaco scuba facility. The on-site restaurant and bar (Conch Inn Café and Conch Out Bar) are under independent management and are recommended separately in "Where to Dine."

## BUNGALOW RENTALS

### The Lofty Fig Villas

P.O. Box AB20437, Marsh Harbour, Abaco, the Bahamas. ☎ and fax **809/367-2681**. 6 villas. A/C. Dec 15–Sept 15, $95 per day or $570 per week for two. Extra person $15. Sept 16–Dec 14, $75 per day or $450 per week for two. Extra person $10. (EP rates.) MC, V. Free parking.

This family-owned bungalow colony across from the Conch Inn overlooks the harbor. Built in 1970, it stands in a tropical landscaping with a freshwater pool. All units are air-conditioned and equipped for housekeeping. Rooms have one queen-size bed and a queen-size hide-a-bed sofa, a fully tiled bathroom, a dining area, a kitchen, and a private screened-in porch. Maid service is provided Monday through Saturday. A gazebo with a barbecue is also at poolside. The location is about a 10-minute walk to a supermarket and shops, and restaurants and bars lie just across the street. Marinas, a dive shop, and boat rentals are also close at hand.

### Pelican Beach Villas

Pelican Shores, P.O. Box AB20304, Marsh Harbour, Abaco, the Bahamas. ☎ **809/367-3600** or toll free 800/642-7268; 912/437-6220 in Darien, Georgia. Fax 912/437-6223 in Darien, Georgia. 5 cottages. A/C TEL. Year-round, $160 daily or $975 weekly for two. Extra person $15. (EP rates.) MC, V. Free parking for cars and boats.

In a double waterfront location—a beach in front and a lagoon in back—this cottage colony offers five pink two-bedroom, two-bath accommodations, all fronting on the sea. Every unit has a fully equipped kitchen and sleeps up to six with sleeper sofas. An 87-foot-long dock on the lagoon side of the property accommodates rental boats and is ideal for snorkeling or diving. Nestled in a grove of casuarina trees with its own small cove, the cottages are well furnished in a comfortable Bahamian style, with cathedral ceilings. Shaded picnic tables and beachfront hammocks are outside, and it's only a walk to bakeries and liquor and grocery stores. There's an on-site caretaker.

## WHERE TO DINE
### MODERATE

### Conch Inn Café/Conch Out Bar

At the Conch Inn (The Moorings), Bay St. ☎ **809/367-2319**. Reservations not necessary. Lunch salads, sandwiches, and platters $7–$12; dinner appetizers $3–$6; main courses $9.25–$22. MC, V. Breakfast daily 8–11am; lunch daily 11am–4pm; dinner Tues–Sun 6–9pm (last order). BAHAMIAN/INTERNATIONAL.

This is probably the most amusing, sophisticated, and international restaurant in Marsh Harbour. Set adjacent to the Conch Inn and the upscale marina facilities of the Moorings, it attracts whatever yachting enthusiast happens to be on-island at the time, and counts among its roster of visitors a surprising array of professional sports players as well as boaters from as far away as Newport, Bristol (England), and the Azores. The walls are decorated in virtually every kind of yachting memorabilia you could imagine (including fishnets, glass buoys, and the pennants of yacht clubs around the world), and the menu is appropriately laden with fish dishes. These include shrimp and crabmeat salad, lobster salad, seafood platters, at least four different preparations of grouper and snapper, and just about everything a chef could conceivably concoct from a conch. And if you're frittering away a few hours before your plane ride out of Marsh Harbour and want to drop in for a drink? Consider a Conch Killer ($4.50), whose yellow color derives from a potent mixture of rums and fruit juices.

## ✪ Island Oasis

In the Great Abaco Beach Hotel, Marsh Harbour. ☎ **809/367-2158.** Reservations recommended for dinner. Appetizers $3.50–$5; main courses $15–$25. AE, MC, V. Breakfast daily 7–10:30am; lunch daily 11:30am–2:30pm; dinner daily 6:30–10pm. BAHAMIAN/INTERNATIONAL.

At the Boat Harbour, overlooking the Sea of Abaco, this establishment is the main restaurant in the previously recommended hotel. The restaurant has a nautical theme and a Bahamian decor. Dock pilings rise from the water, and the place is open and airy. In the corner of the restaurant is the popular Penny's Pub. The menu changes daily, but fresh seafood is always featured, along with a well-chosen selection of meat-and-poultry dishes. Begin with chilled papaya soup or perhaps the lobster-and-crab pâté. For a main course, try hogfish and shrimp with a broccoli and basil cream sauce. Desserts are homemade. On Thursday, a buffet is presented, with such dishes as curried conch, fried chicken, and barbecued ribs. The cost is $20 per person, or $10 for children under 12.

## The Jib Room

Marsh Harbour Marina, Pelican Shores. ☎ **809/367-2700.** Reservations not required. Appetizers $3.50–$4.50; main courses $10–$15. MC, V. Lunch daily 10am–3pm; dinner Wed–Sun 6:30–10pm. BAHAMIAN/AMERICAN.

This restaurant is the drinking arena of local residents and boat owners who like its welcoming spirit. The Jib Room Restaurant is downstairs, and the Jib Room Bar is upstairs, with a ceiling canopy. The canopy is called "the yellow glow," since at night the roof acts as a yellow beacon to boaters in the harbor. Some nights are theme nights—for example, the place to be on Sunday is at the Jib's steak barbecue, with a live band. About 300 steaks are served that day. Wednesday is another favorite night, with baby-back ribs and live music on the agenda. Thursday, Friday, and Saturday nights are also special, with slightly more refined fare. Dishes include seafood platter, New York strip steak, and broiled lobster.

## Mangoes Restaurant

Front St., Marsh Harbour. ☎ **809/367-2366.** Reservations required. Appetizers $4.50–$6; main courses $15.50–$23; lunch $4.75–$10. AE, MC, V. Lunch daily 11:30am–2:30pm; dinner daily 6:30–9pm. Bar, daily 11:30am–midnight. Closed Sept–Nov 15. BAHAMIAN/AMERICAN.

Mangoes is one of the best restaurants, and certainly one of the most popular, on the island, attracting both yachties and residents. Set near the harborfront, it is also one of the town's most distinctive buildings. It also boasts a cedar-topped bar and a cathedral ceiling that soars above a deck jutting out over the water. Within the pink-and-white dining room you can order such appetizers as mozzarella sticks, fritters, chowders, and pizzas. Main dishes at lunchtime include a pasta special of the day, salads, sandwiches, and grilled and blackened filets of dolphin or grouper. Main evening courses include grilled steaks, swordfish, chicken stuffed with crabmeat, and baby-back ribs.

## Wally's

E. Bay St., Marsh Harbour. ☎ **809/367-2074.** Reservations required for dinner. Appetizers $3–$6; main courses $7–$10; set dinner $28 Mon, $14–$18 Sat. AE, MC, V. Lunch Mon–Sat 11:30am–3pm (bar open until 5:30pm); dinner Mon 7pm, Sat 6pm. Closed six weeks during Sept and Oct. BAHAMIAN/INTERNATIONAL.

Wally's competes with Mangoes as one of the island's most popular luncheon stop-overs. It occupies a well-maintained pink colonial villa on a lawn dotted with begonias across the street from the water. There's an outdoor terrace, a boutique, and an indoor bar and dining area filled with Haitian paintings. The special drinks are daiquiris, Bahama Mamas, and Goombay Smashes, which most visitors accompany with conch burgers, beef burgers, grouper Nantua style, a selection of sandwiches, and such homemade desserts as guava-filled chocolate cake. The only dinner served is on Monday and Saturday, and it is anticipated by local residents as a kind of weekly ritual of fine dining.

## INEXPENSIVE

### ☉ Mother Merle's Fishnet

Dundas Town. ☎ **809/367-2770.** Reservations recommended. Appetizers $3.50–$5; main courses $10–$25. AE, MC, V. Dinner Thurs–Tues 6:30–11:30pm. BAHAMIAN.

More substantial, and far more elaborate than you might have suspected, this restaurant sits about 1 $^1$/$_2$ miles from the main marinas of Marsh Harbour. Dundas Town was created as a settlement by the government in the postwar years. Mother Merle for many years has been known as one of the best local cooks. Behind an unpretentious facade is a pair of raftered rooms dimly lit with flickering candles. You can drink in the lounge before heading in for dinner. The menu includes barbecued chicken, grouper, fresh lobster, conch chowder, and game fish when it's available. Accompanying most meals is peas 'n' rice with hot sauce. For dessert, try key lime pie or coconut ice cream.

## SPORTS A TO Z

All the hotel keepers at Marsh Harbour can help fix you up with the right people to take care of your sporting requirements. For variety, you can also take the ferry over to Hope Town and avail yourself of the facilities offered there.

### BOAT CHARTERS

#### Sunsail

115 East Broward Blvd., Fort Lauderdale, FL 33001. ☎ toll free **800/327-2276** in the U.S. and Canada; 305/524-7553 outside the U.S. and Canada.

If you've got a good track record as a sailor, even of small boats, you can charter a yacht here big enough for the entire family, with just yourself as skipper to sail to all those places you've heard about. Sunsail, based in Marsh Harbour but with bookings arranged at Fort Lauderdale, is the operator of the largest charter fleet in the Bahamas. A bareboat charter is likely to cost you less than a comparable land-based vacation in the Family Islands or in Florida. Of course, you can cook your own meals in the fully equipped galley, complete with icebox (on larger boats, refrigerator and deepfreeze). You can barbecue your steak and fish on a hibachi fixed to the stern rail. You can go where you like, subject to instructions to keep out of shoal waters and stay, with one exception, within the line of the outer cays. Most of the time you cruise in waters 6 to 18 feet deep with the bottom clearly visible.

When you board your boat, you'll find it cleaned, fueled, watered, provisioned, inspected, and ready to sail. Sunsail will give you and your crew a complete familiarization briefing on everything on board from bow to stern—anchors, rigging, sails, engine, radio, lights, navigational aids, cooking equipment, and the outboard dinghy towed astern of every boat. Before you actually sail, they'll give you a chart briefing, warning you of the few dangerous areas, how to "read" the water, and how best to make the Whale Cay ocean passage that takes you to the northern section of Abaco Sound.

Bareboat charters are usually in the range of $995 to $4,995 per week, depending on the vessel and the season. For more information, or reservations, write to Sunsail at the above address.

### Sea Horse Boat Rentals
Great Abaco Beach Resort, Marsh Harbour. ☎ **809/367-2513.**

Boat rentals are offered by this outlet, which used to be at Hope Town on Elbow Cay. In its new location, it offers 18-foot Boston whalers for $94 per day or 20-foot vessels for $99. You can rent a 22-foot Boston whaler for $120 per day. The outlet also rents bicycles here for $8 a day if you'd like to go exploring the relatively flat area around Marsh Harbour. Hours are daily from 8am to 5pm.

## TENNIS

### Great Abaco Beach Hotel
Marsh Harbour. ☎ **809/367-2158.**

Two hard-surface courts are available at this hotel. Nonguests pay $10 for a game.

## WATER SPORTS

### Dive Abaco
Marsh Harbour. ☎ **809/367-2787** or toll free 800/247-5338 in the U.S.

Dive Abaco offers personally guided tours for scuba divers and snorkelers alike. You can explore tunnels and caverns in the world's third longest barrier reef. Resort courses for uncertified divers are all inclusive for $100. Scuba trips, including tanks and weights for certified divers, are $65 or else $35 for snorkel trips. Both dive and snorkel trips depart daily at 9:30am, and afternoon trips are as demand dictates. Shop hours are daily from 8:30am to 5pm. Ask for owner-operator Keith Rogers.

## 6  Great Guana Cay

Longest of the Abaco cays, Great Guana, on the east side of the chain, stretches 7 miles from tip to tip, lying between Green Turtle Cay and Man-O-War Cay. The cay has a 7-mile-long beach, which some consider unsurpassed in the Bahamas. The reef fishing is superb, and bonefish are plentiful in the shallow bays.

The settlement stretches along the beach at the head of the palm-fringed Kidd's Cove, named after the pirate; and the ruins of an old sisal mill near the western end of the island make for an interesting detour. The island has about 150 residents, most of them descendants of Loyalists who left Virginia and the Carolinas to settle in this remote place, often called the "last spot of land before Africa."

As in similar settlements in New Plymouth and Man-O-War Cay, their houses resemble old New England. Over the years the traditional pursuits of the islanders have been boatbuilding and carpentry. They are also farmers and fishers. It won't take you long to explore the village, because it has only two small stores, a one-room schoolhouse, and an Anglican church—and that's about it.

Instead of automobiles, small boats are used for getting around the island. On the cay, small boats are available to charter for a half day or a full day (or a month, for that matter). For example, a 23-foot sailboat, fully equipped for living and cruising, is available for charter, and deep-sea fishing trips can be arranged.

**Albury's Ferry Service,** Marsh Harbour (☎ **809/367-3147**), runs a charter service to the island, a one-way ride costing $85 for one to five passengers.

## WHERE TO STAY & DINE

### Guana Beach Resort

Great Guana Cay (P.O. Box 530218, Miami, FL 33153). ☎ **809/367-3590**. Fax 305/751-9570 in Miami. 8 rms, 7 suites. A/C. Winter, $99–$125 single or double; $150–$210 suite. Off-season, $79–$115 single or double; $115–$175 suite. MAP $35 per person extra. (EP rates.) MC, V. Free parking.

The only hotel on the island, this is a remotely located resort of comfortably furnished units, ideal for boat owners and escapists, who like its barefoot policy. Gordon and Mary Sadler, from Stamford, Connecticut, liked the resort when they first saw it, with its 7 miles of white sandy beaches and coconut palm trees. They purchased it and renovated it, adding such touches as a freshwater pool. Accommodations have their own kitchens. Rooms are furnished in a casual, relaxed, Bahamian style. The resort has a marina, as well as a good Bahamian dining room and bar if you're over only for the day. Conch burgers with cold beer are often served for lunch. Informal local entertainment is often arranged. Babysitting can also be arranged, and laundry facilities are available. Bicycles can be rented for island tours.

## 7 Man-O-War Cay

Visiting here is like going back in time. Man-O-War Cay shares a cultural link with New Plymouth on Green Turtle Cay, but the people here may not have advanced quite so far. The island has some lovely beaches, and many visitors come here to enjoy them—but it's best to leave your more daring swimwear for other shores.

Some find the people here puritanical in outlook. They are deeply religious, and there is no crime—unless you bring it with you. Alcoholic beverages aren't sold, although you can bring your own supply.

Like New Plymouth, Man-O-War is a Loyalist village, with indications of a New England background. The pastel clapboard houses, built by ships' carpenters and trimmed in gingerbread, are set off by freshly painted white picket fences intertwined with bougainvillea.

The people here are basically shy, but they do welcome outsiders to their remote, isolated island. They are proud of their heritage, and many, especially the old-timers, have known plenty of hard times. They are similar to (and related to many of) the "conchs" of Key West, a tough, insular people who have exhibited a proud independence of spirit for many years.

If you look through the tiny listing for this cay in the phone book, you'll see that the name Albury predominates. In this famed boatbuilding capital of the Bahamas, Albury long ago became synonymous with that business. You can still see descendants of the early Alburys at work at a boatyard on the harbor. Albury shipbuilders still make Man-O-War runabouts, so often seen sailing in the waters of the Bahamas.

Tourism has really only begun on Man-O-War Cay. Because of the relative lack of hotels and restaurants many visitors come over just for the day, often in groups from Marsh Harbour.

To reach Man-O-War Cay, you must cross the water from Marsh Harbour. **Albury's Ferry Service** (☎ 809/367-3147 in Marsh Harbour, **809/365-6010** in Man-O-War) leaves from a dock near the Great Abaco Beach Resort there. The round-trip fare is $12 for adults and $6 for children, and the ride takes about 45 minutes. Except for a few service vehicles, the island is free of cars. But if you want to explore—and don't want to walk—ask around and see if one of the locals will rent you a golf cart.

## WHERE TO STAY

### Schooner's Landing
Man-O-War Cay, Abaco, the Bahamas. ☎ **809/365-6072.** Fax 809/365-6285. 4 2-bedroom apts. A/C TV. Oct–May, $850 per week or $150 per day. June–Sept, $995 per week or $175 per day. Three-day minimum stay required. AE, MC, V.

Set within an isolated position on Man-O-War Cay's northeastern edge, this four-unit apartment complex is the only officially designated hotel on the island. At the time of its construction (1985), its architects wisely added a seawall between its lawns and hibiscus shrubs and the crashing surf, requiring a detour for swimmers and snorkelers who meander a short distance down to the sands of a nearby beach. Each unit contains a duplex format of two stories, a kitchen, ceiling fans, two private bathrooms, a TV set whose only reception comes from an adjacent VCR machine, and a summery decor of wicker-and-rattan furniture. There's no bar or restaurant on-site, but either of two grocery stores on the island will deliver whatever a consumer phones for, and most visitors opt to cook in anyway. Facilities include a private dock for anyone who arrives by private boat, and barbecue facilities lie within a gazebolike structure on the grounds.

## WHAT TO SEE & DO

**Joe's Studio,** (☎ 809/365-6082), on the harborfront, sells an inventory of island-related odds and ends that make this an appealing stopover. Favorite items for sale here are the half-rib models of local sailing dinghies crafted from mahogany and mounted in half profile on a board. They're a substantial but durable souvenir of your visit. Other items include original watercolors, handcrafted woodwork from native woods, and nautical souvenirs and gifts.

Perhaps the most unusual store and studio on the island, **Albury's Sail Shop** (☎ 809/365-6014), occupies a house at the eastern end, overlooking the water. Part of the floor space is devoted to the manufacture (and the other half to the display) of an inventory of brightly colored canvas garments and accessories. The cloth that is universally used—8-ounce cotton duck—once served as sailcloth for the community's boats. When synthetic sails came into vogue, four generations of Albury women put the cloth and their talents to use. Don't stop without chatting with the Albury women. Hours are Monday through Saturday from 7am to 5pm.

# 8 Elbow Cay (Hope Town)

Elbow Cay, noted for the many white sandy beaches that attract hundreds of visitors to its shores, is connected by a regular 20-minute, $12-round-trip **ferry** or **water-taxi** service to Great Abaco at Marsh Harbour. Call Albury's Ferry Service at **809/367-3147** for more information. The cay's largest settlement is **Hope Town,** a little village with a candy-striped 120-foot lighthouse, the most photographed attraction in the Family Islands. The kerosene-powered light is still in service.

## WHAT TO SEE & DO

You can climb to the top of the lighthouse for a sweeping view of the surrounding land and water. From the time construction on this beacon first began in 1838, it came under a great deal of harassment from the Abaco wreckers, who lived on salvaged cargo from wrecked and foundered ships. Seeing an end to their means of livelihood, they did much to sabotage the light in the early days.

Hope Town, often called a "time-warp" hamlet, like other offshore cays of the Abacos, was settled by Loyalists who left the new United States and came to the Bahamas to remain subjects of the British Crown, spreading out from the now long-vanished settlement of Carleton near Treasure Cay. The town will evoke thoughts of old Cape Cod. It has clapboard saltbox cottages weathered to a silver gray or painted in pastel colors, with white picket fences setting them off. The buildings may remind you of New England, but this palm-fringed island has a definite South Seas flavor.

Over the years Hope Town has attracted many famous visitors, some of whom, such as Dr. George Gallup, the pollster, liked it so much that they built "homes away from home" here.

The island is almost free of vehicular traffic. In exploring Hope Town, you can take one of two roads: "Up Along" or "Down Along," the latter running along the water.

Malone seems to be the most popular name here. The founding mother of the town circa 1783 (perhaps 1775) was Wyannie Malone, who came here as a widow with four children. Her descendants are still a big part of the population of 500 full-time residents. A **museum** on Queen's Highway (no phone) is dedicated to Wyannie's memory, containing exhibits tracing the rich history of the cay. It's generally open from 10am to noon but you can't be sure. Donations are welcome.

**ESSENTIALS**  **Drugstore** Try the Clear View Drug Store (☎ **809/365-6217**).

**Post Office**  There is a local post office (☎ **809/365-6214**), but expect mail sent from here to take a long time. The location is at the head of the upper public dock.

## WHERE TO STAY
### MODERATE

#### Abaco Inn

Hope Town, Elbow Cay, Abaco, the Bahamas. ☎ **809/366-0133** or toll free 800/468-8799 in the U.S. Fax 809/366-0113. 12 rms. A/C. Winter, $125 single; $135 double. Off-season, $105–$115 single; $115–$125 double. MAP $35 per person extra. MC, V. Free parking.

This is the area's most sophisticated and desirable resort. It nestles on a ridge of sandy soil on the narrowest section of Elbow Cay, about 1 1/2 miles south of Hope Town. As you stand on the ridge, you'll find yourself on a strategically important land bridge between the crashing surf of the jagged eastern coast and the sheltered waters of White Sound and the Sea of Abaco to the west. An informal "barefoot elegance" and welcoming enthusiasm prevail. The resort's social center is in a modern and rambling clubhouse with a fireplace and the most appealing bar on the island.

Each of the accommodations, which are scattered between the palms and sea grapes of the sandy terrain, has a hammock placed conveniently nearby for quiet afternoons of reading or sleeping, a ceiling fan, private bath, and a comfortable decor of white wooden walls and conservative furniture. When you tire of your cabin with its carefully maintained privacy, you can dream of faraway places from a perch in the cedar-capped gazebo, which sits between the saltwater pool and the rocky tidal flats of the Atlantic.

## Club Soleil Resort

Western Harbourfront, Hope Town, Elbow Cay. ☎ **809/366-0003.** Fax 809/366-0254. 6 rms (all with bath). A/C MINIBAR TV. Winter, $115 single or double; $125 triple; $135 quad. Off-season, $110 single or double; $120 triple; $130 quad. MAP $35 per person extra. MC, V. Free parking.

Because of its isolated position near the lighthouse on the mostly uninhabited western edge of Hope Town's harbor, you'll have to arrive here by boat. If you bring your own, you can moor it at this establishment's marina, but if you happen not to have one, a phone call to the owners can quickly arrange a free waterborne transfer from any nearby coastline you designate. Rooms are contained in a two-story motel-like annex, whose windows overlook a swimming pool as well as the boats that moor at the wooden pier. Each room contains two double beds, coffee-making equipment, and a small refrigerator stocked with beer and soft drinks. The restaurant is covered separately in "Where to Dine," below.

## Hope Town Harbour Lodge

Hope Town, Abaco. ☎ **809/366-0095** or toll free 800/316-7844. Fax 809/366-0286. 21 rms (all with bath). A/C. Winter, $100–$115 single; $110–$125 double. Discounts of around $10 per room in off-season. Breakfast from $8–$10 extra. MC, V. Closed Sept–Oct. Free parking.

Set on a hilltop overlooking the hamlet of Hope Town, the core of this much-renovated inn began its life as a private home during the 1950s. Today, it's the domain of the Gale and Kenyon families, whose yacht rental service (Island Marine) is one of the larger enterprises in the Abacos. Accommodations consist of 14 rooms in the main house (whose windows overlook Hope Town's harbor), and about 7 prefabricated cottages (without kitchens) scattered around the swimming pool, within a garden. Each of these overlooks the Atlantic and lie across the road from the main building. Accommodations are comfortable but simple, each decorated in colors which emulate Bahamian flowers: pink, fuchsia, blue, and yellow. Each room was renovated in 1993, and each has a ceiling fan. Restaurants on-site include an upper-floor restaurant within the main building whose view includes both the harbor and the Atlantic; and a less formal eatery beside the hotel's swimming pool that serves only breakfast and lunch. (Appetizers at dinner in the more formal restaurant range from $4.50 to $9; main courses cost from $17 to $26.) Facilities include a marina and a staff who can arrange most water sports.

## VILLA RENTALS

### Hope Town Hideaways

Hope Town, Elbow Cay, Abaco, the Bahamas. ☎ **809/366-0224.** Fax 809/366-0434. 5 units. A/C TV. Year-round, $225 daily. On 1-week rentals $175 daily. Extra person $20. (EP rates.) AE, MC, V. Free parking.

These villas attract families, couples, and fishing buddies. Each unit has a large kitchen. The villas lie on 11 acres bordering the water. Each villa has a large deck, dining room, living area with two single daybeds, and two bedrooms with queen-size beds and deck entrances. Each of the master bedrooms includes custom built-in beds, dressers, makeup vanities, as well as reading lamps, a large bath with shower, and a private entrance deck. Each unit sleeps one or two couples (the limit is six guests per villa). Furnishings are elegant and attractive. The most recent addition is a honeymoon cottage with a gazebo shower and an outside garden. The villa cluster lies in the shadow of the lighthouse, overlooking boats moored in the harbor and the clapboard houses of Hope Town. Owners Chris and Peggy Thompson do everything from overseeing housekeeping to arranging rental boats, guided fishing trips, picnics, island-hopping excursions, and scuba-and-snorkeling trips.

### Sea Spray Resort & Marina

White Sound, Elbow Cay, Abaco, the Bahamas. ☎ **809/366-0065.** Fax 809/366-0383. 6 villas. A/C. Year-round, $700–$950 per week for one to four persons. (EP rates.) AE, V. Free parking.

On six acres of landscaped grounds, these one- and two-bedroom villas are owned and operated by Monty and Ruth Albury, who run them in a welcoming, personal way. The Albury's share their vast experience of what to see and do on Elbow Cay and in the Abaco area. You can bicycle, sail, go deep-sea fishing, snorkel, bonefish, or explore nearby deserted islands.

Villas have comfortable Bahamian tropical furnishings, with full kitchens and decks overlooking the water. They also operate an informal clubhouse restaurant, serving Bahamian dishes. Sea Spray offers many extras, including daily maid service, unlimited Sunfish use, a private barbecue pit, and free boat dockage up to 23 feet, as well as a freshwater swimming pool. The location is 3 1/2 miles south of Hope Town along the coastal road.

## WHERE TO DINE

### Abaco Inn

Hope Town. ☎ **809/367-2666.** Reservations required. Appetizers $3–$6; main courses $16–$26; lunch $4–$10. MC, V. Breakfast daily 8–10:30am; lunch daily noon–2pm; dinner daily 6:30–9pm. BAHAMIAN/AMERICAN.

The best food is served in the clubhouse of the previously recommended hotel, within view of the crashing surf and a weathered gazebo. The chef prepares such lunch dishes as conch chowder, lobster salad, pasta primavera, and salads with delectable homemade dressings laced with tarragon and other herbs. There is a changing dinner menu of seafood and meats, each expertly seasoned and well prepared. Typical meals are likely to begin with seafood bisque or vichyssoise, followed by broiled lobster, grilled tuna with béarnaise sauce, or broiled red snapper with a light salsa sauce. The key lime pie or coconut pie is delectable. The inn will send a minivan to collect you from other parts of the island if you phone in advance.

### Club Soleil Resort

Western Harbourfront, Hope Town. ☎ **809/366-0003.** Reservations recommended for dinner. Lunch main courses $4–$10; dinner main courses (including appetizers, salad, soup) $21.50–$24. MC, V. Breakfast daily 8–10am; lunch daily noon–2pm; dinner daily 6:30–8:30pm. BAHAMIAN/SEAFOOD.

This pleasant restaurant, on the premises of a marina, lies within a sunny building set on piers, on the western side of Hope Town's harbor. To reach it, you'll arrive either by private yacht or by phoning the owners in advance. (They'll send a boat to meet you wherever you specify.) Lunch might include conch burgers, cheeseburgers, and an array of such salads as niçoise and lobster. The more elaborate evening meals include snapper, grouper, or kingfish served with a butter and garlic sauce. The broiled seafood platter with lemon and garlic is the house specialty. Other tempters include rack of lamb Provençale, steaks, and surf and turf.

### Harbour's Edge

Hope Town. ☎ **809/366-0087**. Reservations not accepted. Appetizers $5.50–$9.50; main courses $17–$21; lunch from $8. No credit cards. Lunch Wed–Mon 11:30am–2:30pm; dinner Wed–Mon 6–9pm. Closed mid-Sept to mid-Oct. BAHAMIAN.

One of the town's most popular restaurants is set on piers above the water, in a clapboard house next to the post office. A bar is found near the entrance, with an adjacent waterside deck for watching the passage of boats. There's also a tile-floored dining room, where the crackle of VHF radio is always audible. Boat owners and local residents reserve tables on the short-wave radio, Channel 16. Lunch includes conch fritters, conch chowder, hamburgers, sandwiches, and conch platters. Dinners include plain yet well-prepared food, such as panfried pork chops, char-grilled grouper, New York strip steak, and fried chicken.

### Rudy's Place

Center Line Rd., Elbow Cay. ☎ **809/366-0062**. Reservations required. Three-course fixed-price dinners $20–$25 each, plus drinks. MC, V. Dinner Mon–Sat 6:30–8:45pm (last order). Closed Sept–Oct. BAHAMIAN.

Because of its isolated position in a wooden house in a valley in the center of the island, this restaurant provides free transportation before and after dinner. It's owned by Rudy Moree, who prepares recipes handed down by his Bahamian grandmother. These, adapted to the tastes of his international clientele, might include crayfish tails baked with parmesan and butter, broiled shrimp in a white wine and garlic sauce, or roasted duck in an orange sauce. You'll dine in a modern dining room sheathed with knotty pine.

## SHOPPING

Of course, no one comes to Hope Town just to shop, but once you're here you might want to buy a souvenir or gift. At Kemp's Straw Market, Hope Town, you can find some gift items made by local residents.

### Ebb Tide Gift Shop

Hope Town. ☎ **809/366-0088**.

The best-stocked gift shop in town is found in a white clapboard house with yellow trim, one block from the harbor. Inside, an employee sells Androsia batiks, jewelry, T-shirts, fabric by the yard, engravings, maps, baby-size quilts, and suntan lotion. Hours are 9am to 4:30pm Monday through Saturday. Closed from mid-September to November 1.

### Native Touches

Hope Town. ☎ **809/366-0053**.

Several of the items sold here are handcrafted. The selection includes hand-painted T-shirts, jewelry, framed maps, gift items, and Bahamian fashions. Hours are Monday through Saturday from 9:30am to 4:30pm.

## SPORTS A TO Z

### Island Marine

Parrot Cay, Hope Town. ☎ **809/366-0282**.

Rental boats can take you to the boatbuilding settlement on Man-O-War Cay, to sculptor Randolph Johnston's bronze foundry in Little Harbour (see below), to the abandoned remains of Wilson City, and to many uninhabited cays and deserted beaches where you can go shelling, beachcombing, exploring, and picnicking.

Charter boats are available for bonefishing, reef fishing, and deep-sea fishing. Bonefish, grouper, snapper, wahoo, yellowtail, dolphin, kingfish, and others are abundant in the local waters, and resident Bahamian guides can show you where they are. A 17-foot Boston whaler rents for $80 per day. The office operates daily from 8am to 5pm.

## 9  Little Harbour

In the Abaco gift and souvenir shops you'll see a remarkable book, *Artist on His Island*, detailing the true-life adventures of Randolph and Margot Johnston, who lived a *Swiss Family Robinson*–type adventure with their three sons. Arriving on this southerly point of the Abacos aboard their old Bahamian schooner, the *Langosta*, they lived in one of the natural caves on the island until they eventually erected a thatched dwelling for themselves.

That was some time ago—in 1951. Now the Johnstons have achieved international fame as artists and sculptors while still living on their own Little Harbour island, a cay shaped like a circle, with a white-sand beach running along most of it.

If you ask at your hotel in Marsh Harbour, chances are that an arrangement can be made for you to visit the island, which is serviced by Albury's Ferry. This is the southernmost stop of the ferry line. Since the island is private property, you are asked to treat it as if it's someone's home you're visiting—as indeed it is.

On the island is a foundry in which Mr. Johnston, using an old "lost-wax" method, casts his bronze sculptures, many of which are in prestigious galleries today. Mrs. Johnston creates porcelain figurines of island life—birds, fish, boats, and fishermen. She also works in glazed metals. They welcome visitors at their studio daily from 10 to 11am and 2 to 3pm. It's also possible to purchase their art, which comes in a wide price range.

# 9

# Eleuthera, Harbour Island & Spanish Wells

**F**ounded in 1648, Eleuthera Island was the first permanent settlement in the Bahamas. It is considered the "birthplace of the Bahamas," a sort of Bahamian Plymouth Rock. In search of religious freedom, the Eleutherian Adventurers came here from Bermuda, finding and colonizing the long, narrow island that still carries their name (Greek for freedom). The locals call it "Cigatoo."

What these adventurers found was an island 100 miles long and a bow shot wide (an average of two miles), lying on the eastern flank of the Bahamas. Today Eleuthera is an island of white- and pink-sand beaches edged by casuarina trees, high, rolling green hills, sea-to-sea views, dramatic cliffs, sheltered coves, old villages of pastel-washed cottages, and exclusive resorts built around excellent harbors.

Eleuthera begins 70 miles east of Nassau and can be reached by a 30-minute air flight. It encompasses about 200 square miles. The island is known for its ocean holes that swirl saltwater into land-locked rock formations.

The population today, estimated at 10,000, is a medley of farmers, shopkeepers, and fisherpeople. Roads run along the coastline today, but if you engage in any extensive touring, you'll find that some of them are not adequately paved.

**Eleuthera** rivals the Abacos in its lure for the foreign visitor. Along with the Abacos, it has the largest concentration of resort hotels outside of Nassau/Paradise Island and Freeport/Lucaya.

Of the 10 destinations recommended in this chapter, **Harbour Island** gets my vote as the number-one choice. Dunmore Town on Harbour Island was the original capital of the Bahamas, and is the island's oldest and most charming settlement. Many visitors who have traveled all over the Bahamas consider Harbour Island the most beautiful in the archipelago.

**Spanish Wells** is another small island just off the north end of Eleuthera. Spanish galleons put sailors ashore to fill the ships' casks with fresh water after long sea voyages—hence the present-day name of the island.

The fishing and diving in the waters around Eleuthera are top-notch. The islands offer a wide choice of coral gardens, reefs, drop-offs, wrecks, and drift dives. Fishers come to Eleuthera for bottom, bone-, and deep-sea fishing, testing their skill against the

---

## What's Special About Eleuthera & Its Environs

Beaches
- Harbour Island beaches, three miles of powdery pink sands, considered the most beautiful beaches in the Bahamas.
- Windermere Island beaches, centering at Savannah Sound, with its sheltered sands and facilities for water sports.

Great Islands & Villages
- Harbour Island, or Briland as locals call it, off the northern coast, settled before the United States became a nation.
- Spanish Wells, called "the quiet corner of the Bahamas," founded by the Loyalist Eleutherian Adventurers.
- Governor's Harbour, a thriving port for generations, now sleepily nestled in Cupid's Cay where the Eleutherian Adventurers landed.
- The Current, in North Eleuthera, with some houses built on low piles—inhabitants said to have descended from a "lost tribe" of Native Americans.

Nature
- The Cave, south of Gregory Town, said to have been frequented by pirates—local guides take you on a trip of eerie exploration, bats and all.
- Glass Window, narrowest point on Eleuthera—a narrow bridge linking two sea-battered bluffs, separating Governor's Harbour from North Eleuthera.

---

dolphin, the wahoo, the blue or white marlin, the Allison tuna, and the amberjack. Charter boats are available at Powell Point, Rock Sound, Spanish Wells, and Harbour Island. Sunfish, sailboats, and Boston Whalers for reef fishing can also be rented.

## GETTING THERE

**BY PLANE**   Eleuthera has three main airports. North Eleuthera Airport, obviously, serves the north along with two major offshore cays, Harbour Island and Spanish Wells. Governor's Harbour Airport serves the center of the island, and Rock Sound International Airport handles traffic to South Eleuthera. Make sure, when making your reservations, that your flight will arrive at the right airport; one visitor flew into Rock Sound Airport, only to face a $100 ride and a water-taxi trip before reaching his final destination of Harbour Island in the north.

Bahamasair (☎ 800/222-4262) offers daily flights between Nassau and the three airports, North Eleuthera, Governor's Harbour, and Rock Sound. Bahamasair also flies in from Miami daily.

In addition, several commuter airlines, with regularly scheduled service, fly from the Florida mainland with either nonstop or one-stop service. Many private flights use the North Eleuthera Airport, with its 4,500-foot paved runway. It is an official Bahamian port of entry, and a Customs and Immigration official is on hand.

USAir Express (☎ 800/428-4322) operates what might be the most popular way of reaching two of Eleuthera's airports directly from the mainland of Florida. Flights depart once a day from Fort Lauderdale flying nonstop to North Eleuthera, then continuing on after a brief unloading of passengers and baggage to Governor's Harbour.

**BY MAIL BOAT**   Several mail boats from Nassau, leaving from Potter's Cay Dock, visit Eleuthera, but their schedules are subject to change because of weather conditions. For more details of sailings, consult the dockmaster at Potter's Cay Dock in Nassau (☎ **809/393-1064**).

The MV *Current Pride* goes from Nassau to Current Island, serving lower and upper Bogue. It departs Nassau at 7am Thursday, returning on Tuesday.

The MV *Bahamas Daybreak II* leaves Nassau, heading for North Eleuthera, Spanish Wells, and Harbour Island. Departures are on Thursday at 6am from Nassau, with a return on Monday.

The MV *Lady Frances* leaves Nassau on Tuesday (returning on Sunday) heading for Central Eleuthera: Hatchet Bay and Governor's Harbour. The same vessel goes from Nassau to South Eleuthera: Davis Harbour and Rock Sound. It leaves Nassau on Monday, returning on Tuesday.

# 1  Rock Sound

In South Eleuthera, Rock Sound is a small, tree-shaded village, the principal center of the island and its most exclusive enclave. To the south of Tarpum Bay, it opens onto Exuma Sound. The town is at least two centuries old, and it has many old-fashioned homes with picket fences out front. Once it was notorious for the wreckers who lured ships ashore with false beacons. In those days it was known as "Wreck Sound."

Besides having an airport, Rock Sound also boasts a modern shopping center. Many residents who live in South Eleuthera come here to stock up on supplies.

A lot of famous people have visited here, including the Mountbattens, titans of industry, and an occasional movie star.

The Ocean Hole to the east is about $1\frac{1}{4}$ miles from the heart of the town. This is a saltwater lake that eventually links to the sea. You can walk right down to the edge of the water. This is one of the most attractive spots on Eleuthera. The "hole" is said to be bottomless. Many tropical fish can be seen here; they seem to like to be photographed—but only if you feed them first.

## FAST FACTS

**Car Rentals**   Ask at your hotel for what's available. No national car-rental agencies operate here. Dingle Motor Service, King's Street (☎ **809/334-2031**), might rent you a vehicle at $60 a day.

**Church**   Rock Sound has an Anglican church, near the water.

**Medical Care**   A doctor and four resident nurses form the staff of the Rock Sound Medical Clinic (☎ **809/334-2226**).

**Police**   Telephone **809/334-2244** to call the police.

**Shopping**   If you're looking for gifts and souvenirs, try Goombay Gifts, Market Place King (☎ **809/334-2191**). Buy liquor at Sturrup's Liquor Store, Queen's Highway, Market Place (☎ **809/334-2219**).

## WHERE TO STAY

For an explanation of rate symbols, refer to "Tips on Accommodations" in Chapter 3. As of this writing, the famous Cotton Bay Club—the reason "Who's Who in America" went to Rock Sound in the first place—remains closed, with no announced date for its reopening. What remains to house guests are one or two places so simple they can be recommended only to the most undemanding clients.

# Eleuthera, Harbour Island & Spanish Wells

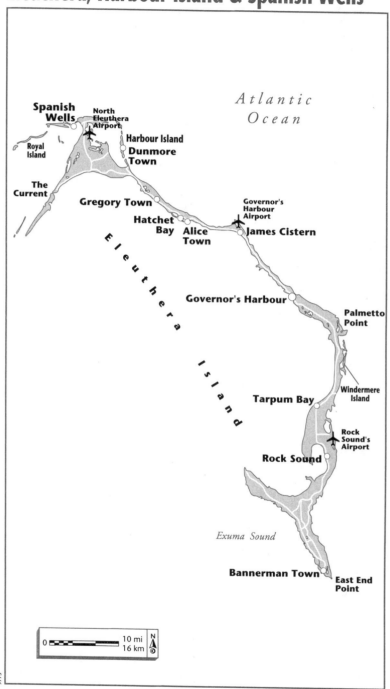

### Edwina's Place

P.O. Box 30, Rock Sound, Eleuthera, the Bahamas. ☎ **809/334-2094.** 9 rms. A/C. Year-round, $60 single; $75 double. (Rates include continental breakfast.) No credit cards. Free parking. Closed Sept–Oct.

This Bahamian-owned place is just a mile south of Rock Sound airport. Its utter simplicity is balanced by the enthusiastic hospitality of Mrs. Edwina Burrows, who vows to carry on in spite of the spectacular drop-off in tourism in South Eleuthera. Set directly on the water, her guest rooms are furnished plainly. No one in the area has much money for state-of-the-art maintenance. There is a restaurant on the premises (see "Where to Dine," below).

All village facilities are within walking distance of the motel, and if you want to go farther afield, Mrs. Burrows says that if you'll put some gas in her old car, "you can take off," but you'll be charged for the privilege. Most of the guests live in their swimsuits, so dress is decidedly casual. Tennis, snorkeling, scuba diving, deep-sea fishing, and boating can be arranged by the management.

## WHERE TO DINE

### Edwina's Place

A mile south of Rock Sound International Airport. ☎ **809/334-2094.** Reservations not required. Appetizers $2–$3.50; main courses $8–$18; lunch $12. No credit cards. Breakfast daily 7–10am; lunch daily noon–2pm; dinner daily 6–8pm. BAHAMIAN.

The hospitable, hardworking owner of this simple little roadside restaurant and adjoining motel (see "Where to Stay," above) will prepare you her acclaimed conch fritters, cracked conch, or perhaps a baked fish based on the catch of the day. She sometimes uses produce from her own garden. I've enjoyed her five-bean salad, and her stuffed tomatoes are delicious. Prices for a main course include appetizers. Lunch can be simple fare, such as fish sandwiches. Top off the meal with Mrs. Burrows' coconut pie, or try her rum cake or guava duff. Try to go for dinner before 8pm.

### Sammy's Place

Albury's Lane, Rock Sound. ☎ **809/334-2121.** Reservations recommended only for special meal requests. Bahamian breakfasts $7, appetizers $2–$5; main courses $11–$21. AE. Daily 8am–10pm. BAHAMIAN.

Set on the northeastern approach to the settlement, in a neighborhood that even the owner refers to as "the back side of town," this is one of the largest restaurants in Rock Sound. Opened in 1987 by entrepreneur Sammy Culmer (who's assisted by Margarita, his daughter), it's contained within a two-story, white-sided building constructed of cement blocks. Inside, within a peach-colored decor whose only view overlooks the street outside, you can order drinks which include Bahama Mamas and rum punches ($3.50 each), conch fritters, conch chowder, marinated conch salads, creole-style grouper, breaded scallops, pork chops, and lobster. If you happen to drop in before around 11am, you might be tempted by a Bahamian breakfast of stewed fish with johnnycakes or a selection of egg dishes or omelets. Everything is very simple here, but many visitors prefer it for its almost complete lack of pretensions.

A quartet of simple, bare-boned bedrooms lie upstairs. Each costs $60 per night, single or double occupancy. Breakfast is extra.

## The Eleutherian Adventurers

Long before the first English colonists arrived, Eleuthera was inhabited by Native Lucayans. However, around the mid-16th century Spaniards came this way, capturing the peaceable people and shipping them out to the Caribbean as slaves.

Pirates plied the waters off Eleuthera and its adjacent islands, but after the removal of the Lucayans there were no inhabitants here for a century, until Capt. William Sayle led the Eleutherian Adventurers here from Bermuda to start a new life. The founding party consisted of about 70 people. They had a rough time of it. Dangerous reefs on the north coast of the island caused their ship and cargo to be lost. Trapped, they had to live off the land as best they could, initially inhabiting a cave (for a description, see "The Current," below). Many of them nearly starved, but they nevertheless drew up their own constitution, promising justice for all. Help came from Virginia colonists who sent food to the little band of adventurers.

Life on Eleuthera proved too much for many of the founding party, however. Many, including Captain Sayle, later returned to Bermuda. But reinforcements were on the way, both from Bermuda and from England, some bringing slaves with them. A permanent settlement had been founded. Freed slaves also came to this island and established settlements. The next wave of settlers were fleeing Loyalists leaving the new United States in order to continue living under the British Crown. These settled principally in two offshore cays, Harbour Island and Spanish Wells.

# 2  Windermere Island

Windermere is a very tiny island, connected by a bridge to "mainland" Eleuthera. It is midway between the settlements of Governor's Harbour and Rock Sound.

This island couldn't be more discreet. "We like to keep it quiet around here," one of the staff at the presently closed Windermere Island Club once told me. But, regrettably for this once deluxe and snobbish citadel, that wasn't always possible. When Prince Charles first took Princess Di here in the 1980s, she was photographed in her swimsuit, even though pregnant, and the picture gained wide notoriety, much to the horror of the club.

Prince Charles himself had first heard of the club long ago, through his great-uncle, Earl Mountbatten of Burma, who was assassinated in 1979 while sailing off Ireland. He was one of the island's more frequent visitors and one of its major enthusiasts.

Aristocrats on both sides of the Atlantic, not only the Mountbattens but the Astors and the Biddles, have flocked to this club, along with an occasional visiting head of state and tycoons of industry.

At press time, the Windermere Club is closed, but check with a travel agent about its status, as properties in South Eleuthera have a long history of suddenly closing and just as suddenly reopening.

Even without its chief attraction, Windermere Island is worth a day trip all on its own, especially Savannah Sound, which has lovely sheltered beaches and facilities for waterskiing, sailboating, snorkeling, and skin diving. There are also excellent beaches for shelling. Frequent picnics are arranged at West Beach on Savannah Sound, and there is good bonefishing, with some catches more than 10 pounds.

## SPORTS A TO Z

Visitors can enjoy a number of activities from **bonefishing** to **windsurfing.** The dockmaster at West Beach is well qualified to guide and advise about bonefishing, or perhaps you'd like to go **deep-sea fishing** for white marlin, dolphin, grouper, wahoo, Allison tuna, and amberjack, just a few of the big fish found in these waters.

West Beach, a good place for sunning and swimming (great for children), is about a 10-minute walk from the shut-down Windermere Club. The beach is on Savannah Sound, the body of calm, protected water separating Windermere from the main island of Eleuthera.

## 3 Tarpum Bay

If you're looking for an inexpensive holiday on high-priced Eleuthera, head here. A waterfront village, some nine miles north of Rock Sound, it has a number of guest houses that take in economy-minded tourists who aren't too demanding. This tiny settlement with its many pastel-washed houses is a favorite of artists who have established a small colony here.

It was once flourishing as a pineapple-export center. That's when many of the present clapboard homes with their gingerbread trim were constructed. Nowadays an air of nostalgia pervades this old community. It's also good for fishing.

The community's artistic patriarch is a Scottish-Irish sculptor and painter who since 1957 has occupied an oceanfront house on the northern edge of the hamlet. Bearded, psychic, and gracious, Peter MacMillan-Hughes, at his **MacMillan-Hughes Gallery and Castle** (☎ 809/334-4091), has sold paintings to an impressive array of patrons, including Lord Mountbatten. His pen-and-ink tinted maps, drawings of birds, and hand-lettered poems and histories are displayed in many prominent homes. He built the tower of the limestone castle that rises from the center of town, a short walk from his studio. Soft-spoken and accessible, Mr. MacMillan-Hughes, might be the single most interesting tourist attraction at Tarpum Bay. Visitors are welcome to show up at his door during daylight hours.

## WHERE TO STAY

### Cartwright's Ocean Front Cottages

Bay St., Tarpum Bay, Eleuthera, the Bahamas. ☎ 809/334-4215. 5 cottages. Year-round, $70 single; $80 double; $95 quad; $160 three-bedroom cottage for six. (EP rates.) No credit cards. Free parking.

Cartwright's is a cluster of two- and three-bedroom cottages right by the sea, with fishing, snorkeling, and swimming at your door. This is one of the few places where you can sit on your patio and watch the sunset. The cottages are fully furnished, with utensils, stove, refrigerator, and pots and pans. Maid service is also provided. The establishment is within walking distance of local stores and restaurants. The owners, Iris and Hervis Cartwright, are helpful. Hervis operates an informal taxi business and will meet you at Rock Sound airport, seven miles away.

### Hilton's Haven Motel and Restaurant

Tarpum Bay, Eleuthera, the Bahamas. ☎ **809/334-4231**. 10 rms, 1 apt. Year-round, $45 single; $55 double; $60 triple; $65 apartment for four. Breakfast $5 extra. (EP rates.) No credit cards. Free parking.

This is a modern Bahamian two-story structure with covered verandas. Comfortably furnished apartments, each with its private sun patio and bath, are rented. The units come with either air-conditioning or ceiling fans. What makes this place special is Mary Hilton herself, everybody's "Bahama Mama." In fact, as a professional nurse, she has delivered some 2,000 of Eleuthera's finest citizens.

If you arrive hot and thirsty, she'll get a fresh lime off a tree and make you a drink. To provide a retirement income for herself, she started Hilton's Haven. "Hilton is my God-given name," she says. "I never met Conrad."

The main tavern-style dining room, with a library in the corner, provides well-cooked food; the cuisine puts its emphasis on freshly caught fish. You can order grouper cutlets with peas 'n' rice, steamed conch, and an occasional lobster. There is also a well-stocked bar. Lunches, costing from $10 each, are served from 12:30 to 2:30pm, and dinners, from $18 each, are offered from 6:30 to 8pm.

# 4  Governor's Harbour

After passing through Tarpum Bay, the next destination is Governor's Harbour, which, at some 300 years old, is the island's oldest settlement. This is believed to have been the landing place of the Eleutherian Adventurers. The largest settlement in Eleuthera after Rock Sound, it lies about midway along the 100-mile island. It has an airport where Bahamasair comes in on both morning and evening flights from Nassau.

The town today has a population of about 750, with some bloodlines going back to the original settlers, the Eleutherian Adventurers, and to the Loyalists who followed some 135 years later. Many old homes—waiting for "discovery"—can still be seen, showing the wear and tear of decades. A quiet nostalgia prevails amid the bougainvillea and casuarina trees.

Leaving Queen's Highway, you can take a small bridge to Cupid's Cay. The bridge to the cay is thought to be about a century and a half old. As you're exploring, you'll come upon one of the most interesting buildings in the area, an old Anglican church with its tombstone-studded graveyard.

The long-ago opening of the Club Med brought renewed vitality to the sleepy village. Tourism has unquestionably altered Governor's Harbour.

## FAST FACTS

If you're staying outside the town in one of the housekeeping colonies, you may find much-needed services and supplies in Governor's Harbour or at nearby Palmetto Point.

**Bank**   Governor's Harbour has a branch of Barclays Bank International, Queen's Highway, P.O. Box 22 (☎ **809/332-2300**). It is open Monday through Thursday from 9:30am to 3pm and Friday from 9:30am to 5pm.

**Car Rental**   If you need a car, try Ronnie's Rent-a-Car, Cupid's Cay, Governor's Harbour (☎ **809/332-2307**). The cost is from $60 for one day, maybe more, depending on the car.

**Medical Care**   On Queen's Highway are both the Governor Harbour's Medical Clinic (☎ **809/332-2001**) and the dentist's office (☎ **809/332-2774**).

**Police**   To telephone the police, call **809/332-2111**.

**Post Office**   Governor's Harbour has a post office on Haynes Avenue (☎ **809/ 332-2060**).

**Shopping**   For gifts or souvenirs, try Norma's Gift Shop, Haynes Avenue (☎ **809/332-2002**), which sells batik dresses, blouses, skirts, beachwear, swimwear, and men's shirts, as well as jewelry. Some of the clothing is handmade on the premises. Hours are Monday through Saturday 9am to 5:30pm.

Nearby is another place to shop, Brenda's Boutique, Haynes Avenue (☎ **809/ 332-2089**). This two-room store occupies a clapboard-sided building a few steps away from the only traffic light in Eleuthera. Inside is a large inventory of T-shirts, sundresses, bathing suits, and such Bahamian souvenirs as conch jewelry. Hours are Monday through Saturday 9am to 5:30pm.

## WHERE TO STAY

For an explanation of the rate symbols, see "Tips on Accommodations" in Chapter 3.

### EXPENSIVE

#### Club Mediterranee

French Leaves, P.O. Box 80, Governor's Harbour, Eleuthera, the Bahamas. ☎ **212/750-1687** in New York City or toll free 800/CLUB-MED. Fax 809/332-2691. 300 rms. A/C. Winter, $800–$1,300 per person double; $520–$780 per child aged 2–11 sharing parents' room. Off-season, $870 per person double; $565 per child aged 2–11. Rates are all-inclusive and per week. AE, MC, V. Free parking.

Along an unspoiled beach of fine sand and hardy vegetation, you'll find a cluster of peach-colored twin-bedded bungalows built in two- and three-story colonies. Built on the Atlantic side, the club replaced the first hotel on Eleuthera, French Leave, which once stood on this site. There's heavy emphasis here on social life for families with children. Activities include day-long picnics, nightly entertainment, disco, organized games in the resort's centerpiece free-form swimming pool (set in a garden), and taped classical music concerts after sunset.

Each room contains bright colors, furniture crafted from bamboo, and a private bathroom. Three full meals a day, including free unlimited beer and wine at lunch and dinner, plus most water sports and evening entertainment, are included in the rates. Tariffs are all-inclusive, except for drinks consumed at hours other than mealtimes; there are several bars scattered throughout the property. The club is heavily booked by French groups in midsummer, with more North Americans in wintertime.

The club's scuba program is not geared to experienced divers—only to beginners. Those just taking up the sport go through a series of four lessons before their first deep dive in the nearby harbor. All equipment and instruction are provided. Waterskiing, snorkeling, sailing, bicycling, tennis (eight courts, two lit for night play), picnics, aerobics, and jogging on the pale pink sands of the beach are ways most members spend their days. Children enjoy the club's Circus School, where a team of instructors teach fundamentals of tightrope walking, low-level trapeze work, trampolining, greasepaint makeup, and costuming. At the end of their stay, children perform in the club's weekly circus performance.

## INEXPENSIVE

### Cigatoo Inn

Haynes Ave., P.O. Box 86, Governor's Harbour, Eleuthera, the Bahamas. ☎ **809/332-2343.** Fax 809/332-2159. 30 rms. A/C TV. Winter, $55–$84 single; $72–$114 double. Off-season, $49–$84 single; $55–$84 double. AE, MC, V. Free parking.

Set on a hillside, this motel-like cluster surrounds a small swimming pool with a terrace. Cigatoo, which is the Arawak name of Eleuthera, is one of the most reasonably priced inns (both for accommodations and food) in the Governor's Harbour area. You enter between two rows of Christmas palms to reach the hotel. Set on grounds planted with such tropical foliage as hibiscus, the inn rents streamlined, functional bedrooms, all with double beds, private baths, and patios overlooking the distant sea or the hotel's pool. The beach is about a 5-minute walk away, and there is a tennis court.

The hotel's restaurant serves a combination of Bahamian and American dishes, costing from $18 or $12 at lunch. If you're exploring Governor's Harbour for the day, you can drop in seven days a week from noon to 2pm and 6 to 9pm for a meal. The inn also has a bar serving such drinks as piña coladas and Goombay Smashes. Local entertainment is often provided.

### Laughing Bird Apartments

Haynes Ave./Birdie St., P.O. Box 25076, Governor's Harbour, Eleuthera, the Bahamas. ☎ **809/332-2012.** Fax 809/332-2358. 4 apts. A/C. $60–$90 single or double; $100 triple; $110 quad. (EP rates.) MC, V. Free parking.

In the center of Eleuthera, these apartments lie near the Cupid's Cay section. These units are best for people who want to settle in for a week or so rather than those seeking an overnight stopover. The location is within walking distance of many shops, and sports facilities lie nearby. Arrangements can be made for waterskiing, surfing, fishing, sailing, tennis, golf, and snorkeling.

Efficiency apartments come with a living/dining/sleeping area, with a separate kitchen and a separate bath. Apartments, which front the beach, sit on an acre of landscaped property. Facilities include a beach and garden, plus tables and chairs for outdoor eating, along with a garden barbecue. Hammocks and a thatched beach cabana make for the easy life.

### Wykee's World Resort

Queen's Hwy., P.O. Box 25176, Governor's Harbour, Eleuthera, the Bahamas. ☎ **809/332-2701.** Fax 809/332-2123. 4 villas. Winter, $135–$220 single or double. Off-season, $110–$175 single or double. (EP rates.) No credit cards. Free parking.

This is a snug and cozy retreat on a private estate, set in a landscape of coconut palms and tropical plants. Lying three miles north of Governor's Harbour, the resort was once owned by a former prime minister of the Bahamas, Sir Roland Symonette. Four well-equipped stone-built villas, each one different but each with an ocean view, are rented all year. The least expensive is the Hibiscus House, with two bedrooms, two baths, a kitchen, a separate dining room, a living room, and a screened-in porch. Some villas offer views of the ocean; all have ceiling fans.

The estate has a saltwater pool, and beaches are on the Atlantic Ocean. Snorkeling, fishing, windsurfing, and tennis can be arranged. Laundry facilities, babysitting, a maid, culinary services, and rental cars and scooters can be arranged.

## WHERE TO DINE

### Kohinoor

Queen's Hwy. ☎ **809/332-2668.** Reservations recommended but not required. Appetizers $3–$5; main courses $10–$25. MC, V. Lunch Tues–Sat 11:30am–2pm; dinner Tues–Sat 5–10pm, Sun 1–10pm. BAHAMIAN/INTERNATIONAL.

Located 3¹/₂ miles north of Governor's Harbour and 3 miles south of Governor's Harbour Airport, this restaurant occupies a veranda-fronted modern building. Guests can also eat in the big-windowed dining room. The fare includes spiny lobster, cracked conch, red snapper, broiled grouper, and pasta dishes. The owners occasionally present entertainment on Sunday afternoon.

---

# 5  Palmetto Point

On the east side of Queen's Highway, south of Governor's Harbour, North Palmetto Point is a little hamlet where visitors rarely venture (although you can get a meal there). Far from the much-traveled tourist routes, this laid-back town will suit visitors seeking an escapist retreat.

Also south of Governor's Harbour, on the western coast of Eleuthera, the beach-fronting South Palmetto Point has some inexpensive housekeeping units.

## WHERE TO STAY

### Palmetto Shores Vacation Villas

P.O. Box EL-25131, Governor's Harbour, Eleuthera, the Bahamas. ☎ **809/332-1305.** Fax 809/332-1305. 10 villas. A/C. Winter, $90 one-bedroom villa for one or two; $180 two-bedroom villa for up to four. Off-season, $80 one-bedroom villa for one or two; $100 two-bedroom villa for four. (EP rates.) AE, V. Free parking.

The creation of a local builder, this resort is a good choice for a housekeeping holiday. Asa Bethel rents villas suitable for two to four guests. Units are built in Bahamian style, with wraparound balconies, and they open directly onto your own private beach. Furnishings are simple but reasonably comfortable, maid service is included, and the villas lie within walking distance of local shops and tennis courts. Some units contain TVs, and a one-bedroom villa has a living room and kitchen. Deep-sea fishing and waterskiing are available. Free Sunflower sailboats are also provided. You can rent a flipper, mask, and snorkel, and car rentals can be arranged.

### Unique Village

North Palmetto Point, the Bahamas (send mail to P.O. Box 25187, Governor's Harbour, Eleuthera, the Bahamas). ☎ **809/332-1830.** Fax 809/332-1838. 10 rms (all with bath), 2 1-bedroom apts with kitchenettes, 2 2-bedroom villas with kitchens. A/C TV. Winter, $100–$120 single or double; $140 one-bedroom apartment for two; $170 two-bedroom apartment for up to four. Extra person $25 extra per day. Off-season discounts of $20 per category listed above. MAP $35 per person per day. MC, V. Free parking.

This hotel is the creative statement of a Palmetto Point businessman whose most visible ventures included the local hardware store (Unique Hardware). Built in 1992, the hotel prides itself on offering a wider range of different types of accommodations (everything from conventional single or double rooms to two-bedroom self-catering villas) than virtually any other hotel on the "mainland" of Eleuthera.

The hotel consists of a cluster of buildings whose roofs, exterior and interior walls, tiled floors, and amenities are mostly white. There's a bar and restaurant (the Unique) on-site where main courses range from $10 to $30, but few other sporting amenities. (Although there are no sailing, scuba, or tennis courts on-site, the staff can direct enthusiasts to other facilities that lie within a reasonable drive. Access to them will almost certainly require a car.) Part of the appeal of this place is affected by its position on a steep rise above the Atlantic coast of Eleuthera. The beach is accessible after a 2-minute descent via a flight of wooden steps. A sandy cove prefaces an oceanfront dotted with coral reefs whose bulk breaks up much of the Atlantic surf. Bring a book and/or a friend for a sojourn where there are few, if any, scheduled activities.

## WHERE TO DINE

### Mate & Jenny's Pizza Restaurant & Bar

South Palmetto Point, right off Queen's Hwy. ☎ **809/332-1504.** Reservations not required. Pizza $7–$22; snacks and main dishes $3–$10. MC, V. Wed–Sat noon–10pm; Sun 6:30–10pm. PIZZA.

This popular pizza restaurant (known for its conch pizza) has a jukebox, video games, and pool table along with a dartboard. The Bethel family will also prepare panfried grouper, cracked conch, or light meals, including snacks and sandwiches. Many patrons come here just to drink. Try their Goombay Smash, rumrunner, or piña colada. Ever had Bahamian Kalik beer?

### ⊗ Muriel's Home Made Bread, Restaurant, and Grocery

North Palmetto Point. ☎ **809/332-1583.** Reservations required for dinner. Appetizers $1.50–$5; main courses $5.50–$10. No credit cards. Lunch Mon–Sat noon–2pm; dinner Mon–Sat 6–8pm. BAHAMIAN.

If you're an adventurer, a good place to go is Muriel Cooper's operation. She operates a bakery, a take-out food emporium, and a grocery store. Her rich and moist pineapple or coconut cake is some of the best you'll find in the Family Islands. A limited menu includes full dinners, such as chicken with chips, cracked conch, conch chowder, and conch fritters. A dining room, decorated with family memorabilia, is available for clients who want to eat inside. If you want a more elaborate meal, you'll have to stop by in the morning to announce your arrival time and menu preference.

## 6 Hatchet Bay

Twenty-five miles north of Governor's Harbour, Hatchet Bay was once known for its plantation that raised prize Angus cattle. But that operation now produces poultry-and-dairy products. The unused chicken parts are thrown to devouring fish at "Shark Hole."

Hatchet Bay Harbour is one of the finest in the Bahamas, a favorite port of call for hundreds of private yachts and charter boats. Full docking facilities and moorings are available. The area is known for its high, rolling green hills, sea-to-sea views, pink- and white-sand beaches, and excellent fishing on both shores. You may want to veer off Queen's Highway and take one of the side roads, such as Lazy Road or Smile Lane.

## WHERE TO STAY

### Rainbow Inn

P.O. Box 25053, Governor's Harbour, Eleuthera, the Bahamas. ☎ **809/335-0294** or toll free 800/688-4752 in the U.S. Fax 809/335-0294. 9 units. A/C MINIBAR. Year-round, $90 for one or two in a studio; $125 one-bedroom apartment for four; $150 two- or three-bedroom villas for four to six. Continental breakfast $5 extra. MC, V. Free parking. Closed Sept 15–Nov 15.

Two miles south of Alice Town, the Rainbow Inn is an isolated collection of cedar-sided bungalows, each designed in the shape of an octagon. The bar/restaurant has a high beamed ceiling and a thick-topped bar where guests down daiquiris and piña coladas. Dinner costs from $25 per person. The popular restaurant features live Bahamian music and one of the most extensive menus on Eleuthera. Local Bahamian food includes fish, conch chowder, fried conch, fresh fish, and Bahamian lobster, and international dishes feature French onion soup, escargots, and steaks, followed by key lime pie for dessert.

There are simple but comfortable accommodations. Each has a private bath, lots of exposed wood, and a ceiling fan. All of the units also contain kitchenettes. There's a sandy beach a few steps away, plus a tennis court. Free tennis balls and rackets are provided, along with snorkeling gear and bikes. Free guided tours of the Hatchet Bay Caves are offered. Rental cars are available at the inn.

## 7  Gregory Town

Gregory Town stands in the center of Eleuthera against a backdrop of hills, which breaks the usual flat monotony of the landscape. A village of clapboard cottages, it was once famed for growing pineapples. It still grows them, but not as it used to. However, the local people make a good rum out of the fruit, and you can visit the Gregory Town Plantation and Distillery, where pineapple rum is still produced. You're allowed to sample it, and surely you'll want to take a bottle home with you.

## WHERE TO STAY

### The Cove Eleuthera

Queen's Hwy., P.O. Box 1548, Gregory Town, Eleuthera, the Bahamas. ☎ **809/335-5142** or toll free 800/552-5960. Fax 809/335-5338. 24 units. A/C. Winter, $99–$119 single; $109–$129 double; $119 triple. Off-season, $79–$89 single; $89–$99 double; $99 triple. Children under 12 stay free in parents' room (maximum of two). MAP $33 per person extra. AE, MC, V. Free parking.

On a private sandy cove, this year-round resort is set on 28 acres partially planted with pineapples. The resort consists of a main clubhouse and seven tropical style buildings nestled on the oceanside. The comfortable rooms with tile floors are furnished in pastel fabrics and rattan furniture. Each has a private bath or a porch. The restaurant (see below) serves three meals a day, and the lounge and poolside Pineapple Patio is open daily for drinks and informal meals. Kayaks, bicycles, and a freshwater pool compete with hammocks for your time. No TV or phones are there to distract you. The Cove lies 1 1/2 miles northwest of Gregory Town and 3 miles southeast of the Glass Window.

## WHERE TO DINE

### The Cove

Queen's Hwy. ☎ **809/335-5142**. Reservations not required. Breakfast $4.50–$9; main courses $10–$22; lunch $5–$12. AE, MC, V. Breakfast daily 8–10:30am; lunch daily noon–2:30pm; dinner daily 6–9:30pm. BAHAMIAN/AMERICAN.

In this previously recommended hotel, lying 1 1/2 miles north of Gregory Town, this spacious dining room is your best bet for dining in the area. The restaurant is spacious and decorated in a light tropical style. On the daily changing menu, you are likely to find the inevitable conch chowder. Later you can go on to rib eye steak, grilled grouper, the local spiny lobster, or perhaps pasta Alfredo or spare ribs. Local seafood and vegetarian fare are always available. Rosemary's pineapple-apple crisp is the recommended dessert. The owners invite you to come early to enjoy the sunset from the patio, surrounding a freshwater pool overlooking the serene coves.

## Monica's Restaurant

Shirley St. ☎ **809/335-5053.** Reservations required. Appetizers $3; main courses $10–$20. No credit cards. Dinner Mon–Sat 7–9pm. BAHAMIAN/AMERICAN.

While in Gregory Town, follow your nose: A tantalizing aroma of freshly cooked food will draw you here. Not only do the locals come to Monica's for their conch fritters and hot patties, but visitors flock here as well. You might begin with conch chowder, then follow with stuffed spiny lobster, pigeon peas 'n' rice, grouper fingers, or barbecued chicken. Dishes are often accompanied by scalloped potatoes or tossed salad. For dessert, try a coconut cream pie, or better yet, the acclaimed pineapple pie. Always call first before heading here since Monica's has been known to close for long periods of time when business is slow.

## WHAT TO SEE & DO

Dedicated surfers have come here from as far away as California and even Australia to test their skills on the "second-best wave in the world." (The best is in Hawaiian waters.)

An increasingly popular activity here is spelunking (exploring and studying caves). South of the town on the way to Hatchet Bay are several caverns worth visiting, the largest of which is called simply the **Cave.** It has a big fig tree out front, which the people of Gregory Town claim was planted long ago by area pirates who wanted to conceal the cave because they had hidden treasure in it.

Local guides (you have to ask around in Gregory Town or Hatchet Bay) will take explorers through this cave. The bats living inside are considered harmless, even though they must resent the intrusion of tourists with flashlights. At one point the drop is so steep—about 12 feet—that you have to use a ladder to climb down. Eventually you reach a cavern studded with stalactites and stalagmites. At this point, you're faced with a maze of passageways leading off through the rocky underground recesses. The cave comes to an abrupt end at the edge of a cliff, where the thundering sea is some 90 feet below.

After leaving Gregory Town and driving north, you come to the famed **Glass Window,** chief sight of Eleuthera. This is the narrowest point of Eleuthera. Once a natural rock arch bridged the land, but it is gone, replaced by an artificially constructed bridge. As you drive across it, you can see the contrast between the deep blue of the ocean and the emerald green of the shoal waters of the sound. The rocks rise to a height of 70 feet. Often, as ships in the Atlantic are being tossed about, the crew has looked across the narrow point to see a ship resting quietly on the other side. Hence the name Glass Window.

## 8 The Current

At a settlement called the Current, in North Eleuthera, some houses are built on low piles. The inhabitants are believed to have descended from a tribe of Native

Americans. A narrow strait separates the village from Current Island, where most of the locals make their living from the sea or from pleating straw goods.

The **Boiling Hole** is in a shallow bank that boils at changing tides.

This is a small community where the people often welcome visitors. There are no crowds and no artificial attractions. Everything focuses on the sea, which is a source of pleasure for the visiting tourists but a way to sustain life for the local people.

From the Current, you can explore some interesting sights in North Eleuthera, including **Preacher's Cave.** This is where the Eleutherian Adventurers found shelter in the mid-17th century when they were shipwrecked with no provisions. However, if you want to be driven there, know that your taxi driver may balk. The road is treacherous on his expensive tires. If you do reach it, you'll find a cave that has been compared to an amphitheater. The very devout Eleutherian Adventurers held religious services inside this cave, which is penetrated by holes in the roof, allowing light to intrude. The cave is not too far from the airport, in a northeasterly direction.

## WHERE TO STAY

### Sandcastle Apartments

The Current, Eleuthera, the Bahamas. ☎ **809/333-0264.** 1 duplex apt (with bath and kitchenette). A/C. Year-round $70 for one to three, extra persons $10 each. No credit cards. Free parking.

Even the most embittered victim of Hurricane Andrew agrees that some benefits eventually derived from that destructive storm. What had been a pair of hastily built cottages catering to the tourist trade were so badly damaged that a complete rebuilding rendered them substantially better than before. For escapists looking for an outlet in a location far removed from the usual tourist circuit, this simple but airy accommodation might be a good bet. The Symonette family emphasizes its appeal for families because of the on-site kitchen, the easy access to a simple grocery store within a 5-minute walk, and the self-contained nature of the modest accommodations. There's a double bed in the bedroom, a queen-sized pullout bed in the living room, and a view over shallow offshore waters where children can wade safely for a surprisingly long distance offshore. The unit lies just across the road from the sea.

## 9  Harbour Island

One of the oldest settlements in the Bahamas, founded before the United States was a nation, Harbour Island lies off the northern end of Eleuthera, some 200 miles from Miami. It is 3 miles long and half a mile wide.

Affectionately called "Briland," Harbour Island is studded with good resorts and is famous for its spectacular pink-sand beach, which runs the whole length of the island on its eastern side. The beach is protected from the ocean breakers by an outlying coral reef, which makes for some of the safest bathing in the Bahamas. Except for unseasonably cold days, you can swim and enjoy water sports year-round. The climate averages 72 degrees Fahrenheit in winter, 77 degrees in spring and fall, and 82 degrees in summer. Occasionally they have cool evenings with a low of around 65 degrees from November to February.

For years, inhabitants of Harbour Island were engaged in farming and boatbuilding, along with fishing and sponge diving. Farming is still done today on the main body of Eleuthera on land given to the Brilanders by Andrew Devereaux, a colonel in the British army back in 1783. The Civil War in the United States brought an economic boom, as the Brilanders prospered by running the blockade that the Union had placed on shipping to and from the Confederate states.

By 1880 Dunmore Town had become the second most important town of the Bahamas. It not only was a port of entry, but also had a major shipyard turning out vessels as large as four-masted schooners, as well as a trio of sugar mills—and it produced rum. It eventually fell on bad times, but with Prohibition in the United States, another boom era came to Dunmore Town and rum-running became a major source of income.

The Brilanders suffered a great financial setback with the repeal of the Prohibition amendment, and then came the Great Depression and World War II. Finally, tourism has again brought prosperity.

## GETTING THERE & GETTING AROUND

By plane, Harbour Island is only 1¹/₂ hours from Fort Lauderdale or Miami and a 30-minute flight from Nassau. To get here, you take a flight to the North Eleuthera airstrip, from which it's a 1-mile ride to the ferry dock, costing $4 per person. The final lap is the 2-mile direct ferry ride to Harbour Island, at a cost of $4 per person. Most people don't need transportation on the island. They walk to where they're going or take a golf cart. Some hotels have these for rent.

If you want to go some distance on the island, call **Reggie's Taxi** at **809/ 333-2116** or **Big M Taxi Service** at **809/333-2043.**

**Michael's Cycles** in the Straw Market on Bay Street rents bikes, motorbikes, and golf carts, with free delivery to your hotel. His shop is open Monday through Saturday from 8am to 5pm. Call **809/333-2384** to reserve some wheels.

### FAST FACTS

**Bank**   The Royal Bank of Canada, just up the hill from the city dock (☎ **809/ 333-2250**), is open Monday through Thursday from 9:30am to 3pm and Friday from 9:30am to 5pm.

**Hospital**   The Harbour Island Medical Clinic, at Dunmore Town (☎ **809/ 333-2227**), handles routine medical problems.

**Pharmacy**   Harbour Pharmacy Health Care and Prescription Service lies on the waterfront four blocks north of the fig tree (☎ **809/333-2174**). In addition to health-and-beauty aids, it fills prescriptions and offers over-the-counter drugs. Hours are daily from 7:30am to 10:30pm.

**Police**   The police can be called at **809/333-2111.**

## WHERE TO STAY
### EXPENSIVE

#### ✪ Dunmore Beach Club

Colebrook Lane, P.O. Box 27122, Harbour Island, the Bahamas. ☎ **809/333-2200.** Fax 809/333-2429. 12 units. A/C. Nov–May, $340 double. June–Aug, $290 double. (AP rates.) No credit cards. Free parking. Closed Sept–Oct.

This colony of cottages is an elegant oasis placed in a tropical setting of trees and shrubbery on well-manicured grounds along the 3-mile pink sandy beach. The Bahamian-style bungalows are an attractive combination of traditional furnishings and tropical accessories. Excellent Bahamian and international meals are served in a dining room with a beamed ceiling, shutter doors, and windows with views. Breakfast is offered in a garden terrace under pine trees with a clear view of the beach. Dinner is served at one sitting at 8pm, when men are required to wear coats and ties in winter. Nonresidents can call for reservations, paying $45 per person. A clubhouse is the focal point for socializing, and a living room with a library and a fireplace is another cozy nook, as is a bar-lounge with rattan furniture.

## MODERATE

### Coral Sands

Chapel St., P.O. Box 23, Harbour Island, the Bahamas. ☎ **809/333-2350** or toll free 800/ 468-2799 in the U.S. and Canada. Fax 809/333-2368. 25 rms, 8 suites. A/C. Winter, $125 single; $150 double; $190 suite for two. Off-season, $100 single; $110 double; $140 suite for two. Extra person in suite $15. MAP $38 per person extra. (EP rates.) AE, DC, MC, V. Free parking. Closed U.S. Labor Day–Nov 14.

Coral Sands is the beachfront lair of two remarkable people, Brett and Sharon King. Theirs is a self-contained, all-purpose resort built on 14 hilly and tree-covered acres overlooking a beach of pink sand and lying within walking distance of the center of Dunmore Town.

Brett King had an adventurous life before coming to Harbour Island. A wartime flyer and veteran of 134 combat missions in Europe and Africa, and winner of many medals for his bravery and daring, he later became an actor. He worked with Bette Davis, John Wayne, and Robert Mitchum and dated, among others, Elizabeth Taylor. He came to Harbour Island to complete plans for the resort, which had been envisioned by his father before his death. Brett stayed and the rest of the story is now part of Harbour Island lore.

Since their opening in 1968, the world has come to their door. Sharon, a gracious hostess, runs between phone calls and welcoming guests as if to her own private party, which at times it becomes. California born and bred, Sharon is known for her style and vivacity.

Each of the rooms has been refurbished in a Caribbean motif. The main building contains singles and doubles. The suites, which have ocean-view patios, sleep four persons and are ideal for families.

**Dining/Entertainment:** The food is one of the reasons for staying here. It's like good home cooking, with a selection of American, Bahamian, and international dishes. For example, if you take lunch at the Beach Bar Sun Deck, order a bowl (not a cup) of some of the best-tasting conch chowder in the islands, served with a slice of freshly made coconut bread. You might follow with a toasted lobster sandwich, which other hotels have tried to imitate. Dinner at the Mediterranean Café might be preceded by one of the potent rum drinks in the Yellow Bird Bar. Your appetizer might be conch fritters, and your main course might be a fresh Bahamian fish, such as grouper, prepared in a number of ways. Outsiders who call for a reservation can order dinner from 7 to 8pm at a cost of $38 per person. Entertainment is often provided in the nightclub in the park, where you can dance under the stars.

**Services:** Beach umbrellas and chaise longues provided; picnic lunches available should you desire to explore some uninhabited islands nearby. Laundry, babysitting.

**Facilities:** Tennis court lit at night; sailboats, rowboats, surf riders, and snorkeling equipment; all water sports, including boats and gear, can be arranged.

## Romora Bay Club

Colebrook St., P.O. Box 146, Harbour Island, the Bahamas. ☎ **809/333-2325** or toll free 800/327-8286 in the U.S. For reservations, contact the Romora Bay Club, P.O. Box 7026, Boca Raton, FL 33431 (☎ 305/427-4830 in Florida). Fax 809/333-2324. 29 rms, 9 suites. A/C. Winter, $125–$140 single; $160–$190 double; $200–$270 suite. Off-season, $90–$100 single; $120–$150 double; $160–$215 suite. Extra person $20. MAP $38 per person extra. Children under 10 stay free in parents' room. (EP rates.) AE, MC, V. Closed Mid-Sept to Nov 1.

Fronting both the beach and harbor, this beach club, owned by Bill and Nancy Steigleder, is an intimate resort of well-furnished bedrooms and suites. Created from a former private estate, the T-shaped main house is the center of social activities. The club stands in a decades-old semitropical garden with tall coconut palms, filmy pine trees, and beds of flowering shrubbery.

The accommodations assure more privacy than most, and only yards away is a harbor where you can swim in clear waters. Each unit is comfortably furnished, containing a private patio or balcony. Rooms are classified as standard, superior, and deluxe, each carrying a different price tag.

**Dining/Entertainment:** Buffet luncheons are served at the waterfront patio and bar. Home cooking is a feature, with continental, Bahamian, and American cuisine served. The homemade breads and pastries are superb.

**Services:** All flights are met at the airport by taxis for the 1-mile drive to the ferry dock. There's a 2-mile ferry ride direct to the club's private dock. Picnic trips, including an "X-rated one for honeymooners," is offered to a nearby uninhabited island. Laundry, babysitting.

**Facilities:** Sunfish rentals, deep-sea fishing, tennis courts.

## Runaway Hill Club

Colebrook St., P.O. Box 27031, Harbour Island, the Bahamas. ☎ **809/333-2150** or toll free 800/327-0787 in the U.S. Fax 809/333-2420. 10 rms. Winter, $165 single; $185 double. Off-season, $140 single; $160 double. MAP $40 per person extra. No children under 16. (EP rates.) AE, MC, V. Free parking. Closed Sept 5–Nov 12.

This small, intimate hotel overlooks the pink sands of Briland's beach. The resort, built in 1947 as a private home, was later sold to two sisters from New Zealand who ran it as a small inn. After they sold the property, the hotel remained closed for several years. In 1983 a group of Brilanders renovated the property and opened it to the public. The hotel has 7 acres of beachfront and a huge lawn, separated from Colebrook Street by a wall. The mansion's original English colonial dormers are still prominent, as are the four stately palms set into the circular area in the center of the driveway. In winter, a crackling fire is sometimes built in the hearth near the entrance.

Each bedroom is different, giving the impression of lodging in a private home, as this used to be. Accommodations are in the two buildings that the hotel occupies.

**Dining/Entertainment:** Dinners are served on the breeze-filled rear porch overlooking the swimming pool, and nonresidents are welcome.

**Facilities:** Freshwater swimming pool set into a steep hillside and surrounded by plants, pink sandy beach; fishing trips and water sports can be arranged.

## Valentine's Yacht Club & Inn

Harbourfront, P.O. Box 1, Harbour Island, the Bahamas. ☎ **809/333-2142.** Fax 809/333-2135. 21 rms. A/C. Winter, $115–$135 single; $125–$145 double. Off-season, $75–$85

single; $90–$105 double. MAP $32 per person extra. (EP rates.) AE, MC, V. Free parking.
Closed Sept 3–Nov 14.

Valentine's is a low-slung, rustic-modern, comfortable place near the sea. It's also
a 40-slip marina complex, totally rebuilt after Hurricane Andrew. You register in
the wood-paneled main building. In back, in view of the dining room, there's a
swimming pool where first-time divers may have just finished their introductory
lessons. Simple accommodations sit bungalow style, each with its own private veranda, in a somewhat hilly flowering garden. If you plan to arrive by yacht, you'll
be in good company, since the likes of Barbara Mandrell and Mick Jagger have also
moored their vessels here.

**Dining/Entertainment:** The Bahamian cuisine served in the restaurant is usually preceded by drinks in the comfortably intimate wood- and brass-trimmed bar.
Dinner is served by candlelight at tables where artificial gold coins sparkle beneath
laminated surfaces and hanging ships' lanterns—each an antique—cast an intimate
glow. Either before or after dinner, you might enjoy one or two of the bartender's
almost hallucinogenic Goombay Smashes. The bar area often provides live entertainment, becoming one of the social centers of town.

**Services:** Full-service marina with everything you could need for your yacht,
including a "yacht-sitting" service, which makes this dock one of the focal points
of the marine activities on Harbour Island.

**Facilities:** Swimming pool, hot tub/Jacuzzi. For information on the Dive Shop,
which offers everything a scuba or snorkeling aficionado could want, see "Sports
A to Z," below.

## WHERE TO DINE
### MODERATE

#### ✪ Runaway Hill Club
Colebrook St. ☎ 809/333-2150. Reservations required. Fixed-price dinner from $40.
AE, MC, V. Dinner Mon–Sat at 8pm. Closed Sept 5–Nov 12. BAHAMIAN/AMERICAN.

Known for its well-prepared food, this dining room enjoys a sweeping view over
the sandy slope stretching down the beach. Inside, in a green-and-white decor accented with polished wood and nautical accessories, you can enjoy evening meals.
The restaurant is contained in a hotel (see "Where to Stay," above), but outside
guests are welcome for the single-service meal. The kitchen prepares marinated
London broil, suprême of chicken piccata, spaghetti with conch, crabmeat soup
with scotch, spicy lobster bisque, and many versions of local fish. Dessert might
be French chocolate pie with a meringue crust and walnuts.

#### Valentine's Yacht Club & Inn
Harbourfront. ☎ **809/333-2142.** Reservations not required. Appetizers $2.50–$5; main
courses $15–$30; fixed-price dinner $30; lunch $10; breakfast from $8. AE, MC, V.
Breakfast daily 8:30–10am; lunch daily noon–2pm; dinner daily at 7:30pm. Closed Sept 3–
Nov 14. BAHAMIAN/AMERICAN.

Don't even think of a meal here without stopping for a drink in the bar before-
hand. Surrounded with nautical accessories and burnished paneling, you can while
away the predinner hours with denizens of the island's boating crowd. The fare in
the dining room includes steamed pork chops, steak or grouper cutlets, asparagus
soup, baked stuffed grouper, and roast leg of lamb. When the main bar closes at
9pm, you can walk out to the more raucous bar on the marina (known as the
Reach Bar), which remains open until midnight on most nights.

## INEXPENSIVE

### Ⓢ Angela's Starfish Restaurant

Dunmore and Grant Sts. ☎ **809/333-2253.** Reservations recommended. Appetizers $3–$6; main courses $12–$20; lunch $7–$10; breakfast from $6. No credit cards. Daily 9am–8:30pm. BAHAMIAN.

Angela's is one of the simplest and also one of the most popular eating places in Harbour Island. Residents as well as visitors literally plan their Sunday around an evening meal here, although it's equally crowded on other nights. Run by Bahamians Angela and Vincent Johnson, the house sits on a hill above the channel in a residential section somewhat removed from the center of town. Angela can often be seen in the kitchen baking.

Cracked conch and an array of seafood are specialties, and chicken potpie and pork chops are frequently ordered. You can dine on the palm-dotted lawn with its simple tables and folding chairs, although for chilly weather there's an unpretentious dining room inside near the cramped kitchen. Some of the best local food is offered here. It can get quite festive at night, after the candles are lit and the crowd becomes jovial. Dinner is served on tables where conch shells are usually the centerpiece.

# WHAT TO SEE & DO

Harbour Island's historic old ✪ **Dunmore Town,** with its pastel clapboard houses, often with whitewashed picket fences, was once the capital of the Bahamas. It's one of the oldest settlements in the archipelago, and even today remains one of the most colorful villages in the Family Islands. It evokes thoughts of waterfront vacation spots in the Carolinas.

Titus Hole, a cave with an open mouth that looks out onto the sheltered harbor, is said to have been the first jail on Harbour Island. Also worth seeing is the **Loyalists Cottage,** dating back to 1790. Vestiges of colonial architecture can be seen in other old houses that were built during the latter part of the 19th century.

The town was settled by English religious dissidents who came here in the 17th century. They were joined about 135 years later by Loyalists coming from the new United States, where they had become unpopular during the American Revolution for their support of British sovereignty. Dunmore Town was named for Lord Dunmore, an 18th-century royal governor of the Bahamas.

# SPORTS A TO Z

The diving in this part of the Bahamas is considered among the most diversified in the region, with visibility in midsummer reaching as much as 200 feet on good days. A 197-foot steel freighter, the *Carnarvon* (also spelled *Caernarvon* and pronounced in endlessly different variations by the locals), sank in 1917 and is considered today one of the highlights of the region. Nearby are the badly rusted chassis of a half-dozen railway boxcars reportedly captured by Confederate soldiers from the Union army during the Civil War and sold to the owner of a sugar plantation in Cuba. Hit by a hurricane during their southbound transit, the barge containing them was sunk, scattering the boxcars along the sea bottom. Today, only the wheelbases remain visible above the reef fish and kelp that have made the site their home.

The most spectacular pastime of all, however, judged among the 10 top dive sites in the world and visited by scuba enthusiasts from as far away as Europe, is the **Current Cut Dive.** Considered one of the fastest (nine knots) drift dives in the world, it involves the descent of a diver into the fast-moving current racing between the rock walls that define the underwater chasm between Eleuthera and Current Island. Swept up in the underwater currents with schools of stingrays, mako sharks, and reef fish, divers are propelled along a half mile of underwater distance in less than 10 minutes. The dive is defined as one of the highlights of a diver's career.

## Romora Bay Club
Colebrook St. ☎ **809/333-2325.**

This club is fully geared for a wide array of water sports. The sandy bottom of the sheltered bathing precincts off the hotel (see "Where to Stay," above) serves as the learning area for the introductory scuba lessons. An introductory lesson followed by a half-day dive trip costs $65, with equipment included; those who prefer snorkeling can join a half-day expedition for $15 per person. Guided scuba trips cost $25 per tank in daytime, $36 for night dives. Call to agree on departure time.

Experienced divers can rent any piece of scuba equipment they need. Bill Steigleder, the owner of the hotel, is an experienced diver. He is assisted by two PADI instructors. The Romora Bay Club offers dive packages that make combined MAP, housing, and diving less expensive.

## Valentine's Dive Center
Harbourfront. ☎ **809/333-2309.**

Valentine's has a full range of dive activities. The dive center is in a wooden building near the entrance to Valentine's Marina. Lessons in snorkeling and scuba diving for beginners are given daily at 9:30am. Snorkeling from a boat costs $20 for a half-day tour. A full certification course for scuba is taught for $350. Single-tank dives, daily at 9:30am and 1:30pm, cost $30; two-tank dives go for $55; and night dives (four divers minimum) cost $45 per person. Underwater cameras, with film included, rent for $15 for a half day, $25 for a full day. The guides at Valentine's are proud to point out the wreck of the *Carnarvon* (mentioned above).

# 10  Spanish Wells

Called a "quiet corner of the Bahamas," Spanish Wells is a colorful cluster of houses on St. George's Cay, half a mile off the coast of northwest Eleuthera. It is characterized by its sparkling bays and white beaches, sleepy lagoons, and a fine fishing and skin-diving colony.

The Eleutherian Adventurers were the first people to inhabit St. George's Cay after the Spanish had exterminated the original residents, the Arawaks (Lucayans). However, it was prominent on the charts of Spanish navigators as the final landfall for galleons heading home from the New World laden with plunder. The Spaniards early on sank a well here from which to replenish their potable water before setting off across the Atlantic. Hence the name "Spanish Wells." Ponce de León noted this stopover, where he was able to get water, if not the youth-giving liquid for which he was searching.

After the American Revolution, Loyalists joined the descendants of the Eleutherian Adventurers in Spanish Wells. Some of these, particularly those from southern plantations in America, did not stay long on St. George's Cay, however, as the Spanish Wellsians were adamantly opposed to slavery. Since slaves had been brought by the new wave of immigrants hoping to start island plantations, they were forced to move on to other parts of the Bahamas with their African bondsmen. The people of Spanish Wells still have strong religious beliefs, and there's a bounty of churches on the island.

The towheaded, blue-eyed people of this little town number fewer than 1,500 souls, which makes it a white enclave in a predominantly black country. More than half the people on the island are named Pinder. As the saying goes, "We was Pinders before we married, and we're Pinders now." The names Albury, Higgs, Sawyer, and Sweeting are also prominent. The islanders' patois blends old English with the accents of others who have settled on the island over the centuries. For years they have been known as good seamen and spongers, and some of them are farmers. Because of the infertile soil on St. George's Cay, however, they have to do their planting on "mainland" Eleuthera.

Over the centuries the Spanish Wellsians have tried their hand at many economic ventures, from growing cotton and pineapples for export to shipbuilding, lumbering, and fishing. Of these, fishing and some agriculture have been lasting moneymakers, joined today by tourism. Many have grown rich on harvesting spiny lobster.

You can walk or bicycle through the village, looking at the houses, some more than 200 years old, which have New England saltbox styling but bright tropical coloring. You can see handmade quilts in many colors, following patterns handed down from generations of English ancestors. No one locks doors here or removes ignition keys from cars.

There are those who suggest that the island doesn't offer much to do, but this is disputed by those who just want to snorkel, scuba dive, fish, sunbathe, read, or watch the sun set. You'll also have a choice of tennis, sailing, volleyball, shuffleboard, or windsurfing.

## GETTING THERE

**BY FERRY**   To reach the island, you can fly to the airstrip on North Eleuthera, from which taxis will deliver you to the ferry dock. Regardless of the time of day you arrive, a ferryboat will either be waiting for passengers or about to arrive with a load of them. A memorable skipper of one of them is Caleb Sawyer, who runs a well-maintained speedboat, the *Moldie Crab* (☎ **809/333-4254**). The boat runs between Gene's Bay in North Eleuthera to the main pier at Spanish Wells. The ferries depart whenever passengers show up. The cost is $12 per person round-trip.

## WHERE TO STAY

### Spanish Wells Yacht Haven

Harbourfront, P.O. Box 27427, Spanish Wells, the Bahamas. ☎ **809/333-4255.** Fax 809/333-4649. 3 rms, 2 apts. A/C. Winter, $85 single or double; $105 apartment for up to four. Off-season, $75 single or double; $95 apartment for up to four. (EP rates.) AE, MC, V. Free parking.

One of the most modern marinas in the islands is now owned by the Nassau Yacht Haven, which also rents apartments and rooms for the boating crowd or any other visitors to Spanish Wells. As for the marine facilities, they include a self-service laundry, hot and cold showers, an ice machine, a saltwater swimming pool, and a lounge and restaurant. You can also get Exxon marine fuels and lubricants. Should you not happen to have a yacht to service, you'll find a quintet of rentable rooms. Each of them has servicable furniture and a private bath. Two of them contain small kitchenettes.

## WHERE TO DINE

### D-J'S Restaurant
Harbourfront. ☎ **809/333-4782.** Reservations recommended. Appetizers $2.50–$6; main courses $13–$21; lunch from $12. AE, MC, V. Breakfast daily 8–10am; lunch daily noon–2pm; dinner daily 6:30–9:30pm. BAHAMIAN.

This is one of the few places to eat on the island. Visitors mingle with a yachting crowd from around the world in the lounge and restaurant, which is decorated with a few nautical artifacts and overlooks the marina. Naturally, the emphasis is on seafood here, including lobster "right out of the water and into the pot." You can order such Bahamian fish as grouper, prepared several different ways. Conch is prepared in a number of ways as well, including a tasty chowder.

### The Sea View
Harbourfront. ☎ **809/333-4219.** Reservations not required. Main courses $11–$20. No credit cards. Daily 10am–10pm. BAHAMIAN.

This little place stands along the waterfront on the way to Spanish Wells Yacht Haven. It's known for its home cooking and Bahamian foods. Many hungry boaters come here just to sample the fish fingers. Painted in pink and white with red lettering, it is a simple but welcoming little place. It offers the usual array of sandwiches and hamburgers. But you can also order some good local dishes. Cracked conch is invariably offered, as is conch chowder. However, everything depends on what is available locally on any particular day.

# The Exuma Islands  10

The Exuma island chain is considered to be one of the prettiest in the Bahamas. Some liken its beauty to that of Polynesia. Shades of jade, aquamarine, and amethyst in deeper waters turn to transparent opal near sandy shores: the water and the land appear almost inseparable. Sailors and their crews like to stake out their own private beaches and tropical hideaways, and several vacation retreats have been built by wealthy Europeans, Canadians, and Americans.

Most of my resort recommendations are in and around pretty, pink George Town, on Great Exuma, the capital of the Exumas. A community of some 900 residents, it was once considered a possible site for the capital of the Bahamas because of its excellent Elizabeth Harbour (see below).

The cruising grounds around the Exumas, which are scattered over an ocean area of 90 square miles, are perhaps the finest to be found in the Western Hemisphere, if not in the world, for both sail- and powerboats. If you don't come in your own craft, you can rent one here, from a simple little Daysailer to a fishing runabout, with or without a guide. The annual regatta in April in Elizabeth Harbour has attracted such notables as Prince Philip and the ex-King of Greece, Constantine. The Exumas are often referred to by yachting people as "where you go when you die if you've been good."

Snorkeling and scuba-diving opportunities draw aficionados from around the world to the Exuma National Land and Sea Park, a vast underwater preserve, and to the exotic limestone and coral reefs, blue holes, drop-offs, caves, and night dives. Dive centers in George Town and Staniel Cay provide air fills and diving equipment.

Fishing is top grade here, and the "flats" on the west side of Great Exuma are famous for bonefishing. You can find (if you're lucky) blue marlin on both sides of Exuma Sound, as well as sailfish, wahoo, and white marlin, plus numerous others. Other popular activities include playing tennis, windsurfing, and waterskiing.

The Exumas are among the friendliest islands in the Bahamas, the people warmhearted and not (yet) spoiled by tourism. They seem genuinely delighted to receive and welcome visitors to their shores. They grow a lot of their own food, including cassava, onions, cabbages, and pigeon peas on the acres their ancestors worked as slaves. Many fruits grow on the cays, including guavas, mangoes, and avocados. You can watch these fruits being loaded at Government

## What's Special About the Exuma Islands

Beaches
- Great Exuma beaches, stretching for miles and miles, secluded and dotted with coconut palms. Water shades range from deep turquoise to pale aqua.

Great Towns & Islands
- George Town, capital of the Exumas and its biggest town, opens onto yacht-filled Elizabeth Harbour.
- Little Exuma, southernmost of the Exuma Cays, with beaches of white sand.
- Staniel Cay, an 8-mile chain of uninhabited islets, sandy beaches, coral reefs, and bonefish flats.
- Stocking Island, in Elizabeth Harbour, off the coast of George Town, a long, thin barrier island with some of the finest white sandy beaches in the Bahamas.

Nature
- Exuma National Land and Sea Park, sea gardens with spectacular reefs, stretching for some 22 miles northwest of Staniel Cay.
- The waters of the Exumas, one of the finest cruising areas in the world. Yachting people called the upper Exumas "a nature wonderland," filled with a wide array of wildlife, including iguanas and exotic birds.

Special Events
- Family Island Regatta in April in Elizabeth Harbour, attracting some of the world's classiest yachts and the international yachting set.

Film Locations
- Staniel Cay, north of Great Exuma, with a grotto where the James Bond thriller *Thunderball* was filmed in part. Scenes from *Never Say Never Again* and *Splash* were also shot here.

Wharf in George Town for shipment to Nassau. The sponge industry is being revived locally, as the product of the sea is found in shallow waters and creeks to the south side of the Exumas.

A spiny, sandy chain of islands, the Exumas, which begin just 35 miles southeast of Nassau, stretch more than 100 miles from Beacon Cay in the north to Hog Cay and Sandy Cay in the south. These islands have not been developed like the Abacos and Eleuthera, but they have much to offer, with gin-clear waters on the west around the Great Bahama Bank and the 5,000-foot-deep Exuma Sound on the east, plus uninhabited cays ideal for picnics, rolling hills, ruins of once-great plantations, and coral formations of great beauty. Although it's crossed by the Tropic of Cancer, the island has average temperatures ranging from the mid-70s to the mid-80s.

On most maps this chain is designated as the "Exuma Cays," but only two of the main islands—Great Exuma and Little Exuma—bear the name. A single-lane bridge connects those two cays, where the major communities are concentrated.

## GETTING THERE

**BY PLANE**  The most popular way to visit the Exumas is to fly there aboard **Bahamasair** (☎ **800/222-4262**), which has daily service from Nassau.

**Gulfstream** (☎ 800/992-8532) also flies between Miami and George Town.

**American Eagle** (☎ 800/433-7300) serves Exuma from Miami twice daily on Friday through Saturday and once a day Monday through Thursday.

Exuma has some private airstrips, but its major commercial airport—the new Exuma International Airport—is 10 miles from George Town, the capital. (For flights to the private airstrip at Staniel Cay, refer to Section 4 of this chapter.)

**BY MAIL BOAT**   Several mail boats leave from Potter's Cay Dock in Nassau, stopping at various points along the Exumas.

The MV *Grand Master* goes from Nassau to George Town. Departures are on Tuesday at 2pm. It returns to Nassau on Friday morning.

Since hours and sailing schedules are subject to change because of weather conditions, it's best to check with the dockmaster at Potter's Cay Dock in Nassau (☎ 809/393-1064).

## GETTING AROUND

After your arrival at the airport in George Town, chances are you'll meet Kermit Rolle. He's known by everybody. You can stop in at **Kermit's Airport Lounge,** Exuma International Airport (☎ 809/345-0002), which is just across from the airport terminal building. Kermit, who runs things up in Rolleville, knows as much about the Exumas as anyone else (maybe more). You'll be lucky if Kermit is free, and you can negotiate a deal with him to take you in his car for a tour of the

---

### In Search of the Red-Legged Thrush

Under the protection of the Bahamas National Trust, ✪ Exuma National Land and Sea Park begins at Conch Cut in the south and extends northward to Wax Cay Cut, encompassing Halls Pond Cay, Warderick Wells, Shroud Cay, Hawksbill Cay, Cistern Cay, and Bell Island, as well as numerous other small, uninhabited islands. It lies to the northwest of Staniel Cay.

The park is some 22 miles long, and much of it is a sea garden with reefs, some only 3 to 10 feet beneath the water's surface. The park is reached only by chartered boat, and is very expensive to visit.

This is an area of natural beauty that can be enjoyed by skin divers and yachties, but it's unlawful to remove any plant, marine, or bird life. Before 1986, visitors were alowed to fish for spiny lobster, hog fish, conch, and such, but the park is now designated a marine replenishment nursery.

Many bird-watchers visit the park, looking for the red-legged thrush, the nighthawk, even the long-tailed "Tropic Bird," plus many, many more winged creatures.

This was once the home of the Bahamian iguana, which is now found only on Allan's Cays, a tiny island group just north of Highborne Cay. The government is taking belated steps to protect this creature, which is found nowhere else in the world. If a person kills or captures an iguana, the penalty on conviction is a fine of as much as $300 and/or imprisonment for a term as long as six months.

Exumas. He's filled with local lore (see "Where to Dine" for a description of his lounge).

**BY TAXI** If your hotel is in George Town, it will cost about $24 to get there in a taxi from the airport. Rides often are shared. The island has only a few taxis. Most of them wait at the airport. Hotels can usually get you a taxi if you need to go somewhere and don't have a car. There are no taxi-service telephone numbers to call, other than that of Kermit's Airport Lounge.

**BY CAR** It's also possible to rent a car during your stay. Try Exuma Transport, Main Street, George Town (☎ **809/336-2101**). They have cars to rent for $60 per day and up or $300 per week. A $200 deposit is required.

## FAST FACTS

Much factual information regarding George Town and the Exumas is also applicable to the rest of the Bahamas and appears under "Fast Facts: The Bahamas" in Chapter 3. The information here is aimed at helping you on matters more specific to this area.

**Banks** In George Town, a branch of the Bank of Nova Scotia, Queen's Highway (☎ **809/336-2651**), is open Monday through Thursday from 9am to 1pm, on Friday from 9am to 1pm and 3 to 5pm.

**Churches** If you're a Protestant churchgoer, you'll be warmly welcomed at St. John's Baptist Church, Queen's Highway, George Town (☎ **809/336-2513**).

**Customs** The Bahamian Customs office (☎ **809/345-0071**) is at the Exuma International Airport.

**Docking** If you come to the Exumas aboard your own boat, Exuma Docking Services, Main Street, George Town (☎ **809/336-2578**), has slips for 52 boats, with water and electricity hookups. There's a restaurant on the premises, and you can replenish your liquor stock from the store here. Also they have a Laundromat, fuel dock, land-based fuel pumps, and a store selling supplies for boats and people.

**Dry Cleaning** To get dry cleaning done, go to Exuma Cleaners, Queen's Highway, George Town (☎ **809/336-2038**), open Monday through Saturday from 9am to 5pm.

**Medical Care** The government-operated medical clinic in George Town can be reached by phone (☎ **809/336-2088**).

**Police** To call the police in George Town, dial **809/336-2666,** but only for any emergency or special services.

## 1 George Town

The tropic of Cancer runs directly through George Town, the capital and principal settlement of the Exumas, located on the island of Great Exuma. Some 900 people live in this tranquil seaport village, opening onto a 15-mile-long harbor. George Town, part in the tropics and part in the temperate zone, is a favorite port of call for the yachting crowd. Its one road runs parallel to the shoreline of the harbor. Flights from Nassau, Miami, and Fort Lauderdale come into nearby Exuma International Airport.

Sometimes the streets of George Town are nearly deserted, except when the mail boat from Nassau arrives at Government Wharf, bringing everybody out. If you've rented a housekeeping unit on the Exumas, you can come here to buy fresh fish when the fishers come in with their catch.

# The Exumas

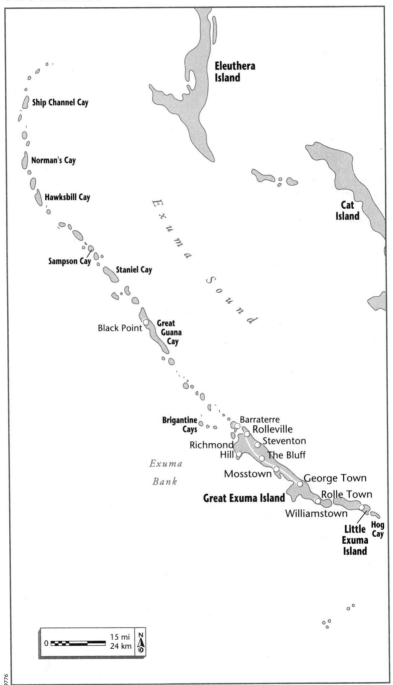

Eleuthera
Island

Ship Channel Cay

Norman's Cay

Hawksbill Cay

*E x u m a*

Cat
Island

Sampson Cay

Staniel Cay

*S o u n d*

Black Point  **Great
Guana
Cay**

Brigantine
Cays

Barraterre
Rolleville
Steventon
Richmond
Hill  The Bluff
Mosstown
George Town
**Great Exuma Island**  Rolle Town
Williamstown
**Little
Exuma
Island**  **Hog
Cay**

*Exuma
Bank*

0    15 mi
24 km

N

If you need to stock up on supplies, George Town is the place, as it has more stores and services than any other place in the Exumas. There are dive centers, marinas, and markets, as well as a doctor and a clinic.

George Town often doesn't bother with street names, but it is so small that everything is easy to find.

## WHERE TO STAY

For an explanation of rate symbols, see "Tips on Accommodations," in Chapter 3.

### MODERATE

#### ✪ Club Peace and Plenty

Queen's Hwy., P.O. Box 29055, George Town, Great Exuma, the Bahamas. ☎ **809/ 336-2551** or toll free 800/525-2210 in the U.S. and Canada. Fax 809/336-2093. 35 units. A/C. Winter, $120–$150 single or double. Off-season, $90–$110 single or double. MAP $30 per person extra. (EP rates.) AE, MC, V. Free parking.

In the heart of George Town is this attractive and historic waterside inn. Once it was a sponge warehouse and later the home of a prominent family before it was converted into a hotel in the late 1940s, making it the oldest in the Exumas. It was named for a vessel that brought Loyalists from the Carolinas to the Exumas. The two-story pink-and-white hotel has dormers and balconies opening onto a water view. The units are all tastefully furnished.

The grounds are planted with palms, crotons, and bougainvillea. Peace and Plenty fronts on Elizabeth Harbour, which makes it a favorite of the visiting yachting set, including Prince Philip. The hotel faces Stocking Island and maintains a private beach club there, offering food and bar service as well as miles of sandy dunes. A free boat makes the run to Stocking Island for hotel guests. There is a small free-form freshwater pool on the patio of the hotel; drinks are served here. There are also two cocktail lounges. One of these lounges, converted from an old slave kitchen, is filled with nautical gear, including lanterns, rudders, and anchors. Food consists of continental, Bahamian, and American specialties.

Dining is both indoor and outdoor. Calypso music is played on the terrace. Naturally, the sporting life holds forth here, and Sunfish sailing, fishing, diving, and boating are all the rage. The resort will rent you snorkeling gear and Windsurfers, even arrange snorkeling trips to nearby reefs. Fishing packages can also be arranged for bonefishers. The staff here can also arrange bookings in their Peace and Plenty Bonefish Lodge, also in George Town. All-inclusive packages are sold to bonefishers who book in here on 4- or 5-day blocks.

#### ✪ Coconut Cove Hotel

Queen's Hwy., P.O. Box 29299, George Town, Great Exuma, the Bahamas. ☎ **809/ 336-2659.** Fax 809/336-2658. 10 rms, 1 suite. A/C MINIBAR. Winter, $108–$133 single; $128–$153 double; $206–$226 suite. Off-season, $80–$105 single; $100–$125 double; $178–$198 suite. MAP $38 per person extra. (EP rates.) MC, V. Free parking.

Set on an acre of palm-dotted sandy soil, one mile west of George Town, in a neighborhood known as the Jolly Hall District, this 10-unit hotel began its saga as the private home of Thomas Chimento and his wife, Pamela Predmore. Built as a home in the mid-1980s, its main building is a long (96-foot), single-story rectangular bungalow whose ocean-facing side is composed almost entirely of sliding glass doors. Inside, mahogany doors and panels glow. Many were built by Tom himself, a former New York–based manufacturer of doors and panels.

Accommodations include beachfront rooms with private terraces, plus other rooms overlooking an aquatic pond and tropical gardens. These also have private terraces. All accommodations have a view of the ocean and are equipped with private baths. The Paradise Suite is the special place to stay, furnished with a Jacuzzi, an oversize bath, and a private hot tub on the terrace. All the accommodations have queen-size beds, bathrobes, fully stocked minibars, toiletries, and both air-conditioning and ceiling fans. The club also has a beachfront freshwater pool, plus a "Sandbar" for poolside drinks. See below for a separate recommendation of its restaurant. Stocking Island, a sand spit, lies within a 5-minute boat ride offshore, and shelters the hotel from the direct action of the surf. Good snorkeling lies all around.

## The Palms at Three Sisters

Mount Thompson, P.O. Box EX 29215, Georgetown, Great Exuma, the Bahamas. ☎ **809/ 358-4040** or toll free 800/688-4752. Fax 809/358-4043. 12 rms, 2 villas. A/C TV. Winter, $115 single or double; $135 triple. Off-season, $90 single or double; $105 triple. Extra person $15 each. Breakfast from $8 extra. MC, V. Free parking.

In December of 1994, a resort opened on an isolated spot 7 miles from its nearest neighbor, adjacent to a 1,200-foot stretch of one of the best beaches in the Exumas. Set on 6½ acres of windswept oceanfront about 9 miles northwest of George Town, the property benefitted from thousands of dollars worth of improvements to what had, until then, been a somewhat rundown resort. Its manager is Welsh-born Treffor Davies, former manager of George Town's Peace and Plenty resort, who directs his 15-member staff in the day to day details of opening what promises to be one of the most interesting resorts in the Exumas. A dozen bicycles are available for the use of guests. Rooms lie within a two-story motel-like building and have English colonial details and simple, summery furniture. Meals and drinks are served in a low-slung annex, with views stretching out over the Atlantic. There's a flowering patio with live music presented every Friday, a tennis court that is lit for night play, an on-site swimming pool, and plenty of opportunity for calm, low-key seclusion and privacy. Look for an enlargement of this property during the lifetime of this edition, and what promise to be good reports about its performance.

The resort, incidentally, is named after a trio of rocks (the Three Sisters) whose composition is radically different from the coral that comprises the rest of the Exumas. They jut about 15 feet above sea level just offshore from this resort's beach and serve as a beacon for picnic excursions by motor launch that the hotel arranges to a sandy cay offshore. Snorkeling is excellent in the shallow waters offshore, and rental of fishing boats and fishing equipment is easily arranged.

## Peace and Plenty Beach Inn

Harbourfront, P.O. Box 29055, George Town, Great Exuma, the Bahamas. ☎ **809/ 336-2550** or toll free 800/525-2210 in the U.S. and Canada. Fax 809/336-2253. 16 rms. A/C. Winter, $130 single or double. Off-season, $98 single or double. Continental breakfast $6 extra. (EP rates.) AE, MC, V. Free parking.

You can also stay at the previously mentioned hotel's annex, the Peace and Plenty Inn, located a mile west of George Town. It opened in 1991. It contains first-class and well-furnished double rooms that open onto 300 feet of white-sand beach, with a bar, restaurant, swimming pool, and dinghy dock. The bedrooms have Italian tile floors as well as balconies overlooking Bonefish Bay and Elizabeth Harbour.

An adjacent structure housing the bar and restaurant was designed to reflect the colonial flavor of George Town. A freshwater pool offers an alternative to ocean bathing, and Sunfish rentals are available if you'd like to explore Elizabeth Harbour. Scuba diving, snorkeling, and fishing excursions can be arranged. There's a free shuttle service running between the Beach Inn and Club Peace and Plenty.

## INEXPENSIVE

### Regatta Point

Regatta Point, Kidd Cove, P.O. Box 2906, George Town, Great Exuma, the Bahamas. ☎ **809/336-2206** or toll free 800/327-0787 in the U.S.; 081/876-1296 in London. Fax 809/336-2206. 5 units. Winter, $114–$138 single or double; $170 two-bedroom apartment for up to four. Off-season, $96–$114 single or double; $146 two-bedroom apartment for up to four. Extra person $15. (EP rates.) AE, MC, V. Free parking.

Regatta Point lies on a small cay just across the causeway from George Town. The cay used to be known as Kidd Cay, named after the notorious pirate. Overlooking Elizabeth Harbour, the present complex consists of five efficiency apartments. This little colony hums with action in April during the Family Island Regatta. Your hostess, American Nancy Bottomley, does much to ease your adjustment into the slow-paced life of the Exumas. She discovered this palm-grove cay—really bush country—in 1963, and opened the little colony of efficiencies in 1965. She even had to build the causeway herself. Each of the pleasantly furnished units has its own kitchen.

There is a little beach for the use of guests, and Mrs. Bottomley will help with arrangements for water sports and outings. One guest liked the place so much he stayed for seven years. Ceiling fans keep the place fairly cool. Those guests who don't want to cook for themselves can take dinner out in George Town. They have a choice of the already-recommended hotels in town or one of the local restaurants. Grocery stores are fairly well stocked if you want to do it yourself, however. The hotel staff will direct you to their whereabouts.

### Two Turtles Inn

Main St., P.O. Box 29051, George Town, Great Exuma, the Bahamas. ☎ **809/336-2545.** Fax 809/336-2528. 12 rms. A/C. Winter, $88 single or double; $92 triple; $96 quad. Off-season, $68 single or double; $72 triple; $76 quad. MC, V. Free parking.

Set opposite the village green, midway between the town's harborfront and a salt-water estuary known as Victoria Pond, this pleasant hotel is as popular for its drinking and dining facilities (see "Where to Dine," below) as for its accommodations. Originally built of stone and stained planking in the early 1960s, these are arranged around a courtyard, the centerpiece of which is the enormous Norfolk pine that is the envy of gardeners throughout the island. Each room has a ceiling fan and a private bath. Beach enthusiasts and water-sports aficionados head for the facilities of Peace and Plenty, a short walk away. Tennis, sailing, boating, snorkeling, and scuba diving can be arranged through other nearby hotels.

## WHERE TO DINE

In general, the best places to take meals in George Town are the main hotels, reviewed above, although there are exceptions.

## MODERATE

### Club Peace and Plenty Restaurant

In the Club Peace and Plenty, Queen's Hwy. ☎ **809/336-2551.** Reservations recommended. Appetizers $3.50–$5; main courses $14–$24; lunch $10; breakfast $6. AE, MC, V. Breakfast daily 7–9am; lunch daily noon–2:30pm; dinner daily 6:30–9:30pm. FRENCH/ITALIAN/BAHAMIAN/AMERICAN.

Club Peace and Plenty has one of the finest island dining rooms, where there is good home cooking and enough of it so that no one leaves unsatisfied. Who knows who might be seated at the next table? In days of yore, it might have been an ex-king, Constantine of Greece, or maybe Jack Nicklaus. You might begin with conch salad or one of the salads made with hearts of palm or hearts of artichoke, then follow with local lobster or a rack of lamb. You sit under ceiling fans, looking out over the harbor, at a table right off the hotel's Yellow Bird Lounge. Windows on three sides and candlelight make it particularly nice in the evening.

But you can also visit for lunch. You have a selection of such dishes as home-made soups, followed by, perhaps, a conch burger, a chef's salad, or deep-fried grouper. For breakfast you're given a selection of such dishes as french toast or scrambled eggs and sausage. But if you want to go truly Bahamian, you'll order the breakfast of boiled fish and grits.

### Coconut Cove Hotel Restaurant

Queen's Hwy. ☎ **809/336-2659.** Reservations recommended. Appetizers $5–$7; main courses $16.50–$27. MC, V. Breakfast daily 8–10am; dinner Tues–Sun 6–9pm. CONTINENTAL.

Although it's a casual place during the day, this is the most formal dining choice in the evening, with "white glove" service from its position overlooking Elizabeth Harbour. It is also the preferred choice for "dining with a view." The menu varies daily, but the chef has won awards for his fine cuisine. Fresh produce such as "treasures from the sea" are always available, and dining is either in the main restaurant or al fresco on the terrace. Cuisine may also be prepared according to your own specifications, and dietetic foods are also available upon request. Gourmet picnic baskets can also be packed for you here if you'd like to go on a boat ride to one of the uninhabited cays for the day.

### The Palm

At the Palms at Three Sisters Hotel. ☎ **809/358-4043.** Reservations not required. Break-fast $4.25–$9; lunch platters and sandwiches $5–$10; dinner appetizers $3.75–$7.50, dinner main courses $14–$25. MC, V. Breakfast daily 7–10am; lunch daily 11:30am–3pm; dinner daily 6–9pm. INTERNATIONAL.

Set beside a sandy, isolated beach, nine miles northwest of the Exuma capital, this airy, ocean-facing restaurant is associated with one of the island's newest resorts. Breakfasts are the kind of hearty steak-and-egg fare appreciated by serious mariners, although such dishes as Bahamian coconut pancakes, Exuma-style stewed fish with grits or johnnycakes, and omelets with grilled tomatoes are also featured. Lunches include lobster salads, conch chowder, grouper fingers, burgers, and sandwiches. Dinners are more formal, and include flame-broiled grouper, chinese stir-fries, and porterhouse steaks.

## INEXPENSIVE

### Kermit's Airport Lounge

Exuma International Airport. ☎ **809/345-0002.** Reservations not accepted. Platters from $4.75; cheeseburgers $4.50; beer $3. No credit cards. Daily 8am until the last airplane takes off. BAHAMIAN.

Owned by one of the island's most entrepreneurial taxi drivers, Kermit Rolle, this simple but appealing place lies across the road from the entrance to the island's airport. Views from inside encompass the sight of airplanes taking off and landing, and help to define this as a semiofficial waiting room for most of the island's flights. Food items include platters of fish with beans, rice, and johnnycake and sandwiches, cheeseburgers, and an array of tropical drinks.

### Sam's Place

Main St. ☎ **809/336-2579.** Reservations not required. Appetizers $2.50–$2.75; main courses $10–$18.50; breakfast from $5; lunch from $6. MC, V. Daily 7am–10pm. BAHAMIAN.

If Bogie were alive today, he'd surely head for this second-floor restaurant and bar overlooking the harbor in George Town. It opened in 1987 and is one of the best restaurants in Great Exuma, popular with the yachting set. The decor has been called "Bahamian laid-back." Sam Gray, the owner, offers breakfasts to catch the early boating crowd. Lunches could include everything from freshly made fish chowder to spaghetti with meat sauce. You'll also be able to order an array of sandwiches throughout the day. The dinner menu changes daily, but you're likely to find such main courses as Exuma lobster tail, roast lamb, Bahamian steamed chicken, and panfried grouper. Of course, you can always get native conch salad. At dinner the talk here is of one of everybody's dreams—that of owning a private utopia, one of those uninhabited cays still remaining in the Exuma chain.

## WHAT TO SEE & DO

There isn't much to see here in the way of architecture except the confectionary pink-and-white **Government Building,** which was "inspired" by the Government House architecture in Nassau. Under an old ficus tree in the center of town there's a straw market where you can talk to the friendly Exumian women and perhaps purchase some of their handcrafts.

George Town has a colorful history, despite the fact that it appears so sleepy today (there's so little traffic, there is no need for a traffic light). Pirates used its deep-water harbor in the 17th century, and then what was called the "plantation aristocracy," mainly from Virginia and the Carolinas, settled here in the 18th century. In the next 100 years **Elizabeth Harbour,** the focal point of the town, became a refitting base for British men-of-war vessels, and the U.S. Navy used the port again during World War II.

The greatest attraction is not George Town but ✪ **Stocking Island,** which lies in Elizabeth Harbour. It faces the town across the bay, less than a mile away. This is a long, thin barrier island with some of the finest white-sand beaches in the Bahamas. Snorkelers and scuba divers come here to explore the blue holes, and it is also ringed with undersea caves and coral gardens. Boat trips leave daily from Elizabeth Harbour heading for Stocking Island at 10am and 1pm. The cost is $5 per person one-way. However, guests of the Peace and Plenty hotel ride free.

**Mystery Cave** is a famous dive site, tunneling for more than 400 feet under the hilly, 7-mile-long island with its palm-studded beaches.

If you'd like to go shelling, walk the beach that runs along the Atlantic side. You can order sandwiches and drinks at the beach club on the island, which is run by Club Peace and Plenty (see above). Stocking Island used to be a private enclave for guests at Club Peace and Plenty, but it is now used by all visitors. They reach the island on high-speed Boston Whaler runabouts (ask at your hotel desk for departure times). The boats leave from Government Wharf in George Town.

The landlocked **Lake Victoria** covers about two acres in the heart of George Town. It has a narrow exit to the harbor and functions as a diving-and-boating headquarters.

# Why Everyone Is Named Rolle

The history of the Exumas is not much documented before the latter part of the 18th century. It is assumed that the island chain was inhabited by Lucayans at least until the Spaniards wiped them out. Columbus didn't set foot on this chain of islands. However, from the northern tip of Long Island, he is believed to have seen Little Exuma, naming whatever was in the area "Yumey." At least, that's how the island chain appears on a map of the New World from 1500.

By the late 17th century, Great Exuma had become a major producer of salt, and permanent settlers began to arrive. The sailing vessels of the salt merchants were constantly harassed by pirates, but some families from Nassau must have looked on this as the lesser of two evils. On New Providence they were subjected to the terrorism inflicted by both the pirates and the Spanish, and in the latter part of the 17th century and the first of the 18th they fled to the relative peace of the Exumas (they still do!).

Some Loyalist families, fleeing the newly established United States of America after British defeat, came to the Exuma Cays in 1783, but nothing like the number that came to settle in Harbour Island, New Plymouth, and Spanish Wells. In the 18th century, cotton and salt were "king" on the Exumas. English plantation owners brought in many slaves to work the fields, and many of today's Exumians are direct descendants of those early bond servants, who were mostly of African origin. The "king" did not stay long on the throne. Insects went for the cotton, and salt lands such as those of the Turks and Caicos Islands proved much too competitive for those of the Exumas, so these pursuits were eventually abandoned.

Most of the white owners went back to where they came from, but the slaves, having no such option, stayed on, subsisting by working the land abandoned by their former owners and taking the names of those owners as their own. A look through the George Town directory turns up such names as Bethel, Ferguson, and especially Rolle, the same as those of the long-gone whites.

It becomes immediately apparent, however, that every other person is named Rolle. One elderly woman, sitting in front of her little shanty painted in florid tricolors, and wearing a Bahama Mama T-shirt, confided, "You're born a Rolle, all your cousins are called Rolle, you marry a Rolle and have children called Rolle, and you are a Rolle and all the mourners at your funeral, related or not, are called Rolle." She claimed that since everyone in the Exumas keeps track of their blood relatives, the locals know which Rolle is "real family" and which is not related by blood. "That's got to be kept in mind," she said, "when it comes time to get married."

At one time Lord John Rolle held much of the Exumas under a grant from the British Crown, giving him hundreds of acres. He is reported to have owned 325 slaves who worked this acreage, but Lord Rolle never set foot on his potentially rich plantation. Stories vary as to what happened to the slaves—whether they were, as some claim, freed by Lord Rolle and given the land by him, or whether, upon being released from bondage by the United Kingdom Emancipation Act in 1834, they took over the land, with or without Rolle's approval. Whichever, descendants of those same slaves are important Exumians today.

One of the offshore sights in Elizabeth Harbour is Crab Cay, which can be reached by boat. This is believed to have been a rest camp for British seamen in the 18th century.

In April, the ✪ **Family Island Regatta** draws a yachting crowd from all over the world to Elizabeth Harbour. It's a rollicking week of fun, song, and serious racing when the island sloops go all out to win. It's said that some determined skippers bring along extra crewmen to serve as live ballast on windward tacks, then drop them over the side to lighten the ship for the downwind run to the finish. The event, a tradition since 1954, comes at the end of the crawfish season. The George Town regatta is considered the most popular of all the traditional sloop races held in the archipelago.

## SPORTS A TO Z

### Club Peace and Plenty
Queen's Hwy. ☎ **809/345-5555.**

Many visitors come to the Exumas just to go bonefishing. The best arrangements can be made at Club Peace and Plenty, from which you can go out for a half day. The Exumas offer miles of wadeable flats (shallow bodies of water), and trained guides accompany you. Fly instruction and equipment are also offered.

### Exuma FantaSea
P.O. Box 9261, Queen's Highway, George Town. ☎ **809/336-3483** or toll free 800/760-6700 in the U.S.

The lectures and oral commentary offered by this fine diving outfit are probably as articulate and scientifically grounded as anything you'll find in the Bahamas. The company is run by Ed Haxby, a Florida-born marine biologist who is assisted by his Inagua-born wife, Madeline. They specialize in taking groups of six or fewer divers into the offshore reefs and mysterious blue holes, explaining before and after the dive what was seen and offering ecologically conscious narratives on underwater life. PADI instruction is available from a resort course, priced at $90 for those interested in sampling the scuba experience for the first time, and from certification courses ranging from basic open water diving up through advanced courses. They emphasize specialized certification in a wide variety of areas, including underwater naturalist, night diving, and underwater photography. While the specialty courses range in price, certified divers can join one tank "eco-dives" for $55 and two tank dives for $85. The company maintains two dive boats, 20 and 25 feet in length, plus a 15-boat fleet of Boston Whaler rental boats you can drive yourself with daily rates of $75 for a 17-footer to $105 for an 18-footer. Weekly rates are also available.

## SHOPPING

Unless you're one of the islanders who resides permanently in Great Exuma, chances are you won't visit George Town just to shop. However, there are a few places where you can purchase souvenirs and gifts.

### Exuma Liquor and Gifts
Queen's Hwy. ☎ **809/336-2101.**

Perhaps the most popular store in town, this place sells liquor, wine, and some souvenirs. Hours are Monday through Friday from 9am to 5pm.

## Peace and Plenty Boutique

Queen's Hwy. ☎ **809/336-2551.**

This boutique stands next to the Sandpiper and across the street from the previously recommended Club Peace and Plenty, which owns it. Its main draw is its selection of Androsia batiks for women. Androsia cloth is also sold by the "yard" (a yard measures 43 inches wide). You can also find the usual practical items such as film and suntan oil.

A line of saltwater flyfishing equipment and sports clothing is also sold. Hours are Monday through Saturday from 9am to noon and 2 to 5pm.

## The Sandpiper

Queen's Hwy. ☎ **809/336-2084.**

The Sandpiper stands across from Club Peace and Plenty. Its highlights are the original serigraphs by Diane Minns, but it also offers a good selection of Bahamian arts and crafts, along with such items as Bahamian straw baskets (or other handcrafted works), sponges, ceramics, silk-screen fabrics, Seiko cameras, and postcards. It is open Monday through Saturday from 8am to 1pm and 2 to 5pm.

# EASY EXCURSIONS

**Queen's Highway,** which is still referred to as the "slave route," runs across Great Exuma, and you may want to travel it, in either a taxi or a rented car, to take in the sights in and around George Town.

**Rolleville,** named after Lord Rolle, is still inhabited by descendants of his freed slaves. It is claimed that his will left them the land. This land is not sold but is passed along from one generation to the next.

Rolleville is 28 miles to the north of George Town. As you travel along the highway, you'll see ruins of plantations. This land is called "generation estates," and the major ones are Steventon, Mount Thompson, and Ramsey. You pass such settlements as Mosstown (which has working farms), Ramsey, the Forest, Farmer's Hill, and Roker's Point. Steventon is the last settlement before you reach Rolleville. Rolleville is the largest of the plantation estates. There are several beautiful beaches along the way, especially the one at Tarr Bay and Jimmie Hill.

Some visitors may also want to head south of George Town, passing Flamingo Bay and Pirate's Point. In the 18th century Captain Kidd is said to have anchored at Kidd Cay (here you can stay at the Regatta Point, recommended previously).

**Flamingo Bay,** the site of a hotel and villa development, begins just half a mile from George Town. It's a favorite rendezvous of the yachting set and bonefishermen.

## WHERE TO DINE

### Iva Bowe's Central Highway Inn Restaurant & Bar

Queen's Hwy. ☎ **809/345-7014.** Reservations not required. Appetizers $1.50–$3; main courses $8–$18. No credit cards. Daily 10am–10pm. BAHAMIAN.

You might stop at this roadside tavern operated by Mrs. Lorraine Bowe-Lloyd. Located a quarter of a mile from the entrance to the International Airport, and about 6½ miles northwest of George Town, it specializes in very tender cracked conch. The conch is marinated in lime, pounded to make it tender, and than fried with her own special seasonings. You might also try her crawfish salad or shrimp scampi. Her food is good Bahamian cookery.

### Kermit's Hilltop Tavern

Rolleville. ☎ **809/345-6006.** Reservations required for dinner, not required for lunch. Lunch platters $8; three-course dinners $18–$21. No credit cards. Lunch and snacks daily 8am–9pm; dinner by prior arrangement only. BAHAMIAN.

Originally built in the 1950s by members of the Rolle family, this stone-sided social center sits atop the highest point in Rolleville, with a view over the rest of the town. Today, it's open as a tavern and general meeting place for almost everyone in town, as well as for people passing through. Lunch and drinks are served continuously throughout the day and early evening, but more formal meals of chicken, fish, or lobster should be arranged by phone in advance. Try Kermit's curried mutton, steamed conch, or panfried grouper. Some of the produce comes fresh from his farm. The place lies about 20 miles north of George Town.

## EN ROUTE TO LITTLE EXUMA

On the road to Little Exuma, you come to the hamlet of Rolle Town, which is another of the generation estates that was once, like Rolleville in the north, owned by Lord Rolle and is filled with what are called his "descendants" today. This sleepy town has some houses about a century old. In an abandoned field, where goats frolic, you can visit the Rolle Town Tombs, burial ground of the McKay family, who died young. Capt. Alexander McKay, a Scot, came to Great Exuma in 1789 after he was granted 400 acres for a plantation. His wife joined him in 1791, and they had an infant child. However, tragedy struck in 1792, when Anne McKay and her child died. She was only 26. Perhaps grief stricken, her husband died the following year. Their story is one of the romantic legends of the island.

The village claims a famous daughter, Esther Rolle, the actress. Her parents were born here, but they came to the United States before she was born.

## 2 Little Exuma

This is a faraway retreat, the southernmost of the Exuma Cays. It has a subtropical climate, despite being actually in the tropics, and beaches of white sand. In some places, sea life is visible from about 60 feet down in the clear waters. The island, about 12 square miles in area, is connected to Great Exuma by a 200-yard-long bridge. It's about a 10-mile trip from the George Town airport.

## WHAT TO SEE & DO

Less than a mile offshore is **Pigeon Cay,** which is uninhabited. Visitors often come here for the day and are later picked up by a boat that takes them back to Little Exuma. You can go snorkeling and visit the remains of a wreck, some 200 years old, right offshore in about six feet of water.

On one of the highest hills of Little Exuma are the remains of an old pirate fort. Several cannons are located near it, but documentation is lacking as to when it was built or by whom. Pirates didn't leave too much data lying around.

Coming from Great Exuma, the first community you reach on Little Exuma is called **Ferry,** so named because the two islands were linked by a ferry service before the bridge was put in. See if you can visit a private chapel of an Irish family, the Fitzgeralds, erected generations ago.

When you come onto Little Exuma, you might ask a local to direct you to the cottage of Gloria Patience, the "most unforgettable character of the Exumas." Her house, called Tara, lies on the left side of the road after you come over the bridge.

She is famous and much publicized as the **Shark Woman.** Now in her 70s, she earns her living collecting sharks' teeth, which she sells to jewelers. Called the "Annie Oakley of the Family Islands," this barefoot septuagenarian has some tall fish stories to tell, and she's told them to such people as Peter Benchley, author of *Jaws.* She's also appeared on television with Jacques Cousteau. She discounts some modern theories that sharks are kindly souls with a bad press. Take it from the woman who's bagged at least 1,800 of them single-handedly: "They're vicious." The biggest deadly choppers, she claims, are found in the jaws of the female hammerhead. She sells the flesh of her prey to restaurants, although she says she doesn't eat shark meat herself. Her home, a house split by the tropic of Cancer, is like a museum, and you can come here on a shopping expedition, not only for shark teeth, but for all the flea-market stuff and more valuable pieces she's collected over the years. She's a remarkable woman.

Along the way, you can take in **Pretty Molly Bay,** site of the now-shuttered Sand Dollar Beach Club. Pretty Molly was a slave who committed suicide by walking into the water one night. The natives claim that her ghost can still be seen stalking the beach every night.

Many visitors come to Little Exuma to visit the **Hermitage,** a plantation constructed by Loyalist settlers. It is the last surviving home of the many that once stood in the Exumas. It was originally built by the Kendall family, who came to Little Exuma in 1784. They established their plantation at **Williamstown** and, with their slaves, set about growing cotton. They then encountered so many difficulties in having the cotton shipped to Nassau that in 1806 they advertised the plantation for sale. The ad promised "970 acres more or less," along with "160 hands" (referring to the slaves). Chances are you'll be approached by a local guide who, for a fee, will show you around. Ask to be shown several old tombs in the area.

Also at Williamstown (look for the marker on the seaside), you can visit the remains of the **Great Salt Pond.**

Finally, the explorer who has to "see everything" can sometimes get a local to take him or her over to **Hog Cay,** the end of the line for the Exumas. This is really just a spit of land, and there are no glorious beaches here. As such, it's visited mainly by those who like to add obscure islets to their chain of exploration.

Hog Cay is in private hands, and it is farmed. The owner seems friendly to visitors. His house lies in the center of the island. There is also an old lookout tower with a 5-foot cannon at its base. At one time it stood guard for ships coming and going into Elizabeth Harbour.

## WHERE TO DINE

### Gordy's Palace

At Gray's Ville, William Town. No phone. Reservations not required. Appetizers $2–$3.50; main courses $9–$13. No credit cards. Daily 9am–10:30pm. BAHAMIAN.

The "hot spot" of the island is Gordy's Palace, although it's certainly no palace, and if you drop in here on a sleepy afternoon you might think only the weather is hot. You could, in fact, interrupt a poker game. Nevertheless, things get lively around here, especially on Friday and Saturday disco nights. The place is popular mainly with locals, although it gets an occasional visit from a member of the U.S. military stationed in the area. You get typical island fare here, including grouper fingers, conch fritters, or cracked conch, served in modest surroundings. You can also visit just to drink and soak up the laid-back Little Exuma atmosphere. Beer costs $3.

# 3 Barraterre

For years linked to the world only by boat, Barraterre during the 1980s became connected to "mainland" Great Exuma by a road. The area is now open for development, but no one here expects that to happen soon. The place is no more than a sleepy hamlet, and everybody seems to be named McKenzie. As you're heading north, instead of continuing to "end of the line" Rolleville, turn left in the direction of Stuart Manor. You pass through Alexander and keep going until you reach the end of another road, and there lies little Barraterre, asleep in the sun. For the boating crowd, it is the gateway to the Brigantine Cays, which stretch like a necklace to the northwest.

Here you'll see how the "life of the cays" is lived, with the biggest event being the arrival of the mail boat, which is a vital link to the outside world. No one, not even any of the McKenzies, is absolutely certain how the place got its name. Perhaps it came from the French, *bar terre,* or "land obstruction."

The Barraterrians live in a hilly community, with vividly painted houses (many in decay).

## WHERE TO DINE

### Fisherman's Inn

Barraterre. ☎ **809/355-5017.** Reservations not required. Appetizers $2–$3.50; main courses $8–$12. MC, V. Daily 7am "until the last person leaves." BAHAMIAN.

Luckily, your only choice is a good one. Fisherman's Inn is the social center of town, presided over by Mr. and Mrs. Norman Lloyd. The place has a large dance floor, where reggae music often fills the night, and a pool table. It is especially active during those homecoming parties when Barraterrians return, often in August, from either Nassau or the United States with their newfound ways. Everybody seems to have a good time, and the kitchen promises that "fish eaters make better lovers." Conch is the specialty here, and you can order it in fritters, cracked, scorched, and even steamed. You can also ask for grouper fingers and fried chicken. No one will look askance if you want only a hot dog. The specialty of the kitchen is turtle, which, of course, is an endangered species.

# 4 Staniel Cay

Staniel Cay lies at the southern end of the little Pipe Creek archipelago 80 miles southeast of Nassau, which is part of the Exuma Cays. This is an 8-mile chain of uninhabited islets, sandy beaches, coral reefs, and bonefish flats. There are many places for snug anchorages, making this a favorite yachting stopover in the mid-Exumas. Staniel Cay, known for years as "Stanyard," has no golf course or tennis courts, but it's the perfect island for "The Great Escape." It was described by one yachting visitor as lying "in a sea of virtual wilderness."

## GETTING THERE

Before the coming of the airplane, it took days to reach the island from Miami or Nassau, but now it has a 3,000-foot paved airstrip. Some of the vacation homes on Staniel Cay today are owned by pilots. A telecommunications center links the island with both the Bahamas and the United States.

Air service from Fort Lauderdale can be arranged by calling **Island Express** at **305/359-0380.**

## WHAT TO SEE & DO

An annual **bonefishing festival** is sponsored here on July 10, during the celebration of Bahamian Independence Day.

The Happy People Marina (☎ **809/355-2008**) arranges sportsfishing trips with local guides as well as snorkeling trips.

There are about 100 Bahamians living on this island, and there's a local **straw market** where you can buy handcrafts, hats, and handbags. The little cay was settled in the mid-18th century. Its oldest building is a 200-year-old shell.

Just off Staniel Cay is the *Thunderball* **grotto,** where some sections of the famous James Bond movie were filmed. Divers can explore this grotto, but removal of anything but yourself is forbidden, as it is under the protection of the Bahamas National Trust. At low water, it's possible to swim here; a blowhole in the roof illuminates the cave. Tropical fish can be seen in their natural habitat. Another James Bond flick, *Never Say Never Again,* was also partially filmed at this grotto, as, more recently, was *Splash.*

## WHERE TO STAY

The traditional place to stay, Staniel Cay Yacht Club, established in 1959, was involved in major litigation among its owners at press time. Check with travel agents or determine its status before booking in here.

### Happy People Marina

Staniel Cay, the Exumas, the Bahamas. ☎ **809/355-2008.** 12 rms. Year-round, $70 single or double. No credit cards.

This marina is operated by an Exumian, Kenneth Rolle (one of the many descendants of slaves who once belonged to Lord Rolle). His mother was the famous Ma Blanche, who had a mail boat named for her. He offers motel-like rooms on the water, as well as a restaurant and bar, a swimming pool, and a private beach. There are dockage facilities, but no ability to fuel or service the majority of the island's visiting yachts. The prevailing atmosphere is casual, and all of the rooms face the waterfront.

Meals and drinks are served in a separate building closer to the center of town, within a 3-minute walk of the marina. Known as the Royal Entertainer Lounge, it sometimes welcomes local bands and serves meals according to a flexible schedule. Lunches cost from around $8 to $12 per person, dinners around $14 to $18.

## 5 Sampson Cay

In the heart of what has been called the "most beautiful cruising waters in the world," tiny Sampson Cay has a certain charm. It lies directly northwest of Staniel Cay and just to the southeast of the Exuma National Land and Sea Park. It has a full-service marina and some accommodations (see below), as well as a small dive operation. Along with Staniel Cay, Sampson Cay has the only marina in the Central Exumas. To fly to it, you must go to Staniel Cay, unless you arrive on your own boat, as do most visitors. Local guides take out sportfishers for the day; this can be arranged at the club. Sampson Cay lies 67 nautical miles southeast of Nassau, and is considered one of the safest anchorages in the Exumas and a natural "hurricane hole." The cay lies near the end of Pipe Creek, which has been called a "tropical Shangri-la."

## WHERE TO STAY

### Sampson's Cay Colony

Sampson Cay, the Exumas, the Bahamas. ☎ **809/355-2034.** Fax 809/355-2034. 4 units. A/C. Year-round, $115 beachfront villa single or double; $150 hilltop villa single or double. Breakfast from $6. (EP rates.) No credit cards.

Your host here is Mrs. Rosie Mitchell, whose husband, Marcus, is well known in these parts for his marine salvage company, which rescues yachts foundering on nearby rocks and reefs.

Each of the establishment's units has a tiny kitchenette (with a hot plate, sink, and refrigerator, but no oven). The hilltop villa is larger and more spacious than the beachfront villas, carrying a higher price tag. The most noteworthy of the accommodations is contained within a stone-sided, two-story tower—probably the most prominent building on the island.

Guests are quickly absorbed in the community's main pastime, which involves running the grocery store and commissary, the fuel and dockage facilities of the marina, and the bar and restaurant favored by visiting yachtspeople. Its nautically decorated clubhouse serves drinks and sandwiches anytime of the day to anyone who shows up, but reservations are required before 4pm for the single-seating dinner, which is served nightly between 7 and 8pm. A fixed-price meal costs $22 per person. (Reservations can be made via ship-to-shore radio on Channel 16 VHF.)

On the premises, a pair of 13-foot Boston Whalers can be rented for $45 per half day.

## 6 Norman's Cay

Throughout the Exumas, you'll see islands with NO TRESPASSING signs posted. In some cases this is meant with a vengeance. In the early 1980s, at least on one island, you could have been killed if you had gone ashore!

On a long-ago summer day, the boat containing my party sailed by Cistern Cay. Back then, we were told that Robert Vesco owned part of that island. "He likes to keep it *very, very private* here," our guide cautioned, heading for friendlier shores. (Vesco, of course, is the financier much wanted by the U.S. government.) Even though the fugitive is long gone, people around here still like to keep it quiet.

Perhaps the most bizarre Out Islands episode in all the Bahamas centers around Norman's Cay, one of the northernmost islands in the Exumas, 44 nautical miles southeast of New Providence Island. At one time when I stayed at the former hotel there, Norman's Cay Club, this was a South Seas island–type outpost. Reportedly it was once the retirement home of the pirate Norman.

This was always a very special cay. It isn't flat, since parts rise to 50 feet above sea level. It is heavily wooded with lignum vitae, royal poinciana, palmetto, tamarind, and casuarina, and it used to be considered a bird-watcher's paradise. Snorkeling and scuba diving on the coral heads were among the best in the Exumas, with vertical drop-offs, black-coral forests, spectacular cuts, and wrecks. The location is adjacent to the Exuma National Land and Sea Park.

In the old days you might have run into Ted Kennedy, Walter Cronkite, or William F. Buckley, Jr., enjoying the pleasures of Norman's Cay. The remote outpost enjoyed great popularity with a Harvard/Boston clique.

However, in the 1980s the situation changed drastically when a German-Colombian, Carlos Lehder (pronounced *Leader*) Rivas (his mother's name), purchased most of the island. The story of his purchase of Norman's Cay was mentioned in the 1985 *Newsweek* article "Empire of Evil," documenting the horrors of cocaine smuggling. A short time after Lehder's purchase of the property, the Colombian flag was flying over Norman's Cay, and many of the wintering wealthy fled in horror from the island when they returned to find their homes broken into and "trashed."

Norman's Cay, experts have stated, became the major distribution point for drug export to the United States. Millions of dollars worth of cocaine was flown from Colombia and deposited in hangars at Norman's Cay before being smuggled into the United States. It is estimated that some 30 pilots crashed attempting to fly in their illegal cargoes. You can still see the wreckage of a C-46 that went down in the bay.

When an undersecretary of state arrived from Washington and landed on the island, he was ordered off at gunpoint by a Colombian commando. He left, but when he returned to the U.S. capital, he launched a major protest. Apparently, strong, hard pressure was applied by the U.S. government on the Bahamian government to "clean up the act" at Norman's Cay.

Lehder fled Norman's Cay for further adventures in Colombia, where he was captured and extradited to the United States (he was later tried, convicted, and imprisoned).

Norman's Cay may one day realize its tourist potential again, but for the moment it remains relatively abandoned.

# 11 The Southern Bahamas

This cluster of islands on the southern fringe of the Bahamas might be called the "undeveloped islands." Some of them are proud to proclaim that "we are as we were when Columbus first landed here."

But their history hasn't been that uneventful. In the 18th century Loyalists from the Carolinas and Virginia came here with slave labor and settled onto many of the islands. For about 20 years they had thriving cotton plantations until a blight struck and killed the industry. A second and perhaps more devastating "blight" from the planters' point of view was the freeing of the slaves in 1834. The Loyalists moved on to more fertile ground, in many cases leaving behind the emancipated blacks, who were left with nothing. Many people in the southern Bahamas have had to eke out a living as best they can "Farmin' and Fishin'."

With some notable exceptions, such as on Long Island, tourism developers have stayed clear of these islands, although their potential is enormous, as most of them have excellent beaches, good fishing, and fine dive sites.

If you consider visiting any of these islands, be forewarned that transportation will be a major problem. Also, except for two or three resorts, accommodations are severely limited. For these and other reasons, yachties have been the primary visitors up to now.

Many changes may be in the wind for the southern Bahamas. But if you want to see things the "way they used to be," as they say in those Jamaica ads, go not to Jamaica but to Mayaguana Island. That's *really* how things used to be in the Bahamas. No traffic, no banks, no lawyers.

*Note:* For an explanation of rate symbols used in accommodations listings, see "Tips on Accommodations" in Chapter 3.

## 1 Cat Island

Untainted by tourism, the sixth-largest island in the Bahamas, fishhook-shaped Cat Island, is some 48 miles long and 1 to 4 miles wide, comprising some 150 square miles of land area about 130 miles southeast of Nassau and 325 miles southeast of Miami. This is not—repeat *not*—Cat Cay. The cay is a little private island near Bimini. The location of Cat Island—named after the pirate Arthur Catt—is near the Tropic of Cancer, between Eleuthera and Long

## What's Special About the Southern Bahamas

Beaches
- Fernandez Bay, Cat Island, is a picture-postcard beach—brilliant white sand against a turquoise blue sea. Lined with casuarina trees, this spot is for seekers of tranquillity.
- Long Island beaches, dreamy for swimming in calm coves. Best bets include Deal's Beach, Cape Santa Maria Beach, Salt Pond Beach, Turtle Cove Beach, and the South End beaches, the latter offering miles of waterfront with powdery white or pink sands.
- San Salvador beaches, miles and miles of sandy shores with rarely a bather in site—ideal for shelling, swimming, or snorkeling. Try Bamboo Point, Fernandez Bay, Long Bay, or Sandy Point.

Intriguing Islands
- Cat Island, sixth largest in the Bahamas, shaped like a fishhook—underpopulated, undeveloped, and filled with virgin beaches.
- San Salvador, where many historians believe Columbus made his first landfall in the New World—easternmost island in the Bahamian archipelago.
- Long Island, the third island to which Columbus presumably sailed, with the tropic of Cancer running through its long, thin sliver of land.
- Acklins/Crooked Island, little tropical islands so undiscovered they remain Bahamian frontier outposts.
- Great Inagua, most southerly and third-largest Bahamian island, home to the endangered Bahamian flamingo.

Ancient Sites
- Arawak Indian Caves at Columbus Point on Cat Island.

Island. Its climate is one of the finest in the Bahamas, with temperatures in the high 60s during the short winters, rising to the mid-80s in summer, and with trade winds making the place more comfortable. Some 2,000 residents call it home.

With its virgin beaches, Cat Island is considered one of the most beautiful islands in the Bahamas, and it is visited by so few people it could be called "undiscovered." Even though it has remained relatively unknown to mainstream tourism, many local historians claim that it was Cat Island that first saw Columbus. The great explorer himself was believed by some to have been first welcomed here by the peaceful Arawaks.

Cat Island remains mysterious to some even now. It's known as a stronghold of such strange practices as *obeah* (West Indian witchcraft) and of miraculously healing bush medicines. Its history has been colorful. Regardless of whether or not Columbus stopped off here, the island has seen a parade of adventurers, slaves, buccaneers, farmers, and visionaries of many nationalities.

A straight asphalt road (in terrible shape) leads from the north to the south of the island. Along the way you can select your own beach, and chances are you'll have complete privacy. These beaches also offer an array of water sports, and visitors can go swimming or snorkeling at several places. The island's north side is considered wild, untamed shoreline. Diving lessons are possible for the novice, and the experienced will find boating and diving among the reasons to go to Cat Island.

Arthurs Town, in the north, is the major town and the boyhood home of actor Sidney Poitier. (He has many relatives still living on the island, including one or two amazing look-alikes I recently spotted.) Poitier shared memories of his childhood home in his book *This Life.*

## GETTING THERE

**BY PLANE**   A commercial flight on **Bahamasair** (☎ toll free **800/222-4262** in the U.S.) leaves Nassau for Arthurs Town on Sunday and Thursday at 8:40am, but that could change, so check locally. There is also an airport near the Bight, the most beautiful village on the island.

**BY MAIL BOAT**   Cat Island is also serviced by mail boat. The MV *North Cat Island Special* (☎ **809/393-1064**) departs Potter's Cay Dock in Nassau weekly, heading for Bennett's Harbour and Arthurs Town. It leaves on Tuesday at 2pm and returns to Nassau on Thursday. Another vessel, MV *Sea Hauler* (☎ **809/393-1064**), departs Potter's Cay in Nassau on Tuesday at 2pm, going to Old and New Bight, with a return on Saturday.

## GETTING AROUND

There is no taxi service available on Cat Island. Hotel owners, if notified of your arrival time, will have someone drive to the airport to pick you up. You can, however, rent a car from **Russell Brothers,** Bridge Inn, New Bight (☎ **809/342-3014**), to go exploring on your own.

## WHERE TO STAY & DINE

### Bridge Inn
New Bight, Cat Island, the Bahamas, ☎ **809/342-3013.** Fax 809/342-3041. 12 rms. MINIBAR TV. Winter, $70 single; $80 double; $95 triple. Off-season, $60 single; $70 double; $85 triple. Continental breakfast $7 extra. (EP rates.) No credit cards. Free parking.

The Bridge Inn is managed by Allan Russell, who is ably assisted by a group of family members. The inn offers babysitting services so that parents can play tennis or go diving, windsurfing, jogging, bicycling, fishing, or just sightseeing with the knowledge that their youngsters are being carefully tended and are having fun, too. Bedrooms are in the modest motel style. Each unit can house three to four guests. Room service is available, and there are a full bar and a restaurant serving Bahamian and international cuisine. Local jam sessions ("rake and scrape") are easily arranged for your entertainment, usually on Friday night. As manager Russell points out, you'll learn that life can be "no problem, mon, on Cat Island."

### Fernandez Bay Village
3 miles north of New Bight, Cat Island, the Bahamas. ☎ **809/354-5043** or toll free 800/940-1905; 305/474-4821 in Plantation, Florida. Fax 809/354-5051 or 305/474-4864 in Plantation, Florida. 10 units. $180–$210 villa for two; $210 cottage for two. Off-season, $170–$195 villa for two; $185 cottage for two. (MAP rates.) AE, MC, V. Free parking.

Here on Fernandez Bay, you can enjoy the same water and sun activities as at big resorts without the hassle of crowds and constant coming and going. Fernandez Bay Village has been in the Armbrister family since it was originally established on a plantation in 1870. It's a place where rusticity and seclusion are part of the charm, and yet, if you wish, you can get acquainted with other guests with similar interests (or even watch video movies). Right on the beautiful white-sand beach of the bay, nestled among the casuarina trees, are eight full housekeeping

# The Southern Bahamas

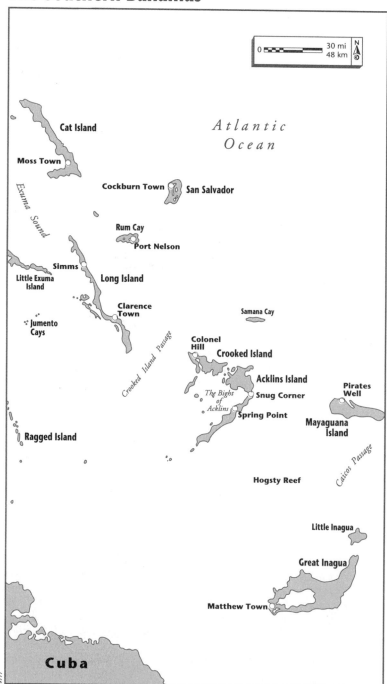

0  30 mi
   48 km

N

*Atlantic Ocean*

Cat Island

Moss Town

*Exuma Sound*

Cockburn Town  San Salvador

Rum Cay
Port Nelson

Simms

Little Exuma
Island

Long Island

Clarence
Town

Jumento
Cays

Samana Cay

Colonel
Hill

Crooked Island

*Crooked Island Passage*

Acklins Island

*The Bight
of
Acklins*

Snug Corner

Spring Point

Pirates
Well

Mayaguana
Island

Ragged Island

*Caicos Passage*

Hogsty Reef

Little Inagua

Great Inagua

Matthew Town

**Cuba**

9777

villas, each of which sleeps up to six people, as well as two double-occupancy cottages, built of stone, driftwood, and glass. Full maid service is provided. Because of the lack of nearby dining facilities, most clients opt for accommodations with MAP, which in this case means either breakfast or lunch ("because so many people don't even eat breakfast") and dinner. Fernandez Bay Village often has visiting yachtspeople who moor in the waters offshore (there are no marina facilities), taking advantage of the resort's general store and the fresh supplies to be found there. Nearby is Smith's Bay, one of the best storm shelters in the region, where even the government mail boats take refuge during hurricanes.

Breakfast and lunch are served in a clubhouse decorated with antiques, Haitian art, a sitting library area, stone fireplace, and overhead fans, opening onto a view of the beach and sea. Dinners are served on a beach terrace adjacent to a thatched roof tiki-bar that is run on the honor system.

There is free use of Zuma sailboats and bicycles, and snorkeling and waterskiing are also on the agenda. Also offered are scuba and fly-fishing services. Rental vans are available from Jason's Car Rental at $85 for 24 hours. You can picnic on deserted beaches around the island, then dine on authentic island cuisine at the resort's restaurant, after which on many nights a blazing bonfire near the water is the focal point for guests who want to listen to island music.

The resort will supply air transportation from Nassau on request (usually in the private plane owned and operated by the manager himself). Flights land at the nearby New Bight Airport.

For reservations and information, write to Fernandez Bay Village, 1507 S. University Dr., Suite A, Plantation, FL 33324 (☎ 305/474-4821).

### ⊛ Hotel Greenwood Inn

Port Howe, Cat Island, the Bahamas. ☎ **809/342-3053** or toll free 800/343-0373. Fax 809/342-3053. 20 rms. Year-round, $79 single; $99 double; $119 triple. Children under 12 stay free in parents' room. Free meals for children up to 6 years old. (EP rates.) AE, MC, V. Free parking.

Hotel Greenwood Inn, open year-round, is a group of modern buildings on the ocean side with a private sandy beach on the most isolated section of the island. There are spacious oceanview double rooms, all equipped with full baths and showers and their own terraces. There is an all-purpose bar and a dining room. The staff meets each Bahamasair flight when it arrives. Make time for some comfortable chats with fellow guests before jumping into the swimming pool. The inn has a 40-foot motorboat for diving excursions. Its Tabaluga Diving Base has complete equipment for 20 divers at a time.

## WHAT TO SEE & DO

There's an interesting Arawak cave at Columbus Point on the southern tip of the island. In addition, you can see the ruins of many once-flourishing plantations. Some old stone mounds are nearly 200 years old. Early planters, many of them Loyalists, marked their plantation boundaries with these mounds. These include the **Deveaux Mansion,** built by Col. Andrew Deveaux of the fledgling U.S. Navy, who recaptured Nassau from the Spanish in 1783. Its heyday was during the island's short-lived cotton boom. Yet another mansion, **Armbrister Plantation,** lies in ruins near Port Howe.

You can hike along the natural paths through native villages, past exotic plants. Finally, you reach the peak of **Mount Alvernia,** the highest point in the Bahamas at 206 feet above sea level, and are rewarded with a splendid view. The mount is capped by the Hermitage, a religious retreat built entirely by hand by the late Father Jerome, the former "father confessor" of the island, who was once a mule skinner in Canada. Curiously, the building was scaled to fit his short stature (he was a very, very short man). Formerly an Anglican, this Roman Catholic "hermit priest" became a legend on Cat Island. He died in 1956 at the age of 80, but his memory is kept very much alive here and he's known even among young people born long after his death.

The boating activities reach their peak at the **Annual Three-Day Regatta,** usually conducted at the end of July. That's when Cat Island receives its biggest collection of visitors, and its inns prove inadequate to receive them.

## 2  San Salvador/Rum Cay

This may be where the New World began. It has for some years been believed that Christopher Columbus made his first footprints in the Western Hemisphere here, although this assertion is still strongly disputed. The easternmost island in the Bahamian archipelago, San Salvador lies 200 miles southeast of Nassau. It is some 60 square miles in area, much of which is occupied by water. There are said to be 28 landlocked lakes on the island, the largest of which is 12 miles long and serves as the principal route of transportation for most of the island's 1,200 population. A 40-mile road circles the perimeter of San Salvador.

The tiny island keeps a lonely vigil in the Atlantic. The Dixon Hill Lighthouse at South West Point, about 165 feet tall, can be seen from 90 miles away. The light is a hand-operated beacon fueled by kerosene. Built in the 1850s, it is the last lighthouse of its type in the Bahamas. The highest point on the island is Mount Kerr at 138 feet.

### GETTING THERE

Club Med (see below) solves transportation problems for its guests by flying them in on weekly charter planes from Miami or Eleuthera. Otherwise, Riding Rock Inn (see below) has charter flights every Saturday from Fort Lauderdale. You can also rely on public transportation by land or sea; but if you do you'll have to wait a long time before getting off the island.

**BY PLANE**   Bahamasair (☎ 800/222-4262) has lots of flights to the island because of the location of Club Med there. Departures include Monday at 10:30am, Wednesday at 9:15am, and Thursday, Friday, and Sunday at 11:30am.

**BY MAIL BOAT**   The MV *Lady Francis* goes from Potter's Cay Dock in Nassau to Rum Cay and San Salvador. It departs Nassau weekly on Thursday at 2pm and returns on Saturday. The North Island Special leaves on Tuesday at 2pm and returns on Thursday. For details about sailing, contact the dockmaster at Potter's Cay Dock in Nassau (☎ 809/393-1064).

### GETTING AROUND

**Taxis** meet arriving planes and will take you to Riding Rock Inn, (see below), where you can rent a car for $85 a day to explore the island on your own. You can also rent **bicycles** at $8 a day. The latter are the most popular means of transport for visitors. If you pedal energetically, you can traverse all of San Salvador in about an hour.

## The Columbus Question

In 1492 a small group of peaceful Lucayan Natives (Arawaks) went about their business of living on a little island they called Guanahani, which they and their forebears had called home for at least 500 years. This is the island that scholars believe Columbus first landed on. It is said that Columbus knelt and prayed—and claimed the land for Spain.

Unfortunately, the event was not so propitious for the reportedly handsome natives. Columbus later wrote to Queen Isabella that they would make ideal captives—perfect servants, in other words. It wasn't long before the Spanish conquistadores cleared the island—as well as most of the Bahamas—of Lucayans, sending them into slavery and early death in the mines of Hispaniola (Haiti) in order to feed the Spanish lust for gold from the New World.

No lasting marker was placed by Columbus on the sandy, sun-drenched island he had come to, resulting in much study and discussion during the last century or so as to just where he really did land. Some say that it was on one of the cays of the Turks and Caicos Islands; others claim that it was on Cat Island.

In the 17th century, an English pirate captain, George Watling, took over the island and built a mansion to serve as his safe haven. The island was listed on maps for about 250 years as Watling's (or Watling) Island.

In 1926 the Bahamian legislature formally changed the name of the island to San Salvador, feeling that enough evidence had been brought forth to support the belief that this was the site of the landing of Columbus. Then in 1983, artifacts of European origin (beads, buckles, and metal spikes) were found here together with a shard of Spanish pottery, plus Arawak pottery and beads. It is unlikely that the actual date of these artifacts can be pinned down, although they are probably from about 1490 to 1560. However, the beads and buckles fit the description of goods recorded in Columbus's log.

*National Geographic* magazine published a meticulously researched article in 1986 written by its senior associate editor, Joseph Judge, with a companion piece by the former chief of the magazine's foreign editorial staff, Luis Marden, setting forth the belief that Samana Cay, some 65 miles to the southeast of the present San Salvador, was Guanahani, the island Columbus named San Salvador when he first landed in the New World. The question may never be absolutely resolved, but there will doubtless be years and years of controversy about it. And nevertheless, history buffs still flock here every year hoping to follow in the footsteps of Columbus.

## ESSENTIALS

**HOSPITAL**  The San Salvador Medical Clinic (☎ 809/331-2105) services the island's residents, but serious cases are flown to Nassau.

**POLICE**  To call the police, dial **919.** (Phones are rare on the island, but the front desk at Riding Rock Inn will place calls for you.)

## WHERE TO STAY & DINE

### ✪ Club Med-Columbus Isle

2 miles north of Cockburn Town, San Salvador, the Bahamas. ☎ **809/331-2458** or toll free 800/CLUB-MED. Fax 809/331-2458. 270 rms. A/C MINIBAR TV TEL. Winter, $1,150–$1,700

per person per week. Off-season, $1,050 per person per week. No discounts for children. Children under 12 not admitted. Rates include all meals, drinks, and most sports activities. AE, MC, V. Free parking.

This is one of the newest, most ecologically conscious, and, by many accounts, the most luxurious Club Med in the Western Hemisphere. Set at the edge of one of the most pristine beaches in the archipelago (two miles of white sand), about two miles north of Cockburn Town, the resort is by anyone's estimate the most visible and splashiest entity on the entire island. (Its promoters estimate that more than 30% of the island's population works within the club.)

Mostly prefabricated in Alabama, individual buildings were barged to the site beginning in 1991. The resort is built around a large free-form swimming pool whose waters, because of the color selected for the tile sheathing, are said to almost exactly match the color of the nearby ocean. The public rooms are graced with some of the most lavish and cosmopolitan decors in the country, with art and art objects imported from Asia, Africa, Oceania, the Americas, and Europe and assembled by a battalion of well-trained designers. Bedrooms each contain a private balcony or patio, furniture that was custom-made in Thailand or the Philippines, sliding glass doors, and feathered wall hangings crafted in the Brazilian rain forest by members of the Xingu tribe. Each room is large (among the largest in the entire chain) and decorated in shades of blue and green. Unlike many other Club Meds, this one does not encourage children, and deliberately offers no particular facilities for their entertainment.

**Dining/Entertainment:** The main dining room, where meals are an ongoing series of buffets, lies in the resort's center. Within a pair of oceanfront outbuildings lie two specialty restaurants—serving Italian and grilled food, respectively—where meals are served by the staff. Eating en masse is not the only option. Nonfat, low-calorie, and vegetarian dishes are offered. Nightly entertainment is offered in a covered, open-air theater and dance floor behind one of the bars.

**Services:** Dozens of multilingual GOs (guest relations organizers, or *gentils organizateurs*) on hand to help initiate newcomers into the resort's many diversions.

**Facilities:** 10 tennis courts (3 lit for night play), the largest scuba facility in the Club Med chain, windsurfing, kayaking and kayak-scuba-diving, and a miniarmada of Hobie Cats and other sailing craft.

## Riding Rock Inn

Cockburn Town, San Salvador, the Bahamas. ☎ **305/359-8353** in Florida or toll free 800/272-1492 in the U.S. Fax 305/359-8254 in Florida. 42 rms. A/C. Year-round, $87 single; $87–$135 double. Continental breakfast $7 extra. Dive packages available. (EP rates.) MC, V. Free parking.

San Salvador's second resort is the Riding Rock Inn, which is almost exclusively (95%) patronized by divers and underwater enthusiasts. Each accommodation faces either a pool or the open sea. The most recent improvement to the inn is an 18-room oceanfront building, where the bedrooms are decorated in a tropical

### Impressions

*The island is fairly large and very flat. It is green, with many trees and several bodies of water. There is a very large lagoon in the middle of the island and there are no mountains. It is a pleasure to gaze upon this place because it is all so green, and the weather is delightful.*

—Columbus's log, October 13, 1492

decor, with two double beds, satellite TV, a refrigerator, telephone, and, of course, air-conditioning. The resort specializes in week-long packages that include three dives a day, all meals, and accommodations. Packages begin and end on Saturday and, if a client pays a $255 supplement, can include specially chartered round-trip air transportation from Fort Lauderdale. Although most of this resort's clients are already experienced and certified divers, beginners can arrange a $95 resort course for the first day of their visit, and afterward participate in most of the community's daily dives. Full PADI (Professional Association of Dive Instructors) certification can also be arranged for another supplement of $375.

Accommodations contain simple tropics-inspired furnishings and ceiling fans. An island tour is included in the rates, but after that, most clients find that the best way to navigate is by bicycle (the hotel rents them, plus scooters). On the premises are a restaurant and a bar whose seating area juts above the water on a pier.

# WHAT TO SEE & DO

Among the settlements on San Salvador are Sugar Loaf, Pigeon Creek, Old Place, Holiday Track, and Fortune Hill. United Estates, the one with the largest population, is a village in the northwest corner near the Dixon Hill Lighthouse. The U.S. Coast Guard has a station at the northern tip of the island.

Bonefishers are attracted to Pigeon Creek, and some record catches have been chalked up there. San Salvador is mainly visited by the boating set who can live aboard their craft, but if you're visiting for the day, you'll find one or two local cafés. They all serve seafood.

### Chicago Herald Monument
Crab Cay.

If a preponderance of monuments is anything to go by, this is the San Salvador visited and named by the historic explorer. The *Chicago Herald* installed a monument to the explorer in 1892, but it is not probable—indeed, it's almost impossible—that any landing was made at that site. It opens onto reefs along the eastern shore, surely a dangerous place for a landing.

### Olympic Games Memorial
Long Bay.

This memorial to Columbus—three miles south of Cockburn Town, was erected in 1968 to commemorate the games in Mexico. Runners carrying an Olympic torch circled the island before coming to rest at the monument and lighting the torch there. The torch was then taken to Mexico on a warship for the games. A fourth marker is underwater, supposedly where Columbus dropped anchor on his *Santa Maria.*

Just north of the monument stands the **Columbus Monument,** where on December 25, 1956, Ruth Durlacher Wolpher Malvin, a Columbus scholar and widow of Hollywood producer David Wolpher, established a simple monument commemorating the landfall of Columbus in the New World. Unlike the *Chicago Herald* monument, this spot is actually supposed to be the place where Columbus and his men landed.

### Watling's Castle
French Bay.

Watling's Castle, also known as Sandy Point Estate, has substantial ruins that are about 85 feet above sea level and some 2¹/₂ miles from the "Great Lake," on the southwestern tip of the island. Local "experts" will tell you all about the castle and its history. Only problem is, each "expert" I've listened to—three in all, at different times—has had a conflicting story about the place. Ask around and perhaps you'll get yet another version. One of the most common legends involves a famous pirate who made his living either by salvaging the wreckage from foundered ships or by attacking them for their spoils.

### Farquharson's Plantation
West of Queen's Hwy., near South Victoria Hill. Admission free. Open anytime.

In the early part of the 19th century some Loyalist families moved from the newly established United States to this island, hoping to get rich from farmland tended by slave labor. That idea ended when the United Kingdom Emancipation Act of 1834 freed the slaves. The plantation owners, having been compensated for their bond servants' value, moved on, but the former slaves stayed behind.

A relic of those times, Farquharson's Plantation, is the best-known ruin on the island. People locally call it "Blackbeard's Castle," but it's a remnant of slavery days, not of the time of pirates. You can see the foundation of a great house, a kitchen, and what is believed to have been a punishment cell.

### Cockburn Town

San Salvador is one of the most unspoiled of the Bahamian Family Islands—not that much has changed since Columbus landed except the Club Med. It has wooded hills, lakes, and white-sand beaches. Its people are hospitable. Some still practice obeah and bush medicine.

The island's capital, Cockburn (pronounced *Coburn*) Town, is a harbor village that also has an airstrip. It takes its name from George Cockburn, who is said to have been the first royal governor of the Bahamas who cared enough about this remote island to visit it. That was back in 1823.

Look for the town's giant, landmark almond tree. Whatever is happening at San Salvador generally takes place here, especially the Columbus Day parade held every October 12.

### New World Museum
North Victoria Hill. No phone. Admission free. Open anytime during the day.

This museum has relics dating back to Indian times, but you'll have to ask until you find someone with a key if you want to go inside. The museum lies just past Bonefish Bay in the little village of North Victoria Hill. It's part of a large estate, called "Polaris-by-the-Sea" and is owned by Ruth Durlacher Wolpher Malvin, widow of Hollywood producer David Wolpher. The museum is on her estate.

### Holy Saviour Roman Catholic Church
Cockburn Town.

The very first Christian worship service to be held in the New World was conducted according to the Catholic rites. It thus seems fitting that the Roman Catholic Diocese of the Bahamas in 1992 dedicated a new church on San Salvador on the eve of the 500th anniversary of the Columbus landfall.

Holy Saviour Roman Catholic Church (San Salvador in Spanish) serves a congregation of about 200 members. The construction of the church was funded by the Knights of Columbus of North America.

## SPORTS A TO Z

Associated with the Riding Rock Inn (see above), **Guanahani Dive Ltd.** (☎ 809/ 331-2631) offers dive packages, as well as snorkeling, fishing, and boating trips. One-, two-, and three-dive trips cost from $40, $55, and $75, respectively.

Riding Rock Inn also has a tennis court where guests can play for free.

## 3 Long Island

Most historians agree that the Long Island of the Bahamas (which has nothing to do with that 100-mile landmass at the southern tip of New York State) was the third island to which Columbus sailed during his first voyage of discovery. The Lucayans (Arawaks) who lived there at the time (and who had come from South America via Cuba) called their island Yuma, but Columbus renamed it Fernandina, in honor of King Ferdinand, and claimed it for Spain.

Loyalist plantation owners came here in the 18th century from the Carolinas and Virginia, bringing with them their slaves and their allegiance to the British Crown. There was a brief cotton boom, but when the slaves were freed in 1834, the owners abandoned the plantations and left the island. Inhabited by the former slaves, Long Island slumbered for years, until German resort developers began investigating its resources in the 1960s.

The tropic of Cancer runs through this long, thin sliver of land, located 150 miles southeast of Nassau. It stretches for some 60 miles running from north to south, and averages 1 1/2 miles wide. It's only 3 miles wide at its broadest point.

Having only recently emerged as a minor tourist resort, Long Island is characterized by high cliffs in the north, wide and shallow sand beaches, historic plantation ruins, native caves, and Spanish churches. It is also the site of the saltworks of the Diamond Crystal Company. The island's present population numbers some 3,500 people. Offshore are famed diving sites, such as the Arawak "green" hole, a "bottomless" blue hole of stunning magnitude.

In June, the sailors of Long Island participate in the big event of the year, the **Long Island Regatta.** They've been gathering since 1967 at Salt Pond for this annual event, which lasts for four days. In addition to the highly competitive sailboat races, Long Island takes on a festive air with calypso music and reggae and lots of drinking and partying. Many expatriate Long Islanders come home at this time, usually from Nassau, New York, or Miami, to enjoy not only the regatta but rake-and-scrape music (accordion playing).

## GETTING THERE

**BY PLANE**    There are two airstrips here, which are connected by a bad road. The Stella Maris strip is in the north, and the other, called Deadman's Cay, is in the south, north of Clarence Town. **Bahamasair** (☎ 800/222-4262 in the U.S.) wings from Nassau, connecting the two airports. Nassau departures are Wednesday at 12:15pm and Friday and Sunday at 10am.

**BY MAIL BOAT**    Mail boats service Clarence Town weekly, with service to Deadman's Cay and Stella Maris once a week or every other week. The MV *Mia Dean* leaves from Potter's Cay Dock in Nassau, but there is no set schedule. For information on sailing, days and times and costs, get in touch with the dockmaster at Potter's Cay Dock, Nassau (☎ 809/393-1064).

## GETTING AROUND

The **Stella Maris Resort Club** (☎ **809/336-2106**) can make arrangements to have you picked up at the airport upon arrival and can also arrange for a rental car.

## ESSENTIALS

POLICE    The police at Clarence Town can be reached by calling **809\337-0444.**

## WHERE TO STAY & DINE

### Stella Maris Inn

Ocean View Dr., P.O. Box 30105, Long Island, the Bahamas. ☎ **809/336-2106** or toll free 800/426-0466 in the U.S.; 305/359-8236 for the Florida booking office. Fax 305/359-8238 in Fort Lauderdale. 37 rms, 13 cottages and bungalows. A/C. Winter, $105–$130 single; $125–$150 double; $220–$490 cottage. Off-season, $95–$115 single; $110–$135 double; $250–$285 cottage. Continental breakfast $7 extra. (EP rates.) AE, MC, V. Free parking.

On the Atlantic, overlooking the coastline, is the Stella Maris Inn, built on the grounds of the old Adderley's Plantation. Courtesy transportation is provided to a 3-mile beach reserve. Accommodations vary widely—rooms, studios, apartments, and cottages consisting of one to two bedrooms. Rentals are all in individual buildings, including cottages and bungalows, set around the clubhouse and a trio of hotel pools.

Each accommodation has its own walk-in closet and fully equipped bath. Some bungalows are 100 feet from the water, others are directly on its edge. The inn serves Bahamian cuisine, as well as continental specialties. Dress here is informal.

The inn provides rum punch parties, cave parties, barbecue dinners, Saturday dinners, and dancing. There are two hard-surface tennis courts, and water sports are excellent here. Divers and snorkelers have a wide choice of coral head, reef, and drop-off diving, along the protected west coast of this island and at the north and all along the east coast, around Conception Island and Rum Cay. Waterskiing and bottom and reef fishing are also offered; there are three good bonefish bays close by. Some 12-foot Scorpion and Sunfish sailboats are free to hotel guests.

For more information or reservations, write to Stella Maris Inn, 1110 Lee Wagener Blvd., Fort Lauderdale, FL 33315 (☎ **305/359-8236**).

### Thompson Bay Inn

Main Rd., Thompson Bay, P.O. Box 30123, Stella Maris, Long Island, the Bahamas. 8 rms. Year-round, $55 single; $65 double. Continental breakfast $5 extra. (EP rates.) No credit cards. Free parking.

Located at Salt Pond, 12 miles south of Stella Maris, Thompson Bay Inn is a modest two-story stone inn. Other than the Stella Maris Inn, it is one of the few commercially viable gathering places on the island. Its bar, lounge, dance hall, and restaurant serves such Bahamian dishes as conch, grouper, and peas 'n' rice. Dinners cost $15 each. Rooms are simply furnished, and the inn's four baths are shared.

*Note:* To telephone the inn you must call the Deadman Cay's operator (☎ **809/ 337-0099**). The operator will call the inn on the VHF radio and deliver your message.

## WHAT TO SEE & DO

Most of the inhabitants live at the unattractively named **Deadman's Cay.** Except for Burnt Ground, other settlements have colorful and somewhat more pleasant names: Roses, Newfound Harbour, Indian Head Point, and at the northern tip of the island, Cape Santa Maria, generally believed to be the place where Columbus landed and from which he looked on the Exumas (islands that he did not visit). My favorite name, however, is Hard Bargain. No one seems to know how this hamlet got its name. Hard Bargain, now a shrimp-breeding farm, lies 10 miles south of Clarence Town.

Try to visit **Clarence Town** in the south, 10 miles below Deadman's Cay, along the eastern coastline. It was here that the stubby little priest, Father Jerome, who became known as the "father confessor" of the islands, built two churches before his death in 1956—one, St. Paul's, an Anglican house of worship, and the other, St. Peter's, a Roman Catholic church. The "hermit" of Cat Island, where you can visit his Hermitage, was interested in Gothic architecture, and he must also have been of a somewhat ecumenical bent, having started his ministry as an Anglican but embracing Roman Catholicism along the way.

The days when local plantation owners figured their wealth in black slaves and white cotton are recalled in some of the ruins you can visit. The remains of **Dunmore's Plantation** at Deadman's Cay stand on a hill with the sea on three sides. There are six gateposts (four outer and two inner ones), as well as a house with two fireplaces and wall drawings of ships. At the base of the ruins is evidence that a mill wheel was once used. It was part of the estate of Lord Dunmore, for whom Dunmore Town on Harbour Island was named.

At the village of Grays stand **Gray's Plantation** ruins, where you'll see the remnants of at least three houses, one with two chimneys. One is very large, and the other seems to have been a one-story structure with a cellar.

**Adderley's Plantation,** off Cape Santa Maria, originally occupied all the land now known as Stella Maris. The ruins of this cotton plantation's buildings consist of three structures that are partially intact but roofless.

Two underground sites that can be visited on Deadman's Cay are **Dunmore's Caves** and **Deadman's Cay Cave.** You'll need to hire a local guide if you wish to visit these attractions. Dunmore's Caves are believed to have been inhabited by Lucayans and later to have served as a hideaway for buccaneers. The cave at Deadman's Cay, one of two that lead to the ocean, has never been fully explored. There are two native drawings on the cavern wall in the one you can visit.

## 4  Acklins Island & Crooked Island

These little tropical islands approximately 240 miles southeast of Nassau comprise an undiscovered Bahamian frontier outpost. Columbus came this way looking for gold. Much later Acklins Island, Crooked Island, and their surrounding cays were retreats of pirates who attacked vessels in the Crooked Island Passage, which is the narrow waterway separating the two islands through which Columbus sailed. Today a well-known landmark, the Crooked Island Passage Light, built in 1876, guides ships to a safe voyage through the slot. A barrier reef begins near the lighthouse, stretching down off Acklins Island for about 25 miles to the southeast.

These are neighboring islands, which, although separate, are usually mentioned as a unit because of their proximity to one another. Together the two islands form the shape of a boomerang. The northern one, Crooked Island, is 70 square miles in area, while Acklins Island, to the south, occupies 120 square miles.

In his controversial article in *National Geographic* in 1986, Joseph Judge identifies Crooked Island as the site of Columbus's second island landing, the one he named Santa Maria de la Concepción.

It is estimated that by the end of the 18th century there were more than three dozen working plantations on these islands, begun by Loyalists fleeing mainland North America in the wake of the revolutionary war. At the peak plantation period, there could have been as many as 1,200 slaves laboring in the 3,000 "doomed" acres of cotton fields (which were later wiped out by a blight).

## GETTING THERE & GETTING AROUND

A government-owned ferry service connects the two islands; it operates daily from 9am to 4pm. It links Lovely Bay on Acklins Island with Browns on Crooked Island. The one-way fare is $4. Both these islands have magnificent white-sand beaches, and good fishing and scuba diving are possible. Both islands are inhabited mainly by fishermen and farmers.

An airport lies at Colonel Hill on Crooked Island, and there is another airstrip at Spring Point, Acklins Island. If you arrive on one island and intend to go to the other, you can use the ferry, mentioned just above.

**Bahamasair** (☎ toll free **800/222-4262** in the U.S.) has two flights a week from Nassau, on Tuesday at 9:30am and Saturday at 10:15am, to Crooked Island and Acklins Island, with returns to Nassau scheduled on the same day.

There is also mail-boat service aboard the MV *Windward Express.* It leaves Potter's Cay Dock in Nassau, heading for Acklins Island, Crooked Island, Long Cay, and Mayaguana Island each week. Check on days of sailing and costs with the dockmaster at Potter's Cay Dock in Nassau (☎ **809/393-1064**).

Once you arrive at Crooked Island, there is a taxi service available, but because of the lack of telephones, it's wise to advise your hotel of your arrival—they will probably send a van to meet you.

## FAST FACTS

**Banking**   If you're visiting these islands, take care of all your banking needs before you arrive, as there is no banking service on either Crooked Island or Acklins Island.

**Hospitals**   There are two government-operated clinics. Phones are few on the island, but your hotel desk can reach one of these clinics by going through the operator. The clinic on Acklins Island is at Spring Point and Chesters Bay, and the one on Crooked Island is at Landrail Point.

**Police**   The police station on Crooked Island can be reached by dialing **809/344-2197**.

## WHERE TO STAY & DINE

### Caribe Bay Ltd. at Pittstown Point Landing

Landrail Point, Crooked Island. ☎ **809/344-2507.** Fax 809/344-2507. For reservations and information, contact Caribe Bay Ltd., 300 Mariner's Plaza, Suite 303, Mandeville, LA 70448. ☎ toll free 800/752-2322 in the U.S. and Canada. 12 rms. Year-round, $165 single; $220 double. (Rates include all meals.) MC, V. Free parking.

This hotel lies in a position so isolated, at the extreme northwestern tip of Crooked Island, that it's easy to forget the world outside. For most of the early years of its life, it was a well-guarded secret shared mostly by the owners of private airplanes who flew in from the mainland of Florida for off-the-record weekends. Even today, about 80% of the clients arrive by one or two-engine aircraft that they fly themselves as part of island-hopping jaunts around the Bahamas. The island maintains its own 2,300-foot hard-surface landing strip, which is completely independent from the one used for the twice-per-week flights from Nassau on Bahamasair.

In 1994, a group of Louisiana-based investors upgraded the place, taking great care not to change the raffish, escapist allure that made it so appealing in the first place. Surrounded by scrub-covered landscape at the edge of a turquoise sea, it lies $2^1/_2$ miles north of the hamlet of Landrail Point (population 60 souls), on a sandy peninsula jutting seaward. Within easy access are some of the most weirdly historic sites in the Bahamas, including the sunbaked ruins of a salt farm (Marine Farms Fortress) that was sacked by American-based pirates in 1812.

Accommodations lie within a trio of low-slung, cement-sided buildings that, since the 1994 takeover, are painted a soft Nassau pink. They lie directly on the beach, usually with screened-in porches prefacing a view of the sea. Because of the constant trade winds blowing in, bedrooms contain no air-conditioning, only large paddle-shaped ceiling fans and private bathrooms. The entire resort shares only one telephone/fax, which is reserved for calls of great urgency.

Meals are served in a stone-sided building that was originally erected late in the 1600s as a barracks for the British West Indies Naval Squadron and later served as the region's post office. The restaurant serves seafood and a menu composed of North American and Bahamian specialties. Hotel residents always arrive on the MAP plan, but since this establishment is considered one of the most appealing hotels and restaurants on the island, you're likely to find a scattering of yacht owners or aviators who drop in spontaneously for refreshment.

### Crooked Island Beach Inn

Cabbage Hill, Crooked Island, the Bahamas. ☎ **809/344-2321.** 6 rms (all with bath). Year-round $50 single; $60 double. Breakfast from $5 extra. (EP rates.) No credit cards. Free parking.

Built of cement and cinderblock in the early 1980s, this simple and isolated ocean-view hotel lies directly on the sands of the beach, about a 5-minute drive north of the island's airport. Bedrooms open directly onto a veranda and are about as basic as you can get, although few visitors check in expecting luxury. Each contains a ceiling fan, a private bathroom, and a scattering of bare-bones furniture. Although there is no formal restaurant, breakfast can be arranged by expressing your wishes the night before, and lunch and dinner can be prepared if you request it in advance.

## WHAT TO SEE & DO

Crooked Island opens onto the Windward Passage, the dividing point between the Caribbean Sea and the Bahamas. Whatever else he may have named it, it is said that when Columbus landed at what is now Pittstown Point, he called it Fragrant Island because of the aroma of its many herbs. One scent was cascarilla bark, used in a native liqueur, which is exported. For the best view of the island, go to Colonel Hill, if you didn't land at the Crooked Island Airport (also known as the Colonel Hill Airport) when you arrived.

Guarding the north end of this island is the **Marine Farms Fortress,** an abandoned British fortification that saw action in the War of 1812. It looks out over Crooked Island Passage and can be visited (ask your hotel to make arrangements for you).

Also on the island is **Hope Great House,** with its orchards and gardens, dating from the time of George V of England.

Other sights include **French Wells Bay,** a swampy delta leading to an extensive mangrove swamp rich in bird life, and the **Bird Rock Lighthouse,** built a century ago.

**Fortune Island,** south of Albert Town, lies off the coast of Crooked Island. Based on the research done for the article in *National Geographic* mentioned above, Fortune Island (sometimes confusingly called Long Cay) is the one Columbus chose to name Isabella, in honor of the queen who funded his expedition. Once it had a thriving salt and sponge industry, now long gone. Albert Town, classified as a ghost town, officially isn't. There are some hardy souls still living there. Fortune Hill on Fortune Island is the local landmark, visible from 12 miles away at sea. This small island got its name from the custom of hundreds of Bahamians who went there in the two decades before World War I. They'd wait to be picked up by oceangoing freighters, which would take them as laborers to Central America—hence, they came here to "seek their fortune."

At the southern end of Acklins Island lies **Castle Island,** a low and sandy bit of land where today an 1867 lighthouse stands. Pirates used it as a hideaway, sailing forth to attack ships in the nearby passage.

Acklins Island has many interestingly named hamlets—Rocky Point, Binnacle Hill, Salina Point, Delectable Bay, Golden Grove, Goodwill, Hard Hill, Snug Corner, and Lovely Bay. Some Crooked Island sites have more ominous names, such as Gun Point, Cripple Hill, and Landrail Point.

## 5  Mayaguana Island

"Sleepy Mayaguana" it might be called. It seems to float adrift in the tropical sun, at the remote extremities of the southeastern "edge" of the Bahamas. It occupies 110 square miles and has a population of about 500. It's a long, long way from the powers at Nassau, who rarely visit here.

Standing in the Windward Passage, Mayaguana is just northwest of the Turks and Caicos Islands, coming up in Part Two. It's separated from the British Crown Colony by the Caicos Passage. Around the time of the American Civil War, inhabitants of Turks Island began to settle in Mayaguana, which before then had dozed undisturbed for centuries.

Acklins Island and Crooked Island lie across the Mayaguana Passage. Mayaguana is only 6 miles across at its widest point, and about 24 miles long. It has most enticing beaches, but you'll rarely see a tourist on them, except sometimes an occasional German. A few tourism developers have flown in to check out the island, but so far no activity has come about.

Mayaguana has hardwood forests, and because of its remote location, the United States has opened a missile-tracking station here.

Its southern location makes it ideal in winter, and if you seek it out as a place to retreat from cold weather, no one will ever think of looking for you here. Summers are scorchingly hot, however.

## GETTING THERE

**BY PLANE**   Getting to Mayaguana presents a problem. **Bahamasair** (☎ **800/222-4262** in the U.S.) flies in here to a little airstrip, but only the most adventurous of travelers seek the place out. A plane wings in from Nassau Monday at 8am, Wednesday at 10:15am, and Friday at 1pm.

**BY MAIL BOAT**     From Nassau, the MV *Lady Mathilda,* going also to Crooked Island, Acklins Island, and Fortune Island (Long Cay), makes a stop at Mayaguana. For information on the days and times of departure and return from Nassau, check with the dockmaster at Potter's Cay Dock in Nassau (☎ **809/393-1064**).

## WHERE TO STAY & DINE

If you should find yourself on the island, ask to be shown to a little café and guest house belonging to Doris and Cap Brown (no phone) at Abraham's Bay. They'll feed you some locally caught seafood and, maybe, put you up for the night. They're at Abraham's Bay, the biggest and most populated place on the island.

## 6 Great Inagua

The most southerly and third-largest island of the Bahamas, Great Inagua, some 40 miles long and 20 miles wide, is a flat land that is home to 1,200 people. It lies 325 miles southeast of Nassau. Henri Christophe, the self-proclaimed Haitian king, is supposed to have had a summer palace built for himself here in the very early part of the 19th century, but no traces seem to be in evidence today. This island is much closer to Haiti than it is to the Bahamian capital.

In 1687, long before the coming of Christophe, a Captain Phipps discovered 26 tons of Spanish treasure from sunken galleons off these shores.

This is the site not only of the Morton Salt Crystal Factory, here since 1800, but also of one of the largest nesting grounds for flamingos in the Western Hemisphere. The National Trust of the Bahamas protects the area around Lake Windsor, where the birds breed and the population is said to number 50,000. Besides the pink flamingo, the Bahamian national bird, you can also see roseate spoonbills and other bird life here.

Flamingos used to inhabit all of the Bahamas, but the bird is nearly extinct in many places, and the reserve can only be visited with a guide.

Green turtles are raised here, too, at Union Park. They are then released into the ocean to make their way as best they can; they, too, are an endangered species. The vast windward island, almost within sight of Cuba, is also inhabited by wild hogs, horses, and donkeys.

The settlement of Matthew Town is the chief hamlet of the island, but it's not of any great sightseeing interest. Other sites have interesting names, such as Doghead Point, Lantern Head, Conch Shell Point, and Mutton Fish Point, and Devil's Point (which makes one wonder what happened there to give rise to the name). There's an 1870 lighthouse at Matthew Town.

Little Inagua has no population. It's just a little speck of land off the northeast coast of Great Inagua, about 30 square miles in area. It has much bird life, including West Indian tree ducks, and wild goats and donkeys live there.

## GETTING THERE & GETTING AROUND

**Bahamasair** (☎ **800/222-4262** in the U.S.) flies to Matthew Town Airport from Nassau on Monday at 8am, Wednesday at 10:15am, and Friday at 1pm.

You can also go by mail boat, the MV *Windward Express,* which makes weekly trips from Nassau to Matthew Town (schedule varies). Call the dockmaster's office (☎ **809/393-1064**) at Potter's Cay in Nassau for details.

**Taxis** meet incoming flights from Nassau. A guest house is on Great Inagua at Matthew Town on the southwest coast, 1¹/₂ miles from the airport.

## ESSENTIALS

**HOSPITAL**   The Inagua Hospital can be called at **1249.**

**POLICE**   The police can be reached by dialing **1263.**

## WHERE TO STAY

### Main House
Matthew Town, Inagua, the Bahamas. ☎ **809/339-1267.** 4 rms (2 with bath). A/C. Year-round, $45 single; $55 double; $60 triple. (EP rates.) No credit cards. Free parking.

Main House is owned by Morton Bahamas Ltd., the salt people. This place is for the willing recluse or the devotee of flamingos, which abound on the island. Only four bedrooms are rented, and the furnishings are modest. Two of the rooms have private baths. The dining room is simply furnished, and the cook prepares meals with an emphasis on locally caught fish. Life is casual and decidedly informal.

### Walkine's Guest House
Gregory St., Matthew Town. Inagua. ☎ **809/339-1612.** 5 rms (all with bath). A/C TV TEL. $50 single; $60 double. AE. Free parking.

Set a half-mile south of Matthew Town, this simple guest house took great pains to paint its exterior blue and its bedrooms a rosy tone of shell pink. Your hosts are Eleanor and Kirk Walkine, who built their establishment in 1984 across the road from the beach. There are no dining facilities on-site, but a simple restaurant (the Cozy Corner) lies nearby; it serves breakfast every morning for around $5 each.

# 7  Ragged Island & Jumento Cays

This, the most remote territory recommended in this guidebook, might come under the classification of "faraway places with strange-sounding names." The area is visited by very few tourists, except for a few stray people who come in on yachts.

The thing that's truly memorable here is the sunset, which, except in the rare times when clouds obscure the sky and the horizon, bursts forth in some of the most spectacular shades of gold, purple, red, and orange—and sometimes with a green flash reflecting in the gin-clear waters.

This island group, a miniarchipelago, begins with Jumento Cays off the west point of Long Island and runs in a half-moon shape for some 100 miles down to Ragged Island; Little Ragged Island is the southernmost bit of land at the bottom of the crescent. They comprise the southeastern limit of the Great Bahama Bank.

Ragged Island and its string of uninhabited cays could be called the backwater of the Bahamas, since most of them are so tiny and so unimportant they don't often appear on maps. However, visitors who return from this area talk of the remarkable beauty of these little pieces of land and coral.

Sailing in this area in bad weather is considered dangerous because of the unrelenting winds. Otherwise, the cays would probably be better known among the boating crowd. In summer it's usually a good place to cruise the waters.

Like nearly all the islands considered in this chapter, Ragged Island knew greater prosperity when hundreds of inhabitants worked its salt flats. Today Duncan Town, the little hamlet still standing on the island, evokes a faraway memory. Some of its people are hardworking and weather-beaten, and many have a

---

## Pink Flamingos

Inagua, the most southerly of the Bahamas, and third-largest in the chain, lies just off the eastern tip of Cuba. Partially because of its isolation, it's home to some of the best-stocked bird colonies in the Western Hemisphere. In fact, its human population of 1,200 is outnumbered by the island's vast colonies of pink flamingos. Seen as an ensemble, they present a surreal vision. They're so plentiful on Inagua, that some of them even roost on the runway of the island's airport, as well as at thousands of other locations throughout the flat, heat-blasted landscape.

Dedicated bird-watchers who are willing to forego the usual comforts usually trek inland to the edges of the many brackish lakes in the island's center. About half the island is devoted to a National Park; the island's most viable industry involves distilling salt from the local salt flats. For detailed information on bird-watching on Inagua, ornithologists can contact the Bahamian National Trust (administrators of about 270 square miles of the island's bird-breeding interior) at P.O. Box N-4105, Nassau, the Bahamas (☎ **809/322-8333**). Matthew Town, the island's largest hamlet, offers the island's only bona-fide hotel rooms, and even these are among the most basic accommodations in the Bahamas. Despite the hardships and inconveniences, a view of the pink flamingos of Inagua is considered an ornithologist's dream. The most desirable season for viewing them is from November until June.

---

difficult time making a living. Nassau seems to have forgotten this outpost of the nation.

Some of the little cays, from Jumento Cay around the semicircle toward Ragged Island, have names such as No Bush Cay, Dead Cay, Sisters, Nurse Cay, Double-Breasted Cay, and Hog Cay. There's a Raccoon Cay, as well as a Raccoon Cut. A light tower stands on Flamingo Cay.

Visitors are so rare that anybody's arrival is treated as an event, and the townspeople are eager to help in any way they can. There's a 3,000-foot paved airstrip here, but it's only accessible to private planes, so it's not used much.

A **mail boat**, MV *Emmipt and Cephas,* leaves Potter's Cay in Nassau on Tuesday at 2pm en route to Ragged Island. It returns on Thursday. For details about costs and sailing, contact the dockmaster at Potter's Cay Dock, Nassau (☎ **809/393-1064**).

Regrettably, there are no hotel facilities for tourists.

# Turks & Caicos Islands 12

**A** recent discovery of sun-seeking vacationers, the Turks and Caicos Islands (or "Turks and Who?" as they're often called) have long been called the "forgotten islands," but there is now talk of a "second Bahamas" in the making. Although they are actually a part of the Bahamian archipelago, they are under a separate government and are tucked away to the east of the southernmost islands of the Bahamas. Directly north of Haiti and the Dominican Republic, they lie at the crossroads of the Caribbean and the Americas. This obscure outpost is technically not the Caribbean but on the fringe of the Atlantic. *La Figaro* once quoted a developer, and I concur, that "these islands will be the only place left where the jet set, tired of Florida and the Bahamas, will be able to take refuge. They already are!"

The Turks take their name from a local cactus with a scarlet blossom, which resembles the Turkish fez. The word *caicos* is probably derived from the word *cayos*. Spanish for cays or small islands.

Grand Turk and Salt Cay (which constitute the Turks Islands) and Cockburn Harbour (South Caicos) are ports of entry.

Many of the islanders today work in the salt-raking industry; others are engaged in the export of lobsters (crayfish) and conch, as well as conch shells. But more and more the citizens of this little country feed off the tourist industry.

The mean temperature in these islands is 82 degrees Fahrenheit, dropping to 77 degrees at night, but the cooling breezes of the prevailing trade winds prevent the climate from being oppressive, a fact that vacationers are learning and taking advantage of. Perhaps the first VIP to recognize the attractions of these islands for a holiday retreat was Haiti's self-proclaimed king, Henri Christophe, who is rumored to have made excursions to South Caicos in the early 19th century.

The Turks and Caicos Islands are a coral-reef paradise, shut off from the world, free of pollution and crowds. Even with the increasing development of a tourist mecca under way, the beauty and tranquillity of this little island chain are sure to be maintained for the foreseeable future.

The inns of the Turks and Caicos Islands, except those on Providenciales, are small and personally run, very casual, and island entertainment is most often impromptu. The islands have no TV, no daily papers, but there is a radio station. Most visitors are

---

### What's Special About Turks & Caicos

Beaches
- Governor's Beach, a strip of sand—long and white—on Grand Turk, one of the nation's finest beachfronts.
- Provo Beach, a magnificent white sandy beach that goes on for a dozen or so miles along the northeast coast of Providenciales.
- Sapodilla Bay Beach, at the northwest point, is another gem of a beach.
- Big Ambergris Cay, draws the boating crowd. A splendid beach at Long Bay lures visitors to this uninhabited cay.
- East Caicos, also uninhabited, attracts boaters who want to sample its white sandy beach, stretching for 17 miles along the north coast.
- Pine Cay, an upmarket stamping ground, has one of the most acclaimed beaches in the country—stretching for $2^1/_2$ miles.

Great Islands
- Grand Turk, whose capital is Cockburn Town, the capital of Turks and Caicos, its financial and business hub, but also worthy of tourism.
- Salt Cay, nine miles south of Grand Turk, no longer a center for "white gold" (salt), but the perfect getaway for those seeking beauty and tranquillity.
- North Caicos, northernmost of the major islands, a cay of nearly deserted soft white sandy beaches and crystal clear waters.
- Providenciales—affectionately called "Provo"—seat of all the major tourist development, a 38-square-mile island with white sandy beaches. This island has the most to offer in food, nightlife, hotels, and attractions.

A Museum
- Turks and Caicos National Museum on Grand Turk, the country's only museum, displays the wreck of a Spanish caravelle that sank sometime before 1513.

---

interested in skin diving and scuba diving, fishing, sailing, and boating. Divers still dream of finding that legendary chest of gold hidden in the coral reefs or underwater caverns.

What has made Turks and Caicos a belated tourist destination for those who have already "done" both the Bahamas and the Caribbean is its some 225 miles of beaches. Sometimes the beaches of white sand run for miles; others are small and found at secluded coves. Most of the beaches of the little archipelago are made of a white sand of soft coralline. Of course, nude sunbathers and others prefer some of the uninhabited cays for their skinny-dipping.

*Note:* These islands are recommended only to those readers who dare to venture off the beaten track.

## A LITTLE HISTORY

The Arawaks first settled the Turks and Caicos Islands, and in time Ponce de León sighted the little chain in 1512, although there are those who believe that Columbus landed here, not at San Salvador (Watling Island) or Samana Cay in the Bahamas. It was not far to the south, in the waters off the north coast of Hispaniola (the part that is now Haiti), that the *Santa Maria,* the flagship of the discovery fleet of Columbus, sank on Christmas night, 1492.

# The Turks & Caicos Islands

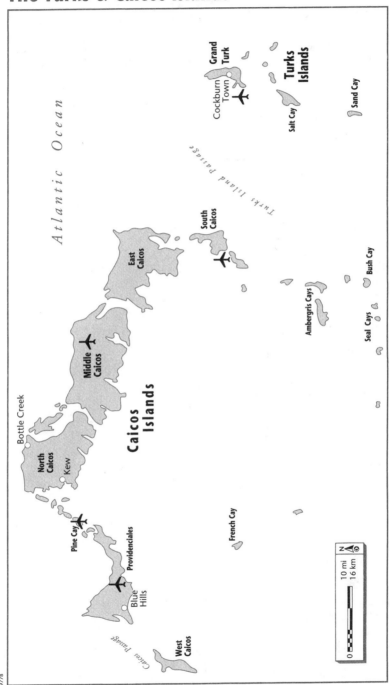

The claim that Columbus landed here has received the endorsement of eminent Caribbean historians in recent years. Symposiums on the subject have presented supporting data. The assertion is that Grand Turk was the site of the first landfall of Columbus, on October 12, 1492, and that he set foot on the island's western shores later that same day. He was supposedly greeted by the natives, the Arawaks, who called the island Guanahani.

Pirates marauding on the Spanish Main learned of the hidden coves of the Turks and Caicos Islands and used them when they ventured out to plunder Spanish galleons sailing out of Cuba and Haiti. This nest of cutthroats was called "Brothers of the Coast." The most famous of these was Rackam the Red, an Englishman.

After the Arawaks were removed to their doom in the mines of Hispaniola, the islands had no permanent inhabitants until 1678. In that year the Bermudians, who had built ships and were searching for goods to trade with the American colonies, established the salt-raking industry. The Spanish drove the Bermudians away in 1710, but they soon returned and thereafter repelled attacks by both Spain and France. Their ranks were augmented during and after the American Revolution by Loyalists who fled America, bringing slaves; this move increased the island population of bond servants of African ancestry.

Bermuda finally lost out in 1799, when representation in the Bahamian assembly was given to the little island neighbors to the southeast. This attachment to the Bahamas ended in 1848. The people of the Turks and Caicos Islands petitioned to withdraw from the assembly that met in Nassau. They said the Bahamian government had paid no attention to them except to send collectors of the salt tax, and that they saw the mail boat only four times each year.

The islands were allowed to break their ties with their northern relatives and to have their own president and council, supervised as a separate colony by the governor of Jamaica. After a quarter of a century, however, they were annexed by Jamaica as a dependency. It was not until 1962, when Jamaica became independent, that the little group of islands became a separate British Crown Colony.

The Turks and Caicos Islands are mainly self-governing today. Queen Elizabeth selects a governor to be her representative in island affairs; this governor appoints the chief minister who, in turn, appoints minor ministers.

Generally, **dress** on these islands is informal. Light cotton clothing is the most comfortable, although beachwear is best left for the beach. Jackets or ties are not required in the evening for men in bars or dining rooms. A light sweater is advisable for breezy evenings. It is customary to greet people you encounter walking along the roads.

The **food** specialties are whelk soup, conch chowder and fritters, lobster, and special types of fresh fish. If you're interested in **shopping,** you can purchase native straw and shellwork, sponges, and rare conch pearls here and there on the islands.

## GETTING THERE
### BY PLANE

Miami is the only U.S. gateway for flights into the Turks and Caicos, and from Miami, **American** (☎ 800/433-7300) is the only carrier flying from the U.S. mainland. American offers daily nonstop service to Providenciales, a flight time of 1 hour 39 minutes. It departs late enough in the day (11:15am) to permit easy transfers from any of the hundreds of flights winging into Miami from virtually everywhere every day. The return flight from Provo to Miami departs every day at 3:30pm, landing in Miami around 5pm, in time for connections onto flights heading to all points of North America and Europe. Round-trip tickets for passengers who reserved at least 14 days in advance and who remained abroad for between 3 and 30 days range from $279 to $321, depending on the day of the week and the season.

**Turks & Caicos Airways** (☎ **305/871-7169** or **800/946-4255**) doesn't fly from the U.S. mainland; however, it offers flights from other points in the Bahamas and the Caribbean. These include nonstop flights on Monday, Wednesday, Friday, and Saturday from Nassau to Provo, and a once-a-week flight from Freeport in the Bahamas to Provo. In the Caribbean, the little airline flies back and forth three times a week from Grand Turk to Puerto Plata in the Dominican Republic.

## GETTING AROUND

Getting around can be a problem. Car-rental agencies are few and far between (most visitors don't use this means of transport, but see below). Each of the islands has taxi drivers with just-adequate vehicles.

### BY TAXI

Taxis are found at the three airports—on Providenciales, South Caicos, and Grand Turk. They'll quote you a fixed price to and from the various hotels. They'll also deposit you on an isolated beach and return at a predetermined time to pick you up. Don't be surprised if your ride is shared (the government is trying to save fuel). Ask your hotel to make arrangements for you.

### BY CAR

Because of the island's large size and the far-flung nature of its hotel and restaurant locations, you might find a car on Providenciales useful. There are some local outfits, but advance reservations with them, and easy settlement of any possible dispute in the event of an accident, can be very difficult. The only U.S.-based car-rental agency with a franchise in the Turks and Caicos Islands is on Providenciales itself. It's **Budget Rent-a-Car,** Butterfield Square, near the airport (☎ **809/946-4079** or **800/527-0700** in the U.S.). A Mitsubishi Precis with automatic transmission rents for $234 per week, with unlimited mileage. A Suzuki Swift, automatic, air-conditioned, and two-doored, costs $264 a week. This contract requires a 24-hour advance booking from the North American mainland, and also requires that drivers be at least 25 years of age. Collision-damage insurance costs $10 a day, but even if it's purchased, the holder of such a policy is still liable for the first $500 worth of repair costs to the vehicle. (If you don't buy the policy, you'll be liable for up to the full value of repair costs to the car if you damage it.) A slightly bigger vehicle, a Mitsubishi Mirage, also with air-conditioning and automatic transmission, costs $294 per week. The local government will collect a $10 tax for each rental contract, regardless of the number of days you keep the car.

For information once you arrive on Providenciales, Budget's phone number is **809/946-4079.** Because the company's main office lies in the commercial center of the island, a short drive from the airport, a representative will come to meet your flight at the airport if you notify them in advance of your arrival.

*Note:* In the British tradition, *cars throughout the country drive on the left.*

## BY PLANE

Some visitors opt to visit the country's outlying islands because of their marine life and get-away-from-it-all sense of isolation. The most leisurely way to do this is by boat, but barring your access to a yacht, you can travel on one of the eight- or nine-passenger propeller planes operated by **Turks & Caicos Airways** (☎ 305/ 871-7169 in Florida or **809/946-4255**). Most convenient are the airline's "patch flights" that operate 10 daily flights. Eastbound, they fly from Providenciales to North Caicos, Middle Caicos, South Caicos, and terminate at Grand Turk. Westbound, they fly the same itinerary in reverse, touching down briefly after only a few minutes' flight time at each of the above-mentioned islands, depositing passengers, luggage, and supplies en route. In addition, the airline offers daily flights that touch down only in the country's most populous islands, Provo and Grand Turk. (The total number of daily flights between Provo and Grand Turk is 10 per day. The price, each way, is $50). Most passengers traveling to Salt Cay arrive by boat, but those who prefer to fly opt for the Monday, Wednesday, and Friday flights (two round-trip flights on each of those days) between Grand Turk and Salt Cay. Small islands, such as Pine Cay, are serviced only by specifically prearranged charter flights.

## FAST FACTS: Turks & Caicos Islands

**American Express**　　American Express is not represented anywhere on the Turks and Caicos Islands.

**Area Code**　　The area code for the Turks and Caicos Islands is 809, which can be dialed directly from the North American mainland.

**Banks**　　For cashing of traveler's checks and other banking services, head for Barclay's Bank (☎ **809/946-4246**) or for the Bank of Nova Scotia (☎ **809/ 946-4750**), both in the Butterfield Mall on Providenciales. On Grand Turk, both Barclay's Bank (☎ **809/946-2831**) and the Bank of Nova Scotia (☎ **809/ 946-2831**) are located on Front Street.

**Business Hours**　　Banking hours are 8:30am to 2:30pm Monday through Thursday and 8:30am to 12:30pm and 2:30 to 4:30pm on Friday. Most business offices are open Monday through Friday from 8:30am to 4 or 4:30pm.

**Climate**　　The islands receive approximately 21 inches of rainfall annually. The Turks and Caicos mean monthly temperature is 80 degrees Fahrenheit, and the winter water temperature ranges from 72 degrees to 80 degrees.

**Currency**　　The U.S. dollar is the coin of the realm here.

**Customs**　　On arriving, you may bring in 1 quart of liquor, 200 cigarettes, 50 cigars, or 8 ounces of tobacco duty free. There is no restriction on cameras, film, sports equipment, or personal items provided they aren't for resale. *Absolutely no spearguns are allowed,* and the importation of firearms without a permit is also prohibited. Illegal imported drugs bring heavy fines and lengthy terms of imprisonment.

　　Each U.S. citizen is eligible for a $400 duty-free exemption if he or she has been out of the country for at least 48 hours and if a period of 41 days has elapsed since that privilege was last exercised. This allowance may include 1 quart of liquor. In addition, you can mail home a number of unsolicited gifts to friends and relatives amounting to $50 or less per day and not to include more than 4 ounces of liquor or 1 ounce of perfume.

**Dentist**   See "Hospitals," below.

**Doctors**   See "Hospitals," below.

**Drugstores**   On Grand Turk, go to the Government Clinic, Grand Turk Hospital, Hospital Road (☎ 809/946-2040). In Providenciales, go to the Providenciales Health Medical Center, Leeward Highway and Airport Road (☎ 809/946-4201). Actually, it's best to arrive on the islands with whatever prescribed medication you think you will need.

**Electricity**   The electric current on the islands is 120 volts, 60 cycles, AC.

**Emergencies**   Most emergencies are handled by the police on the various islands (see "Police," below).

**Entry Requirements**   U.S. and Canadian citizens must have a birth certificate, a photo ID, and a return or ongoing ticket to enter the country. The photo ID could be an official driver's license with a photograph or a voter's registration card with a photograph. Of course, valid passports are always acceptable. Passports and visas are required for all aliens except nationals of certain countries, which include the U.K., Commonwealth countries of the Caribbean, the Republic of Ireland, and specific European countries. Visas for the Turks and Caicos Islands may be obtained from the British High Commission or various consulate offices in the United States.

**Holidays**   The actual dates of some of these observances may vary from year to year. If the date of a particular celebration falls on Saturday or Sunday, the actual observance may not take place until the following Monday. Holidays include *New Year's Day, Commonwealth Day* (March 11), *Good Friday, Easter Day, Easter Monday, Birthday of Her Majesty the Queen* (June 15), *Emancipation Day* (August 1), *Columbus Day* (October 12), *International Human Rights Day* (October 24), *Christmas,* and *Boxing Day* (December 26).

**Hospitals**   Should you become ill, the islands are served by three medical practitioners and a qualified nursing staff. There is a 20-bed hospital on Grand Turk, Grand Turk Hospital, Hospital Road (☎ 809/946-2333), with x-ray facilities, an operating theater, and a pathology laboratory. In Providenciales, there is the Providenciales Health Medical Center, Leeward Highway and Airport Road (☎ 809/946-4228). There are clinics on South Caicos (☎ 809/946-3216) and North Caicos (☎ 809/946-7194). All the islands are served by one dentist, who can be reached at the Providenciales health center. Anyone critically ill is transferred to Grand Turk for hospital treatment or evacuated to Nassau, Miami, or Jamaica for specialist treatment. Should you become ill, your hotel will locate the nearest medical facility.

**Information**   The Turks and Caicos Sales and Information Office, Front Street, Cockburn Town, Grand Turk, BWI (☎ 809/946-2321, or toll free 800/441-4419 in the U.S.), is open Monday through Thursday from 8am to 4:30pm, on Friday from 8am to 4pm.

**Language**   The official language is English.

**Police**   In Grand Turk, call **809/946-2299;** in Providenciales, **809/946-4259;** and in South Caicos, **809/946-3299.** On North Caicos call **809/946-7116;** on Middle Caicos, **809/946-6111.**

**Post Office**   The General Post Office is on Grand Turk ( ☎ **809/946-2801**), and there are suboffices on South Caicos, Salt Cay, Providenciales, Bottle Creek, and Middle Caicos. They are open Monday through Thursday from 8am to 4:30pm, on Friday from 7am to 1:30pm. Collectors consider Turks and Caicos stamps valuable, so there is a philatelic bureau that operates separately from the post office to take care of the demand. It is the Turks and Caicos Islands Philatelic Bureau, Front Street, Grand Turk, Turks and Caicos Islands, BWI.

**Religious Services**   The islanders are deeply religious, and details of church services are available from your hotel.

**Safety**   Although crime is minimal in the islands, petty theft does take place, so protect your valuables, money, and cameras. Don't leave luggage or parcels in an unattended car. Beaches are vulnerable to thievery, so don't take chances.

**Taxes**   There is a departure tax of $15, payable when you leave the islands. Also, the government collects a 7% occupancy tax, applicable to all hotels, guest houses, and restaurants in the 40-island chain.

**Telephones, Telegrams & Fax**   It's not too difficult to keep in touch with the outside world—if you really want to. Cable & Wireless Ltd. provides a modern diversified international service via submarine cable and an earth station. There are automatic exchanges on Grand Turk, South Caicos, and Providenciales. Incoming direct dialing is available from the United States, the U.K., and most countries in the world. Outgoing direct dialing is being introduced.

   Most hotels in the country have fax machines. Your hotel's staff will probably offer to send and receive faxes for you. Telex service is fully automatic, operating 24 hours a day. The international-operator telephone service is available 24 hours a day and the telegraph service from 8am to 4:30pm Monday through Friday from the company's main office on Front Street, Cockburn Town, Grand Turk ( ☎ **809/946-2222**).

**Time**   The islands are in the eastern time zone and daylight saving time is observed.

**Tipping**   Hotels usually add 10% to 15% automatically to handle service. If individual staff members perform various services for you, it is customary to tip them something extra. In restaurants, 10% to 15% is appropriate unless service has already been added. If in doubt, ask. Taxi drivers like at least a 10% tip.

**Water**   Don't drink from the tap and avoid ice in your drinks that was made from tap water. Don't even use tap water to brush your teeth. Remember that water is precious on the islands. Try to conserve it. Hotels provide safe drinking water.

## 1  Grand Turk

The most important of the island chain, Grand Turk (Cockburn Town), with its Government House, is the capital of the Turks and Caicos Islands. Cockburn (pronounced *Coburn*) Town is also the financial-and-business hub. The largest concentration of population in the colony, 3,500 people, is here.

## What the Symbols Mean

**AP (American Plan):** Includes three meals a day (sometimes called full board or full pension).

**BP (Bermuda or Bahamas Plan):** Popularized first in Bermuda, this option includes a full American breakfast (sometimes called an English breakfast).

**CP (Continental Plan):** A continental breakfast (that is, bread, jam, and coffee) is included in the room rate.

**EP (European Plan):** This rate is always cheapest, as it offers only the room—no meals.

**MAP (Modified American Plan):** Sometimes called half board or half pension, this room rate includes breakfast and dinner (or lunch if you prefer).

**Cockburn Town** might remind you of New Plymouth on Green Turtle Cay, but there's more bustle here because of the larger number of inhabitants. The harbor road is called Front Street, like the one in Hamilton, the capital of Bermuda.

Grand Turk is rather barren and windswept. There is little vegetation, so don't come here expecting to find a lush tropical island.

Once this was the teeming headquarters of a thriving salt industry. Today there are those who want to restore the economy of the colony by making Grand Turk an offshore banking center like the Cayman Islands, but that may be difficult. There are many problems to face with both the British and the U.S. governments.

Grand Turk was in the limelight in 1962, when John Glenn, the first American astronaut to orbit the earth, alighted in the ocean about 40 miles offshore and was brought in by helicopter to the U.S. Air Force base here, to be welcomed by Vice President Lyndon Johnson.

Chances are, if you come here for your vacation, you'll land at Grand Turk. You'll find **Governor's Beach** near—you guessed it—the governor's residence on the west coast of the island. It's the best for swimming. If you are going on to another of the islands, at least take time to tour the town's **historic section,** particularly Duke and Front Streets. Here, three-story houses built of wood and limestone stand along the waterfront.

Many scholars believe that Grand Turk was the site of the first landfall of Columbus in 1492. They maintain he set foot on the western shores of the island late on the day of October 12. The Native Arawaks were there to welcome him to their island of "Guanahani," although they were later to pay a terrible price for that hospitality, as they were sold into slavery in the Caribbean.

At the tourist office (see "Information" in "Fast Facts," above), the National Parks of Turks and Caicos produce a guide to the marine parks, nature reserves, sanctuaries, and historical sites of the island nation.

There are several protected historical buildings on the 7-square-mile island of Grand Turk, one of which is used in the hotel industry—Turks Head Inn. Other buildings include the police station and Government House.

## WHERE TO STAY

As mentioned, hotels add a 10% to 15% service charge, plus a 7% government occupancy tax, to the rates quoted below.

## MODERATE

### Coral Reef Beach Club

Lighthouse Rd., P.O. Box 156, Grand Turk, Turks and Caicos, BWI. ☎ **809/946-2055.** Fax 809/946-2911. 16 rms, 5 suites. A/C TV TEL. Winter, $105 single or double. Off-season, $90 single or double. Year-round, from $105 suite. Continental breakfast $7 per person extra. (EP rates.) AE, MC, V. Free parking.

Coral Reef Beach Club lies on a stretch of beachfront on the eastern coast. As you negotiate the steep access road that winds down to it, a sweeping expanse of the sea seems to surround the property. This pleasantly isolated inn was originally created by two Texans. Stretched end to end along the beachfront, and interconnected with a sunny boardwalk, the ocean-view accommodations contain fully equipped kitchenettes and are designed like comfortably furnished studios and suites. Each was prefabricated in the United States, then constructed on the site. There is maid service.

An attractive dive package is offered for $665 per person for seven nights' accommodation, double occupancy, with 10 tank dives included. The hotel has its own on-the-premises dive operators, named Blue Water Divers. Guests can use a small freshwater pool and play on a floodlit tennis court. The hotel also has a beach bar and restaurant plus a gym and a Jacuzzi.

### Guanahani Beach Resort

Pillory Beach, Grand Turk, Turks and Caicos, BWI. ☎ **809/946-2135.** Fax 809/946-1460. 16 rms. A/C TV TEL. Year-round, $1,625 double. Children under 12 free in parents' room. (Rates include airport transfers.) AE, MC, V. Free parking.

Two Canadians, Sheila and Brian Boundey, have remodeled and brightened up this place and now offer weekly packages. Composed of a handful of hip-roofed villas set directly on the sands of one of the finest beaches on the island (supposedly, according to local lore, where Columbus made one of his landfalls), this hotel is almost exclusively devoted to enjoyment of the sun, sand, and sea. Only a decorative wooden railing separates its sandy grounds from unobstructed ocean views. Concrete walkways connect each of the accommodations to the hotel's pair of bars, its square-sided swimming pool, and its restaurant.

Each room has a private balcony and a collection of simple tropical furniture appropriate to the accommodation's beachside location. Off-white, coral, and turquoise are the dominant color themes. The hotel lies a 25-minute drive north of Cockburn Town. Laundry and babysitting are provided, and room service is offered daily from 9am to 9pm.

In the restaurant, Stardust, three meals a day are served. The cuisine is local, and sometimes bands are brought in to entertain guests (see "Where to Dine," below).

### Hotel Kittina

Duke St., P.O. Box 42, Grand Turk, Turks and Caicos, BWI. ☎ **809/946-2232.** Fax 809/946-2877. 23 rms, 20 suites. A/C TEL. Year-round, $75–$130 single; $95–$130 double; $150–$220 suite. Extra person $15. Children under 2 free in parents' room. Children 2–12 sharing room $5. Dive packages available. (EP rates.) AE, MC, V. Free parking.

Owned by a bank, this is the largest hotel on Grand Turk. The hotel straddles two sides of the main street leading through the center of town. The older section is a low-slung building covered with trailing vines and bougainvillea. It contains a bar and restaurant. The Sandpiper is the hotel dining room (see "Where to Dine," below).

Across the street rise the modern two-story town houses containing the newer accommodations. Each of these has a ceiling crafted from varnished pine, carpeting, a kitchen, a veranda with a view of the sea, and ceiling fans. The units on the upper floors benefit from high ceilings and more space. These rooms have sheltered everyone from Mariel Hemingway to Princess Alexandra.

You can snorkel or swim near the white sands of the hotel's beach. If you're sailing, be sure to ask one of the staff members for instructions on the best places to moor your sailboat.

### Salt Raker Inn

Duke St., P.O. Box 1, Grand Turk, Turks and Caicos, BWI. ☎ **809/946-2260.** Fax 809/946-2817. 10 rms, 3 suites. A/C. Year-round, $45–$75 single; $75–$95 double. (EP rates.) AE, MC, V. Free parking.

Lying a 1-mile taxi ride from the airport, a short walk from the island's busiest docks, the informal Salt Raker Inn occupies a clapboard house that was originally built in 1810 by a Bermudian shipwright. Its English-colonial style is visible in its front veranda, where guests can rock in chairs overlooking the ocean and a garden filled with bougainvillea. The main house, set close to the road paralleling the sea, contains a wide front hallway, a guest library, the establishment's office, and the three best accommodations. Each of the rooms has a private bath and a ceiling fan. Seven sea-facing rooms have a phone, and each has a minifridge. The two large upstairs suites have verandas overlooking the sea. The downstairs accommodation has a large screened porch. Several others are in two motel units spread end to end on either side of the garden.

The Salt Raker Inn is also one of the most popular dining choices in town (see separate recommendation under "Where to Dine," below).

### INEXPENSIVE

### Turks Head Inn

Duke St., P.O. Box 58, Grand Turk, Turks and Caicos, BWI. ☎ **809/946-2466.** Fax 809/946-2825. 7 rms. A/C TV. Year-round, $65 single; $80 double. Continental breakfast from $5. (EP rates.) AE, MC, V. Free parking.

About as charming as anything you'll find on the island, this old-fashioned hotel was originally built in 1840 as a private home by Bermudian shipwrights. Once it was the governor's private guest house and later the American consulate. Today, most of its business comes from its bar and restaurant (see "Where to Dine," below). However, a handful of bedrooms lie upstairs, behind a two-level veranda

---

### 👬 Family-Friendly Hotels

**Hotel Kittina**   *(see p. 308)* A local landmark, this hotel is the family favorite on Grand Turk. Families prepare simple island meals in the units with kitchens.

**Ramada Turquoise Reef Resort & Casino**   *(see p. 322)* Provo's best answer for families, this resort on Grace Bay puts up an extra person in the room for $25 a night. A separate staff coordinates activities for children.

**Le Deck Beachclub and Hotel**   *(see p. 322)* Near one of Provo's best white sandy beaches, families like to rent these villalike condos. Kids delight in the freshwater swimming pool on the premises.

whose ornate balustrades are painted in bright tropical colors. Owned by French-born Xavier Tonneau (sometimes known to his friends as "Froggie"), the inn lies in a mature garden with towering trees and a shady terrace with outdoor tables. Be warned in advance that if you stay here, you'll basically occupy your room and be left alone by a management that's busy running its food-and-beverage facilities. For clients not interested in the facilities of a resort hotel, however, that might prove appealing. Two of the bedrooms have access to an open second-floor veranda in front, while four have access to the somewhat more private enclosed veranda overlooking the back. Each has a private bathroom, ceiling fan, an old-fashioned kind of high-ceilinged spaciousness, and antique or period furnishings. All contain queen-size beds, two of which are four-posters.

## WHERE TO DINE

### MODERATE

#### ⑤ The Pepper Pot
Front St. No phone. Visit to make arrangements for dinner. Meals $15–$25. No credit cards. Dining time (usually 7:30 or 8pm) to be arranged in advance. CARIBBEAN.

Guests are served on battered plastic tables amid crepe-paper streamers and the kind of decor that might have adorned a 1930s high-school prom. Despite its drawbacks, diners retain a happy memory of this place. It's the domain of a hardworking member of the island's Anglican church, Philistina Louise ("Peanuts") Butterfield. Born in North Caicos, she has attracted an ardent array of fans. Her conch fritters, carefully frozen and packaged, accompany diners back to the United States, where they've been served at receptions on Fifth Avenue.

To dine here, you must visit in the evening of the day before your arrival, since there is no phone. Any taxi driver in town will conduct you to the clean but simple cement-sided house and pick you up at a prearranged time at the end of your meal. The menu depends on whatever Peanuts produced that day. It's likely to be lobster with all the fixings. Full meals are served only at dinner at a time mutually agreed upon.

In a pinch, try calling Ms. Butterfield's daughter, Vera Kennedy, at **809/946-1225.** Although, as stated above, it's always better to speak directly to Ms. Butterfield; in some cases, Ms. Kennedy might be able to establish contact for you.

#### Salt Raker Inn
Duke St. ☎ **809/946-2260.** Reservations recommended for dinner Wed and Sun only. Lunch platters $3.50–$7; dinner appetizers $2.75–$6.50; dinner main courses $12.50–$19.50. AE, MC, V. Daily 7am–9pm (last order). CARIBBEAN/SEAFOOD.

Contained beneath the corrugated tin roof of the previously recommended hotel, this comfortably unpretentious restaurant remains open throughout the morning and afternoon for anyone who happens to wander in hungry from the nearby wharves and beaches. Many guests prefer to dine in the rear garden.

You can get lunch at virtually anytime of the morning or afternoon, consisting of club sandwiches, cheeseburgers, fish-and-chips, or cracked conch. Evening meals are somewhat more elaborate, with grouper cooked island style (with onions and peppers), grilled swordfish, and the house favorite, broiled lobster with butter sauce. You might also try such specialties as an award-winning version of local Junkanoo-style (spicy) barbecued spareribs.

### The Sandpiper

In the Hotel Kittina, Duke St. ☎ **809/946-2232.** Reservations recommended. Appetizers $4–$8.50; main courses $12–$18. AE, MC, V. Dinner only, daily 6:30–9:30pm. CARIBBEAN/ AMERICAN.

Contained on the lobby level of the main (beachfront) building of a previously recommended hotel, this restaurant overlooks the ocean through sliding glass doors. It is simply decorated in white. This is one of the best-known restaurants on the island, offering a combination of American and local dishes with an emphasis on freshly caught seafood such as lobster or red snapper. The conch chowder is invariably good. A main dish specialty also involves conch—conch steak à la Kittina, a local delicacy. It is queen conch marinated in special herbs and spices, then deep-fried a golden brown and served with the house's spicy seafood sauce. Other "fresh from the sea" dishes include fresh filet of grouper and broiled lobster tail. If not fish, then you can try one of their down-home dishes such as southern fried chicken. Finish off with one of their homemade pies.

### Stardust Restaurant

In the Guanahani Beach Resort, Pillory Beach. ☎ **809/946-2135.** Reservations recommended. Breakfast $4.95–$8.95; lunch $4.95–$12.95; dinner $12.95–$22.95; gourmet dishes $49. AE, MC, V. Breakfast daily 8–10:30am; lunch daily noon–3pm; dinner daily 5–9:30pm. INTERNATIONAL.

Contained within the most isolated and remote hotel on the island, this restaurant lies on the north shore, about a 25-minute drive from Cockburn Town. By many estimates, it's one of the most consistently popular restaurants on the island.

Decorated in tones of off-white with large French windows, the restaurant offers sweeping maritime views. On one side is the restaurant and on the other is a lounge with a library and comfortable chairs. There you can order rum punches and piña coladas. The menu features well-prepared seafood. Although steaks are offered, the most frequently requested dishes include grilled grouper served with tartar sauce, cracked conch, lobster with butter and bread crumbs, and any of the array of freshly caught fish that happen to have arrived that day from local fishing craft. If you plan an evening meal here, you might try to time your visit to catch the final rays of sundown, an event that is especially well framed from the restaurant's outdoor terrace.

### Turks Head Inn

Duke St. ☎ **809/946-2466.** Reservations recommended on Fri night only. Lunch platters $6–$8; dinner appetizers $4–$4.50; dinner main courses $7–$19. AE, MC, V. Daily 7am– 10pm. INTERNATIONAL.

This is the island's oldest and busiest pub, a landmark to the many divers, dockworkers, writers, and eccentrics living in Grand Turk. Set within the previously recommended inn, it contains an indoor dining room, raffish and tropical, and a thatch-roofed annex that shelters outdoor diners from the sun and rain. The well-flavored food is served informally, in large portions, according to whatever happens to have arrived from mainland suppliers that week. Specialties are recited by a waitress, and, depending on the mood of Xavier Tonneau, the French-born chef and owner, might include baked grouper, steak, and lobster, or steak and lobster on the same platter. The establishment's bar is open continuously every day throughout the afternoon until midnight, serving drinks to whatever dockworker or barefoot contessa happens to need a drink.

### Water's Edge Restaurant

Duke St., Grand Turk. ☎ **809/946-1680.** Reservations not necessary. Appetizers $4–6; main courses $7.50–$30. MC, V. Daily 10am–10pm (last food order); bar open daily 10am–1:30am. SEAFOOD.

It's fun, it's informal, and its chef and staff pride themselves on preparing at least a half-dozen kinds of fish in virtually any way you can think of. It occupies a brightly painted blue and pink wooden house beside the beach and has a waterfront terrace that is one of the most consistently popular in town. Even if you don't opt for a bistro-style meal here, consider dropping in during happy hour (every day from 5 to 7pm) when drinks are slightly reduced in price, or for Thursday night disco or Friday night karaoke. Annie and Curtis will welcome you, offering such drinks and dishes as rum punch, fish-and-chips (made with island grouper), at least four different preparations (blackened, grilled, stewed, or steamed) of snapper, kingfish, wahoo, lobster, and (for meat eaters) roast leg of lamb.

## INEXPENSIVE

### Regal Begal

Hospital St. ☎ **809/946-2274.** Reservations not required. Soups and fritters $1.50–$3; sandwiches and salads $5.50–$6; platters $5.50–$10. No credit cards. Lunch Mon–Sat 11am–3pm; dinner Mon–Sat 5:30–10pm. CARIBBEAN.

Located beside the road, about a 3-minute drive from the center of Cockburn Town, this is one of the simplest and least pretentious restaurants on the island. Its name was made famous on the long-running hit TV comedy series, *Three's Company.* There's a bar to quench your thirst, and a handful of plain tables where such dishes as lobster salad, several variations of conch, chicken or fish with chips, and pork dishes are served.

## WHAT TO SEE & DO

Other than doing nothing, or perhaps snorkeling, swimming, or scuba diving, Grand Turk doesn't dazzle with a lot of attractions—except one, previewed below.

### Turks & Caicos National Museum

Guinep Tree Lodge, Front St., Cockburn Town, Grand Turk. ☎ **809/946-2160.** Admission $5 nonresidents, $2 full-time island residents. Mon–Tues and Thurs–Fri 9am–4pm, Wed 9am–6pm, Sat 10am–1pm.

Established in 1991, this is the first (and only) museum in the country. It lies within a 150-year-old residence (Guinep Tree Lodge), which was originally built by Bermudian wreckers out of the salvaged timbers of ships that had been demolished on nearby reefs. Today, about half of its display areas are devoted to the remains of the most complete archaeological excavation ever performed in the West Indies, the wreck of a Spanish caravelle (sailing ship) that sank in shallow offshore water sometime before 1513. Used for enslavement of the local Arawak tribe, it was designed solely for exploration purposes and is similar to types of vessels built in Spain and Portugal during the 1400s. The original finders of the wreck were treasure hunters who announced it as the *Pinta* of the fleet of Columbus to attract financial backers for their salvage and to guarantee a value to the otherwise valueless iron artifacts if there proved to be no gold. However, there is no proof that the *Pinta* ever came back to the New World after returning to Spain from the first voyage. Researchers from the Institute of Nautical Archeology at Texas A & M University began excavations in 1982, although staff members never assumed that the wreck was the *Pinta.* Today, the remains are referred to simply as the Wreck of Molasses Reef.

Today, although only 2% of the hull remains intact, the exhibits contain a rich legacy of the everyday (nonbiodegradable) objects used by the crews and officers.

The remainder of the museum is devoted to exhibits about the island's salt industries, its plantation economy, the Pre-Columbian inhabitants of the island, and the island's natural history. The natural history exhibit features an 8-by-20 feet three-dimensional reproduction of a section of the Grand Turk Wall, the famous vertical reef. Also included are displays on the geology of the various types of ecological niches in the islands and information on the reef and coral growth.

## SPORTS A TO Z

### Blue Water Divers
Coral Reef Beach Club, Lighthouse Rd., Grand Turk. ☎ **809/946-2055.**

This outfit offers single dives, PADI registration, and dive packages that include accommodations in the hotel that contains it, the Coral Reef Beach Club (see previous hotel recommendation about a dive-package deal).

### Sea Eye Diving
Duke St., Grand Turk. ☎ **809/946-1407.**

This outfit is located between the Kittina Hotel and the Salt Raker Inn and is convenient to most other hotels as well. It offers two-tank morning dives at $45 on a prepaid package or $55 if purchased separately. An afternoon single-tank dive costs $30 and a single-tank night dive goes for $35. Rental equipment is also available. NAUI and PADI courses at all levels are offered. A full certification course goes for $350, including training equipment and boat checkout dives. Dive packages with accommodation are arranged with a hotel if you wish. Snorkeling and cay trips are available for nondivers.

## 2  Salt Cay

Just nine miles south of Grand Turk, this sparsely settled cay is named for its salt ponds, a once-flourishing industry that may be revived. In its day it was known for this "white gold," and some 100 vessels a year sailed from here and Grand Turk with their heavily laden cargoes bound for the United States. It is estimated that during the American Revolution more than 20 Bermudian privateers were running salt on a regular schedule from the Turks Islands past British blockades to Washington's battered armies. Salt was the chief preservative of meat for the colonial army.

In 1951 the government took control of the 300-year-old industry, and in 20 years managed to destroy it completely through bureaucratic mismanagement. Salt Cay fell into a long slumber and has only been revived in 1990 with the arrival of chic guests visiting the Windmills Plantation (see below).

The cay has a landmass of 3¹/₂ square miles, with a beautiful beach bordering the north coast. It has been designated as a historical site by the National Park Service of Turks and Caicos.

You can walk down to the salinas and see the windmills that once powered the salt business, and you can stroll past the 150-year-old "White House," built by a Bermudian salt raker. In addition, you can visit the ruins of an old whaling station and learn how fearless seamen caught whales in the early 19th century. It's also possible to drop in at the local school, where the children are likely to greet you with island calypso songs.

Essentially, Salt Cay is peaceful, quiet, and colorful—the perfect relaxation spot to get away from it all. Since there are only four automobiles on the island, traffic jams aren't a problem.

## GETTING THERE
### BY PLANE

For a long time, residents of Salt Cay were dependent on their small sailboats for communication with the outside world, and the island is still often reached by private boat. But with the opening of a 3,000-foot landing strip, located 575 miles southwest of Miami, the island is connected to the wider world once again. For information about the 5-minute flight from Grand Turk, call Turks & Caicos Airways (☎ 809/946-4255) for departure times. (See "Getting Around" earlier in this chapter).

## WHERE TO STAY

### ⑤ Mount Pleasant Guest House

Dockland, Salt Cay, Turks and Caicos, BWI. ☎ **809/946-6927** or toll free 800/441-4419 in the U.S. Fax 809/946-6927. 10 rms. $65 single; $85 double. Continental breakfast $6 extra. All-inclusive week-long dive packages, with lodging, meals, three daily boat dives, and unlimited beach dives, $795 per person double occupancy, $895 per person single occupancy. (EP rates.) MC, V. Free parking

Set across the street from the island's main docks, this friendly oasis of cost-conscious charm lies within the stone walls of what was originally built in the 1830s as the home of a salt merchant. Established in 1991 by Bryan and Emily Sheedy, refugees from New York City and Wyoming, respectively, the place caters almost exclusively to divers who usually opt for the week-long all-inclusive packages described above.

In addition to a likable restaurant (described below), the hotel maintains the only horseback-riding stables in the country, with four horses that guests of the hotel can ride for free, and which otherwise rent for around $20 for a half-day jaunt. Accommodations lie for the most part within a modern two-story annex built across the street. Rooms contain ceiling fans, comfortably unpretentious furniture, and simplified accessories. Day-trippers or residents of other hotels are welcome to use the hotel's dive facilities. Dives cost $25 per tank, with all equipment included, while a resort course for beginners goes for around $75. Recently discovered by the Sheedys is one of the most celebrated dive sites in the region, the as-yet-unsalvaged wreck of a British warship that sank in 1790 in shallow waters far from shore. Still visible are 9-foot cannons and a quartet of massive anchors.

Visitors planning to stay here usually inform the hotel of their time of arrival in Grand Turk, and are then ferried by the hotel's supply boat from a point near the airport to Salt Cay.

### ✪ The Windmills Plantation at Salt Cay

N. Beach Rd., Turks and Caicos, BWI. ☎ **809/946-6962** or toll free 800/822-7715 in the U.S. Fax 809/845-2982 or 410/820-9179 in the U.S. 4 rms, 4 suites. Year-round, $345 single; $490 double; $660 suite. (AP rates, including service, airport transfers, and all drinks.) AE, V.

Set in the midst of 17 acres of scrubland beside a white-sand beach on the north side of the island, this hotel was entirely built by local artisans using centuries-old building techniques. Each of the dozen or so buildings within the compound has been designed in a whimsically derivative colonial style that differs from that of its neighbor. These styles, best defined as "Caribbean vernacular," include plantation-inspired influences from the French, English, Dutch, and Spanish colonies of 200 years ago. Their design by architect/owner Guy Lovelace was the culmination of years of research by a man who—until recently—made a career of designing other people's Caribbean resort hotels. The Windmills Plantation is the highly creative result of a dream come true. Its centerpiece is a trio of dramatically proportioned swimming pools, which include a 50-foot lap pool and a "fun pool" only 4 feet deep centered around a mermaid-shaped fountain.

Each of the resort's accommodations contain a tasteful selection of antique reproductions (mostly handmade in the Dominican Republic or in Haiti), a veranda, a cathedral ceiling with a ceiling fan, and a white-with-splashes-of-tropical-color decor. Four of the accommodations are considered suites, and two of these have their own plunge pools. All drinks are included in the rates (the hotel maintains a constantly open bar for its clients). Tax (but not service) is extra.

For reservations and information, contact the establishment's Maryland address, Windmills Plantation at Salt Cay, P.O. Box 635, Easton, MD 21601.

**Dining/Entertainment:** Meals feature a culinary tour of the Caribbean, with a visit to a different island for lunch and dinner every day. Festive or native dishes of a particular island are featured.

**Services:** Room service.

**Facilities:** Swimming pool, lap pool, 2-mile nature trail, mangrove trail, historic salt tour, bicycles, snorkeling on 2-mile reef.

## WHERE TO DINE

### Mount Pleasant Guest House

Dockland, Salt Cay. ☎ **809/946-6927.** Reservations not required. Appetizers $1.50–$3; main courses $6.50–$12. MC, V. Breakfast daily 7:30–9am; lunch daily noon–2pm; dinner daily 6–9pm. AMERICAN/BAHAMIAN.

Contained on a patio beside the previously recommended hotel, this is one of the most consistently popular and unpretentious restaurants on the island. Food is well prepared and served in copious portions that are much appreciated by the establishment's clientele of serious scuba divers as well as by well-intentioned locals. Seafood is especially popular, much of it freshly caught several hours previous to its preparation. Don't overlook a before-or-after-meal libation at the establishment's Gazebo Bar.

## 3 North Caicos

North Caicos is the most northern of the major islands in the archipelago. This 41-square-mile island is strictly for people who want to get away from it all. If you're seeking deserted soft white-sand beaches and crystal-clear water, then this is the place. No one dresses up here, so leave your jacket and tie at home. It contains miles and miles of uncrowded sandy beaches and is surrounded by a sea teeming with fish—an ideal place for scuba divers and snorkelers. Experienced guides can take you fishing for snapper, barracuda, or bonefish. Beach picnics, boating excursions, and fish cookouts on deserted cays are easily arranged. You can snorkel on a barrier reef or tour the island by taxi. Ask to be taken to **Flamingo Pond,** located south of Whitby, which is a nesting place for these elegant pink birds. You'll also be shown the ruins of old plantations and such tiny hamlets as Sandy Point and Kew.

A resort in the making, North Caicos is slated for development.

## GETTING THERE & GETTING AROUND

The local airline, **Turks & Caicos Airways** (☎ **809/946-4255** or 305/871-7169 in Florida), runs connecting flights to the island's terminal. If you disembark at Providenciales, the airline takes only six minutes to fly you to North Caicos.

The best way to see the island is to have your hotel arrange a taxi tour at the rate of about $25 per hour.

## WHERE TO STAY & DINE

### Club Vacanze/Prospect of Whitby Hotel

Whitby, c/o Kew Post Office, North Caicos, Turks and Caicos, BWI. ☎ **809/946-7119.** Fax 809/946-7114. 24 rms, 4 suites. A/C. Dec–Apr and Aug–Sept, $165 per person double occupancy. May–July and Oct–Nov, $150 per person double occupancy. (MAP rates.) AE, MC, V. Free parking.

Originally established in 1974, this beachside hotel was named after one of the most historic Thames-side pubs of London, the Prospect of Whitby. Repaired and renovated, and working hard to regain a niche in the touristic marketplace, the hotel is surrounded by vegetation considered verdant for the Turks and Caicos Islands, and is near the white sands of a highly desirable beach. Each of the half-dozen buildings that compose this complex is painted a soft pink. The units contain a scattering of art, a ceiling fan, comfortable furnishings, and a view of the sea.

The establishment's bar and restaurant are popular with yachties who moor their sailing craft off the expansive north-coast beach on which the hotel sits. The hotel's Italian-born managers imbue the cuisine with a European flair, and they help to arrange excursions to nearby cays. Many different water-sports activities, including scuba diving, windsurfing, snorkeling, and sailing, can be organized by the staff.

### Ocean Beach Hotel

Whitby, North Caicos, Turks and Caicos, BWI. ☎ **809/946-7113.** Fax 809/946-7386. (For information and reservations, write to RR#3 Campbellville, Ontario L0P 1B0. ☎ 905/336-2876. Fax 905/336-9851.) 10 units. Year-round, $98 single; $110 double; $140–$195 double suite; $155–$215 triple suite; $175–$255 quad suite. Extra person $40. Children under 12 free in parents' room. MAP $35 per person extra. (EP rates.) MC, V. Free parking.

This resort sits on a fine beach, a 6-mile taxi ride from the airport and 1 mile from the center (such as it is) of Whitby. A hotel condo, it features individual rooms or two- and three-bedroom suites. Each suite offers a fully equipped kitchen, a full linen service, and safe drinking water. Sliding glass doors and picture windows open onto an ocean view, and the rooms are cooled by trade winds. Furnishings are in the typical Florida tropical style, nothing fancy. Guests can purchase groceries and drinks at the commissary, or else patronize the dining room and lounge, offering local and American dishes. Sometimes the place takes on a house-party atmosphere, with barbecues, patio dancing, or beach picnics.

Facilities include a pool, tennis court, and night club, and deep-sea fishing, scuba diving, and snorkeling can be arranged.

## Pelican Beach Hotel

Whitby, North Caicos, Turks and Caicos, BWI. ☎ **809/946-7112.** Fax 809/946-7139. 12 rms, 2 suites. Winter, $130 single; $165 double; $230 suite. Off-season, $110 single; $130 double; $165 suite. (MAP rates.) AE, MC, V. Free parking.

Set a few steps above the high-water mark of one of the finest beaches on North Caicos, this hotel is the culmination of a dream of Clifford Gardiner, a native of North Caicos who has always believed in the island's touristic potential. It lies on the island's western coastline, midway between the settlements of Kew and Bottle Creek, isolated from almost everything except the sand and the sea. Opened in 1985, the hotel caters to isolationists who usually arrange transport on and off the island with Mr. Gardiner's charter-airline service, the Island Flyers. The airline's twin-engine, six-passenger aircraft charges about $50 round-trip for passage to and from the international airport at Provo.

Bedrooms lie within one- and two-story wings of the original core and are furnished in a Spartan, functional, modern style. Each has a ceiling fan and a minimum of other accessories. During the day, especially in summer, the rooms may be too hot for you, but at night they are generally comfortable. Shortly after its opening, Mr. Gardiner won praise from the then chief minister, who came here to acknowledge the "blood, sweat, and tears" he expended in getting the hotel launched.

You can also take your meals here, and not everything has to be shipped in, as North Caicos grows a lot of its fruit and vegetables. Conch, lobster, and locally caught fish are available. Try such dishes as okra soup, made with pig tail, vegetables, pigeon peas, dumplings, salt beef, and, of course, okra. Occasional "jump up" evenings are staged to entertain fellow guests and locals.

The hotel offers skin-diving and snorkeling trips. You can snorkel for a full day, with lunch included, for $40. Scuba dives and fishing trips can be arranged.

# 4 Middle Caicos

Called Grand Caicos by some islanders, Middle Caicos is the largest island in the archipelago, consisting of 48 square miles (it's 15 miles long). Secluded beaches and towering limestone cliffs that protrude into the sea along the north coast give Middle Caicos the most dramatic coastline of the islands. Conch Bar, on the north side of the island, offers cathedral-size **limestone caves** once used by the Lucayans, as the artifacts found within have proved. In the 1880s these caves were the site of a thriving guano (fertilizer) export industry. With their clear underground salt lakes, the caves have been called a "natural museum" of stalagmites and stalactites. Nearby wild cotton plants derive from the 18th century, when Loyalists from the southern colonies in the new United States came to try their hand at establishing plantations.

Middle Caicos men were some of the most expert boatbuilders in the island nation. They made their vessels from pine taken from the middle island's pine groves. The boats were used by fishermen to work the waters around many of the cays and to gather conchs for shipment to Haiti.

Bring an insulated cooler packed with food and supplies, which you can procure on Provo. Pack whatever meats, milk, butter, bread, beer, staples, and more beer you think you'll need. When you return home to Provo, use the cooler to pack whatever fish or lobster you catch offshore, or use it as an easy mode of carting conch shells back from Middle Caicos. Middle Caicos has about a half-dozen simple mom-and-pop food outlets, but their inventory is limited to dried or canned foods such as cornmeal, flour, sugar, salt, and powdered milk.

Big real estate plans are slated, and there is wide speculation of major developments in this now sleepy place, including a causeway linking its mangrove swamps and scrub-covered landscapes to the booming developments of nearby Provo.

## GETTING THERE

Most visitors come to Middle Caicos on a private-boat tour for a 1-day visit to the caves. Ask at your hotel in North Caicos if any fishing or supply boats will be going there during your stay. (Larger boats usually avoid Middle Caicos because of the shallow waters that surround it.)

The cheapest and easiest way to reach this largely undeveloped island is to fly to Provo any way you can and then transfer to one of two regional airlines. The more obvious of these is **TCA (Turks & Caicos Airlines)** (☎ **305/871-7169** in Florida or **809/946-4366**), which stops at Middle Caicos several times a day as it "island-hops" between Provo and Grand Turk. The one-way cost (for the 15-minute flight) to Middle Caicos from Provo is $30.

## WHERE TO STAY

### Eagles Rest Villas

Reality Subdivision, Bambarra Beach, Middle Caicos, Turks and Caicos, BWI. ☎ **809/ 946-6122.** (For reservations, call or write Eagle Enterprises, 240 Pebble Beach, Suite 712, Naples, FL 33962. ☎ toll free 800/484-1882, code 7177. Fax 813/793-7157.) 2 2-bedroom villas. A/C TV. Winter, $900–$1,000 per week for up to six. Off-season, $750 per week for up to six. Cook and maid available for $35 extra per day. No credit cards. Free parking.

This pair of seafront villas represents the only overnight accommodations on Middle Caicos. Although they were originally built as part of a real-estate speculation by a Florida-based developer, their appeal has proven so successful that they will probably remain on the rental market for many years to come.

Both of them are the centerpiece of what's eventually intended as an upscale community of about a hundred private homes whose building lots have been subdivided into parcels of about an acre each. Although only about five homes had been built at press time, it's one of the several developments on the Caicos Islands that will probably bear close attention as the island continues to develop. (The island's only paved road is a 10-mile stretch that runs adjacent to the property.)

The developer of the fledgling community, Richard Zebo, is justifiably proud of his role as the first white person to own and build anything on Middle Caicos in more than 172 years. Since his initial interest, more than 30,000 plants have added touches of verdant growth to a landscape that is otherwise covered only in stunted trees, mangroves, and casuarinas.

Don't even think of coming here unless you want lots of seclusion, peace, and quiet. Rental cars and a quartet of fishing boats can be rented from an on-site manager, and a limited selection of scuba supplies lies nearby. Other than that, however, there's very little to do except read, reflect, sunbathe, snorkel, and fish. Each of the villas is a white-walled single-story structure with a red hip roof, its own fully equipped kitchen, two air-conditioned bedrooms, two bathrooms, a VCR-TV, ceiling fans, and summer-style rattan and wicker furnishings. A local resident from the nearby hamlet of Bambarra (about three-fourths of a mile to the south) can be employed on a daily basis as a cook and maid, but if you don't want to see anyone, this setting will provide the seclusion you need in ample amounts.

Be warned that most of the provisions you consume will need to be imported, probably from Provo in a cooler.

## 5 South Caicos

Some of the finest **diving** and **snorkeling** in the Bahamas, as well as in this Crown Colony, are found on South Caicos, an 8½-mile island with numerous secluded coves and panoramic coral reefs. Long Beach is a beachcomber's paradise. One visitor wrote, "This is like escaping to another era." There are always locals available to take you sailing, boating, or fishing for a small fee. Bonefishing here is the best in the country.

Some 600 miles southeast of Miami and 22 miles east of Grand Turk, South Caicos can be reached by **Turks & Caicos Airways** (☎ **809/946-4255**). There is a 6,500-foot paved and lit jetport, where passengers disembark as they head for Cockburn Harbour, considered the best natural harbor of the island nation. It is the site of the annual **Commonwealth Regatta** in May.

Although the island may appear nearly deserted, there are 1,400 permanent residents and what one local described as "about 65 vehicles and a few wild horses and donkeys in the bush." Some of the residents use their cars as taxis and meet visitors at the airport.

## WHERE TO STAY & DINE

### Club Carib Harbour & Beach Resort

South Caicos, Turks and Caicos, BWI. ☎ **809/946-3444** or toll free 800/722-2582 in the U.S. Fax 809/946-3446. 21 rms, 9 suites. Winter, $75–$125 single or double; $140 suite. Off-season, $50–$100 single or double; $115 suite. Extra person $10; children 2–12, $5. Children under 2 free. MC, V. Free parking.

This resort is comprised of two hotels: one is situated on the water at Cockburn Harbour and the other is located about 1½ miles to the east, at beachside. The isolated beachside hotel offers clean, no-frills accommodations for rest and relaxation. The rooms have private baths, kitchenettes, and ceiling fans, but they have no air-conditioning.

The harbor hotel is located across the street from an old salt warehouse where salt shipments were weighed and loaded for the ocean-bound vessels anchored in the harbor. The rooms have private baths, air-conditioning, TV, and telephones. The harbor site offers guests great snorkeling, but for swimming it's best to stick to the pool. The Club Carib Café is also here, serving international fare.

Although room service is only available at the harbor site, both entities have daily maid service and can arrange for babysitting, laundry, and bicycle rentals. Along with your stay you may want to partake in such water sports as paddle boats and windsurfing.

## 6 Providenciales

Affectionately known as Provo, this 38-square-mile island has white-sand beaches that stretch for 12 miles along the northeast coast. It also has peaceful rolling hills, clear water, a natural deep harbor, flowering cactus, and a barrier reef that attracts swimmers, divers, and boaters. The roads may not always be paved, but you'll still find some stores and two full-service banks. The island is served by an airport capable of handling wide-body jets and has good marina and diving facilities.

Provo is the most built-up island in the Turks and Caicos chain; its development began with the opening of the Club Med "Turkoise" (see below) at the cost of $27 million. Once known mainly to a group of millionaires headed by Dick du Pont, Provo has now developed a broader base of tourism.

It was first discovered by the rich back in the 1960s, but word just had to get out, and now the bulldozers are there in full force. Throughout most of the 1970s it was known as a "pedigreed playground." Other celebrities have arrived more recently, including Dick Clark, *American Bandstand* idol, who liked the place so much he bought property.

Provo is the headquarters for PRIDE, a nonprofit organization for the Protection of Reefs and Islands from Degradation and Exploitation. PRIDE assists residents and visitors with conservation education and management.

To reach the island, see "Getting There," at the beginning of this chapter.

# WHERE TO STAY
## EXPENSIVE

### ✪ Club Med Turkoise
Grace Bay, Providenciales, Turks and Caicos, BWI. ☎ **809/946-5500** or 800/CLUB-MED in the U.S. Fax 809/946-5500. 300 rms. A/C. Winter, $1,130–$1,650 per person weekly. Off-season, $850 per person weekly. (AP rates.) AE, MC, V. Free parking.

Set on 70 acres of sun-blasted scrubland, 11 miles from the airport, this resort was inaugurated in 1984 as the most widely publicized and upscale resort in the Club Med chain. Although its preeminence has since then been supplanted by more recently established newcomers, it remains an appealing oasis of verdant charm and communal diversion. Set on a bleached-white strip of beachfront overlooking Grace Bay, it was initially built for a total cost of $27 million. A self-contained irrigation system, with an in-built desalinization plant, keeps the arid landscape green. Unlike certain other Club Meds, this one does not particularly go out of its way to entertain children with a barrage of special programs—that is, it is not designated as a Club Med "Family Village." The ambience is among the most casual and most loosely structured of any member of its chain, a fact that seems to appeal to the more laid-back members of its French and North American clientele.

The village-style cluster of two- and three-story accommodations are painted a pastel pink and capped with cedar shingles imported from Sweden. All meals and most sports are included in the weekly package rates. Drinks, which cost extra, are paid for with pop-off beads from a necklace.

The resort contains 600 beds, each twin size, in ultrasimple rooms designed with beachfront lifestyles in mind.

**Dining/Entertainment:** Most meals are served buffet style and consumed at long communal tables, in a system not unlike those at a summer camp. Table wine and beer is provided at mealtime for free. Two specialty restaurants have waiter/waitress service, and include a pizzeria and a beachfront entity (the Grill) that specializes in late breakfasts, late lunches, and late suppers. A disco keeps residents active, if they wish, from 11:30pm to at least 3am nightly.

**Facilities:** Scuba diving, which is not included in the package price, is offered on a space-available basis. Activities that are part of the package include windsurfing, sailing, waterskiing, and daily sessions devoted to arts and crafts. There are two Jacuzzis on the property and eight tennis courts, four of which are lit for night play.

## ✪ Grace Bay Club

Grace Bay Rd., P.O. Box 128, Providenciales, Turks and Caicos, BWI. ☎ **809/946-5757** or 800/946-5757 in the U.S. Fax 809/946-5758. 22 suites. A/C TV TEL. Winter, $335–$375 single or double; $455–$495 one-bedroom suite; $595–$655 two-bedroom suite; $725 penthouse. Extra person $85. Off-season, $255–$285 single or double; $345–$375 one-bedroom suite; $445–$495 two-bedroom suite; $555 penthouse. Extra person $65. (EP rates.) AE, MC, V. Free parking.

Established late in 1992, this Swiss-owned and managed development is ringed with about 200 palm trees imported from Florida and Nevis. The hotel lies on five landscaped acres of what used to be sun-blasted and barren scrubland on Provo's North Shore, midway between the larger and better-known resorts, Club Med and the Ramada.

Designed in the spirit of an Andalusian village at the edge of a white-sand beach, the hotel is mostly contained within a three-story building inspired by the architectural traditions of Iberia. Capped with terra-cotta tiles and partially sheathed with sculpted coral stone, it was built around a courtyard in whose center stands a splashing fountain imported from Spain.

Each accommodation has an eclectic kind of elegance well suited to its water-loving clientele and can be configured as an individual room or as an extended suite simply by opening or closing inner doors. Each bedroom contains a king-size bed with a carved headboard imported from Mexico, carpets from Turkey or India, tables and armoires from Mexico or Guatemala, artwork from Haiti or Brazil, ceiling fans, safes, and cable TV with VCR. Suites and penthouses each have their own kitchens, washing machines, and dryers. Bathrooms throughout the resort contain hand-painted Mexican tiles and lots of mirrors.

**Dining/Entertainment:** The hotel's restaurant, the Anacaona (separately recommended in "Where to Dine," below) lies on three thatch-covered and interconnected satellites of the main building. The gracefully furnished bar area contains its own artificial waterfall and meandering stream and a wide selection of tropical drinks. Live music is presented several times a week. For other types of entertainment, guests usually walk for about seven minutes along the beachfront to the casino and nightlife options at the Ramada.

**Services:** Room service from 7am to 9pm, babysitting, concierge.

**Facilities:** Swimming pool, free use of equipment for Sunfish sailing, two tennis courts lit for night play, snorkeling, and windsurfing; availability of waterskiing, bonefishing and deep-sea fishing, boating excursions, deserted island picnics, and parasailing, and a small library with books and video games.

## Ocean Point/Chalk Sound Villas

Between Sapodilla Bay and Taylor Bay, Providenciales, Turks and Caicos, BWI. (For information and reservations, write P.O. Box 550509, Atlanta, GA 30355. ☎ **404/351-2200.** Fax 404/351-2615.) 9 villas. TV TEL. Year-round, $1,200–$3,800 per week. AE, DC, MC, V. Free parking.

Many visitors to Provo prefer to avoid accommodations in hotels in favor of the more private, and infinitely more isolated, pleasures that only a self-contained villa can afford. Between the early 1980s and around 1992, two villa compounds were developed on Provo's arid and windswept southern coast, midway between Sapodilla Bay and Taylor Bay. Each building within the compound is built of imported Canadian cedar, fir, glass, concrete, and (in one case) local stone; each blends into the rocky, scrub-covered landscape that surrounds it. Angled toward sweeping views over turquoise-colored waters, each features a veranda-ringed design based on West Indian or creole models. Although their position on a half-acre or more of seafront land transmits a sense of isolation, grocery stores lie within a 15-minute drive, and since each unit contains a kitchen, many visitors opt to prepare most of their meals on-site. Some of the villas boast their own piers, others have serpentine staircases that wind down to the water's edge from hilltop positions looking over the sea. Each has a scattering of tasteful and surprisingly expensive furniture and many of the amenities you'll need for an escapist vacation. All have ceiling fans; most also have air-conditioning, and some come with fax machines. Each has a satellite TV hookup with at least 32 channels to while away the moonlit nights when you're not otherwise occupied with your Significant Other. All rental arrangements are made through the Atlanta address that is listed above, and the availability of any particular villa will vary with the schedule and priorities of each villa's individual owners.

## Ramada Turquoise Reef Resort & Casino

Grace Bay, P.O. Box 205, Providenciales, Turks and Caicos, BWI. ☎ **809/946-5555** or 800/854-7854 in the U.S. Fax 809/946-5522. 226 rms, 2 suites. A/C TV TEL. Winter, $190–$230 single or double; from $435 suite. Off-season, $125–$160 single or double; from $240 suite. MAP $35 per person extra. (EP rates.) AE, MC, V. Free parking.

Set on 15 acres of flat sandy land, with a 900-foot beachfront along the island's northeastern coast, this resort opened in 1990. It was built with touches of style and offers fairly priced accommodations that seem even better during its seasonal promotions. Managed (but not owned) by Ramada International, it is the first of the island's properties to contain a casino, and offers probably more glitter and flash than any of its competitors. The resort has been designed with prominent balconies in a modern hip-roofed compound, the buildings of which are symmetrically arranged around a landscaped garden and central swimming pool.

Each of the resort's bedrooms contains clay-tile floors, wicker furniture, ceiling fans, a private balcony or patio, with splashes of color partly provided by framed illustrations.

**Dining/Entertainment:** The resort's most upscale restaurant, the Portofino, features grilled seafood and steaks, with an emphasis on Italian cuisine. Less formal dining and daytime drinks are available beside the pool and beach, at Buddy's Bar. Especially convenient is the laissez-faire simplicity of the Coral Terrace Restaurant and Lounge, the resort's coffee shop. After dark, at 7pm, with live music beginning at 9pm Monday to Saturday, clients congregate in the Portofino Nightclub. It features musicians imported from the Caribbean and the U.S. mainland. Entrance is free, with drinks priced from $4 each.

**Services:** Babysitting, massage, room service (7am to 10am and 6 to 10pm), guest activities coordinator for adults and children respectively.

**Facilities:** Health club with exercise machines and Jacuzzi, swimming pool, two tennis courts lit for night play, dive shop with facilities for underwater photography, tour desk, scooter-and-bicycle rental, in-house car rental, and duty-free shop for the purchase of perfumes, jewelry, and liquor. Entrance is free to the island's only casino (the Port Royale), which opens every night from 4pm to 2am.

## MODERATE

### Le Deck Beachclub and Hotel

P.O. Box 144, Grace Bay, Providenciales, Turks and Caicos, BWI. ☎ **809/946-5547.** Fax 809/946-5770. 23 rms, 2 suites, 2 1-bedroom condos. A/C MINIBAR TV TEL. Winter, $153 single or double; $198 suite; from $225 condo. Off-season, $119 single or double; $154 suite; from $198 condo. Continental breakfast $6 extra. (EP rates.) AE, MC, V. Free parking.

Set a few steps from the very white sands of the island's eastern beaches, this hotel opened in 1989. It benefits from its location, a 10-minute walk from the larger and better-accessorized Ramada. Guests frequently walk over to the bigger resort to patronize its facilities, including its restaurants and gambling casino. Each accommodation has a ceiling fan, a private bathroom, and a comfortable decor of beach-inspired furniture and Caribbean colors. There's also a villalike condominium that sits a short distance from the rest of the hotel.

Arranged in a U-shape around a deck that serves as a social center (and gives the establishment its name), the hotel is painted pink and white and contains on its premises a curve-sided freshwater swimming pool, a wood-trimmed clubhouse-bar-restaurant with big windows and sea views, and a full array of water-sports options.

## Erebus Inn

Turtle Cove, Providenciales, P.O. Box 238, Turks and Caicos, BWI. ☎ **809/946-4240.** Fax 809/946-4704. 25 rms, 4 chalets. MINIBAR TV TEL. Winter, $100–$150 single or double; $100 chalet. Off-season, $100–$120 single or double; $80 chalet. MAP $45 per person extra. AE, V. Free parking.

Erebus Inn occupies a hillside above Turtle Cove on the northern shore of the island. Its 10 studio apartments face the marina at the bottom of the hill. Additional accommodations are in a long and narrow stone-sided annex whose breeze-filled central hallway evokes an enlarged version of an old Bahamian house. Twenty-two rooms are air-conditioned. Ringing both sections of the hotel are dry-weather plants such as cactus and carefully watered vines such as bougainvillea.

The social center is the big-windowed Spinnaker Bar, the perimeter of which offers a view of the marina and the gulf. There is also an open-air terrace surrounded by walls of chiseled stone. Facilities include two pools (one saltwater), two clay tennis courts, and a health club. The inn also has one of the best restaurants on the island, Mama Mia (see "Where to Dine," below).

## Island Princess Hotel

The Bight, Providenciales, Turks and Caicos, BWI. ☎ **809/946-4260.** Fax 809/946-4666. 72 rms. A/C TEL. Year-round, $70–$100 single; $80–$100 double. Continental breakfast $6 extra. (EP rates.) AE, MC, V. Free parking.

In 1979 an enterprising American engineer returned after years of building roads and dams in Iran to an island he vaguely remembered from a brief stopover many years before. Today the domain of Cal Piper includes pleasant rooms, a popular bar, and a sunny dining room with a view of the sea. The hotel sits on some of the best beachfront on Provo, lying 6$^1$/$_2$ miles northeast of the airport. Built of local stone and designed in a zigzagging labyrinth of two-story annexes, the property contains acreage devoted only to gardens, plus a water-sports kiosk where visitors can rent sailboats and snorkeling equipment. There are two swimming pools. The hotel has amply proportioned sheets of glass, which are angled for the best views of the sea and the sands of the beach.

The hotel has a helpful staff and often hosts Canadian tour groups. Each of its motel-like bedrooms has a ceiling fan, a patio or balcony, wall-to-wall carpeting, a private bath, and big windows. Reasonably priced dive packages are available, allowing divers to take advantage of the hotel's location at the edge of the "Walls," which drops 6,000 feet into uncharted waters a short distance offshore. Meals are served in an airy dining room. The chef prepares concoctions of island seafood and international specialties. If you catch a conch or lobster during your explorations in the water, it can be prepared for your dinner.

### Sun Worshippers Hotel

Sapodilla Point, Providenciales, Turks and Caicos, BWI. ☎ **809/946-4488.** Fax 809/946-4488. 25 rms. A/C. Winter, $90–$95 single or double; $105 triple. Off-season, $65 single or double; $75 triple. AE, MC, V. Free parking.

Uncluttered simplicity is the byword of this informal hotel, principal decor of which are the sweeping sea vistas around it. It stands three miles southeast of the airport. The only object interrupting the panorama is a Shell Oil unloading dock, a concrete-and-steel giant jutting into the sea at the bottom of the slope supporting the hotel. Even the dock, however, has a form of isolated grandeur about it. The owners have worked hard to turn the locale into an oasis of flowering plants. These grow around the bases of the villas containing the accommodations. The social center is the sundeck, where palms and parasols shade the planked boardwalks.

Accommodations are basic, unfussy places, with ceiling fans, bathrooms, and modern lines. However, if the season is slow, this place might be closed for several months at a time. Always check before planning to visit.

### Turtle Cove Inn

Turtle Cove Marina, Suzie Turn Rd., Providenciales, Turks and Caicos, BWI. ☎ **809/946-4203** or toll free 800/887-0477 in the U.S. Fax 809/946-4141. 29 rms, 1 suite. A/C MINIBAR TV TEL. Winter, $95–$125 single or double; $150 suite. Off-season, $85–$110 single or double; $125 suite. (EP rates.) AE, MC, V. Free parking.

Originally built of local stone and white stucco in 1983, and enlarged and upgraded in 1990, this pleasant and cheerful hotel is built in a U-shaped format around a swimming pool. A few feet away, boats dock directly at the hotel's pier, which juts into Seller's Pond amid the many yachts floating at anchor. Near the pool lie the tables of the separately recommended Tiki Hut Cabana Bar & Grill. Upstairs, open for dinner only, is Jimmy's (see separate recommendations for restaurants). Each bedroom is simply but comfortably furnished, with views over either the pool or the marina.

Although it doesn't have a beach of its own, many guests don't consider this a problem because of the ferryboat shuttle that carries guests from the hotel's wharf across the pond to the sands of a nearby beach. There is also a swimming pool. You'll find two tennis courts, lit for night play, on the premises. Dive packages are available.

## WHERE TO DINE
### EXPENSIVE

#### ✪ Alfred's Place

Suzie Turn Rd., above the Turtle Cove Marina. ☎ **809/946-4679.** Reservations recommended. Lunch platters $6.50–$8; dinner appetizers $4.50–$8; dinner main courses $12.50–$24. AE, MC, V. Lunch daily noon–2pm; dinner daily 7–9pm. FRENCH.

Considered by some as the most innovative restaurant on the island, this is the domain of Austrian-born Alfred Holzfeind, who worked for many years as a chef on an upscale cruise line. It occupies a pavilion-style building high on a hillside above the Turtle Cove Marina, with an outdoor terrace that by anyone's standards is breathtaking.

Cuisine is a blend of modernized French recipes and includes such dishes as Thai-style shrimp salad; carpaccio with walnut oil; seafood fritters; salads made of fresh basil, fresh tomatoes, and mozzarella; roast rack of lamb with either blueberry sauce or goat cheese; veal briard nestled in a bed of applesauce and melted Brie; grilled swordfish prepared in the fiery style of Thailand; and grilled tuna with anchovy and tomato sauce. Lunches are less complicated, featuring such dishes as prime rib or lobster sandwiches, chicken or fish in pita bread, and club sandwiches.

## ✪ Anacaona

In the Grace Bay Club, Grace Bay Rd. ☎ **809/946-5757.** Reservations required. Lunch salads, sandwiches, and platters $11–$20; dinner appetizers $8–$13; dinner main courses $28–$35. AE, MC, V. Lunch daily 12:30–3pm; dinner daily 7–10pm. FRENCH/CARIBBEAN.

The unlikely name of this restaurant translates from a dialect of the Native Lucayan tribe as either "feather of gold" or "flower," depending on its context. Set in three thatch-roofed and interconnected "pods" that serve as outbuildings of a previously recommended resort, this culinary charmer is lighthearted, fun, and elegant.

You might enjoy one of the frothy drinks in the bar before crossing over an artificial stream to the restaurant. There, a lunchtime menu of lobster salads, sandwiches, and well-prepared platters of fish gives way in the evening to more elaborate food inspired by the French colonial tropics. This might include snapper amandine or baked *en papillotte,* many preparations of lobster, and whatever fresh fish happens to have arrived from the sea that day. The thatched "palapa" which covers the rooftop of this restaurant, incidentally, was woven by Native Seminoles especially imported from Florida in 1992 during its construction.

## ✪ Banana Boat Restaurant

Turtle Cove Marina. ☎ **809/941-5706.** Reservations recommended. Appetizers $6; main courses $9.95–$16. AE, DC, MC, V. Daily 11am–10pm. INTERNATIONAL.

Sheltered by a low-slung hip roof and lined with louvered shutters, Banana Boat Restaurant is the most popular independent restaurant on the island. It was established in 1981 Since then there's hardly been a yachtsperson on Providenciales who hasn't enjoyed at least one of the establishment's island meals and potent drinks, such as Wilbert's Wet and Wild Wonder, costing $5. For a main course, you might try rib-eye steak, cracked conch, or some freshly caught local fish. At lunch, favorites include lobster or tuna salads, along with half-pound

---

### ⊕ Family-Friendly Restaurants

**Tiki Hut Cabana Bar & Grill**  *(see p. 327)* At Provo's Turtle Cove Inn, this cabana-style restaurant places tables around the pool and offers children American breakfasts, sandwiches, or fresh pasta dinners.

**Salt Raker Inn**  *(see p. 309)* On Grand Turk, this simple family restaurant offers familiar fare at lunch (burgers, fish-and-chips, sandwiches), and at night grills "the catch of the day" for its largely boating crowd, many of whom are with their families.

**Hey José Cantina**  *(see p. 327)* Two Californians welcome the family trade at this Provo hotspot and feed their diners well on burritos, tacos, quesadillas, and the best pizzas on the island.

burgers. Dessert might be carrot cake or key lime pie. A choice perch is on the timber-and-plank veranda jutting on piers above the water of Turtle Cove.

## Hong Kong

Leeward Hwy., Grace Bay. ☎ **809/946-5678.** Reservations recommended. Appetizers $2–$4.50; main courses $10–$17. AE, MC, V. Mon–Sat 11am–10pm, Sun 5–10pm. CANTONESE.

Contained within a white-painted cement-sided building on the highway, midway between the Ramada and Club Med, this simple hole-in-the-wall serves some of the best Chinese food on the island. Many of the cooks are immigrants from China. In one of a pair of dining rooms, you can enjoy a medley of Cantonese dishes served with such sauces as black bean, hot pepper, soya, sweet and sour, and lobster sauce. A popular dish inspired by local culinary tastes includes sweet-and-sour conch. The owner, Bosco Chan, named his establishment after his native city of Hong Kong.

## Mama Mia

In the Erebus Inn, Turtle Cove. ☎ **809/946-4240.** Reservations recommended. Pizzas $9.50–$17; lunch $4.50–$22; dinner appetizers $5; dinner main courses $9.50–$22. AE, MC, V. Lunch daily noon–2pm; dinner daily 6–10pm. ITALIAN/WEST INDIAN/INTERNATIONAL.

Set on a hillside overlooking the yachts that bob at anchor in the Turtle Cove Marina, this terraced restaurant offers outdoor platforms that some visitors claim are among the best on the island for the evening ritual of sunset watching. The bar here enjoys an enthusiastic clientele in its own right and serves two-fisted versions of rum punches and piña coladas ($5.50 each) that are well-known throughout the neighborhood.

The adjoining restaurant offers 20 kinds of pizza, along with such dishes as lobster, grilled pork chops, steaks, and a wide array of fish and pastas. The decor is typically Italian with long guest tables and benches covered in blue and white checkered tablecloths.

## Portofino

In the Ramada Turquoise Reef Resort & Casino, Grace Bay. ☎ **809/946-5555.** Reservations required. Appetizers $4.50–$7; main courses $12.50–$28. AE, MC, V. Dinner daily 6–11pm. ITALIAN.

Inspired by the decor and cuisines of Italy, this is considered the most elegant Italian restaurant in Provo. Set adjacent to its own seafront terrace overlooking Grace Bay, in a previously recommended hotel, it sports modern furniture, subtle lighting, a formally dressed staff, and a soothing color scheme of turquoise and pale pink. Your meal might include any of about 10 varieties of pasta, including the chef's proposed pasta of the day, served either as main courses or (in lesser quantities) as appetizers. Main courses include strips of veal sautéed with morels and chanterelles in a vermouth sauce, roast pheasant with shiitake mushrooms and a mushroom sauce, a medley of shrimp and scallops with mushroom and Italian seasonings served in a piquant béchamel sauce, and prime tenderloin of beef rubbed with fresh peppercorns and served in a cognac cream sauce.

## MODERATE

### Dora's Seafood Restaurant

Leeward Hwy. ☎ **809/946-4558.** Reservations not required. Breakfast $5.50; lunch $6.50–$8; appetizers $1.50–$3.25; main courses $10–$15. AE, MC, V Daily 8am–midnight. SEAFOOD.

Contained within a white-painted single-story cement building beside the main highway, this restaurant is the domain of Dora Lightbourne, born on remote South Caicos. There's a bar area to quench your thirst, as well as a handful of tables where local dishes are served. Your meal might include conch fritters or conch chowder, followed by grouper fingers, chicken, several different preparations of lobster or cracked conch. There's a seafood buffet served every Monday and Thursday night from 7 to 10pm, priced at $22 per person, which will include transportation to and from whatever hotel you happen to be staying in.

### Jimmy's

In the Turtle Cove Inn, Suzie Turn Rd., South Shore. ☎ **809/941-5575**. Reservations recommended. Appetizers $5–$7; main courses $10–$20. AE, MC, V. Mon–Sat 5pm–midnight, Sun 5–10pm. INTERNATIONAL.

Its virtues include a decor that might remind you of home (flowered curtains and lots of books), a well-stocked bar, white napery, and a view over the trees that flank the edge of a marina and a white-sand beach. Hosts Jimmy and Dodie McLean are hospitality personified, giving you a cheerful welcome ("Eat, eat, eat—don't go away hungry.") Rum punch ($4.95) is a specialty at the bar, and if you can't find a congenial person to talk to, you can always browse through the lending library that occupies one corner of this establishment's interior. Menu items include lobster, lasagne, broiled snapper or grouper with lemon-spice marinade, ribs, New York steaks, and assorted pizzas and pastas.

### Tiki Hut Cabana Bar & Grill

In the Turtle Cove Inn, Turtle Cove Marina. ☎ **809/941-5341**. Reservations not required. American breakfast from $4.50; lunch platters $4.50–$11; dinner appetizers $3–$6; dinner main courses $8.50–$13. AE, MC, V. Breakfast daily 7–11am; lunch daily 11am–5pm; dinner daily 6–11pm. AMERICAN/CARIBBEAN/PASTA.

This open-air cabana-style restaurant arranges its tables beside the pool of a pleasant hotel that sits next to one of the island's biggest marinas. This restaurant was established in 1993 after its owner split away from the hugely successful Banana Boat Restaurant next door. The Tiki Hut serves full-fledged American-style breakfasts; lunches that include salads, fresh fish platters, and sandwiches; and dinners that consist almost completely of pasta and fresh fish. Culinary specialties include jerked grouper (slow-cooked with spices in the Jamaican style), panfried or grilled catch of the day served with fresh dill and caper-tartar sauce, and the traditional favorite, English-style fish-and-chips, prepared with your choice of swordfish, grouper, snapper, or dolphin. The house drink, a Banana Slammer, costs $5.

## INEXPENSIVE

### Hey José Cantina

Central Square, Leeward Hwy. ☎ **809/946-4812**. Reservations not required. Lunch platters $6–$10; pizzas $5.50–$20; dinner appetizers $3–$11; dinner main courses $6–$14; margaritas $3.50 each. AE, MC, V. Mon–Sat noon–10pm. Bar Mon–Sat noon–11pm. MEXICAN/PIZZA/AMERICAN.

Set in the center of the island, as one of the focal points of a small shopping center, this lighthearted eatery is the creative statement of Larry Klein. Within a decor of burnt orange, greens, and yellows, you can enjoy the best margaritas in Provo, as well as a wide array of Mexican food. Menu items include burritos, tacos, quesadillas, chimichangas, and a selection of barbecued steaks and chicken. Also popular, especially with expatriate North Americans who have had their fill of an island diet of fish and cracked conch, are the richly accessorized pizzas. Available in three sizes, they culminate with a variety known as "the kitchen sink," where virtually everything you can think of is included among its ingredients.

### Pub on the Bay

Blue Hills. ☎ **809/941-5309.** Reservations not necessary. Breakfast $4.50–$7.50; lunch platters $5–$10; dinner appetizers $3–$5; dinner main courses $10–$22.50. AE, DC, MC, V. Daily 9am–10pm (last order). BAHAMIAN/INTERNATIONAL.

Most of its clients categorize this place as a pub/bistro with stiff drinks, well-prepared food, and a congenial staff who will prepare virtually anything you want at virtually anytime of the morning, noon, or night. It lies within a modern, wood-sided building (peach colored, with brown trim), across the road from Northside Beach, within a 40-minute drive west of the Grace Bay Club and the Club Med.

You'll find a handful of tables on the sands of the beach, across the road from the restaurant's core, but be warned in advance that service there is usually a bit slower than that offered within the main building. Breakfasts here are always competently prepared, with focus on ham and eggs, grits, and omelets, but on weekends many local residents come here for the local (i.e., ethnic) breakfasts, priced at $7.50 each, which include such dishes as boiled fish, chicken souse, and johnnycakes. (These are available only on Saturday and Sunday mornings from 9 to 11:30am.) Lunchtime platters include sandwiches, salads, peas 'n' rice, grilled fish, and pork-chop platters. Evening meals include virtually everything a cook could concoct from a conch and a repertoire of straightforward but flavorful dishes that include barbecued pork, chicken, sirloin steaks, and local Provo lobster, either broiled or minced. During midwinter, the place sometimes presents live music on Saturday night.

### Tasty Temptations

In the Butterfield Square Shopping Center, Leeward Hwy. ☎ **809/946-4049.** Reservations not accepted. Pastries and turnovers $1.50–$2; sandwiches $4–$6.25. No credit cards. Mon–Fri 6:30am–3pm; Sat 6:30am–noon. Closed Sept. DELI.

No one would ever consider coming here for a full-fledged meal, but for a morning cup of espresso or cappuccino, bagels with smoked salmon and cream cheese, and any of about a dozen kinds of lunchtime sandwiches, the place is an excellent choice. It's arranged deli style, with prominent sandwich boards, oil paintings of nautical subjects from a nearby art gallery, and glass-fronted display cases where you collect your food on trays or in paper bags for take-away. If you opt to eat on the premises, there's an outdoor terrace. The place is popular with the office workers from Provo's administrative headquarters, and with anyone assembling the components of a picnic. (The place sells cold cuts and deli foods by the pound.) Run by an expatriate from French-speaking Canada, the establishment lies within a 10-minute drive west of Provo's airport.

## WHAT TO SEE & DO

The national treasure of Provo is a famous Atlantic bottle-nosed dolphin, **JoJo,** who has lived and played around these waters since 1983. What makes this wild dolphin unusual is that he chose to leave his pod and seek out the company of people. He cavorts and plays with the children of the residents of the Bight, on the northern shore of Provo, giving them rides out to the reef and back. Very few dolphins have ever adopted such a people-oriented lifestyle on their own.

---

### ❓ Did You Know?

- A world survey once found that Turks and Caicos had the least name recognition of any nation on earth.
- The infamous Caicos Banks, south of the Caicos Islands, claimed much of the Spanish fleet lost in the Caribbean from the 1500s to the 1700s.
- The 7,000-foot-deep, 22 mile-wide Turks Island Passage is used by thousands of North Atlantic humpback whales heading south to their breeding grounds.
- The inhabitants of Turks and Caicos were descended from African slaves brought by colonists to work plantations, all of which failed.
- More than 100 species of native plants have been identified on Provo—ranging from fragrant frangipani to red mangrove to the infamous strongback (alleged to enhance male sexual powers).
- Lucayans came all the way from South America to settle Turks and Caicos some seven to nine centuries before the arrival of Columbus in 1492.

---

**Chalk Sound,** a landlocked lagoon west of Five Cays Settlement, has been turned into a public park. The hamlet of Five Cays itself boasts a small harbor and a modern airport.

### Caicos Conch Farm
Leeward Hwy. ☎ **809/946-5849.** Admission $6 adults, $3 children under 12. Mon–Fri 9am–5pm (last tour).

Located on the isolated eastern end of the island, amid a flat and sun-baked terrain of scrub and sand, this establishment was founded in 1984 by a consortium of investors from Miami and Canada. It is considered a pioneer (the only one of its kind in the West Indies) for the commercial production of the large edible mollusk known as conch. Its techniques are not commercially viable, but this place could spark breeding techniques that could change the way the mollusk is cultivated worldwide. Its staff will show a 20-minute video to visitors, and give them a walk-through tour of the breeding basins. Admission includes a tour of the hatchery and the laboratories. There's a snack bar selling conch fritters and soft drinks. In the gift shop, you can buy rare conch pearls, shell jewelry, and commemorative T-shirts.

## ORGANIZED TOURS
**Executive Tours** (call **809/946-4524** for information and reservations) is the largest ground-transport company in Provo, exclusively responsible for transporting Club Med clients. However, when they are not busy with their Club Med obligations, they take visitors from all hotels on island tours in an eight-passenger minivan. Tours last half a day and cost $10 per person.

## SHOPPING
### Bamboo Gallery
Leeward Hwy., Provo. ☎ **809/946-4748.**

If shopping for paintings is one of the diversions you enjoy when you're on holiday, you might enjoy browsing through the artworks of one of the leading art galleries of Provo. Its inventories include woodcarvings, ceramic sculptures, and the kinds of colorful oil paintings which, if they don't come directly from Haiti, were at least inspired by that island's traditions.

### Greensleeves
Central Square. ☎ **809/946-4147.**

This is one of the leading craft and souvenir shops on Provo. Its merchandise features paintings and ceramics by local artists, and such craft items as baskets, jewelry, and sisal mats and bags.

### Tropical Fashions
Turtle Cove, Provo. ☎ **809/946-4343.**

Well-made clothing, often inspired by the fashions you might have expected in Miami's stylish South Beach neighborhood, are sold at this popular boutique. Missing a sarong or a bathing suit, or did you leave your sandals on the beach during last week's midnight swim? This store will probably stock more or less what you need.

## SPORTS A to Z

### Art Pickering's Provo Turtle Divers Ltd.
Turtle Cove. ☎ **809/946-4232** or toll free 800/328-5285 in the U.S.

Provo Turtle Divers Ltd., with headquarters directly in front of Erebus Inn on the water, is a dive operation offering personalized service. It is the oldest dive operation in the islands. Dive experts have considered Provo "one of the finest sites for diving in the world," because of a barrier reef that runs the full length of the island's 17-mile north coast. At Northwest Point there is a vertical drop-off to 7,000 feet.

There are scuba tanks for rent, plus ample backpacks and weight belts. Snorkel equipment is also available. A single dive costs $40. A PADI open-water certification course is $350. Provo Turtle is a PADI training facility, with full instruction and resort courses.

### Dive Provo
In the Ramada Turquoise Reef Resort, Grace Bay. ☎ **809/946-5040** or toll free 800/234-7768 in the U.S.

Dive Provo has one of the best scuba programs on the island. Its Grace Bay dive boat leaves the Ramada pier daily at 8:30am. It also offers PADI open-water certification courses, along with snorkeling trips, glass-bottom boat rides, equipment rental, Windsurfer or sailboat instruction, and sailing excursions. A two-tank scuba dive costs $60, with a PADI certification course going for $350. Snorkeling trips go for $20, and Windsurfers or sailboats can be rented for $20 per hour.

### Provo Golf Club
Grace Bay Rd., Provo. ☎ **809/946-5991.**

Opened with much fanfare late in 1992, this is the only golf course in the country. Developed by the local water board, whose desalinization plants provide the water to irrigate it, the 6,529-yard, par-72, 18-hole course was designed by Karl Litten, of Boca Raton, Florida. Young palms and colorful bougainvillea, rocky outcroppings and powdery sand traps, help make the course a challenge to the serious golfer or a lovely day on the links for the beginner or novice. Four sets of tees allow golfers to tailor their game to their level of expertise. For those who want to sharpen specific elements of their game, a driving range and putting greens

## Diving Paradise

A reef system 65 miles across and 200 miles long; a great range of diving spots whales; playful dolphins who show up unexpectedly; countless varieties of fish and coral—these are the undersea attractions of the Turks and Caicos Islands.

The Turks and Caicos Islands promise to be much more than the latest "hot dive spot." Dive operators can take visitors to spots popular with other divers or customize a trip of discovery to virgin territory.

For example, off the northwest corner of the island of Providenciales, known locally as "Provo," is Smith's Reef, a walk-in dive to a seascape of brain and fan corals, purple gorgonias, anemones, and sea cucumbers, active with sergeant majors, green parrot fish, long-nosed trumpet fish, the odd, ominous-looking green moray, an occasional southern ray, and a visiting hawksbill turtle or two.

From the shore at Grace Bay, a sweep of powdery white beach that is graced by some of Provo's most highly regarded resorts, visitors can see where the sea breaks along 14 miles of barrier reef. But the reef is much more than the natural breakwater that makes this beach so accommodating, it is also the teeming undersea home of sea life ranging from swarms of colorful schools of fish to the singleton feeding barracuda to large, rotund grouper.

Around Grand Turk, there are miles and miles of drop-off diving. Here you can enjoy one of the underwater world's great experiences, a night dive on a wall where the colors of the day become the phosphorescent illumination of the night.

Ledge and wall dives are the attractions around South Caicos. Here divers can literally select the level of their vertical descent, then glide horizontally among the multicolored, multishaped corals and drift through schools of trumpets, hamlets, basslets, and more.

Off Salt Cay, divers can explore the wreck of the HMS *Endymion,* which went down in a storm in 1790. Two centuries later, Brian Sheedy, a local diver and inn operator, discovered the wreck. Today, while the reef has reclaimed the hull and all else that was biodegradable, divers can nonetheless get a close-up look at its cannons and four huge anchors lying about.

But Salt Cay is more than the final resting place of a ghost ship. Between January and March each year, the humpback whales come here to play. Visitors can watch their antics from shore, boat out among them, or don dive equipment and go below. To reach these underwater treasures of West Caicos, a handful of dive boats make hour-long transits (each way) from the southern tip of Provo (Sapodilla Bay) several times a week. Once they're below the water's surface, divers are usually awestruck at the more than two miles of sheer coral walls whose edges begin less than a quarter-mile from the West Caicos shoreline. The most popular dive sites are Boat Cove, Sunday Service, and Isle's End.

Packages are available with international airlines serving the Turks and Caicos Islands and local hotels (with or without meals). Dive certification courses are also offered.

are available. The clubhouse contains a bar and a restaurant serving breakfast and lunch. Starting times are daily from 7:15am to 4pm. Greens fees are $80 per person for 18 holes, a price that includes the use of a golf cart, which is mandatory. Golf clubs can be rented for $15 per set.

# 7 Pine Cay

This exclusive territory, a private island in the West Indies, is owned and managed by members of the Meridian Club, who rightly praise its 2$^1$/$_2$-mile talcum-powder beach, which is among the finest in all the islands.

Pine Cay is one of a chain of islets connecting Providenciales and North Caicos. Two miles long and 800 acres in land area, it is a small residential community with a large area set aside for a park. It has its own 3,900-foot airstrip with scheduled local air service, as well as dock-and-harbor facilities. No cars are allowed, and transportation is by golf cart or bicycle. There is just enough fresh water, and the cay has its own generating plant.

Once a private club, Pine Cay still has members but they now join the public guests for swimming, sunning, and shelling along the white-sand beach. Snorkeling and diving are possible in an unspoiled barrier reef. Explorers look for Arawak and British colonial remains. There is also a wide range of birds and plants.

The islands' possibilities were recognized by Ferdinand Czernin, son of the last prime minister of the Austro-Hungarian Empire. It is said he was looking for an "intellectual Walden Pond" when he discovered this unspoiled, pristine retreat.

## GETTING THERE

To reach Pine Cay, fly to Miami and then take another flight to Providenciales (see the "Getting There" section at the beginning of this chapter). There, an air taxi can be arranged to meet you for the 10-minute flight to Pine Cay.

## WHERE TO STAY & DINE

### ✪ The Meridian Club

Pine Cay, Turks and Caicos, BWI. ☎ **toll free 800/331-9154** or 212/696-4566 in the U.S. Fax 809/946-5128. 12 rms. A/C. Winter, $425–$515 single; $485–$575 double. Off-season, $335 single; $395 double. No children under six. (AP rates.) No credit cards.

The Meridian Club is an environmentally sensitive resort that includes a main clubhouse that faces the beach and a freshwater pool. The club, barefoot elegance at its best, has a delightful dining room, a comfortable library, and an intimate bar with a panoramic terrace for sunset cocktails. A dozen accommodations are offered, with bed- and sitting-room areas, dressing rooms, outdoor showers, and terraces facing the beach.

For reservations and information, contact the Meridian Club, c/o Resorts Management, Inc., 201$^1$/$_2$ E. 29th St., New York, NY 10016 (see the toll-free number above).

**Dining/Entertainment:** The Meridian Club has one dining room and two bars, one of which is poolside. The open-air dining room offers full American breakfasts, buffet-style lunches served poolside, and dinners by candlelight. The food is a Caribbean/continental cuisine, the high standard of which is complemented by the extensive use of local produce, especially lobster, conch, and snapper. Guests can enjoy poolside barbecues and a band once or twice weekly.

**Services:** Laundry, room service for breakfast only.

**Facilities:** One tennis court, large freshwater swimming pool, variety of nature trails. There are activities planned daily, such as offshore snorkeling trips or boat trips to neighboring islands. Boats, snorkeling gear, tennis rackets and balls, and fishing tackle are available, as are fishing guides and experienced boatmen.

# Index

The following Frommer's guides are available from your favorite bookstore, or you can use the order form on the preceding page to request them as part of your membership in Frommer's Travel Book Club.

## FROMMER'S COMPLETE TRAVEL GUIDES

*(Comprehensive guides to sightseeing, dining and accommodations, with selections in all price ranges—from deluxe to budget)*

| | | | |
|---|---|---|---|
| Acapulco/Ixtapa/Taxco, 2nd Ed. | C157 | Jamaica/Barbados, 2nd Ed. | C149 |
| Alaska '94-'95 | C131 | Japan '94-'95 | C144 |
| Arizona '95 | C166 | Maui, 1st Ed. | C153 |
| Australia '94-'95 | C147 | Nepal, 3rd Ed. (avail. 11/95) | C184 |
| Austria, 6th Ed. | C162 | New England '95 | C165 |
| Bahamas '96 (avail. 8/95) | C172 | New Mexico, 3rd Ed. | C167 |
| Belgium/Holland/Luxembourg, | | New York State, 4th Ed. | C133 |
| 4th Ed. | C170 | Northwest, 5th Ed. | C140 |
| Bermuda '96 (avail. 8/95) | C174 | Portugal '94-'95 | C141 |
| California '95 | C164 | Puerto Rico '95-'96 | C151 |
| Canada '94-'95 | C145 | Puerto Vallarta/Manzanillo/ | |
| Caribbean '96 (avail. 9/95) | C173 | Guadalajara, 2nd Ed. | C135 |
| Carolinas/Georgia, 2nd Ed. | C128 | Scandinavia, 16th Ed. | C169 |
| Colorado '96 (avail. 11/95) | C179 | Scotland '94-'95 | C146 |
| Costa Rica, 1st Ed. | C161 | South Pacific '94-'95 | C138 |
| Cruises '95-'96 | C150 | Spain, 16th Ed. | C163 |
| Delaware/Maryland '94-'95 | C136 | Switzerland, 7th Ed. | |
| England '96 (avail. 10/95) | C180 | (avail. 9/95) | C177 |
| Florida '96 (avail. 9/95) | C181 | Thailand, 2nd Ed. | C154 |
| France '96 (avail. 11/95) | C182 | U.S.A., 4th Ed. | C156 |
| Germany '96 (avail. 9/95) | C176 | Virgin Islands, 3rd Ed. | |
| Honolulu/Waikiki/Oahu, 4th Ed. | | (avail. 8/95) | C175 |
| (avail. 10/95) | C178 | Virginia '94-'95 | C142 |
| Ireland, 1st Ed. | C168 | Yucatán '95-'96 | C155 |
| Italy '96 (avail. 11/95) | C183 | | |

## FROMMER'S $-A-DAY GUIDES

*(Dream Vacations at Down-to-Earth Prices)*

| | | | |
|---|---|---|---|
| Australia on $45 '95-'96 | D122 | Ireland on $45 '94-'95 | D118 |
| Berlin from $50, 3rd Ed. | | Israel on $45, 15th Ed. | D130 |
| (avail. 10/95) | D137 | London from $55 '96 | |
| Caribbean from $60, 1st Ed. | | (avail. 11/95) | D136 |
| (avail. 9/95) | D133 | Madrid on $50 '94-'95 | D119 |
| Costa Rica/Guatemala/Belize | | Mexico from $35 '96 | |
| on $35, 3rd Ed. | D126 | (avail. 10/95) | D135 |
| Eastern Europe on $30, 5th Ed. | D129 | New York on $70 '94-'95 | D121 |
| England from $50 '96 | | New Zealand from $45, 6th Ed. | D132 |
| (avail. 11/95) | D138 | Paris on $45 '94-'95 | D117 |
| Europe from $50 '96 | | South America on $40, 16th Ed. | D123 |
| (avail. 10/95) | D139 | Washington, D.C. on $50 | |
| Greece from $45, 6th Ed. | D131 | '94-'95 | D120 |
| Hawaii from $60 '96 (avail. 9/95) | D134 | | |

# FROMMER'S COMPLETE CITY GUIDES

*(Comprehensive guides to sightseeing, dining, and accommodations in all price ranges)*

| | | | |
|---|---|---|---|
| Amsterdam, 8th Ed. | S176 | Minneapolis/St. Paul, 4th Ed. | S159 |
| Athens, 10th Ed. | S174 | Montréal/Québec City '95 | S166 |
| Atlanta & the Summer Olympic | | Nashville/Memphis, 1st Ed. | S141 |
| Games '96 (avail. 11/95) | S181 | New Orleans '96 (avail. 10/95) | S182 |
| Atlantic City/Cape May, 5th Ed. | S130 | New York City '96 (avail. 11/95) | S183 |
| Bangkok, 2nd Ed. | S147 | Paris '96 (avail. 9/95) | S180 |
| Barcelona '93-'94 | S115 | Philadelphia, 8th Ed. | S167 |
| Berlin, 3rd Ed. | S162 | Prague, 1st Ed. | S143 |
| Boston '95 | S160 | Rome, 10th Ed. | S168 |
| Budapest, 1st Ed. | S139 | St. Louis/Kansas City, 2nd Ed. | S127 |
| Chicago '95 | S169 | San Antonio/Austin, 1st Ed. | S177 |
| Denver/Boulder/Colorado Springs, | | San Diego '95 | S158 |
| 3rd Ed. | S154 | San Francisco '96 (avail. 10/95) | S184 |
| Disney World/Orlando '96 (avail. 9/95) | S178 | Santa Fe/Taos/Albuquerque '95 | S172 |
| Dublin, 2nd Ed. | S157 | Seattle/Portland '94-'95 | S137 |
| Hong Kong '94-'95 | S140 | Sydney, 4th Ed. | S171 |
| Las Vegas '95 | S163 | Tampa/St. Petersburg, 3rd Ed. | S146 |
| London '96 (avail. 9/95) | S179 | Tokyo '94-'95 | S144 |
| Los Angeles '95 | S164 | Toronto, 3rd Ed. | S173 |
| Madrid/Costa del Sol, 2nd Ed. | S165 | Vancouver/Victoria '94-'95 | S142 |
| Mexico City, 1st Ed. | S175 | Washington, D.C. '95 | S153 |
| Miami '95-'96 | S149 | | |

# FROMMER'S FAMILY GUIDES

*(Guides to family-friendly hotels, restaurants, activities, and attractions)*

| | | | |
|---|---|---|---|
| California with Kids | F105 | San Francisco with Kids | F104 |
| Los Angeles with Kids | F103 | Washington, D.C. with Kids | F102 |
| New York City with Kids | F101 | | |

# FROMMER'S WALKING TOURS

*(Memorable strolls through colorful and historic neighborhoods, accompanied by detailed directions and maps)*

| | | | |
|---|---|---|---|
| Berlin | W100 | Paris, 2nd Ed. | W112 |
| Chicago | W107 | San Francisco, 2nd Ed. | W115 |
| England's Favorite Cities | W108 | Spain's Favorite Cities (avail. 9/95) | W116 |
| London, 2nd Ed. | W111 | Tokyo | W109 |
| Montréal/Québec City | W106 | Venice | W110 |
| New York, 2nd Ed. | W113 | Washington, D.C., 2nd Ed. | W114 |

# FROMMER'S AMERICA ON WHEELS

*(Guides for travelers who are exploring the U.S.A. by car, featuring a brand-new rating system for accommodations and full-color road maps)*

| | | | |
|---|---|---|---|
| Arizona/New Mexico | A100 | Florida | A102 |
| California/Nevada | A101 | Mid-Atlantic | A103 |

# FROMMER'S SPECIAL-INTEREST TITLES

| | | | |
|---|---|---|---|
| Arthur Frommer's Branson! | P107 | Frommer's Where to Stay U.S.A., | |
| Arthur Frommer's New World | | 11th Ed. | P102 |
| of Travel (avail. 11/95) | P112 | National Park Guide, 29th Ed. | P106 |
| Frommer's Caribbean Hideaways | | USA Today Golf Tournament Guide | P113 |
| (avail. 9/95) | P110 | USA Today Minor League | |
| Frommer's America's 100 Best-Loved | | Baseball Book | P111 |
| State Parks | P109 | | |

## FROMMER'S BEST BEACH VACATIONS

*(The top places to sun, stroll, shop, stay, play, party, and swim—with each
beach rated for beauty, swimming, sand, and amenities)*

| | | | |
|---|---|---|---|
| California (avail. 10/95) | G100 | Hawaii (avail. 10/95) | G102 |
| Florida (avail. 10/95) | G101 | | |

## FROMMER'S BED & BREAKFAST GUIDES

*(Selective guides with four-color photos and full descriptions of
the best inns in each region)*

| | | | |
|---|---|---|---|
| California | B100 | Hawaii | B105 |
| Caribbean | B101 | Pacific Northwest | B106 |
| East Coast | B102 | Rockies | B107 |
| Eastern United States | B103 | Southwest | B108 |
| Great American Cities | B104 | | |

## FROMMER'S IRREVERENT GUIDES

*(Wickedly honest guides for sophisticated travelers
and those who want to be)*

| | | | |
|---|---|---|---|
| Chicago (avail. 11/95) | I100 | New Orleans (avail. 11/95) | I103 |
| London (avail. 11/95) | I101 | San Francisco (avail. 11/95) | I104 |
| Manhattan (avail. 11/95) | I102 | Virgin Islands (avail. 11/95) | I105 |

## FROMMER'S DRIVING TOURS

*(Four-color photos and detailed maps outlining
spectacular scenic driving routes)*

| | | | |
|---|---|---|---|
| Australia | Y100 | Italy | Y108 |
| Austria | Y101 | Mexico | Y109 |
| Britain | Y102 | Scandinavia | Y110 |
| Canada | Y103 | Scotland | Y111 |
| Florida | Y104 | Spain | Y112 |
| France | Y105 | Switzerland | Y113 |
| Germany | Y106 | U.S.A. | Y114 |
| Ireland | Y107 | | |

## FROMMER'S BORN TO SHOP

*(The ultimate travel guides for discriminating
shoppers—from cut-rate to couture)*

| | | | |
|---|---|---|---|
| Hong Kong (avail. 11/95) | Z100 | London (avail. 11/95) | Z101 |